DATE DUE

CRIMINAL JUSTICE ILLUMINATED

Community Corrections and Human Dignity

Edward W. Sieh

Department of Criminal Justice
St. Cloud State University
St. Cloud, Minnesota

JONES AND BARTLETT PUBLISHERS

Sudbury, Massachusetts

BOSTON   TORONTO   LONDON   SINGAPORE

World Headquarters
Jones and Bartlett Publishers
40 Tall Pine Drive
Sudbury, MA 01776
978-443-5000
info@jbpub.com
www.jbpub.com

Jones and Bartlett Publishers Canada
2406 Nikanna Road
Mississauga, ON L5C 2W6
Canada

Jones and Bartlett Publishers International
Barb House, Barb Mews
London W6 7PA
United Kingdom

Jones and Bartlett's books and products are available through most bookstores and online book-sellers. To contact Jones and Bartlett Publishers directly, call 800-832-0034, fax 978-443-8000, or visit our website www.jbpub.com.

Substantial discounts on bulk quantities of Jones and Bartlett's publications are available to corporations, professional associations, and other qualified organizations. For details and specific discount information, contact the special sales department at Jones and Bartlett via the above contact information or send an email to specialsales@jbpub.com.

Production Credits
Publisher, Public Safety Group: Kimberly Brophy
Acquisitions Editor: Chambers Moore
Production Director: Amy Rose
Associate Production Editor: Carolyn F. Rogers
Marketing Associate: David Weliver
Cover and Text Design: Anne Spencer
Photo Research: Kimberly Potvin
Cover Image: photo © Bob Daemmrich/PhotoEdit;
    column © Ron Chapple/Thinkstock/Alamy Images
Chapter Opener Image: © Masterfile
Composition: Carlisle Publishers Services
Printing and Binding: Malloy, Inc.
Cover Printing: Malloy, Inc.

Library of Congress Cataloging-in-Publication Data
Sieh, Edward Wallace, 1946-
    Community corrections and human dignity / Edward W. Sieh.
        p. cm.
    Includes bibliographical references and index.
    ISBN 0-7637-2905-1 (hardcover : alk. paper)
    1. Community-based corrections—United States. 2. Community-based corrections—United
    States—History. 3. Probation—
United States. 4. Parole—United States. 5. Dignity. I. Title.
    HV9304.S53 2005
    364.6'8'0973—dc22
                                                                    2005007149

Printed in the United States of America
09 08 07 06 05   10 9 8 7 6 5 4 3 2 1

Contents

Having recently completed my thirty-second year in the community corrections business, I remain amazed at the apparent intractability of certain professional problems. The attitudes of probation officers towards those under their control is one of the most important. I have been most fortunate to have held positions as president of The American Probation Association, assistant commissioner of a department of corrections, chairman of a parole board, and numerous other prominent positions in various professional associations. I feel most fortunate to have served in line-level positions and to have worked my way through the community corrections career ladder.

It is my line-staff vantage point, coupled with active involvement in community corrections efforts in no less than 46 states, Canada, and Western Europe, that has enabled me to clearly see and to understand the importance of human dignity in my beloved profession. Sadly, I have at the same time come to realize how little progress has been made in establishing value for human dignity in all facets of community corrections work. This book is the first scholarly attempt to connect the relevance of human dignity to probation. Even more important is the clear and concise manner in which the entire matter of human dignity is relevant to a civilized society and the public safety interests of law-abiding citizens.

Historically, there has been a disconnect between the philosophical ideals of corrections and actual practice. While it is true that there have been and continue to be noteworthy exceptions with regard to the disconnect, these anecdotal examples have not been incorporated into correctional practice on anything close to a grand scale.

Yes, it is true that some corrections professionals come to the defense of the field when faced with what may be perceived as criticism of their collective values and beliefs. In fact, I expect to hear from at least a few of them after they read this Foreword. Notwithstanding, any corrections professional that has spent even a few years in the business would be less than honest in denying that there is a "human dignity" crisis in the profession. In this regard, correctional insiders should reflect on the many ways that correctional clients are routinely talked about, handled, and supervised—many of which are not appropriate for publication here.

I suspect that even the more subtle manifestations of human disrespect are equally damaging—perhaps more so! These subtle manifestations are embraced by organizational norms across the nation's correctional spectrum. Some of the most commonplace examples of the diminution of respect for human dignity in correctional environments involve simple things like referencing inmates by number rather than name, referring to halfway house inmates as residents, probationers and parolees as "the subject," "the defendant," the probationer/parolee, etc. And, things really start to get interesting when agencies

Foreword

begin to debate whether individuals under correctional control are clients or something closer to sub-citizens. With regard to this last point I have witnessed staff grievances and line-staff attempts to publicly ridicule, or otherwise politically embarrass, agency administrators for trying to cast the "bad guys" in a better light.

The foregoing examples, though they are only the tip of the human dignity iceberg, illuminate the depth of the values crisis that pervades the corrections profession in America. Why the profession has not paid more attention to staff value for human dignity is perplexing, especially when the success or failure of correctional treatment endeavors turns on this core staff value.

The findings of the "what works" research on effective correctional programming is clear—firm, fair, mutually respectful, and caring relationships between those delivering and those receiving treatment services are essential for recidivism reduction to be achieved. Is it possible that treatment services can be delivered in this manner by individuals who have little or no regard for the human dignity of individuals under correctional control? The field of psychology has long recognized that the attitudes and values of therapists is at least as important as treatment modalities, when it comes to ameliorating personal and social problems. Corrections professionals must emphatically and unanimously come to the same professional conclusion if the field is to accomplish its public safety mission through recidivism reduction.

The major point of the pages that follow is that effective correctional treatment cannot be delivered unless the individuals providing these services value human dignity. The author makes the point that human dignity is valuable in itself. That is to say that even if the utilitarian goals of justice and public safety were removed from correctional treatment endeavors, the inherent nature of human dignity in all of society's citizens is in itself a sufficient justification for mentoring, nurturing, or otherwise trying to help everyone—even, perhaps especially, violators of the law. However, if one's ideological bent is contrary to the advancement of human dignity for secular humanistic reasons, human dignity in correctional settings must still be pursued because it is inextricably linked to the public safety interests of all law-abiding citizens. In short, a mean-spirited or disrespectful approach to the delivery of correctional services renders them less effective, and therefore more perilous, than would otherwise be the case.

The fact that this book pays considerable attention to probation services provides me with the justification to turn my attention to some specific issues relevant to probation supervision. Probation services include treatment services, and these are best viewed as a means to the end goal of public safety. No other probation supervision strategies have been shown to be as successful (e.g., increased contacts, surveillance, curfews, electronic monitoring, etc.). In the face of the evidence, it becomes compelling for probation officers to strive to be as effective as they can be in the delivery of treatment services.

This effectiveness, as has already been stated, turns in large part to the values of the probation officers themselves. Moreover, failure to be effective translates into more victimization by errant probationers than would have otherwise have been the case. Thus, the orientation of the probation officer toward human dignity has a significant impact on probation's primary goal—public safety. Therefore, hiring, training, and retaining staff with a strong positive view toward human dignity is critical to a probation agency's success.

The time has come in the professional development of probation services to recognize that not all values and skill sets are appropriate to the mission of probation organizations. Moreover, deficient attitudes and values are resistant to change through in-service training or education. The probation profession has virtually ignored the needed, but extremely sensitive, discussion on values and has instead chosen to devote its attention primarily to training and staff development as the panacea for recidivism reduction.

In countless candid discussions I have had, and continue to have, with probation professionals, there is widespread agreement that more needs to be done to hire the "right" people, fire the "wrong" people, and groom those who possess the basic foundational values but who need to mature and develop. Increasingly, I hear it said that ". . . there are not good and bad programs, just good and bad staff and organizations." While this may be an oversimplification of the problem, the statement serves to focus us on what is, in my opinion, the main reason for the lack of success—and the basis for the crisis of credibility by and within the community corrections profession in general.

Since human dignity plays such an important and compelling role in the recidivism public safety process, probation agencies are faced with two options:

1. Ensure congruity between the values of the agency's leaders and staff and the vision and mission of the agency.
2. Address any incongruity between the personal values of agency leaders and staff and the vision and mission of the agency, by assuring that the leaders and staff are committed to putting their personal views aside in order to effectively deliver treatment services and hence increase public safety.

Congruity between personal and agency values about human dignity, especially as codified in local statutes, administrative codes, and policies, is the ideal. When personal and agency values are incongruous in this regard, the best that can be hoped for is that probation practitioners "act as if" they embrace human dignity as a societal goal. Clearly, the latter set of circumstances is a very distant second to the ideal. Nevertheless, and as a practical matter, it is the latter scenario that is most common in the practitioner world. As Sieh correctly notes, it is this less than ideal scenario that is at the root of probation's inability to maximize its public safety effectiveness.

There is much to be learned from a well thought out discussion on human dignity. After reading this book, I reflected on how disregard for human dignity is related to the objectification of individuals and, ultimately, a lack of empathy for those with whom we live, work, and recreate. In fact, the de-objectification and empathy issues involved in the human dignity values of probation officers are similar to those that are integrated into the thinking and behaviors of criminals. Probation officers' objectification of probationers—and the resultant lack of probationers' human dignity—is a process that is akin to that employed by criminals in order to facilitate lack of responsibility and a diminished sense of guilt for harm caused to individuals and communities. Who shall break this insidious cycle of objectification and victimization? When you are finished reading this book, you will realize that the responsibility rests with America's corrections systems, and that each and every one of us must insist on it!

Mario Paparozzi
Pembroke, North Carolina

Today thousands of children die each day across the world because of malnutrition or disease, mass murder and cruelty are inflicted in the name of national security, and people are valued for possessing qualities that seem superficial and ephemeral. Women and children are exploited or denied basic rights. And while the United Nations in 1948 promulgated an International Declaration of Human Rights, there still is no basic principle that once born, someone has the right to live. Today, the United States has more people in prison than at any time in its history. Billions of dollars are spent punishing men, women, boys, and girls. How a nation treats those who have committed crimes is a measure of the level of civilization that nation can claim to have achieved.

After working in corrections and teaching in this field for over twenty-five years, I would like to challenge society by asking three basic questions: What is actually happening in probation and parole? What should be happening? And, why does anyone care about the offender at all? Answers to these questions originated in my earlier research into understanding workplace crime and deviance. This research led me to recognize that probation officers are similar to all other occupations in that some officers work hard, treat offenders with respect, and care about the probationer's success, while other probation officers have little interest in doing a good job, care little for the offender, and are guilty of ethical violations or even crimes.

There are times when an officer will deny a probationer's human dignity. When this occurs, the probationer is not seen as having worth or value as a human being. These sentiments may result from deficient recruitment practices, a lack of training, failure to hold officers accountable, or burnout. These officers create other problems that affect office support staff and other officers. In fact, these officers can make the work of good officers that much more difficult.

This text offers an overview of probation and parole as it is practiced in the United States. It is based on research conducted in two counties, each having a population of more than one million people. One was on the East coast and the other was in the Midwest. In total, over 50 officers holding positions that ranged from the lowest-ranking and newest officers to experienced probation directors were interviewed for this project. Direct observation of field and office visits has been augmented with the most recent research in community corrections. The task proved to be both interesting and enlightening. There is a great deal to learn about probation work than has traditionally been incorporated into textbooks. For example, officers sometimes make decisions contrary to policy and court orders because they are dealing with real people and not abstractions.

This book is comprised of thirteen chapters. Chapter 1 addresses the foundation of human dignity and explains why people have value and worth: because of their potential for good and for improvement. The importance of human dignity cannot be underemphasized when considering how much power the state has over convicted offenders. Offenders can be punished for what they have done but they should not needlessly be treated badly.

Chapter 2 offers a detailed perspective on the early history of probation. Probation in 1840 came into existence in the United States when many other significant changes were occuring in this country. Immigration, advancements in the arts and cultural institutions, and various social movements affecting slavery, education, women's rights, and the consumption of alcohol were all under way at this time. Probation was established amid controversy and concern. John Augustus proved to be worthy of his assumed responsibilities of providing sound practical support for those who came before the court. It was an amazing time.

In Chapter 3, the fragile nature of probation as an institution is underscored. During the time when Americans prohibited the consumption and sale of alcohol the very viability of federal probation was brought into question when a challenge was made to the powers of the court to suspend the imposition of a prison sentence in lieu of community supervision. If the courts lacked the power to put someone on probation, then what is to become of the offender? Eventually politicians and officials realized that probation was the appropriate mechanism for handling violators of the prohibition against alcohol. The public had neither the desire nor finances to build the prisons that would be necessary to handle all violators of the Volstead Act. This chapter also details the transformation of probation policy over the decades. As the institutionalization of probation went forward the knowledge base on which probation relied expanded. Probation moved into an era where its professional stature became well entrenched. At the same time officials felt that probation should emphasize offender reintegration, a theme that runs through corrections even to this day.

Chapter 4 addresses the social and economic context of community corrections. Probation officers work in communities and with offenders who have a variety of problems. All kinds of people are arrested, convicted, and put on probation. Many of these people are women and children. These people in turn are often very poor and have many needs. This chapter talks about their needs ranging from drug and alcohol rehabilitation to treatment for mental illness. Many offenders come from communities that have few resources. Offenders in turn have few friends they can rely on and possess few skills that can aid them in resolving their problems. These problems are exacerbated by a racially divided society that has huge income differentials.

Chapter 5 deals with probationers. We often hear discussions of probationers, but until recently have not had a detailed description of who is on probation. A great range of people are on probation, including professionals and working folks. There are property, public order, and violent offenders on probation. There are people who make a lot of money and those who live on the streets. Understanding who these people are makes the job very interesting. Understanding the human side of the offender is vital to succeeding in the task of community supervision.

Probation would not be possible if the probation officer failed to attend to offender incapacitation. In many ways this is central to the mission of probation. To achieve a measure of incapacitation offenders are subjected to risk-needs assessments. Chapter 6 discusses the devices used to establish the level of attention the offender is to receive and how many contacts he or she is to have. Once the level of risk has been established we can work out the needs assessment. In assessing needs probationers must be matched to the appropriate treatment program if we expect to have any chance of success.

Risk-needs assessment is central to probation supervision. Chapter 7 examines offender supervision. Attention is given to the presentence report, violations, and discharges. Most important is developing an understanding of the process of offender supervision beginning with advocacy and intake, and then on to the final step of evaluation. It is paramount to correct the denial of offender responsibility and to offer help in directing offenders to discuss important issues that affect them and others. It is time to evaluate not just special programs but the day-to-day activities of probation. For the officer to be successful it is important for him or her to provide an appropriate model for the offender. Teaching offenders to respect others begins with the probation officer's behavior toward the offender.

A major theme in probation work today is restorative justice. Chapter 8 offers a detailed analysis of the principles, hopes, and problems with restorative justice. Since this model calls for a major paradigm shift in handling the offender and the victim, some departments have adopted only portions of the process. Restorative justice plays an important role in promoting human dignity.

The handling of probation technical violations is a major problem. This is a problem that deserves careful consideration. Chapter 9 offers an analysis of technical violations and then offers a theory for handling them. It is believed that there are so many technical violations that probation officials would overwhelm the corrections systems if those who deserved to be sent to prison were actually sent. In this chapter a theory for handling such violators is presented—violations are handled in a fashion similar to a regulatory process where compliance with the rules rather than exacting a pound of flesh for punishment is the chief concern.

The data indicate that many crimes are committed by individuals while on probation. Probation needs to be accountable for the actions of the officers as well as the offender. Chapter 10 discusses probation in terms of public safety, crime prevention, community involvement, and performance-based measures for assessing probation activities. Without these activities probation has proven to be ineffective in providing real public safety. In the future probation's role in crime prevention will provide an important measure of public safety. Community partnerships will prove essential.

Juveniles, it seems, are the bedrock of the probation movement. Juvenile probation, as discussed in Chapter 11, has played an important part in local correctional activities. Juvenile offenders deserve our utmost attention. The principle of parens patriae must be properly implemented. If the state is to assume the role of the parent, then the state should do everything it can to help the juvenile offender. Of critical importance is the notion that juveniles deserve to be given the best treatment possible for their problems so that they are capable of doing good in the future.

Chapter 12 provides an account of the role of parole in the correctional enterprise. With all of the attention given to paroled sex offenders the public hears little of offenders who have to deal with work, family, housing, mental health, and stigma issues. It is very important to realize that the parolee has served time and deserves to be treated with dignity. For he, too, has value and worth and is not the sum total of his worse deeds.

This book concludes in Chapter 13 with a discussion of the future of probation. There are serious concerns about the direction that probation and parole may take in the future. Probation may be adequately funded or it might become a vast regulatory agency concerned with minor offenders who are kept in line but are not corrected. If they committed a serious crime they go off to prison.

It is hoped that a discussion of human dignity will bring some measure of kindness back into the system. We cannot teach people to treat others with dignity if they are not themselves treated with dignity.

Acknowledgments

Mario Paparozzi deserves special appreciation for having contributed the foreword. Chambers Moore, Acquisitions Editor; Deidre Schaefer, copyeditor; and Carolyn Rogers, Associate Production Editor, each deserve a note of appreciation for their support and patience. I would also like to thank Barbara Brooks for reviewing earlier drafts. Lastly, I would like to thank my wife, Christina, whose support truly made this project possible.

Jones and Bartlett Publishers would like to express its gratitude to Charles E. Reasons of Central Washington University; Mario Paparozzi of the University of North Carolina at Pembroke; and Linda Fleischer of the Community College of Baltimore County at Essex, who, during the development of the project, reviewed the manuscript.

Introduction

1

Chapter Objectives

In this chapter you will learn about:

- The philosophical foundation of human dignity
- The problems with prison and human dignity
- The role of less eligibility
- The role of prison overcrowding
- The role of deficient health care
- The importance of human dignity to rehabilitation
- The role of violence in prisons

The nicest compliment I have ever received from a probationer was when he told me that he appreciated that I had treated him with dignity.

Probation Officer

The code of ethics of the American Probation and Parole Association (APPA) promotes a high standard of conduct for probation and parole officers to follow in their work with offenders. In part it states (APPA, 2004):

> *I will strive to be objective in the performance of my duties, recognizing the inalienable right of all persons, appreciating the inherent worth of the individual, and respecting those confidences which can be reposed in me.*

Inherent in this code is the concept of human dignity. <u>**Human dignity**</u> is comprised of various elements of respect, personal worth, and perfection. Human

human dignity is comprised of various elements of respect, personal worth, perfection, and the Kantian rationalist perspective that sees any individual as having worth because of the person's ability to think and make choices about personal actions and goals.

dignity is based on the acknowledgment that a human is equipped with reason, uniqueness, freedom, morality, originality, and self-determinism. Human dignity is often subsumed under such terms as *fairness* or *due process*. If discussed at all, human dignity stems from a consideration of ethics. Ethics is important in any field. When applied to sentencing, as a society, each is concerned with the morality of punishment. When applied to probation, each is interested in the reasons an offender receives a measure of respect even though he or she has inflicted serious harm.

■ Human Dignity

Gerald Lynch (1996), as president of John Jay College, gave a speech on human dignity in which he praised the fact that the school was offering a course in its international curriculum on human dignity and the police. According to Lynch, the course provided a clearer understanding of human dignity as an innate quality possessed by all humans regardless of race, color, creed, sex, country, or social status, thus granting them a right to respect, fair treatment, and personal dignity. Lynch stated that the course focused on the police as a part of the larger society and that both the police and society were mutually dependent, requiring mutual respect and understanding.

Various probation departments, along with the APPA, have vision, mission, and value statements supporting the concept of human dignity (Mickel 1994). Maricopa County, Arizona, for example, states that one of its principal values is that people are treated with dignity and respect. Other departments have done likewise. Despite such statements, it is apparent that other than stating a concern for human dignity, there is little further explication of the term nor are there any measures used to assess its role in the agency especially when it is paid lip service but denied in practice.

Definition

The Latin word *dignitas* translates into English as "merit, worth, esteem, and honor" (Latin–English Dictionary 2004). The *Oxford English Dictionary* defines dignity as the quality of being worthy or honorable (OED 1979). It is not that all humans are morally praiseworthy, but humans are, by their nature, worthy of a special level of respect fundamentally above that of nonhuman animals (Cheshire 2004). At its core, human dignity is a metaphysical concept that has a reality in the very substance of the human being. Cheshire also states that dignity is inseparable from human nature when it is understood intuitively rather than through reason. As a result, most everyone expects to be treated with dignity but he or she cannot explain why. Cheshire (2004) defines human dignity as the exalted moral status that every human being uniquely possesses. Human dignity is a given reality, intrinsic to the human substance, and not contingent upon any functional capacity that varies. Evidence of this is found in reasoning, language, conscience, and free will, which humans have the capacity to exercise and develop unless restricted by disease, coercion, or will. Possessing human dignity carries with it certain moral obligations to treat other human beings with the respect due them.

There is much discussion of the concept of human dignity in Holy Scripture, where humans are to be treated according to the biblical ideal of worthiness. This requires each one to treat another in a manner that is pleasing to God. Human dignity is expressed in Genesis 1:26; it is explained that humanity's likeness to the Divine stresses the essential holiness and, by implication, dignity of all, without distinction. Human dignity has played an increasingly important role in secular society. Officers who served during the American Revolution in 1783 formed the Society of the Cincinnati, a fraternal order advancing the principle to preserve human rights and liberties, without which the rational being is cursed instead of blessed. More recently, the *Universal Declaration of Human Rights* (United Nations 1948) stipulates that all human beings are born free and equal in dignity and rights. Likewise, the principle of individual autonomy that flows from much of the bioethical literature is founded on a fundamental appreciation of human dignity (Cheshire 2004).

Philosophical Basis

Only within a truly cross-cultural dialogue will ideas of human dignity be finally meaningful. It is assumed that such a dialogue is possible between cultural and religious traditions. By situating any discussion of human rights on religious traditions, the focus of any discussion of human rights provides a larger understanding of the common good and of ultimate purpose (Strain 1995). One of the implicit understandings of this work is that a cross-cultural dialogue on human rights and the environment has become an essential requirement at the end of the 20th and at the beginning of the 21st centuries. In Western theology, traditional human dignity is rooted in the creative act of God. For Buddhists and traditional Native Americans, on the other hand, it is the embededness of human beings in the wider context of reality that grounds human dignity. In other words, human beings are inextricably interrelated with other beings and do not have a privileged place among them (Dalton 1959, 31).

Religious Philosophies

The Prophet Jeremiah calls people to recognize dignity, not just of God through their ritual observance, but also of human beings through social justice (Jones 1968):

> For if you truly amend your ways and your doings, if you do not oppress the alien, the orphan, and the widow, or shed innocent blood in this place, and if you do not go after other gods of your own heart, then I will dwell with you in this place.

Jeremiah calls the worshippers to recognize the dignity of all people, particularly the marginalized in society, the people with no voice, namely, resident aliens, orphans, and widows. He calls these people to perform deeds of righteousness that ameliorate the conditions of the poor (Scullion 1999, 20). The prophets also challenge the individual to identify and condemn the subtle and not-so-subtle acts of violence in society. Violence is destructive whether in the form of oppression, infanticide, anger, vengeance, or hatred. According to Scullion, people of violence are not imagining God. Jesus' death on the cross revealed the victimization mechanism of scapegoating and the deceit of violence.

It is necessary to expose modern attempts to make scapegoats and the deceit of violence (Scullion 1999, 25).

While Islam, Judaism, and Christianity are all concerned with the excesses of materialism, Buddhism, Hinduism, and Native American traditions appear to be largely nonmaterialistic. It is interesting that the mystics from each tradition seem to be experiencing and talking about the same thing: the idea that life is always in transition, that things are often not what they seem, that it is essential to love God and serve the truth. The great wisdom traditions all say that the meaning of life is not found in what is possessed but the kind of person each one is. Whether literally incarcerated in a prison, most are at one time or another hostages to the inner person dominated by fear and anger. The way to liberation is through love, compassion, and peace while the way to remaining in the inner prison is through attachment to such things as the accumulation of wealth, attainment of success, and the grasping for power. Those who live out these traditions show by their lives the way to peace is difficult but simple, inviting, but not compelling. They show that love, kindness, peace, humility, and determination are much more valuable than financial security. This requires service and sacrifice. Peace, love, and happiness do not exist in some reconstructed sense of social utopia but within the person.

Human dignity stems from what a person essentially is. Aristotle argued that man is a political and a rational animal (Hutchins 1988). Human nature indicates that each is intelligent and capable of exercising free will. Aristotle also believed that humans were essentially unequal beings in the sense that he believed in a meritocracy where people with appropriate gifts and talents should lead a nation. He is famous for saying that certain people should rule who are able to rule best. These attributes reveal a spiritual dimension in the human being and uncover the human nature that is quite dynamic in its development. The duty to respect and affirm human dignity involves definite and specific obligations. Human dignity should be respected and affirmed without question or hesitation, as a matter of course, and as though the alternative is unthinkable (Boxill 1992). Human dignity requires respect for the "real person." The term *real person* is a label used to identify the dignity consequent upon the human's nature (Cronan 1955, 4). The question of the value of a human is the standard measure of how each should treat the other (Cronan 1955, xiv).

St. Thomas Aquinas The Thomistic synthesis, which is a compilation of St. Thomas Aquinas's commentaries, reaches its full bloom in *Summa Theologica*. In *Summa Theologica*, Aquinas (Encyclopedia Britannica 1988) argues that human dignity is brought about by the perfect union of body and the soul. A perfect union is considered complete. Dignity is embedded in the substance of the person and not determined by any particular quality in the person. Saints and sinners alike are bestowed with the same level of dignity. Furthermore, people have the ability to rationally consider problems and solutions and to make choices on how they want to live. People can be self-determining. Free will would be senseless if it did not at the same time mean people have the capability to recognize good and have the will to choose it (Roos 1998, 55). *Goodness* is an other-regarding activity in that one is altruistic and cares to see others do well.

The Renaissance

The Renaissance, and especially the Enlightenment of the 17th and 18th centuries, represented a fundamental turning point in the foundations of the Western conception of human rights. The base for modern human rights theory was laid at that time (Mayer 1995, 37). With the Renaissance, Reformation, and Enlightenment, the individual became more central in religious as well as political thinking. The dignity of the person became identified with the dignity of the individual. According to Powers et al. (1995), Pico della Mirandola (1463–1494), during the Italian Renaissance, argued that human dignity is recognized in a person's rational powers, the moral choices each makes, and his or her ability to develop a vision of a better world. Earlier doctrines of human duties gave way to the conviction that human rights should be central in political theory. Human beings were now understood to be autonomous and in possession of certain inalienable rights. Universal standards and values were discernable by rational beings and these are inherent to the human condition (Powers et al. 1995, 5). These ideas influenced such documents as the English Petition of Rights (1627), the Habeas Corpus Act (1679), the Declaration of Independence (1776), the U.S. Constitution (1787), the Declaration of the Rights of Man and of the Citizen (1789) (Pollis and Schwab 1979, 2).

The Age of Reason

The main complaint of the Age of Reason was the moral injustices of a wrongful conviction (Johnson 1988, 119). One of the key concerns was the denial of the offender's dignity as played out in the excessively harsh law and the reliance on the use of torture to extract confessions. Enlightened thought on criminal procedure sprang from a new view of the relationship of the individual to society: In the words of Montesquieu (Carrithers 1977, 158):

> . . . in moderate governments, . . . the life of the meanest subject is deemed precious, . . . and no one can be deprived of honor or property except after a long inquiry during which he has been given every possible opportunity to make a defense.

Kant Rationalist Perspective

Immanuel Kant (1724–1784), a German philosopher during the Age of Enlightenment, defined the principle of human dignity this way in 1785: "Act so that you treat humanity, whether in your own person or in that of another, always as an end and never as a means only" (Kant 1996). In other words, Kant insists that people are not to be manipulated by the pretense of human dignity as a means to an expedient outcome. Kant's view of human dignity assumes an ideal world in which his imperative would be relatively easy to follow. In the real world, it should be strongly considered as an aspiration to consider in the treatment of others.

Bedau (1992) elaborates further on Kant's notion of human dignity. According to Bedau, dignity is granted because people are seen to have the capacity to do good. It is their human potential, not what they deserve or have done that matters. Individual persons do not vary in their dignity or worth. Human dignity is shared equally, essentially as a form of moral egalitarianism. Under the law, everyone assumes an equal amount of responsibility and obligation; no one can act with impunity. Human dignity respects the fact that people possess autonomy. This autonomy is analogous to a captain sailing a ship on the Atlantic Ocean. The captain determines when to begin the voyage. He also sets the direction the ship is headed, assesses from time to time whether the ship is on course, makes the appropriate changes in the compass settings by issuing orders to the crew, and reflects on how well the crew is doing in meeting its scheduled arrival. Probation officers, farmers, lawyers, teachers, construction workers, parents, and all other humans do the same thing. Autonomy is aided by rational thought that enables people to understand the world they live in and how to maximize their self-interests within it.

Although the Kantian notion of human dignity may be nothing more than a secular counterpart to the religious conception of human dignity offered earlier by Aquinas, Kant's ideas, nonetheless, were fairly radical for their time because they claimed ordinary people had a value when slavery and aristocratic doctrine said otherwise. The inherent value of the individual played a part in both the American and French revolutions. By virtue of possessing human dignity, persons deserve certain kinds of treatment, a form of treatment that clearly indicates the person has worth. Personal worth, whether in ourselves or in others, is indicated by the respect accorded them.

Modernist Perspectives

Charles Abel (2004) outlines various modernist arguments in favor of inherent human dignity. Existentialists believe that humans commit themselves to an equality of human life prospects; therefore, equality is neither a goal nor a right but an artifact of social existence. Libertarians emphasize that freedom gives humans value because it separates humans from other animals. The pragmatist suggests that human worth is an expression of an attitude humans have toward other people. Rational agency is based on the argument that freedom and well-being are dependent on the exercise of independent thought processes and therefore is a fundamental right. John Rawls in *A Theory of Justice* (1971) argues in favor of the original position elaborated of total equality; no one would agree to have less dignity than another because that would not be in one's self-interest. The legalist would argue that the rule of law may be yet another means of protecting personal freedom. Observance of the rule of law is necessary if the law is to respect human dignity. Human autonomy may be limited by personal ignorance of the various options, an inability to decide as to what to do or to select choices, or having no choices at all (Raz 1983). In addition, Taboada (2003) states that morality is not about ethical principles, commandments, or laws but primarily about the proper response to the person's essential dignity.

A Code of Ethics

The APPA code of ethics challenges probation officers to treat their charges with as much dignity as humanly possible within the context of the complexities of the real world. Probation officers must recognize the potential in each of their probationers. Probation officers must recognize that people are far more than the sum total of their worst actions. According to Karp and Clear (2002), probation officers who emphasize social integration have to balance individual freedoms of expression with expectations of conformity especially with youth, minorities, and nonconformists in general. Consequently, the probation officer must walk a thin line between careful supervision and allowing the offender to experiment with decision making. Courts must become comfortable with a degree of experimentation. Ultimately, a rehabilitated offender is one who can make appropriate decisions on his or her own. Despite a pattern of poor choices, probationers are self-conscious, rational individuals whose thoughts must be understood as a rational story or explanation of what happened and how they feel and think. It is when one rejects this presentation of the probationer as someone offering an honest appraisal of himself or herself that one is most inclined to deny his or her essential dignity. Too often it is assumed that an explanation is a justification or excuse when it is actually all someone has to offer. It is the purpose of probation to develop a greater understanding of the self.

Obligations of Human Dignity

Human dignity is a normative principle. Goolam (2001) proposes that the fundamental values promoted by the South African courts today are human dignity, equality, and freedom. Goolam goes on to say that human rights laws must serve the purpose of effectively protecting the rights and human dignity of the members of society by making moral demands on the state. This is an imperative assertion that flows from an attribute of life itself; thus the people through the state are duty bound to uphold human dignity. The universal recognition of human dignity promotes a greater sense of tolerance. *Tolerance* is an active attitude that is prompted by the recognition of universal human rights and fundamental rights of individuals, groups, and states.

The duty to respect and affirm human dignity involves definite and specific obligations. One might conclude that any threat to a person's capacity to be human is a threat to his or her dignity. If anything diminishes, eradicates, or ignores the capacity to imagine, feel, think, or will, it diminishes human dignity (DiSanto 1999, 59). Recognizing the qualities present in human dignity leads one to respect another. Some people are respected, for example, because they hold a prestigious office. When prestigious office holders leave office, they no longer are so highly esteemed because they no longer have the power that goes with the office. Others are respected because people recognize their inherent dignity. *Respect,* as applied to probation, consists in an affirmative, rationally grounded recognition of and regard for a status that all human beings have by virtue of their inherent dignity. Respect is displayed in an attempt to understand another's culture, lifestyle, and modes of thought. Lack of respect is an indignity.

Indignity

One particular form of indignity that often impacts a probationer is disrespect. **Disrespect** is found among officers who view offenders as different from themselves in terms of the possession of one (or more) negative attribute, thus conferring inferiority upon the offender. Disrespect is conveyed in words and deeds. It occurs in probation work when officers reduce human beings to certain simple and fixed types, usually distinguishable by a single attribute such as race,

disrespect is found among officers who view offenders as different from themselves in terms of the possession of one (or more) negative attribute, thus conferring inferiority upon the offender. Disrespect is conveyed in words and deeds.

skin color, religion, sexual orientation, gender, wealth, intelligence, or social status. Mockery is but another form of disrespect. If people are accorded human dignity, they are respected and taken seriously but mockery denies these assumptions and presents them as foolish, vain, and absurd (Boxill 1992, 103). The probationer is reduced to being judged on grounds that have nothing to do with moral character (Parent 1992, 61). Lastly, as in the case of probation, officers have an abundance of power over the probationer, much of it based on knowledge of an offender's human frailties. While under supervision, probationers relinquish autonomy, independence, reasoning, freedom, and self-determinism. This knowledge carries with it the ability of the officer to either heal or harm. When used inappropriately, it causes much harm by putting support and understanding further out of reach. Such degradation can inflict psychic wounds and also impose tangible and material harms. The imposition of stigma upon the offender not only reflects fear of those who are different, but also fear of elements within one's self. Organizations that permit degradation by not reacting forcefully against it degrade themselves (Minnow 1992). The legal code is an instrument of justice but it also guards against corruption of the heart that occurs when probation officers no longer care about the offender. The rule of law furthers the cause of justice by providing everyone with an understanding of what to expect when under the control of the law.

Peacemaking

Human dignity comes into actuality in community corrections when considering its application through peacemaking. Braswell, Fuller, and Lozoff (2001) have written an insightful work on what is needed for an officer to treat offenders with dignity by attending to the concept of peacemaking. **Peacemaking** is a valuable process, a personal transformation the officer undergoes in order to achieve a positive state of well-being that allows him or her to address the needs of the offender. If one wants the offender to become a good person, one must first treat them as a good person. Peace is not found in the acquisition of things but about truth and love. The meaning of life is found in the kind of person one is, not what is displayed.

Various aspects of peacemaking have been supported by many of the world's religions. They support the notion that each must die to the personal self to do good for others and to consider living simple lives to aid the transformations. These transformations must be deep, genuine, personal, and spiritual, putting individual plans on hold and thinking of the needs of others. Each person must view the world as a community and not as a source of anger, hatred, and discrimination. If the officer employs a peacemaking philosophy in his or her work, the officer will promote nonviolence, social justice, and inclusion, employ the correct means to achieve the end, use objective criteria to assess achievement of the goals, and emphasize Kant's categorical imperative.

Peacemaking is founded on nonviolence; peacemakers believe that violence begets violence. Peacemakers also address social justice in that they are willing to take a comprehensive view of the underlying conflict inherent in the offense

peacemaking is a personal transformation the officer undergoes in order to achieve a positive state of well-being that allows him or her to address the needs of the offender. If one wants the offender to become a good person, one must first become a good person.

and believe in repairing the relationship that causes suffering. Inclusion means the probation officer is concerned that everyone affected by the problem participates in its solution. This means consideration is given to the offender, victim, community, and the criminal justice system. Offenders should have some say in their own sentencing. By employing the correct means, an attempt is made to protect the offender's rights and to engage in a process that has a chance for success. Many problems are caused when the criminal justice system is not a paragon of fairness and virtue. By employing objective criteria to assess various peacemaking practices, a person allows others to accept and understand how peacemaking works and how it has affected them. Lastly, peacemaking calls for a level of moral reasoning; this suggests that each one treats others well because each in turn will be treated well. A person cannot be indifferent to those under supervision if he or she hopes to have them take their supervision seriously.

Goal Conflict

Many introductory texts on community corrections discuss the probation officer's dilemma inherent in trying to accomplish the goals of crime control versus client welfare. Probation officer professional goal conflict is a factor that has been noticed by many writers. (For instance, see: Allen et al. 1985; Czajkoski 1973; Ellsworth 1990; Glaser 1969; Jacobs 1990; Klockars 1972; Lipsky 1980; McCleary 1978; Ohlin et al., 1956; Tomaino 1975; Whitehead 1989). The professional goals of a probation officer can lead to problems with human dignity. The conflict is expressed in interactions with probationers. Organizational and work-related research indicate that most probation officers are caring and respectful individuals (Jacobs 1990). They treat their clients with dignity and assist them in making significant changes in their lives.

However, a vast body of organizational and occupational research suggests that anyone in a position of power is capable of exploiting a relationship or succumbing to personal weaknesses that take advantage of a subordinate. Raz (1983) suggests that one way that the individual's autonomy is limited is through the use of an insult, enslavement, or manipulation. An insult offends a person's dignity if it consists of or implies a denial that a person is an autonomous person or that he or she deserves to be treated as one. An action enslaves someone if for all intents and purposes the environment is so manipulated so as to deny another person any choice of action. Manipulation of a person occurs when someone is subject to changing tastes, beliefs, or the ability to act or decide.

Deliberate indifference to the rule of law can violate someone's dignity (Raz 1983). The violation of the rule of law leads probationers to a sense of uncertainty or frustrated or disappointed expectations about the conditions of probation. Uncertainty is problematical because people are unable to plan for the future. This, too, again denies people their autonomy, thus denying them their dignity. More typically, a person violates the autonomy (dignity) of another when exercising patronizing and condescending supervision and control over the other or (worse yet) manipulates the other by using force or fraud in order to achieve some good or end chosen without regard to the other's welfare or capacity for autonomy. Such patronizing or manipulative behavior is insulting, undignified, and an affront to the other person's status as a human being.

Probation officers are not immune from this practice. Some officers are cynical, burned out, frustrated, and overworked and are experiencing sympathy fatigue (an exhausted sense of concern for others where the person is unable to have compassion for another person's problems). Others, due to personal weakness or personal problems, succumb to the manipulations of the client. Officers may deny the dignity of the probationer in numerous ways. Some examples include pocketing a probationer's restitution money, having sex with a probationer, applying unreasonable force on the probationer, using drugs with a probationer, cursing a probationer, directing racial slurs at the probationer, sending probationers to a poorly performing program for the sole purpose of punishment, sending probationers to expensive programs the probationer cannot afford, misinforming the probationer as to what might happen in the future, scheduling appointments with little possibility of the probationer keeping them, lying to a judge about the behavior of the probationer, failing to give the probationer time when the probationer reports on schedule, making the probationer wait unnecessarily for a meeting, sharing professional confidentialities with unauthorized persons, and putting something in the presentence report that cannot be verified.

Degradation Rituals

<u>Degradation rituals</u> are personal affronts to the individual's dignity that are used to further humiliate the person. A degradation ritual might involve taking a urine sample or conducting a strip search of the offender. All of these practices form a paradigm of degradation when they are converted to repeated stories about probationers. As officers are promoted through the ranks, it is likely that some of these stories are passed on to the upper ranks in the department, causing similar reciprocal problems for the hierarchical supervisor who must not only treat those below him or her with dignity but also ensure that officers in turn treat others with dignity. The probation officers' objectification of the probationer, resulting from a lack of respect, is a process that is akin to that employed by offenders to deny the essence of the victim. That process suggests the crime was the victim's fault or that he or she had it coming; it facilitates a lack of responsibility and thus diminishes the sense of guilt for the harm caused to individuals and communities.

Treatment Value

The principles of human dignity are essential to any effective treatment program. It is difficult to develop a set of behaviors consistent with social expectations when the exhibiter is not doing what is expected of everyone else. This is true of teachers, clergy, sports stars, political leaders, police officers, and probation officers. If the probationer is treated as though he or she has worth, the probationer can learn to treat others as though they, too, have worth. Through the use of modeling behavior, and by teaching the probationer to respond constructively to comments about his or her own behavior, behavior can be corrected

degradation rituals are personal affronts to the individual's dignity that are used to further humiliate the person. A degradation ritual might involve taking a urine sample or conducting a strip search of the offender.

Figure 1.1 Human dignity requires the officer to teach the offender how to engage in a self-assessment process: how to reflect properly on one's own behavior in terms of one's actions, the outcome of these actions, and the meaning it holds. *Source: Photo courtesy of Edward Sieh.*

that does not respect others. It is not enough to simply expose someone to anticriminal modeling; one needs to exhibit support for prosocial values through thought, word, and deed.

Modeling

Modeling is the key to effective learning, as indicated in research on offenders, parenting, and aggression. Modeling also has importance relative to the cognitive learning processes associated with one's thoughts, beliefs, values, and perceptions (Bandura 1977). Good modeling and good interpersonal skills prove most effective, especially for probation officers. Andrews (1980) found that probation officers who modeled anticriminal behaviors and sentiments and possessed good relational skills had the lower recidivism scores. Officers who scored low on relational measures and failed to model prosocial behavior and sentiments tended to have clients who had higher rates of recidivism. Even the officers who had good relational skills but failed to appropriately model their behavior had higher recidivism scores. The officers who had low relational scores but were strong on anticriminal modeling did not achieve the desired recidivism reduction.

A growing body of research shows the qualities of good role modeling. According to Bandura and others (Bandura 1965, 1977; Bandura et al. 1963; Bandura and Walters 1963), these factors are attractiveness, competence, and receiving rewards for one's behavior. Andrews and Bonta (1998) noted good models are enthusiastic, open, and flexible and afford others a chance to express their feelings and opinions. They also present vivid models that reward compliance and achievement. The relationship qualities involve maintaining an environment of mutual liking, respect, and caring in which openness, warmth, and understanding are offered within clearly understood interpersonal boundaries. This does not mean the probation officer does not get angry with the probationer who skips treatment. The officer can be honest about his or her anger and yet limit his or her comments to the behavior and its consequences. The officer retains the belief in the client's ability to succeed and in his or her inherent worth as an individual.

Positive Reinforcement Positive reinforcement is conveyed through emphatic and immediate expressions of warmth and understanding but also by using eye contact, hand shakes, smiles, the sharing of experiences, the holding of timely meetings, and making every effort to give the probationer undivided attention when in the office. Conversely, probationers should receive a clear explanation of the counselor's reasons for approval or disapproval with suggestion for the appropriate behavior as an alternative (Van Voorhis 2000, 152). Office politics and cynicism must not be allowed to interfere with maintaining a warm and professional relationship. The probation officers must defeat any expeditious, ends-justify-the-means thinking that denies the significance of the victim or the presence of any victim at all. In an excellent list of examples of distorted cognitive thinking, Samenow (1984, 1989) points out that offenders often blame others for their crimes; deny responsibility for their actions; fail to understand the concept of injury; fail to empathize with the victim; fail to put enough effort forward to accomplish goals; assume ownership of others' property; fail to understand what is trustworthy behavior; expect others to adopt to their way of thinking; make rash decisions; refuse to let their pride suffer for a mistake; have flawed understanding of the time and effort needed for success; refuse to accept criticism; deny occasions of real fear; use anger to control others; and seem overzealous in their efforts to obtain power. In sum, offenders experience a great deal of distorted thinking, which functions as a considerable impediment to change.

In the modeling process and in conjunction with efforts to attack dysfunctional thoughts, beliefs, and attitudes, special consideration should be made to support and encourage ideas promoting human dignity in consideration of past actions and future behavior. Probationers should be encouraged to attend to personal statements that express disrespect. Appropriate recognition should be given to statements expressing individual value and worth. Such expressions are particularly relevant as they pertain to the victim. True progress is indicated when the offender uses positive expressions about helpful social institutions such as schools and treatment programs. This may be the most difficult of assignments.

Underpinning effective behavior modeling is human dignity. Despite the crime, the probation officer must respect the probationer. This respect occurs when the offender is viewed as a person and this attitude is exhibited in moments of concern and kindness. Many probationers are simply looking for someone to care about them. There is also a sense among experienced officers that almost anyone can find his or her way onto probation. Such officers develop a strong but unofficial sense of moral egalitarianism. Under moral egalitarianism, everyone is subject to the same code of behavior and to the same punishments. Most importantly, moral egalitarianism accepts the notion that everyone makes mistakes, no one is perfect, and that all need forgiveness and understanding provided by probation.

Self-Correction

One of the critical components of human dignity is the recognition that humans are self-correcting. Human dignity requires the officer to teach the offender how to engage in a self-assessment process: how to reflect properly on one's own behavior in terms of one's actions, the outcome of these actions, and the meaning it holds. When properly developed, probationers should become comfortable with self-activating, self-directing, self-criticizing, self-correcting, and self-understanding processes that can not only help keep them free of crime, but make them better people as well. In other words, the experience of rehabilitation and change provides tools that allow the offender to view himself or herself as others do and thus correct the impression the offender provides others of his or her own behavior.

A fully rehabilitated person is capable of effectively evaluating his or her actions. More importantly, one is able to organize one's life, predict future events, and explain one's actions or conjecture about what will happen under various courses of action. This requires the officer to recognize when this is happening. Due to the inherent need to emphasize offender surveillance, there is a tendency in probation to overlook positive change and focus on negative performance. Due to the pressures of the caseload, many officers eventually come to see the need for increased probationer autonomy. With increased autonomy comes infrequent contact and reduced levels of supervision and reinforcement. Incorrectly, some officers with large caseloads assume that decreasing contact will somehow accomplish what more frequent contact could not provide. How one treats another reflects more on who the person is than on the character of the person receiving the treatment.

Implementation

Many kinds of organizations consider it important to treat clients with dignity. As stated earlier, the mission statement for the community corrections agency in Maricopa County, Arizona, clearly calls for treating clients with respect, but there is always the question of whether they go beyond providing lip service to the concept. Various measures can be employed to provide an atmosphere in which human dignity is promoted in the workplace. First, this is a proposal that must be supported by top management. Initially, those wishing to promote this notion must begin by gaining the support of top political figures and the probation officers' association. These two should see that human dignity is expressly valued in the vision and mission statements, policy directives, and procedural manuals. Second, the program supporting human dignity must be viewed in terms of the entire organization. If human dignity is to become an important workplace value, it must be applied throughout the entire organization including support staff, professionals, and probationers. Human dignity must become a hallmark of the general management style of the organization and employed equally with people regardless of age, gender, race, ethnicity, or status. It is taken for granted in human resource departments that the most important employee decision is whether to hire someone. An important beginning point is to utilize hiring procedures that assess personal views on human dignity. Various screening mechanisms could be put into place to test the applicant's attitudes on the matter. The goal is to hire personnel who place value on human dignity and are willing to express their views on it. To further support a dignified work environment, periodic assessment and training programs could be instituted. Assessments could be made to determine if the officers' attitudes have deteriorated over time. It would be important to keep data on the officers' stance over time, especially because cynicism affects many criminal justice jobs around the seventh year. Some officers may not be aware that their attitude has changed with the additional work experience. One aspect of the training would encourage officers to have experiences with minority group members or marginalized populations who are not having trouble with the law.

Work environments are complex systems displaying a variety of values and attitudes each day. In community-based corrections, it is hoped that the dominant values express concern for the victim, offender, community, and agency. However, many work environments have a culture that expresses values about the victim or the offender that are part of the daily colloquial interplay in the office. For example, probationers may be denigrated informally by their race, offenses, sexual preference, or mental state thus developing a label transmitted throughout the office. The problem occurs when private discussions using these terms are overheard by someone who is concerned with the application of the term.

Respecting the dignity of all humans is morally, ethically, socially, and politically correct. Dignity will not become a priority unless there are procedures in place to enforce abuses of it. Reporting mechanisms must be available for those who feel they have been mistreated, impartial investigations need to be undertaken, and appropriate and fair reactions should be put into place. It should also be emphasized that these things are not done to achieve any so-called political correctness but to express values inherent in people regardless of where they fall on the political spectrum. Human dignity is expressed in the values promoted by restorative justice and peacemaking. In fact, the most important thing associated with restorative justice are the values that promotes vindication, healing, and resolution.

■ Prisons and Human Dignity

If one is to understand community-based corrections, one needs to understand institutional corrections and associated problems. The Bureau of Justice Statistics (Glaze and Palla 2004) reports that as of July 2004 there were 6,889,800 persons under correctional supervision in the United States. This country has undergone a tremendous growth in prison population over the last 25 years. According to Glaze and Palla, in 1980, there were 1,118,097 probationers; 183,988 jail inmates; 319,598 prison inmates; 220,438 parolees; and a total of 1,842,100 persons under correctional supervision. By year end 2003, there were 4,073,987 probationers; 691,301 jail inmates; 1,387,269 prison inmates; and 774,588 parolees for a total of 6,732,400 persons under correctional supervision. This expansion in the number of offenders led to a huge increase in the number of prisons. The number of state prison facilities increased from 600 prisons in the mid-1970s to over 1,000 prisons by the end of 2000 (Lawrence and Travis 2004).

It is clear that after nearly 200 years of operation, prisons have proven themselves incapable of maintaining the human dignity of their incarcerated residents. The crime rate has gone down but the correctional populations have continued to expand. For some, this seems anomalous; however, prisons have historically been overcrowded (Sieh 1989a).

Why continue to send so many people to prison? For several decades now, the United States has conducted a war on drugs and has put numerous first-time offenders in prison with lengthy sentences. Mauer, Potler, and Wolf (1999) at the Sentencing Project (a nonprofit organization based in Washington, D.C.) point out that since the 1980s, women are being sent to prison at a rate that is double that of men. Drug offenses accounted for 50 percent of the increase in the number of women sent to prison between 1986 and 1996. Also contributing to this problem are sentencing guidelines, especially at the federal level, that require mandatory minimum sentences for crimes that if prosecuted at the state level would lead to an intermediate sanction such as probation, restitution, or community service. In addition, these sentencing guidelines have imposed lengthy sentences that have contributed to the buildup of the prisoner population. At some point in the future, the rate of admissions might match the rate of releases from prisons at which point the prison population should stabilize. Another contributing factor is the general public's attitude supporting the growth of prison populations. In the not-too-distant past, various community groups vigorously opposed the building of a prison in their communities. Now, rural communities in the northern rust-belt states experiencing an exodus of businesses welcome any effort to revitalize the economy. In these communities, someone who has been an assembler at a windshield-wiper plant might become a correctional officer.

In addition to the considerations just discussed, there is one further matter that is often overlooked: level of criminal activity measured by FBI data reports. Police efficiency is measured by the clearance rate, the ratio of number of arrests to the number of reported crimes. Clearance rates do not approach 100 percent, even for murder. In the Federal Bureau of Investigation reports for 1999, a 21 percent crime index clearance rate, excluding arson, was recorded for law enforcement agencies nationwide. In 1999, 50 percent of violent crimes were cleared as compared to 18 percent of property crimes. Clearance rates are generally higher for violent crimes than for property offenses. The murder clearance rate was 69 percent; aggravated assault, 59 percent; forcible rape, 49 percent; and robbery, 29 percent. For property offenses, 19 percent of the larceny thefts, 15 percent of the motor vehicle thefts, and 14 percent of the burglaries were cleared (FBI 1999, 201). It seems clear that the prisoner population generated by these arrest statistics could increase 79 percent, if the crime rate stabilized and the authorities arrested all the people for the crimes they committed. If this were true, the number of people incarcerated could reach 3,627,606 persons. The country is not prepared to house that many offenders.

Prison overcrowding leads to increased instances of theft, looser control over inmates, and a breakdown in inmate solidarity. Classification and work assignments are also hindered with an overabundance of workers and too much idleness. Inmates sometimes become frustrated and attack each other or staff members. Official forms of violence increase because the guards do not know how to handle problems without special training or additional staff. As a result of high population counts, prisoners have health-related problems, especially mental health issues; prisoners do not receive the rehabilitation they require; prison violence continues; and there are serious effects on the outside community (Sieh 1989).

Cost of Punishment

Stephan (2004) reports that the cost of incarceration is considerable: States spent $29.5 billion for prisons in 2001. This is a 150 percent increase over the $11.7 billion spent on imprisonment in 2001. Prison operation consumed 77 percent of state correctional costs in fiscal year 1986. The average cost of operating state prisons in fiscal year 2001 was $100 per U.S. resident, up from $90 in fiscal year 1996. According to Stephan, California reported the largest prison expenditure, $4.2 billion, and North Dakota the smallest, $26.8 million. The average cost per inmate in fiscal year 2001 was $22,515. The spending on medical care totaled $3.3 billion or 12 percent of the operating cost of these prisons.

Probation and parole are attractive penal measures if for no other reason than the fact that they are less expensive than incarceration. According to Camp and Camp (1999), the average per diem cost of probation is $2.35, parole is $5.62, and the cost for probation and parole combined is $3.65. When one considers the different forms of supervision, per diem, regular supervision is $5.86, intensive is $9.65, electronic monitoring is $9.49, and special caseload supervision is $7.39. As indicated, intensive supervision, the most expensive form of supervision, costs $3,522.25 per annum per client. Intensive supervision, the most expensive form of community supervision, is one-tenth as costly as imprisonment (Camp and Camp 1999).

Less Eligibility

Programs intended for prisoners are always subject to careful scrutiny. The public is often concerned that prisoners are given things they do not deserve. The public neglects to take into account the fact that the life of a prisoner is dangerous and difficult. Prisoners have been considered lower in status than slaves because they are viewed as blameworthy and thus have little value to the rest of us.

Inasmuch as prisoners are considered blameworthy, they are in vulnerable positions. For years, the infliction of whatever treatment was deemed necessary in the name of punishment carried little fear that these measures were excessive. As a result of the notion of punishment, prisoners were subject to the principle of less eligibility. The principle of **less eligibility** stipulates that if imprisonment is to act as a deterrent, the treatment given the prisoner should be perceived as not superior to that provided a member of the lowest significant social class in the free society (Sieh 1989b, 159). For a marginalized member of society, regardless of how bad prison is for others, prison may be a relief from the hardships on the outside. Less eligibility is a powerful concept that has greatly influenced the policies and operations of the correctional system (Sieh 1989b, 159). It certainly has provided justification for not supporting rehabilitative efforts underway in this country's prisons. What this means is that the prisoner's

less eligibility stipulates that if imprisonment is to act as a deterrent, the treatment given the prisoner should be perceived as not superior to that provided a member of the lowest significant social class in the free society.

quality of life should not be better than the working poor. Prisoners should not be eligible for high-quality free education, health care, meals, and housing. This also means that any amenity provided the inmate could be granted and then taken away when conditions shift on the outside. It also means that technological changes must gain universal acceptance before they are introduced into the prison, and only if they are proven not to create a security risk.

Prison Value

The principal value prisoners have is most evident in the communities where the prison is a major employer. Without the prisoners, there are few jobs. Once prisons are built, they are kept full but never demobilized. The public pays for expensive secure constructions and for their operations but most would prefer that prisons not exist. For many people, prison inmates might as well be from outer space. Other than what they see in movies or read in books, most people do not have much knowledge of what it is like to be in prison. Rarely does the general public venture inside the walls for a tour or to visit someone. It is assumed by most that prisoners are treated well and, in some cases, treated too well. Careful examination of the actual treatment given to prisoners reveals an altogether different world. Prison is difficult, dangerous, and, for many offenders, ineffective in reducing pro-criminal attitudes. Beliefs are beginning to change. It is argued here that if offenders are to change, it is essential that they be treated with dignity—the type of dignity befitting a human being.

History of Prisons

Prior to the advent of the penitentiary, public forms of punishment were quite hideous. Brutal measures of punishment were intended to make an impression on the illiterate minds of the superstitious masses coming to witness a public execution in a town square. Public executions could involve a hanging, beheading, drawing and quartering, a vivisection, and impalement on a stake followed by a burning. At one time, the English had over 200 different offenses for which anyone could be put to death (Hirsch 1992). A death sentence 300 years ago, or even 100 years ago, was a common experience. Life was cheap and ephemeral. According to Hirsch, inasmuch as prison sought to rehabilitate offenders, supporters viewed it as a more benevolent solution to crime than the bloody alternatives such as capital punishment, corporal punishments that relied on deterrence, and incapacitation.

The prison was invented as a rational response to these brutal measures. Prisons were, in part, originally conceived as a rational means of punishment inasmuch as the offender served a penalty commensurate with the seriousness of the crime (Hirsch 1992). More importantly, imprisonment was intended as an egalitarian punishment in which everyone would experience the passage of time in a similar fashion regardless of social standing. Hirsch also pointed out that the prison would be a major improvement in the punishment of the offender and would begin to offer some measure of reformation. It was thought that the prison, instead of reintegrating the offender back into the community, would draw the offender out of the criminal subculture.

Prisoner Privileges

Prisons are environments in which everything on the outside that is taken for granted is inside considered a privilege. Prisoners find that all decisions are made for them. As a result, prisoners who have trouble making law-abiding decisions do not have any chance to make their own decisions. This may be considered an appropriate denial of freedom but, as has occurred in such places as Eastern Europe, Russia, and Africa, it is difficult to teach anyone the intricacies of democracy if the person has been socialized in a dictatorial regime. The importance of the rule of law has to be reestablished—and to further highlight the importance of the state's power over each offender, each state now has one "impregnable" institution in the guise of a super-maximum prison. The facilities are intended to house the "worst of the worst." For the most part, as with the Oakpark Heights prison in Minnesota, much of it is comprised of redundant security measures, offering little in the way of residual function.

It may be surprising to many that a majority of all persons sent to prison, even the high-rate offenders, aspire to a relatively modest conventional life and hope to prepare for that while in prison. This point should be carefully considered because very little is done in prison to equip prisoners for conventional life on the outside (Irwin and Austin 1997, 137). To replace rehabilitation with punishment as the principal goal of imprisonment makes sense only if no one is released from prison. The released prisoner's decision to stay free of crime has more to do with the offender being older and maturing out of crime than it has with any sense of punishment or rehabilitation provided to the offender. The propensity to commit crime declines with the advance of age regardless of sex, race, country of origin, ethnicity, or offense. Glaze and Palla (2004) report that the younger the prisoner released on parole from prison, the higher the rate of recidivism. For example, over 80 percent of those under 18 were rearrested, as compared to 45 percent of those 45 or older.

Problems of Prisons

Over the last 20 years, community-based corrections have received considerable attention, resulting in the need to find alternatives to the high cost of prison overcrowding. More offenders are going to prison than ever before, principally for drug offenses. The problem is that many states realize they can overextend their budgets if they do not seek effective alternatives to imprisonment.

Health Concerns

Hammett (1998) has studied the health problems of inmates. Prisoners have significantly more medical problems than the general public because of the lack of attention given to their health before their arrest and because, once in prison, they live in crowded conditions, tend to be economically disadvantaged, and have high rates of substance abuse. Hammett also points out that inmates, when compared to the general public, have higher-than-average rates of infectious diseases such as HIV and AIDS; sexually transmitted diseases (STDs) such as syphilis, gonorrhea, and chlamydia; and tuberculosis (TB) all of which can be made more lethal by insufficient discharge planning and the lack of follow-up medical services. It is generally understood that these diseases will become more immune to treatment if the treatment protocol is not continued after discharge from prison. The prisoner not only has the disease but the disease becomes more virulent and harder to control. Evidence of this is found in New York State where, in 1991, a multidrug-resistant TB was identified, necessitating a series of collaborative efforts between public health and corrections (Hammett 1998).

Overcrowding

Prison overcrowding is another concern. Thornberry and Call (1983) note the connection between overcrowding and prison riots, violence, and assaults. Cobb (1985) also points out other problems associated with overcrowding. These include problems with high temperatures, poor ventilation, high noise levels, diminished hygiene standards, and higher incidences of communicable diseases. Prisoners living in crowding conditions are known to have elevated blood pressure levels and psychological problems that can lead to violence. Privacy is interrupted and older inmates develop other health maladies including increased levels of suicide (Thornberry and Call 1983).

The Elderly

Another problem faced by prisons is the number of elderly offenders serving time. Thousands of offenders are serving extremely long sentences. The National Center on Institutions and Alternatives (NCIA) (1998) reports that the number of offenders 55 years old or older grew from 6,500 in 1979 to over 50,000 in 1999. This means there are 7.5 times as many elderly offenders as there once were. It also notes that elderly offenders spend twice as much time in medical facilities as younger prisoners. The center notes that older prisoners consume medical dollars at a rate that is 3.1 times the rate of younger prisoners. Elderly prisoners in need of treatment for a chronic condition can have medical bills as high as $250,000 and the estimates of the yearly average cost to incarcerate an elderly inmate range from $60,000 to $80,000. Over $2.1 billion is spent annually to incarcerate inmates over 55 years old (NCIA 1998).

Finally, one must note the importance of prisoner mental illness. Camp and Camp (1997) report that there are nearly 42,000 inmates taking part in mental health programs in prison. Prisoners can develop a mental illness any time during a period of incarceration. This is especially true with the longer periods of incarceration so common today. What must be considered is that eventually all of these offenders will be released on supervised release and the supervising officer will have to find services for the ex-offender.

Rehabilitation

Rehabilitation in prison has not received the attention it was initially intended to receive. The underlying problem was that expectations ran high when correctional institutions were first put into place. Officials had promised programs and rehabilitation services but did not deliver them. According to Robert Johnson (1996), prison officials simply did not know how to implement these programs nor did they have sufficient resources and staff. More importantly, officials knew more about punishment and executions than they did about rehabilitation. These officials simply were not prepared to conduct a correctional enterprise.

For the most part, rehabilitation has, at best, been more a token than a reality for most prisoners. Considerable resentment developed among prisoners who were held in correctional institutions. For many confined to the correctional institution, the rehabilitation regime included a combination of vocational training, educational programming, and psychological treatment. It is understood that many of these programs were offered as mere tokens with few opportunities for all inmates to participate. Frequently, vocational programs were anachronistic to the outside world. As far as education in general was concerned, there was never a complete effort to ensure that all inmates left the prison with a high school diploma or its equivalent. Too often, the prisoner presented educational disabilities that could not be addressed by the institution's resources. In order to accommodate therapeutic needs, prisoners were given group therapy offered by guards or other prison staff who knew little about the inmate dynamic. In other words, prisoners in large therapy groups were asked to discuss problems that inmates felt were best kept secret from the staff. For example, prisoners may be asked to discuss a knifing that had recently occurred on the cellblock. Rather than discussing the incident and what precipitated the knifing, the group leader might hear a series of complaints about the lack of hot water or the poor medical care. The prisoners knew they risked being labeled a snitch by addressing prisoner violence in a group setting.

The Medical Model

medical model views the problem in terms of basic constitution, physical ailment, or to apply the model to social-adjustment problems in terms of identifying the problem, proscribing a treatment, and assessing when the cure has been effected.

Central to prisoner rehabilitation was the application of the **medical model**. The medical model assumed that an offender broke the law because of some defect or social or psychological pathology. The medical model views the problem in terms of basic constitution, physical ailment, or to apply the model to social-adjustment problems in terms of identifying the problem, proscribing a treatment, and assessing when the cure has been effected (Enos and Southern 1996). The medical model presumes the expert's responsibility is to first diagnose the disease or problem such as alcoholism or crime, discover the causes and clarify the symptoms, design the treatments, and determine when the person has been "cured."

The Indeterminate Sentence

The indeterminate sentence was conceived in the 1870s as a means of regulating the release of the rehabilitated offender. It was thought the authorities would identify offenders who had undergone rehabilitation and then release them. The medical model has been criticized on numerous grounds, especially because it was implemented in conjunction with the indeterminate sentence. The medical model alone is difficult to defend. First of all, social behavior in some circumstances is indicative of defective thinking and in other cases it is not. Killing someone in cold blood is qualitatively different from killing someone in self-defense. The medical model is also subject to attack because of who is making the decisions and how the offender is viewed. The values and ideologies of the decision maker clearly impact this process. In *Asylums* (1961), Goffman clearly identified the problems associated with stereotyping someone who is considered mentally ill. Another issue is that the model requires the cooperation of the patient, client, or prisoner. The prisoner can still be quite resistant. Furthermore, the prison is a difficult place to conduct treatment, especially since the setting is so artificial. There is little room to test reality. In relation to the indeterminate sentence, there is the issue of how one determines the prisoner is rehabilitated in a prisonized environment. How does one define rehabilitation and what techniques are employed to critically assess such actions? Attendance at church may indicate a religious conversion but it also may mean the prisoner simply finds the church as safe place away from the more predatory prisoners. Lastly, the model calls for society to understand what crime is and how it is caused. Most of the successful criminals in this world are never caught and those who are studied are the failures.

The indeterminate sentence, the principal means for implementing the medical model, has been attacked for several years. Most of the assault has been directed at the arbitrary way in which sentences are determined. Offenders appeared before a parole board and were denied parole for reasons that seemed unrelated to the crime and their performance in prison or the prisoners did not know the reason why they were denied or granted parole (Manocchio and Dunn 1970). In some cases, prisoners were told they needed to participate in more programs when few were available.

Rehabilitation

Prisons have taken a beating when it comes to assessing their rehabilitative functions. Institutional rehabilitation, designed to assist offenders, has been attacked as either hopeless naiveté put into practice or as merely another guise for exercising social control over inmate populations (Whitehead et al. 2003). In many cases, it has been more rhetoric than fact (Martinson 1974). Anyone who is writing on imprisonment must address the essential problems associated with three issues: the lack of support for rehabilitation; dominance of a prison culture that does not trust rehabilitation; and the failure of the medical model.

Violence

Prisons are certainly violent places. Silberman (1995) identifies violence as associated with riots that have occurred from 1950 to the present day. Some periods such as the early 1950s, late 1960s, and early 1970s were particularly riotous. Mass prison violence is but one form of prison violence. The New Mexico prison riot was targeted at hated inmate informants. Informants in general are often targets of violence. Silberman also notes violence directed toward correctional officers.

Institutional violence is certainly exacerbated by prison overcrowding, but there are other factors that also make the prison dangerous. Silberman (1995) argues that the violence stems from a destabilization of prison conditions and norms brought about by a shift in correctional policy. It must also be noted that many of the men and women who enter prison come there with prior experience as victims of violence. The Bureau of Justice Statistics (Harlow 1999) reports that 10 percent of the men under correctional supervision said they had been physically or sexually abused. About 3 percent of the men said they had been raped before their incarceration. It was reported that almost half of the women in the jail or prison had been physically or sexually abused before imprisonment. A third of the women in state prisons, a quarter in local jails, and a fifth of the women in federal prisons said they had been raped before their incarceration. Abused state prisoners were more likely than those not abused to have ever served a sentence for a violent crime. Among male inmates, 76 percent who were abused and 61 percent who had not been abused had a current or past sentence for a violent offense. Among female offenders, 45 percent of the abused and 29 percent of those not abused had served a sentence for a violent crime (Harlow 1999).

Bowker's *Prison Victimization* (1980) is a powerful account of the concerns with prison violence, sexual assault, rape, and other forms of prisoner violence. Younger prisoners are raped, sodomized, and terrorized by other inmates if for no other reason than to offer an expression of power. In Davis' study (1968) of Philadelphia's 2,000 sexual assaults that occurred in its correctional system during a particular period, only 156 were documented. Of the 96 that were reported to institutional authorities, 32 were not mentioned in the prison records. Only 40 of the 64 cases mentioned in prison records resulted in disciplinary action against the aggressor (Bowker 1980, 2). Prisons are also places where there is a strong likelihood of physical victimization by threat or physical assault; sexual victimization or manipulation; economic victimization by which prisoners are exploited in order to obtain some of life's basic essentials; social victimization whereby prisoners are attacked because of their color, sexual orientation, age, or citizenship; and victimization by correctional staff (Bowker 1980).

Prison Gangs

Gang activity is another institutional drawback and have been a part of prison life since the 1960s. Knox studied gangs in prisons and in a 2004 report gave statistics on a 1999 survey of gangs in correctional institutions. He estimates that there are over 47,000 gang members in one-third of the correctional institutions in America. About 32.7 percent of the inmates could be expected to be members of a gang or a security threat group (STG). An STG is any group or gang within a prison that is considered a threat to institutional order and discipline. About a third of all adult correctional institutions report gang members as a problem in terms of assault on staff. Many prisoners join a prison gang on the basis of political, racial, or neighborhood solidarity for protection. Prisoners join neo-Nazi hate groups because they share similar attitudes. Some prisoners join racial or ethnically specific gangs for the benefits derived from the gang and its ties to the old neighborhood. Younger prisoners who belonged to gangs on the outside or have been moved from a youth prison where gangs are present find joining a gang easy. Other prisoners have to prove themselves.

Gangs are comprised of core members and affiliates. The core members stay together, planning their daily activities including robbing other prisoners, dealing drugs, controlling homosexuals, and carrying on feuds with other gangs. The presence of gangs and the related social group tensions means that inmates tend to be more preoccupied with finding a safe place than with long-term self-improvement. Gang associates play a low-key role in the gang's activities. The associates are expected to support the gang when called upon to provide a large measure of support or to help when drugs are smuggled into prison or weapons are hidden. In return for their support, they are provided protection and share in some of the spoils of the gang (Irwin and Austin 1997).

Authorities respond to these gangs by transferring the reputed leaders and by placing them in segregation. Some leaders are put into special housing units where they have limited contact with the outside. Despite these efforts, much of the activity continues unabated. The better-organized gangs have made plans for such contingencies by bringing in or assigning another person to be leader. New gangs are forming all the time as a means of dealing with the various forms of deprivation imposed upon the prisoner. Without some form of organization, such as a prisoner's union, even the law-abiding prisoner finds there is safety in numbers and joining a gang provides some assurance that tangible help is there when needed.

Indirect Imprisonment Effects

There are various indirect effects of imprisonment on prisoners' later lives. Imprisonment is a terrible experience for the family of offenders. While some families may be relieved a family member is out of the house, imprisonment leads to the breakup of families and social relationships and to less parental involvement with children (Hagan and Dinowitzer 1999). Some prisoners may try to stay involved with the family and in the growth of their children but many fathers do not care to stay involved and, if they do so, they recognize how superficial it is for the children. It can be frustrating knowing one can do little good for one's children. Imprisonment also reduces ex-offenders' subsequent incomes and employment. In addition, the prisoners' civil rights are limited. Various state and federal laws deny ex-offenders the right to vote or hold office and deny them the opportunity to engage in certain occupations and to receive public assistance and services (Fellner and Mauer 1998). The negative effects of restricted employment opportunities impact income, employment, and family involvement and can lead to increased offenses in the future. It is well known that prisons are schools for crime and that the younger and less-experienced prisoners are socialized into antisocial and oppositional attitudes and thus leave prison better educated in crime and a more highly motivated offender.

Prison expansion has also meant that fewer dollars are directed toward other social and economic programs. Public education, programs, and services have diminished in some communities as a result of the building of prisons. Also, money needed for development is directed to small, rural communities where new facilities are being built. Some communities are severely impacted by the large number of young males who are sent to prison or are prevented from marrying, parenting, working, or becoming contributing members of the community (Mauer 1999). With so many men going to prison, imprisonment no longer holds the stigma it once did, and in fact, may be treated as a right of passage by some.

Prisons also are known to minimally reduce crime rates through deterrence and incapacitation (Nagin 1998). One of the drawbacks of deterrence and incapacitation is a misunderstanding of the connection between behavior and consequences. With so many offenders going to prison for drug violations, society would expect that drug use would decline appreciably—but it hasn't. Despite the war on drugs, most drug offenders believe they will not be caught because their experiences suggest otherwise. Many believe that by employing the proper safeguards, they can continue as always. Many authorities have no idea of the extent of drug use or its general availability in some communities.

Increased dollars for incarceration have not meant an increase in funding for rehabilitation programs. Fewer programs and fewer incentives to participate mean that fewer prisoners leave prison having addressed their work, education, and substance abuse problems. Although prison-sponsored drug programs have expanded, minimal numbers of inmates have participated.

■ Conclusion

Supporting human dignity is important because one cannot afford the loss of civility that comes with ignoring its importance. Humans need to understand that all people, whether newborns or the elderly, have value. It is not just the person's potential that matters but it should mean something that in the past one has contributed some good to society. Being incapable of doing good should not be reason to deny respect. To ignore human dignity furthers crimes against people who have done nothing to deserve such treatment. Too often, in the name of progress, religion, or greed, people have been treated expediently, as though those who lack use or appear blameworthy can be simply rejected. Furthermore, recognizing the importance of human rights promotes the spread of empathy, combats cruelty, and protects the weak from oppressors. Society can only benefit from understanding murderers, sex offenders, and drug offenders as real people who share much in common with all humanity. The principles and ideals of fairness suffer whenever the ability to find common ground with the offender is downplayed.

The concept of human dignity can be summarized as such: People possess human dignity and worth because man and woman are made in the image of God and thus are perfection in the form of the unity of body and soul. Humans have worth because of the excellence found within the person. This excellence takes the form of goodness that draws people to those who are good. Due to their rational nature, people are capable of making choices about both the means and the ends of various actions. Autonomous humans are free to make moral choices and form their own moral habits. These habits will be actualized in the company of others who share equal rights. Rational humans are self-activating, self-directing, self-criticizing, self-correcting, and self-understanding. Such self-possession results in the ability to evaluate, calculate, organize, predict, explain, and conjecture on human events. If the reasoning process is conducted meaningfully, society will find that individuals are then given the full respect and accorded the human dignity they deserve.

Treating the offender with dignity is an essential value for a well-functioning correctional system. To operate otherwise only perpetuates a life of crime and expense. Correctional officials have to be careful in dealing with offenders inasmuch as they have a great deal of power and discretion and few restraints. The prisoner knows full well that there are procedures available to guards that are not controlled by policy or law that will lead to further punishment. Probationers know they must please their probation officer if they expect to be released from supervision early. Some officers have been known to act unethically when dealing with their clients. Essentially, society requires these officials to respect the dignity of their charges despite the powers they possess.

Prisoners are put into a vulnerable position in that they deserve to be punished for their crime but there is a limit to what this punishment can be. Punishment must be carefully regulated to protect the dignity of the prisoner. Based on the criteria set aside by Justice William Brennan in establishing what is cruel and unusual punishment (Bedau 1992), it is clear that it is an affront to the dignity of the person to be forced to undergo catastrophic harm at the hands of another in the name of punishment. Second, it offends the dignity of a punished person when the punisher arbitrarily selects one offender over another so that only a few are punished severely when all deserve the same punishment. Third, it offends the dignity of the punished person when society shows by its actual conduct that it no longer regards such severe punishment as appropriate. Finally, it is an affront to human dignity to impose an extremely severe punishment on an offender when it is known that a less-severe punishment will achieve the same purposes (Bedau 1992, 160–161).

According to the notion of a social contract (see Barker 1962), each one has a right to be treated with human dignity. Human dignity is a corollary of the agreement by which one limits one's liberty in exchange for the benefits derived from formal governments. The government has an obligation to treat its citizens with dignity under all circumstances inasmuch as the citizens have given the state immense power to be used for public safety. It is agreed that conflicts are to be resolved peacefully through various institutions or through the political process.

It seems clear that prisons should be considered the institution of last resort for most of society's offenders. There are too many problems with overcrowded and expensive facilities to suggest that it not worry about what lies ahead. As a whole, society needs to understand the connection among increased health risks, diminished rehabilitative actions, increased violence, and the negative effects visited on the family if we are to provide sufficient reason to consider other means of punishment such as probation. Other countries continue to pursue the notion of rehabilitation without increasing the level of punitive action directed at prisoners. The Swedes, for example, have left the probation officer, along with the police, to focus on the control of the offender's behavior, while the role of assistance is left for other experts such as alcohol and drug-abuse agencies. In addition, room is left for client volition. Even with the strictest level of supervision, the probationer is involved as an agent in his or her own life (Fogel 1988, 233). Society must remember that most of these offenders will return to free society one day and citizens must have confidence that they are fully rehabilitated. The evidence thus far suggests that this is not likely to happen.

Society needs to carefully consider what community-based alternative corrections have to offer in making effective use of resources. Punishment does not have to be unjust to be effective. If society releases prisoners into the community who are illiterate, unemployable, not rehabilitated but rather increasingly sophisticated as far as crime is concerned, then it would be wiser to give considerable attention to alternative means of punishment.

The remainder of this book offers a view of community-based sanctions that attempt to provide a view of human dignity as it is applied to community-based corrections. The book continues with a discussion of the history of probation in the 19th and 20th centuries, followed by chapters on the socioeconomic-political context, probationers, probation work, offender treatment, restorative justice, regulatory probation, alternative sentencing, and probation in the future.

REFERENCES

Abel, C. 2004. The issue of human dignity. www.sfasu.edu/polisci/Abel/Apt/Dignity/html1.

Allen, H., C. Eskridge, E. Latessa, and G. Vito. 1985. *Probation and parole in America.* New York: Free Press.

American Probation and Parole Association. 2004. Appanet.org/about%20appa/codeof.htm.

Andrews, D. 1980. Some experimental investigations of the principles of differential association through deliberate manipulation of the structures of service system. *American Sociological Review* 45: 448–462.

Andrews, D., and J. Bonta. 1998. *The psychology of criminal conduct,* 2nd ed. Cincinnati, OH: Anderson.

Bandura, A. 1965. Influence of model's reinforcement contingencies on the acquisition of imitative responses. *Journal of Personality and Social Psychology* 1: 589–595.

Bandura, A. 1977. Self-efficacy: Toward a unifying theory of behavioral change. *Psychological Review* 94: 191–215.

Bandura, A., D. Ross, and S. Ross. 1963. Vicarious reinforcement and imitative learning. *Journal of Abnormal and Social Psychology* 67: 601–607.

Bandura, A., and R. Walters. 1963. *Social learning and personality development.* New York: Holt, Rinehart and Winston.

Barker, E. 1962. *Social contract: Essays by Locke, Hume, and Rousseau.* New York: Oxford University Press.

Bedau, H. 1992. The Eighth Amendment, human dignity, and the death penalty. In M. Meyer and W. Parent, 1992. *The constitutional rights: Human dignity and American values.* Ithaca, NY: Cornell University Press, 153–154, 160–161.

Bowker, Lee H. 1980. *Prison victimization.* New York: Elsevier.

Boxill, B. 1992. Dignity, slavery and Thirteenth Amendment. In M. Meyer and W. Parent, 1992. *The constitutional rights: Human dignity and American values.* Ithaca, NY: Cornell University Press.

Braswell, M., J. Fuller, and B. Lazoff. 2001. *Corrections, peacemaking, and restorative justice.* Cincinnati, OH: Anderson.

Camp, C., and G. Camp. 1999. *The corrections yearbook 1999. Adult corrections.* Middletown, CT: Criminal Justice Institute.

Camp, C., and G. Camp. 1997. *The corrections yearbook 1997. Adult corrections.* Middletown, CT: Criminal Justice Institute.

Carrithers, D., ed. 1977. *Charles Louis de Secondat, Baron de la Brede et de Montesquieu, the spirit of laws.* Berkeley: University of California Press.

Cheshire, W. 2004. Guest editorial: Toward a common language on human dignity. *Ethics and Medicine* 18(2): 7–10.

Cobb, A. 1985. Home truths about prison overcrowding. *Annals of the American Academy of Political and Social Science* 478: 73–85.

Cronan, E. 1955. *The dignity of the human person.* New York: Philosophical Library.

Czajkoski, E. 1969. Functional specialization of probation and parole. *Crime and Delinquency* 15: 238–246.

Dalton, M. 1959. *Men who manage.* New York: Wiley.

Davis, A. 1968. Sexual assaults in the Philadelphia prison system and sheriff's vans. *Trans-Action* 6: 8–16.

DiSanto, R. 1999. The threat of commodity-consciousness to human dignity. In R. Duffy and A. Gambatese, eds. *Made in God's image.* New York: Paulist Press.

Ellsworth, T. 1990. Identifying the actual and preferred goals of adult probation. *Federal Probation* 54: 10–15.

Encyclopedia Britannica. 1988. Aquinas, T., *The summa theologica.* I–II., Chicago: Great Books of the Western World.

Enos, R., and S. Southern. 1996. *Correctional case management.* Cincinnati, OH: Anderson.

Federal Bureau of Investigation. 1999. Uniform crime reports, 1999. Section III, Crime index offenses cleared. www.fbi.gov.

Fellner, J., and M. Mauer. 1998. Nearly 4 million Americans denied vote because of felony convictions. *Overcrowded Times* 9(5): 1, 6–13.

Fogel, D. 1988. *On doing less harm.* Chicago: University of Illinois at Chicago.

Glaser, D. 1969. *The effectiveness of a prison and parole system.* Indianapolis, IN: Bobbs-Merrill.

Glaze, L., and S. Palla. 2004. *Probation and parole in the United States 2003.* Washington, DC: U.S. Department of Justice, Bureau of Justice Statistics.

Goffman, E. 1961. *Asylums: Essays on the social situation of mental patients and other inmates.* Garden City, NY: Anchor Books.

Goolam, N. 2001. Human dignity: Our supreme constitutional values. Paper delivered to the International Conference on Development in the Contemporary Constitutional State, Potchefstroom University, South Africa. November 2–3, 2000. www.puk.ac.za/lawper/2001.1/goolam.html.

Hagan, J., and R. Dinowitzer. 1999. Collateral consequences of imprisonment for children, communities, and prisoners. In *Prisons,* Michael Tonry and Joan Petersilia, eds. Chicago: University of Chicago Press, 121–162.

Hammett, T. 1998. *Public health/corrections collaborations: Prevention and treatment of HIV/AIDS, STDs, and TB.* National Institute of Justice Center for Disease Control and Prevention.

Harlow, C. 1999. Prior abuse reported by inmates and probationers. *Bureau of Justice Statistics.* Washington, DC: U.S. Department of Justice.

Hirsch, A. 1992. *The rise of the penitentiary.* New Haven, CT: Yale University Press.

Hutchins, R. (Ed.) 1988. *Great books of the western world: The works of Aristotle, volume I and II.* Chicago: Encyclopedia Britannica.

Irwin, J., and J. Austin. 1997. *It's about time: America's imprisonment binge.* Belmont, CA: Wadsworth.

Jacobs, M. 1990. *Screwing the system and making it work.* Chicago: University of Chicago.

Johnson, H. 1988. *History of criminal justice.* Cincinnati, OH: Anderson.

Johnson, R. 1996. *Hardtime: Understanding and reforming the prison.* Belmont, CA: Wadsworth.

Jones, A. (Ed.) 1988. The prophets: Jeremiah. *The Jerusalem Bible.* Garden City, NY: Doubleday.

Kant, I. 1785. *The metaphysics of morals.* Translated by Mary Gregor (1996). New York: Cambridge University Press.

Karp, D., and T. Clear (Eds.). 2002. *What is community justice?: Case studies of restorative justice and community supervision.* Thousand Oaks, CA: Sage.

Klockars, C. 1972. A theory of probation supervision. *Journal of Criminal Law, Criminology, and Police Science* 63: 550–557.

Knox, G. 2004. A national assessment of gangs and security threat groups (STGs) in adult correctional institutions: Results of the 1999 adult corrections survey. www.ngcrsc.com/ngcrc/page8.htm.

Latin–English Dictionary. 2004. www.arts.cuhk.edu.hk/Lexis/Latin/.

Lawrence, S., and J. Travis. 2004. The new landscape of imprisonment: Mapping America's prison expansion. www.urban.org/url.cfm?ID410994.

Lipsky, M. 1980. *Street-level bureaucracy.* New York: Russell Sage.

Lynch, G. 1996. Police training in human dignity. Policing in Central and Eastern Europe: Comparing firsthand knowledge with experience from the West. www.ncjrs.org/polcing/dig41.htm Slovenia: College of Police and Security Studies.

Manocchio, A., and J. Dunn. 1970. *The time game.* Beverly Hills, CA: Sage.

Martinson, R. 1974. What works? Questions and answers about prison reform. *The Public Interest* 10: 22–54.

Mauer, M., C. Potler, and R. Wolf. 1999. *Women, drugs, and sentencing policy.* Washington, DC: Sentencing Project.

Mauer, M. 1999. *The crisis of the young African American male and the criminal justice system.* Washington, DC: Sentencing Project.

Mayer, A. 1995. *Islam and human rights: Tradition and politics,* 2nd ed. San Francisco: Westview.

McCleary, R. 1992. *Dangerous men: The sociology of parole.* New York: Heston.

Mickel, K. 1994. A little TLC: Maricopa county's transitional living center. In *Topics in community corrections annual issue 1994: Mentally ill offenders in the community.* Washington, DC: U.S. Department of Justice, National Institute of Corrections.

Minnow, M. 1992. Equality and the Bill of Rights. In M. Meyer and W. Parent, *The constitutional rights: Human dignity and American values.* Ithaca, NY: Cornell University Press.

Nagin, Daniel. 1998. Criminal deterrence research at the outset of the twenty-first century. In Michael Tonry, ed., *Crime and justice: A review of research,* vol. 23. Chicago: University of Chicago Press.

National Center on Institutions and Alternatives. 1998. Imprisoning elderly offenders: Public safety or maximum security nursing homes. www.ncianet.org/ncia.

OED. 1979. *The compact edition of the Oxford English Dictionary,* Oxford University.

Ohlin, L., H. Piven, and D. Pappenport. 1956. Major dilemmas of the social worker in probation and parole. *National Probation and Parole Association Journal* 2: 21–25.

Parent, W. 1992. Constitutional values and human dignity. In M. Meyer and W. Parent (Eds.). *The constitutional rights: Human dignity and American values.* Ithaca, NY: Cornell University Press.

Pollis, A., and P. Schwab. 1979. *Human rights: Cultural and ideological perspectives.* New York: Praeger.

Powers, G., D. Christensen, and R. Hennengsen. 1995. *Peacemaking: Moral and policy challenges for a new world.* Washington, DC: Georgetown Press.

Rawl, J. 1971. *A theory of justice.* Cambridge, MA: Belknap.

Raz, J. 1979. *The authority of law.* Oxford: Clarendon Press. 1983.

Roos, L. 1998. Institutions of social organization: Family, private property, and state. In David Boileau, ed., *Principles of Catholic social teaching.* Milwaukee, MN: Marquette University Press.

Samenow, S. 1984. *Inside the criminal mind.* New York: Times Books.

Samenow, S. 1989. *Before it's too late: Why some kids get into trouble and what parents can do about it.* New York: Times Books.

Scullion, J. 1999. Creation-incarceration: God's affirmation of human worth. In Regis Duffy and Angelus Gambatese. *Made in God's image.* New York: Paulist Press.

Sieh, Edward W. 1989a. Less eligibility: The upper limits of penal policy. *Criminal Justice Policy Review* 3(2): 159–183.

Sieh, Edward W. 1989b. Prison overcrowding: The case of New Jersey. *Federal Probation* 53: 41–51.

Silberman, M. 1995. *A world of violence: Corrections in America.* Belmont, CA: Wadsworth.

Stephan, J. 2004. State prison expenditures, 2001. Bureau of Justice Statistics Special Report. www.ojp.usdoj.gov/bjs/abstract/spe01.htm.

Strain, Chareles. R. 1995. Social engaged Buddhism's contribution to the transformation of Catholic social teaching on human rights. *Journal of Buddhist Ethics* (online conference on Buddhism and human rights, October 1–14, 1995). www.//jbe.gold.ac.uk/1995conf/strain.txt.

Taboada, P. 2003. The sources of human dignity. International Association for Hospice and Palliative Care. www.hospicecare.com/ethics/monthlypiece/pom_april03.htm.

Thornberry, Terrence P., and J. E. Call. 1983. Constitutional challenges to prison overcrowding: The scientific evidence of harmful effect. *The Hastings Law Journal* 35: 313–351.

Tomaino, L. 1975. The five faces of probation. *Federal Probation* 39: 41–46.

United Nations. 1948. *Universal declaration of human rights.* Geneva, Switzerland: Office of High Commissioner for Human Rights, United Nations Department of Public Information.

Van Voorhis, P. 2000. Social learning model. In P. Van Voorhis, M. Braswell, and D. Lester (Eds.). *Correctional counseling and rehabilitation.* Cincinnati, OH: Anderson.

Whitehead, J. 1989. *Burnout in probation and corrections.* New York: Praeger.

Whitehead, J., J. Pollock, and M. Braswell. 2003. *Exploring corrections in America.* Cincinnati, OH: Anderson.

KEY POINTS

1. Human dignity is based on the acknowledgment that a human is equipped with reason, uniqueness, freedom, morality, originality, and self-determinism.

2. Various probation departments, along with the American Probation and Parole Association, have vision, mission, and value statements supporting the concept of human dignity.

3. The government has an obligation to treat its citizens with dignity under all circumstances inasmuch as the citizens, on their behalf, have given the state immense power to be used for public safety.

4. One way in which probation officers deny probationers' dignity is through a lack of respect.

5. Human dignity is intimately related to human autonomy and rationality in which one is self-activating, self-directing, self-reflective, self-criticizing, self-correcting, and self-understanding.

6. The writings of the Prophet Jeremiah, Aristotle, St. Thomas Aquinas, and Immanuel Kant have discussed the importance of human dignity.

7. One of the principal reasons in support of human dignity is that people have the potential to do good.

8. Peacemaking is a contemporary concept in community corrections that suggests that offenders should be treated with dignity.

9. Human dignity is essential to treatment in that if the offender is treated with dignity he or she can learn to treat others with dignity as though they have worth.

10. Human dignity is denied in prison and is further denied through the principle of less eligibility.

11. Prisons are inappropriate for all but the most dangerous offenders because of overcrowding, health concerns, ineffective rehabilitation, violence, and gang activity.

KEY TERMS

degradation rituals are personal affronts to the individual's dignity that are used to further humiliate the person. A degradation ritual might involve taking a urine sample or conducting a strip search of the offender.

disrespect is found among officers who view offenders as different from themselves in terms of the possession of one (or more) negative attribute, thus conferring inferiority upon the offender. Disrespect is conveyed in words and deeds.

human dignity is comprised of various elements of respect, personal worth, perfection, and the Kantian rationalist perspective that sees any individual as having worth because of the person's ability to think and make choices about personal actions and goals.

less eligibility stipulates that if imprisonment is to act as a deterrent, the treatment given the prisoner should be perceived as not superior to that provided a member of the lowest significant social class in the free society.

medical model views the problem in terms of basic constitution, physical ailment, or to apply the model to social-adjustment problems in terms of identifying the problem, proscribing a treatment, and assessing when the cure has been effected.

peacemaking is a personal transformation the officer undergoes in order to achieve a positive state of well-being that allows him or her to address the needs of the offender. If one wants the offender to become a good person, one must first become a good person.

REVIEW QUESTIONS

1. What are some examples of how a probation officer might deny the human dignity of an offender?

2. Discuss the points in support of human dignity.

3. Comment on the following statement: No one is the sum total of his or her worst deeds.

4. What role does respect play in human dignity?

5. What is the value of human dignity in the treatment of probationers and parolees?

6. List the problems that institutional corrections have with the implementation of human dignity.

The History of Probation: From Augustus to the Progressives

The history of punishment over the last 200 years has given considerable attention to the deplorable conditions found in various jails or prisons. Housing men, women, and children, they were characterized by overcrowding, idleness, mental illness, abuse, exploitation, and persistent criminality. Frequently, jailers exploited the situation to their full advantage by siphoning off prior funds for their personal benefit. The Pennsylvania silent system, while intending to reform the offender, fostered insanity instead. The Auburn system of congregate living offered some improvement by allowing prisoners to work together in groups. However, discipline in this system was maintained through cruelty and violence.

Recognizing the importance of keeping prisoners busy meant that officials required inmates to do meaningless work, participate in endless military exercises, or be leased out to those who had little interest in the prisoners' well-being. As a result, prisoners became sick or injured but received only rudimentary support. Southern prisons were even worse. While the prisons during this era were considered an improvement over the use of torture and mutilation, they nevertheless failed to work out the problem of how to treat the undeserving minor offender when imprisonment is excessive.

■ Probation Practices

This chapter provides an account of the various practices that preceded the modern forms of community corrections and outlines some of the forces behind the changes that took place to bring about modern-day probation. Attention will be given to the peace oath, benefit of clergy, suspended sentencing, and recognizance, as well as the social changes brought about by the Enlightenment, changing religious sentiment, and general bureaucratic developments. Many of these practices originated before the advent of probation, had concurrent histories, continued after its development, and in some form or other are continued even today.

Probation, as it is known today, is an extension of English common law (United Nations 1951) and like many other correctional innovations, an updated version of earlier practices. In the history of criminal policy, the development of probation and related measures became an integral part of the movement away from traditional fearful approaches to punishment and toward more humanitarian and utilitarian thoughts (United Nations 1951, 82).

Peace Oaths

The germ of the British system of probation is found in the proclamation of 1195. At that time, an oath to keep the peace was sworn by all persons above the age of 15 years. The justice of the peace was given the authority to supervise the peace and to report any violator to the general sessions of the peace. It was recognized that it was sometimes possible to impose a conditional threat of punishment directed at future acts (Timasheff 1941b, 284). Those found guilty were required to swear oaths binding them to a certain course of action and to refrain from certain actions. An especially powerful oath was the purgatory oath, purging or clearing the person from presumptions, charges, or suspicions standing against him or her (Black 1979, 966). It may be assumed that probation was conditioned by the practice of imposing peace through such oaths. However, there is no direct correlation between the imposed peace and the advent of probation. In some countries they took place almost simultaneously; in others there were centuries between them, and yet in others, there was no connection whatsoever (Timasheff 1941b, 285).

Benefit of Clergy

The benefit of clergy is another interesting phenomenon. As an expression of the power of the church's authority over worldly affairs and the fact that for centuries there was little separation of the church and state, the clergy benefited when charged with wrongdoing by having their cases turned over to church authorities. The benefit of clergy exempted clergy men from the jurisdiction of the secular courts for particular cases. It applied neither to high treason nor to misdemeanors. The privilege was claimed after conviction by offering a motion asking for an arrested judgment. In other words, the offender was put on trial and instead of finding the person guilty or innocent, the court simply made no judgment at all. As a means of testing clerical character, the defendant was usually given Psalm 51 to read: "Have mercy on me, O God, in your goodness, in your great tenderness wipe away my faults; wash me clean of my guilt, purify me from my sin." Upon reading it correctly, the person was turned over to the ecclesiastical courts to be tried by the bishop or jury of 12 clerks. The bishop's court heard any case in which sin was alleged. Sin was synthesized from Roman law: breach of contract, injuries to the person or property, the withholding of property belonging to another, fraud, and so forth (Berman 1983, 452). This court heard the accused and the witnesses under oath, all of whom attested to the accused's innocence.

Initially the benefit of the clergy was granted only to the clergy, but later, it was extended to all who were connected officially to the church in even the slightest way, and still later, to any one who could read the Latin verse. Besides church officials, the upper classes, educated persons, and anyone clever enough to memorize the verse benefited. The importance of this plea was a function of the need to work out practical solutions to modifying the severity of the law (United Nations 1951). In 1790, an act of Congress abolished it in the United States (Black 1979, 144). By 1827, abuses forced the English also to do away with it. Although not a direct antecedent of probation, the concept of benefit of clergy illustrates the extent to which the authorities were willing to mitigate the severe penalties required by law.

Suspended Sentencing

Suspended sentencing, which continues to this day, provides the accused with a chance to appeal a decision and convince the court he or she has been reformed and deserves another chance or provides the offender a chance to offer new evidence. Suspended sentencing is seen in the filing of cases and in the judicial reprieve. The filing of cases originated in Massachusetts. It consisted of suspending the imposition of the sentence on the consent of the defendant and prosecutor after a guilty verdict subject to the conditions set by the court. The case could be opened any time at the request of either party (Henningsen 1981, 14).

The **judicial reprieve** was a temporary suspension of either the imposition or the execution of the sentence. It was used to permit the accused a chance to seek a pardon when the judge was not satisfied with the verdict or when the evidence was suspicious. Under 19th-century common law at the time, the person had no right to appeal, so this was an important consideration. While this measure was, for the most part, considered temporary, in some cases it led to an abandonment of prosecution. The judicial reprieve was not to be offered as an indefinite suspension of sentence. The judicial reprieve was important later because it formed the basis of the claim advanced by many American courts to the right to indefinitely suspend sentences (United Nations 1951, 16).

A **suspended sentence** means either the withholding or postponing of the sentencing of a prisoner after conviction, or postponing the execution of it after the sentence has been pronounced. In the latter case, it may, at the discretion of the courts, be indefinite or during good behavior of the person (Black 1979, 1223). The suspension of sentences should be considered a form of probation, as long as the resumption of the punishment is determined by the violation of another law. Moreover, this situation does not change if the offender has been released on his or her **recognizance** prior to appearing at court. If the person fails to appear and has violated the recognizance, the legal consequence is the forfeiture of bail. The forfeiture is invalidated if the offender is acquitted when he or she finally appears (Rotman 1990, 4). In the 1920s, there was much use of suspended sentences in federal courts.

Recognizance

The most complete precursor to modern-day probation was recognizance. Recognizance for good behavior was an obligation with sureties entered into before

judicial reprieve was a temporary suspension of either the imposition or the execution of a prison sentence. It was used to permit the accused a chance to seek a pardon when the judge was not satisfied with the verdict or when the evidence was suspicious.

suspended sentence means either the withholding or postponing of a sentencing of a prisoner after conviction or postponing the execution of a sentence after it has been pronounced.

recognizance for good behavior was an obligation with sureties entered into before the court or magistrate. Entering into a recognizance (with or without sureties) created a debt to the state that became enforceable over a period of time when specified conditions were not met. If a violation occurred, the person was required to appear in court, and if found guilty, to forfeit a certain sum of money.

the court or magistrate (Allen et al. 1979; Carter et al. 1984). Entering into a recognizance (with or without sureties) created a debt to the state that became enforceable over a period of time when specified conditions were not met (United Nations 1951, 83). If a violation occurred, the person was required to appear in court, and if found guilty, to forfeit a certain sum of money (Black 1979, 1143). The authorities realized that the threat of future punishment offered sufficient general and specific deterrence (Timasheff 1941b, 284).

Recognizance was used widely throughout Europe (Rotman 1990). Early practices were found in England, France, Germany, Switzerland, Italy, Hungary, and Russia (Timasheff 1941b). The practice of granting recognizance arose in the 16th century on the basis of the general powers granted the justice of the peace (Rotman 1990). For centuries the courts of England released minor offenders on their own recognizance with or without sureties. Edward Cox, an English recorder, published a work closely tying recognizance to bail. Cox suggested the offenders should be released on their own recognizance, with sureties, as a substitute for punishment. Nothing further was to be done in the case unless the person violated the law and had not taken into account the significance of the original punishment (United Nations 1951). Similarly, instances of this practice can be found in the records of the American colonies (United Nations 1951, 84). In the 17th century, the Court of Assistants of the Massachusetts Bay Colony tried Henry Norton, John Emerson, and John Stretson. In each case, they were placed on their good behavior for a period of time and asked to provide a surety. In Virginia, first offenders and offenders convicted of drunkenness and rioting were given a second chance (Timasheff 1941b, 289). Once the practice of releasing the offenders on their own recognizance was formally approved for juveniles and minor offenders by Massachusetts in 1836, other states took up similar measures (Henningsen 1981, 14). Because the concept of recognizance contained prescribed conditions restricting the behavior of the offender, there was some supervision present in the process that allowed a friend to make a financial commitment to the good behavior of the offender. This person was to ensure the offender obeyed the conditions of the recognizance. If no one was willing to provide sureties, then it was understood that the offender was in need of further self-reformation (Killinger and Cromwell 1978).

The use of sureties on conditionally released offenders, either on their own recognizance or on bail, indeed seems to have been, in a very real sense, the first rudimentary stage in the development of probation (United Nations 1951). Dressler (1959) believes that in these early procedures are found suspension of sentence, freedom in lieu of incarceration, conditions set for such freedom, and the possibility of incarceration or payment of a fine if a violation of a condition occurs. In general, these procedures usually resulted in more lenient sentences. Nowhere were these inventions fixed except in Massachusetts.

■ The Early Years of Probation

About the time probation was introduced, people were becoming aware that brutal imprisonment was offering little in the way of social protection. Instead it was converting relatively harmless individuals into incorrigible offenders

(Timasheff 1941a, 2). The choice of probations, as the response to this problem, could take place only under the momentum of a broad social trend that brought about curbing the use of the death penalty, renewed interests in prison reform, and the desire to create special institutions for juvenile delinquents (Timasheff 1941a, 2).

In 1841, the first sustained services resembling modern-day probation were provided in Birmingham, England, and Boston, Massachusetts. In England, escalating social unrest during the 1830s and 1840s led some people to fear that the nation was on the verge of civil war. The industrial towns could not accommodate many of the impoverished laborers brought in to work in the factories. Employment was irregular and the wages were extremely low. Child laborers forced wages down; fathers competed with their own children for work. Workers, including children, were subjected to alternating periods of extreme overwork and utter destitution. Living conditions were miserable and epidemics were common. Sanitary conditions were dreadful. People were starving to death for lack of adequate diet. In Liverpool, an unemployed poor youth could expect to live, on average, to the age of 15 (Hamlin 1998). In Manchester, around half of all children died before they were 5 years old. As the spirit of rebellion spread across the north of England, unemployed factory workers were forming armed gangs. A target of much of the criticism was the 1834 New Poor Law, which denied unemployed workers relief unless they entered the squalid workhouses, which were like prisons, only worse. Some workers preferred to starve than to enter the workhouse. Reformers believed that the cause of so much death and illness among the poor was poverty and the resultant hunger. This was the beginning of the public health movement in England (Hamlin 1995, 862).

In Britain, the first use of probation occurred with the Warwickshire magistrates. Matthew D. Hill is credited with being the first English probation officer (Timasheff 1941a; Rotman 1990). He was born in 1792 and had a varied career as a British barrister, one-time member of House of Commons, and penologist. Hill worked as a recorder in Birmingham from 1841 to 1856 during which time he provided services to the court that were similar to the work of a probation officer. He is credited with recommending many important penal reforms that were enacted into law during his lifetime. His most important work, *Suggestions for the Repression of Crime,* was published in 1858 (Goetz 1989).

John Augustus

John Augustus, born in Woburn, Massachusetts, in 1785, is considered to be the father of American probation. He prospered as a cordwainer (cordovan shoemaker) and boot maker in Lexington and then moved to Boston, hoping to improve his fortunes even further (Chute and Bell 1956, 37). While in Boston, Augustus was a member of various reform societies and religious groups. By 1841, Augustus was active in the Washington Total Abstinence Society, the Anti-Slavery movement, the Moral Reform association, and other similar groups. He also belonged to various religious groups including the Methodists, Universalists, Baptists, and Unitarians. Augustus had long since given up on formal sectarian religions but he was not left unaffected by them inasmuch as he was motivated by the religious impulse to rescue the sinner (Chute and Bell 1956,

49). His association with these different groups led him to develop an interest in reclaiming drunkards and in saving people from the law (Chute and Bell 1956, 44). It is probable that Augustus first began to visit the courts because of his membership in these various groups. Although others worked before him, Augustus was the first to develop a sustained service (Chute and Bell 1956, 38).

In 1841, John Augustus, while attending police court in Boston, decided to stand bail for a common drunkard. The court permitted Augustus to return the man to court in 3 weeks at which time Augustus would report on the person's general conduct. Upon their return, the offender showed remarkable signs of reform. Instead of being sent to a house of corrections, the man was given a nominal fine and ordered to pay court costs.

Probation, as conceived by Augustus, was the execution of concrete measures aimed at helping the offender stay out of further trouble (Diana 1960, 190). Augustus originally took under supervision male first offenders but later expanded his efforts to include women and juveniles. His method was to provide bail during a suspension or postponement of sentencing, during which time he counseled and assisted his charges in such practical ways as finding housing, securing employment, attending school, and adjusting to family difficulties. At the end of the probation period, he brought the offender back to court. If no further complaint had been lodged, the judge imposed a nominal fine with costs. If a person was too poor, Augustus advanced a loan, sometimes to his personal disadvantage when the offender failed to show up later. By 1846 and 1847, he was giving all of his time to his new vocation (Chute and Bell 1956, 38). As a result of John Augustus' hard work, it soon became the rule of the court in Boston that a person charged with being a common drunkard could be granted probation.

Opposition to His Efforts

Augustus met with a great deal of opposition. Criticism came from the press, politicians, and especially criminal justice personnel. He was called a fanatic and a fool. Politicians, civic leaders, and the press accused him of upholding crime and not offering sufficient deterrence. Augustus replied that people too easily identify a particular class of individuals as evil when only a few of them are such. Jailers resisted Augustus' efforts because they were compensated according to the rate of occupancy (Champion 1990, 13). The county attorney occasionally found Augustus troublesome because postponements cluttered the court's docket (Chute and Bell 1956, 45). Court officials sometimes excluded him from the dock and put him among the criminals, which often worked to Augustus' advantage in that he was able to spend more time with the accused offenders (1972, XXVII):

> By being driven back I was not infrequently brought in contiguity
> with the prisoner and this was the very object I desired. Here then,
> were two points gained, - to take my place with members of the bar,
> and to occasionally whisper a word of hope to the desponding heart
> of some unfortunate and perhaps innocent person.

Occasionally, his effort cost him dearly and forced him to face the realities of urban law enforcement. For example, Augustus described one incident involving a woman he bailed out of jail who was charged with running a house of prostitution. He put up surety to gain her release and told her to return to court later where she would likely receive a small fine. The woman moved out of state and could not be reached, and Augustus found that he was subject to arrest and forfeiture of a remitted $100 bail (Augustus 1972, 22):

> So I had actually paid one hundred dollars for breaking up a den of vice, and making an effort to reform the abandoned, by which in various ways I have saved the county and the Commonwealth at least two or three thousand dollars, to say nothing of removal of bad influences. I then became aware that it was useless to attempt to break up a den of vice of this kind, as the strongarm of the law was adverse to such an act.

Others Join to Help

Augustus did not stand alone. Influential people, including Horace Mann, Theodore Parker, and Wendell Phillips, gave him both moral and financial support (Chute and Bell 1956, 48–49). Horace Mann wrote, "Your labors favor all classes, they tend to reform the prisoner; they render property more inviolable; they give additional security to every man's person, and every man's life" (Augustus 1972, 61). In a very rational and utilitarian sense Augustus believed that many more were saved from crime by his methods than could ever be saved by cruel techniques of punishment (Chute and Bell 1956, 46–47).

Augustus restricted his attention to those he felt worthy of rehabilitation and to those exhibiting the greatest likelihood of refraining from further criminal activity (Champion 1990, 13). He did not assume responsibility for just any offender but only after investigating the case and looking into the history and character of each individual. To achieve this understanding, it was necessary to take into account the person's character, age, and future influences. To accommodate the court, Augustus agreed to make an impartial report to the court whenever required. His personal records indicate he was successful in changing the lives of over 2,000 persons during his 18 years of service (United Nations 1951).

During that same period, Augustus attracted several philanthropic volunteers who performed similar probation services. Estimates are that many benefited as a result of these voluntary services (Champion 1990, 11). When Augustus died in 1859, various prisoners' and children's aid societies, many religiously based, continued to volunteer their services to the courts for the purpose of supervising convicted offenders on probation (Krajick 1980).

After Augustus died, Rufus Cook, a chaplain working at the Suffolk county jail and a member of the Boston Children's Aid Society, along with other volunteers, continued his work. Their work continued the essential features of probation investigations, regular reports, and home visits. However, they viewed the work as a "rescue," thus limiting their commitment and involvement in the process. This meant their investigations were meager, probationary periods were extremely short, and their records, plans for treatment, and close supervision were lacking (United Nations 1951). By 1869, volunteers were partially superseded by state-visiting agents. Although no provisions for these agents were made in any law concerning probation, they could, however, make suggestions as to the disposition of the case and used that opportunity to "suggest the release of children on probation to friends" (Timasheff 1941b, 11).

The Settlement Solution

Beside the visiting agents, workers engaged in the settlement movement augmented probation services (Linder and Savarese 1984). The settlement movement was an attempt to preserve human values in crowded urban environments by having university men settle in working-class neighborhoods where they could help relieve poverty and despair by easing entry for new immigrants. Between 1886 and 1900, a number of settlement houses were established for the purpose of assisting the poor and improving the lot of the disadvantaged. Settlement workers were natural candidates to supervise probationers by virtue of their knowledge of the community and their skills in studying living conditions, providing personal intervention, procuring employment, and offering a continuous presence with the client (Linder and Savarese 1984, 8; Sullivan 1990, 28).

One organization that earlier had conducted background investigations and supervised persons placed on suspended sentence was the Prison Association of New York. Representatives of this association had worked in the courts and in the Tombs Prison in New York City for more than 50 years, interviewing prisoners, conducting investigations, and furnishing information to the judges upon request (Chute and Bell 1956, 76). Friendly supervision and guidance of juveniles was common during the last quarter of the 19th century. This activity was characterized by the creation of various prisoner aid societies, children aid societies, and societies for the prevention of cruelty toward children.

Attention Given to Juveniles

By 1869, the Massachusetts legislature provided for the appointment of a state agent to investigate cases of children tried before the courts, to attend such trials, and to receive the children for placement if the courts so ordered. The state agents exercised supervision according to the common law practices of probation (United Nations 1951). Later on, the societies provided for paid agents to appear in court on behalf of the children. These activities coincided with the development of the boarding-out system that diverted children from imprisonment by placing them in the homes of good citizens who volunteered to care for the children (Timasheff 1941a, 5).

During the 19th century, officials often chose to acquit juveniles who committed minor offenses (Fox 1970, 1194). Authorities were confronted with a dilemma when punishing juveniles; either they could put the juvenile in prison or they could choose to do nothing. Incarceration was considered too harsh, but doing nothing was considered out of the question. Both options seemed to increase crime among juveniles (Bernard 1992, 87). Incarceration was considered shocking and scandalous because it flew in the face of cultural conceptions of childhood (Garland 1990). The child savers, or those dedicated to reforming juveniles, instituted reform campaigns resulting in probation and juvenile reform (Garland 1990, 201–202).

It is generally accepted that juvenile courts began in Illinois in 1899 with the passage of the Act to Regulate the Treatment and Control of Neglected and

Delinquent Children (Rotman 1990, 45). However, it should be noted that separate hearings for juveniles were held for the first time in Massachusetts as early as 1875. New York held separate hearings for juveniles in 1893 (Rotman 1990, 45). The establishment of the juvenile court was thought to be the result of clear-headed men and women of good will who were concerned with the growth of delinquency and the inadequacy of treatments available to them (Rotman 1990, 45). Platt (1977) argues that the child-saving movement was not a humanistic enterprise on behalf of the working class: "On the contrary, its impetus came primarily from the upper and middle classes who were instrumental in devising new forms of social control to protect their power and privilege, as society moved from inefficient repression to welfare state benevolence."

Adult Probation

After its early philanthropic stage, adult probation was taken over by the state (Rotman 1990, 157). In 1878, probation also came to be regulated by statute. At that time, Massachusetts provided for paid probation officers to work in the courts. The legislature was careful to see that only persons expected to be reformed without punishment should be selected for probation. Equally important was the lack of any limitation on the offenders (youthful, first offenders, etc.) or for what offenses could be put on probation.

The Massachusetts Administrative Statute of 1878 was designed to handle the appointment and duties of the probation officer. The Boston probation officer was selected and appointed annually by the mayor of Boston, who was to choose a suitable person from the ranks of the police department or from the citizens at large. The first paid probation officer, a former police officer, was E. H. Savage (Timasheff 1941a, 17). The probation officer was then under the general supervision of the chief of the police (United Nations 1951, 91). The statute prescribed their duties as including court attendance, the investigation of the cases of persons charged with or convicted of crimes or misdemeanors, the making of recommendations to the courts about using probation, the submission of periodical reports to the chief of police, visiting probationers, and rendering such assistance and encouragement to probationers as necessary to prevent future crime. To strengthen their power, probation officers were given the authority to make arrests without a warrant but with the approval of the chief of police. "Generally speaking the previously existing common law practice of probation remained unaltered, the only significant innovation being the official nature of the new arrangements for the exercise of probationary supervision" (United Nations 1951, 91).

The early history of probation follows a pattern of statutory enactment of what had been common law practices. It was through judicial experiment, believed to be within the common law powers of Massachusetts's judges, that the principle of probation was applied experimentally in practice. Gradually the practice became so generally approved that the legislature provided for its development on a broader scale (Grinnell 1917, 610). By combining the elements of suspension of punishment, personal care, and supervision, probation owes its origins less to legal doctrines, despite its statutory development, than to the recognition of the importance of the social needs emerging from the practical considerations (Grunhut 1948, 298).

■ Allied Forces of Change

The rise in probation has to be understood in the broad terms of changes in modes of punishment, the development of social institutions in general, and changes in the social context and in the forces working to formalize the process.

Penal Measures

An early driving force supporting a move toward the use of peace oaths, the benefit of clergy, suspended sentencing and recognizance was the obliteration of the social order brought on by the plague. Bubonic and pneumonic plagues, or what came to be known as the Black Death, ravaged Europe between 1347 and 1351, taking a greater toll on life than any previously known epidemic or war. Recurrences occurred up to the 15th century. Entire families and communities were annihilated. Many people felt insecure and sought assurances in mysticism, the occult, and various heresies (Goetz 1989, 253). A slump in economic trade immediately followed, but the more serious problem was the drastic reduction in the amount of land under cultivation brought on by labor shortages throughout Europe. This proved to be the ruin of many landowners but a bonanza for laborers as their services became more valuable and their wages increased. This change brought with it a general social fluidity along with a new appreciation of life and of the worth of the individual. Of great importance for punishment was the fact that bloody and punitive punishments were seen as wasteful. It made no sense to maim an offender so severely he or she was unable to work the fields. At least for a time, efforts were directed toward reducing the severity of punishments for the youthful or minor offenders through employing benefit of clergy, suspended sentences, recognizance, and later, the friendly supervision of offenders by benevolent persons and charitable societies. Prior to 1841, these practices occurred only sporadically (Timasheff 1941a, 2).

To reach the point where probation could takes its place among other major social institutions, some important changes needed to take hold. Probation came about due to three important influences:

1. a philosophical movement that provided support
2. the rise of a complex social structure
3. the growth of a bureaucratic organization permitting the formalization and continuation of probation

The Enlightenment

During the 17th and 18th centuries, a European intellectual movement, the Enlightenment, took hold. The **Enlightenment** concerned ideas relative to God, reason, nature, and humans synthesized into a world-view that drew wide interests and instigated revolutionary developments in the arts, philosophy, and politics. Central to this movement was the celebration of reason, the powers that humans use to understand their world and improve their condition (Goetz 1989). It became possible to imagine a better world to live in. Obviously later, throughout the 18th and 19th centuries in the United States, there was a visible change in the manner of production. The industrial revolution produced greater efficiency

Enlightenment is a European intellectual movement in which ideas concerning God, reason, nature, and humans were synthesized into a world-view that drew wide interests and instigated revolutionary developments in the arts, philosophy, and politics.

in agriculture and manufacturing. With the aid of new roads and canals, markets expanded and people began to travel more and learn new ideas.

Between the 16th century and the start of the 19th century, most punishments were very punitive and exceptionally bloody (Timasheff 1941b, 294–295). By 1820, the English had over 200 different capital offenses (Hay 1975). As fairness and equality began to find expression, people started to think severe punishment was no longer necessary to achieve the goals of punishment (Garland 1990, 205). Montesquieu (1988, 37–38) believes that with moderate governments, conviction alone offered sufficient punishment, and thus, it did not require much force and severity. Cesare Beccaria (1764), another important figure of the Enlightenment, argued that punishments should be selected to make the biggest impression on the person, but also, to have the least torment on the body. Beccaria claimed that it is far more important to have certainty of punishment than severity of punishment. Reform legislators took up Beccaria's ideas across Europe and North America. Under the pressure of the Enlightenment, earlier forms of punishments gave way to the arguments put forward by Beccaria. His formalized, rational approaches to punishment emphasized uniformity, proportionality, and equality under the law and the strict application of rules. The views of Montesquieu, Beccaria, and their followers eventually won a complete victory in the battle to dominate the theory and practice of criminal law.

In *The Leviathan*, Thomas Hobbes (1990) characterized human life in the state of nature as solitary, poor, brutish, and short. In the absence of any overriding power, people are naturally competitive, insecure, and mutually defensive, but they are also rational enough to see that they must form a social compact to protect their own interests. People were essentially equal as they insist on respect and honor from one another. People formed social contracts that emphasized social and political equality. The Enlightenment was important for probation because it reflected the changing social structure. It gave a voice to philosophers who earlier had promoted a new concept of the person and it required a reconsideration of the notion of punishment.

The Enlightenment was in part about rational moral principles in the aid of the poor. The idea was to free people from official care and oversight. Adam Smith in the *Wealth of Nations* (1776) and Marquis de Condorcet in *A Sketch for a Historical Picture of the Progress of the Human Mind* (1795) both argued that justice toward the poor demands that their welfare take priority over all else. The government responsibility was to secure justice but people were to make what they could of their own lives in their own way (Ryan 2001, 43). The Enlightenment offered a new set of values supported by the 18th-century humanists who believed in the innate dignity of the individual (Martindale 1981, 35). These humanists, fortified with their religious views, shared a belief that all are tied together in universal brotherhood. These humanists were certain that reason alone could solve most problems. For them, society was not established for the ends of individuals but was an instrument to perfect the human existence (Martindale 1981, 37). Humanists emphasized personal progress and hope for greater social equality. The industrial revolution and the age of Enlightenment brought with them many changes and what had once been seen as the proper method of application of justice was by 1820 considered scandalous and unjust (Garland 1990, 206).

Transcendentalism

Intellectual ferment and social reform in New England during the early 19th century increased with the rise of transcendentalism (Green 1967, 42). This movement laid heavy stress on the divine in each person and the individual's ability to reach truth by applying a technique called *spiritual intuition*. Among its beliefs was the unity of creation, the goodness of humanity, and supremacy of insight over logic and reason. It was a philosophy that rejected the whole established order because people could establish their own kind of society. It was a liberating philosophy that broke up old orthodoxies (Hofstadter 1992, 33). It was a philosophy that recognized that each offender must be treated with some dignity despite the offense.

The Enlightenment gave way to transcendentalism because various ideas behind the Enlightenment were not completely integrated into the larger society. Much of this problem stemmed from conflicting religious world-views. Most vexing was the conflict between the world-view of the Calvinists and the Enlightenment rationalists. The Calvinists stressed the human's depravity and untrustworthiness, and the enlightened rationalists, who were called deists or Unitarian and Universalists, stressed innate goodness, free will, and reasonableness (McLoughlin 1978, 99). The need for individual treatment of the offender came to be recognized in the changes brought on by altering social and cultural systems.

The Enlightenment also interrupted the movement toward probation, which had been observed during the previous centuries. If previously the development of probation was checked by the lack of humanitarian concerns, during the period of Enlightenment, uniformity and equality before the law reduced the possibility for judicial discretion and individualized punishment (Timasheff 1941b, 295). A reaction, however, against the extreme rationalism, egalitarianism, and formalism in the law represented in the Enlightenment was necessary before probation could be rediscovered (Timasheff 1941b, 295).

Social Sentiments

Ferdinand Tonnies (1971) points out that one of the evolutionary stages of modern society is the movement from the gemeinschaft to the gesellschaft society. Gemeinschaft societies are based on primary relations, tradition, consensus, informality, and kinship. Gesellschaft societies are dominated by secondary relationships that are formal, contractual, expedient, impersonal, and specialized. This modern gesellschaft society has a weak family structure, and emphasizes utilitarian goals and impersonal and competitive social relationships. To further elaborate on this change, Emile Durkheim (1968, 1983) argues that as a society becomes more advanced, the intensity of punishment diminishes. Simple mechanical societies resort to severe measures because the intensity of the collective conscience sees any violation of a law as violating an important religious precept. Violations occurring in the modern or more complex organic society are formalized into criminal offenses that have varying degrees of severity of punishment attached to them. The offended sentiments in advanced societies are, except for the most serious of offenses, less demanding and occupy a less prominent place in social life. What is unique in the modern era is the notion of criminal intent that allows for a distinction between penalties. Modern organic societies have morally diverse character, have a division of labor, have differentiated statuses among the individuals, and have a system of shared beliefs that emphasizes the value of individuality, freedom, dignity, reason, tolerance, and diversity.

Different periods in American history have brought great social change. The 1840s were one such period. Other periods would include the Progressive era from the 1890s to 1914, the 1950s and 1960s and the civil rights movement (1950–1970), and the current era of globalization and computerization of life from 1980 to the present.

By the 19th century, social institutions had become more complex. The 1830s and 1840s were remarkable for New England's economic growth, cultural expansion, and great reform movements. By 1835, the New England Renaissance became the era of Poe, Emerson, Hawthorne, Melville, Thoreau, and Audubon (Alden 1963, 329). In fact, in the 1840s, major institutions were established in many parts of the country. For example, at the time the Smithsonian Institution came into existence in Washington, D.C., the Philharmonic Orchestra was founded in New York City.

A Turning Point

The election of 1828 is commonly considered to be a turning point in American politics (Goetz 1989). Andrew Jackson was the first president elected from west of the Appalachians. His campaign, organized in the West, won the support of the new mass voters. Jackson benefited from rising social sentiment in favor of greater political democracy. The admission of six new states to the union, five of which provided for male suffrage, along with the extension of suffrage in the older states, weakened the power of the established political machines (Goetz 1989, 456). The Jacksonian presidency was a period of great excitement, promise, and change.

The Jacksonians' conception of the causes of crime, for both juveniles and adults, focused on the person's upbringing. The importance of family discipline in a community pervaded with vice characterized practically every spokesperson's statement on delinquency. In conjunction with the building of houses of refuge came the family social history. Parental neglect was targeted as the primary cause of deviance. The movement from petty to serious crime was as inexorable as the climb from the house of refuge to the prison. Saloons, theatres, and houses of prostitution were all blamed for corrupting youth. The Jacksonian analysis of the origins of crime became the rallying cry for action (Rothman 1971, 27–28).

Social Changes

At the time that John Augustus moved to Boston, it was undergoing many changes. Boston earlier made an attempt to create a city without vice, lawlessness, and disease (Green 1967, 41). Prior to 1840, it had no slums and remarkably little crime. This picture was altered when, by 1845, a wave of immigrants hit the city and brought with them intemperance, poverty, criminality, and immorality (Green 1967). Few people recognized the real economic causes for these conditions. Snaring immigrants in the law enforcement process was a reaffirmation of traditional values and an assertion that resident Americans were morally superior

(Fox 1970, 1202). Nonetheless, during this time, a reform effort created sympathy for the lowest classes. True to their Puritan traditions, some Bostonians experienced a deep sense of social responsibility. These people felt responsible for the destiny of the alien, and the socially and educationally underprivileged (Green 1967, 46). In practical terms, the people of Boston believed in the infinite capacity of human nature (Green 1967, 43). Some Bostonians, however, saw these conditions as an invitation to reform their existing institutions, especially in the areas of religion, philosophy, education, and literature.

Various cultural patterns or practices emphasizing the reforming influence of religion and humanitarianism were clearly evident at the time Augustus lived in Boston. This new outlook reached its zenith in the great reform movement underway in New England in the 1840s when Augustus began his work. At the time of Augustus, the Protestant passion for reform was insatiable. It reached into every nook and cranny of American life while it searched for every public vice, every secret blemish. It was not "reform" as considered today—a strenuously secular and liberal spirit of social improvement—but rather was full of the redemptive ardor found in the Protestant Reformation (Smith 1981, 686).

Changing attitudes toward the lawbreakers could not have occurred until the people of Boston moved away from much of the severity, narrowness, and intolerance of inherited Puritan attitudes. Incarceration for debt was forbidden by one state after another, a change heartily welcomed by the working man of that time (Alden 1963, 337). The emphasis on punishment was gradually replaced, in part, by reform or "correction." The most prominent feature of this movement was the emphasis on the practical needs of the person (Brace 1961, 114–115). The leaders of this movement included Horace Mann, Dorothy Dix, Theodore Parker, and William Lloyd Garrison (Alden 1963, 329). These reformers had experiences in various crusades including the abolition of slavery, the temperance movement, the abolition of capital punishment, the women's movement, the mental health reform movement, and the prison reform movement (Alden 1963; Chute and Bell 1956; Smith 1981). These reformers led a nationwide fight against capital punishment 10 years earlier in the 1830s (Smith 1981, 694). Each movement, in its own way, combined humanitarianism with faith in the perfectibility of humans. Many of the leaders had strong religious convictions and were deeply committed to freedom as a necessary attribute of all Americans. The lack of freedom was most obviously noticeable among slaves. The fact that slavery existed in a nation pledged to freedom and equality seemed particularly hypocritical and generated harsh condemnation (Johnson 1988, 149–150).

Religious Fervor

Probation could not have taken hold or started were it not for a series of changes taking place throughout the United States. One of these changes was a rise in religious fervor. These religious awakenings allowed speakers to attack social problems and inequalities in various areas. John Augustus heard these messages as he participated in the various religious institutions in which he found some value in all of them.

Human resistance to change and to the unknown gave way to the desire to convert the dreams of the American Enlightenment to reality (Fox 1970, 1188). As the economy continued to expand in the early 19th century, the middle class grew in numbers, too. The middle class was becoming better educated, expressed values that reflected various sectarian groups they belonged to, and found that their power to vote influenced many areas of society. Many of these people had emigrated from countries where excessively brutal penal codes were in effect. The middle-class white male sought other forms of punishment that were not quite so cruel and wasteful of human labor. Labor shortages made prisoners important economic instruments. Furthermore rapid economic growth created a labor shortage that often meant that permanently eliminating the worker ultimately hurt industrial growth. New forms of punishment were demanded that were considered fairer and just to all classes. These concerns were particularly important for the reformers of the 18th and 19th centuries whose religious convictions and humanitarian sensibilities tended to play a crucial part in the reformative process (Garland 1990, 203). These evangelicals were in the vanguard of the alternative to the imprisonment movement (Garland 1990, 204). They demanded punishment that was both just and reformative.

As America's first age of liberal reform was underway in the 1840s, New England pulpits and podiums rang with denunciation of slavery, poverty, and illiteracy. The spirit of reform seemed on the rise everywhere. Doubtlessly, behind all the good works was an element of self-interest. The propertied classes welcomed an influx of cheap labor but they also worried that in the absence of educational and economic opportunities, immigrants would bring with them the unrest threatening Europe. A crisis between capitalist owners and labor was indicated by Karl Marx and Frederick Engles (Wood 1980). There was an awareness that ignoring the worse inequities could create conditions that required more radical remedies. The individual no longer existed for the benefit of the state.

The First Great Religious Awakening

The first great religious awakening occurred during the 18th century. As McLoughlin reports (1978), the **second great religious awakening** in this country occurred from 1800 to 1830. By 1800, new fears and doubts about the direction the country was taking began to surface. The new nation struggling to develop its own institutions and sense of direction seemed to be losing its revolutionary fervor and commitment. There was general agreement on the nation's achievements and its potential but considerable disagreement about how to proceed. Should slavery, for example, be allowed to expand into new territories? At another level, there was considerable disagreement between those who believed in the rule by the elite educated, rich, and well-born and those who thought the common people should dominate and control their representatives.

The Second Great Religious Awakening

The second great religious awakening was not so much an intellectual movement as it was an organizing process that helped to give meaning and direction to people suffering in various ways (McLoughlin 1978, 98). However, more importantly, it brought into focus a sentiment that was a harbinger of things to come. According to McLoughlin, a new social consensus developed that in-

second great religious awakening was not so much an intellectual movement as it was an organizational process that helped to give meaning and direction to people suffering in various ways.

cluded, among other things, the belief that Americans were a peculiar race, uniquely chosen by God to perfect the world. This was the nation's manifest destiny. Participants in the second great awakening saw themselves as a new and special race that was to uplift inferior peoples (McLoughlin 1978, 106).

The second awakening, which began in Appalachia, had its biggest influence in New England where its institutions, wealth, intellectual, and political leadership were a powerful force around the nation. However, at the turn of the 19th century, New England was thoroughly disillusioned with the course of the nation (McLoughlin 1978, 108). Under the direction of higher education, the young people of this region chose to experiment with religion and political practices. Many of them became missionaries or joined voluntary societies. Congregationalists and the Methodists were particularly active. These churches worked for temperance, Sabbath observance, blue laws (i.e., laws that closed businesses on Sunday), and the arrest of gamblers and prostitutes—and against dueling. Their missionaries promoted a new zeal for reform that supported the republican ideal of the virtuous citizen. After 1830, these religious zealots sometimes became revolutionary as they fought against slavery and alcohol usage and promoted the women's rights movement. With reduced patriarchal influence, children were no longer in awe and fear of their parents, but loved them more and were more respectful (McLoughlin 1978, 115).

The influence of the various socioreligious theories, however, was not enough to foster the further development of probation. To avoid disintegration, institutions needed to regulate and formalize their actions.

Bureaucratic Growth

It is clear that during the 19th century, probation exhibited a rudimentary form of bureaucracy. According to Chambliss and Seidman (1971, 468) "Theorists have identified the bureaucracy as the single most important variable determining the actual functioning of the legal system."

With the passage of laws expanding probation to other communities, the importance played by state law and increased formalism is noted. The rudimentary bureaucracy is both a function of the growth of probation and an indication of the changes society was undergoing. Although the bureaucracy did not achieve complete dominance during the 19th century, there was an effort to consolidate probation operations. From the beginning, an incredibly fragmented probation system, which varied greatly from one court to another, was clearly evident.

Understanding the bureaucracy requires an explication of sociologist Max Weber's theory of domination. In a relationship determined by power, the dominant person believes that he or she has the right to impose his or her will on others and the subjects consider it their duty to obey. In legal domination, the belief in the rule of law is granted because people accepted the procedure that established the law. The typical organizational structure corresponding to the legal type of domination is the bureaucracy. Impersonal rules possessing legal authority determine the course of interaction. These rules delineate the hierarchy of the apparatus, the rights and duties of each position, and the method of recruitment, promotion, and so fourth (Mouzelis 1969, 15–17).

By considering the growth of probation from a volunteer service to a formal organization, one can see a system of laws promulgated to regulate probation as caseloads expanded. These laws determined who was subject to probation, who could be employed as an officer, and what the officer could do with the client. Discipline was assured by a set of rules that are meant to maximize productivity (Mouzelis 1969, 18–19). By taking the common law practices of probation and formalizing them under the rubric of statutory law, the informal practices received formal recognition.

For Max Weber, the existence of written rules triggered the action of administrative staff who formed the core of the bureaucratic administration of justice. It is believed that in the first days of probation, the need to organize a rational system for administering services was an important force. The whole structure of the organization is consciously designed according to rational principles. What Weber called "formal rationality" in law emphasized a purely logical application of written rules by impartial officials (Littrell 1979, 21). Impartiality, for example, in probation work is exhibited in deciding whom to recommend for probation. Impartiality also manifests itself in the form of equality. All probationers deserve similar treatment. These officials are, for the most part, performing specialized functions. The bureaucracy favors the employment of specialists where great attention is given to competence, proficiency, and professionalism in the field (Bensman and Rosenberg 1963, 511). Technical specialists, such as probation officers, were chosen because of their prior experience in law enforcement or social work. The role of the probation officer was to be carefully defined and limited.

Historically, the bureaucracy was said to evolve out of the actions of a charismatic figure (Mouzelis 1969). One such charismatic figure was John Augustus, even though he did not lead an organization. Weber's concept of the historic movement and the trend toward increasing rationalization creates tension between charisma—representing the creative, spontaneous forces of the individual in the group and routine—and the drive toward organizational conformity. The helping orientation of the probation bureaucrat can require a great deal of spontaneity that possibly runs counter to the organization's needs for internal order. Because official probation interactions are often judgmental, probation officers are not free to give themselves unreservedly to clients. Work is hindered by large caseloads, limited resources, and the requirement to treat all clients equally (Lipsky 1980, 74).

■ Conclusion

This chapter explains the forces that influenced a major shift in public sentiments that allowed for the development of probation. First considered were the influences operating during the 19th century. This process began with a change in the concept of the offender, particularly as represented in the cultural forms that expressed society's regard for offenders.

Probation was made possible when rationality, human dignity, and social equality came to importance during the Enlightenment, especially when it became possible to argue that horrific punishments were both unnecessary to prevent future crime and were wasteful of human resources. With this recognition, each individual assumed a new importance, and when combined with discretionary decision making, probation could provide help to people in meeting their practical requirements for daily existence.

Augustus was a man who, in many ways, reflected the excitement of his time when major social movements were simmering in New England. Powerful social, political, and religious forces were operating, to shape probation during its early years. It was a time greatly influenced by the Enlightenment, humanitarian and religious ideals, and a rekindling of interest in the practical problems of humanity, and less on the saving of the person's soul. Probation was springing up not only in Boston, but at the same time in England and on the continent. As a result of these pressures, it is probable that if John Augustus had not provided his assistance, eventually someone else would have done so. John Augustus belongs with the pantheon of other leaders who made significant changes during this period.

Chapter Resources

REFERENCES

Alden, J. R. 1963. *Rise of the American republic.* New York: Harper and Row.

Allen, H., E. Carlson, and E. Parks. 1979. *Critical issues in adult probation.* Washington, DC: U.S. Government Printing Office, U.S. Department of Justice.

Augustus, J. 1972. *John Augustus: First probation officer.* Montclair, NJ: Patterson Smith.

Beccaria, C. 1764. *On crimes and punishment.* Translated by H. Paolucci, 1963. New York: Macmillan.

Bensman, J., and B. Rosenberg. 1963. *Mass, class and bureaucracy.* Englewood Cliffs, NJ: Prentice Hall.

Berman, H. 1983. *Law and revolution.* Cambridge, MA: Harvard University Press.

Bernard, T. J. 1992. *The cycle of juvenile justice.* New York: Oxford University Press.

Black, H. C. 1979. *Black's law dictionary.* St. Paul, MN: West.

Brace, C. L. 1961. The new and practical movement. In R. E. Pumphrey and M. W. Pumphrey, eds., *The heritage of American social work.* New York: Columbia University, pp. 114–115.

Carter, R., D. Glaser, and L. Wilkens. 1984. *Probation, parole, and community corrections.* New York: Wiley.

Chambliss, W., and R. Seidman. 1971. *Law, order, and power.* Reading, MA: Addison & Wesley.

Champion, D. J. 1990. *Probation and parole in the United States.* Columbus, OH: Merrill.

Chute, C. L., and M. Bell. 1956. *Crime, courts and probation.* New York: Macmillan.

Delbanco, A. 2001. An experiment in darkness. *New York Review of Books* 48 (14): 36–39.

Diana, L. 1960. What is probation? *Journal of Criminal Law, Criminology, and Police Science* 51: 189–208.

Dressler, D. 1959. *Practice and theory of probation and parole.* New York: Columbia University Press.

Durkheim, E. 1983. The evolution of punishment. In S. Lukes and A. Scull, eds. *Durkheim and the law.* Stanford: Stanford University Press, pp. 98–118.

Durkheim, E. 1968. *The division of labor.* New York: Free Press.

Fox, S. J. 1970. Juvenile justice reform: An historical perspective. *Stanford Law Review* 22: 1187–1239.

Garland, D. 1990. *Punishment and modern society.* Chicago: University of Chicago.

Goetz, P., ed. 1989. *The new Britannica encyclopedia,* II and IV. Chicago: Encyclopedia Britannica.

Green, M. 1967. *The problem of Boston: Some readings in cultural history.* New York: Norton.

Grunhut M. 1948. *Penal reform: A comparative study.* Oxford: Clarendon Press.

Grinnell, F. W. 1917. Probation as an orthodox common law practice in Massachusetts prior to the statutory system. *Massachusetts Law Quarterly* 2: 601–612.

Hamlin, C. (1995). Could you starve to death in England in 1839: The Chadwick-Farr controversy and the loss of the "social" in public health. *American Journal of Public Health* 85 (6): 856–866.

Hamlin, C. (1998). Revolutions in public health: 1848, and 1988. *British Medical Journal* 317: 587–591.

Hay, D. 1975. Property, authority and criminal law. In D. Hay, P. Linbaugh, J. Rule, E. Thompson, and C. Winslow. *Albion's fatal tree.* New York: Pantheon, pp. 17–63.

Henningsen, R. 1981. *Probation and parole.* New York: Harcourt Brace Jovanovich.

Hobbes, T. 1990. Thomas Hobbes from *The Leviathan.* In R. Solomon and M. Murphy. *What is justice: Classic and contemporary readings.* New York: Oxford University Press, pp. 80–100.

Hofstadter, R. 1992. *Social Darwinism in American thought.* Boston: Beacon.

Johnson, H. 1988. *History of criminal justice.* Cincinnati, OH: Anderson.

Krajick, K. 1980. Probation: The original community program. *Corrections Magazine* 6: 6–12.

Killinger, G., and P. Cromwell. 1978. *Corrections in the community.* St. Paul, MN: West.

Linder, C., and M. R. Savares. 1984. The evolution of probation: University settlement and the beginning of statutory probation in New York City. *Federal Probation* 48: 3–12.

Lipsky, M. 1980. *Street-level bureaucracy.* New York: Russell Sage.

Littrell, B. 1979. *Bureaucratic justice: Police, prosecutors and plea bargaining.* Beverly Hills, CA: Sage.

Martindale, R. 1981. *The nature and types of sociological theory,* 2nd ed. Boston: Houghton Mifflin.

McLoughlin, W. 1978. *Revivals, awakenings and reform.* Chicago: University of Chicago Press.

Montesquieu, B. 1988. *Great books of the western world: Montesquieu - Rosseau.* Robert Hutchins, ed. Chicago: Encyclopedia Britannica.

Mouzelis, N. P. 1969. *Organization and bureaucracy: An analysis of modern theories.* Chicago: Aldine.

Platt, A. 1977. *The child savers: The invention of delinquency.* Chicago: University of Chicago Press.

Rotman, E. 1990. *Beyond punishment: A new view of the rehabilitation of criminal offenders.* New York: Greenwood.

Rothman, D. 1971. *The discovery of the asylum.* Boston: Little, Brown.

Ryan, A. 2001. Economic sentiments: Adam Smith, Condorcet, and the Enlightenment by Rothchild, Emma. *New York Review of Books* XLVIII (11): 42–45.

Smith, P. 1981. *The nation comes of age*, vol. IV. New York: McGraw-Hill.

Sullivan, L. E. 1990. *The prison reform movement*. Boston: Twayne.

Timasheff, N. S. 1941a. *One hundred years of probation 1841–1941.* New York: Fordham University Press.

Timasheff, N. S. 1941b. Probation and imposed peace. *Thought* 16: 275–296.

Tonnies, F. 1971. *On sociology: Pure, applied, and empirical.* Chicago: University of Chicago.

United Nations. 1951. The legal origins of probation. In R. Carter and L. Wilkins, eds. *Probation, parole, and community corrections.* New York: John Wiley.

Wood, A. 1980. The Marxian critique of justice. In Marshall Cohen, Thomas Nagel, and Thomas Scanlon, eds. *Marx, justice and history.* Princeton, NJ: Princeton University Press, pp. 3–41.

KEY POINTS

1. The germ of probation is found in peace oaths, the benefit of clergy, suspended sentences, and recognizance practices found in Europe.

2. In 1841, the first sustained services resembling modern-day probation were provided in Birmingham, England, and Boston, Massachusetts.

3. John Augustus, a Boston boot maker, known as the father of probation, utilized concrete measures to improve the lives of his probationers.

4. Augustus was opposed by the press, politicians, and criminal justice personnel working in the court.

5. Augustus had the support of other progressive movements including the temperance movement, the women's movement, the mental health reform movement, the prison reform movement, those who wanted to abolish slavery, and those who wanted to abolish capital punishment.

6. During a time when labor was in short supply, society found brutal punishments to be wasteful.

7. The Enlightenment was important for probation because it reflected the changing social structure. It gave voice to philosophers who earlier had promoted a new concept of the person, and it required a reconsideration of the notion of punishment.

8. Probation could not have taken hold were it not for the great religious awakening taking place in the eastern and southern portions of the United States.

9. The bureaucratic growth of probation as a formal organization began in Massachusetts and is a reflection of the historic movement of the time and toward increasing rationalization of processes.

KEY TERMS

Enlightenment is a European intellectual movement in which ideas concerning God, reason, nature, and humans were synthesized into a world-view that drew wide interests and instigated revolutionary developments in the arts, philosophy, and politics.

judicial reprieve was a temporary suspension of either the imposition or the execution of a prison sentence. It was used to permit the accused a chance to seek a pardon when the judge was not satisfied with the verdict or when the evidence was suspicious.

recognizance for good behavior was an obligation with sureties entered into before the court or magistrate. Entering into a recognizance (with or without sureties) created a debt to the state that became enforceable over a period of time when specified conditions were not met. If a violation occurred, the person was required to appear in court, and if found guilty, to forfeit a certain sum of money.

second great religious awakening   was not so much an intellectual movement as it was an organizational process that helped to give meaning and direction to people suffering in various ways.

suspended sentence   means either the withholding or postponing of a sentencing of a prisoner after conviction or postponing the execution of a sentence after it has been pronounced.

REVIEW QUESTIONS

1. What were the main forces behind the changes that took place in the bringing about of how probation is practiced today?

2. Discuss the importance of recognizance in the development of modern-day probation.

3. What influence did John Augustus have on probation in the 1800s?

4. Explain how and why probation changed in 1878.

5. Explain how probation would be viewed during the Enlightenment. What might be the nature of the punishment?

6. How did the religious awakening and socioeconomic changes in the 18th and 19th centuries affect the development of probation?

Twentieth-Century Probation

Chapter Objectives

In this chapter you will learn about:

- The state taking primacy over the individual
- The offender becoming a source of scientific inquiry
- How various probationary practices limit human dignity
- The increasing concern for human dignity in society

Probation is a 150-year-old institution that has been marked by piecemeal growth and showered with ideas that may or may not be reflected in practice. Lacking strong professional leadership, the field became fragmented, isolated, and unresponsive to community values. Some departments came to use new ideas under the rubric of casework while others continued to emphasize the more rigid notion of supervision and conformity. As the field evolved, the debate over the policing versus counseling function continued, but the field also adopted new theoretical concepts relative to offender management, surveillance, assessment, and casework.

By 1900, numerous states recognized the professional status of probation by implementing various practices to ensure the maintenance of high standards. From the start, state legislation made it possible for probation to be administered by either the state or the county. In 1897, Missouri, following the example of Massachusetts, became the second state to enact a probation law. In 1898, Vermont enacted county-based probation statutes while Rhode Island enacted state-based statutes (Smith and Berlin 1979). Thirty-seven states, including Illinois and the District of Columbia, had a children's court by 1910. Forty states also had introduced probation for juveniles. By 1925, probation for juveniles was available in every state, but this was not achieved for adults until 1956 (President's Commission 1967, 27).

Progressives were interested in a variety of social program reforms including safety and sanitation codes, worker compensation laws, 8-hour workdays, and abolition of sweatshops. Prison and reform schools also came under scrutiny.

Progressivism was a reform movement the like of which had not been seen since the 1840s. This reform effort was in response to the belief that social problems were too complex for the current governmental institutions to solve. Various schemes to ensure popular control of the government were enacted into law including the initiative, referendum, and recall.

It is important to ask what has happened over the course of the 20th century to a punishment that was designed to provide care and treatment of the minor offender. To develop this understanding, society needs to consider the roles played by the <u>Progressives</u>, organizational and statutory developments, federal initiatives, the drive for professionalism, post-war probation, radical nonintervention, the justice model, and current perspectives.

■ The Progressives

Hardly had the 20th century dawned when the nation was consumed by <u>Progressivism</u>, a reform movement the like of which had not been seen since the 1840s (Bailey 1961). This reform effort was in response to the belief that social problems were too complex for the current governmental institutions to solve. Various schemes to ensure popular control of the government were enacted into law including the initiative, referendum, and recall. The Progressives were interested in a variety of social program reforms including safety and sanitation codes, worker compensation laws, 8-hour workdays, and abolition of sweatshops. Prison and reform schools also came under scrutiny (Bailey 1961, 665).

The emergence of the land grant state universities in 1870 brought the expertise of the social scientist to bear on various social problems (Hofstadter 1955). Many progressive programs were formed by philanthropic-minded college graduates who came from curricula that included courses on the punishment of criminality and public and private charities (Rothman 1980, 46). Many shared optimistic theories that at once clarified the origins of deviant behavior and suggested strategies for controlling this behavior. The Progressives possessed great faith in the American system (Rothman 1980, 5). Increasingly, from the 19th century onward, penal practices were influenced by a variety of academic disciplines, in the shape of scientific criminology, penology, psychology, medicine, and so on. This knowledge expresses itself as specific cultural forms (Garland 1990, 209). These cultural forms found expression in probation.

The Progressives and Probation

The Progressives did not ignore probation; in fact, it came to be their quintessential form of punishment. Progressives were not enthusiastic supporters of incarceration nor were they believers, as some penologists, that a well-ordered asylum was essential in assuring social stability. The Progressives were the culmination of a process that first viewed the underclass as in need of pity, then in need of understanding, and finally, in need of coercion (Rothman 1978). This is not considered an appropriate expression of support for the human dignity of people, if for no other reason than the idea denies human autonomy and their ability to make moral choices. Essential to the Progressive ideology was a belief in the primacy of the state as a parent; offenders were treated like children. Individual needs had primacy over individual rights. Accordingly, state intervention involved wide-ranging actions designed to bring the downtrodden into the middle class. In order to achieve this goal, force was to be used only as the last resort. With the adoption of probation, society had the means to provide for someone's needs but if the probationer chose to reject the offer of help, then force was to be used to gain compliance to the system's master plan. The idea was to provide legitimacy to community corrections while maintaining an abiding belief that the state would carry out this agenda in good faith (Cullen and Gilbert 1982, 77–81).

Lacking faith in prisoner reform, the Progressives saw probation as a chance to try out new techniques and theories (Sullivan 1990, 28). Of central importance was a case-by-case analysis employed by many treatment specialists, especially in probation, whose task was to understand the life history of each offender and then devise a specific remedy (Rothman 1980, 5). The life history of the person was understood by employing one of two interpretations: The environmentalist located the problem in the wretched milieu, while the psychologist focused on the mind-set of the person. Both schools agreed, nonetheless, that each case had to be analyzed and responded to on its own terms and that some offenders were best treated in the community, hence the need for probation (Rothman 1980, 5). Initially, the Progressive foray into treatment, especially popular from 1900 to 1915, was spearheaded by the environmentalists, who cast the probation officer as a "friend." The officer's task was to develop confidence and friendship through helpful oversight and encouraging advice (Rothman 1980, 64). This strategy was to become the modus operandi of the probation officer for years to come.

Discretion

The centerpiece of the Progressive strategy was the exercise of discretion (Rothman 1980, 6). To the Progressives, permitting greater discretion met the requirements of justice, the aims of therapy, the welfare of the individual, and the security of society (Rothman 1980, 6). The Progressives adopted the discretionary model offered by the medical profession (Rothman 1980) in the hope of strengthening their position as professionals. They were not entirely successful because they were not wholeheartedly accepted by the court and the police (Hagan and Leon 1977) as the new officers were often considered "new fangled" reformers (Linder 1992, 49). Probation eventually won these people over because judges came to see the officer as providing an important resource for decision making. The judge now had the help of a person whose specific job was to look into the defendant's situation and character. The first offender, caught in the tangles of justice, had a chance to escape imprisonment through the vast discretionary powers of the probation officer and judge (Friedman 1993, 407).

Progressives Success

The success of the Progressives was limited in that the promise of the new social sciences proved insufficient in addressing crime and punishment. Furthermore, while the reforms and practices supported by the Progressives have been heavily criticized, they, nonetheless, provided a means for developing a focal point of consistent action permitting the testing of new ideas. Opposition to the formalization of probation was found at both the state and federal levels.

According to Scull (1983), Progressive innovations were transformed into harsh caricatures of themselves. They served merely to advance the self-interest of caretaker professionals, or as with social work, virtually to create the profession that perpetuated them. For example, the introduction of probation and the indeterminate sentence increased the inducement to "cop a plea," and the plea bargaining enabled judges and prosecutors to shorten trials, ease crowded court calendars, and raise the conviction rate, as well as to insulate both their own and police conduct from further judicial scrutiny and review. The Progressives, despite their efforts to formalize the process by making it more rational, created a criminal justice system that lost sight of the person in the offender. No longer was the offender to be treated as an individual with powers to make his or her own decision but was soon converted into an item for scientific inquiry. As a result, the offender lost all sense of autonomy and was treated as a specimen. His or her human worth was denied when the goal became to unlock the key that explained his or her behavior without suggesting that society had any responsibility for what had taken place.

■ Organizational and Statutory Developments

Popular pressure in support of probation led to its authorization in New York in 1901. The passage of this law was spearheaded by Samuel Barrow, a Unitarian minister and practical humanitarian who was concerned about the abuses of imprisonment (Chute and Bell 1956, 74). Soon thereafter, in 1902 and 1903, bills were passed authorizing probation supervision for children and extending the probation system to courts throughout New York. Buffalo established the first children's court in New York State as a separate division of its city court. From its inception, probation saved money for the state by not sending offenders off to state prisons, but not for the locality who had to pick up the cost (Sullivan 1990). The Buffalo Probation Department, from the beginning, had excessive caseloads and poor physical facilities. Among the early probation officers were volunteer social workers assigned from private and religious agencies, and police and court officers temporarily assigned to probation duties (Chute and Bell 1956, 75; Linder 1992, 45). It was not until 1904 that the first salary appropriations were made.

New York provides further indications of the growth of probation as a bureaucracy. In 1907, New York pioneered in establishing the first permanent state probation commission. At that time, there were as many systems of probation in the state as there were courts using the probation law. The commission was required to study the probation system, receive and publish reports from all probation officers, prescribe record keeping, and raise standards throughout the state. When the commission began its work, 1,672 probationers were supervised by 35 salaried officers. By 1913, the probationers numbered 8,607 and the salaried officers had increased to 157. These jobs were filled by civil service examinations (Chute and Bell 1956, 79; McGinnis 1960).

In 1926, a state crime commission made additional proposals. The commission did not go so far as to recommend complete state control but urged the following steps: the creation of the division of probation in the department of corrections to replace the state probation commission; the merging of the New York City central probation bureau; and the recodification of probation laws (Chute and Bell 1956, 80–81).

In 1928, the state division of probation assumed authority to provide leadership in the state's system. The division had offices located throughout New York that provided supervision and service to the local offices. The local offices were instructed in how to collect data, deal with special problems, conduct special studies, sponsor legislation, and revise rules regulating probation (McGinnis 1960). The evolution and development of probation did not go unopposed.

Opposition to Probation

This opposition and limits to probation came from those who feared the competition, those who opposed the use of police officers, and those who didn't know what to do with women. Serious resistance came from the New York Society for the Prevention of Cruelty to Children. The society felt any new law would infringe on their monopoly over existing children's services and threaten their viability (Chute and Bell 1956, 75). Their opposition caused the law to be limited to adults. Furthermore, the society contended that existing laws were adequate for the care of delinquent children, although as a matter of fact, little supervision was provided. The use of police as probation officers was opposed by settlement workers. They charged that this practice permitted a corrupt police officer to monitor the activities of novice criminals (Linder and Savarese 1984; Sullivan 1990). Officials initially tried to establish separate procedures for female probationers. Some agencies excused female probationers from reporting for a number of reasons: to discourage commingling with other probationers, to prevent exploitation by males who loitered in the waiting areas, and to prevent traveling the city after dark (Linder 1992, 50). Such concerns about probation were not limited to New York.

In Ohio, Reginald Smith and Herbert Erhmann, participants in the 1917 Cleveland Crime Survey, were bitterly critical. Probationers, they argued, were a bad lot, the dregs of the process—those with anything in their favor had been filtered out before trial or by pleading to a misdemeanor—yet the offenders went practically unpunished. The fault also lay, they thought, in the weak, understaffed probation department where offenders were paroled to relatives, detectives, clerks, and even stenographers in the prosecutor office. As a result, probation was a "joke" (Friedman 1993, 408–409).

Efforts continued to restrict those eligible for probation in New York, too. As early as 1922, in New York a bill was introduced, but not passed, that stipulated no person previously convicted of a crime could be placed on probation. Then in 1928, a law was passed that prohibited the use of probation by anyone convicted of his or her fourth felony, as well as anyone who committed a crime with a weapon. In 1930, fearing abuses in probation, the prosecuting attorney was given the opportunity to be heard and the reasons for granting probation were then to be entered into the court's minutes (Timasheff 1941, 55).

By 1960, probation existed in all but four counties in New York and a unified system of probation was in place in all but 18 counties (McGinnis 1960, 106). Today, all New York counties have some form of probation and are working from a unified model for administration; moreover, there are over 120,000 people on probation in New York and the state employs over 1,000 officers (Camp and Camp 1989).

Federal Initiatives

Over 150 years ago, the federal theory of criminal justice, in common with the times, was punitive. It held that the primary function of the federal courts was to establish guilt and impose punishment as a form of retribution and as a deterrent to crime. Consequently, long before there were any probation laws on the books, the federal courts found themselves struggling with the harsh penalties they were compelled by statute to impose upon wrongdoers (Meyer 1952, 713).

Experience demonstrated that imprisoning an offender took the individual out of circulation but only temporarily protected society. Judges gradually came to discard the theories of retribution and deterrence. Instead, they adopted the view that social protection was best gained through the methods of correctional treatment that promoted social adjustment and a useful and law-abiding citizen, thereby benefiting not only the criminal and his or her family but society as a whole. The only problem was that the judges had no statutory authority to do this (Meyer 1952, 713).

Federal judges had employed various techniques to modify the penalties including (Meyer 1952, 713)

1. partial suspension of sentence
2. suspension of the sentence in its entirety
3. continuances to a later date
4. suspension with provision for oversight
5. unclassified suspension

Laws on the books at the time did not say that the judge had the right to suspend judgment or sentence, but many of the federal courts reasoned that what the law did not forbid the law permitted. Before 1916, many federal judges opposed a probation statute as unnecessary as long as they could suspend sentences and as uneconomical because they were not required to hire probation officers. By 1916, thousands of federal offenders were serving suspended sentences. All of this activity was done without any proper supervision of the offender (Meyer 1952, 713). This problem came to a head with what became known as the *Killits* case.

The 1916 *Killits* Case

This case (Exparte United States, 242 U.S. 27) brought to the forefront the lack of legal authority under which federal courts had operated. According to Timasheff (1941), Federal District Court Judge John M. Killits sentenced a man guilty of embezzlement with 5-year suspension of the execution of the sentence during the good behavior of the defendant. The federal prosecutor moved to set aside Killits' order on the grounds that it was not a mere temporary suspension of the sentence but a permanent suspension based upon considerations extraneous to the legality of the conviction or duty to enforce the sentence. Judge Killits' failure to recognize the government's motion resulted in the case being carried to the U.S. Supreme Court. The Supreme Court's decision denied the existence of an inherent power in courts to grant an absolute suspension of sentence and argued that ascribing such power to the courts was contrary to the constitutional principle of separation of powers. The decision of the Supreme

Court was, for a time, disastrous to the development of federal probation. There were three immediate consequences: First, the president "pardoned" about 5,000 offenders placed on probation by the federal courts. Second, federal judges began to look for new devices that would allow for the application of probation despite the decision of the Supreme Court. In extreme cases, judges adjourned their decision for an indefinite period and required the offenders to report at stated times and to submit to certain conditions. Finally, they imposed minimum sentences, such as 1 day in jail.

After the *Killits* decision, the federal courts were hard put to find some method of showing leniency where merited. The problem became particularly acute with the passage of the National Prohibition Act or the Volstead Act that enforced the prohibition of alcohol. Andrew Volstead, as chairman of the House of Representatives' Judiciary Committee, insisted that no leniency be shown liquor violators. This is especially evident in that the penal provision of the prohibition act made no mention of probation at all and instead offenders were to be fined or jailed. The failure to recognize the role of probation in the Volstead Act created additional pressures on the courts and jails, further necessitating the acceptance of probation.

By 1925, the federal courts were given the power to suspend the imposition or execution of the sentence and to place the defendant on probation when it appeared that justice and the best interests of the public, as well as those of the defendant, would be served in doing so. No personal restriction was imposed on the discretionary powers of the courts. The courts were also given the power to determine the length of probation (but not beyond 5 years), to impose such terms and conditions of probation as they thought best, and to revoke or modify such conditions. The conditions might be payment of a fine, restitution or reparation to the aggrieved party, or support of the family (Timasheff 1941, 65).

As a result of the *Killits* case, an interruption of 8 years, the federal probation system basically had to be reconstructed. The new federal act that was created charged probation officers with the duties of investigating cases, making reports to the courts, and supervising probationers. No provisions were made for centralized supervision of the activity of any federal probation officers. Salaried officers were to be appointed after a competitive examination that was to be held in accordance with the laws and regulations of the civil service. One salaried probation officer could be appointed in each court. The appropriations for salaries were so small that the use of volunteers continued to be a necessity. Volunteer probation officers were widely used. After an initial period of enthusiasm, the volunteers' services were so restricted that federal probation threatened to degenerate into a system of suspended sentences without any supervision of the behavior of probationers (Timasheff 1941, 65). In 1930, the federal government dropped the civil service requirement and the limitation on the number of salaried probation officers. The U.S. Attorney General was given the power to prescribe report forms and to supervise the officers' work. Appropriations for probation increased from $25,000 to $200,000 and a probation supervisor was appointed to create order in the system (Timasheff 1941, 66). By 1940, there were 233 probation officers throughout the country.

Ironically, the *Killits* decision had a favorable impact on the spread of probation. When the Supreme Court held that the judiciary could not unilaterally suspend sentences indefinitely, it also ruled that the legislature could authorize the court's use of the indefinite suspensions of sentence by the courts. In other words, if indefinite sentences were permitted under statute, they were legal. By thus resolving the original dispute concerning court authority to order probation and providing an acceptable legal basis for the practice, the *Killits* decision was a positive influence on the development of probation (Henningsen 1981, 17).

The *Killits* case was another effort by the conservative element in this country to abolish probation or at least limit its application. By bringing the case to court, the supporters of tough sentences hoped that the whole notion of probation would be viewed as unconstitutional and, therefore, abolished or put under tight limitations. The liberalization of society brought on by the Progressive movement finally found support in the court after the tremendous pressure put on the system by Prohibition.

Professionalism

Initially, probation was conceived not as therapeutic treatment applied by expertly trained individuals but as a humanitarian penal undertaking. Early on adult probation was set up to help the nonprofessional criminals who had committed offenses without evil intent. The motivation behind probation was to offer an alternative to exposing the offender to the contaminating influence of the prisons. The criterion for selection of the first candidates was whether the offender was a risk to the community as determined by an assessment of the violator's character. The selection process became more sophisticated with the application of a **deterministic theory of crime**. It argued crime was the result of antecedent conditions that predisposed the offender to take certain action. Among professionals, determinism had replaced individual free will (Lehman 1975, 51). Cesare Lombroso, an Italian criminologist and organically oriented psychiatrist, developed the concept that criminals were motivated by some organic disease or congenital defect. Under the influence of scientific methodology, criminals were to be classified as either "congenital" or "occasional" offenders (Lehman 1975). Probation officers of the period (circa 1910) were encouraged by the belief that if crime was a manifestation of a disease, then scientific knowledge could give them the treatment they needed to be effective.

deterministic theory of crime states that crime was the result of antecedent conditions or events that preceded the action.

Diagnosis of a Delinquent

By 1918, probation leaders believed they possessed the required tools to make a comprehensive diagnosis of a delinquent (Lehman 1975, 53). Imbued with the philosophy of social work and encouraged by the "scientific methodology" (meaning establishing a theory, hypothesis development, prediction, experiment, and evaluation), Edwin Cooley, a leading social reformer, had great hopes for the future of probation. With the blessing of the archdiocese of New York, he established an experimental program emphasizing the individualized approach, supposedly to be conducted under ideal conditions including an adequate number of social work staff, proper equipment, and other resources. The upshot of this experiment was that Cooley proposed 60 standards for treatment, evaluation, and practice. Most of these standards were to be adopted later by other agencies. Any problem with the client or a lack of reformation was assumed to be due to the failure to meet these professional standards. The high rate of initial success for probation may, however, have had less to do with the treatment program and more to due to the quality of the person on probation (Lehman 1975, 54). The key to success was not the diagnosis and treatment but the selection of the proper candidate.

After World War I as probation services further expanded, there was an increased demand for professionally educated people, especially trained social workers, to serve as probation officers. The training of social workers, in turn, was profoundly influenced by the introduction of psychiatric and psychoanalytic theory. The diagnosis was primarily concerned with the individual's emotional problems and deficiencies (President's Commission 1967, 30); thus, the treatment emphasized psychotherapy. Therefore, the professional probation caseworker came to be valued for the ability to offer individually oriented therapy (President's Commission 1967, 30). To this day, psychodynamic treatment methods continue to be used by probation officers working with sex offenders (Sampson 1994, 21).

■ The Medical Model

From the 1920s onward, there was a gradual acceptance of the **medical model** that consisted of the diagnosis of the symptoms, a treatment aimed at the problem or symptoms, and a cure, or amelioration, of the problem. The medical model assures a "cure" if proper diagnosis is followed by equally proper treatment (Rose 1975, 58). This model gained prominence due to its association with the growing prestige of the medical profession (Lehman 1975, 47). The status of the professional social worker–probation officer was supposedly enhanced by adopting the practices of the medical professional. If true, then perhaps much of the criminal justice system's faith in the medical model rests not with its efficacy, but with its association with the medical profession. Any reluctance to change this approach is evident when considering the fact that probation administrators often appealed to this approach when emphasizing to funding sources the professional nature of their work (Lehman 1975, 54–55). What affinity probation officers could not find with the medical profession they found in social work (Lehman 1975, 53).

medical model was used for analyzing and addressing the antecedent conditions associated with the offense consisting of the diagnosis of the symptoms of the crime; a treatment aimed at the problem or symptoms; and a cure, or amelioration, of the problem.

Criticisms of the Model

Over the years, the medical model received a great deal of criticism. One of the main concerns is the *doctrine of specific etiology* (Rose 1975). This doctrine assumes that it is possible to identify a single causal factor associated with a particular phenomenon. The single causal model unquestionably has been constructive for medicine but this cannot be said for those laboring in the field of social science. Human behavior is far too complex, frequently reflecting unconscious motives and elaborate rationalizations. There are too many past and present internal and external factors influencing behavior for any one person to completely understand a specific course of action at a particular moment in time.

The medical model, furthermore, has been attacked because of various inconsistencies in the application of the concept, whether it is in the definition of the crime, the diagnosis, the treatment, or in the conclusion that the person is cured. Most importantly, the medical model has been attacked because of the power it granted those who were responsible for implementing it. A major complaint against probation officers in the past has been a treatment model that allowed them unchecked sway over the lives of probationers (O'Leary 1987, 10). This problem is particularly vexatious when inadequately trained individuals make decisions exercising unbridled discretion. Today, few people are naive enough to believe broadly exercised discretion can achieve probation's goals without promoting a sense of injustice. This discretionary power fails abysmally because it denies the essential qualities of human dignity in the offender. The model denies the offenders' powers to reason and act with a measure of self-determinism. The offender is consistently viewed as lacking the ability to be self-activating, self-directing, self-criticizing, self-correcting, and self-understanding. No longer is the offender capable of independently evaluating, calculating, organizing, explaining, conjecturing, or justifying his or her actions in a way that reflects the offender's inherent self-worth. What this means is that society has lost sight of the person in the offender. When technology is brought to play through psychological testing and through classification schemes that focus on unchangeable factors, the offender is put in the position being forced to operate in a "clockwork orange" environment, where punishment and behavior modification are the norm.

Deficiencies of the Model

Offenders need educational and vocational skills, job opportunities, and adaptation of conventional values and goals (Palmer 1994, 109). Many of these factors are related to the person's socioeconomic status and may be intractable at the individual level.

As a result of these deficiencies, the medical model—specifically, the diseased entity or fundamentally deficient and defective view of the offender—has seldom been invoked since the mid-1970s. Thus, when it is currently referred to as a basis for criticizing or characterizing various psychologically or socially/psychologically weighted accounts of offenders, it comprises a largely obsolete argument (Palmer 1994, 189). The problem becomes one of explanation when the behavioral sciences are drawing closer to the natural sciences and the medical field, and the medical model is drawing on explanations for crime that still bear a good deal of sociological learning theory (Palmer 1994).

In the abstract, there is ample evidence for critiquing the medical model as applied to the probation setting. Probation officers are confronted daily with a myriad of social, psychological, and economic problems that require attention. Probation officers are continuously asked what should be done with a probationer who is not complying with the conditions of probation. The officer has either a probationer who is seeking help or a parent who would like some advice. This requires diagnosis, treatment, and determination of cure. The officer needs to understand why this is happening, what can be done about it, and when the problem is no longer a concern. It is also important to recognize that for some people this would simply be called casework: the identification of problem, the application of solution, and the recognition of problem rectification.

There are some additional similarities between probation and the medical field. Although the medical profession practices, for the most part, natural science where probabilities are quite high, it must also be recognized that the medical field does not deal in complete certainties. As with the social scientist, the medical professional must assign a probability to any diagnosis and treatment. Not all treatments work with the same high degree of certainty. The one advantage the medical profession has is that frequently it is dealing with a specific etiological condition that can be identified with a high degree of certainty. Sometimes this is not possible, either. A final point is that the treatment given both the patient and the probationer is similar in that in both cases one waits in the waiting area for a long time to speak to an authority figure for only a few minutes. Much of that discussion focuses on what should be done when the person leaves the office. Quite often what is required is that the patient or probationer refrain from doing something or is asked to do something that other people are freely doing, too. For example, both the physician and the probation officer may ask the person to stop drinking.

■ Post-War Probation

The 1950s and 1960s represented the apotheosis of the American spirit. Having ended World War II with the atomic bomb, the United States possessed a sense of technological arrogance that would achieve its zenith with the landing on the moon. The civil rights movement took on a power of its own as it was led by Martin Luther King, Malcolm X, and others. A theme that has consistently run through their discussions was the importance of respecting human dignity. More importantly, the civil rights movement let people conclude that anyone could share in the American dream. There was a belief that any problem could be solved if enough resources were poured into it.

A More Humane Justice System

In retrospect, the 1950s and 1960s represented a movement to make criminal justice more humane and offer greater dignity. According to O'Leary (1987), probation agencies employed standardized case development and reporting techniques. Essentially, probation was understood to be a matter of counseling and referral to community agencies. Presentence reports were designed to identify the causes of the offender's behaviors and to delineate the appropriate intervention. All of this action was contrived to prepare the probationer for release and a future free from crime. The problem was that whether incarcerated or placed on probation, whether given psychotherapy, group counseling, job training, or no assistance at all, the proportion of offenders who returned to crime seemed to be about the same—roughly one in three (Silberman 1980, 505).

When immediate results were not forthcoming and problems seemed more intractable than originally thought, people looked for a change. Simultaneously, a wave of conservatism swept the country. Its roots can be found, perhaps, in the great fear and hatred of crime but also as a function of the myth of rugged individualism that permeated this country for decades. This belief ultimately meant that each person is individually responsible for his or her own condition. Some people, it was thought, could benefit from assistance, some could do well enough without it, and for some, no level of assistance would make any difference. The crime rate and the failure of various programs simply came to symbolize this belief in more concrete terms. With this information, and with the failures delineated by the Lipton, Martinson, and Wilks (1975) report, to both conservatives and moderates alike, there was not much to be sanguine about when it came to reform of the criminal. If the truth be known, treatment does work in some cases. The problem is one of trying to expand a successful treatment to a client population for which the treatment is basically inappropriate. Despite this knowledge, enormous pressure came to bear on politicians to do something about the crime problem (Friedman 1993, 305).

According to O'Leary and Clear (1984), caseload management and counseling are the bread and butter of probation work. The problem is that the caseload-counseling approach rests on assumptions about change processes that may be untenable. Most significantly, it assumes that one person can handle the broad range of problems present in a normal caseload. It seems, beyond dispute, that many probation officers lack the skills to deal adequately with all of these problems. The fact that the setting is authoritarian further militates against this approach. It is now widely accepted that little is accomplished when the treatment is coerced. Furthermore, the use of discretion suggests that it is nearly impossible to carefully balance the role of helper with the need to enforce conditions. This may be why research has had a hard time finding support for its usefulness. However, due to administrative convenience, this approach continues.

The Rehabilitation Model

rehabilitation model provides the only justification of punishment that requires the state to care for the offender's needs and welfare.

Despite these findings, the treatment model, or the belief that offenders can become productive citizens with the appropriate help, continues to hold great importance. The rehabilitation model, according to Cullen and Gilbert (1982), is still quite useful. The **rehabilitation model** provides the only justification of punishment that requires the state to care for the offender's needs and welfare. Rehabilitation provides a measure of balance against the conservative notion that increased punishment will reduce crime. Rehabilitation still receives a considerable amount of support among the public. Lastly, rehabilitation has historically been an important motive underlying the requirement that those in the system must be treated humanely.

There is concern with punishing the deserving but there is also the recognition that some offenders are more deserving than others. In conjunction with this, there is a greater use made of multiple supervision levels. Most departments are moving toward gradations of caseloads in which there exists large caseloads for those judged to be low risk and small intensive caseloads for high-risk offenders. This is best understood as *differential supervision*. Differential supervision provides various levels of supervision for the offender on the basis of the offender's assumed risk and needs. Rules were established that enunciate how a person moves from a high-risk to a low-risk caseload. With these high-risk caseloads, society also gets greater accountability. The officer must identify the specific objectives for each probationer. In order to make all of this work, there is a growing trend to develop elaborate computerized information systems to aid in case management (O'Leary 1987).

Whatever might be said about the benefits of rehabilitation under the guise of humane treatments, some humiliating and terrible things have taken place. For one, the employment of discretion is handled in such a way that permits both the rich and poor to experience a dual system of criminal justice: The rich get probation and the poor get prison.

■ Modern Models

Now consider three models used for probation during the 20th century. The *reintegrative model* emphasizes rehabilitation, the *radical nonintervention model* emphasizes doing less harm, and the *justice model* emphasizes fairness.

The Reintegration Model

Rehabilitation, according to O'Leary and Duffee (1971), has various correctional policy models that offer a different emphasis but nonetheless do overlap. The *rehabilitation model* places a high emphasis on the offender and a low emphasis on the community; the basis of influence is the offender's identification with the staff or peers. In the **restraint model**, the agency's concern is with the maintenance of the organization as a "comfortable" situation for both staff and offender, without regard to changing anyone. The **reform model** emphasizes compliance with the values of the community through the coercive measures available to an authoritarian administration. Finally, the **reintegration model** assumes that a high emphasis can be given to the welfare and goals of the offender and to the protection of the community (Conrad 1973, 12).

Community Corrections

Community corrections include building or rebuilding solid ties between the offender and community, integrating or reintegrating the offender into community life by restoring family ties, obtaining employment and education, and securing a larger sense of place in the routine functioning of society. This requires that efforts be directed toward changing the individual offender and in mobilizing community institutions, as well (President's Commission 1967, 7). Offender reintegration refers to helping the offender readjust and fit into the community. It is believed that if the offender is helped to reintegrate, then the offender will be less likely to recidivate and the community/society is better served (Masters 1994, 7). Reintegration has been an important offender treatment goal for almost 30 years. Successful readjustment required personal reformation and the presence of the conditions within the community that would support and encourage these activities. More specifically, probation services employed diversion, psychotherapy, family therapy, school programs, and job programs. This point of view did not deny the importance of increasing individual capacity, but it did make clear that correctional techniques were nearsighted when they failed

restraint model where "restraint" is the model, the agency's concern is with the maintenance of the organization as a "comfortable" situation for both staff and offender, without regard to changing anyone.

reform model emphasizes compliance with the values of the community through the coercive measures available to an authoritarian administration.

reintegration model was developed in response to the identifiable failures of the medical model. Instead of viewing the offender in medical terms as "sick" and in need of a "cure," the offender is now viewed, according to the sociological paradigm, as disorganized and thus can be dealt with most appropriately by the development and nurturing of positive ties to the community.

community corrections include the building or rebuilding of solid ties between the offender and community, integrating or reintegrating the offender into community life by restoring family ties, obtaining employment and education, and securing a larger sense of place in routine functioning in society.

to take into account the needed changes in an offender's social and cultural milieu (President's Commission 1967, 30).

Social Disorganization

The reintegration model was developed in response to the identifiable failures of the medical model. Instead of viewing the offender in medical terms as sick and in need of a cure, the offender is now viewed, according to the sociological paradigm, as disorganized and thus can be dealt with most appropriately by the development and nurturing of positive ties to the community. Reintegration was influenced by the work of the Chicago School of Sociology beginning in the 1930s up through the 1960s. The Sutherland and Cressey (1966) criminology work is a comprehensive overview of the various theories coming out of this school. The central focus was on the slum dweller and those suffering social and economic disadvantages. These people, if organized at all, had the potential to become a powerful political force as displayed in revolutionary Russia. The underlying premise of this school of thought was that crime and delinquency are symptoms of failures and disorganization of the community, as well as the individual offender. These failures prevent the offender from contact with the institutions that are responsible for assuring the development of law-abiding conduct, including sound family life, good schools, employment opportunities, recreational opportunities, and desirable companions, among others. These anticriminal influences give way to deleterious habits, standards, and associates, all of which promote criminal activities (President's Commission 1967, 7). Through the use of concerted efforts to economically develop the community, expanded opportunities for all of its inhabitants, and with schools and families promoting anticriminal beliefs and attitudes, community reintegration took hold as a strategy for change.

Achieving Objectives

McCarthy and McCarthy (1991) suggest that to achieve the objectives of reintegration, community-based correctional programs must be located within and interact with the local community. The program must take place in a nonsecure environment. Services should be provided by the local community. Offenders should have an opportunity to assume normal roles in the community and to engage in a process of personal growth. Staff in reintegrative community-based correctional programs act as **resource brokers**, linking offenders to the appropriate services and to monitor their progress. They should also work to ensure that the offender's rights are protected and to ensure that a high quality of service delivery is maintained (McCarthy and McCarthy 1991, 3). Accordingly, Allen, Carlson, and Parks (1979) suggest the process includes assessing the personal and social conditions of the offender, providing information and recommendations to the court, designing and delineating a plan of action, providing an appropriate level of supervision, continually modifying the plan as necessary, and conducting research that will develop and improve on the reintegrative technique.

According to the President's Commission (1967), the reintegration approach is based on several assumptions, some of which are familiar to contemporary experts on community justice. First of all, it is assumed that by placing probation officers in satellite offices located in high crime areas, the probation officer will

resource brokers are probation officers who link offenders to appropriate services and monitor their progress after assistance is initiated.

develop ties to the probationer's community and, in some cases, would likely offer an expanded first-hand understanding of these problems. Second, it is assumed that it is possible to divert many offenders to treatment programs before they are entrenched in the criminal justice process. Third, it is assumed that an understanding of the social-economic conditions of the probationer will add greater understanding to the person's problems and permit the officer to work within the community to deal with the problems. Last, it is assumed that quality resources are available in the community. Full support of reintegration requires efforts directed toward the offender and also mobilization and change of the community and its institutions.

The reintegrative model is consistent with the training and capabilities of the average probation officer—that is, someone who has earned a baccalaureate degree in the social sciences and has some additional training. Reintegrative theories influenced the training of probation officers as they were encouraged to place greater emphasis on developing the offender's effective participation in the community's social institutions. The reintegrative approach is also appropriate for the kind of work probation officers do. Many officers do not have the time to engage in protracted treatments with the probationer. Their caseloads are too high and they have too many interruptions during their meetings with the probationer.

The reintegrative model also considers it necessary to attend to the importance played by the court in the process by considering its decisions and responsibilities. It also emphasizes the responsibility to treat each probationer as an individual, to develop a supervision plan that considers the needs of each probationer, to monitor the progress of each probationer, and to modify the plan as warranted (Allen et al. 1979). Probation officers have continued to individualize their interactions with the offender, particularly as they perform risk assessments, needs assessments, counseling, and various control measures. Officers have undergone a job enrichment of sorts by branching out into areas, especially community organizing, that were more familiar to the early pioneers of probation. The officers assumed responsibility for the probationer's housing, work, schooling, remedial tutoring, vocational training, and guidance and counseling.

Problems of Reintegration

Reintegration suffers from several problems that may to some appear intractable and suggest to others that it has failed to achieve its promise. It is difficult to identify a probation system that consistently bases its daily practices on reintegration. Many departments may support the reintegration concept but swing back and forth in light of probationer requirements. This means any application of the model is inherently unstable and coercive. Increasing instability and heightened coercion are evident in many areas of probation today.

Today, programs are not administered in a fashion that supports reintegration. Probation officers can be centrally located so as to be convenient to the courts, the remainder of the criminal justice system, and other actors involved in the process. Much use is made of nonsecure facilities but electronic monitoring has made the system more intrusive. Concerns that reintegration entails an element of paternalism are important inasmuch as one seeks to nurture the moral autonomy of the individual. Finally, opportunities for personal growth are limited because of the system's recent intolerance for mistakes. It is difficult to convince a client that he or she should deny himself or herself certain amenities when others, including the government, are spending beyond their means.

Reintegration is wedded to the belief that there is a community and the probationer needs to take advantage of existing opportunities. This might be possible if there is a real community and a fair distribution of opportunities. Barriers to reintegration, however, have been erected. These hurdles reflect to some degree the risks and harm posed by these individuals. Full community support of the reintegration approach is difficult to achieve due to these various barriers. Businesses and unions have opposed liberal social programs because they believe that the changes threaten the status quo. State laws also make it difficult for the offender to achieve bonding and licensing. More importantly, many urban centers are being abandoned by the private sector, and the major employer of last resort has become the government. Governmental agencies have traditionally barred offenders from employment. Family problems, insufficient pay for work, and a lack of education continue to play a major part in many lives. Urban opportunities for advancement have diminished and a consensus on what the community should provide, and to whom, has eroded (Harrell and Peterson 1992, xvii).

The Family The reintegrative approach emphasizes the importance played by the family as a source of strength. Today's family is undergoing an assault not unlike that which it experienced during the upheaval of the industrial revolution. Healthy childrearing practices and coping skills are not given sufficient attention under these conditions. Governmental help is also not available. Many states are considering altering their social benefits packages to families. California, for one, cut benefits for the family by 10 percent. Coupled with previous cuts, California ultimately cut benefits by 40 percent (Davey 1995, 33). These problems are compounded by a decrease in federal public housing funding and a rise in homelessness. States are reluctant to fill the void by providing meaningful subsidies because they believe larger amounts might draw even more dependent citizens to their states. Two facts that researchers agree on is that there are far more homeless people today than there were in 1980, and an increasing number of homeless people are children (Davey 1995, 40). Schwartz, Ferlauto, and Hoffman (1988) believe that much homelessness in America can properly be labeled "government issue."

Employment Employment is the second area to receive emphasis by the reintegrationist. If society wants to keep the offender free from crime, he or she needs a job. The problem is that many jobs pay too little and provide no health benefits. Employment is fundamental to anyone's self-concept and in many ways determines the kind of life the person leads. Current economic transformations have made it difficult for people to find secure employment that provides a living wage, or the wage a full-time worker would need to earn to support a family above the federal poverty line, and health insurance. Federally sponsored programs designed to develop businesses in economically depressed communities have been tried for years; some of them have been successful but others have been failures. There is much debate about the role that the government should play in these programs. The liberals would like to see more job training, particularly for the recently laid-off workers and for those who live in conditions of chronic unemployment. The conservatives would like to see wages kept low through the availability of a large pool of workers. Conditions may reach the point that only through raising wages is it possible to provide sufficient buying power to maintain economic strength.

Education The third area of concern is education. The public school is often the most stable influence in a youth's life. The problem is that anytime people believe they have the means for handling youthful offenders, it is somehow related to using the school. One of the latest ideas is to open the school for year-round programming and to use gymnasiums for late evening recreation. The school has its limitations, however. Many juveniles drop out of school and are not subject to its influence. Schools also have the ability to escalate delinquency and crime. Schools are quite proficient at labeling students from the first days of school. Extensive records are carried for years on youth with discipline problems and other difficulties. Many of these students are encouraged, either directly through warnings on expulsion or indirectly through suggested outside placements, to seek schooling at another institution. Many schools find they are incapable of dealing with the truly troublesome student. Instead they limit their work to addressing the basic educational needs of their students because they no longer have the funding necessary to provide ancillary programs wealthier schools districts can afford.

In many cases, the services and community institutions that offenders need simply are not there. There is little sense in getting an offender readmitted to a slum school so poor that he or she will not profit from it; funds for the purchase of clinical services are useless if there is no clinic to which to go (President's Commission 1967, 10). What this says is that there is little sense in promoting a reintegrative agenda when it is clear the offender is offered services to which other members of the community do not have access.

The "Underclass"

According to Julius Wilson (1990), the *underclass* is a heterogeneous group of families and individuals who inhabit the core of the nation's central cities. A fundamental transformation has taken place in ghetto neighborhoods. The middle class has moved out and those who have remained are more socially isolated. This group is battered by violence, drugs, AIDS, poverty, family breakdowns, and other problems (Wilson 1990). Extreme marginalization from mainstream institutions and counterproductive behavior had, by the mid-1970s, reached catastrophic proportions in the inner cities (Auletta 1982; Nathan 1987; Reischauer 1987; Wilson 1990). Almost all of the descriptions of the underclass indicate a weak labor force attachment, far greater than formally documented. Also noted are persistently low incomes, welfare dependency, school drop-outs, and out-of-wedlock births (Harrell and Peterson 1992; Jencks 1989; Myrdal 1962; Sjoquist 1990). When all of these attributes exist concurrently within households, they repeat themselves and substantially diminish the economic fortunes of affected members (Wilson 1990). Is it possible that the United States has a permanent underclass and it possesses a major political threat to anyone who ignores it, or is this underclass so self-medicated with illegal drugs and alcohol that they are unable to take any effective action?

Gaubatz (1995) has argued that the offender, as a member of the underclass, is considered to be *beyond the pale*. Beyond the pale refers to someone who is outside the mainstream of society and who is not likely to be brought back into it. The key to understanding what is happening with those who believe incarceration, as opposed to probation, is the best means for dealing with crime is that they have placed criminal offenders beyond the pale. Those who support incarceration do not claim the offender is acting in good intention, nor do they find similarity between offenders and ordinary citizens. Forgiveness may be an important standard for the commerce of everyday life—but the forgiveness of the criminal is not a part of that daily activity (Gaubatz 1995, 165).

The Radical Nonintervention Model

An ancient principle in the discussion of justice is the desire to limit harm. Basically put, if one cannot be sure when one is acting justly, one should do what one can to avoid acting unjustly. During the 1970s, this notion came to be associated with the belief that the criminal justice system should do no harm. In this vein, Conrad (1980, 85) asserted that the criminal justice system "has a responsibility to do as little damage as possible to the citizens it is required to punish." In matters of criminal justice, this meant that the state must not use its awesome powers to ensure social peace at the risks of unfairly depriving citizens of their liberty. Instead, the state should use the least restrictive measure possible. Liberals believed the state should seek to help offenders overcome the social and psychological forces that compelled them to move outside the law. Rehabilitation and not merely punishment—doing good rather than inflicting pain—should be the ultimate goal of state legal intervention (Travis and Cullen 1984, 29). In more practical terms, various states undertook efforts to deinstitutionalize all types of populations. This involved using traditional mechanisms such as probation and parole that were thought capable of quickly returning previously incarcerated offenders to the community (Scull 1977, 45).

With the coming of the 1960s, institutional modes of social control became far more costly and difficult to justify (Scull 1977, 135). Incarceration had come to symbolize punishment but as fiscal pressures on states intensified during the 1960s and 1970s, noninstitutional techniques for coping with the miscreant came to exert an ever-greater fascination for criminal justice planners and policy makers. The plan was to expand the use of "community-based" programs instead of building large, expensive institutions and to try to keep the prison population below 300,000 (Scull 1977, 3). Diversionary programs, in particular, enjoyed increased popularity (Scull 1977, 135).

During this time, the creation of the Law Enforcement Assistance Administration offered sizable financial incentives for the development of community corrections programs. Partly in response to these actions, and partly as a reflection of local initiatives, there was a tendency to fine offenders, to reduce felonies to misdemeanors, and to ignore certain crimes rather than sending someone to an institution (Scull 1977, 45). By 1972, there were 11 percent fewer people in state and federal prisons than there had been in 1961, despite a nearly two-and-one-half fold increase in the number of serious crimes (Silberman 1980, 505). Beyond all doubt, the data reveal that from the late 1960s onward, probation and parole were used in unprecedented ways. From 1930 to 1960, the probation population increased from 72 to 173 per 100,000 general population (Sutherland and Cressey 1966, 483).

Besides flooding community programs with new clients, this least restrictive approach also had another important consequence. In practice, the "do-no-harm" strategy appears to have entailed a "do-nothing approach." In other words, there was a substantial withdrawal from the policy-making arena. Doing nothing applied to only those who had adopted a stance of minimizing damage while those who continued to hold another view, such as incarcerating offenders, saw no reason to step back. Those who were not concerned with the negative consequences of institutionalization had not abdicated their roles as lobbyists and formulators of policy. Rather, they moved with considerable haste to mold justice policy (Travis and Cullen 1984, 29).

The nonintervention model has problems with human dignity because it fails to do anything useful for the offender. In fact, by specifying that nonexistent treatment take place in the community, probationers are denied their essential equality and their right to be treated as others.

The Justice Model

Sentencing during the 1950s and 1960s seemed to be totally irrational, relying entirely on the whims of the prosecutor and judge. This highly discretionary system was thought to undermine deterrence and crime control objectives but also fed probationer and prisoner resentment and impeded rehabilitation. Probation was portrayed as something less than a penalty inasmuch as it was seen as an inadequate expression of community-directed reprobation (Bishop 1988, 119). Conservatives viewed probation as a symbol of public tolerance. Probationers were dealt with too leniently, let off, or excused. During the early 1990s, probation seemed incapable of reversing its image and to some it was not clear how this could be achieved (Zimring and Hawkins 1991, 188).

Climbing out of the ashes of various prison riots were the proponents of the justice model who focused their attention on limiting or structuring sentencing discretion. Few people complained of sentencing disparity, especially as it related to probation. More politicians, however, were now using rising crime rates as indications of the failures of the criminal justice system. In any event, firm, immovable sentences seemed like a step in the direction of "law and order," as well as a step toward justice. This was a potent political combination (Friedman 1993, 412).

The movement to set limits on judicial sentencing discretion, as expounded in the justice model, was connected, politically and ideologically, with new explanations for crime and the repeal of indeterminate sentencing. Rational choice theory postulates that the criminal chooses to engage in crime because of the expected utility of that activity. A key component of the theory is the expected utility hypothesis thus dispensing with special theories of anomie, psychological inadequacies, or inheritance of special traits (Becker 1968, 170). Many offenders, it was believed, were not ipso facto sick and examples of deep-seated pathology (Palmer 1994, 112). According to the justice model, probation officers should address clients as volitional and responsible individuals. Probation officers, therefore, should not be responsible for providing intensive specialized services nor should probationers be judged on their success or lack of success in completing such treatment. Successful treatment will occur when the client is ready to complete it. There should be voluntary acceptance of the treatment modality in order to avoid officer coercion and client manipulation (Thomson 1984, 102).

The postulates of the justice model for probation, which put emphasis on the dignity of the offender, are (Fogel 1984, 72)

No accurate etiological theory of crime is possible.

Punishment is measured in proportion to the harm inflicted on the offender.

Probation is a criminal sanction.

Justice-as-fairness, as an aspiration, is central to the process.

Probationers should be addressed as responsible and volitional human beings.

Unbridled discretion undermines the law.

Probation as a sentence must be made explicit.

The presentence report should be treated as a legal document.

Judges should have the discretion to consider the victim in setting the conditions of probation.

Probation itself is a summary punishment.

Treatment, if provided, must be voluntarily accepted.

The standard of proof for revocation should be set as "beyond a reasonable doubt."

The needs of the victim should be explicitly taken into account.

The justice model proposed that the presentence report should be discoverable and used to aid the victim. The judge should provide a sentence, be flexible in the conditions, and remain undogmatic in what assistance can be given to the victim. This is a major component of restorative justice.

retrospectivity is a focus on what the person has done.

proportionality matches the severity of the sanction to the seriousness of the harm.

Essential to the justice model of corrections are **retrospectivity**, a focus on what the person has done, and **proportionality**, matching the severity of sanction to the seriousness of the harm. This requires an assessment of the culpability of the offender and the imposition of a range of a sanctions. Although a retrospective view requires a careful assessment of the facts, proportionality suggests that like events are to be treated alike. The principles of retrospectivity and proportionality draw their strengths from common concerns they share with fairness or evenhandedness in the administration of punishment. Accordingly, this model grants punishment, especially incarceration, limited value; the individual, however, as either a victim or an offender, has increased value due to the unique qualities the person possesses as a human being. Furthermore, after punishment society must also prepare to welcome the offender back into the community. It was recognized that the justice model for criminal justice can only provide a service if it, too, is a model for greater social justice (Thomson 1984, 102).

Critics of the Justice Model

The justice model is not without its critics. Longer sentences, whether incarcerative or probationary, are being handed down. Although probation proponents would like to see these penalties reduced for humanitarian reasons, the only argument that can made in support of just desert and reduced penalties is one of parsimony, an argument suggesting that it is a needless use of resources to punish the offender beyond what is required to achieve the goals of punishment. Once one accepts the argument that the justice model applies to probation, one is left in the difficult position of ascertaining whether the seriousness of the harm corresponds with the penalty. Can society deliver a penalty that is both internally meaningful to the offender and externally meaningful to the public? The offender and the public may disagree over the whole range of penalties. Research from Tonry and Morris (1990) and Taxman (1994) indicate that there are great variations on the relative value of sentences even among probation officers. It is only when the penalty is applied on the personal level does its appreciation rise above the abstract.

The effort to reform sentencing in some ways has caused devaluation in the worth of community supervision. Much of the motivation for developing and maintaining a professional staff was expended with the loss of rehabilitation. However, despite the ambiguity of purpose, most agencies have continued on as always.

Alternative Programs

Those agencies that chose not to implement the justice model for probation took another path. Many of them became interested in intensive supervision. In response to accusations of lax supervision, various states—beginning with New Jersey and Georgia—developed intensive supervision programs (ISPs). To some degree, these programs provided sufficient deterrent and incapacitation functions. Research found many offenders preferred to serve a jail sentence than to participate in an ISP. Pearson (1988) reported that 15 percent of the applicants to ISPs in New Jersey withdrew their application once they understood what it meant. The Rand Corporation reported that in a study conducted in Oregon of randomly selected nonviolent offenders about a third of those eligible for ISPs chose prison instead of the community's ISPs (Petersilia 1990).

Departments not interested in the justice model were also given a boost by the drug war. The large number of drug offenders on probation belies the argument that the case management approach is dead. When innovative ideas (community resource management, intensive supervision, team supervision, and newer risks assessment and classification techniques) are taken into consideration, the case method remains essentially a "needs deprivation" model. Whatever the resources available, probation continues to deploy community assets in a fashion that centers on the offender (client) and sees the probation officer (therapist) as responsible for developing, through referrals and brokerage activities, the resources necessary to meet the client's needs. Convicted offenders may be shown leniency because the diagnosis (presentence report) is optimistic about their prognosis for law-abiding behavior provided a treatment plan (the Rx) is implemented. It is, therefore, a theory that focuses on the offender, rather than the offense.

The Debate Continues

The debate over treatment versus control that rages today in probation is part of the maturation process of this institution. The debate is simply more public and participatory than in the past. Throughout the 20th century, there were certain officers who were more interested in law enforcement than in casework. Only recently have these officers felt free to express their views. Well-organized groups foster elaborate arguments to represent different sides of the debate. There is pressure to ensure that the information gathered in the presentence investigation (PSI), the conditions imposed, and the officer's behavior has a direct relationship to specific sentencing goals. With the use of additional conditions, officers are often asked to provide not only evidence of sobriety but indications the offender has paid restitution and performed community service. The use of risk control is evident.

Over the last few years, the probation bureaucracy has attempted to deal with the changes in the field through a three-prong attack. First of all, the field has tried to emphasize the professional nature of the endeavor. This is a strategy that repeats itself from time to time throughout the history of probation. This time around, instead of emphasizing the professional qualifications of the staff, the emphasis is on the execution of techniques. A good example of this is the article on recidivism rates and outcome measures by Matthews, Boone, and Fogg (1994). The belief is that the system only needs to adopt strategies that provide some standards for measuring professional performance and outcome other than recidivism.

Another area that has been emphasized is the notion of planning. Particular emphasis is given to mission statements and developing a vision of what probation should be like now and in the future. The concern is with a planning process that establishes a mission or goal. From a holistic perspective, officials are asked to consider using more technology and adopting a restorative notion of the offender that includes a greater emphasis on education, victim support, and community concern. Community partnerships are considered important, particularly as they relate to human resource agencies and the educational system. Officers must be aware of the diversity that exists in society and what that means for themselves and their clients. No longer is there a stereotypical offender.

Probation is becoming more interested in prevention both in terms of community factors and individual considerations. Isolated solutions do not work when the interrelationship with other etiological factors are ignored. Officer safety is another important issue. The job cannot be done without proper concern for what it means to go into the community today. Community corrections is not shying away from the political system. Leaders in probation are more willing to involve themselves with the political establishment. The police have been doing this for some time and community corrections cannot set itself apart any longer. Lastly, probation is engaging the public in this process. If probation wants public support, it must be willing to open up the process and permit the public to have its say, too.

What is happening to probation today is what would have been expected had one carefully considered the mandate of the Law Enforcement Assistance Administration. This agency poured billions of dollars into the criminal justice system and made society much more aware of the implications of viewing criminal justice as a system. With systems theory, one sees the interrelationships and inconsistencies in its practices. One must look beyond the immediate borders and consider the implications of one's actions both in the short and long term. Society is left with a system that promised much more than it can deliver.

Reinventing Probation

Probation thus may be destined to reinvent itself according to its past images. A study of the cyclic nature of correctional reform (Murton 1976) indicates society tends to reinvent its institutions and only permit real change to occur as long as it does not threaten the status quo or the existing agenda of the power elite. Despite probation's pulse on the community, it has never been a strong advocate of community action programs or programs that empower community leaders.

When all other social agencies want nothing to do with someone, the criminal justice system finds that it is required to deal with this person on some level. What is more, probation agencies continue to serve a population of people who refuse to "go away" but require attention because other agencies, both public and private, have the luxury of being able to ignore or reject them as clients. Probation should not apologize for its accomplishments and for its efforts to humanize a potentially dangerous and highly punitive system. Furthermore, most politicians are aware of the advantages offered by a system that responds to concerns for mitigating punishments.

■ Summary

The 20th century was characterized by increased professionalism and court recognition of probation; it was an interesting time for probation. It started off with the Progressives working to reform government of its abuses. Universities began to teach courses specifically directed toward the solution of social problems. There was a belief that, with enough information, various social problems could be dealt with using an appropriate amount of discretion. The Progressives, despite their efforts to formalize the process by making it more rational, created a criminal justice system that lost sight of the person in the offender.

With the aid of the work of the Progressives, one sees formalization of probation as it was instituted by the state. Still there was opposition from various volunteer associations. Nonetheless, opposition did not become critical until the *Killits* federal case. The continuance of probation was not decided until the court denied the right of the lower court to suspend a sentence. In response, Congress was forced to address the question through legislation authorizing the development of probation. During this period, the conservative forces in support of probation went all out to put probation on the shelf. The fact that the public believed probation served an important public function must be recognized.

With the support of federal legislation and state authorization, probation was free to become further professionalized through the adoption of the same procedures applied by the medical profession as offered by social work. In this effort to increase the ability of the probation officers to address client problems, too often discretion is granted to untrained officers. Following the identified problems of the medical model, the emphasis shifted to offender reintegration as a model that incorporates offender rehabilitation on a variety of fronts. Reintegration of the offender continues to be a major factor in offender treatment but not without problems relative to family, work, and education. Probation then shifted away from providing the type of services that would guarantee real offender integration to limiting programs specifically directed toward offenders and their families. Because this approach was inadequate and continued to emphasize discretionary practices, a strategy of doing little for the offenders was found in the radical nonintervention movement. This approach considered doing as little as necessary for the offender in recognition that intervention in the past may have done more harm than good.

As research uncovered increased sentencing disparity, new efforts were made to promote a justice model for probation. The justice model emphasized the fact that, because there was no single explanation of crime, offenders acted volitionally, treatment should be voluntary, victims should be given a say in the process, punishment should be proportionate to the offense, and revocation should be based on a legal standard of beyond a reasonable doubt. Probation had to prove that it could offer a punishment that was a deterrent and protective of the community. Increased emphasis on supervision became the norm.

REFERENCES

Allen, H., E. Carlson, and E. Parks. 1979. *Critical issues in adult probation*. Washington, DC: U.S. Government Printing Office, U.S. Department of Justice.

Auletta, K. 1982. *The underclass*. New York: Random House.

Bailey, T. 1961. *The American pageant*. Boston: D.C. Health.

Becker, G. S. 1968. Crime and punishment: An economic approach. *Journal of Political Economy* 76: 169–217.

Bishop, N. 1988. *Non-custodial alternatives in Europe*. Helsinki, Finland: Institute for Crime Prevention and Control.

Camp, C., and George Camp. 1989. *The corrections yearbook 1999. Adult corrections*. Middletown, CT: Criminal Justice Institute.

Chute, C. L, and M. Bell. 1956. *Crime, courts and probation*. New York: Macmillan.

Conrad, J. P. 1980. There has to be a better way. *Crime and Delinquency* 26: 83–90.

Conrad, J. 1973. Reintegration: Practice in search of a theory. In M. Danzinger, ed. *Criminal justice monograph*. Washington, DC: Department of Justice.

Cullen, F. T., and K. E. Gilbert. 1982. *Reaffirming rehabilitation*. Cincinnati, OH: Anderson.

Davey, J. D. 1995. *The new social contract: America's journey from welfare state to police state*. Westport, CT: Praeger.

Fogel, D. 1984. The emergence of probation as a profession in the service of public safety: The next ten years. In D. McAnany, D. Thomson, and D. Fogel, eds. *Probation and justice*. Cambridge, MA: Oelgeschlager, Gunn & Hain, pp. 65–99.

Friedman, L. 1993. *Crime and punishment in American history*. New York: Basic Books.

Gans, H. 1972. Positive functions of poverty. *American Journal of Sociology* 78: 275–289.

Garland, D. 1990. *Punishment and modern society*. Chicago: University of Chicago Press.

Gaubatz, K. 1995. *Crime in the public mind*. Ann Arbor: University of Michigan.

Hagan, J., and J. Leon. 1977. Rediscovering delinquency: Social history, political ideology, and the sociology of law. *American Sociological Review* 42: 587–598.

Harrell, A., and G. Peterson. 1992. *Drugs, crime and social isolation*. Washington, DC: The Urban Institute.

Henningsen, R. J. 1981. *Probation and parole*. New York: Harcourt Brace Jovanovich.

Hofstadter, R. 1955. *The age of reform*. New York: Vintage.

Jencks, C. 1989. What is the underclass—And is it growing? *Focus* 12: 14–31.

Killits 1916 (Exparte United States, 242 U.S. 27).

Lehman, P. E. 1975. The medical model of treatment—Historical development of an archaic standard. In E. Peoples, ed., *Readings in correctional casework and counseling*. Pacific Palisades, CA: Goodyear, pp. 47–56.

Lindner, C., and M. R. Savarese. 1984. The evolution of probation: University settlement and the beginning of statutory probation in New York City. *Federal Probation* 48: 3–12.

Lindner, C. 1992. The probation field visit and office report in New York State: Yesterday, today, and tomorrow. *Criminal Justice Review* 17: 44–60.

Lipton, D., R. Martinson, and J. Wilks. 1975. *The effectiveness of correctional treatment: A survey of treatment evaluation studies*. New York: Praeger.

Masters, R. 1994. *Counseling criminal justice offenders*. Thousand Oaks, CA: Sage.

Matthews, T., H. Boone, and V. Fogg. 1994. Alternative outcome measures: The concept. *Perspectives* Winter: 11–12.

McCarthy, B. R., and B. J. McCarthy. 1991. *Community-based corrections*. Pacific Grove, CA: Brooks/Cole.

McGinnis, P. D. 1960. *Manual for probation officers in New York state,* 6th ed. Albany, NY: New York Department of Correction.

Meyer, C. Z. 1952. A half century of federal probation and parole. *Journal of Criminal Law, Criminology, and Police Science* 42: 707–728.

Murton, T. 1976. *The dilemma of prison reform*. New York: Holt, Rinehart and Winston.

Myrdal, G. 1962. *Challenge to affluence*. New York: Pantheon.

Nathan, R. 1987. Will the underclass always be with us? *Society* 24: 57–62.

O'Leary, V. 1987. Probation: A system in change. *Federal Probation* 51: 8–11.

O'Leary V., and T. Clear. 1984. *Directions for community corrections in the 1990s*. Newark, NJ: National Council on Crime and Delinquency Collection.

Chapter Resources

O'Leary, V., and D. Duffee. 1971. Correctional policy—A classification of goals designed for change. *Crime and Delinquency* 17: 373–386.

Palmer, T. 1994. *A profile of correctional effectiveness and new directions for research.* New York: State University of New York Press.

Pearson, F. 1988. Evaluation of New Jersey's intensive supervision program. *Crime and Delinquency* 34: 437–448.

Petersilia, J. 1990. When probation becomes more dreaded than prison. *Federal Probation* 54: 23–27.

President's Commission on Law Enforcement and Administration of Justice. 1967. *Task force report: Corrections.* Washington, DC: U.S. Government Printing Office.

Reischauer, R. 1987. *The geographic concentration of poverty: What do we know?* Washington, DC: Brookings Institute.

Rose, S. 1975. The fallacy of the medical model as applied to corrections. In E. Peoples, ed., *Readings in correctional casework and counseling.* Pacific Palisades, CA: Goodyear, pp. 57–60.

Rothman, D. 1978. The state as parent: Social policy in the Progressive era. In W. Gaylin, I. Glasser, S. Marcus, and D. Rothman (Eds.). *The limits to being good.* New York: Pantheon, pp. 67–98.

Rothman, D. 1980. *Conscience and convenience: The asylum and its alternatives in progressive America.* Boston: Little, Brown, and Co.

Sampson, A. 1994. *Acts of abuse: Sex offenders and the criminal justice system.* New York: Routledge.

Schwartz, D., R. Ferlauto, and D. Hoffman. 1988. *A new housing policy for America.* Philadelphia: Temple University Press.

Scull, A. 1977. *Decarceration.* Englewood Cliffs, NJ: Prentice Hall.

Scull, A. 1983. Community corrections: Panacea, progress or pretense? In D. Garland and P. Young, eds., *The power to punish.* London: Heinemann.

Silberman, C. E. 1980. *Criminal violence, criminal justice.* New York: Vintage.

Sjoquist, D. 1990. Concepts, measurements, and analysis of the underclass. Unpublished manuscript. Georgia State University. Atlanta.

Smith, A. B., and L. Berlin. 1979. *Introduction to probation and parole.* St. Paul, MN: West.

Sullivan, L. E. 1990. *The prison reform movement.* Boston: Twayne.

Sutherland, E., and D. Cresey. 1966. *Principles of criminology.* New York: Lippincott.

Taxman, F. S. 1994. Correctional options and implementation issues. *Perspectives* 18: 32–37.

Thomson, D. 1984. Prospects of a justice model for probation. In P. D. McAnany, D. Thomson, and D. Fogel, eds., *Probation and justice.* Cambridge, MA: Oelgeschlager, Gunn, Hain, pp. 101–135.

Timasheff, N. S. 1941. *One hundred years of probation: 1841–1941.* New York: Fordham University Press.

Tonry, M., and N. Morris. 1990. *Between prison and probation.* New York: Oxford University.

Travis, L., and F. T. Cullen. 1984. Radical nonintervention: The myth of doing no harm. *Federal Probation* 48: 29–32.

Volstead Act. 2004. www.historicaldocuments.com/volsteadact.htm.

Wilson, W. J. 1990. *The truly disadvantaged: The inner city, the underclass and public policy.* Chicago: University of Chicago.

Zimring, F. E., and G. Hawkins. 1991. *The scale of imprisonment.* Chicago: University of Chicago Press.

KEY POINTS

1. Progressivism was in response to the belief that social problems were too complex for the current government institutions to solve. However, its theory focused on the primacy of the state as a parent: Offenders were treated as children.

2. The emergence of the land grant universities in 1870 brought the expertise of the social scientist to bear on various social problems, especially through the offender's life history.

3. From its inception, probation saved the state money but did not save the locality money.

4. In 1928, the New York State office directed local probation officers to collect information on special offender problems and conduct studies, sponsored legislation, and revised the rules regulating probation.

5. Federal judges employed various techniques to modify the offender's sentence including partial suspension of sentence, suspension of the sentence in its entirety, continuances to a later date, suspension with the provision of oversight, and unclassified suspension.

6. As a result of the U.S. Supreme Court decision in the *Killits* case, the president "pardoned" about 5,000 offenders placed on probation by the federal courts. Second, federal judges began to look for new devices that would allow for the application of probation despite the decision of the Supreme Court. In extreme cases, judges adjourned their decision for an indefinite period and required the offenders to report at stated times and to submit to certain conditions. Finally they imposed minimum sentences, such as 1 day in jail.

7. The medical model with the definition of the offense, the diagnosis, the treatment, and the decision the offender was "cured" was at the start a key driving force in the treatment of offenders but later became a liability because of its lack of conceptual clarity.

8. Through offender reintegration it is understood that crime and delinquency are symptoms of failures and disorganization of the community as well as failures on the part of the offender, who can only be dealt with by the development of positive ties to the community.

9. The radical nonintervention theory opened the door for conservatives to push their more punitive correctional agenda, including intensive supervision, because noninterventionist and other liberals withdrew from the policy arena.

10. The justice model for probation rejected the notion that the offender was necessarily sick but was instead quite volitional. Thus the model was based on what the offender did rather than what might happen in the future.

11. Probation agencies continue to serve offenders who refuse to go away and demand to be treated with dignity.

KEY TERMS

community corrections include the building or rebuilding of solid ties between the offender and community, integrating or reintegrating the offender into community life by restoring family ties, obtaining employment and education, and securing a larger sense of place in routine functioning in society.

deterministic theory of crime states that crime was the result of antecedent conditions or events that preceded the action.

medical model was used for analyzing and addressing the antecedent conditions associated with the offense consisting of the diagnosis of the symptoms of the crime; a treatment aimed at the problem or symptoms; and a cure, or amelioration, of the problem.

Progressives were interested in a variety of social program reforms including safety and sanitation codes, worker compensation laws, 8-hour workdays, and abolition of sweatshops. Prison and reform schools also came under scrutiny.

Progressivism was a reform movement the like of which had not been seen since the 1840s. This reform effort was in response to the belief that social problems were too complex for the current governmental institutions to solve. Various schemes to ensure popular control of the government were enacted into law including the initiative, referendum, and recall.

proportionality matches the severity of the sanction to the seriousness of the harm.

reform model emphasizes compliance with the values of the community through the coercive measures available to an authoritarian administration.

rehabilitation model provides the only justification of punishment that requires the state to care for the offender's needs and welfare.

reintegration model was developed in response to the identifiable failures of the medical model. Instead of viewing the offender in medical terms as "sick" and in need of a "cure," the offender is now viewed, according to the sociological paradigm, as disorganized and thus can be dealt with most appropriately by the development and nurturing of positive ties to the community.

resource brokers are probation officers who link offenders to appropriate services and monitor their progress after assistance is initiated.

restraint model Where "restraint" is the model, the agency's concern is with the maintenance of the organization as a "comfortable" situation for both staff and offender, without regard to changing anyone.

retrospectivity is a focus on what the person has done.

REVIEW QUESTIONS

1. Discuss the Progressive reform movement relative to its positive and negative effects on the development of probation.

2. Outline the development of probationary practices in New York.

3. Why was the *Killits* case carried to the U.S. Supreme Court and how did this decision affect the development of federal probation?

4. What are the pros and cons of utilizing the medical model as a treatment for corrections?

5. Explain the reintegration model in terms of
   a. development
   b. objectives
   c. assumptions on which it is based
   d. problems associated with this model

6. What influenced the development of the justice model? What is its premise?

The Social Context of Probation

4

Chapter Objectives

In this chapter you will learn about:

- The complex social context of probation work
- Census 2000 data as it relates to the offender and family characteristics
- Concepts of capital value

Probation officers perform their duties in an extremely complex social environment. As they work toward the amelioration of individual problems and antisocial behavior, officers come to recognize that a host of economic, social, psychological, and political factors affect probationers. In order for probation officers to do their work effectively, a clear understanding of this complex environment is necessary. Doing so not only facilitates relating to probationers, but it also provides a basis for planning and organizational development, policy, training, and hiring at the agency level.

This chapter offers an understanding of the social context in which probation officers do their work. Consideration is given to U.S. Census Bureau demographic data on family life, education and training, household income inequality, and characteristics of those in poverty. Public attitudes toward crime and Uniform Crime Report data on arrests are addressed. Information about some of the more common offenders on probation, including drunk drivers, mentally ill probationers, and drug offenders is given. An exploration of the capital value of the person, including **physical capital**, **social capital**, and **human capital**, is discussed. Finally, this chapter considers racial divisions, income levels, and poverty levels.

physical capital refers to the attributes of a physical object such as roads, houses, buildings, tools, or machines. These include stadiums, arenas, restaurants, good roads, and transportation.

social capital refers to goodwill, fellowship, sympathy, and social intercourse among the individuals and families that make up social units. The individual is helpless without social networks.

human capital refers to the properties of individuals such as training, education, and experience that enhance individual productivity.

■ Population Statistics

Numerous community problems arise as populations expand and migrate; towns, cities, and their surrounding rural areas grow rapidly; and levels of poverty and disparities between rich and poor increase. These developments have already led to problems of national and international security in many countries. Currently, between 40 percent and 55 percent of the world's populations live in urban centers (Shaw 2001), and this proportion is expected to rise to 70 percent by 2020. Levels of poverty have risen in many Western countries despite increasing overall wealth. Throughout the world, income disparities between the rich and poor have increased. In developing countries, the poor tend to be concentrated in particular areas. In developed countries, conditions in urban cores have declined while poverty rates in rural areas have increased. A greater number of women are living in poverty in both developed and developing countries. The number of single mothers has increased and they will likely continue to face problems with finding jobs that allow them to care for their children and to find affordable housing. In fact, across the world we are also likely to see minority populations everywhere living in higher rates of poverty than the majority populations regardless of which ethnic group they represent (Shaw 2001). Migration, immigration, and rapid growth are bringing about major changes to the ethnic character of urban populations. In many countries, the concentration of poverty and social and economic problems in particular areas has led to talk about social exclusion. In Europe, especially in Great Britain, France, and Germany, increasing economic disparity and concentration of poverty have been restricted to certain areas of these countries (Dubet and Lapeyronnie 1994; Pheiffer and Wetzels 1999; and Social Exclusion Unit 2000).

Families living in these areas are often the poorest in the nation. Quite often, as a result of their minority status and patterns of discrimination, people in these areas are excluded from taking part in the employment, health, safety, and prosperity encountered by others in the country. These residents are left with an assortment of ills, including poor health, crime, vandalism, drugs, unsupervised young people, litter, pollution, and lack of services, including a lack of safety and security.

In the United States, African-American communities often are concentrated in inner cities. These cities have experienced huge increases in youth crime, violence, and youth homicides. In some communities, generations of youth are growing up without fathers, and as imprisonment rates increase for women, many children are without parental care (Mauer et al. 1999a, 1999b). This has resulted in a reduced network of social controls involving parents, employees, friends, and neighbors. Poverty in the United States has also become a major problem outside of the larger cities, affecting the white majority in those smaller communities. Although crime has decreased in many communities, it continues to increase in the rural communities along the Texas/Mexico border (Shaw 2001, 5). It is also true that in the United States, as reported by the National Center on Addiction and Substance Abuse (2000), substance abuse was higher in the rural communities than in the urban areas. Drug use was higher among young teens in mid-sized cities and rural areas than in larger metropolitan centers.

Eighth graders in rural areas were 83 percent more likely to use crack cocaine and 70 percent more likely to have been intoxicated than their urban counterparts.

As the world experienced an economic decline following the 9/11 attacks, employment opportunities suffered. Changing labor and trade markets involving the global economy, technological developments, and the loss of unskilled jobs increased the probability, extent, and duration of unemployment. In an effort to drive down wages and increase profits, international corporations have moved business operations from one third-world country to another until the highest profit margin can be achieved. This has contributed to a great deal of social and economic instability. In particular, young people have been affected, increasing their vulnerability to drugs, gangs, illness, and crime. A greater number of adolescents are not at school, at work, or in job training. In the United States, youth unemployment continues to remain especially high among African-American and Hispanic youth who have reduced educational skills (Shaw 2001). Unemployment is in part explained by the buzzwords *deindustrialization* and *outsourcing*. *Deindustrialization* is the process by which local industrial enterprises are replaced by service economy jobs. Windshield wiper blade production is replaced by jobs in a local prison. *Outsourcing* means that jobs are sent overseas where wages are lower, working conditions are not well regulated, and union activity is limited.

Numbers from the 2000 Census

United States Census 2000 data (www.census.gov) indicates that the number of people living "traditional" family lifestyles has fallen dramatically over several decades. In 1947, two-parent families comprised 87 percent of all households, whereas in 2000, the number fell to 51 percent. According to Census 2000, there were over 57 million men and women who were never married, 4.7 million who were separated, and another 9 million men and 12 million women who were divorced.

As of 2004, the U.S. Census Bureau indicates that the United States had an estimated population of 291 million people. Of these, 51 percent were female and 49 percent were males. In rounding out these figures, for those who reported their race, 75 percent were white, 12 percent were African-American, 1 percent were American Indian or Alaskan Native, 4 percent were Asian, 1 percent were native Hawaiian or Pacific Islander, 5 percent were some other race, and 2 percent were of two or more races. Latinos or Hispanics, who can be of any race, comprised 12.5 percent of the people in the United States.

According to the American FactFinder (factfinder.census.gov), a family includes the householder and one or more people living in the same household who are related to the householder by birth, marriage, or adoption. All people in a household related to the householder are regarded as members of his or her family. A family household may contain people not related to the householder, but those people are not included as part of the householder's family in census tabulations. Thus, the number of family households is equal to the number of families, but family households may include more members than do families. A household can contain only one family for purposes of census tabulations. Not all households contain families, since a household may comprise a group of unrelated people or one person living alone.

Census 2000 reports that there were 104,724,456 households in the United States in 2000 and the average size of those households was 2.61 people. Families comprised 68 percent of the households in 2000. As mentioned earlier, 51 percent of the households were comprised of both couple (husband and wife) families. Other families comprised 17 percent. Non-family households made up the remaining 32 percent of the households in the United States. Most of those households were people living alone (26 percent) but some, 6 percent, were people living in households maintained by non-relatives.

Eleven percent of the people living in the United States were foreign born (Census 2000). Eighty-nine percent were native to this country, including 67 percent who were born in the state of residence. Among people at least 5 years of age, 18 percent spoke a language other than English at home. Sixty percent of those people spoke Spanish; 40 percent spoke a different language. Forty-three percent of those who spoke a language other than English reported they did not speak English "very well."

As for mobility, 84 percent reported they were living in the same residence for 1 year prior to the census count. Another 10 percent had moved within the same county. Three percent moved into another county, another 3 percent to another state, and 1 percent moved abroad (Census 2000).

At that time, the employment picture in this country was quite diverse. According to the U.S. Census Bureau (2004), 41 percent of the people worked in the service industries, 14 percent in manufacturing; and 12 percent in the retail trades. Seven percent of the employed population worked in each category of construction, communication and transportation, and finance and real estate. Regarding specific occupations, 33 percent worked in management, professional, and related jobs; 27 percent in sales and office occupations; 15 percent in service, production, transportation, and material moving; and 9 percent in construction, extraction, and maintenance occupations. Eighty percent of the people were employed by the private sector, 14 percent were government employees, and 6 percent were self-employed.

These jobs produced a median income of $41,343. Eighty-one percent received earnings and 17 percent received retirement income other than social security, and 12 percent received social security. This income allows 66 percent of the people to live in a single-unit structure, 27 percent to live in multi-unit structures, and 7 percent to live in mobile homes. There were over 530,658 housing units that lacked plumbing and 625,602 units that lacked kitchen facilities. Three percent of the units did not have a telephone. The cost of housing is a substantial burden for many people. Census 2000 reports that some people spent 30 percent or more of their income on mortgages, 27 percent were owners with mortgages, 11 percent were owners without mortgages, and 41 percent were renters. The cost of housing is a critical problem.

■ Public Attitudes

The Gallup organization (Gallup 2004a) has conducted various surveys on crime and the public attitudes toward the criminal justice system. In 1972, when asked if there was more crime in the area than a year ago, 51 percent of those polled indicated yes. By 1992 the number had grown to 54 percent. Things began to change in 1998 when the poll indicated that only 31 percent of the public believed there was more crime in their area than there was a year ago. By 2004, 37 percent of the public believed that crime was up, 37 percent believed that crime was down, and 22 percent believed that crime was the same.

Since 1989, the Gallup poll (Gallup 2004b) has been asking Americans whether crime should be fought by attacking social and economic problems that lead to crime or by deterring crime through improved law enforcement with a greater number of police, judges, or prisons. They have found that over the course of time, people continue to support efforts to reduce crime through attacking social and economic problems. In 1994, 42 percent of those polled believed that crime should be attacked through law enforcement and 51 percent believed that these problems should be attacked through social and economic means. By 2003, 69 percent of those surveyed believed that the best way to lower crime was to attack social and economic problems, while 29 percent believed that crime was best attacked through tougher law enforcement. This was good news for community corrections.

The Gallup survey (Gallup 2004b) also learned that 83 percent of the public wanted stiffer penalties for hate crimes. The public supported hate crime legislation designed to protect racial minorities, women, homosexuals, and religious minorities. An overwhelming number of respondents, 95 percent, believed that crime was still a serious problem. When asked about their own neighborhood, though, most people, 53 percent, believed that crime was not a serious problem. Then again, when asked if the criminal justice system was tough enough on crime, 22 percent felt it was about right and 70 percent believed it was not tough enough despite the fact that the United States, as the major industrial power, has some of the highest rates of imprisonment and some of the longest prison terms in the world. When asked if the criminal justice system was fair in dealing with people, most people, 67 percent, felt the system was very or somewhat fair and 29 percent believed the system was unfair.

Environmental Behaviors

It is well known today that environmental factors greatly influence behavior. Healthy children come from healthy environments. Neighborhoods with high levels of social capital tend to be good places to raise a child. *Social capital* refers to goodwill, fellowship, sympathy, and social intercourse among the individuals and families who make up a social unit such as a neighborhood. Neighborhoods characterized by low levels of trust, weak social networks (a series of interconnected social relationships), and little citizen engagement where people meaningfully connect with others in the community translate into unsafe neighborhoods. Ecological theories of crime which study people and their environment, especially theories that emphasize social disorganization and the breakdown of social institutions, have considered this notion. For example, Shaw and McKay and others from the Chicago School of Sociology have focused on social disorganization as a key factor in the development of crime. Social disorganization is evident in communities where population turnover is high, neighbors live anonymously, ethnic groups are uneasily mixed, local organizations are rare, and disadvantaged youth are trapped in subcultures cut off from the adult world (Putnam 2000, 307).

Sampson (1995) argues that even when attempting to control for poverty and other factors that encourage criminal behavior, communities face increased risks of crime and violence when they have limited control of public space, weak organizational structures in the community, and low resident participation in community activities. Jane Jacobs (1961) in *The Death and Life of Great American Cities* argues forcefully that crime is lower in communities where the layout and design of the neighborhoods permit people to regularly and casually interact so they may develop a sense of concern and respect for each other. These informal relations form a system of social concern and social control. People develop a measure of respect, trust, and an appreciation of the value of each person. When needs arise, the community responds. Communities with higher levels of social capital exhibit lower rates of crime (Putnam 2000, 308). Often, this environment is lacking in disorganized communities.

An extensive body of research (Putnam 2000) has examined crime and delinquency. This research concludes that people with similar problems tend to share neighborhoods. It is also clear that families play a major role in this process. Scholars have been able to demonstrate that beyond their individual predispositions to engage in risk behaviors, youth who live among other risk-taking youth are more likely to take risks themselves. In other words, if one lives somewhere where there is a high probability that other youth in the neighborhood will take risks associated with drugs, sex, danger, and violence, it is likely that child will also. These studies indicate people are profoundly affected by their own choices and the choices of others.

Researchers have come to believe that individuals connected to one another through trusting social networks and common values help to facilitate enforcement of positive standards for youth and offers them access to mentors, role models, educational sponsors, and job contacts outside of the neighborhood.

Crimes by the Numbers

There are differing points of view about the increase or decrease of crime, but what remains clear is that authorities must address considerable numbers of offenders who require presentence investigations and supervision. The Federal Bureau of Investigation (2000) reports that over 7 million males were arrested for all types of offenses during 2000. Juveniles comprised a considerable proportion of these offenders. Males 17 years and under comprised 15.9 percent of all arrests. Offenders between the ages of 18 to 29 comprised 42.8 percent of all arrests. There were 2 million female arrests. Twenty-one percent of the females were 17 or younger and 37 percent of the females were between the ages of 17 and 29. Women were most often arrested when they were between the ages of 25 and 39, comprising 36.7 percent.

An analysis of **Table 4-1** indicates the overrepresentation of African-Americans in certain categories of arrest. According to Census 2000, whites comprise 75 percent of the population, African-Americans 12 percent, Native Americans 0.9 percent, and Asians and Pacific Islanders, 3.7 percent. While Caucasians are underrepresented in many areas, they come close to matching their expected rate of offending in burglary, arson, forgery, vandalism, drug offenses, and liquor

Table 4-1 Uniform Crime Reports Arrest Data 2000

Offense	Male	Female	Males Under 18	Females Under 18	Percent White	Percent Black	Percent American Indian/ Alaskan Native	Percent Asian/ Pacific Islander
Murder	7,783	926	715	91	47.1	49.8	0.5	2.6
Rape	17,712	202	2,903	34	63.1	35.4	0.8	0.7
Robbery	65,026	7,294	16,592	1,696	41.4	56.1	0.7	1.8
Aggravated assault	25,2921	63,709	33,633	10,246	60.9	36.6	1.0	1.5
Burglary	164,165	25,178	55,278	7,279	72.9	24.6	1.0	1.5
Larceny-theft	501,106	280,976	153,381	90,342	70.2	26.2	1.4	2.2
Motor vehicle theft	83,149	15,548	28,196	5,620	55.3	41.3	1.3	2.1
Arson	9,065	1,610	4,965	670	79.5	18.4	1.0	1.1
Other assaults	661,210	197,175	107,044	47,870	64.9	32.7	1.2	1.3
Forgery	43,483	27,785	2,804	1,421	77.2	20.0	0.6	2.3
Fraud	117,922	95,906	4,551	2,094	63.4	33.9	0.8	1.8
Embezzlement	6,284	6,293	685	614	62.0	34.7	0.2	3.2
Stolen property	64,971	13,714	15,491	2,882	60.2	37.2	0.9	1.7
Vandalism	155,872	28,628	65,485	9,352	81.8	15.8	1.2	1.2
Weapons	96,831	8,510	22,307	2,570	67.0	30.6	0.8	1.6
Prostitution	23,237	38,146	418	506	57.4	39.3	1.7	1.5
Sex offenses	56,656	4,516	10,581	818	70.9	26.9	0.8	1.4
Drug abuse	858,633	183,701	115,013	19,567	70.2	28.1	0.7	1.0
Gambling	6,408	789	968	41	11.7	86.4	0.3	1.6
Offenses against family	70,853	20,444	3,626	2,172	77.5	19.8	0.8	2.0
DUI	765,680	150,251	10,839	2,242	92.9	4.7	1.5	1.0
Liquor laws	335,618	100,054	69,738	31,899	91.9	4.6	2.8	0.7
Drunkenness	367,825	55,485	11,598	2,829	91.2	7.5	0.6	0.7
Disorderly conduct	324,465	96,077	78,532	30,823	65.9	32.4	0.9	0.8

Source: Federal Bureau of Investigation, U.S. Department of Justice. *Uniform Crime Reports.* Washington, DC: U.S. Government Printing Office, 2000.

violations, including driving under the influence (DUI). African-Americans are arrested at a disproportionate rate in all offense categories except for DUI, liquor law violations, and arrest for drunkenness. Arrest figures for blacks exceed those for whites for murder, robbery, and gambling. Native Americans are arrested at a rate close to what is expected based on population size. The areas where they are most susceptible to arrest are for liquor law violations, theft, and assaults. Pacific Islanders and Asians are underrepresented in all arrest categories.

■ Drunk Driving

A Bureau of Justice Statistics (BJS) study authored by Maruschak (1999) reports on people who were on probation and in prison for drunk driving. The study estimates that more than 512,600 people in 1997 were under some form of correctional supervision as a consequence of driving under the influence of alcohol; this compares with 270,000 in 1986. According to the BJS study, there were 454,000 on probation, 41,000 in local jails, and 17,600 in prison. The number of DUI offenders under correctional supervision nearly doubled between 1986 and 1997. BJS interviews with jailed DUI offenders revealed a pattern of heavy drinking. Half of the DUI offenders in jail said they consumed the equivalent of 12 beers or 6 glasses of wine prior to their arrest. Half of those on probation said they consumed the equivalent of at least 8 beers and 4 glasses of wine. Thirty-four percent of the jail inmates and 8 percent of those on probation reported three or more prior arrests for driving while intoxicated. Two percent of the probationers, 12 percent of the jail inmates, and 6 percent of the state prison inmates said they had been previously sentenced five or more times for driving while intoxicated.

Maruschak (1999) goes on to report that these drinkers had other problems in addition to those related to driving a vehicle. Sixty-six percent of the jail inmates and 55 percent of the probationers reported their involvement in a domestic dispute while under the influence of alcohol. Thirty-one percent of the probationers reported they drank daily, as did almost 40 percent of those jailed. Thirty-seven percent of the probationers and 47 percent of the jail inmates indicated signs of alcohol dependency. Twenty-four percent of the probationers and 38 percent of the jail inmates reported having a drink first thing in the morning.

As far as treatment is concerned, the Maruschak study (1999) reported that probationers fared better than others. Forty-six percent of the probationers reported they had received treatment from a trained professional for their alcohol abuse since being sentenced, but only 4 percent of the jail inmates reported being in treatment. Sixty-two percent of the probationers and 17 percent of the jail inmates had participated in Alcoholics Anonymous or peer group counseling since their sentencing. About three-quarters of these DUI offenders had taken part in such programs or had received treatment in the past. Compared to other offenders under correctional supervision, DUI offenders were more commonly white, male, older, and better educated. Two-thirds of those convicted were white and non-Hispanic. Seventeen percent of the probationers were women, as were 7 percent of the jail inmates and 6 percent of the state prison inmates. Their average age ranged from 36 to 38 years old, depending on the population. According to the study, 37 percent of those on probation, 18 percent of those in jail, and 16 percent of those in prison had attended at least some college.

Depressing Statistics

The National Commission Against Drunk Driving (NCADD) offers important information relevant to drunk driving. National surveys indicate that in an average 1-year period, between 17 percent and 27 percent of people in the United States drive shortly after consuming a least some alcohol (NCADD 2001). The

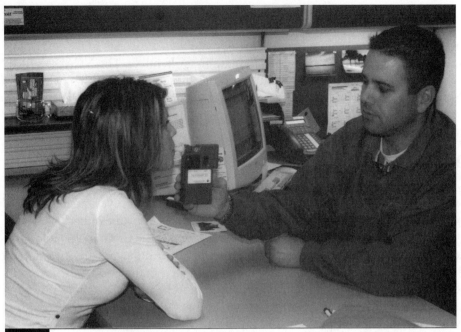

Figure 4.1 When meeting with their probation officer, probationers are often required to submit to a breathalyzer test. *Source:* Courtesy of Edward Sieh.

1996 National Household Survey on Drug Abuse revealed that, in 1995, 23 percent of drivers 16 and older drove within 2 hours of drinking, 4 percent after using both alcohol and other drugs. Non-Hispanic whites had the highest reported rates of driving after alcohol use (26 percent), followed by Hispanics (17 percent), and non-Hispanic blacks (13 percent). Nearly 40 percent of drivers who admitted to driving after alcohol use were estimated to have blood alcohol content (BAC) levels of at least .02, with 8 percent estimated at least .08. A greater number of males than females drove after consuming alcohol. When the percentage of drivers at .02 to .079 and .08 or higher were examined, greater percentages of women were estimated to be in these two categories.

These findings are complemented by the results of the 1996 National Roadside Survey, which revealed that 9 percent of drivers had a measured blood alcohol content (BAC) of at least .005, with 5 percent having a BAC of .05 to .099, and 3 percent having a BAC of at least .10. For whites in the last two categories, the number declined only slightly from 1986 to 1996. For African-American drivers, these same percentages have decreased even though more were driving. Hispanic drivers had the highest percentage of all drivers in both the .05 and .10 categories. The number of women driving after drinking at both the .05 and greater and the .10 levels increased slightly during this time. Because the number of women drivers on the roads during weekend evening hours has nearly tripled in the last 10 years, the small increase in percentage of impaired women drivers represents a substantial increase in actual number of women driving with positive BACs (National Roadside Survey 1996).

In a compendium of research, the NCADD provides some useful information. Studies show that approximately one-third of all drivers arrested for DUI are repeat offenders and that one in eight drunk drivers in a fatal crash has had a DUI conviction in the past 3 years (NCADD 2001). Approximately 2,300 innocent victims are killed each year due to drunk drivers. These drivers are also more likely to have a significantly greater number of arrests and spend more time in jail for nontraffic violations than do first offenders. The NCADD (2001) shows almost half of the persistent drinking drivers have a father who has a drinking problem. Due to the severity and chronicity of the repeat offenders with alcohol problems, traditional legal sanctions have not effectively deterred drinking and driving in this group.

DUI Deterrents

A variety of measures have been employed to deter drunk drivers. Special and unpredictable DUI patrols and checkpoints may be more effective in detecting and apprehending chronic drunk drivers. Other strategies might be of use.

NCADD (2001) also reports that the majority of the driving-age public believes that the probability of being arrested for a drinking and driving incident is in accordance with this perception; it is estimated that a person drives drunk between 200 and 2,000 times before being apprehended. The most prevalent sanctions levied against DUI offenders are license suspension and incarceration. While the threat of suspension and jail time has been an effective deterrent for the general population, the research is unclear regarding these sanctions for multiple offenders. Some offenders do stop drinking and driving during the sanction period but offenders who are alcoholics continue to drive and so do some offenders while they await trial. In some cases, this can be close to a year's time. Rodgers' (1994) study of license impoundment in Minnesota is revealing. First of all, Rodgers reports that when the law was first passed it was implemented in only 65 percent of the cases in which it was possible to do so. Secondly, the recidivism rate of DUI offenders was much lower if the officer impounded the auto plates immediately than if the offender received a letter from the department of public safety with instructions to turn the plates in to the authorities. The overall results of the study indicated that impoundment may be helpful in reducing drunk driving for the multi-offending drunk driver.

The National Commission Against Drunk Driving (2001) estimates that 80 percent of chronic drinking drivers continue to drink and drive after license suspension. The probability of getting caught is very low. Jail time, public service, and attendance at victim impact panels do little to stop chronic drinking drivers from drinking and driving after release. Long-term incarceration would overwhelm the correctional system. There is virtually no difference in recidivism rates between those who receive jail time or public service and those who do not. In response to the ineffectiveness of previously employed strategies, jurisdictions have begun to employ alternative sanctions such as ignition interlock devices and electronic home monitoring.

Ignition interlocking systems appear to reduce recidivism at least for a period of time. A Maryland study (Beck, Rauch and Baker 1997) of multiple DUI offenders who had successfully completed treatment for alcohol problems indicated that offenders assigned to the interlock program had recidivism rates that were one-third lower than the control group's. Rates climbed once the person was no longer in the program. To combat this tendency, it is suggested that the device remain effective for a longer period of time and that the offender be required to pay a portion of the cost. Various alternative sanctions could be employed to ensure the safety of the mechanism and to promote continued attendance at treatment where personal assessment, education, and employment are combined in a meaningful way over an extended period of time.

■ Mental Illness

According to the U.S. Surgeon General's (Satcher 1999) report on mental health, mental illness touches many families in the United States. According to current epidemiological estimates, at least one person in five has a diagnosable mental disorder during the course of a year. In general, 19 percent of the adult U.S. population has a mental disorder in 1 year, 3 percent have both mental and addictive disorders, and 6 percent have addictive disorders. Consequently, about 28 to 30 percent of the population has either a mental or an addictive disorder.

The epidemiology of mental disorders is somewhat handicapped by the difficulty of identifying a "case" of mental disorder. *Case* is an epidemiological term for someone who meets the criteria for a disease or disorder (Satcher 1999). It is not always easy to establish a threshold for a mental disorder, particularly in light of how common the symptoms of mental illness are and, in some cases, the lack of objective, physical symptoms. It is often difficult to determine when a set of symptoms rises to the level of mental disorder, a problem that affects other areas of health. In many cases, symptoms are not of sufficient intensity or duration to meet the criteria of a disorder and the threshold may vary from culture to culture.

<u>Diagnosis of mental disorders</u> is made on the basis of a multidimensional assessment that takes into account observable signs and symptoms of illness, the course and duration of the illness, response to treatment, and degree of functional impairment. One of the problems with diagnosis is that there is no clearly measurable threshold for functional impairments (Satcher 1999). Efforts are currently underway in the study of mental disorders to create a threshold, or agreed-upon minimum level of functional limitation, that should be required to establish a case (i.e., a clinically significant condition). Reflecting the state of psychiatric classifications during the past two decades, epidemiology has focused primarily on symptom clusters and has not uniformly applied—or, at times, even measured—the level of dysfunction. Ongoing analysis of existing epidemiological data is expected to yield better understanding of the rates of mental disorder and dysfunction in the population.

diagnosis of mental disorders is made on the basis of multidimensional assessment that takes into account observable signs and symptoms of illness, the course and duration of the illness, response to treatment, and degree of functional impairment.

Treatment of Mental Health

Another limitation of contemporary mental health knowledge is the lack of a standard measure of "need for treatment," particularly that which is culturally appropriate (Satcher 1999). Such measures are at the heart of the public health approach to mental health. Current epidemiological estimates therefore cannot definitively identify those who are in need of treatment. Other estimates indicate that some individuals with mental disorders are in treatment and others are not; some are seen in primary care settings and others in specialty care. In the absence of valid measures of needed services, rates of disorder estimated in epidemiological surveys serve as an imperfect proxy for the need for care or treatment.

The cost for the treatment of mental illness is exceedingly high (Satcher 1999). The direct cost of mental disorders services in the United States in 1996 totaled $69 billion. This figure represented 7.3 percent of the total cost of medical treatment. Another $17.7 billion was spent on Alzheimer's disease and $12.6 billion on substance abuse treatment. Direct costs correspond to spending for treatment and rehabilitation nationwide, but indirect costs are substantial as well. In 1990, the indirect cost was estimated to be $78.6 billion (Satcher 1999). Much of this cost is related to lost productivity at the workplace and school as well as financial support of those who are disabled and in prison.

According to the U.S. Department of Justice, mental illness is a significant problem for probationers (Ditton 1999), as shown in **Table 4-2**. Based on the 1995 survey of adult probationers, Ditton reports that 6 percent were identified as mentally ill, 13.8 percent reported a mental or emotional condition, and 8.2 percent admitted to an overnight stay at a mental hospital. Furthermore, the estimated number of mentally ill probationers reporting a mental or an emotional condition was 547,800. Another 281,200 admitted to having stayed overnight in a facility for mental health treatment. In terms of which probationers were identified as mentally ill, females (21.7 percent) were more likely to be identified than males (14.7 percent); whites (19.6 percent) more than blacks (10.4 percent) or Hispanics (9.0 percent); and probationers who are ages 45 to 54 (21.2 percent) more than probationers younger than age 24 (13.8 percent), 25 to 34 (13.8 percent), 35 to 44 (19.8 percent), and 55 or older (16 percent) (Ditton 1999).

When comparing the most recent serious offense of the mentally ill probationers with other probationers in Table 4-2, the mentally ill probationers are

Table 4-2	Mentally Ill Probationers	
Offense	**Mentally Ill Probationers (in percent)**	**Other Probationers (in percent)**
All Offenses	100	100
Violent Offenses	28.4	18.4
Murder	.5	.9
Sexual assault	6.8	4.1
Robbery	2.0	1.4
Assault	14.0	10.5
Property Offenses	30.4	28.5
Burglary	6.4	4.3
Larceny/theft	5.3	8.8
Fraud	11.7	9.2
Drug Offenses	16.1	20.7
Possession	7.2	11.0
Trafficking	6.7	9.2
Public Order Offenses	24.7	31.6

Source: Paula M. Ditton. "Mental Health and Treatment of Inmates and Probationers." Washington, DC: U.S. Department of Justice, Bureau of Justice Statistics, July 1999.

more likely to commit a violent offense other than murder. They also commit more assaults, sexual assaults, and robberies than other probationers. This holds true of burglary and fraud. However, other probationers are more likely to have committed larcenies, drug offenses, and public order offenses.

Ignoring the problems associated with persons with mental illness (PWMIs) opens agencies up to many dangers, including increased failure rates, liability issues associated with the failure to provide appropriate treatment (Cohen 1993), the "duty to protect" (the moral and legal obligation to shield from harm those who are incapable of shielding themselves) (Monahan 1993), and externally driven policies in response to crisis situations. This reactive posture toward mentally ill probationers leads to detrimental effects on the personal well-being of these offenders and inevitably increases costs for the agency. In contrast, knowing more about the nature and prevalence of mental illness through improved data collection will result in informed decision making, enhancement of individual case management, and the improvement of broad organizational practices for PWMIs (Fulton 1996).

Right to Treatment

An important consideration for probation is the **right to treatment** (Fulton 1996). Once offenders have been identified as mentally ill, appropriate treatment and services must be provided. A method for obtaining data supporting these resource needs and for tracking offender treatment will assist agencies in resource development and will provide legal protection. Due to the wide range of social and human service needs of persons with mental illness, interagency collaboration is a core principle of effective programming for this population (Dvoskin et al. 1994). Hence, tracking, recording, and communicating assessment and case information are essential.

right to treatment means that once offenders have been identified as mentally ill, appropriate treatment and services must be provided.

One example of such a program is the Maricopa County Adult Probation Department (MCAPD). Mickel (1994) describes how the MCAPD uses agency data to advocate for resources to meet the supervision needs of persons with mental illness. After the identification of a probationer with mental illness and the need for assistance during the period of distress, the department establishes a specialized supervision unit for that person. When the need for additional resources was noted by the MCAPD, it was able to secure funding for transitional living for those awaiting appropriate community placements. The agency then contracted with local nonprofit agencies for their services, which were designed to provide full medical and psychiatric evaluations, to prescribe appropriate medications, to initiate referrals for applicable benefits and entitlements, and to identify follow-up placements and treatment strategies. A review of treatment outcomes indicated that out of 144 offenders served during the course of a year, 63 percent were successfully placed in the community. As a result of this program, the county saved $81,000.

It is important that the officers who serve in the MCAPD have the training and skills in dealing with the mentally ill. Even when the staff have specialized training and are given special caseloads of offenders with mental illness, it is appropriate for mental health and other related agencies to be the primary service providers for these clients. These relationships should not be based on referrals alone but on partnerships for the offender whose psychological problems, social deficits, and legal troubles are intertwined. An integrated approach is essential (Clear 1996).

■ Drug Offenders

The Columbia University Center on Addiction and Substance Abuse (CASA) National Survey of American Attitudes on Substance Abuse (2000) revealed that for the sixth straight year, drugs were the most important problem teens said they face. The percentage of teens expecting to never try an illegal drug in the future dropped from 60 percent in 1999 to 51 percent in 2000. Twenty-eight percent of teenagers knew a friend who had used methylenedioxymethamphetamine (MDMA), also known as Ecstasy. Ten percent said they had attended rave parties; MDMA is available at 70 percent of raves.

Drug use among teens and younger people has been increasing for the past several years. A 1998 National Center on Addiction and Substance Abuse survey demonstrated that teen marijuana use was up almost 300 percent since 1992. According to the Monitoring the Future Study (2001), 15 percent of eighth graders, 32 percent of tenth graders, and 37 percent of twelfth graders had used pot in the last month. This trend is fairly steady, but cocaine and heroin use were down. A troubling trend is that the number of eighth graders who believe that daily marijuana use is bad for you has fallen from 74 percent to 72 percent. Potency is also an issue.

The problem of increased drug use is exacerbated by the increased purity of these drugs. For example, the Drug Enforcement Administration (Casteel 2003) reports that average commercial grade potency of marijuana is up and overall heroin purity in smaller quantities has remained over 50 percent. Furthermore, the Office of National Drug Control Policy (2002) reports on the number of hospital emergency room visits brought on by drugs. Often these drugs are taken in doses that are too high and the person overdoses. Between 1990 and 2001 the number of admissions for marijuana and hashish rose 604 percent, from roughly 15,700 to 110,500, and heroin episodes increased 180 percent from 33,800 to 93,000, but the number of amphetamine episodes decreased during this time.

Drugs and Crimes

According to Anne Stahl (2001), drug abuse violations had the highest arrest rate in 1999. As indicated in Table 4.1, over 1 million arrests were made for drug violations. The number of juvenile court cases involving drug offenses more than doubled between 1993 and 1998. In 1998, juvenile courts across the country handled an estimated 192,000 delinquency cases in which a drug offense was the most serious charge. The number of drug offense cases processed during 1998 was 108 percent greater than in 1993 and 148 percent greater than 1989. Males have accounted for the majority of drug offenses: 81 percent. In 1998, white youth were involved in 68 percent of the cases. For black youth, this proportion was only 29 percent. The proportion of youth held in detention for drug violations was 22 percent, representing 43,000 youth. Another 148,000 youth were not detained. The majority of formally processed drug cases (63 percent) resulted in the juvenile being an adjudicated delinquent, and in 23 percent of these cases, the most severe disposition was residential placement. The courts ordered probation in 59 percent of the adjudicated cases. Furthermore, in 1998, most formally adjudicated petitioned drug cases that were not waived or adjudicated were dismissed (67 percent). In 16 percent of these cases, the juvenile agreed to informal probation and in another 15 percent to other dispositions. About 2 percent of these cases involved voluntary out-of-home placement (Stahl 2001).

■ Capital Value

Community corrections do not occur in isolation but must take place in a dynamic environment. This environment is constantly changing and varies considerably from place to place. Some communities have extremely robust economies, highly effective schools, and an array of alternative support services at their disposal. Other communities have lackluster economies, mediocre-to-poor schools, and few resources to call upon to help with their probationers. It is difficult to make any generalization today without completely misstating the circumstances of a community.

It is possible, nonetheless, to make a few claims that are valid for everyone and that have a good chance of representing the current state of affairs. If probation is to have an effective system of reintegration, an understanding of the concept of *capital value* is essential. The concept of "capital" can be broken down into three areas: physical capital, social capital, and human capital. It is advantageous for agencies and probation officers to consider capital value as an underlying theme for their work with probationers who come from all walks of life. By doing so, the human dignity of each probationer can be more effectively maintained and nurtured.

Physical Capital

Physical capital refers to the attributes of a physical object such as a community's roads, houses, buildings, tools, or machines. The more modern and plentiful the physical capital, the better it is for its citizens. According to Bruce Kratz in *Reviving Cities: Think Metropolitan* (1998), if one is to accept the latest popular views on the matter, after 50 years of decline, U.S. cities have been reborn as safe and exciting places, places to visit for entertainment. Crime and unemployment rates are at their lowest since the 1970s. With investment in new stadiums, arenas, sports palaces, restaurants, entertainment districts, and gentrified housing, city budgets were for a time balanced and most of the problems of the recent past have gone away. What is also true is that there are fundamental changes occurring in the suburbs as well. In the suburbs and smaller communities, there is a rapid conversion of farmland into an array of housing developments, shopping plazas, and industrial or office parks. The decentralization of people, jobs, and services is an important factor to consider in the changing urban and suburban landscape.

Katz (1998) has argued that these larger patterns of metropolitan growth are fiscally, socially, and environmentally damaging and unsustainable. The benefits of the new economic prosperity are not shared equitably. Rapidly developing new suburbs, built since the early 1970s on the outer fringes of metropolitan areas, are capturing much of the new employment and population growth. Low taxes and quality services are evident but affordable housing is extremely limited, thus excluding families of modest means—many from racial or ethnic minorities—from living there. Without adequate transportation systems, these suburbs are characterized by social isolation and social and economic homogeneity. Cities and older suburbs find it difficult to compete with these new suburbs for businesses and middle-class residents. Urban emigration leads to reduced tax bases, leaving many cities without sufficient resources to address the problems of minority poverty, joblessness, family fragmentation, and failings schools.

Federal and state policies contribute to the migration to the suburbs. Transportation monies earmarked for highway construction have paved the way for strip malls and housing subdivisions while neglecting the mass transit or road repair work needed for the cities and older suburbs. Katz (1998) is quite critical of federal and state policies and administrative practices that have concentrated the poor in urban areas where they are isolated from the economic enterprise. The lack of a policy supporting affordable housing in all communities means that suburban communities can establish exclusionary zones setting themselves off from the poor in their metro areas. Low- and moderate-income families are trapped in decaying inner cities and older suburban neighborhoods where they are denied good schools and services (Katz 1998, 2)

Combined with white families moving to the suburbs, the city has become the repository of a disproportionate share of a region's poor people. Many of the nation's urban areas, whether in the rust belt or in such once desirable places as Los Angeles, are in the midst of profound and deleterious transformations. Decentralization of services, work, and living arrangements has caused many cities to go dead at their core. Urban sprawl has resulted in the end of locally available taxes, shrinking retail trade, and the loss of hundreds of thousands of manufacturing jobs (Flannagan 1993, 76). These cities, previously the centers of culture and civilization, have become hollow shells, abandoned by the working and middle classes (Katz 1989) and have been characterized as disordered (Skogan 1990). Disordered communities are an affront to community values with a high amount of public drinking, loitering youth, street harassment, sale and use of drugs, noisy neighbors, homeless and mentally ill people, commercial sex (for sale through shows, movies, and prostitution), physical decay, vandalism, dilapidation and abandonment, and rubbish. Anger, fear, intergroup conflict, and demoralization are the identified consequences. Consistent with all of these is a general lack of civility. This sense of disorder may also serve as an indicator that community self-controls no longer protect residents and passersby (Skogan 1990, 48).

Under these conditions, the mechanism of moral reliability dissolves and there is no assurance that anyone will uphold earlier standards except through direct threats of violence. Moral reliability is the accumulated trust that develops when, over time, people repeat actions that have proven to be beneficial to others. People can be relied upon when shared reciprocal expectations are met, and when they are not, people can expect to be disciplined. Because of the heterogeneity of city life, there is a premium on moral reliability and knowing whom one can trust (Lewis and Salem 1986).

In the years prior to 1950, cities became convergent places where employees drove into a center city for business and entertainment by using transportation corridors carrying them from their homes and urban villages. These central districts lacked a stable residential population but provided housing in an area high in delinquency, predatory crime, and other social problems. These areas were afflicted with the presence of a high number of psychotics, people afflicted with infectious diseases, alcoholism, truancy, school problems, housing problems, and unemployment (Felson 1994, 52).

Social Capital

In recent years, social scientists have framed concerns about the changing character of American society in terms of the concept of *social capital*. (The idea of social capital is that social networks have value.) Social capital affects the productivity of individuals and groups and refers to goodwill, fellowship, sympathy, and social intercourse among the individuals and families who make up a social unit. The individual is helpless socially if left alone. If the person comes into contact with a neighbor, and then with other neighbors, there will be an accumulation of social capital. This may immediately satisfy social needs and may bear a social potentiality sufficient to the substantial improvement of living conditions in the whole community (Putnam 2000, 19).

Social capital can also have externalities that affect the wider community, so that not all costs and benefits of social connection accrue to the person making the contact. This is played out in the concern a neighbor has for a vacant home or apartment. A well-connected person in a poorly connected society is not as productive as a well-connected individual in a well-connected society. Even a poorly connected individual may derive some of the spillover benefits from living in a well-connected community (Putnam 2000, 20).

Social Networks

Social connections developed through social capital are important for the rules of conduct they support. Networks involve mutual obligations: they are not interesting as mere contacts. Networks of community engagement foster norms of reciprocity. Sometimes reciprocity is specific. Most important is the norm of generalized reciprocity. The predominant thought is "I will do this without expecting anything in return with the full knowledge that someone else will do something for me." A society characterized by general reciprocity is more efficient than a distrustful society. Trustworthiness lubricates social life. Frequent interaction among a diverse set of people tends to produce norms of generalized reciprocity. Civic engagement and social capital entail mutual obligation and responsibility for actions facilitating cooperation for mutual benefits (Putnam 2000).

Social capital makes sense for those inside the network but those outside a specific network may utilize their own network for completely different purposes. Social capital can be directed toward malevolent, antisocial purposes, just like any other form of capital. Therefore, it is important to ask how the positive consequences of social capital—mutual support, cooperation, trust, and institutional effectiveness—can be maximized and the negative manifestations—sectarianism, ethnocentrism, and corruption—minimized. Of all the dimensions along which forms of social capital vary, perhaps the most important is the distinction between bridging or inclusion and bonding or exclusion. Some forms of social capital are inward looking and tend to reinforce exclusive and homogeneous groups. <u>**Bonding networks**</u> include ethnic fraternal organizations, church-based women's reading groups, and fashionable country clubs. Bonding networks are good for undergirding specific instances of reciprocity and mobilizing solidarity. These networks can provide crucial social and psychological support for the less fortunate members. <u>**Bridging networks**</u> are outward looking and include civil rights groups, youth groups, and ecumenical religious organizations that are useful for external

bonding networks include ethnic fraternal organizations, church-based women's reading groups, and fashionable country clubs.

bridging networks are outward looking and include civil rights groups, youth groups, and ecumenical religious organizations that are useful for external assets and for information diffusion.

assets and for information diffusion. External ties are preferable to internal bonding ties. Bonding is getting by, but bridging is getting ahead where broader identities and reciprocity are possible. It must be understood that groups are not oriented toward complete forms of bonding or bridging but must be considered in terms of more or less of one form over the other (Putnam 2000, 23). This is expressed in the positive form of mutual support, cooperation, trust, and institutional effectiveness. Some forms of social capital involve multistranded networks such as people who meet repeatedly but in different contexts. Bonded social capital reinforces exclusive identities and homogeneous groupings. This involves specific reciprocity and mobilizing solidarity (Putnam 2000, 23).

A Push Forward

According to Putnam (2000), society must reestablish a measure of social capital by renewing its civic engagement. Each member needs to develop responses to the eroding effectiveness of civic institutions and overcome the tendencies to privately prefer a vibrant community. However, when no one else seems willing to participate at that level, society falls back on achieving private aims. Both collective and individual initiatives must be employed. The single most important cause of this country's current plight is a pervasive and continuing generational decline in almost all forms of civic engagement. In order to achieve this measure of social capital, citizens need to emphasize bridging capital—capital that extends social relationships. First, the goal is to increase participation and deliberation in a variety of civic institutions. This starts with programs in the schools that explain the civic process, the need to participate and the opportunities to participate. Second, society needs to find ways to make the work environment more worker-friendly so that there are time and opportunity for the development of social capital. Work schedules should be family- and community-friendly. Many of the benefits of employment that encourage social capital formation such as stronger families, more effective schools, safer neighborhoods, and a more vibrant public life tend to affect the community more than the work site. Employers see their investment as providing little return (Putnam 2000, 406). Third, the metropolitan settlements have imposed heavy personal and economic costs, including pollution, congestion, and lost time. In many ways this sprawl damages the fabric of communities. Employees need to spend less time traveling to and from work and more time connecting with neighbors. Integrated and pedestrian-friendly neighborhoods are needed where casual socializing can occur more often. Urban experiments need reassessment to learn what is working to bring people closer. Policies are needed to assure a good quality of life but also to balance population concentration against urban sprawl. Fourth, religion has played a major role in any civic renewal. Putnam believes members of society should be more involved in their faith communities while at the same time be more tolerant of the beliefs of others. Each must be careful that bridging capital is developed through community connections if one is to succeed in helping to build a stronger community. Fifth, society must spend less time before electronic entertainment and more time actively engaging each other in meaningful discourse; each needs to learn to speak the language of others. Last, Putnam advocates greater civic participation by using the arts to bridge the social barriers set for one another.

Human Capital

Human capital refers to properties of individuals such as training, education, and experience that enhance individual productivity. It amounts to the level of personal expertise. The 2000 census reported that 82 percent of the people who were at least 25 years old had earned a high school diploma or its equivalent. Twenty-five percent of these people had earned at least a bachelor's degree or higher. Among people 16 to 19 years of age, 11 percent were high school dropouts, were not currently enrolled, and had not graduated from high school.

Table 4-3 indicates that the percentage of blacks, Hispanics, and whites who have completed high school has increased dramatically for all categories of persons. Particularly dramatic positive changes have occurred with blacks; in 1960 one in five graduated from high school. Now we find that one in five blacks do *not* graduate from high school. Hispanics continue to have the lowest level of graduation. What is also interesting is that whites have also increased their rate of graduation from high school.

Table 4-4 indicates the percentage of high school dropouts starting in 1970 and ending in 2002. There was a steady decline in the percentage of all student dropouts. Between 1970 and 2002 the overall total of dropouts declined by 33 percent; for whites the rate dropped 19 percent; for blacks the rate dropped 54 percent; and for Hispanics, the dropout rate fell 27 percent. This data does suggest that there has been some success with educational achievement and an increase in social capital.

Table 4-3	Percent of High School Graduates, Persons 25 Years and Older, by Race and Hispanic Status				
	Percent High School Graduates				
	1960	**1970**	**1980**	**1990**	**2003**
All persons	41.1	52.3	66.5	77.6	84.6
Blacks	20.1	31.4	51.2	66.2	80.0
Hispanics	Not available	32.1	44.0	50.8	57.0
Whites	43.2	54.5	68.8	79.1	85.1

Source: U.S. Census Bureau. 2004. *Statistical Abstract of the United States, Education, 2004–2005.*

Table 4-4	High School by Race and Hispanic Origin, 1970–2002				
Dropouts	**1970**	**1980**	**1990**	**1995**	**2002**
Total	12.2	12.0	10.1	9.9	8.8
Whites	10.8	11.3	10.1	9.7	8.7
Blacks	22.2	16.0	10.9	10.0	10.1
Hispanics	Not available	29.5	26.8	24.7	21.5

Note: Percent of the population which has not completed high school and not enrolled.
Source: U.S. Census Bureau. 2004. *Statistical Abstract of the United States, Education, 2004–2005.*

The American Management Association (AMA 2001) found that more than 38 percent of job applicants failed reading tests. The AMA points out that new technology requirements have raised the minimum requirements for a basic skills position. A few years ago, the only requirements for warehouse work were minimal literacy, good health, and a willingness to do the work. Today, the employee must also understand how to use a handheld scanner to check for inventories. Work will require higher levels of cognitive skills but society also has fewer workers who possess such skills needed in the workforce (AMA 2001).

One indication of human capital is the certificates of training awarded people of different races. The Census Bureau reports important information about the vocational certificates of various types of people.

Table 4-5 is an indication of the human capital present in the workforce by ethnicity and race. The data is based on 6.5 million whites, 834,000 blacks, and 584,000 Hispanics. It is clear that whites, blacks, and Hispanics have significant numbers of vocational-certified workers in each category. Whites are more likely

Table 4-5	Vocational Certification Field Given by Race and Ethnicity, 1996 (in thousands)					
	White		**Black**		**Hispanics**	
Field	*No.*	*Percent*	*No.*	*Percent*	*No.*	*Percent*
Total	6,499		834		584	
Agriculture	52	.001	6	.007	14	**.023**
Auto mechanic	275	.042	24	.028	27	**.046**
Aviation	106	.0006	12	.014	13	**.022**
Business office	1,191	.183	147	.176	124	**.212**
Computer	237	.036	55	**.065**	36	.061
Construction	216	.033	17	.020	38	**.061**
Cosmetology	644	**.099**	62	.074	43	.073
Drafting	76	.011	12	**.014**	4	.006
Electronics	370	.056	48	.057	46	**.078**
Food service	71	.010	14	**.016**		.000
Health care	1,274	**.196**	145	.173	69	.118
Home economics	18	.002	9	**.010**	3	.005
Hotel restaurant	20	.003	17	**.020**	11	.018
Marketing	30	.004	11	**.013**		.000
Metal working	162	**.024**	8	.010	7	.011
Police protection	57	.008	11	**.013**	8	**.013**
Refrig. heating	154	**.023**	9	.010	14	**.023**
Transportation	60	.009	26	**.031**		.000
Other	1,484	.228	193	.231	148	**.253**

Source: U.S. Census Bureau. 2001. Table 3A: Vocational Field by Sex, Race and Ethnicity, and Age, 1996. Available online at: http://www.census.gov/population/socdemo/education/p70-72/tab03a.txt.

to have more people in cosmetology, health care, metalworking, and refrigeration and heating but blacks and Hispanics lead in the other categories, thus reflecting considerable influence in these trades.

■ Racial Divisions

A July 2001 Gallup poll indicated broad differences between the views of black and white Americans about the state of race relations (Ludwig 2004). Six in 10 blacks were dissatisfied with the way people of their race were treated by society. This contrasts with the 64 percent of whites who say they were personally satisfied with the way blacks were treated in society. The overall assessment from blacks about their personal lives was generally positive. Close to 9 in 10 blacks said they were satisfied with their lives. Blacks, however, were more dissatisfied than whites when it came to issues such as personal safety, employment, housing, and the communities in which they lived.

Similar differences exist between whites' and blacks' assessments of equal educational and housing opportunities in their communities. Eight out of 10 whites but only half of blacks view the educational opportunities for black and white children as equal. Over several years, measurements conducted by the Gallup organization revealed that blacks have become more pessimistic about equal educational opportunities than they had been in the early and mid 1990s. There is a 36-point difference between whites and blacks on this issue, a difference that is almost identical to what it was nearly 40 years ago (Ludwig 2004).

The gap between blacks' and whites' perception of equal housing opportunities also has increased. In 1989, a 20-point gap was recorded. In July 2001, the gap stood at 35 points—the largest it had ever been—with 83 percent of all whites but only 48 percent of blacks perceiving equal housing opportunities in the communities (Ludwig 2004).

Gallup also found that blacks are much more likely than whites to perceive unfair treatment of blacks in several settings in their communities (Ludwig 2004). In particular, 35 percent of white adults as compared to 66 percent of blacks believe blacks are treated less fairly by the police in their community. Race relations in general have deteriorated. Forty percent of whites, but only 9 percent of blacks, say that blacks are treated the same as whites in the nation. A majority of blacks express pessimism about whether the solution to the problem of black/white relations in the United States will ever be reached. Indeed, black Americans have been as pessimistic as they have been since the question was first asked in 1993. As an indication of a growing social distance, whites are expressing less pessimism about the same issue. At the time of this survey (2001), 45 percent of the whites indicated race relations would always be a problem. The 21-point gap between white and black Americans' expectations for the future of race relations is the largest that Gallup has recorded. Nearly half of black Americans (47 percent) feel they were treated unfairly because of their race in the past month. More than one in four (27 percent) say they were treated unfairly when shopping.

Profiling

The Gallup poll results indicated that racial profiling is a particularly acute problem (Ludwig 2004). Twenty-one percent of the black adults overall, and 31 percent of black men, reported unfair treatment in the past 30 days at the hands of the police. Large differences between black and white Americans' perceptions of police fairness underscore the importance of this issue in understanding the racial divide. Nearly 9 out of 10 whites feel they are treated fairly by state and local police; only just over half of all blacks feel this way. This gap in perception of treatment by the police is significantly larger than that recorded in 1999, when blacks were much less likely to claim unfair treatment. Forty-four percent of blacks feel that, at some point in their lives, the police have stopped them because of their race or ethnic background. The practice of racial profiling is believed to be widespread by 83 percent of blacks, but by only 55 percent of whites.

■ Income

The U.S. Census Bureau reported in 1999 that the real median income of households in the United States had risen for the fifth consecutive year. Real median income reached its highest level since the census bureau began compiling statistics in 1967. The median income was the highest ever recorded for white non-Hispanic, black, and Hispanic households and equaled the highest level achieved by Asians and Pacific Islanders. American Indians had household incomes higher than blacks, the same as Hispanics, but lower than white non-Hispanics and Asians and Pacific Islanders. The median income for men working full-time year-round continued to rise to $36,000 but women working full-time year-round found their income had not changed. In fact, the gap between men's and women's wages continued to increase. A woman made a median income of $26,000 per year, which was 72 percent of the average man's wage. The number of women joining the workforce continues to increase. In fact, an increase in the number of married women in the workforce contributed to a 150 percent increase in real median income of married-couple families between 1947 and 1997. Since 1950, the proportion of married women in the workforce has nearly tripled.

In 1997, men who were college graduates had a median income of $47,000, a 22 percent increase since 1963. Less-educated men showed a decline in income. The census bureau used two different measures related to the distribution of income and income inequality. Generally, the long-term trend has been toward income equality; the income made by educated persons has increased faster than those of the less educated.

Since 1969, the share of aggregate family income controlled by the lowest income quintile decreased from 4.1 percent to 3.6 percent in 1999, while the share gained by the highest one-fifth of the population increased from 43 percent to 49.4 percent, as shown in **Table 4-6**. Most noticeably, the share of income controlled by the top 5 percent of households increased from 16.6 percent to 21.5 percent.

Table 4-6	Share of Aggregate Income by Family					
1999	Lowest Fifth Income	Second Fifth Income	Third Fifth Income	Fourth Income Income	Highest Fifth Income	Top Five Percent
Black	3.2	8.7	15.0	24.3	48.9	19.3
Hispanic	4.3	9.7	15.2	23.4	47.5	19.7
White	4.6	10.2	15.7	22.8	46.6	20.2
All races and ethnic groups	3.6	8.9	14.9	23.2	49.4	21.5

Source: U.S. Census Bureau. 2001. *Historical Income Tables – Families.* Available online at: http://www.census.gov/hhes/income/histinc/incfamdet.html.

Wage Distribution

Wage distribution has become increasingly unequal, as the workers at the top of the economic structure have seen some real wage gains and those at the bottom have experienced some significant wage losses. These changes reflect shifts in the demand for specific forms of labor, which are differentiated on the basis of education and skill: human capital. Meanwhile, long-term changes in living arrangements have exacerbated differences in household incomes. Divorce, separations, out-of-wedlock births, and later marriages have led to fewer married couple households and more single-parent households. These non-married couples and single parents tend to have lower income (U.S. Census, *Income Inequality,* 2004).

Gary Burtless (2001) has offered some useful information on income inequality, which can be measured by the <u>Gini index</u>. Income inequality can be calculated by arranging family income in rank order, from the poorest to the richest; dividing the hierarchy into fifths (quintiles); computing the average income per quintiles; and then comparing the shares of income. In making comparisons with a single index, economists have devised the Gini index (coefficient, ratio, or number). Gini is calculated by comparing the possible pure equal distribution of income, where each quintile has 20 percent of all the income, with the actual distribution of income across the five quintiles. The higher the Gini index, the greater the distance between the equal distribution of wealth curve and the actual distribution of this curve across the five quintiles. In a perfectly unequal society, in which one person had all the income, the curve would look like an "L" and its value would be 1.000. In practice, the Gini index usually falls between 0.200 and 0.450. The United States calculates a Gini curve based on a sample of 60,000 households polled by the Census Bureau every March as part of its Current Population Survey (Left Business Observer 2004).

From 1969 to 1999, the Gini index, a measure of the concentration of wealth, rose 17.4 percent to its 1997 level of .459 (U.S. Census 2000). A Gini measure of 1.0 would again indicate the wealth is in the hands of one person. A measure of .01 would mean it is spread evenly throughout the population. Measuring change as

Gini index of income inequality is a measure of the degree to which a population shares that resource unequally.

a percentage of movement is just one indicator of its use. For purposes here, this indicates money is becoming increasingly concentrated in the hands of a few in this country. Those making higher incomes find they are taking home a larger share of the economic pie. Since 1945, the Gini index of income inequality has taken some interesting turns. Income inequality was at its lowest point on this index in 1967 when President Johnson's "war on poverty" was at its height. Beginning with 1968, there is a continuous process of expansion of the Gini index. In other words, since the late 1960s, income in this country has become steadily concentrated in the hands of fewer and fewer individuals. American inequality rose sharply after 1979. It rose both in terms of family earnings and in terms of workers' earnings. Although the rise in income disparities slowed after 1993, the level of money income inequality was as high at the end of the 1990s as at any time since the end of the Great Depression (Burtless 2001).

Poverty

Figure 4.2 indicates that the number of people living in poverty changed from a high of 40 million in 1959 to 34.6 million in 2002. It is clear is that the number living in poverty is quite unstable. In 1974 there were only 23 million people living in poverty. The percentage of people who live in poverty fell from roughly 23 percent in 1959 to 12.1 percent in 2002. Over the last 40 years, the percentage of the population living in poverty has been in the 10 to 15 percent range regardless of the presidential administration and whether there was an economic recession. As indicated by the shadowing, the poverty rates spike during an economic recession, which is what is happening during this jobless market boom. This is largely true except for the jump in poverty found in 1993 when 40 million people lived in poverty.

Note that the poverty rates are highest among children under 18, which does not bode well for their future (**Table 4-7**). Ethnicity reports indicate that the highest rates of poverty are found among full-blooded African-Americans and those who in-

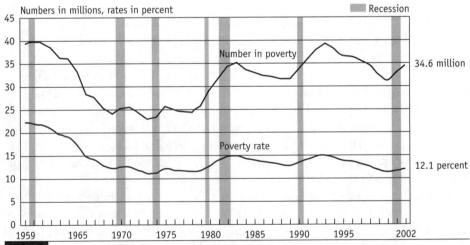

Figure 4.2 Poverty trends, 1959–2002.

Source: U.S. Census Bureau. 2003. *Current Population Survey, 1960–2003 Annual Social and Economic Supplements.*
Note: The data points represent the midpoints of the respective years.

dicate racial or ethnic ties to another group. The rate is slightly smaller for people of Hispanic origin. The lowest rates of poverty are found among whites and
Asians. Poverty rates are highest for people living in central cities followed by
those living outside of metropolitan areas. The lowest levels are found in the
suburbs, the areas outside of central cities. Due to family problems associated
with alcoholism, mental illness, unemployment, along with other factors,
poverty exists in most communities.

Particularly troubling is the poverty levels for families (**Figure** 4.3). The lowest level of poverty is found with married couples where one or both work. Working obviously reduces poverty but not for everyone. Poverty is greatest where no
member of the family works, especially for female householders. Of all families,
the percent living in poverty is 10.4. In married couple families, the rate is only
6.1 percent but rises to 28.5 percent in female-headed households, 13 percent in
male-headed households. Understandably, the rate of poverty jumps considerably

Table 4-7	Poverty Rate Among Individuals by the Official Poverty Measure, 2002	
Characteristic	**Number (in thousands)**	**Poverty Rate (in percent)**
All	34,570	12.1
Age		
Under 18	12,133	16.7
18–64	18,861	10.6
65 and over	3,576	10.4
Race/Ethnicity		
White, not Hispanic	15,567	8.0
Black alone or in combination*	8,136	22.7
Black alone	8,602	24.1
Hispanic origin+	7,997	21.4
Asian alone or in combination*	1,243	10.0
Asian, Native Hawaiian, and other Pacific Islander, either alone or in combination	1,378	10.2
Asian alone	1,161	10.1
Residence		
Inside metropolitan areas	27,096	11.6
In central cities	13,784	16.7
Outside central cities	13,311	8.9
Outside metropolitan areas	7,474	14.2

*The 2003 Current Population Survey on which these estimates are based asked respondents to choose one or more races.
+Persons of Hispanic origin may be of any race.

Source: U.S. Census. 2003. *Poverty in the United States: 2002*, P60–222, Tables 1 and 2.

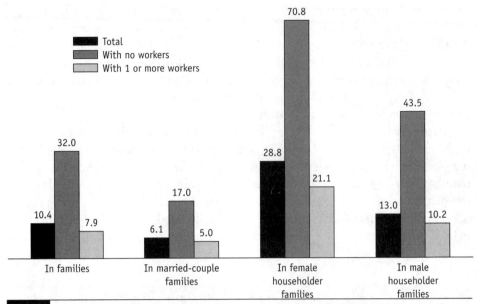

Figure 4.3 Poverty rates of people in families by family type and presence of workers: 2002 (in percent). *Source:* U.S. Census Bureau. *Current Population Survey, 2003 Annual Social and Economic Supplement.*

when there are no workers: in all families, 32 percent; in married couple families, 17 percent; in female householder families, 70.8 percent; and in male householder families, 43.5 percent. Even when there is at least one or more workers in the family, poverty continues. In all families, the rate is 7.9 percent; in married couple families, 5 percent; in female-headed households, 21.1 percent, and in male-headed households, 10.2 percent. Poverty exists under a variety of circumstances and there are a considerable number of working poor.

Prior to welfare reform, long-term welfare mothers tended to belong to racial minorities, had never been married, and were high school dropouts (Wilson 1987). Wilson also noted that the average poor black child is in the midst of a poverty spell that will last almost 2 decades. Almost one in three (32 percent) young black males in the age group 20 to 29 years are under some type of correctional control (incarceration, probation, or parole), as is one in eight young Hispanic males (Mauer 1999). Having the male out of the house may have some benefit, especially because some of these men have brought trouble to their families. Nontraditional families can be successful but are not as successful as two-parent households (Roberts 1995, 45). Due to the reduced pool of marriageable men, many poor women have little realistic hope of becoming wives and mothers in conventional marriages. It becomes more rational to have children out of wedlock; raise them in single-parent, female-headed households; and maintain informal extramarital relations. According to J. D. Greenstone (1991), the apparent pathological behavior should be understood not as a cultural aberration but as a symptom of racial and cultural inequality (p. 402).

The proportion of U.S. families in which men are the sole breadwinners has declined from 42 percent to 15 percent since 1960. One reason is the worsening economic position of younger men since the mid 1960s, particularly those handicapped in the labor market by low education and minority status (Wilkie 1991). Between 1960 and 1990, the proportion of 18- to 24-year-olds still living at home increased from 43 to 53 percent. The proportion forming their own families dropped from 42 to 22 percent. More men than women are living at home (Roberts 1995, 47). Delayed marriages, deferred childbirths, and a continued high rate of divorce have meant that many young adults are remaining in or returning home. Housing and educational costs, combined with declining wages, have forced these adults to return to their parents' home (Roberts 1995, 48).

Undeserving Poor

A 1995 major welfare reform law has mandated the termination of Aid to Families with Dependent Children. Despite the overall effect of such a change, poor people will continue to struggle with the problems of keeping a job because their social network is as bereft as they are of resources. Friends can provide only so much help. Finding and keeping full-time work with benefits for a single mother has proven difficult for not just the poor but for other sectors of economy. Major problems occur when someone gets sick and can't be left alone, a car has to go in for repairs, school conferences are scheduled, and the rent is due. Many of these struggles would overwhelm someone in the middle class but the poor have proven to be resilient.

According to Herbert Gans (1995), for much of America's history, the country has been waging war against the poor. This war is waged utilizing various weapons, including withholding the opportunities for decent jobs, schools, housing, and the necessities required for a modest standard of living. Among students of poverty, there is little disagreement that a fairly distinct black and white **underclass** or undeserving poor exists and that this underclass generally feels excluded from society, rejects commonly accepted values, and suffers from behavioral as well as income deficiencies (Auletta 1982, xiii). According to Auletta (1982), terms such as "middle class" and "underclass" often are used because occupation, income, educational credentials, cognitive skills, criminal record, out-of-wedlock childbearing, and other personal characteristics are somewhat correlated with one another. People possessing positive attributes live better than those who do not. Those who do not possess these positive attributes are likely to be stereotyped, stigmatized, and harassed. The labeling of the poor as morally inferior encourages the blaming of the poor for the ills of the American society and economy, reinforces maltreatment, dehumanizes them as mere expendables, increases their misery, and exacerbates their alienation from society. The poor are blamed for their condition. If they continue to seek support, they are labeled as undeserving of any economic assistance. This further minimizes their chances of escaping poverty.

Limiting the benefits received by the poor is conceptualized under the **principle of less eligibility** (Sieh 1989). Accordingly, the poor must be motivated in part to seek work by limiting their benefits to an amount not exceeding the standard of living experienced by the lowest significant social class, the working class. To exceed this measure creates a disincentive to seek out work and increases dependence.

underclass is a sector of society that is generally considered poor and excluded from society, rejects commonly accepted values, and suffers from behavioral as well as income deficiencies.

principle of less eligibility states that the poor must be motivated in part to seek work by limiting their benefits to an amount not exceeding the standard of living experienced by the lowest significant social class. Exceeding this amount creates a disincentive to work.

Mainstream America Versus the Poor

According to Gans (1995), the war against the undeserving poor has been justified on the basis of at least four points. First, if poor people do not behave according to the rules set by mainstream America, they must be undeserving. They are undeserving because they believe in and practice bad values. Continuing to express these bad values over time only confirms the belief that they do not want to be part of mainstream America. The bad values and practices associated with the undeserving are the central cause of poverty. Poverty will decline when they begin to give up these values and mainstream America will welcome the undeserving into mainstream society.

Second, it is thought that the men among the undeserving poor are lazy and unable to learn the cultural importance of work and its requirements; in some cases, their negative values turn them into street criminals. As street criminals, they heighten the sense of fear, insecurity, and concerns for the public's safety. In response, people limit their social activities. When Americans are frightened, and the dark side of the culture takes over, concern for the offender's interests is not allowed to impede the search for greater safety (Tonry 1995, 138). Moreover, in response to increased drug use and failed intervention programs, broad-based support for increasingly punitive correctional measures is noted for programs that are far more costly than welfare or drug treatment.

The poor are often unjustly portrayed as a dangerous class, waiting for the opportunity to prey on the weak. For this to happen, the criminal justice system must not only associate crime with poverty, but it must also fail to reduce crime so that it remains a real threat (Reiman 1995, 161). If the criminal threat can be portrayed as coming from the poor, then the punishment of the poor criminal becomes a morality play and the probation officer's job is to provide absolution (Reiman 1995, 162). The identification of crime with poverty has not produced sympathy but has produced hostility toward the poor. Few Americans believe poverty to be a cause of crime (6 percent of those surveyed, while 21 percent think unemployment is a cause). Instead, says Reiman, crime and poverty are merged in the explanation to which they are considered a sign of poor or weak character (pp. 162–163) and in the end both the rich and the poor, the criminal and welfare recipient, are said to get what they deserve.

Third, according to Gans (1995), it is felt women among the undeserving poor have an unhealthy and immoral taste for early sexual activity and for having babies as adolescents. If they waited until they were sufficiently mature and ready to find work as well as find husbands who sought work, they and their children would not need to be poor, and poverty might end with the current generation.

Last, by not altering their values and practices voluntarily, the undeserving poor must be coerced into compliance by ending welfare payments, placing illegitimate children in foster care or orphanages, and meting out other punishments. Because ultimately these punishments benefit the victims by eliminating their dependency, it is assumed that any negative effects, such as breaking up families, increasing homelessness, and discovering higher rates of physical and mental illness, should be ignored, even if the better-off segments of society have to pay higher cost later (Gans 1995, 6–7).

■ Welfare and the Poor

There are several explanations and variations on a theme for what is happening in the welfare system.

The *individual model* emphasizes attitudinal, motivational, and human capital explanations. Essentially, this model focuses on the poor person's lack of thrift, effort, ability, and talent; loose morals; and drunkenness. They remain on welfare because they lack the motivation to get off. These people are just not working hard enough (Gilder 1981). The human capital explanation attends to the lack of training, education, experience, skills, and so on. The labor market is correctly viewed as competitive, in which wages are determined by supply and demand, as well as the resources people bring to work. The people who do well do so because of what they are able to bring to their work. This model assumes that poor people lack these strengths and abilities and thus are unable to effectively compete. To reduce the welfare roles, society should improve the skills and abilities of the poor (Rank 1994, 27).

The individual argument is, for the most part, a blaming-the-victim explanation. Many of the poor are fully cognizant that they are homeless and unable to control their substance abuse. Others fail to see that others have contributed to their problems as enablers by providing excuses for the person's behavior when, instead of excuses, the person should have been held accountable. Well-intended families, friends, and workmates have all contributed to this problem.

The <u>**social isolation explanation**</u> is offered by Julius Wilson. He suggests that the increasing problems found among the truly disadvantaged are due to the social transformation of the inner city. This has resulted in a disproportionate concentration of the most disadvantaged segments of the urban black population, creating a social milieu significantly different from the environment that existed in these communities several decades ago (Wilson 1987, 58). Communities of the underclass are plagued by massive social problems and social disorganization, and therefore tend to be avoided by outsiders. Consequently, the residents of these areas have become increasingly socially isolated from the mainstream pattern of behavior, whether women and children on welfare or aggressive street criminals (Wilson 1987, 58). Furthermore, Wilson argues that these social conditions minimize opportunities and impose structural constraints (p. 158):

social isolation explanation is a disproportionate concentration of the truly disadvantaged segments of the population creating a social milieu significantly different from the environment that existed in these communities decades ago.

> *Its seems to me that the most realistic approach to the problems of concentrated inner-city poverty is to provide the ghetto underclass families and individuals with the resources to promote social mobility through better schools and opportunities for employment. Social mobility leads to geographic mobility. We need to enhance the social capital of the inner-city resident and also eliminate segregated housing.*

The <u>**dual labor market theory**</u> was developed in reaction to the apparent failures of the human capital theory. The dual labor theory posits that there are two distinct labor markets operating by two different sets of rules. The

dual labor market theory suggests that there are two different labor markets operating by two different set of rules. In the primary market, there are good jobs, high wages, and effective unions, while in the secondary market one finds menial work, poor working conditions, and low wages.

primary market has good jobs, high wages, and effective unions in large organizations (Gordon 1972). The secondary market is characterized by menial work, poor working conditions, and low wages. It exists primarily within the competitive sector and tends to be small, labor intensive, and less productive and to utilize local markets. People are poor not because they are unemployed or do not participate in the economy but because of the way in which they participate in the economy. Because of the instability of jobs in the secondary labor market, workers often experience occasional unemployment and turn to welfare programs in order to survive lean times. In addition, these jobs often pay low wages, which workers may supplement periodically with benefits from a public assistance program. (Rank 1994, 43).

The contempt with which the underclass is viewed is evident in some of the more commonly discussed solutions, which range from increased numbers of police and prisons to a strict approach to welfare where fathers are required to pay child support, where mothers must work or attend school under threat of losing their welfare benefits, and where adolescents are expected to say no to drugs and sex and yes to studying hard and staying in school (Devine and Wright 1993, 126). If the conditions of life are improving for a growing black middle class and yet the relative differences between blacks and whites on many social indicators continue to increase, it is still difficult for poor black Americans who are not moving into the mainstream.

For the individual probation officer who must confront the problems of the undeserving poor on a day-to-day basis, how he or she treats the probationer often reflects the officer's understanding of the poor. Some officers recognize the importance that poverty plays, while others who may have once shared this view have now become less sympathetic and more demanding. Employment plays such a significant role that, for some officers, finding work for the probationer is the most important priority. In some cases, this is nearly impossible and the officer must devote an extraordinary period of time finding work for the probationer. Some officers have used work-supported programs designed to train someone who has no work history to find work and to learn what to expect from the job. It is now clear that institutions responsible for social control must learn to deal with people using more realistic solutions involving controlled experimentation (Jencks 1991, 98). It remains vitally important that despite the offender's social standing and employment status, the probationer deserves to be treated with respect. Human dignity of all people needs to be protected and guarded as work with probationers continues. Bear in mind that everyone must be treated with respect, regardless of what he or she has done.

■ Conclusion

This chapter has considered the social context in which probation must operate. It has been shown that the public supports continuing efforts to prevent crime and social problems over the construction of new prisons and jails. It was also shown that many different people are involved in crime and many of them come from middle-class backgrounds, especially the drunk driver. A considerable proportion of probationers are mentally ill who need and deserve special treatment. Considerable attention has been given to the urban drug offender but scant attention has been given to rural users and to what extent they are involved in the criminal justice system. Drug offenders comprise a considerable proportion of offenders on probation.

The higher the value a person has to society is one indication of his or her ability to address problems he or she faces. Several tables and graphs have been presented that underscore the fact that the number of those living in poverty is increasing, that minorities continue to fare poorly, that single mothers are often the poorest of the poor, and while there has been an increase in education among African-Americans, there are still problems. It has been shown that the poor and the middle class are not as well off as they once were. Some of these problems seem intractable.

In the final analysis, probation officers are confronting people who are poor in body, mind, and spirit. Some substance abusers are so consumed by their addictions that they care not for themselves and the people they affect. What must be done is to find a way of dealing with the abusive alcoholic husband who has not worked for years and, because of the way that probation fees are arranged and child support is collected, has no interest in getting a formal job but works only on the cash-based underground economy. These offenders operate with impunity but at the same time require a measure of dignity so that they can learn to at least offer support to those who seek them for some comfort.

REFERENCES

American Management Association (AMA). 2001. Skills testing and psychological measurement. Available online at: http://www.amanet.org/research/archive_2001.

Auletta, K. 1982. *The underclass.* New York: Random House.

Beck, K., W. Rauch, and E. Baker. 1997. Proceedings of the 14th International Conference on Alcohol, Drugs, and Traffic Safety, Annecy, France, September 21–26, 1997. *Alcohol, Drugs and Traffic Safety – T. 97,* Volume 1, 1997.

Burtless, 2001 speech to Center for the Study of Living Standards, January 26–27, 2001, Ottawa, Canada.

Burton, C. E. 1992. *The poverty debate: Politics and the poor in America.* Westport, CT: Greenwood Press.

Casteel, S. 2003. *Illegal drug prices and purity report.* Domestic Strategic Unit of the Office of Domestic Intelligence. Drug Enforcement Administration. Available online at: http://www.dea.gov.

Clear, T. 1996. The challenge of responding to persons with mental illness on community corrections supervision. In A. Lurigio, ed., *Community corrections in America: New directions and sounder investments for persons with mental illnesses and codisorders.* Seattle, WA: The National Coalition for Mental and Substance Abuse Health Care in the Justice System.

Cohen, F. 1993. The legal context for mental health services. In H. Steadman and J. Cocozza, eds., *Mental illness in America's prisons.* Seattle, WA: The National Coalition for Mental and Substance Abuse Health Care in the Justice System, pp. 1–8.

Devine, J. A., and J. D. Wright. 1993. *The greatest of evils: Urban poverty and the American underclass.* New York: Aldine De Gruyter.

Ditton, P. 1999. *Mental health and treatment of inmates and probationers,* Washington, DC: U.S. Department of Justice, Bureau of Justice Statistics.

Dubet, F., and D. Lapeyronnie. 1994. "Im Aus der Vorstad." *Der Ferfall der Demokratischen Gesellschaft.* Stuttgart, Germany.

Dvoskin, J. A., T. McCormick, and J. Cox. 1994. Services for parolees with serious mental illness. In *Topics in community corrections annual issue 1994: Mentally ill offenders in the community.* Washington, DC: U.S. Department of Justice, National Institute of Corrections, pp. 14–20.

Federal Bureau of Investigation. 2000. Uniform Crime Reports, 2000. Washington, DC. Available online at: http://www.fbi.gov/ucr/cius.

Felson, M. 1994. *Crime and everyday life.* Thousand Oaks, CA: Pine Forge Press.

Flannagan, W. 1993. *Contemporary urban sociology.* Cambridge, MA: Cambridge University Press.

Fulton, B. 1996. Persons with mental illness on probation and parole. In A. Lurigio, ed., *Community corrections in America: New directions and sounder investments for persons with mental illnesses and codisorders.* Seattle, WA: The National Coalition for Mental and Substance Abuse Health Care in the Justice System.

Gallup Poll. 2004. Crime. Available online at: http://www.gallup.com/poll/content/.

Gallup Poll. 2004. Public on Justice System: Fair, Still Too Soft. Available online at: http://www.gallup.com/poll/content/.

Gans, H. 1995. *War against the poor: The underclass and antipoverty policy.* New York: Basic Books.

Gilder, G. 1981. *Wealth and poverty.* New York: Basic Books.

Gordon, D. 1972. *Theories of poverty and underemployment: Orthodox, radical, and dual labor market perspectives.* Lexington, MA: Heath.

Greenstone, J. D. 1991. Culture, rationality and the underclass. In C. Jencks and P. Peterson, eds., *The urban underclass.* Washington, DC: Brookings Institute, pp. 399–410.

Jacobs, J. 1961. *The death and life of great American cities.* New York: Random House.

Jencks, C. 1991. Is the American underclass growing? In C. Jencks and P. Peterson, eds., *The urban underclass.* Washington, DC: Brookings Institute, pp. 28–102.

Katz, M. 1998. Reviving cities: Think metropolitan. Policy Brief #33, Brookings Institute, www.brook.edu/comm/policybriefs/pb33.htm.

Katz, M. B. 1989. *The undeserving poor.* New York: Pantheon.

Left Business Observer. 2004. *Gini says: Measuring income inequality: An LBO report, October 18, 1993.* Available online at: http://www.leftbusinessobserver.com/Gini_supplement.

Lewis, D., and G. Salem. 1986. *Fear of crime: Incivility and the production of a social problem.* New Brunswick, NJ: Transaction Books.

Lloyd, J. 2002. *Drug use trends: October 2002.* Office of National Drug Control Policy. Drug Policy Information Clearinghouse. Fact Sheet. Available online at: http://www.whitehousedrugpolicy.gov.

Ludwig, J. 2004. *Gallup social audit on black/white relations in the United States.* Available online at: http://www.gallup.com/poll.

Maruschak, L. 1999. *DWI offenders under correctional supervision.* Washington, DC: U.S. Department of Justice, Bureau of Justice Statistics.

Mauer, M. 1999. The crisis of the young African American male and the criminal justice system. Washington, DC: U.S. Commission on Civil Rights, the Sentencing Project.

Mauer, M., C. Potler, and R. Wolf. 1999a. *The crisis of the young African American male and the criminal justice system.* Sentencing Project. Prepared for U.S. Commission on Civil Rights, Washington, DC.

Mauer, M., Potler, C., and Wolf, R. 1999b. *Women, drugs, and sentencing.* Policy. Sentencing Project. Washington, DC.

Mickel, K. 1994. A little TLC: Maricopa County's transitional living center. In *Topics in community corrections annual issue 1994: Mentally ill offenders in the community.* Washington, DC: U.S. Department of Justice, National Institute of Corrections, pp. 30–32.

Monahan, J. 1993. Limiting therapist exposure to Tarasoff's liability. *American Psychologist* 48: 107–118.

Monitoring the Future. 2001. Monitoring the future survey 2001. www.hhs.gov.news.

National Center on Addiction and Substance Abuse at Columbia University. 2000. *CASA white paper, no place to hide: Rural 8th graders using drugs, drinking and smoking at higher rates than urban 8th graders.* New York, NY.

National Commission Against Drunk Driving. 2001. What research says about chronic drinking drivers and ways to apply this research, www.ncadd.com/tsra/abstracts/chronic.html.

Pheiffer, C., and P. Wetzels. 1999. *The structure and development of juvenile violence in Germany, Forschungsberichte No. 76.* Hanover, Germany: Kriminologisches Forschungsinstitut Niedersachsen.

Putnam, R. 2000. *Bowling alone: The collapse and revival of American community.* New York: Simon and Schuster.

Rank, M. 1994. *Living on the edge: The realities of welfare in America.* New York: Columbia University Press.

Reiman, J. 1995. *The rich get richer and the poor get poorer.* Needham Heights, MA: Allyn & Bacon.

Roberts, S. 1995. *Who we are.* New York: Times Books.

Rodgers, A. 1994. Effect of Minnesota's license plate impoundment law on recidivism of multiple DWI violators. *Alcohol, Drugs and Driving.* Vol. 10, No. 2.

Sampson, R. 1995. The community. In James Q. Wilson and Joan Petersilia, eds., *Crime.* San Francisco: Institute for Contemporary Studies Press, pp. 193–216.

Satcher, D. 1999. *Mental health: A report of the Surgeon General.* U.S. Department of Health and Human Services, Substance Abuse and Mental Health Services, Administration Center for Mental Health, National Institutes of Health, National Institute of Mental Health.

Shaw, M. 2001. *The role of local government in community safety.* Washington, DC: U.S. Department of Justice, Bureau of Justice Assistance.

Sieh, E. 1989. Less eligibility: The upper limits of punishment. *Criminal Justice Policy Review* Winter 1989.

Skogan, W. G. 1990. *Disorder and decline.* Berkeley: University of California.

Stahl, A. 2001. *Drug cases in juvenile court: 1989–1998.* Office of Juvenile Justice Delinquency Prevention. Fact Sheet. U.S. Department of Justice.

Social Exclusion Unit. 2000. *National strategy for neighborhood renewal, report of policy action team 4: Neighborhood management.* London, England: The Stationary Office.

Tonry, M. 1995. *Malign neglect.* New York: Oxford University Press.

U.S. Census Bureau. 2000. *Historical income tables: Share of aggregate income received by each fifth and top 5 percent of all races, whites, black, hispanic origin, 1999.* Available online at: http://www.census.gov/hhes/income/histinc/incfamdet.html.

U.S. Census Bureau. 2004. *Income inquality (middle class) – Narrative.* Available online at: http://www.census.gov.hhes/income/midclass/midlclsan.

U.S. Census Bureau. 2004. *Statistical abstract of the United States, education, 2004–2005.* Available online at: http://www.census2000.gov.

U.S. Census Bureau. 2004. United States Census 2000. Available online at: http://www.census.gov.

Wilkie, J. R. 1991. The decline in men's labor force participation and income and the changing structure of family economic support. *Journal of Marriage and Family* 53: 111–122.

Wilson, W. J. 1987. *The truly disadvantaged.* Chicago: University of Chicago Press.

KEY POINTS

1. Throughout the world, income disparities between the rich and poor have increased as more women are living in poverty in both developed and developing countries. Poverty in America has become a major problem outside of big cities, affecting the white majority community.

2. The number of people living traditional family lifestyles has fallen dramatically over several decades.

3. In 1998, a significant shift occurred in the public's perception of crime when the number of persons who believed there was more crime in an area fell below the number who believed that it was less.

4. Researchers have come to believe that individuals connected to one another through trusting networks and common values facilitate enforcement of positive standards for youth and offer them access to mentors, role models, educational sponsors, and job contacts outside of the neighborhood.

5. The number of DWI offenders under correctional supervision nearly doubled between 1986 and 1997.

6. According to the Department of Justice, mental illness is a significant problem for probationers.

7. The number of juvenile court cases involving drug offenses more than doubled between 1993 and 1998.

8. The lack of a policy supporting affordable housing in all communities means that suburban communities can establish an exclusionary zone setting themselves apart from the poor in metro areas.

9. The idea of social capital is that social networks have value inasmuch as a well-connected person in a poorly connected society is not as productive as a well-connected individual in a well-connected society. However, even a poorly connected individual may derive some of the spillover benefits from living in a well-connected community.

10. Human capital, as reflected in the number of people who have completed high school, has increased dramatically since 1950, especially in the rise in the number of blacks who have graduated from high school.

11. Six in 10 blacks are dissatisfied with the way people of their race are treated by society, especially as played out in racial profiling.

12. Since the late 1960s, income in this country has become steadily concentrated in the hands of fewer and fewer individuals. Particularly hit by poverty are single female parents. Due to the pool of marriageable men in prison, the number of single parents will continue to be high.

KEY TERMS

bonding networks   include ethnic fraternal organizations, church-based women's reading groups, and fashionable country clubs.

bridging networks   are outward looking and include civil rights groups, youth groups, and ecumenical religious organizations that are useful for external assets and for information diffusion.

diagnosis of mental disorders   is made on the basis of multidimensional assessment that takes into account observable signs and symptoms of illness, the course and duration of the illness, response to treatment, and degree of functional impairment.

dual labor market theory   suggests that there are two different labor markets operating by two different set of rules. In the primary market, there are good jobs, high wages, and effective unions, while in the secondary market one finds menial work, poor working conditions, and low wages.

Gini index of income inequality is a measure of the degree to which a population shares that resource unequally.

principle of less eligibility   states that the poor must be motivated in part to seek work by limiting their benefits to an amount not exceeding the standard of living experienced by the lowest significant social class. Exceeding this amount creates a disincentive to work.

right to treatment   means that once offenders have been identified as mentally ill, appropriate treatment and services must be provided.

social isolation explanation   is a disproportionate concentration of the truly disadvantaged segments of the population creating a social milieu significantly different from the environment that existed in these communities decades ago.

underclass   is a sector of society that is generally considered poor and excluded from society, rejects commonly accepted values, and suffers from behavioral as well as income deficiencies.

REVIEW QUESTIONS

1. Why is it necessary to understand the complex social environment in which probation occurs?

2. Formulate two or three assumptions about how the UCR arrest data affects the work of probation.

3. What are the public's attitudes toward crime?

4. What might the right to treat have to do with mentally ill probationers?

5. Discuss the concepts of capital value as it relates to the social context of probation.

6. Why is it important for a probation officer to take racial divisions and poverty into account when dealing with his or her clients?

5

Probationers

Chapter Objectives

In this chapter you will learn about:

- The characteristics of adults on probation
- Probation officers' perceptions of their clients
- The diversity of offenders on probation
- The presence of people on probation who hold status in the community
- The sense of humanity present in each probationer

There is a sense among experienced officers that almost anyone can find his or her way onto probation. Such officers develop a strong but unofficial sense of moral egalitarianism. Under the condition of moral egalitarianism, everyone is subject to the same code of behavior and to the same punishments. Most importantly, moral egalitarians accept the notion that everyone makes mistakes, no one is perfect, and all need the forgiveness and understanding provided by probation.

Probation in the United States

According to the Bureau of Justice Statistics (Glaze and Pella 2004), the nation's combined federal, state, and local adult correctional population reached a new high of almost 6.9 million men and women in 2003—1 in every 32 adults. On December 31, 2003, there were 4,073,987 men and women on probation, 774,588 of them on parole. At the end of 2003, the number of adults under community corrections reached 4.8 million, up from 3.2 million in 1990. Among probationers, 50 percent were convicted of felonies, 25 percent were on probation for drug violations, and 17 percent were on probation for driving while intoxicated. Nationwide, women comprised 23 percent of the adult probationers in 2003, up from 18 percent in 1990. At the end of 2003, more than one-third of probationers were black, while more than half were white. Persons of Hispanic origin, who are of any race, comprised 12 percent of the probation population. Nearly 2 million probationers were discharged from supervision during 2000. Three out of five discharged from probation had successfully completed their term. During the same year, 16 percent of probationers discharged from supervision were reincarcerated because of rule violations or new offenses. At the end of 2003, 4 percent (162,959) were listed as absconders (Glaze and Pella 2004).

It is commonly assumed that a majority of offenders are unemployed, have problems with alcohol and drugs, and have little or no money at the time of arrest. They have insufficient work training and need employment counseling, job training, job placement, substance abuse treatment, and money management training (Lauen 1997, 136). It is important to not lose sight of the fact that these are real people who have real problems. Probation and parole officers can start their careers with a sense of optimism and understanding, but as they are increasingly exposed over time to the more difficult probationers, they can become cynical and even indifferent. What is important is that, despite actual feelings about the probationer, a public posture is adopted that presumes the offender can change and has value and worth. This requires the probation officer to separate his or her personal feelings from his or her job and treat the offender in a completely professional manner, even when he or she thinks the offender does not deserve respectful treatment. Acting in such a way is the essence of being a professional. The probation officer must come to appreciate the chance that offenders treated with dignity can learn to treat others with dignity.

This chapter provides aggregate data offered by a national survey of the characteristics of those on probation. It also includes information provided by probation officers on juveniles, adults, property offenders, substance abusers, and sex offenders. Many of these descriptions support the belief that those who work with offenders are dealing with a diverse mixture of people.

Survey on Probationer Characteristics

The 1995 Survey of Adults on Probation (SAP) conducted by the U.S. Bureau of the Census for the Bureau of Justice Statistics was the first national survey to gather information on individual characteristics of adult probationers. The SAP was a two-part survey consisting of records checks based on probation office administrative records and personal interviews with probationers. The records checks provided detailed information on 5,867 probationers on current offenses and sentences, criminal histories, levels of supervision and contacts, disciplinary hearings and outcomes, and demographic characteristics. It was completed by a probation officer or another person familiar with probation office administration records. Only those on formal probation were included. A subset of 2,030 probationers selected for the records check were interviewed. Information gathered included current offense, supervision, criminal history, alcohol and drug use and treatment, mental health treatment, demographic characteristics, and a variety of socioeconomic characteristics. From this data, some conclusions can be drawn about the population of offenders on probation (**Table 5-1**).

Table 5-1	Characteristics of Adults on Probation		
Characteristics	Number of Adults State and Federal	Percent Known Status 1995	Percent Known Status 1985
Total number of adults on probation	3,096,529	100%	100%
Status of Probation	**1,616,004**	**100%**	**100%**
Execution of sentence suspended	342,441	21	47
Imposition of sentence suspended	69,351	4	8
Direct imposition of probation	891,115	55	44
Split (incarceration with probation)	248,379	15	**
Other	64,718	4	1
Status of Supervision	**2,809,146**	**100%**	**100%**
Active supervision	2,223,413	79	85
Inactive supervision	221,782	8	7
Absconded from supervision	263,618	9	6
Supervised out of state	51,171	2	2
Other	49,162	2	2
Adults Entering Probation	**894,464**	**100%**	**100%**
Probation without incarceration	644,522	72	93
Probation with incarceration	116,124	13	5
Probation with other types	133,918	15	2
Sex of Adults on Probation	**2,446,175**	**100%**	**100%**
Male	1,938,608	79	84
Female	507,567	21	16
Race of Adults on Probation	**2,172,594**	**100%**	**100%**
White	1,541,426	66	70
Black	748,505	32	29
American Indian/Alaskan Native	20,347	1	1
Asian/Pacific Islander	9,269	–	–
Hispanic Origin of Adults on Probation	**1,892,239**	**100%**	**100%**
Hispanic	271,583	14	14
Non-Hispanic	1,620,656	86	86
Type of Offense of Adults on Probation	**2,621,572**	**100%**	**100%**
Felony	1,409,098	54	50
Misdemeanor	724,178	28	49
Driving while intoxicated	430,756	16	**
Other infractions	57,540	2	1

Source: Bonczar, T. 1997. *Characteristics of Adults on Probation.* Washington, DC: U.S. Department of Justice, Bureau of Justice Statistics.

Administrative records were drawn from 167 state, county, and municipal probation agencies nationwide. Offices providing direct supervision were drawn from 16 different types of government agencies (executive or judiciary), levels (state or local), and regions (Northeast, Midwest, South, and West). Offices were selected with probabilities proportionate to their numbers. Only adults with a formal sentence to probation who were not considered absconders were included in the records. Excluded were persons supervised by a federal probation agency, those on parole, those on presentence or pretrial diversion, juveniles, and absconders. Data is reported, however, on probationers who later absconded and were returned to the custody of probation or incarceration.

The report indicates that nearly two out of five probationers were convicted of either a violent or drug offense. In 1995, 17 percent of the adults on probation had been sentenced for a violent offense and 21 percent for a drug offense. The remainder was split between property offenders (29 percent) and public order offenders (31 percent). The most frequent offense among probationers was **driving under the influence (DUI)** (17 percent). Other offenses—including larceny/theft (10 percent), drug possession (10 percent), drug trafficking (10 percent), and assault (9 percent)—account for an additional 39 percent of the adult population on probation.

driving under the influence (DUI) a traffic violation.

Crimes Leading to Probation

Table 5-2 offers some insights regarding offenses committed by those on probation. Males are more likely to be on probation for a public order offense, while females are more likely for property offenses. White and Hispanic probationers are most often on probation for public order offenses, while blacks are on probation for drug offenses. For public order offenses, probationers under 24 years of age commit property offenses, while 25–45 and older, probationers have public order offenses.

These results are quite different than what is found with those going to prison. Probation is applied as a mechanism for regulating the activities of those who are charged with weapons violations, obstruction of justice, traffic offenses, DUI, drunkenness, and other public order offenses. Further analysis of the data indicates that driving while intoxicated is the major offense within the public order offenses. Convictions for DUI bear a strong relationship to age, increasing

Table 5-2	**Most Serious Offense of Adults on Probation by Gender, Race, and Age**								
	Gender (by %)		Race (by %)			Age (by %)			
Offense	Male	Female	White	Black	Hispanic	Under 24	25–34	35–44	45+
Violent	19	9.5	16.5	17.1	19.4	16.5	17	17.4	20.3
Property	25.3	42.6	29.9	28.6	23.8	38.7	27	22.9	24.7
Drug	21.7	20.1	17	30.9	23.1	19.7	23.9	23.2	13.4
Public order	32.3	26.5	35.6	22.2	30.4	22.1	31.5	35.7	40.7
Other	1.3	1.3	1.	1.2	3.2	3.1	.6	.7	.8

Source: U.S. Department of Justice. 1999. *Survey of Adults on Probation—1995.* Bureau of Justice Statistics. ICPSR edition, July. Ann Arbor, MI: Interuniversity Consortium for Political and Social Research.

steadily from 7 percent of those under the age of 25 to 28 percent of those age 45 and older (U.S. Department of Justice 1999). DWI was the single most frequent offense among probationers in each group aged 25 or older. For those who were under age 25, larceny/theft (14 percent), burglary (10 percent), and drug trafficking (10 percent) were the common offenses.

Prior Convictions

Half of all adults on probation had a sentence prior to probation or incarceration; 9 percent of juveniles and 45 percent of adults on probation were in this category. Felons were more likely to have a criminal history. Of particular note is that violent offenders (45 percent) were less likely to have a sentence prior to probation when compared to property (51 percent) or public order offenders (55 percent). Nearly half of the drug offenders had a prior sentence. Violent probationers had the lowest percentage (37 percent) with a record prior to probation and public order offenders the highest (45 percent).

Probation and Prison

Table 5-3 indicates that if put on probation, the probationer has a good chance of serving some jail time; half of them receive a split sentence involving probation and incarceration. Judges sentence offenders to probation but they also make sure that some jail time is attached to increase the punitive nature of the sentence. Offenders who are convicted of misdemeanors (54.4 percent) are slightly more likely to serve a probationary sentence. When offenders have no prior offense, chances of receiving probation only increase to nearly 59 percent. If the criminal has any prior offenses, he or she is likely to be given a split sentence. This holds true whether the offender has served a probationary or jail sentence. It is also interesting to consider prior sentences. Almost one in three offenders on probation were previously in prison; however, those who were incarcerated earlier are likely, in two thirds of the cases, to receive a split sentence with most of the time served in jail.

Table 5-3: Type of Sentence: Adult Probationers by Severity of Current Offense and Prior Sentence, 1995

		Severity of Offense			Prior Sentence		
Sentence	Total (by %)	Felony (by %)	Misdem. (by %)	None (by %)	Any (by %)	Probation (by %)	Incarceration (by %)
Probation only	49.8	45.7	54.4	58.9	40.4	40.8	32.2
Probation/ incarceration	50.2	54.3	45.2	41.1	59.6	59.2	67.8
Jail	37.3	36.5	38.3	28.4	44.5	44.5	52.8
Prison	15.3	20.6	9.0	14.5	18.7	18.1	19.2

Note: Full calculations may lead to more than 100% because some offenders were sentenced to both probation and prison.

Source: U.S. Department of Justice. 1999. *Survey of Adults on Probation—1995.* Bureau of Justice Statistics. ICPSR edition, July. Ann Arbor, MI: Interuniversity Consortium for Political and Social Research.

Probationer Employment

According to the SAP data, probationers hold many different jobs. People on probation work in professional fields, protective services, food services, building trades, farming, forestry, precision production, transportation, heavy equipment, and freight. There are individuals on probation with extensive work histories. There are also probationers who, because of the requirements that they pay a fee for almost all probation-related services they receive, choose to work off the books where there are no records of their work. Probationers earning $500 a week find that because of the total amounts paid for various supervisions assessments (whether for electronic monitoring, restitution, or court fees and various testing fees for drugs and alcohol), maintaining regular employment does not make sense when there is only $40 left in the pocket after payments are made (Feddema 2004).

■ Probation Officers and Probationers

Probationers perceive probation officers as agents who will assist them, while judges are viewed more as agents whose main purpose is to punish offenders for wrongdoing. According to SAP data, probationers are split on the issue of the probation officer providing assistance, because 53 percent of them prefer to seek help from someone else. This implies that substantial barriers must be overcome for some probationers to accept help from the probation officer, particularly around the issue of trust. Probation officers must be aware that they will not always be effective in helping probationers, making it necessary to find outside resources for the probationer to succeed.

Allen (1985) found that although 28 percent of the probationers found nothing useful in probation supervision, another two-thirds felt they received benefits via counseling, encouragement, and supportive intervention. Allen's study also found that probationers felt the officers should be client advocates for increasing employment assistance and be granted more authority outside of the court. It seems most probationers are grateful that they received probation and many expressed concerns that they had made a mistake, increasing the odds they would land in jail (Allen 1985).

Over 50 officers in three different agencies, one in an eastern state and the others in a midwestern state, were interviewed by the author. Two of the departments were responsible for large urban communities. When asked if probation officers believe offenders view probation as punishment, a typical response was

> *To some it is. Some just hate reporting. To some they feel that they have gotten away with something. You can sense it by the way that they talk to you. You can sense the ones that are afraid of probation and the ones that see it as a joke. They know the system. Some of these people tell me what the score is. I am only going to do 90 days or I can bargain this down to this or that. They are attorneys due to their constant interaction with the court.*

violation is when a probationer disobeys one or more of the conditions of probation.

There are few **violations** of the conditions of probation for failing to report or not keeping appointments. It is only after the conviction for a new crime that probation is revoked. Probationers, for the most part, do not consider themselves as criminals, sick, or morally deficient. Quite to the contrary, many probationers understood their circumstances in rational terms and fully expect to continue to live normally in the community once through with probation (Allen 1985).

◼ Probationer Interviews

Probation officers work with people who have a variety of problems. Some probationers are so difficult to work with the officer would just as soon not have anything to do with them. The client may be dangerous, resistant to treatment, or mentally ill or may have committed a particularly reprehensible offense. Some probation officers appreciate the uniqueness of the probationer and may even come to admire the person's daring or alternative lifestyle. Some officers, however, guard against this notion, believing that doing so only makes the job difficult or compromises the officer's ethics. There are officers who have different views of the probationers. The officer may cynically believe that the probationer is a bad person and will display as much on probation and afterwards. The officer may be stoic about the caseload and believe that the probationer will do well while on supervision but will eventually recidivate. The officer may even be cautiously optimistic about the client and believe that there is a chance that the probationer will make it as a law-abiding citizen. And there is the officer who takes the pragmatic approach to the probationer, believing that the road to success will have setbacks and yet the probationer will eventually succeed.

What follows are selected portions of anonymous verbatim interviews with various probation officers. Officers were asked questions about their probationers, their meetings with probationers, and whether they had clients they liked more than others or were considered interesting. The point of these interviews was not to assess the extent to which officers express concerns for human dignity. In fact, readers will find that some officers express attitudes that seem to contradict the notion of human dignity. And while this is true, there were also ample concerns for the dignity of the offender and for his or her problems. Most of all, this chapter is an effort to humanize the offender, to learn something about different types of offenders, and to understand how the officers responded to these offenders. The names used here are pseudonyms. There is no effort to provide a complete description of all clients, nor is there an analysis of the probationer's needs.

Juveniles

Q: What is your caseload like?

A: Juvenile Officer (J.O.) Karl – Most of the kids are pretty much fourteen, fifteen and sixteen. I do get them as young as nine or ten. The vast majority of my kids will be **persons in need of supervision (PINS)** and a small amount will be juvenile delinquents. There are a lot of kids who are going to come to court on a delinquency charge but it will be reduced to a PINS. PINS cases are juveniles who are con-

persons in need of supervision (PINS) Juveniles who are considered to be out of control.

sidered to be out of control. Probably mostly white, 60 percent white, 20 percent black and 20 percent Hispanic and Puerto Rican. Most of mine have parents on welfare. Probably 90 percent of mine are. If you look at the ages of many of the parents you will find that many were children themselves when they had the kids. A lot of parents must have been between 17 and 20 when their kids were born.

Q: **What are probationers like when they come to report?**

A: J.O. Karl – Surprisingly most of them are pretty sweet and have a good attitude when they report. And in general the ones I dislike are the ones that talk too much, so you got a feeling that something is up. Like I tell them I have been hearing all the words but I want to see the evidence. It seems that a lot of the substance abusers really talk a lot to manipulate.

Families on Probation

Q: **Do you have any families on probation?**

A: J.O. Martin – In the morning yesterday I had a court case involving the Westside Church that burned down. I have the younger brother on probation whose older brother has been charged with the arson. The younger brother is being charged with subsequent burglaries related to that church and some other churches. I also have the older sister on probation to me and the oldest brother is in the intensive supervision unit on probation to an officer up here. This is a white family. It is kind of an interesting family in that the dad is a couch potato with a beer in one hand and cigarettes in the other and his Oakland Raiders shirt while his mom is a waitress breaking her ass on a daily basis. And this guy doesn't do crap. He sits home and holds court. He watches cable, watches the movies.

Q: **How does he get away with it?**

A: J.O. Martin – He just does it. He is also a drinker who on occasion has been abusive not so much to the kids, verbally but not physically. And mom is the best enabler in the world that this man will ever meet. And that is the way that family will stay for quite a long time. So we were in court with the kid yesterday and basically what we did, I had the kid on probation as a PINS truant and PINS ungovernable. We went to court on the kid and again we are talking about the best interest of the kid, what we did is that we had him placed with the NYS Division for Youth as a PINS on my violation.

Serial Car Thief

Q: **Juveniles are known to steal a few cars from time to time. Have any?**

A: J.O. Dan – There was a kid that I investigated recently who was in on five separate petitions, totaling about seven different cars and we're only talking about September to November where this kid was stealing cars on average of once a week and got caught every time. So he is not real good at it. The court's way of dealing with it was to move on one petition and to ACD (Adjournment in Contemplation of Dismissal) the rest of them. And the thing that I found most interesting when I interviewed him is that when I am looking for anything that I can hold up to the court that says I am sorry he just kind of gave up, in a generic sense.

But it was real interesting when I was saying to him that you go out and always get arrested. Aren't any one of those times enough to send a message that you could get hurt? I understand that one of the times the police roughed him up and I was looking for something from him indicating that he was pushing this too far. Never once did I get anything like that. And I find that real interesting because usually somebody starts getting caught that much I would like to believe that either they are going to stop it or they are going to get better at it. Neither of them happened here.

Persons in Need of Supervision (PINS)

Q: How about other family problems?

A: J.O. Karen – The other day a mother came in about her fifteen-year-old boy. The parents were divorced maybe three or four years ago. There are five youngsters in the family. At the time of the divorce the father got custody of the two oldest boys. The oldest one was testing any authority. Well, the mother decided two years ago that she wanted her children intact. So she moved into an ex-marital residence. And with that she tried a reconciliation with him and it didn't work. So he moved out and left her with all five kids. Well the oldest boy tried to take over as head of the household which is not unusual. But also he got to the point that he got outright nasty and he would come and go as he pleased, call her every name in the book, running with a tough gang. When she opposed him, he used physical force on her. Not too long ago he and this ten-year old boy were fighting and she went to break it up, he turned on her and beat the hell out of her. And he had been stealing. He is fourteen. She wanted to take him to counseling and he told her to shove it up her nose. So she felt she had to do something about it. And with this physical violence, he spits on her and hits her. Has no respect for her. So she did file a PINS petition against him. But she wants him out. She wants him placed. I don't know what the judge is going to do. It depends upon the judge. We have a judge here who feels we have no bad children so he adjourns many cases with the thought of dismissing it later. A month or two later the parents are back. They wanted a little more than an Adjournment in Contemplation of Dismissal. Then the courts will try probation supervision and if they are violated they will consider placement.

Q: Does this boy see his dad at all?

A: J.O. Karen – No, he has just washed his hands of the whole group. He is still around and working. He is a drinker. So what she was saying is that when he had custody alone, he afforded no discipline and little supervision and that is when this one became really out of control and it is beyond her. He is physically bigger than her. She is scared to death. She works and feels that if she doesn't do something with him, then when it comes to the ten year old and that it is going to be repetition.

Adults

Q: Do you have clients with whom you like to work more than others?

A: Adult Officer (A.O.) Karl – You like the ones that are cooperative of course but then sometimes you wonder if they need to report to an officer anyhow. There are a lot of felony DWI guys who have turned it around. I have seen some since they bought the treatment with their heart and mind and have turned it around. You like to see that. The successes. You don't know then. I don't know if it is due to the personal intervention that has been ordered or mandated and they made the decision to do it and you are just kind of monitoring it.

Q: Do you have some offenders you like to work with more than others?

A: A.O. Ed – I try to do the best that I can for most of the people. Some of them you want to do a lot more for but I don't hold prejudices or grudges. There are some that have the gift of gab and you ask yourself what is he doing here. He seems to be a very affable person but that doesn't mean that I am not going to treat this person any different than another. You have a wide range of people to deal with.

Q: How easy is it to work with this client?

A: A.O. Ed – Initially, your druggies are ok. They come in and they BS the hell out of you while they are talking. Even though this guy may come and oh yea, I am going to do this and I am going to do that. I have turned my life around and I have done this and I have done that. I got a job. You turn around and a couple months later you start making phone calls and you learn that this guy has been BSing you all along.

Q: What kind of criminal backgrounds do people on adult probation have?

A: A.O. Ed – Their criminal histories show that they were PINS and they were juvenile delinquents. There is a lot of drug-related crime, larceny, burglary, possession, alcohol, and DWIs. The majority of them are basically possession and sale. There is a swing now where these people are selling, not selling for profit but to support their habit. The people who are poor don't know how to deal with their problems.

I have about 100 clients on my caseload. They are from 16 to 65 years old. I have had everything. I had one who was 63; he was a DWI. You may get somebody over the age of 45 who has had a long period of no arrests who may commit a misdemeanor and the presentence indicates that he is employed. This crime may have been an isolated incident. You will get a few of those.

The ones that I have here, the majority of them are lucky to have made it through high school. The majority of them have no employment history and are alcohol or narcotic dependents. The more "glamorous" ones that we have here are the felony drug sellers.

We don't get too many 16-year-olds. Usually with the first offense, they don't get probation and we don't recommend it unless it is a hideous or bad crime. If a 16-year-old kid stole a radio from a department store and has no record up to that point, we are going to talk to the family and tell them to take over. The offender pays the fine and the restitution to the store. We supervise them. If we get them again, then he is in trouble.

These offenders are more smart aleck. They definitely know more of their rights. They are out to beat the system. You see more drugs and alcohol. You have more of a chance of changing them at 16 and less at 18; the child's personality is formed by age 7. When you see a 16 and 17 years old, and not doing well, and you see them get their education. That feels good. There is some hope for them.

A lot of the people who are on probation have alcohol problems. They also have not completed an education. Usually the highest is that they completed high school—probably a good 25 percent and it could go as high as 30 percent. About 15 percent are women. I may have fewer women than that. The women are on for DWIs, petty larceny, issuing bad checks. I have one who just turned 18 and they range into the 30s. I have never had an old woman but I have had an old man. He was on for DWIs and petty larceny. He was someone who should have ended his criminal career a little earlier. I am thinking of the guy who was murdered last year. He was 59 years old. He was an alcoholic who got into an argument with someone about some petty thing and the other guy ended up shooting him. The other guy was older too.

Murderer

Q: Any serious offenders?

A: A.O. Kisha – I had a murderer who came in and told me that he killed this guy because he couldn't take it any longer. He was so remorseful for what he did and he was absolutely honest. They had been neighbors and it was one of those long smoldering things. He was sitting home one night and having a couple of beers and they were out on the porch that night. They exchanged words across that porch and he went and got his gun and killed his neighbor.

Robber

Q: One time you talked about a kid who was violated and you had put your neck out for him. Can you tell me about him?

A: A.O. Christina – We are talking about my feelings for young people. He was 21 when he committed the second offense while on probation. He had a pending case prior to being placed on probation. He was put on probation for 3 years and then I had to do a **presentence investigation (PSI)**. He was convicted of the pending case. In my investigation, he was in the holding center. I interviewed him there and

presentence investigation (PSI) is a report given to the court that considers the offender's social history.

my sense from coming out of that interview was that this guy was not a drugee; secondly, he sounded very committed to turning his life around and he had a limited IQ—it was like 85. I did some follow-up and I called welfare. He was on welfare prior to going to the holding center and the caseworker made the statement to the effect that he did a complete about face. He was very aggressive when he walked in to see her and everything and now he was very polite and wanted help, etc. Considering that I wanted to make the recommendation without talking to my supervisor, I told her the score. He had an extensive history of petty larceny; small stuff, juvenile stuff—something that doesn't go over $50 in value. I told her while he has been on probation like 8 or 10 months, he has been arrest free and maybe we should give him a chance. She says that I don't think we should; look at his history and so forth. I said I feel that we should give this guy a chance and she says OK, I will go with your recommendation. It is up to you to make the recommendation. I wrote to the judge asking that this person be continued on probation. I received the new case and the special conditions that I required: that he attend the GED program, that he seek employment, and that he go for counseling. This judge is tough and he didn't see it that way so he gave this guy the **intensive supervision probation (ISP)** program. He had a curfew from 9 P.M. to 6 A.M. We requested that the judge modify it since I already had him on probation. He did fine for a while. He was in a GED program and then all of a sudden he was arrested at a hospital at 11:00 at night.

intensive supervision probation (ISP) is a program developed to provide an alternative for juvenile offenders in lieu of removal from the home.

Q: What was he doing at the hospital?

A: A.O. Christina – He was looking for somebody to rob. He has this compulsion to rob things—that is what it amounts to. When he came in, I told him that I had done the best that I could for him and now I was going to have to write a letter to a judge and violate probation. Last week he didn't show up and right now he is an absconder. We go on a second case in city court and I bet he won't show up either. He is going to do time if they catch him wherever he is. I have a sense that with these warrants that they really don't pursue them.

Q: Is this the first time that you put your neck out to that degree?

A: A.O. Christina – To that degree, yeah. I don't think that I really put my neck out. I told him that but you do just a little bit beyond the norm and in that sense I did go a bit further but not to the sense that I was going to be fired. I think he was legitimate at first but I feel that he has this tendency that he likes to do illegal things and that he likes the thrill. What are you doing in a hospital at 11:00 at night? He gets caught for trespassing often. What do you do with somebody like that?

Auto Thief

Q: Do you have any interesting cases?

A: A.O. Fred – I just did a presentence investigation about a month ago on an individual who committed a crime. He is a parking lot attendant. He didn't want to give me his view of what happened. I told him I was not going to tell anyone but he said that he didn't want it to get back to his employer. Finally, he told me that what he did was to make a duplicate key of a car. He didn't take the car from the parking lot but he found the envelope holding the Insurance Card inside the car and found out where this person lived. On a Friday evening, he went to West Seneca at 8 o'clock and he took the car from the driveway. He kept the car for a full year. He said that he had to go to Chicago to pick up his common-law wife and kid. He said that he kept the car because he said that it had his fingerprints on it. After I did the presentence report, I realized that I had done the wrong thing by not telling him that I wasn't going to call his employer. When I thought about it, I realized that we could be held responsible if he commits an identical crime because I did not call the employer.

Q: Did you tell the probationer that you were going to make the call?

A: A.O. Fred – Well, I didn't have contact with the probationer after that. He was going for sentencing and I did recommend probation for the individual and he is on probation with another officer. I asked the other officer to apologize to him and explain to him why I had to tell his employer. He got fired for what he'd done.

Q: How did he get caught?

A: A.O. Fred – He was double parked and went into a store with a friend and when he came out of the store, there was a police officer who was writing a ticket. He must have panicked because he told the officer that he would move the car and after he gets in, he drives away. Of course the officer hadn't finished writing up the ticket and chased him down. In the course of events, the officer saw an expired registration. She called the car in and found that it was stolen. He got arrested; he had changed the plates on the car.

Auto Thief

Q: Do you have any interesting cases?

A: A.O. Mary – I have one now with a switched vehicle identification number [VIN] on the car. He stole a yellow car and a blue car and made both cars yellow. It had to do with not ruining the good car which was an IROC Camaro. He bought and paid for a regular Camaro and stole an IROC; the difference is about $10,000. He stole it right off the lot. You have to smash the front windshield to change the VIN numbers and he did that. Then he got new glass in the car that he owned. It was absolutely incredible. He was generally a car thief but it was sort of status to have an IROC. I think that it is a very well-organized family and I went back to the district attorney and told him that I thought that the kid was not as culpable as his mother who I believe is the ring leader. She comes off like Pearl Bailey, who you would like a lot. She had a lot of connections.

(ISP) Burglar

Q: Do you have any interesting cases?

A: A.O. Pat – This one man is in jail right now on a burglary. Here is a 44-year-old man who is a college graduate. He presents himself well; always was dressed nicely. He maintained a real nice apartment near the college. You would not know he was a probationer if he were sitting out there. He has an extensive record for breaking and entering primarily because he use to be a heavy drinker. Well, I got him involved in AA; I had him attending a treatment program, group and individual, and he attended them all. He was on house arrest. I came to the house two times a week. He was divorced; he had his girlfriend over. I caught him nipping once and I put the law down to him. He had been through the system and charmed so many people; he is a good talker, intelligent, manipulative. He was refinishing and restoring antique furniture. He was a real smooth talker. He tried to con his way through two counselors. He would come up here with his two girlfriends who were both former *Playboy* bunnies. He got along well because I knew that he was a conniving SOB. I gave him all the rope and he enjoyed talking to me. He told me that I was the first guy who showed him any interest and cared. I said that I cared because my job is to see that he complied with these conditions. I enjoyed talking to him. He was knowledgeable; he had been in the service. He was my age; I could relate to a lot of things that he did. I enjoyed talking to him but I told the SOB if something happened I would be right on his neck. Sure enough he went out to another county and he was burglarizing. He had his [driver's] license revoked for a DWI. He came up to me and wanted my approval to apply for one. I just wouldn't based on the fact that he had a couple of prior DWIs. So he stole a bike and was going to another county and was burglarizing homes. The farmer came home and they were chasing him in the fields. This was a case where I was convinced that I had gotten the guy on the right track. Believe me, I would have bet a paycheck. I was ready to transfer him to a regular caseload, even the counselors were convinced. He had adhered to every condition of probation to the letter of the law. He was in at 9 o'clock. He did this and did that. We had a good rapport and we are right down the tubes. He was just sentenced to two to four years in another county and I am bringing him back on a violation to give him a one to four consecutive sentence.

Welfare Fraud

Q: How about poor people on probation?

A: A.O. Matt – I can do a welfare fraud presentence investigation very quickly (in about 15 minutes) because the facts are in another file and the person is generally extremely cooperative. Most of the time it is cut and dry. They are given a conditional discharge in that they sign a confession of judgment and make restitution. They get a reduced welfare payment for a while; it could be years. If the person is working and it is welfare fraud, you will be lucky to get anything back. Generally it is a stereotypical mother who is trying to get just a little extra. They already are pretty poor. The money is relatively insignificant, and in the few cases where the money is significant, those are generally criminals with premeditated intent that I feel should go to jail but they never do. They may in certain cases get probation with restitution.

Petty Thief

Q: **Any interesting cases?**

A: **A.O. Alisha** – In another interesting case, this guy spent 20 to 25 years in jail. He is 55 years old. He gets out and is rearrested. He is not originally from here but was paroled and wound up here. He had two pending petty larceny charges. I don't know why the police gave him an appearance ticket on one of the petty larceny charges. He evidently stole a credit card, moved from the city mission into the Hyatt Hotel, stayed there 2 days, and ran up a bill of $500. We contacted the victim and they told us he ordered Dom Perignon champagne, shrimp, lobster, and Tangueray gin. I went over to see him and he said that he did it. He has a nice personality but he is going to do 1 to 3. He has been an alcoholic since 1975.

Habitual Offender

Q: **What about the people who are always in trouble?**

A: **A.O. Charlie** – Your habitual criminals, the criminals who have been constantly doing the same thing over and over again, the person who has been on probation for a long time. They have had probation before, but it didn't work out. The probation was revoked. Now all of a sudden, they are on probation again. They have been on parole. They have done time in prison. I don't know why some of the judges put them on probation. It is just a matter of time before you end up violating them. I do work with them. I give them my best shot but keep in mind I think that sooner or later they either abscond or they are re-arrested. A lot of them are druggies, burglars, and that type of thing.

Substance Abuse

DUI Catholic Priest

Q: **Any unusual people on probation?**

A: **A.O. Jack** – I also worked on a presentence investigation of a priest. The priest was arrested while driving intoxicated and crossing the center pavement line. When he was arrested and they were taking him to be breathalized, he asked the arresting officer if he was a Catholic. After the arresting officer replied in the negative, the priest kicked the officer in the groin. He had to be forcibly subdued by four police officers; he just went nuts. When they breathalized him, he was at .18. He is a 240-pound. man so he had a lot [to drink]. The priest was from South Dakota. He sells books; this is his priestly function. He travels around the United States selling these books to different parishes. He pled guilty very quickly. They let him plead guilty to driving with more than .10 percent blood alcohol level. Driving with more than .10 is a DWI but is a separate section. They dismissed driving left of the paving markings and the resisting arrest was also dismissed. When he came in for the presentence interview, he came in with one of the books that he sells and his 1040 showing his income and a picture of himself with the pope as a verification of his priesthood.

I found this kind of interesting so as I was talking to him, he explained to me that he had been in the service for 4 years, got out, and decided to become a priest. He went to Rome to study at the University of St. Thomas Aquinas, which I had never heard of. He allegedly lived there for 6 or 8 years. He met a Filipino bishop who wanted him to become a missionary. He came back to South Dakota and was ordained by the Filipino bishop but not by any American bishop. This was my first suspicion, that there was something here. Then he explains to me that he went to the Philippines where he served for 5 years but developed chronic bronchitis and had to return to the United States because he could not live in that climate. He refuses to be a part of the clergy in the United States. He lives in South Dakota with his mother and together with his sister, they run a mission that prints, distributes, and sells these books. He also claims that he sends the books to the Philippine Islands for free. The Philippine bishop told him not to affiliate with an American parish because they would stop him from doing it.

In the meantime, I have to provide the court with information and verification of what this man has been telling me so they can come up with a sentence. I called South Dakota and asked them if they would try to get some information to verify what this guy had told me. I got a letter back from South Dakota indicating that indeed, the probation officer in South Dakota had talked to the chancery who said that indeed this guy was ordained by a Philippine Bishop in South Dakota. However, he had never practiced in any diocese in the United States and appears to be a persona non grata within the diocese. The priest didn't like the diocese either. As I am doing the investigation, he tells me that he has been on thorazine for 20 years, which I check out later. (When I am doing a presentence investigation, I check into what medications they are taking. When doing a presentence investigation, I believe that medications are important. They say a lot for what is going on with the person.) I look up this medication and it can be for nerves. This guy appears to be a kind of nervous type; he totally denies any relationship with alcohol, saying that he had not had a drink for 6 months prior to coming to the city. He was out socializing at the restaurant because he was lonesome and was overserved. This bartender wanted him to try all of these exotic drinks, so he did. He met a friend at the bar and went to a couple of other restaurants and bars. He denies that he kicked the cop. He was obviously in a blackout which indicates to me a more serious problem than he is relating. When I look up his medication, it says to avoid all alcohol. Now I have to come up with a recommendation. It would be a South Dakota supervision but the man does not stay in the state all the time because he travels 70,000 miles a year selling these books. He is on the road driving a truck pulling a trailer full of books. If you look at the function of probation to protect the community and to rehabilitate the offender, I have to recommend probation for this guy because I think that he needs to have an alcohol evaluation. I am not an alcohol expert, and although I have had some training, I don't consider myself a diagnostician. As I pulled it together, this is a very lengthy report. I am not sure what the court is going to do. He will have to pay a fine anyway. He told me that he had two other DWIs but I can't find them. He had one in Dallas and one in Illinois. Our computer system interfaces with the arrests in other localities but the other ones are not in it. They could be traffic offenses. He also had a disorderly conduct in Minneapolis. This smacks of alcohol. There is something in the back of your mind that doesn't come together.

Q: What happens if you transfer the case and he violates probation?

A: A.O. Jack – I think that he would have to come back to us because supervision is a courtesy kind of thing. The difficult part about recommending probation is that the state that you transfer the case to has to agree to do it, and they are to write back to you and let you know if there is any violation. The offender signs a paper that they agree to return back here if there is a violation. This is cumbersome at best; it has to go through the interstate compact. In terms of paperwork, it is a pain in the neck and in terms of appropriateness, I think the guy needs some supervision or an alcohol diagnosis— somebody to tell him not to drink and take his medication.

He stayed in jail 1 night and then was calling here every day so that he could have his interview scheduled so that he could leave town. He will come back for sentencing. It always surprises me that people do. I think that he might have posted bail. He made $13,000 last year. His mother and sister are employed by the mission. He is very indignant. The guy from South Dakota said that he probably bought a priesthood from the Filipino bishop. There is no record of graduation from a seminary. I believe that he took courses there and did study to become a priest. I don't know if the requirements are the same there as here. He said that the GI bill paid for it. This is another thing that is unusual. This is supposed to be an easy presentence investigation and it turns out to be more time consuming than a second-degree murder. I assume that the mission pays for his expenses.

DUI Offender

Q: Any offenders who are real problems?

A: A.O. Carolyn – We have a 42-year-old client who is under electronic monitoring and has a 15-year-old girlfriend. The parents called to tell the authorities that the girl was over at the guy's house and hiding in the closet. This guy has had a lot of misdemeanors and priors. The thing about this is that he had this girl up there and she lived diagonally across the street. Both families know each other. She is a product of a dysfunctional family herself. The mother wants to hang this guy, and she says that he was selling drugs that night. I asked, "How do you know that?" and she said, "Because I bought some cocaine from him a while ago." The girl really belongs in some kind of protective custody. The sad thing is that this client may have tried to get help because she ran away once before. It is kind of a mess.

The guy works at the mall. He has got a car but he shouldn't drive because he lost his license. His mother drives and his sister drives but every time that he is gone, the car is gone. He even took the car to counseling once. In fact at one court date he wasn't there on time and it was said that he was just looking for a parking spot.

His record goes back to 1965. This is an offense that took place in 1983, and since he has been on probation, he was picked up for another DWI. He did some jail time, like 60 days, but courts are very reluctant for some reason to put DWI offenders in prison—except this judge is about fed up. I came up with the idea about electronic monitoring, and reluctantly he went along with it. He is obeying that for the most part. There are no clear cut violations. I think the guy is driving a car in violation of his conditions but he still hasn't been caught. This gives me the idea: You view the job as a peace officer, which means that you do have to do police-type functions. All I need to do is to see him behind the wheel. It is difficult and boring work. I am more of a bother that he has beaten. I have laid off for a little bit and let him think that everything is OK.

DUI Sentencing, Attorneys, Families, and Victims

Q: Any professionals on probation?

A: A.O. Kelly – Yesterday, I was also on the phone for 45 minutes with an attorney. I normally don't talk to an attorney but he called me. It was another criminally negligent homicide involving a 30-year-old working guy. There was so much notoriety in the paper that although the judge had promised him only 6 months through a plea bargain, if she gave him any more time, he would withdraw his plea and take it to trial. Of course there was much public outcry from the family; they were on the phone with me every day. The judge then gave him more than the bargain; he withdrew his plea and took it to trial. The family continued their crusade and when he went for sentencing before the judge, she gave him 3 to 6 years. I don't think that he should have gotten all that time. He expressed remorse and guilt. It was a hit and run and they really couldn't breathalize him. They placed him at a bar drinking, and they placed him hitting this 19-year-old man and killing him and leaving but they couldn't really prove DUI.

The case that I finished last week was a case where the man didn't run from the scene. He obtained a .22 blood alcohol content. It went to the grand jury and the grand jury didn't indict him for DUI and it was sent back to the lower court for leaving the scene of an accident. Now this man had three prior DUIs. This guy got 60 days. I had to work with that victim's family for days and days; they only wanted a letter of apology. The family was wonderful. They are the most loving family. The kid that was killed was adopted and he was 19 years old and was like a pillar of the community. The man who killed him was so awful and terrible. Through the preliminary hearing he was so arrogant. Through the presentence investigation I had to sit here with my jaws locked. There was like no remorse and no guilt. He blamed this boy for being on the wrong side of the road. He only got 60 days. The DUIs are difficult to deal with emotionally.

DUI Lawyer

Q: Any professional people on probation?

A: A.O. Katherine – I can think of this one woman right now. She is an alcoholic and someone who has completed law school. She had her first arrest and she is in her mid-30s. She got her DUI conviction. There was an accident but she didn't hurt anyone. She has nothing other than this DUI. She ended up getting the DUI because my understanding is that because she didn't want to take a plea, she went to trial and she ended up with a conviction. I don't know if I identify with her because there are so few like her. I mean, she is well-educated. She is in my general ballpark age-wise. She is a very frustrating and aggravating person. I tend to be very sympathetic toward her too.

Q: Why is she frustrating?

A: A.O. Katherine – She is hard to deal with. Her arguments are more sophisticated and take more to counter, plus, I have this very sympathetic feeling toward her. She's sympathetic because you can look at her and say that here but for the grace of God, I could be? That is something; she is very verbal which is refreshing because a lot of them aren't. She also has a really nice sense of humor.

She has an alcohol problem and drug problem too. She took antidepressants and antianxiety medications. She is just a person whom I see with more potential than others. As far as practicing law, she does not want to go back to that. She took the bar exam and failed it. She worked in a law office, but she can't practice law. Failing the bar the first time is fairly common; I didn't know that. I tried to encourage her to give it another try.

As far as her family situation, her father is a drinker. She is not married and lives with her parents and her brother. Her father is never there and her mother, I think, knows what is going on as far as her drinking.

There has been some real arm twisting to get her to counseling. She has been to three different places now, and she is really resisting this. I am in a spot where I am really not moving anywhere. I have a sort of wait and see. I have her on for 3 years, so I have some time and I don't have to rush in and file a violation. She has also appealed her probation, so we have an appeal for the actual sentence that hasn't been scheduled yet. She is saying that she doesn't want therapy. She was seen in one place where they said that her denial was too strenuous; in another place she stormed out, because she got mad at the people there. She just left. She is kind of coming around.

What happened is that she went on vacation for a week and ended up getting some detoxification. I am trying to work with this state of mind that she is in now. She was hospitalized. I don't believe that she has completely stopped drinking. Something happened; I am not going to get into it. Detoxification can last from 3 or 4 days or as long as 28 days. In a hospital they get detoxed and often a residential program is in order. She attributes her blackouts to the antianxiety drugs. She had a high blood alcohol content. I tried to talk to her about what tolerance means. Her blood alcohol was at a .15, and for someone who does not drink regularly, a .05 would have put them on the floor.

She really doesn't want me to talk too much to her mother about it. I said, well, fine, as long as I can deal directly with you. It is tough to know how much you should go into a family situation when you are dealing with an adult on probation and they ask you not to. It is real difficult. How I usually counter it is that some people don't have a "whole" family. A lot of people on probation live by themselves, in apartments, and don't have that much contact with the family. That is some of their problems. With some of the guys, one of the signs that they are going to get better in all ways is having a girlfriend or looking up their fathers. It is just things like that.

She is a woman embarrassed to come to my office. When she started, she tried to disguise herself because she used to work in the place where we met. Here she was among 90 percent men and feeling uncomfortable about it. She never mentioned that she is waiting with a bunch of criminals and things like that but she feels very embarrassed so she would come with sunglasses and a baseball cap. Of course she would be the first one and wait for me by the stairs. She would draw more attention by hovering around and wearing these disguises. She has gotten better about that.

That would be a part too but what is more important is to get her into counseling which the court has mandated that she get into. AA is not mandated but that will be part of it. She was taking therapy and that is part of it.

DUI Parent and Burglar Son

Q: What about the issue of the parents and their contribution?

A: A.O. Ericka – I have a father and son on probation right now. The father is on for a DWI; he is an attorney. He was not disbarred and he could be reinstated to practice, but he is running a legion post. The man makes no money, but he is very happy. He completed his DUI training, paid his fine, and has a volunteer service order that he is doing in a boy's club. This is our one point of contention; I had trouble with him reporting. He is a nice guy. I know where he is. I should come down firmer on reporting but I can get in my car and get him anytime that I want. He is at the legion post or at his home. He is separated from his wife.

His [son] is a young piss pot who has never grown up. He is 19 or 20 years old. We got him on a burglary and he was with a bunch of kids. One of them we got sentenced; another kid went to probation. Another is going to technical college. The son failed to report yesterday. I could have violated him 10 times by now, but if you want to accomplish anything, you have to ask whether you really want this kid in jail. To avoid any kind of legal difficulty, I don't take them back to court for a lecture. The only reason that I violate is that you are going to jail. I make it clear to the kids from the beginning. If you force me to violate you, there is only going to be one recommendation. There are others who take them back to court for reviews, slap their hands; I don't think that accomplishes much.

Q: You don't think this kid is going to work out?

A: A.O. Ericka – No. You got him on a felony which means that the court can give him 1 to 4 [years] at Attica.

DUI Construction Worker

Q: Are there clients whom you find interesting?

A: A.O. Brett – I have this one client who is being discharged soon. I think that it was the type of thing that I grew to like him. He was in his late 30s, working in construction. He was a DUI and he did well. He had no new arrests and he also seemed to gain insight as things moved along which is always appealing. Also it seemed that the changes in his life were making him feel happy and that made me feel happy about him. He has a nice personality; he is easy going. It is always nice when they get into telling you that they are getting to like the therapy; they can see this or when they went to educational stuff about alcoholism. He didn't realize this or that. It is nice to see people discover things and that there is another way to live. It is one of the best parts of the job.

Q: Does that client make the job worth coming to?

A: A.O. Brett – Similar stuff like that is what it is all about. It is not about anything else really.

Bad Checks and Cocaine

Q: Isn't cocaine a big problem?

A: A.O. Anne – I spent a lot of time on the phone on one case. He is a 23-year-old male who had $30,000 in outstanding bad checks. I talked to the bank's loss control officer and the arresting officer. I got a release to schedule a psychological evaluation. It turns out that he was sandbagging me and the psychological program was still in existence. I had him give them a medical release so that they would send me a copy of his psychological evaluation.

Q: How does some guy write up $30,000 worth of bad checks?

A: A.O. Anne – I asked the guy at the bank this, too; I was very concerned about that. I couldn't write a bad check if my life depended on it. What happened is that in the town in which he lives, they know him. He is a likeable guy. He maintains that he needed to do this to maintain his construction business. In reality, I believe, from talking to the people yesterday, that most of this money was spent on drugs. He is a cocaine user but he would not divulge that during the pre-sentence interview. He was very guarded. I would ordinarily send him for an evaluation but nothing would have shown up at this point.

Q: Were these checks written for cash?

A: A.O. Anne – My belief is that he got cash from the people with whom he was doing construction. Instead of taking the cash and depositing it, he would spend it on drugs. Then he would write checks for aluminum screens or doors. He bought a $1,000 stereo. He used a $2,300 check as a down payment for a car. He would use the cash that was incoming for his business and spend that on drugs. He wouldn't have anything to support the checks. In town when he did get a bit of money, he would say that he would deposit it but a day later, he would write a check that was bigger than even what that deposit was. It was always a situation of robbing Peter to pay Paul. The bank is only out of $2,200, therefore each individual person is out.

Q: How much time are you recommending?

A: A.O. Anne – My recommendation is a split sentence because I don't want this guy to think that he has gotten away with it. The most that he could get is 90 days. It would have been great if he could have gotten 6 months and restitution. He is a real wheeler dealer. In the place where he worked before he went into construction, he claimed that he hurt his back. Their compensation doctor said that he could work and he in turn sued them. He then went out and opened up his own construction business which would appear to need some lifting.

Q: He sounds very sophisticated.

A: A.O. Anne – Yeah, and he was really cool in the interview too. He owes $1,000 in one town, $4,200 in another, and $8,900 in a third. He has pending charges in several other towns. I was amazed you could bounce that many checks around.

Burglar and Drug Habit

Q: What about theft and drug use?

A: A.O. Nichole – This case involved an 18-year-old kid involved with burglaries and a $1000-a-day drug habit. He has been in foster care since he was 9 years old. I personally don't think that he is going to make it on electronic monitoring. In fact, I told him that if he takes off, leave the equipment. This guy is one of the worst as far as burglaries. He sat about 7 months in the jail. He kept every drug appointment and follow through but sometimes he is a little too manipulative. He will perform whatever you expect, whatever the goals are to a certain level, then bingo he is gone. They will stop cooperating whether it is too much structure or not. It is sad. If you could see his body with the tattoos all over, and what you saw on the hands. He is in for four different burglary indictments; he was involved with 17 over all that he was arrested for. His criminal history is just unbelievable.

Sex Offenders

Q: What about women sex offenders?

A: A.O. Megan – I have about seven women on for DWI, embezzlement, and I have a woman on for sodomy. This woman and this weird 50-year-old guy sodomized a 16-year-old girl. The offender is attractive, beautiful, and well-educated. She is 25 years old. You rarely get sodomy today because it involves a rape that is pled down to a sodomy. This was sexual molesting. The man and this woman who were living together induced this 16-year-old girl to have sex with the guy and the woman then sodomized her. It was a very interesting case. It is claimed by the sheriff that the guy used the 25-year-old first. He introduced her to sex and she was his partner for many years. The judge put her on probation and ordered counseling. He was going to have her evaluated by the forensic psychiatric unit and try to break up her relationship. He [the 50-year-old man] is serving time.

Q: Do you have juvenile sex offenders?

A: J.O. Danielle – I also have what I consider my small little group of what I call budding sociopaths. They take no ownership for anything. I mean I have a kid right now who has been involved in a tremendous amount of sexual abuse at home—his mother, his younger brother. He has his friends line outside of the bathroom to see his mother coming out of the tub. He goes into her room and tries to pull her pants off while she is sleeping. He barges in on her constantly when she is dressing and undressing. He watches the neighbors undress and things like that. He is a brand-new kid; [for me] in fact I am going to court today, on a review that I requested. There might have been 12 incidences that his mother may have identified. The kid denied literally all 12.

As a matter of fact, I sent the kid in for a clinic evaluation because he took no ownership for anything. The clinician called me back and off the record said that: "You remember when you said you thought this kid was on a different wave length? Well, he is not listening to any station." This kid needs a clinical counseling program.

Pedophile Teacher's Aide

Q: Any sex offenders on probation?

A: A.O. Adam – I have this teacher's aide who's charged with sodomizing four boys age 12 and 14. He is a very nice man and I felt very sorry for him. The ADA feels sorry. The board of education attorney came away liking the guy and feeling sorry for him. He was sexually abused himself at age 11. If you were sexually abused at age 11 and 13, then you start abusing 11- and 13-year-old boys. There is really only one program that has any kind of hope. Before this program, there was nothing for a pedophile; they get no help in the prison. This is something; it is a 5-day-a-week program, 12 months a year. All the information I have read, once you read up on it, once a pedophile always a pedophile. They are great recidivists and once caught, they are more cautious the next time. I think that he is screaming for help. He was probably one of the nicest people that I have ever interviewed—absolutely, totally honest. He never made excuses.

His is a middle-class working family background; a close mother and father. His father is a retired truck driver on a union pension. His mom works as a communication aide for the school board and he has a brother and two sisters. He is the second oldest of the four children. He graduated from high school, but he didn't make it in the marines and he came home. He was a recruit failure at boot camp, honorably discharged.

Q: Does he have a college degree?

A: A.O. Adam – No, he was going to go back to college. He is certainly smart enough. He could do it if he wanted to. He had good letters from everybody about him. His parents have totally stood by him.

Q: How do parents respond to situations like that?

A: A.O. Adam – Each one is different. Some are angry and embarrassed and some don't believe it no matter how hard you try. They are very defensive. This family let him do everything. He is 25 and he has shouldered the burden of everything. Some families will intervene because the person is immature. This guy can handle it.

Q: Has this guy a sense of guilt about what he has done?

A: A.O. Adam – There is no question that there is a sense of guilt there.

Q: But is there also a compulsive tendency as well?

A: A.O. Adam – Yes, but I don't know how much the compulsive tendency is there. I have felt in other cases a stronger compulsion than I do with this guy, that is why I feel that now is the right time for a program. I want you to know that in most cases there is no sense of guilt, or an awareness of the harm and injury in this. This is a big step in the process of change. This is a case where someone started to sexually abuse him at age 11 and it went on with the threat that the abuser would tell his mother that it was his fault if he said anything. He cut himself off from that offender by age 14. An intern moved into the home. They rented out a room in the home and the intern started hitting on this kid. He never said anything to his parents.

Q: Is this process cathartic for the man?

A: A.O. Adam – Yes, I think that it is. He has spent so much time talking to the attorney and others that he really does want this to get out. He didn't take it to trial. He pled guilty instantly within the same week of being charged. That is unheard of.

Q: What is his charge for sentencing?

A: A.O. Adam – It has a mandatory commitment. I think that it is a 3rd degree felony.

Q: Where are you going to try to send this man?

A: A.O. Adam – I told him that I wanted his attorney to call me and I want him to find out everything that he can about the shock treatment program.

Child Abusers

Q: Child abuse is a big problem; any on your caseload?

A: A.O. Bill – I had another one who was doing it with his own natural twin daughters. He was in his 40s. He was a fat 350-pound slob. The father had intercourse with them from the day they were 9 to the day that they were 16. That one really turned my stomach. This guy would not admit to it; he denied it. He disowned the two girls. It was a really shitty situation; it was just terrible. I can honestly say that before I met him, I didn't like him. In our interview, he denied everything and didn't pretend that it was real. But you had to watch yourself too, he had a lawyer.

One of the girls told a classmate who told a teacher. It took 9 years before it came out. That was a long 7 years of hell. I had another female officer interview the girls. The girls were real attractive, nice, and intelligent girls. Now, years later, I think that one is in nursing and another is in college. Back then, they had to go into a foster home. Even on the day of sentencing, he criticized them and had nothing good to say about the two girls.

The mother knew what was going on but never got involved. I think that I had more dislike for her than I did for him, because she sat back and allowed it to happen. In fact, the mother got put on probation because she lied before the grand jury.

I think that he was sick. He might have been an abused individual himself. I dug something up but it didn't materialize. He was dealing with a lawyer who was dealing with his own psychiatrist. You have to watch yourself. He was in an institution but wouldn't sign a release for his records. That is alright. You put it down and let the judge deal with him. He got time. I think that he got 3 to 6 years. That is not a lot of time for what he did.

It was a situation where this guy was just a nasty man. He had a good job too. He got stabbed in the jail. Everyone who was involved in this, the DA, myself, and a couple of caseworkers felt that he got what he deserved. That is a sad thing to say. That was probably the worst one that I had.

Sex Offenders

Q: Any sex offenders who offered interesting stories?

A: A.O. Amanda – I have sex offenders. The interesting thing about sex offenders that I have is when they come in, they are humble as pie. They throw religion at me all the time. There was this child molester who got caught dropping his pants in front of three different girls, masturbating in front of them. Yet he comes in and it is like "God be with you" and that kind of stuff. He is doing this and he is doing that. I have him going to counseling. Your child molesters and your sex offenders are very quiet. Some of them are disturbed.

Mental Illness

Q: How about mentally ill probationers?

A: A.O. Kelly – I do have a crazy client now. He is a physician who was involved in a very serious auto accident and suffered a head injury and has been schizophrenic since then. It is a very tragic kind of case. The problem with him is that in combination with not taking his medication as he should and drinking, he can become violent. He has been assaultive and that is why he is on probation. He is unable to practice medicine because his license has been suspended. It is horrible. His accident was about 20 years ago. He is in his late 50s. He went from the comfortable lifestyle of a physician to living on social security disability in a one-room efficiency-type boardinghouse with no job. The wife divorced him. The kids are in foster care and are in another state. It is horrible and he is very difficult. He has been institutionalized since I have had him under supervision during the past 4 months. He had a relapse.

Q: Does this guy have a chronic problem?

A: A.O. Kelly – Yes, he can be stable for quite a long time. Once a year, he relapses. He knows what he is doing. He is very depressed. Being a physician, having the activity, the social status, and the economic situation and all of it can be a very dynamic go-get-'em type of a life style, and then falling to living in a rooming house on a meager check. He has no employment, friends, or family. And knowing that is it, you are not going to get back into your profession and you are not going to probably do anything. He is on an intensive supervision program with the psychiatric center. They spend a lot of time with him, just day to day to get him through taking care of business. They are real good with him. This brother is retired but not too able to do too much.

Mental health cases can be extremely difficult to deal with. It is real difficult, the way mental health services are now. Unless the person wants treatment or wants to be committed, it is not easy to get by.

I can remember one adult woman she was on probation to me but her mother was mentally ill. She wanted her mother hospitalized but she couldn't accomplish it. She called all kinds of services and unless her mother would willingly go, no one would take her. The lady was seriously ill.

Mentally Ill Veteran

Q: Any veterans on probation?

A: A.O. Karrissa – I think through drugs and alcohol, you get more irrational people and unpredictable people. These are the ones who fall into that category where you have to be very careful. For the most part, I am talking about people with psychiatric problems. To give you an example, I had a guy on probation who was walking down the middle of a street, and he was a complete nut. He was put on probation and we carried him for 2 years. He was pretty good when his father was alive because his father saw that he took his medication but he went off it a couple of times. He came into my office a couple of times and was way out of it. What I do is to call the police and then call the VA hospital and they usually get him in. He was a veteran.

Other Offenders

Dangerous Offenders

Q: Do you have any probationers you consider dangerous felons that are on probation?

A: A.O. Bob – I have one man here who the condition of probation states right on the record that he must remove his two pit bull dogs from the house when the probation officer comes at night. I went in there on a search. I made him take out the dogs; ferocious-looking bastards. He had four or five men in the house. I went into the bedroom to do the search. I felt obligated I had to do it. I don't particularly care to do that type of job. I have AIDS on my mind. When there are four or five strangers around, I wasn't too comfortable. We found two guns there; one was a loaded shotgun and the other was a 30/30. We wrote to the judge; the judge didn't want to do anything. We confiscated the guns and forgot about it. Two months later, the FBI unit was here and they told us that their SWAT team was there. They saw us there and they had us on tape; they thought that we were very conscientious in what we were doing. They wanted to get me to enlist this guy to act as an informant for them. If you met him he was a smooth talker and well-dressed. He attended a community college for 2 years. He was clever and worked in the post office but recognizes that he can make a ton of money out there. He thinks that he is beating the system.

Q: What about felons on probation?

A: A.O. Eric – Another thing is that the outside looking into the criminal justice system is very impressed with the words misdemeanor and felon. They don't mean a damn thing. They mean to a large part the attorney who defended them. What should have been a felony became a misdemeanor. It means very little as far as controlling the individual is concerned. The only difference in the control is the one guy going longer than the misdemeanor. The actual distinction in the behavior is not a whole lot. In fact, other people have probably told you this: Career criminals are the easiest to handle.

Q: Why is that?

A: A.O. Eric – They will not give you a reason to violate them. Your professional burglar, your professional gambler are the easiest to handle and the funniest people to deal with.

Q: Who are the ones whom you like the most?

A: A.O. Eric – Yeah. Bookies. They are colorful; they are night people, they never give you any problems. You ask them to do something and it is done. A fine is paid promptly.

Q: How about people in organized crime?

A: A.O. Eric – They are very easy to deal with. They fall under what I classify as a pro criminal. They are professionals; they are not going to give you any administrative problems. You tell them to be in every day at 9 o'clock in your office, they will be there. They pay their fines immediately. Any conditions, they will immediately contact the counselor. There will be no problems. You are not going to change them or rehabilitate them. Are you going to rehabilitate a guy who is making from $10,000 a week to a guy who makes $850 a week? You are reversing. We have had leaders on the local mafia on probation. We have had their children.

AIDS Cases

Q: What about people with AIDS?

A: A.O. Brian – Well, yes, I am going to be very truthful. I have two people who have the AIDS virus and one of them has the actual AIDS; a very nice person and everything. I kind of shy away from them. I know basically what it is but I have that apprehension. One of them came in the other day with a cold and I said hi, I saw you, good-bye. He has tested positively and he knows it.

Q: Do you expect any more clients like this?

A: A.O. Brian – Given the fact that the zip code area that we handle has a lot of drug-related offenses, I am sure that I expect some more. I am sure that there are a few more than these two and that other officers have others.

Q: This guy has been on probation for a long time?

A: A.O. Brian – One of them started just recently; he is the carrier. He has got the virus. The one from Texas he has been on probation for about a year. He has 4 years of probation. We cannot release him for a while. He has restitution to make in Texas but I can't request a closing. Where is he going to get the money to pay the restitution when he is on disability? He is a guy who has full-blown AIDS and they are requesting restitution of $3,000 or more from a guy who is living on disability. It had something to do with a stolen automobile. This happened after he found out he had AIDS so maybe now the law is meaningless now that he has AIDS.

Q: Do you feel sad about this guy?

A: A.O. Brian – In a way it is a life so you think about the suffering he is going to have to go through and then the eventual death. He is at the point now where he comes to tell me that he has to go to the doctor with lung problems. Also he is at the stage where he doesn't have much wrong with him, depending on how well he takes care of himself. Every time that he comes in, he has a statement about some kind of problem where he had to go to the hospital. Sure, you feel sorry for the individual. This guy is not a drug user. The guy who is the carrier is the drug user. The guy who has the AIDS is gay. The guy who owes the restitution has the AIDS.

■ Conclusion

This chapter has offered some insights about individuals on probation. Although there is no suggestion that it offers a complete list of who probationers are, it does provide some indication of their diversity and humanness. People on probation are under a variety of legal statuses where they have received prison sentences and have been given another chance or they have been assigned to probation directly. Most of these people are under active supervision but there are a sizeable number of offenders who have absconded. Most of the offenders on probation are non-Hispanic white males who have committed felonies but a large number are also convicted of driving offenses.

What is most interesting about the people on probation is the absolute human nature of them all. We see that many but not all officers speak of these people as though they possess some measure of human dignity despite the offense. It is also true that these offenders are interesting for what they have done to get into trouble, how they live, and what they do about their problems. There are no consistent or stereotypical clients. They may be unattractive and there may be an inclination to write some of them off but, for the most part, these are people who made some wrong choices and need carefully considered assistance. There are juveniles who have burned things down, stolen cars, and listed as out of control. Adults have killed people or are robbers, auto thieves, burglars, welfare cheats, petty thieves, habitual offenders, drunks, substance abusers, or sex offenders.

Throughout these interviews, it seems for the most part that offenders are very human people who are not too different from the average citizen. Anyone could find him- or herself stopped for a vehicle violation or in trouble with his or her credit. What is clear is that these offenders are human beings who have made human mistakes. Some of them will become law-abiding citizens someday, but others will continue on their destructive paths. These people, regardless of their offenses or society's frustrations with their irresponsibility, must be treated as though they have some value and potential for good.

REFERENCES

Allen, F. 1985. The probationers speak: Analysis of the probationer's experiences and attitudes. *Federal Probation* 49: 67–75.

Bonczar, T. 1997. *Characteristics of adults on probation 1995*. Washington, DC: U.S. Department of Justice, Bureau of Justice Statistics.

Feddema, T. Probation supervisor, Wright County Probation, Rogers, MN. In discussion with the author, June 2004.

Glaze, L., and S. Pella. 2004. Probation and parole in the United States 2003. Washington, DC: U.S. Department of Justice, Bureau of Justice Statistics.

Lauen, R. 1997. *Positive approaches to corrections: Research, policy, and practice.* Marlboro, MD: American Corrections Association.

U.S. Department of Justice, 1999. *Survey of adults on probation—1995.* Bureau of Justice Statistics. ICPSR edition, July. Ann Arbor, MI: Interuniversity Consortium for Political and Social Research.

KEY POINTS

1. Research findings support the conclusions that those who work with offenders are dealing with an extremely diverse population of offenders.

2. Probation is applied as a mechanism for regulating the activities of those who are charged with weapons violations, obstruction of justice, traffice offenses, driving while intoxicated, drunkenness and morals, and other public order offenses.

3. Half of those on probation have had a sentence prior to probation or incarceration.

4. If placed on probation, an offender also has a good chance of serving some jail time.

5. Probationers hold many different jobs but, because of financial assessments and the like, some choose to work off the books.

6. Probationers are most likely to live in traditional housing (98 percent).

7. Over half of the probationers interviewed said that they would seek help somewhere else than from a probation officer.

8. One of the most interesting aspects of probation work is the clients that an officer works with on a daily basis.

9. A major problem offender is the alcoholic offender.

10. The distinction between felony and misdemeanor means little in terms of how an offender is controlled.

KEY TERMS

driving while intoxicated (DWI)   a traffic violation.

intensive supervision probation (ISP)   is a program developed to provide an alternative for juvenile offenders in lieu of removal from the home.

persons in need of supervision (PINS)   Juveniles who are considered to be out of control.

presentence investigation (PSI)   is a report given to the court that considers the offender's social history.

violation   is when a probationer disobeys one or more of the conditions of probation.

REVIEW QUESTIONS

1. What are the general characteristics of offenders on probation?

2. Based on the interviews with the probation officers in the chapter, describe the qualities of the person that would make an excellent probation officer.

Risk, Needs, and Treatment

6

The prediction of criminal behavior is perhaps one of the most central issues in the criminal justice system. From it stems community safety, prevention, treatment, ethics, and justice, but most importantly, the ability to predict an individual's future criminal behavior may weigh heavily in the probation officer's decision making (Andrews and Bonta 1998, 211). The implications are found in economic considerations, matters of fairness, general deterrence, and public support for the criminal justice system.

■ Establishing Workloads

Probation agencies use mission statements and policy directives to establish agency priorities. A carefully worded policy directive provides the officer with a clear understanding of what the agency expects under different circumstances. A distinction can be made between risk-screening devices that are used for administrative and management purposes and those designed to treat and rehabilitate the offender. Those with management purposes are designed to enhance control and predict criminal offenses. The treatment-rehabilitation systems of classification are based on the concept of differential treatment, which implies that the needs and problems of inmates and those in community supervision must be defined and treated on an individualized basis (Kratcoski 1985, 49).

The treatment-rehabilitation system tries to differentiate offenders on the basis of needs, attitudes, motivation, and attributes and then provide the treatment necessary to bring about the desired changes in values, attitudes, and skills that will inhibit offenders from recidivating.

If a probation director wishes to minimize the problems with the surveillance-service dichotomy, a risk-assessment instrument should be employed that takes into account the risk posed by keeping the offender in the community, as well as the needs the offender has that can be addressed by available resources. With the use of a computerized records system, it is also possible to monitor the progress of the case in such a way as to make sure that both risk and needs assessment are not being ignored. The risk-assessment tool provides a means of structuring the work environment so as to ensure that probation officers have comparable workloads and that clients are dealt with in a way that provides concern for both surveillance and personal needs (Clear et al. 1989). Each case should receive a workload value that represents the amount of work that each case is expected to require. This method helps to objectively assess how much work has accumulated on each caseload. This provides an effective means of distributing the work and reassigning officers to neighborhoods or districts. With the use of computers, it is also possible to monitor the probationer and probation officers (Lauen 1997).

Risk-needs assessment instruments have a number of useful applications (Andrews and Bonta 1995; Aubrey and Hough 1997). First, by offering a structured format for assessing the offender, they promote consistency in practice. Second, their use has been related to improvements in the quality of investigations and supervision plans (Roberts and Robinson 1998). Third, because the assessment is grounded in "scientific" evidence, risk-needs assessment instruments have contributed to the credibility of the assessment (Kemshall 1998). Assessment instruments have proven effective in predicting recidivism (Raynor et al. 2000) and it informs the level of supervision decisions appropriate to the offender. In addition, it allows consideration of the offender to change over the period of supervision (Raynor et al. 2000). Finally, risk-assessment instruments can provide information about changes in the criminogenic needs in the community (Merrington and Skins 2000).

A Clarification System

Without a risk-assessment tool, probation officers develop their own system of classification. Instead of treating all probationers alike, probation officers make an assessment of the probationer and assign each a priority for attention relative to other probationers. They make rough comparisons of the amount of time that can be given to surveillance and to casework based on the amount of time available. Probation officers do this intuitively as a function of managing their work. They make instinctive judgments based on personal experience, punishment ideology, their own view of the offender's problems, and the need for societal protection.

Serious problems, however, can emerge when the classification system is left to individual officers. First, there is no guarantee that bias, prejudice, and caprice will not enter into the classification process. An officer may spend an inordinate amount of time with a probationer the officer would like to see put in prison or with a probationer who is appealing and friendly. There are no assurances that the individual officer's classification system will reflect the goals of the organization (Clear et al. 1989, 186). The officer may be a renegade of sorts, who believes that the current "get-tough" approach to sentencing is nonsense and will continue to classify probationers according to a needs scheme, thereby downplaying the relevance of the risk posed by the probationer.

■ Evolution of Classification

In the last 30 years or so, it has become apparent that offenders are more diverse than previously conceptualized and pose diverse risks, have varying needs, and respond to treatment differently. To ascertain which offenders should be grouped together, correctional systems have used classification systems. This process has been aided by systematic assessment and testing procedures (Van Voorhis et al. 2000, 81). Bonta (1996) categorized risk-assessment measures within a developmental framework. First-generation techniques, **clinical assessments**, were based on clinical intuition and professional judgment. The clinician uses informal, nonobservable criteria for decision making after an interview and review of the case file. Essentially, it is a clinical process in which clinicians use their professional judgment to assess the offender's dangerousness, treatment needs, amenability to treatment, and risk of absconding. Ultimately, this technique proved ineffective. The approach was also considered too nonempirical and subjective for making important decisions and ultimately proved to have little validity (Meehl 1954, 220). This process also came under attack as being time consuming, inequitable, subjective, and discretionary (MacKenzie 1989).

clinical assessments were a clinical process in which clinicians use their professional judgment to assess the offender's dangerousness, treatment needs, amenability to treatment, and risk of absconding.

Warren (1971) points out that many offenders were treated alike and left unassessed because they were not matched to appropriate correctional programs reflecting their needs, characteristics, and circumstances. Quite often, the programs varied according to the case manager (Van Voorhis et al. 2000). Despite these findings, supporters continue to claim that other approaches are antihumanistic and mechanistic. Almost any approach that becomes routine can be accused of similar travesties.

The second-generation assessment devices, **actuarial assessments**, are based on the probability of something happening based on a record of previous occurrences. Scores are used to form the basis of decision making and only on the occasion of a compelling reason is the assessor given the power to override the recommendation. Much of the time these assessments are based on standardized, objective, static criminal-history risk items such as the federal government's Salient Factor Score. Static measures are of little help during classification and treatment because they do not reflect changes in the offender's behavior from time to time. Additional problems with actuarial approaches stem from the belief that they involve too much work, from a fear of statistical procedures, from antiscience training, from ethical misconceptions, and from a defense of one's self-concept as a competent professional (Gendreau et al. 1996, 65). Nonetheless,

actuarial assessments are a second-generation assessment device that relies on the probability of something happening based on a record of previous occurrences.

the actuarial objective-risk measures have proven to be a better classification method than the first-generation techniques. Grove and Meehl's meta-analysis of actuarial and clinical predictions studies (1996) shows that the actuarial approach performed better than the clinical approach in 46 percent of the studies and equally as well in another 48 percent. Only 6 percent of the time did the clinical study prove superior (Andrews and Bonta 1998, 220).

The third generation has developed in yet another direction. Instead of furthering the dispute between clinical and actuarial methods, the discussion now is focused on the identification and assessment of static versus dynamic criminogenic risk factors. Earlier approaches attended to **static risk factors**, or the historical attributes of the offender that do not and cannot change over time or the course of supervision. However, now there are risk prediction measures incorporating dynamic factors. This might include Baird and associates' 1981 Wisconsin System, Motiuk's 1993 Community Risk/Needs Management Scale, and Andrews and Bonta's 1995 Level of Service Inventory—Revised (LSI—R). In a comparison of the ability of dynamic and static instruments to predict recidivism, Gendreau (1996) found that the mean value for the correlation between risk and recidivism for the LSI—R, dynamic assessor, was a value of .35, for the static Salient Factor Score .29 and for the static Wisconsin .27. Gendreau, Goggin, and Paparozzi (1996) have speculated that the LSI—R is a better instrument because, unlike the SFS or the Wisconsin, it assesses a wide range of criminogenic needs.

Andrews, Bonta, and Hoge (1990) in their review of classification schemes put forward three basic assessment principles: risk, needs, and responsivity. The **risk principle** addresses concerns for incapacitation. In terms of community corrections, the risk principle is used to separate out offenders who pose little risk from those who require careful attention.

In a 1994 study, Andrews and Bonta identified four criminogenic factors as key problem areas: parenting, education, antisocial personality, and antisocial attitudes. Gendreau's (1996) meta-analysis revealed antisocial associates, attitudes, personality, and criminal history as criminogenic factors. Andrews and Bonta (1998) report that four of the most common criminogenic needs are antisocial associates, antisocial attitudes and values, history of antisocial behavior, and skill deficiencies, such as poor problem-solving skills, self-management or self-efficacy problems, impulsivity, poor self-control, and irresponsibility. They have also pointed out the necessity of identifying and attacking the need most associated with criminal behavior. Most risk-assessment instruments can be completed quickly by a probation officer if the officer has a completed presentence report and can interview the probationer.

■ Static and Dynamic Risk Factors

As discussed previously, risk instruments employ static and dynamic factors. *Static risk factors* are historical attributes of the offender that do not and cannot change over time or the course of supervision. Race or age at first arrest is one such factor. One such instrument that uses static factors is the U.S. Parole Board's Salient Factor Score (SFS) (Hoffman 1994), which is better suited for

static risk factors are historical attributes of the offender that do not and cannot change over time or the course of supervision.

risk principle is posited on the notion that criminal behavior can be predicted and that the risk of offending can be reduced by matching the level of services to the risk level of the offender, thus bridging assessment and effective treatment.

security and custody than identifying treatment needs. The SFS was developed to assist the Federal Bureau of Prisons, during a time when parole was abolished for newly sentenced federal prisoners. It considers the following matters:

- prior convictions
- prior commitments
- age at current offense
- recent commitment-free period
- probation-parole-confinement-escape status violator
- history of opiate dependence

All of these are static factors. Because the SFS uses static measures for its instrument, an offender who 20 years ago was imprisoned at age 16 for an auto theft while high on heroin would today fall into the poor-risk category. Research indicates respectable predictive validity with correlations of recidivism ranging from .27 (Hoffman and Beck 1984) to .45 (Hoffman 1994). Static factor instruments are not likely to teach much about what resources to direct at the offender as part of the treatment (Andrews and Bonta 1994; Gendreau and Ross 1987).

<u>Dynamic risk factors</u>, or *criminogenic variables,* are personal attributes that are subject to change such as criminal history, employment record, education, marital status, antisocial associates, attitudes, and personality. It is possible to develop a risk instrument that relies on dynamic factors that can be used primarily for treatment (Van Voorhis 2000). Treatment depends on dynamic factors because treatment specialists need to know what they can change and where they can have a significant impact. The dynamic risk variables, or criminogenic need factors, are prime candidates for selection as the target of service programs (Andrews and Bonta 1998, 224). This is most evidently possible when a risk-assessment instrument is applied to offenders over a period of time as they progress through probation. Their risk scores should fall as they involve themselves in change. Recognizing the importance of dynamic factors allows for the predictability of recidivism to be greatly increased through the monitoring of changes in and situation of the offenders.

dynamic risk factors (criminogenic variables) are personal attributes that are subject to change such as criminal history, employment record, education, marital status, antisocial associates, attitudes, and personality.

■ Current Risk-Needs Instruments

Andrews and Bonta (1998) have identified three offender risk-needs instruments in use today:

1. Wisconsin Risk and Needs Assessment Instrument (Baird et al. 1979)

2. Community Risk-Needs Management Scale (Motiuk and Porporino 1989)

3. Level of Service Inventory—Revised (Andrews and Bonta 1995)

Wisconsin Risk and Needs Assessment Instrument

The Wisconsin Risk and Needs Assessment Instrument (Baird et al. 1979; Baird et al. 1989) became the prototype for probation and parole instruments (Van Voorhis 2000). This instrument offers an assessment of the offender's risk, needs, and management classification. Items identifying risk are address changes, time employed in the last 12 months, alcohol problems, drug problems, attitude, age of first conviction, prior probation supervisions, prior revocations, prior felony convictions, juvenile convictions, and convictions for assault.

The needs factors include such items as academic/vocational skills, employment, financial management, family relationships, companions, emotional stability, alcohol usage, drug involvement, mental ability, healthy sexual behavior, and the agent's impression. Probationers are classified as high-, medium-, or low-risk offenders. As with most instruments, the items chosen are statistical predictors of failure while on probation. This actuarial approach is based on closed cases. In the Wisconsin instrument, classification decisions are based on the higher score of either the risk or the needs and not a combination of the two. High-risk probationers are given careful, and if necessary, daily attention, while low-risk offenders are seen once a month or virtually not at all in some jurisdictions with very high caseloads. <u>Differential supervision</u> allows for the use of resources where they are most needed. A primary problem of the Wisconsin instrument is the lack of predictive validity of the needs scale. The needs scale was developed without any appreciation that some offender needs are actually risk factors. The Wisconsin instrument allows the staff to identify needs as problems and the research consisted of tabulating how much time staff devoted to dealing with these problems. Whether these problems had anything to do with criminal behavior was never evaluated by the developers of the Wisconsin instrument (Andrews and Bonta 1998, 227–228).

differential supervision notes offenders that are classified as high, medium, or low risks and are given services reflecting their risks and needs.

Community Risk-Needs Management Scale

The Community Risk-Needs Management Scale was developed for parolees in Canada. The linking of needs with static risk assessment is an important improvement over the Wisconsin classification system. In other words, this instrument uses a single calculation to determine the offenders' level of needs or risks. Research conducted by Motiuk and Porporino (1989) on Canadian parolees indicates an ability to identify low- and high-risk recidivists. Two of the items on the scale—mental ability and health—are similar to those used on the Wisconsin needs instrument but again there is some doubt as to whether they successfully predict parole outcome.

Level of Service Inventory—Revised

The instrument that is receiving most of the praise today is the Level of Service Inventory—Revised (LSI—R). The LSI—R was developed out of a need for probation and parole officers in the 1970s to become more explicit about how decisions were made regarding differential supervision models and types of services provided to probationers. It has the ability to reduce overclassifying or false positives among offenders so that they receive the level of supervision required. During a period of diminished resources, there is a sense that such instruments should be directed toward offenders with high risk and high needs. There is a desire to develop an instrument that could quantitatively aid decision making and could be easily administered. Robinson (2003) offers an interesting discussion of the LSI—R, reporting on officer interests in the use of risk-needs assessment instruments as they improve the consistency and quality of assessments. Her research indicates that officers found a sense of reassurance, security, and a back-up to decisions made as a positive aspect of LSI—R use. It also allows the probation officer to profile the criminogenic needs of the local offender population so as to influence planning and policy decisions.

The LSI—R, as administered by case managers and counselors, is used by probation officers in their daily classification, placement, and treatment decisions (Lauen 1997, 128). There is an expectation that the instrument contains a list of comprehensive items deemed relevant to differential supervision and decision making. The assessment is done through the application of a structured interview (Andrews and Bonta 1995). The LSI—R samples 54 risk-needs factors. Each is scored on a 0–1 scale and distributed across 11 subcategories.

Components of the LSI—R

The LSI—R is comprised of various components: criminal history, employment history, education, financial considerations, family/marital information, living accommodations, recreation, companionship questions, substance abuse, psychological treatment history, and attitude toward crime and law enforcement.

As a Treatment Model

The LSI—R calls for a specific type of treatment model. Attitudes, criminal history, and associates are major correlates of offender populations. These characteristics are also identified in the social learning model. As a classification strategy, the LSI—R fits programs grounded in behavioral, social learning, and cognitive-behavioral treatment strategies. Research indicates that behavioral variables are most likely to respond to change (Andrews 1990; Gendreau 1995; Lipsey 1992; Palmer 1992; Van Voorhis 2000). Behavior variables would include choosing whether or not to drink, look for a job, attend school, or develop a new group of friends. The LSI—R targets important criminogenic needs in a way that can be used by programs known to be the most effective with offenders. Changes in the LSI—R score are associated with changes in recidivism (Andrews and Bonta 1998, 243).

Conducting the LSI—R

The LSI—R requires two separate forms: an interview guide and the LSI—R survey form. The interview guide is quite comprehensive in addressing various areas. The form allows the probation officer to review a number of concerns, score each, and then provide a summary score indicating the level of risk or need indicated for each offender. To achieve answers to these questions the probationer is asked a series of questions from the interview schedule. Although some questions are fairly clearcut such as whether the offender has a prior record or not, there are other questions that consider a wider range of answers.

Interview Guide As with other instruments, the LSI—R instructions warn that offenders cannot be relied on to tell the truth. Offenders certainly have an interest in purposely misrepresenting their situation or in failing to answer fully due to a memory lapse or misunderstanding. Therefore, it is essential to thoroughly investigate and verify any information on the offender. In order to achieve a good understanding of the presence or absence of an attribute identified on the LSI—R schedule, it is necessary for the probation officer to use an interview guide. Probation officer presentence worksheets provide a similar function. Both allow the officer to ask a series of questions to obtain answers providing the basis for scoring on a single item. For example, the family/marital item is concerned with the level of satisfaction with the marriage or equivalent situation and whether relationships with parents and others in the family are rewarding. To obtain some understanding of this situation, the interviewer asks a series of questions related to arguments, sexual activity, infidelity, unwanted pregnancy, child rearing, in-laws, money, companions, leisure time, ex-partners, individual problems, intimacy, communication, dependency, divorce, custody, harassment, and abuse. Further open-ended questions are asked regarding relationships with parents and other relatives.

The emotional/personal section helps identify whether the offender is able to respond to life's stressors and how well the person functions in the "real" world. Particular attention is given to anxiety levels and mild depression and whether the person is receiving appropriate treatment. Those who are suspected of suffering severe problems are studied for indications of active psychosis. Questions are addressed toward emotional stability, thoughts, and urges. To further this process, the interviewer pays attention to body language and the quality of responses. Questions are asked about past and present treatment and any psychological assessment.

In terms of human dignity and restorative justice it is important to develop within the offender a sense of shame for the crime and acceptance of responsibility. The LSI—R interview guide asks the offender to express how he or she feels about the crime. Does the offender feel that it was wrong? Is there any sympathy for the victim? Does the offender have any interest in leading a conventional life involving work and education? Further questions address the appropriateness of any sentence and whether probation is a fair and reasonable punishment.

The LSI—R is not intended to replace the presentence report but can provide a fair assessment of the risk/needs of the offender. If the interview form is thoroughly covered, there is going to be a great deal of information on which to base a risk-needs assessment. It is important for the probation officer to have some understanding of psychological assessment techniques and to stay clear of being overwhelmed by all of the material.

Interpretation

Interpretation of the LSI—R score is based on recognition of the presence of negative attributes or the absence of a positive attribute. Scorers examine the total score to determine what level of risk the offender is. The total score is based on what percentile the offender is placed in by his or her score (which gives the offender's level of risk) and chance of recidivating. Following this, the assessor examines any particular area which has a particularly high score for that area. The last step is to take an even closer look at subcategories that seem troublesome. Groups of offenders achieving a certain score will be assigned a certain level of supervision.

Subcomponents Each major subcomponent has a series of subscales: criminal history, education, and employment have ten subscales, financial has two subscales, marital/family has four subscales, companions has four subscales, drugs and alcohol has nine subscales, emotional/personality has five subscales, and attitudes has five subscales. Combined, these subscales identify, assess, and prioritize criminogenic needs. Dynamic and static items are interspersed throughout the 10 LSI—R subscales. Thirteen of the most dynamic risk factors, found in the subscales, are attached to enhance inter-rater reliability—that is, those who use the instrument have similar scores with similar offenders. The items comprising the LSI—R reflect research that shows theoretical relevance about criminal conduct, including antisocial associates, antisocial attitudes, antisocial personality, and criminal history. These are reflected in the subcomponents of criminal history, companions and attitudes/orientation, and emotional/personal. Other related factors are family, substance abuse, and social achievement. Information gathered on criminal associates determines to what extent these associates reward criminal behavior or attach cost to anticriminal behavior. Distinctions are made between friends and mere acquaintances (Andrews and Bonta 1998, 229). The protocol for scoring these 13 subscales is to first rate the scale according to the anchors in the scoring guide and then to score the item according to the rating. A score of 0 or 1 counts as a "hit," indicating a need for action or intervention; a score of 2 or 3 does not count. In general, a rating of 0 indicates little if any prosocial reinforcement; a rating of 1 indicates some prosocial reinforcement, but an inadequate amount; a 2 is adequate; and a 3 is optimum. By adding up the total score on the 13 items' ratings, one can derive a measure of the protective factors that are inversely related to the individual's risk factors. In other words, those who achieve a high score are a low risk and those who obtain a low score are a high risk. Such scoring helps to identify risk-needs at intake, at various times during probation, and at discharge to learn how an offender is doing or how an overall caseload is doing (Lauen 1997, 128). As with other instruments, the LSI—R provides for the reassessment of the offender's risk score. Reassessment scores can be a valuable tool in assessing program effectiveness and facilitating program release (Van Voorhis et al. 1995).

Problems with the LSI—R

Generally speaking, any prediction of criminal conduct involves four possible outcomes:

1. true positive, where the officer is convinced the offender will reoffend and the offender does
2. false positive, where the officer is convinced the offender will reoffend but the offender does not
3. false negative, where the offender is predicted to not offend but does
4. true negative, where the offender is predicted to not reoffend and the offender does not.

Andrews and Bonta (1998) have generated further calculations of the indices of predictive accuracy. They note that the overall proportion of correct prediction is true positives plus true negatives divided by the number of total predictions. The overall proportion of incorrect predictions is false positives plus false negatives divided by the number of total predictions. It is crucial to understand that predictive accuracy requires more information than any one predictive category. The rates of false positives, false negatives, true positives, and true negatives, as well as the magnitude of the association between the risk predictor and criminal behavior, are all influenced by base rates and selection ratios. In reality, the risk-assessment approach yielding the greatest overall correct predictions may not always be chosen. Changing the cutoff scores or the selection ratios of what is defined as low risk will influence the overall prediction and proportion of errors (Andrews and Bonta 1998, 215).

The prediction of dangerousness is particularly problematical. If the officer is convinced the offender will commit a violent crime, but does not, it is considered a false positive. This person has been treated unjustly. On the other hand, if an offender is released from supervision and commits a violent crime, it is a false negative. These results can be tragic in human and social terms—and because violent crime is such a rare event, accounting for only 10 percent of criminal behavior, making no prediction at all about a person's behavior would lead the officer to be correct in 90 percent of the cases. As a consequence, the standards for predictive accuracy are very high (Andrews and Bonta 1998, 219).

LSI—R at Work

The LSI—R has received much attention with respect to its value as a risk-needs assessment instrument. Most of the comments about the instrument come from the developers. Because there is no perfect instrument, there is a need to discuss various concerns that might come to anyone's attention who uses this instrument (Kinzinger 2002).

Robinson (2003) has reported on officer comments about the LSI—R. When the instrument was first applied, officers expressed a growing sense of professional insecurity around levels of indeterminacy. Probation officers expressed concern that their professional judgment would be minimized in the face of results produced by an exacting instrument. Officers reacted to this perception by continuing to value their own professional assessment of the offender. The instrument was considered a reinforcement of their own professional view of the offender.

Robinson also reports that once incorporated into daily practice, the LSI—R places considerable demands on time and paperwork. The desire for technical proficiency has not been balanced against its user-friendliness. Despite continued positive reinforcement to keep the practitioner on board, Robinson (p. 36) learned that the commitment of many practitioners waned over time. Some officers had come to resent the instrument, especially when they were unable to see how the LSI—R was particularly helpful within their own organization. Consequently, the LSI—R became relatively marginalized within the organization. Some deterioration of support was due to the agency's inability to use the LSI—R information to enhance quality control and procedures (Robinson, 2003). Officers did not receive any feedback on their completed assessments and some felt that their assessments were disappearing into a black hole. What is needed is a database for the capturing of LSI—R data with a management information system feedback mechanism.

There are other areas of concern relative to the LSI—R: one is its standardization and the other is whether or not the instrument meets the offender's needs. In applying the LSI—R, there is a need to standardize and manualize every application. Asking questions differently causes variations in outcome, and yet, asking the same question of a man or woman can result in a different interpretation. Women have special concerns relative to their station in life and their need to care for a family when in the role of principal breadwinner. Another key area concerns self-esteem. Although the LSI—R declares that self-esteem is not a criminogenic need, there is a considerable body of research supporting such concerns among young women. More instruction might be considered to ensure that every assessment is considered to reflect this issue. In addition, the authors of the LSI—R are careful to note that assessors should have an understanding of psychological testing and interpretation. The normative groupings on which individual scores are compared consist of individuals who served time in a Canadian correctional facility. It would be useful to develop normative standards reflecting offender populations drawn from male and female probationers throughout the United States. Furthermore, a good remedy necessitates careful clinical supervision to ensure a proper application. This requires time, training, supervision, and professional expertise. Despite doing this, drift occurs from person to person over time. In other words, not the same interpretation is given to the same facts by the same interpreter at T1 and T2 and T3. Officers may not be aware of drifting but only feel differently about a particular case at various times. They do not recognize a cumulative pattern. Information systems can help an officer overcome such tendencies.

Conducting Assessments

The capacity to conduct formalized risk assessments is directly related to the number of resources a correctional agency has at its disposal (Motiuk 1999, 171). The political nature of state budgets has created unstable service delivery systems, creating problems for professionals and clients alike. Professionals recommending one program over another must take into account whether a specific service will be available from one budget cycle to another. Thus, it is one thing to identify a series of criminogenic needs, and it is quite another to effectively address each of these needs in a timely fashion. Organizational responsivity is a concept reflecting the agency's ability to provide these needed services. The more resources an agency has, the more attention it can give to risk and treatment needs. The offender's needs cannot be determined solely on the LSI—R instrument but must incorporate the use of various supplemental tools brought to bear in the measurement of IQ, learning ability, and behavioral disorders. In conjunction with accumulating this knowledge, it is necessary to transfer knowledge about the assessment to an understanding of criminogenic factors, and once done, to prioritize them. There is a need to not only identify these factors but also to establish some priority of interests and concern. To do this properly requires a user-friendly but sophisticated management information system. All in all, this is a fairly costly process, which can generate a great deal of information requiring careful analysis. Some officers may get caught up in this process and spend inordinate amounts of time poring over data, looking for some clue that unlocks the problem only to see that after all of this time, there is little time for other things. Additionally, it is possible to simply overwhelm the officer with all of this information, so much so that the system is only used in its basic form without regard to its many valuable features. The research and evaluation unit may, in some cases, find greater use for the LSI—R than the officers.

■ Treatment

For treatment purposes, the risk principle requires identification of high-, medium-, and low-risk offenders. There is a need to direct intensive treatment programs at high-risk offenders and reconsider wasting valuable resources on intensive placements and comprehensive treatment programs for low-risk offenders (Andrews and Bonta 1994). Today, offender-assessment systems are used not only to identify the level of offender risk but also to identify the level of offender needs. Consideration of various needs requires attending to the risk, needs, responsivity, and **professional discretion** principles (Andrews and Bonta 1998).

professional discretion is when a probation officer uses his or her own experience and personal understanding to override the assessment findings, which might seem contradicted.

Risk

Until now, risk has been employed to predict dangerous behavior. Presently, there is an effort to match level of treatment services to the risk level of the offender. High-risk offenders are seen as needing more intensive treatment if society is to hope for a significant reduction in recidivism (Andrews and Bonta 1998, 243). The risk principle is posited on the notion that criminal behavior can be predicted and that the risk of offending can be reduced by matching the level of treatment services to the risk level of the offender, thus bridging assessment and effective treatment. Because there are high proportions of felony offenders on probation, programs must be careful to provide intensive and extensive services that appropriately address the offender's condition. It is known that highly intensive programs are effective with high-risk offenders but not low-risk offenders (Andrews et al. 1990).

Need

needs principle is used to determine who should receive certain services based on the presence of various criminogenic needs: antisocial associates, antisocial attitudes and values, history of antisocial behavior, and skill deficiencies, such as poor problem-solving skills, self-management or self-efficacy problems, impulsivity, poor self-control, and irresponsibility.

The **needs principle** is addressed by the case manager in determining who should receive certain services, whether it is drug treatment, job placement, education, counseling, or medical assistance. As stated earlier, Andrews and Bonta (1998) identified four of the most common criminogenic needs. They have also pointed out that it is necessary to identify and attack the need most associated with criminal behavior.

Offender needs come in a variety of forms and differ in place and time. Need assessments cover a variety of issues, including the offender's health, intellectual ability, behavioral/emotional problems, alcohol abuse, drug abuse, educational status, and vocational status. Once again, it is important to attend to dynamic criminogenic needs of the most serious offenders. Attention is to be given to those dynamic needs that can be altered. Noncriminogenic needs may be dynamic and subject to change, too, but according to the current models, they are not going to influence recidivism. Future study may indicate that needs instruments must change to address different technological advances in such areas as street-level drug usage and other behavior such as sexual deviance. Instruments such as the LSI—R are directly relevant to identification of various needs (Andrews and Bonta 1998).

Responsivity

For most of its history, treatment in corrections has involved a search for a panacea that would solve all treatment problems for all offenders (Finckenauer 1982). However, the concept of the *interaction effect*—that most types of treatment are effective for some types of offenders and not others, and that no treatment is effective for everybody—is one of the most widely documented concepts in the field of correctional rehabilitation (Gottfredson 1979; Grant and Grant 1962; Palmer 1976; Ross and Gendreau 1981; Warren 1973).

Responsivity is a term for client-based factors that influence the potential for positive treatment effects (Kennedy and Serin 1997). Simply put, it means that if the offender is in the right program, there is a greater chance of reduced recidivism. The **responsivity principle** refers to the delivery of treatment programs in a style and mode that are consistent with the ability and learning style of the offender. The responsivity principle is based on the belief that offenders are human beings and that behavioral/social and learning/cognitive approaches are the most powerful and influential strategies available in the treatment of offenders. It is now understood that program integrity is not sufficient alone for effective interventions but these interventions must target criminogenic needs, match offenders with treatment modalities, match therapist and offender characteristics, match offender learning styles with relevant programs, and identify sufficient levels of treatment readiness. Several of these principles are central to the treatment of offenders while maintaining their human dignity. Responsivity addresses recognition of the importance of individual qualities in each officer and offender. It is a natural analogue for carrying forward the principles of human dignity. It cannot be forgotten that offenders are autonomous, mostly rational persons deserving of respect because they are capable of moral choices and of assessing their condition in a self-reflective, self-activating, self-directing, self-criticizing, self-correcting, and self-understanding manner. In other words, combining responsivity with human dignity requires treatment of the offender with a measure of respect because the offender has a worth that is not measured by his or her offense but by virtue of possessing characteristics that all people possess. Responsivity requires that after assessment, the offender not be treated as an aggregate of data, ignoring the individual qualities that got the offender in trouble in the first place. It must not be forgotten that combining responsivity and human dignity means that the offender assumes responsibility for the offense and the choices leading up to the offense. To do otherwise treats this person as less than human. Antecedent conditions may be important but it is the reaction to these conditions that is important, not their very presence.

responsivity principle refers to the delivery of treatment programs in a style and mode that are consistent with the ability and learning style of the offender.

Concepts such as amenability, motivation, compliance, treatment response, and treatment gain all contribute to the notion of responsivity (Kennedy and Serin 1997). **Treatability** refers to the clinical determination of how well offenders will respond to certain treatment modalities and environmental conditions. Individual factors affecting responsivity are internal and external. Internal factors such as motivation, personality characteristics (anxiety, depression, self-esteem, and poor social skills), and other demographic factors such as race, gender, ethnicity, and age also play a part in treatment readiness (Dana 1993). Motivation to succeed while on probation is important for offenders who achieve a successful discharge because this may be the first success they have had in their lives. Graduation ceremonies are important reinforcers for them. Some people respond better to professional support. Enhancing offender motivation requires careful assessment of resistance. Motivation and treatment readiness are additional factors. The desire to change is an important but complicated factor. Not everyone shares the same motivations. Voluntary participation in any treatment process is viewed as essential.

treatability refers to the clinical determination of the offenders who will respond most favorably to certain treatment modalities and environmental conditions.

Resistance

Community programs serving the entire community will have many voluntary clients, but obviously, probationers may not be counted among them. According to Masters, "Generally speaking, anyone who feels coerced into counseling will fight back in the form of resistance" (Masters 1994, 165). Resistance is manifested in several ways, including open hostility, aggression, rejection, denial, talking about safe issues, being overly cooperative, never accomplishing anything, setting unrealistic goals, devoting minimal effort, and avoiding responsibility (Egan 1990). Resistance is also manifested in efforts to avoid accountability. This is played out by probationers who point out staff inadequacies, build themselves up by putting others down, tell officers what they want to hear rather than the truth, omit the truth, distort the truth or disclose what can benefit them, are vague, invoke irrelevant issues such as race, and attempt to confuse the officer. Offenders can also minimize the situation, agree to things without meaning it, remain silent, pay attention only when it matters to them, make a scene about minor points, use "I forgot" to deal with obligations not completed, degrade others, quibble over the meaning of things, try to embarrass others, use anger as a weapon, become inattentive, accuse others of misunderstanding, claim that change occurs even if it is only once, use prior experiences as means of accusing the officer of incompetence, and use race, gender, or cultural bias as a means of deflecting attention (Stearns, MN County Probation 2001).

The Officer's Response Probationer resistance can cause problems for an officer, particularly if he or she responds with anger, guilt, irritation, rejection, or panic and turns away from helping the probationer or reemphasizing probationer control. At this point, the officer must recognize there are other people involved with the probationer, too, and that the officer does not have to win the battle alone. Consistency of team play is important. Maintaining patience is essential. The first appropriate reaction is to honestly face the presence of resistance, thus openly facing the probationer's resistance. Second, the officer must confront the probationer with a specific discussion of the resistance as it poses an obstacle to their relationship. Third, it is imperative that the probation officer be realistic and deal with the offender's feelings of coercion. Once identified, it is hoped that the probationer and probation officer can move beyond it (Masters 1994, 167). Fourth, it is necessary to permit the offender to save face by empathizing with the probationer's anger about being coerced into counseling. The probation officer may suggest that mandatory treatment was something the court ordered and is beyond the officer's control. Fifth, the probation officer can try to see if there is some honest reason for what is an apparent case of probationer resistance to treatment. Last, it helps to label the session an office visit or reporting rather than counseling. Whatever the reason, it is important for the probation officer to react slowly to the problems presented by the probationer despite the sense of urgency found with high-volume caseloads. Further movement in the counseling process is possible if the probationer feels some anxiety about the problems before him or her. Anxiety can be created by criticism directed toward the probationer or the officer can wait until the probationer has hit rock bottom to see if help will be welcomed. Probation officers have to be alert to strike while the iron is hot and react to clues that may not be obvious (Harris and Watkins 1987). This final approach is characteristic of motivational interviewing, which is discussed at length in Chapter 7.

Responsivity is based on the notion that there can be potent interactions between the characteristics of individuals and external factors such as the settings or situations (Gendreau and Ross 1979; 1981). Matching the client to the appropriate level of help is not new. The Gluecks (1950), Palmer (1976), and I-Level Classification all have discussed the importance of differential treatment. Responsivity requires attending to the offender's characteristics so that a match can be made with appropriate treatment programs. For example, it would be inappropriate to put a teen with drinking problems in an adult therapy group. Clients differ in many important ways, especially in terms of what they understand about their problems. Some clients need to simply understand themselves better. Reading a book about anger management may be just fine for someone with sufficient reading skills whose anger is not a cause for arrest but was one of the reasons for the use of drugs.

Responsivity also relates to different styles of officer communication. Some officers are more empathetic than others. Some officers clearly are better suited to work with juveniles, women, special-need offenders, or adults. According to Andrews (1994), interaction must be put in a context. Interpersonally anxious offenders, such as juveniles, do not respond well to a highly confrontational and critical interpersonal approach, as might be found in a directive interviewing style.

Matching Officer to Probationer

In conjunction with responsivity is the **matching principle**. The matching principle recognizes that offenders have unique treatment needs, have their own learning style, and are at different stages of readiness to change (Hester and Williams 1995). The three components of responsivity include matching the treatment approach to the learning style and personality of the offender, matching the characteristics of the offender with those of the therapist, and matching the skills of the therapist with the type of program (Gendreau 1994). First, what is needed is a careful assessment of the offender in terms of learning style and motivation. Second, it is necessary to know the special skills of each officer, including counseling styles and supervision methods. Third, there must be a matching of the offender and staff in ways that complement each other. Finally, when brokering with outside services, the officer must be sure the program is capable of providing similar levels of service matches (Lauen 1997). Aside from carefully assessing the probationer, it is necessary to carefully assess the officer and related program treatment staff. Further difficulties arise as offenders change, programs change, staff move on, and cynicism develops among overworked officers.

matching principle recognizes that offenders have unique treatment needs, have their own learning style, and are at different stages of readiness to change.

Responsivity Essentials

Probation officers spend much of their day speaking with people about various matters. Many officers are highly skilled interviewers, facilitators, and problem solvers. Many of them have the ability to enter a crisis and see it through to a successful conclusion. The successful officer has the ability to communicate effectively. Officers should develop a relationship with their clients based on genuine interests, warmth, honesty, humor, assurance, empathy, and intelligence. Essentially the officer must display a high measure of maturity and comfort with him- or herself. To work effectively, the officer must be reflective, directed, resolute, well-ordered, and flexible; exhibit appropriately behavior; and be willing to offer reinforcement. It is also essential that prominence be given to appropriate discretion, dignity, genuine expressions, **congruence**, **empathic functioning**, and **unconditional positive regard**.

Professional Discretion

Discretion plays an important part of any treatment scheme. Prediction and discretion go hand-in-hand. Assuming that a probation officer has a sufficient knowledge base of offender recidivism rates, he or she can feel relatively comfortable making predictions about tendencies toward future criminal behavior. However, sooner or later there is a case that does not fit the paradigm. There are times when the officer utilizes experience and personal understanding to override the assessment findings, which might seem contraindicated. This is what Robinson (2003) referred to as *indeterminacy*. Overrides can be used effectively to bring an assessment in line with the reality of the client population. Scores based heavily on static factors are not likely to change and officers can only hold someone accountable for things he or she can control. Moreover, with the use of management information systems, it is possible to continually assess the progress of various instruments to keep the instruments up-to-date with changing offender characteristics and contemporary reality (Lauen 1997).

Human Dignity and Professionalism

Of central importance is the use of human dignity as it is applied to discretionary decision making relative to any risk-needs assessment device. For example, let's consider the case of a 35-year-old unemployed, divorced, struggling crime-fiction writer who was convicted of assault. He has prior convictions for trespassing when he was 15 and another for a DWI charge when he was 24, for which he was given 3 years of probation along with a 30-day jail sentence. For several years, he has not held a job for longer than a few weeks. He has a record of receiving public assistance, is a graduate of a local college, and holds a bachelor's degree in English. He was married but recently divorced. He does not get along with his ex-wife or with his extended family members. He lives in a low-rent apartment in a high-crime neighborhood. His residence changes every 90 days. He has a variety of friends who have checkered pasts but his friends and associates who have criminal histories have been crime free for some time. He also occasionally uses marijuana and alcohol when he is with friends. He shares their views that the drug laws in this country are ridiculous and cause more trouble than they are worth. He thinks his probation officer paid too much attention to his drug use when he was on probation. Because of his DWI conviction, he has seen a therapist about his drinking and drug use. He does not feel that these drugs interfere with his work or social relations but they do alleviate his depression, which strikes him hard sometimes.

Based on the scoring system devised for the LSI—R, this struggling writer could achieve a score as high as 33. This would suggest that he deserves maximum supervision. On the other hand, one has to ask if this is appropriate in light of the offender's lifestyle and criminal history. A community with little crime

congruence a term coined by psychotherapist Carl Rogers, occurs whenever one's thoughts, speech, and actions are consistent with affect and body language.

empathic functioning refers to the degree to which the counselor can achieve an empathetic understanding of the client's personal frame of reference.

unconditional positive regard is the ability to understand the behavior of the offender while not rejecting the offender in the personal and humanistic sense.

might suggest he is an excellent candidate for probation, but in a high-crime community, he would be placed under moderate supervision at best and possibly even minimum supervision. Professional override is necessary to avoid over-classification but nonetheless the offender shows up in the database as a high risk. Cutoff points are a matter for treatment plans and not for punishment. Despite whatever assessment is made in 10 or 15 minutes, the offender may disagree with the assessment because he knows he is different than the score achieved. Effective change recognizes a measure of self-determinism and self-respect and offenders can be self-correcting individuals, given sufficient time and support. If there is recognition of his autonomy, there can be movement forward as he changes. In the exercise of professional discretion, it is also necessary to realize that respect for the offender's dignity is essential. The offender must be allowed to make mistakes and to experiment in decision making, especially when it comes to granting him a measure of autonomy. As was stated in the introduction, an assessment cannot become a stereotypic instrument, viewing the offender as merely a member of a classification. Respecting the dignity of the offender is essential to the entire process.

Human Dignity and the Probationer

Human dignity is intimately related to recognizing the offender's need for human autonomy as a rational person who will make mistakes. Remember that autonomous beings are self-activating, self-directing, self-criticizing, self-correcting, and self-understanding; they are also self-reflective and should be able to come up with their own plan for action. The strengthening of self is an essential quality of human dignity. As the offender assesses his or her actions and becomes reflective of his or her strengths and weaknesses, he or she can become empowered to change. Therefore, whatever needs assessment instrument is to be used, it should be a self-assessment instrument that is consistent with self-dignity, resulting in the person being self-directing, self-assessing, and self-correcting. Such a procedure leads to greater reality testing and understanding. Offenders begin to understand what took place and begin to ask if they are worthy of the care given them by others (self-esteem). At this point, in a sentencing circle or another restorative process, offenders truly believe they are not going to offend again because they are accepted for who they are and are able to move beyond the woe-is-me phase in their lives, resisting victim status and coming to terms with their actions. They realize that they alone are responsible for their actions and that there are other ways of behaving.

Treatment Direction

Today, treatment is not intended to make the offender an entirely fully-functioning individual; treatment is instead directed at reducing recidivism. This goal is more direct and less obtuse than the general concept of rehabilitation. The supervising agent is given specific, identifiable, and measurable criteria on which to base program actions. Officers are free to ignore a host of problems poor people experience that are related to health and welfare. If the offender has child care needs or AIDS, so be it. Attending to such issues, although very laudable and humanitarian, is not consistent with the need to reduce recidivism. Allowing such an emphasis to become paramount runs the risk of creating a single-minded officer who appears insensitive to the overall needs of the offender and furthers the prospect the offender will be treated with less dignity. One important point to remember is that poor people will not go away if their problems are not addressed, and officers who appear to care for more than criminogenic needs will continue to find there are ample opportunities to direct the offender to various services. For the overburdened officer, such an emphasis will allow better use of existing time and attention.

Dignity

Probationers who are interpersonally anxious do not respond well to highly confrontational or critical exchanges, while the less anxious can respond as long as there is a background condition of caring and respect (Andrews 1994). Probationers must be treated as though they have worth, so they can learn to treat others as if they, too, have worth. Appropriate modeling of behavior through thought, word, and deed teaches the probationer how to assess his or her own behavior, especially behavior that teaches respect. Appropriate modeling is the key to effective learning and to the cognitive learning processes associated with thoughts, beliefs, values, and perceptions (Bandura 1977).

According to Bandura and others (Andrews and Bonta 1994; Bandura 1965, 1977; Bandura et al. 1963; Bandura and Walters 1963), good models display the qualities of attractiveness, competence, enthusiasm, openness, and flexibility and afford others a chance to express their feelings and opinions. A probation officer retains the belief in the client's ability to succeed and in his or her inherent worth as an individual. Good role models also maintain an environment of mutual liking, respect, and caring in which openness, warmth, and understanding are offered within the limits of an appropriate interpersonal boundary (Van Voorhis 2000, 152)

A probation officer who is a good model and has good interpersonal skills can discourage criminogenic factors such as antisocial associates, antisocial attitudes and values, and antisocial behavior and address skill deficiencies, such as poor problem-solving skills, self-management or self-efficacy problems, impulsivity, poor self-control, and irresponsibility. The probation officer must defeat any expeditious, ends-justify-the-means thinking that denies the significance of the victim or the presence of any victim at all. Samenow (1984, 1989) points out that offenders often blame others for their crimes, deny responsibility for their actions, fail to understand the concept of injury, fail to empathize with the victim, fail to put enough effort forward to accomplish goals, assume ownership of others' property, and fail to understand what is trustworthy behavior. Offenders also may expect others to adopt their way of thinking, make rash decisions, refuse to let their pride suffer for a mistake, have flawed understanding of the time and effort needed for success, refuse to accept criticism, deny occasions of real fear, use anger to control others, and seem overzealous in their efforts to obtain power. In sum, offenders experience a great deal of distorted thinking, which functions as a considerable impediment to change. Probation officers who are not treating the offender with dignity will also engage in the same sort of thinking.

Appropriate Modeling

Appropriate modeling reinforces definite expressions of concern. This attitude is exhibited in moments of steadfastness, kindness, charity, forgiveness, understanding, patience, support, and sincerity. Officers can also exhibit trust, warmth, praise, and empathy by eye contact, handshakes, smiles, the sharing of experiences, the holding of timely meetings, and efforts to give the probationer undivided attention when in the office. Conversely, probationers should receive a clear explanation of the counselor's reasons for approval or disapproval, with suggestions for the appropriate behavior if necessary (Van Voorhis 2000, 152).

In the modeling process, and in conjunction with efforts to attack dysfunctional thoughts, beliefs, and attitudes, special consideration should be made to support and encourage ideas promoting human dignity in consideration of past actions and future behavior. Probationers should be encouraged to attend to personal statements that express disrespect. Appropriate recognition should be given to statements expressing individual value and worth, especially as they pertain to the victim. This is accomplished through a self-assessment process. Human dignity requires that the offender be taught how to engage in a self-assessment process: how to reflect properly on the meaning of his or her behavior and in terms of its outcome. When properly developed, probationers should become comfortable with a self-activating, self-directed, self-criticizing, self-correcting, and self-understanding process that not only can keep them free of crime but make them better people as well. When this happens, the officer should grant the offender greater autonomy.

Genuineness

Probation officers have to approach their clients with an openness, a candor, and a directness not found in many other settings. Being genuine is essential if the probationer is to believe what the officer is telling him or her. One cannot talk above or below but right to the probationer. One must be authentic and legitimate. This takes place through self-disclosure where the officer speaks in bits and pieces about his or her own life. This can only be done in a sincere, open, and spontaneous method. Self-disclosure can be a powerful link with the offender. It also presents the probation officer as a human being who has faced and surmounted problems through a socially acceptable method. Care must be used to present only appropriate material that will lead to growth and to display effective use of socially acceptable problem solving. Lastly, the officer has to be careful not to reverse the client-counselor relationship (Enos and Southern 1996, 42–43).

Congruence

Those who lead treatment programs must not only "talk the talk" but "walk the walk." It is difficult to develop a set of behaviors consistent with social expectations when the exhibiter is not doing what is expected of others. There must be a consistency between what the officer thinks, says, and does and his or her outward expressions or body language. Probationers are looking to understand the probation officer as much as they expect the officer to be concerned with understanding them. Reciprocal messages lead to congruence when they are consistently presented. Mixed messages lead to confusion and trouble when one thing is said and another is enforced. Congruence is also about listening.

Listening involves listening to others, listening to oneself, and listening to the essence of things (Barbara 1978). A healthy listener will listen for important statements: what is and is not being said. One asks questions and clarifications, challenging assertions and allegations when necessary. All of this is tied to carefully observing body language, eye contact, and facial movements, to name just a few. Congruence is found in being able to understand what the probationer is trying to say or imply by the message conveyed. Does it have internal consistency and match other experiences?

Empathetic Functioning

This construct refers to the degree to which the counselor can achieve an empathetic understanding of the client's personal frame of reference. Carl Rogers (1951) argues that empathy is central to the successful counselor's ability to bring about change for the client. Counselors need to understand the clients' awareness of life and experiences. This means understanding their private world and what it means for them. The counselor must be able to identify with the client's feelings and to attempt to experience these feelings as though they were the probation officer's own.

Empathy is a powerful tool for understanding the meaning of a various problems. Empathy requires the officer to understand the magnitude of the offender's problems as the offender views them. This does not mean the officer understands how the offender feels about these problems. That would be presumptuous because one can never understand how another person feels. However, the officer can be sensitive about these problems while at the same time trying to offer guidance and structure that will lead to a successful outcome. Probation officers have to be careful not to get caught up in the client's problems. Many of these problems have to be dealt with in another context by professionals specifically geared to handle them. Officers also have to be careful not to be manipulated by the probationer; thus, the officer must be careful to recognize his or her own needs, insecurities, desires, and wishes. The officer must understand what it is like to walk in the shoes of the offender and at the same time maintain a professional approach to this understanding, keeping social and psychological distance between him- or herself and the client.

Unconditional Positive Regard

The last requirement for effective responsivity is for the counselor or probation officer to have unconditional positive regard for the probationer (Enos and Southern 1996). This is important, especially as it relates to recognizing the human dignity of the offender. *Unconditional positive regard* may be defined as the ability to understand the behavior of the offender, while not rejecting the offender in the personal and humanistic sense. The counselor is nonpossessive, caring, and accepting. The counselor has to trust that clients possess the ability to act in order to achieve self-actualization—for example, possess the self-wisdom that can cause them to discover for themselves their inner strengths and resources and the direction their lives should take. The counselor is to be caring but nondirective.

Unconditional positive regard means acceptance of the person. The counselor recognizes the human dignity in each person and while he or she may not approve of the behavior, the counselor nevertheless accepts the person for who the person is in terms of strengths and weaknesses, positive and negative behaviors, and constructive and destructive behaviors. The counselor must simultaneously maintain an appreciation of the innate dignity and personal value of the client while not accepting the person's behavior (Enos and Southern 1996, 45).

■ Conclusion

The whole notion of risk-needs assessment has gone through three transformations over the last 40 years. For a while, it was not known if such instruments were valuable or not. Too much attention was given to static factors the offender could do nothing about; thus, the offender was stigmatized more than helped by the process. Now that there has been a rediscovery of the importance of dynamic factors—factors that can influence change—there is a renewed sense that positive outcomes can be achieved. Attention is given to criminogenic dynamic factors associated with criminal associates, procriminal attitudes, criminal history, and the like. The LSI—R is considered one of the premier tools for identifying such factors. The LSI—R is not without fault, however, especially when officers believe the information collected falls into a black hole. Some still run into the problem of interpreting the presence of criminogenic needs and the problem of providing a mechanism that works equally well with males and females. The LSI—R gives little attention as a criminogenic need to self-esteem, when, in fact, it is known that it plays a major role with females in today's world. To further the process along, the needs component requires attention to offender problems, risks, and responsivity. Needs are important and risk is crucial, but if the offender is unresponsive to treatment or the community is unable to provide appropriate programs that address the offender's problems, negative outcomes ensue. In an attempt to heighten the offender's responsivity to treatment, an officer needs to display warmth, honesty, and genuine concern. He or she needs to allow the offender to take his or her time to accept what is happening to him or her. Officers must be allowed a chance to exercise professional judgment in individualizing their encounters with their clients in order to maximize positive efforts. The officer who treats the offender with dignity allows the offender to assume responsibility for his or her own actions

REFERENCES

Andrews, D. 1994. An overview of treatment effectiveness: Research and clinical principles in results reported in promoting public safety using effective interventions with offenders. Draft. U.S. Department of Justice, National Institute of Corrections.

Andrews, D. A. 1990. Role of antisocial attitudes in the psychology of crime. Paper presented at the Annual Conference of the Canadian Psychological Association, Ottawa, Ontario.

Andrews D., and J. Bonta. 1998. *The psychology of criminal conduct*. Cincinnati, OH: Anderson.

Andrews D., and J. Bonta. 1995. *The level of service inventory—revised*. Tonawanda, NY: Multi-Health Systems.

Andrews, D., and J. Bonta. 1994. *The psychology of criminal conduct*. Cincinnati, OH: Anderson.

Andrews, D., J. Bonta, and R. Hoge. 1990. Classification for effective rehabilitation: Rediscovering psychology. *Criminal Justice and Behavior* 17: 19–52.

Aubrey, R., and M. Hough. 1997. *Assessing offenders' needs: Assessment scales for the probation service*. Home Office Research Study 216. London: Home Office.

Baird, S. 1981. Probation and parole classification: The Wisconsin Model. *Corrections Today* 43: 58–67.

Baird, C., R. Heinz, and B. Bemus. 1979. The Wisconsin case classification/staff deployment project. Project Report No. 14. Madison, WI: Department of Health and Social Services, Division of Corrections.

Baird, C., R. Prestine, and B. Klockziem. 1989. *Revalidation of the Wisconsin probation/parole classification system*. Madison, WI: National Council on Crime and Delinquency.

Bandura, A. 1965. The influence of model's reinforcement contingencies on the acquisition of imitative responses. *Journal of Personality and Social Psychology* 1: 589–595.

Bandura, A. 1977. Self-efficacy: Toward a unifying theory of behavioral change. *Psychological Review* 94: 191–215.

Bandura, A., and R. Waters. 1963. *Social learning and personality development*. New York: Holt, Rinehart and Winston.

Bandura A., D. Ross, and S. Ross. 1963. Vicarious reinforcement and imitative learning. *Journal of Abnormal and Social Psychology* 67: 601–607.

Barbara, D. 1978. *The art of listening*. Springfield, IL: Charles C Thomas.

Bonta, J. 1996. Risk-needs assessment and treatment. In Alan Harland, ed., *Choosing corrections options that work: Defining the demand and evaluating the supply*. Thousand Oaks, CA: Sage.

Clear, T. R., V. B. Clear, and W. D. Burrell. 1989. *Offender assessment and evaluation: The Presentence Report*. Cincinnati, OH: Anderson.

Dana, R. 1993. *Multicultural perspective for professional psychology*. Boston: Allyn and Bacon.

Egan, G. 1990. *The skilled helper: A systematic approach to effective helping*, 4th ed. Pacific Grove, CA: Brooks Cole.

Enos, R., and S. Southern. 1996. *Correctional case management*. Cincinnati, OH: Anderson.

Finckenauer, J. 1982. *Scared straight! And the panacea phenomenon*. Englewood Cliffs, NJ: Prentice Hall.

Gendreau, P. 1994. The principles of effective intervention with offenders. In A. Harland, ed., *What works in community corrections*. Thousand Oaks, CA: Sage.

Gendreau, P. 1995. Technology transfer in the criminal justice field. In T. Backer, S. Davis, and G. Soucy, eds., *Reviewing the behavioral science: Knowledge base on technology transfer*. NIDA Research monograph 155. Rockville, MD: U.S. Department of Health and Human Services, Public Health Service, National Institutes of Health.

Gendreau, P. 1996. Offender rehabilitation: What we know and what needs to be done. *Criminal Justice and Behavior* 23(1): 144–161.

Gendreau, P., C. Goggin, and M. Paparozzi. 1996. Principles of effective assessment for community corrections. *Federal Probation* 60(3): 64–70.

Gendreau, P., and R. Ross. 1979. Effective correctional treatment: Bibliotherapy for cynics. *Crime and Delinquency* 25: 463–489.

Gendreau, P., and R. Ross. 1981. Correctional potency: Treatment and deterrence on trial. In R. Roesch and R. Corrado, eds., *Evaluation and criminal justice policy*. Beverly Hills, CA: Sage.

Gendreau, P., and R. Ross. 1987. Revivification of rehabilitation: Evidence from the 80s. *Justice Quarterly* 4: 349–407.

Glueck, S., and E. Glueck. 1950. *Unraveling juvenile delinquency*. Cambridge, MA: Harvard University.

Gottfreson, M. 1979. Treatment destructive techniques. *Journal of Research in Crime and Delinquency* 16: 39.

Grant, M., and D. Grant. 1962. An evaluation of the community treatment of delinquents. CTP Research Report No. 1, California Youth Authority (August, mimeo).

Grove, W., and P. Meehl. 1996. Comparative efficiency of informal (subjective, impressionistic) and formal (mechanical, algorithmic) prediction procedures. The clinical-statistical controversy. *Psychology, Public Policy, and Law* 2: 293–323.

Harris, G., and D. Watkins. 1987. *Counseling the involuntary and resistant client.* Laurel, MD: American Correctional Association.

Hester, R., and W. Williams. 1995. *Handbook on alcoholism treatment approaches.* Boston: Allyn and Bacon.

Hoffman, P. 1994. Twenty years of operational use of a risk prediction instrument. The United States Parole Commission's Salient Factor Score. *Journal of Criminal Justice* 22: 477–494.

Hoffman, P., and J. Beck. 1984. Burnout—Age at release from prison and recidivism. *Journal of Criminal Justice* 12: 617–623.

Kemshall, H. 1998. Defensible decisions for risk or "it's the doers wot get the blame." *Probation Journal* 45(2): 67–72.

Kennedy, S., and R. Serin. 1997. Treatment responsivity: Contributing to effective correctional programming. *ICCA Journal on Community Corrections* 7: 46–52.

Kinzinger, P. July 2002. Telephone interview. International Community Corrections Association. La Coosse, WI.

Kratcoski, P. 1985. The function of classification models in probation and parole: Control or treatment-rehabilitation? *Federal Probation* 49(4): 49–56.

Lauen, R. 1997. *Positive approaches to corrections: Research, policy and practice.* Lanham, MD: American Correctional Association.

Lipsey, M. 1992. Juvenile delinquency treatment: A meta-analytic inquiry into the variability of effects. In T. Cook, H. Cooper, D. Cordray, H. Hartman, L. Hedges, R. Light, T. Louis, and F. Mosteller, eds. *Meta-analysis for explanation.* New York: Russel Sage Foundation.

MacKenzie, D. 1989. Prison classification: The management and psychological perspectives. In L. Goodstein and D. MacKenzie, eds., *The American prison: Issues in research and policy.* New York: Plenum Press.

Masters, R. 1994. *Counseling criminal justice offenders.* Thousand Oaks, CA: Sage.

Meehl, P. 1954. *Clinical versus statistical prediction.* Minneapolis: University of Minnesota Press.

Merrington, S., and J. Skinns. 2000. Using ACE to profile criminogenic needs. Probation studies unit. *ACE practitioner Bulletin No. 1.* Centre for Criminological Research, Oxford University, Oxford, England, pp. 1–11.

Motiuk, L. 1999. Assessment methods in corrections. In P. M. Harris, ed., *Research to results: Effective community corrections.* Lanham, MD: American Correctional Association.

Motiuk, L., and F. Porporino. 1989. *Offender risk/needs assessment: A study of conditional releases.* Report R-06. Ottawa: Correctional Service of Canada.

Palmer, T. 1976. Martinson revisited. *Journal of Research in Crime and Delinquency* 5: 133.

Palmer, T. 1992. *The re-emergence of correctional intervention.* Newbury Park, CA: Sage.

Raynor, P., J. Kynch, C. Roberts, and S. Merrington. 2000. *Risk and needs assessment in probation services: An evaluation,* Home Office Research Study 211. London: Home Office.

Robinson, G. 2003. Implementing OASys: Lessons from research into LSI—R and ACE. *Probation Journal* 50: 30–40.

Roberts, C., and G. Robinson. 1998. Improving practice through pilot studies: The case of presentence reports. *VISTA* 3: 186–195.

Rogers, C. 1951. *Client-centered therapy.* Boston, MA: Houghton-Mifflin.

Ross, B., and P. Gendreau. 1981. *Effective corrections.* Toronto: University of Toronto.

Samenow, S. 1984. *Inside the criminal mind.* New York: Times Books.

Samenow, S. 1989. *Before it's too late.* New York: Times Books.

Simourd, L., and D. Andrews. 1994. Correlates of delinquency: A look at gender differences. *Forum of Corrections Research* 6: 26–31.

Stearns County, Minnesota, Probation Department. 2001. Handout.

Van Voorhis, P. 2000. Social learning models. In D. Lester, M. Braswell, and P. Van Voorhis, eds., *Correctional Counseling and Rehabilitation,* 4th ed. Cincinnati: Anderson, pp. 149–166.

Van Voorhis, P., M. Braswell, and D. Lester. 2000. *Correctional counseling and rehabilitation.* Cincinnati, OH: Anderson.

Warren, M. 1971. Classification of offenders as an aid to efficient management and effective treatment. *Journal of Criminal Law, Criminology and Police Science* 62(2): 239–268.

Warren, M. 1973. All things being equal. *Criminal Law Bulletin* 9: 483.

KEY POINTS

1. The treatment-rehabilitation system tries to differentiate offenders on the basis of needs, attitudes, motivation, and attributes and provide the treatment necessary to bring about the desired changes in values, attitudes, and skills that will inhibit offenders from recidivating.

2. Risk-assessment instruments are comprised of static and dynamic factors.

3. Risk-assessment instruments can be categorized developmentally as clinical intuition, actuarial, and the static versus dynamic criminogenic risk factors.

4. Central to assessment instruments is the concern for risk, needs, and responsivity.

5. Risk focuses on incapacitation of offenders who require careful attention in the community.

6. Particular factors that deserve attention are parenting, education, antisocial personality, and antisocial attitudes.

7. The dynamic risk factors are criminal history, employment record, education and marital status, antisocial associates, attitudes, and personality.

8. Procriminal attitudes, criminal history, and associates are major correlates of offender populations.

9. LSI—R places considerable demands on time and paperwork which have led some officers to resent the instrument and yet some agencies do not use the information to its fullest effect.

10. The needs principle addresses the dynamic needs that can be altered by attending to the client-based factors that influence the potential for positive treatment.

11. Responsivity matches the offender's learning style to the treatment program, thus respecting the offender's dignity.

12. Human dignity is essential to any treatment program in terms of how the offender is treated while in the program and in the hope of what the offender is to be once the program is completed.

13. Effective modeling of behavior requires that the officer be empathetic, be genuine, and maintain a sense of unconditional positive regard in dealing with the offender.

KEY TERMS

actuarial risk assessment is a second-generation assessment device that relies on the probability of something happening based on a record of previous occurrences.

clinical assessments are a clinical process in which clinicians use their professional judgment to assess the offender's dangerousness, treatment needs, amenability to treatment, and risk of absconding.

congruence a term coined by psychotherapist Carl Rogers, occurs whenever one's thoughts, speech, and actions are consistent with affect and body language.

differential supervision notes offenders that are classified as high, medium, or low risks and are given services reflecting their risks and needs.

dynamic risk factors   criminogenic variables, are personal attributes that are subject to change such as criminal history, employment record, education, marital status, antisocial associates, attitudes, and personality.

empathic functioning   refers to the degree to which the counselor can achieve an empathetic understanding of the client's personal frame of reference.

matching principle   recognizes that offenders have unique treatment needs, have their own learning style, and are at different stages of readiness to change.

needs principle   is used to determine who should receive certain services based on the presence of various criminogenic needs: antisocial associates, antisocial attitudes and values, history of antisocial behavior, and skill deficiencies, such as poor problem-solving skills, self-management or self-efficacy problems, impulsivity, poor self-control, and irresponsibility.

professional discretion   is when a probation officer uses his or her own experience and personal understanding to override the assessment findings, which might seem contradicted.

responsivity principle   refers to the delivery of treatment programs in a style and mode that are consistent with the ability and learning style of the offender.

risk principle   is posited on the notion that criminal behavior can be predicted and that the risk of offending can be reduced by matching the level of services to the risk level of the offender, thus bridging assessment and effective treatment.

static risk factors   are historical attributes of the offender that do not and cannot change over time or the course of supervision.

treatability   refers to the clinical determination of the offenders who will respond most favorably to certain treatment modalities and environmental conditions.

unconditional positive regard   is the ability to understand the behavior of the offender while not rejecting the offender in the personal and humanistic sense.

REVIEW QUESTIONS

1. What are the main reasons for using a risk-assessment instrument?
2. What are the drawbacks of a probation officer doing his or her job without a risk-assessment instrument?
3. Discuss the evolution of classification instruments, including the first-, second-, and third-generation instruments.
4. Discuss the components of the LSI—R and its use and value in corrections.
5. What are the main tenets of risk, needs, and responsivity? Why are they important concepts to consider in probation?

7

Offender Supervision

Chapter Objectives

In this chapter you will learn about:

- Effective supervision
- Probation work
- The role of case management
- Three effective counseling strategies

It is one thing to criticize the oppressive or trivial character of so much of what passes for offender programming, but it is another thing to deny the idea of rehabilitation altogether. Denial of rehabilitation requires one to believe that either criminals (unlike the remainder of society) do not have problems deep enough to require help in overcoming them or that the larger society is not responsible for seeing to it that the offender gets the needed help. This is a clear instance of the unwillingness to confront the fact that people who commit crimes of violence often have a great deal wrong with their lives. To leave them without any service is likely to increase crime and delinquency (Currie 1985, 236).

A New World of Probation

A new paradigm of offender supervision is required today, one emphasizing the value and worth of the offender and one that puts the officer into the community in touch with others who provide support in supervising the offender. This chapter considers several important aspects of probationer supervision. First of all, it considers the need for the officer to connect with the community. Next, it considers some principles of effective supervision, and how the role of human dignity is regarded in the process. Probation work is then analyzed to describe what is it that probation officers actually do; models of supervision such as case management are then considered. Lastly, offender counseling strategies are offered which focus on anticriminal modeling, cognitive therapy, and motivational interviewing.

Effective Supervision

Effective correctional programming requires probation officers to get into the field, to keep an offender in a program long enough to make the program worthwhile, and to have a theory of crime that explains what is taking place so as to understand what is driving the offender into crime. It is necessary for probation officers to have a thorough understanding of where they work and where problem areas in the community are located. Officers can no longer simply understand that they work in a poor neighborhood or that there are a variety of social, economic, and political problems in that area of the community. They need to anticipate problems generated from such circumstances. A great deal of pressure is placed on probation agencies to utilize effective and efficient programs, especially in light of diminishing state resources. Effective supervision is also active, engaged, and community centered. It calls on people in the community to provide additional support for their community members in trouble with the law. Whether it is community justice or renewed community involvement in the traditional model, the officer is to seek community help in establishing a safe and helpful environment.

Officers can reduce communication barriers through the employment of community justice (Karp and Clear, 2002). Getting into the field provides the officer with greater positive visibility and a more direct knowledge of the offender's living arrangement, his or her family, and environment. Officers now have to understand which areas are more dangerous than others; which require two officers during field visits; which have a high concentration of the unemployed, drug offenders, and the mentally ill; and which have good public transportation systems. Effective supervision then is attentive to the social ecology of neighborhood life (Clear and Corbett 1999; Rhine 1998). Offender-based classification schemes are then augmented by place-based classification that address meaningfully the specific crime problems that comprise neighborhood safety and the quality of life of those who live there (MIPR 2003).

Widening Community Involvement

Effective supervision must achieve public safety at a reasonable cost. One means of reducing cost and increasing effectiveness is through the formation of partnerships. By moving beyond traditional case management to form active partnerships with the local police, community members, offenders' families, persons important to the offender, neighborhood associations, and other indigenous organizations and groups, probation is designing a strategy that is more in line with community policing (MIPR 2003). By adopting this type of approach to supervision, probation officers will devote a significant portion of their energies to steering offenders toward socializing institutions and connecting them with prosocial peers, mentors, and other adults. At the same time, probation officers must draw on the informal neighborhood networks and community social control to monitor and respond proactively to the public safety risks presented by those offenders who live there. The probation officers "widen the community

Figure 7.1 One creative solution probation officers have developed is enlisting members of the offender's community, called community guardians, to participate in the supervision of the offender. *Source: Courtesy of Edward Sieh.*

net" by redefining their roles to serve as a catalyst for building relations. (Rhine et al. 1998). In performing such a role, probation officers, in effect, align their efforts where community capacities have the highest probabilities for success in light of the limited internal resources available to probation (Smith and Dickey 1998).

Community "guardians" can play an important role in this strategy. Supervision activities that are community centered must, of necessity, move beyond the monitoring of offenders on probation caseloads toward the establishment of relations with individuals who can serve as "guardians" in the neighborhoods. These are people who would augment probation supervision by taking an interests in the activities of the probationer. Guardians are found by targeting the relationships that significant others have with the probationer (e.g., spouse, family members, parents, employers). The development of active relationships with the guardian can begin where offenders live and at the same time, it represents an invaluable but more complete form of community engagement (Smith and Dickey 1998). Probation is engaging the community and fostering its development in ways that social workers have done in the past and continue to do now.

Clearly by widening the net of community involvement, probation reduces the anonymity offenders all too often enjoy. In sharp contrast to passive case management, active, community-centered supervision requires that probation officers work the neighborhoods with the greatest concentration of offenders. It also means developing preventive capacities to rebuild the informal resources of social control that are lacking in a given neighborhood or community. Last, it means focusing on creative problem solving at the local level, as well as the pursuit of community-enhancing or neighborhood development activities (MIPR 2003).

Lipsey (1989) argues that better programs were identified as having longer treatment durations; were provided outside of a correctional setting; involved treatment being compared to no treatment, not alternative treatments; were behavior oriented; were skill oriented; and were multimodal. The focus of the program was on higher risk cases with treatment that attends to other factors outside of individual concerns. Evaluations concluded that how a program is delivered does influence the results. Structured and focused program delivery when combined with appropriate treatment conditions increase chances for success.

The Psychology of Criminal Conduct

Besides getting into the field and putting offenders into appropriate programs, it is necessary for the probation officer to have a theory of crime that allows a variety of criminal events to be explained. One such clinically relevant approach is the psychology of criminal conduct (Andrews and Bonta 1998). According to the psychology of criminal conduct (PCC), attention should be given to biological, personal, interpersonal, familial, structural-cultural, politico-economic, circumstantial, and the immediate situational factors. One might say this is a new version of the multiple factor approach. The PCC theory is based on the assumption that criminal conduct is a result of someone being in a particular situation at a particular time where the offender is provided with the reason to commit the crime and the ability to neutralize any objections. As a result, rewards for the crime increase and the cost decrease.

PCC may have its merits but it also has its limits. It requires training, support, and a caseload small enough to provide the attention it needs. Criminogenic needs play an important part in the explanation of crime but what is not clear is how particular needs are played out for no one theory accounts for all behaviors. Special needs offenders, such as the substance abusers, have a constellation of problems in which crime is just one of them. As far as theories are concerned, the key assumption is so broad as to be untestable because it is possible to make similar assumptions about almost any action that is undertaken, not just in the commission of a crime. Lastly, PCC needs to be reconciled with the problems made evident with the community justice model. Strategies for dealing with crime must be multifaceted with the expectation that various factors need to be addressed if crime is to be reduced. Probation has the information necessary for this to be done.

Human Dignity

Offender supervision is the main arena in which human dignity may be exhibited. This is where the officer has a chance, possibly for the first time since the arrest, to engage the probationer as a person of real worth. It is an opportunity to teach the offender how to treat others with respect. Such learning opportunities present themselves during initial meetings, when taking reports, on field visits, in handling violations, and in the final discharge of the case. The principles of human dignity are essential to any interaction with the offender. Of import to the probation officer is the understanding that it is difficult to develop a set of behaviors consistent with social expectations when the officer is not manifesting behavior that is expected of everyone else. This is also true of teachers, clergy, sports stars, political leaders, and police officers. If probationers are treated as though they have worth, conversely, the probationer can learn to treat others as if they, too, have worth. This is not easy to achieve nor is it easy to maintain. Where the job becomes more difficult is when the officer is asked to supervise someone considered to have done something extremely wrong and the offender compounds that problem by being someone who appears to have little value and worth and treats others the same. A hypothetical description of one such offender may suffice:

> *Consider a hypothetical 35-year-old male who is a habitual drug user and a convicted pedophile. He sodomized a 12-year-old girl after getting thrown out of a bar. He did some prison time for that offense. He has been on probation several times for minor offenses but also for drug offenses and fighting. His performance while on probation is inconsistent. When he gets drunk, he becomes violent and abusive. Some people have characterized him as a bully. In conversations he becomes openly racist and sexist, especially with regard to African-Americans, Native Americans, Asians, Jews, and women. He has a swastika tattoo on his left forearm. He also has a dirty and unkempt appearance, smokes incessantly, and has a smart-aleck attitude that he displays in a loud voice. He particularly likes to come on to female staff where he can turn the occasion into one of personal dominance. He can be quite authoritarian in his relationships with people he considers his inferiors—women, children, and people of color. He is suspicious of anyone who might pose a threat to him. He has several children with different women. Each one of them is owed child support but he refuses to pay. When asked about payment of child support, he claims he doesn't work and cannot make the payments. When he does work, it is off the books and wages are paid in cash or kind. When he cannot make do by working, he relies on the support of a few friends who are similarly situated. He has lost his driver's license but continues to drive even though he has no insurance. He understands the state's social support system and how to make claims on it. He has little respect for anyone who works for the government or anyone who has an education.*

Any probation officer may find it difficult to supervise resistant, defiant, or passive-aggressive offenders—and despite the current offense, the probation officer has to hold in restraint any objectionable feelings he or she has about the offender. The officer must continue to respect the probationer if for no other reason than there may be a chance to change the behavior. Offender respect occurs when the offender is viewed as a person. This attitude is exhibited in moments of concern, kindness, charity, forgiveness, mercy, understanding, patience, support, solidarity, sincerity, and steadfastness. Experience also helps. The more experienced officers know some offenders come around and others don't. These officers know where and when to expend their energies. There is also a sense among experienced officers that almost anyone can find his or her way onto probation. Such officers develop a strong but unofficial sense of moral egalitarianism. Under the condition of moral egalitarianism, everyone is subject to the same code of behavior and to the same punishments. Most importantly, moral egalitarians accept the notion that everyone makes mistakes, no one is perfect, and each needs forgiveness and understanding.

One of the critical components of human dignity is the recognition that humans are self-correcting. Human dignity requires the officer to teach the offender how to engage in a self-assessment process, how to reflect properly on one's own behavior, the outcome of these actions, and the meaning these actions hold. In the case just noted, the offender may not love the mother of his children but he may love the children nonetheless. What is it that he would like to do for these children and how can one make that possible? Probationers should become comfortable with self-activating, self-directed, self-criticizing, self-correcting, and self-understanding processes that, when properly developed, not only keep them free of crime, but make them better people as well. In other words, the experience of rehabilitation and change provides a tool that allows the offender to view him- or herself as others do and thus correct the impression they provide others. Not all treatment programs provide for equal measures of these factors, especially at the start. It is during the beginning phase that less freedom is afforded the offender but as the person progresses through the program, the individual is rewarded with greater freedom and opportunities. It is during the opening phases that caution is given to ensure the dignity of the individual is not denied completely in an effort to impose change and control. Careful review of procedures must be made. As progress is made in the individual's behavior, opportunities must be present that provide the person with the ability to test reality under conditions that afford more and more freedom. If failure or disappointment should be the outcome, the individual is not necessarily thought to deserve further punishment, but re-education or retraining.

Full rehabilitation or fully habilitated people are capable of effectively evaluating their own actions. More importantly, they are able to organize their lives, predict future events, and explain their actions or conjecture about what will happen under various courses of action. This requires officers to recognize when this is happening. There is a tendency in probation to not pay attention to positive change as much as to negative performances. Negative change is easier to identify; positive change is often viewed with suspicion. Officers, nonetheless, must come to see the need for increased autonomy. With increased autonomy come infrequent contact and reduced levels of supervision and reinforcement. Incorrectly, some officers with large caseloads assume that decreasing contact will somehow accomplish what more frequent contact could not provide. How one treats another reflects more on who one is than on the character of the person receiving the treatment.

■ Probation Work

An understanding of the way in which probation officers treat people is made possible by understanding what probation officers do in their work. In this section, information regarding the attributes of effective officers and the role played by advocacy, intake, assessment, referral, intervention, relapse prevention, and evaluation will be discussed.

The National Institute of Corrections (NIC 1999) recommends that people working in community corrections have the appropriate education, experience, and long-term commitment to the work. They also recommend the staff possess the following personal characteristics: fairness, life experience, empathy, problem-solving skills, and the ability to act firmly but nonconfrontationally. The staff should experience an initial training of 3 to 6 months with in-service training required annually. The staff should also undergo an assessment and evaluation process and have an opportunity for staff input. Staff members should be assessed annually on clinical skills and receive regular clinical supervision. Because of their ability, experience, and training, program employees should also have the ability to have input into programs and modify program structure to reflect changing circumstances. Information gathered by the NIC indicates that 75 percent of service delivery staff have an undergraduate degree and 10 percent have an advanced degree. Three-fourths of these have degrees in the helping profession. A similar proportion has worked in treatment programs with offenders for at least 2 years.

One additional factor not mentioned in the list of National Institute of Corrections personal characteristics is the requirement at the time of hiring that the officer desire to treat the offender with dignity. Developing a measurement device that gets at the essence of human dignity starts with the need to treat the offender with respect and to recognize the offender as having value as a person. One means of gathering data on this is to do an exit survey of discharged probationers.

A better understanding of probation supervision depends upon knowing how daily activities are handled. Probation work has two different aspects to it: case supervision and case treatment. These are not mutually exclusive categories for one goes hand-in-hand with the other. Probation officers provide structure to chaotic lives by supervising their caseloads. Probation officers find opportunities for growth and development through case management and the treatment referrals made through it.

Jacobs (1990) found that contrary to the stereotypical view of the probation officer slavishly attending to office rituals, regardless of the probationer's problems, many officers vigorously pursued the interests of their clients. The officers seemed undaunted by the difficulties presented by the client and felt quit competent in stepping outside well-defined organizational boundaries, as indicated by the emergent system, in order to ensure that sufficient care is give to the probationer.

In this author's nonrepresentative study of 39 probation officers who worked in a large metropolitan probation department, the officers were asked to discuss what might be considered their correctional ideology. They were asked to discuss their beliefs and assumptions about clients and to identify their work-related priorities. Here are two examples:

Juvenile Officer

I think you have to be extremely flexible when you come to work. It is one of the things that I like about the job. I also like the fact that I am my own boss so to speak. I am suppose to be self-motivated enough that when someone calls I know what to do about that situ-

ation and I should be able to make a decision myself. I learn every day from the clients that I have. I learn about myself and I learn what I can be grateful for in my life.

Adult Officer

Yesterday, I dictated a series of cases and compiled my restitution pay out letters. I made a series of phone calls and then I made home visits for 3 hours. I am able to make from 70 to 75 home visits per month. If you work at it, you can find the time.

Presentence Investigations

Probation work begins with the presentence report. In order to develop an accurate description of probation services, it is essential to understand the presentence investigation process (Rosencrance 1987). A good investigation provides a detailed description of someone's life and offers an explanation for the behavior. A good presentence report also presents a picture of the offender as a human being who possesses certain positive and negative attributes. The report does not detail information that is critical but unsubstantiated. It is the sum of someone's life despite whatever failings the person has; thus, it should portray the person as a human being and not a creature deserving of the worse punishments. A good presentence report should be given due consideration by the court. It is the one document the probation officer shares with others, and as such, is a good measure of the officer's abilities, values, and professional orientation.

The presentence investigation is used to provide information used in sentencing. Presentence reports have a variety of formats. The information on a presentence report must tell a story. The narrative must explain who the offender is and what accounts for his or her behavior. The account must follow up on any hint of an important impediment to positive social adjustment. Quite often the report will indicate a series of criminogenic needs meriting attention. It is the officer's job to identify which needs are crucial to the offender, especially if an effort is made to alleviate the condition. Statements need to be factually based and attributable. Rumors or innuendos are not reliable. If the offender is considered to be mentally unstable, then what proof does one have of this condition? Has he (or she) been evaluated? How serious of a problem is it? The officer must write a defensible and justifiable report, one that can stand on its own merits if attacked in court. This is true whether the report is long or short. Whether it is a long report, such as 25 pages, or a short report of only a couple of pages, it is hoped that the officer can present a measure of the essence of the offender and his or her place in the world.

The report also assists in classifying risk and identifying the needs of the offender. Some departments have forsaken their risk assessment instrument and simply considered what the court orders for a sentence (e.g., Hennepin County, Minnesota Probation Officer 1998). Other agencies have very detailed reports that are designed to gather risk-needs assessment information as part of the data-gathering process. Absent sentencing guidelines, the judge's information about the defendant is limited to what is offered in the presentence investigation. In cases where the defendant has pled guilty, one finds that the court often follows the recommendation offered in the report (Allen et al. 1985). Although the probation officer's decision making is limited by plea bargaining, sentencing guidelines, and determinate sentencing (Brewer et al. 1981; Hagan et al. 1979; Kingsnorth and Rizzo 1979; Neubauer 1974; Rosencrance 1987), officers still write independent and discretion riddled reports.

Although many departments attempt to standardize the reports in length and content, the quality of the report in many ways depends solely on the officer's interest in it. Rosencrance (1987) has developed a typology of presentence investigators. Team players are willing to follow departmental policies by writing reports that reflect society's values. Mossback officers, usually older officers who rarely do more than what is required of them as they serve out the remainder of their time, attempt to resolve the matter by considering what needs to be done to move the offender ahead. The hardliner believes it is his or her duty is to protect society through tough sentencing recommendations. The bleeding heart officer takes the perspective that the criminal justice system is unfair and he or she wishes to protect the offender by evening the odds. The maverick officer seeks a form of individualized justice as he or she evaluates each case on its own merits.

Conducting an investigation is the first step in bringing the offender into contact with a probation officer. The initial interview sets the tone for the entire probationary experience. Experienced officers are needed here because of the different forms of information gathered. When the offender reports to the probation officer to discuss the presentence report, the officer will first detail the information that is requested and then explain what use it has for the court. The officer also tries to assure the offender that the information is meant to assist the offender and not punish him or her more than what is deserved. The officer wants the probationer to relax and provide accurate information.

Verification of the criminal record is essential. Because factual information and opinions are often distorted, it is important to have two sources of all information, especially if the information has a strong bearing on the sentence (Clear et al. 1989, 71). The investigative officer interviews the offender and asks a series of questions about his or her crime, prior record, schooling, and employment. Much of the verification involves obtaining the necessary privacy waivers usually through a series of form letters and then to follow up with telephone calls. Form letters are sent out to collect information from school, doctors, employers, and banks. When dealing with families, victims, and neighbors, officers like to interact directly by phone or in person. Verification is central to the process.

Verification is accomplished by interviewing the parents and the offender and obtaining information from them that must be checked against official records. These records include school reports, counseling records, birth certificates, and stubs. When an offender is from a distant large city verifying presentence report information is very difficult, time consuming, and unreliable. Such places as Chicago, Los Angeles, and New York City are considered information black holes in that requests for verified information are presented but little information is received in a timely fashion. Large city departments see such requests as low priorities as they have plenty of work to do.

With respect to recommendations, it is widely known that judges rely heavily on the probation officer to provide at least a reasonable recommendation for the case. Some officers like doing investigations because they view it as one term paper after another. Other officers find that no matter what they write or suggest that a plea deal has been made and some other solution is going to be found for the client. Those who gain some acceptance of their reports have learned to read the judges assigned to the court and anticipate their acceptance of various recommendations. This high rate of acceptance, around 80 percent of the time (Schmolesky and Thorson 1982) is achieved by taking an appropriate amount of time to lay the groundwork for the sentence in the body of the report. This means that the recommendation makes a great deal of sense if someone reads the report from front to back and has all the information offered by the officer. For the more difficult cases, the officer will have the supervisor read the report to gain another perspective and assure that there is a consistency of thought in the document. In many ways, the presentence report investigator is performing a quasijudicial function, because the officer knows far more about the case than the court.

Supervision

Supervision necessitates an organizational structure that enables the agency to protect the community and provide the necessary support to aid the offender. There is much debate as to whether probation should emphasize service delivery, differential supervision, or intensive supervision. Those espousing service delivery would uncouple surveillance from probation responsibilities, leaving the officer free to provide help and assistance to the offender. Essentially this model would abandon the law enforcement functions altogether (Bottom and McWilliams 1979; Fogel 1978). Probation departments in the United States have not implemented the service-only orientation on a systems-wide basis (Rosencrance 1986)—and although this approach has not been widely adopted, some of the officers interviewed certainly took that approach with certain offenders or as a matter of practice for a period of time.

The supporters of differential supervision advocate offender risk assessment (Clear and Gallagher 1985; O'Leary 1985; Wright et al. 1984). The level of supervision is matched to the offender's identified risk, which means that the higher the risk, the more often the probationer reports. The use of objective classification scales lends an aura of rationality to the supervision. Administrators believe that the use of these instruments can lead to scientific management practices and many officers allocate their supervision time as they see necessary (Rosencrance 1986). Risk-needs assessment is one method of controlling organizational drift and a lack of organizational goal clarity. It provides a means for assuring that the officer's unbridled attention to crime control does not overwhelm any concern for the client's needs. It must be kept in mind that when the officer comes into contact with the probationer, the officer may express concern about the client's latest activities but, most importantly, will focus on the client's lawful behavior and any activities that indicate criminal activity. Later on, the officer may consider the needs of the client. By this time, however, there may be little time available for the discussion of the client's needs. These needs may prove to be more important than any marginal client behavior. Moreover, if the officer indicates a lack of interest in the client's problems and suggests the client seek help elsewhere, the client may be back after finding no help there, too. Probationers who have been through the community's support network know the kind of help they are likely to get at different places. The problem becomes one of finding someone who truly has some interest in the probationer's problems, even when they seem to be intractable.

Openings

Openings serve as explanations for the conditions the probationer is to live under. The probationer must have a thorough understanding of what he or she can or cannot do and what will happen if he or she fails to live by this agreement. Openings are an important time to begin to develop rapport. Rapport is achieved, in part, by treating the probationer with a measure of respect and dignity. Openings are crucial because they set the tone for the entire process and prepare the client for working with the officer. If the officer is to treat the probationer with dignity, the probationer is to be considered as someone who can make rational choices, someone who eventually will become self-activating, self-directing, self-criticizing, self-correcting, and self-understanding. This process begins when officers treat the probationer with a measure of respect despite how offensive or indifferent the probationer appears to be at that time.

Openings establish the importance of probation conditions. Following the simplest rules is sometimes the most difficult task for someone who has never before had someone hold him or her to a set of rules. Respect, responsibility, and accountability go hand-in-hand. Some officers begin the opening by being as rigid as possible when they go over the conditions of probation. Consistent with the need to treat everyone with a measure of dignity, each probationer is handled in a similar fashion at the start. This is done for several reasons. First of all, the officer wants to let the offender know that this is serious business. Secondly, the officer knows that it is easier to relax the rules later as a form of reward than it is to tighten them up as a form of punishment. Lastly, this opening is often the point where the officer is given a chance to underscore the importance to attending to the payment of fines and restitution and the necessity of following through with the treatment plan. It must be explained to the probationer that acting responsibly and being treated respectfully are both part of the change process. The treatment plan has to be carefully reviewed so that the probationer understands the importance of following through with it.

Caseload

Caseloads have been going up in all areas of probation except in those restricted by law such as in an intensive supervision unit. Caseloads can be as high as 400 per officer in California to 65 in West Virginia (Maguire and Pastore 1995). Adult officers, who supervised 80 juvenile probationers a few years ago, are now required to supervise 125 probationers.

Cases can be assigned to an officer on a rotating basis. Each officer takes his or her turn handling cases as they arrive. Another method is to assign cases on the basis of caseload maximums. In other words, the officer who has not achieved capacity would have cases assigned to him or her. The third means is to assign cases on the basis of geographic regions. This method is being emphasized with the community justice movement. This model provides the officer with a thorough knowledge of the community factors impinging on the offender but it also means that some officers will have far more cases than others. If that happens, the geographic area should be subdivided. The fourth method is to assign cases on the basis of a single shared characteristic. Officers have specialized caseloads involving drug offenders, sex offenders, drunken drivers, veterans, and mentally retarded offenders. The size of these caseloads will depend on the proportion of offenders who meet these criteria. The fifth technique, the vertical model, is based on the classification level achieved by combining characteristics (Allen et al. 1979, 63). The general conclusion from research conducted on specialized caseloads indicates that they can be relatively effective with the target population if the probationers are referred to appropriate services and they can be offered services that are not otherwise available (Allen et al. 1979, 64).

Another option is the single officer versus team supervision. Single officer supervision attempts to take advantage of the personalized one-to-one relationship established with the probationer. The team supervision model recognizes the diversity of probationer needs and the many skills offered by officers assembled into one team (Allen et al. 1979, 65). Today, this approach is receiving renewed attention in the day reporting center. Computer programs target the cases that need review and remind the officer that attention should be given to them.

Effective caseload management is a real skill and those officers who do well take an interest in each case. Such officers have a desire to see the humanity and worth of each person. This is essential, especially as over time, some officers will become jaded and burnout by the process and unfortunately some may release their frustrations on the offender.

Further problems occur among some officers who continue to carry and leave open cases that should be closed. This problem has been identified as **hooking** the probation officer (Jacobs 1990). The officer continues to supervise someone who is viewed by the unit supervisor as either beyond help or no longer in need of supervision. This happens when the officer gets tied up in other duties such as doing more investigations. This is also attributable to the *squeaky wheel syndrome;* problematic probationers receive attention but successful probationers are ignored. All officers recognize that just one crisis per day is enough to wreak havoc on the caseload. For example, a juvenile who has committed a crime may need special attention because he is arrested, has been released to the custody of his parents but gets thrown out of the home, and has a history of suicide attempts. Or a probationer may be afraid of being mugged at school and refuses to get on the school bus. The officer has to go to the home and speak with parents and the youth, and then take the youth to school where he or she must speak with guidance counselors and principals, and finally meet with a mental health counselor. If the officer is unable to do that, he or she may try to get the parent to follow up on the plan. All of this might take all day.

Another important concept is **working the caseload**, which refers to the officer examining the caseload from time to time to see who can be released. This takes time and effort. There are cases that can be safely discharged and there are cases where there is some element of risk. There are also cases in which risk is not a factor but the probationer is continued because he or she is benefiting from a treatment program. Probationers are also continued because the officer has not reviewed the caseload to see who can be released. In yet another scenario, officers have reviewed their caseloads and believe the administration will only give them more cases than they can manage if they seek the discharge of everyone

hooking occurs when the probation officer continues to supervise someone who is viewed by the unit supervisor as either beyond help or no longer in need of supervision.

working the caseload means the officer examines his or her caseload from time to time to see who can be released.

who might become eligible. These are cases in which the offender is treated unjustly and not granted an appropriate measure of respect.

Reports

The most significant responsibility for a probation agency is supervising offenders (Allen et al. 1985, 170). Reports are set at scheduled times based on how often the probationer is to have contact with the officer. Some probationers will see their officer daily, weekly, or monthly. Some simply send in written reports. Some are taken in central offices or in satellite units. A probation officer will usually devote two or three afternoons per week to taking reports. At that time, he or she hopes to have spoken to everyone on the caseload during the reporting period. Some offenders will report by mail, by phone, or in person. Due to the high caseload numbers, officers have to work hard to make sure they know who is reporting and what is his or her status. Some departments use file photos to ensure there is no misunderstanding. Bar codes will probably be used in the future in some jurisdictions, too. In order to handle the high-volume caseloads, some departments are experimenting with the use of group reporting centers (Parent et al. 1995).

When taking reports, the officers are interested in the probationer's home life, work, school, treatment programs, and required payments and whether any important changes have taken place. Some reports take as little as 5 minutes, especially if the probationer is doing well and has no apparent problems. If there are concerns, however, the conversation may take as long as an hour or more. Of course many problems may be indicated by the report but the officer may believe they are being addressed in the offender's treatment or job training program and the offender may simply need encouragement and not counseling. In a time study of probation officer activity (Jester 1990) one finds that anywhere from 25 percent to 41 percent of the officer's time had been spent on officer-offender interactions. Within this interaction, 14 percent of the interaction was supportive counseling and casework, 8 percent was risk evaluation, 2 percent was service referrals, 2 percent was mandatory service referrals, 3 percent was aggressive enforcement, and 2 percent was material assistance (Jester 1990).

Juvenile Officer Karen

With a lot of kids it is bakery style—first come, first served. And some times you know you may have 10 kids lined up and you got a kid in your office pouring his heart out and it may mean that kids are going to have to wait a little bit.

Intensive Supervision Officer George

I try not to spend a lot of time with each of them. When they come in, I ask them what changes have occurred since the last time that I saw them and find out what their answers are to certain questions. Did they look for work? Did you go to your counseling appointment? Did you go to your drug rehab and your alcohol clinic? What happened? When is your next appointment there? Have you moved? Have you been rearrested? What has changed? A lot of times nothing has changed.

It is also important to have effective treatment programs. Juvenile Probation Officer Fred said: "I don't think it is a question of adequate programs as much as it is the question of the draw. The best programs are progressive and intelligent. There are some who aren't worth a nickel." Juvenile Officer Rich added: "Lots of my kids go to counseling, something that I can't offer. I think that [offering counseling] is inappropriate on my part because I see them only once a week. I used to say that this job is all reality therapy. I think my caseload methods are drawn from all schools of thought." Adult Officer Debra, who is treating her probationers with a measure of dignity, said: "I am a very positive person and I can take the individual who is on probation and say that you have some faults and some weaknesses and we will have to talk about those things but let's talk about your strengths. You have potential here. They made some mistakes and let's eliminate the mistakes and go from there. So I was very fortunate in having success stories."

Community-Centered Field Visits

Field visits provide an important opportunity to look at probation work. Some officers like to get out of the office. However, high caseloads and the danger found in the community are forcing officers to reconsider how they approach their field visits. Many officers find important value in going out into the field. As one said, "I like to be out there working by the seats of my pants going to schools, houses, and agencies." Yet another juvenile officer said: "A majority of my cases are single-parent households and most of them don't understand the concept of parenting so we spend a lot of time on that. I don't think most of them were parented very well. Going out into the field both refreshes the officer and provides him or her with a chance to discuss the case with family members and other professionals who are responsible for the person. In many cases there is a process of cross-fertilization taking place where everyone benefits from the contact."

Community-centered supervision activities call for the development of supervision strategies that carefully monitor, in concert with others, the whereabouts and behavior of offenders. Such activities serve to connect probationers to their local neighborhoods and thereby draw on the influence and leverage presented by the prosocial peers and adults who live there.

Recommendations for Supervision Changes

The Manhattan Institute (2003) has offered some important recommendations for changes in offender supervision. First, traditional working hours need to change so that officers are working hours that make the most sense in terms of work effectiveness. Officers need to understand the environment they are working in to know whether to spend more time later in the day or on weekends. Second, most of the supervision should be actively done in the field in an assigned area for which the officer is responsible. This means getting to where the offender lives, works, and engages in recreational and other activities. The office should be the base of supervision and the field the place of supervision (Clear and Corbett 1999). Firsthand knowledge of the environment is a critical element of meaningful supervision as well as of officer safety. In addition to being in the community, probation should be highly visible and positive in nature

(National Institute of Corrections 1999). As officers become known in the community, they will garner support for their work and create leverage in making changes in these communities. Over time, the officer will assume "ownership" of the area and engage in a more active process of problem solving. Managers and unit supervisors must also become tolerant of flexible schedules and if they treat their staff with dignity, they will learn they can trust their officers to do an effective job. The community can provide the managers and unit supervisors with the appropriate feedback through town meetings, focus groups, and the like. The managers and unit supervisors become problem solvers and ombudsmen for the office. In addition, changes need to be made regarding procedures and qualifications for the hiring of probation staff. Staff representing the different sectors of the community must be hired. Besides the traditional skills, the Manhattan Institute suggests officers will need to be familiar with the principles and practices of human dignity but also will need skills in developing partnerships, community organizing, public relations, and defensive tactics. Human dignity is essential to the process, because it requires that each person be given a respected voice in the course of action. To achieve such changes, senior officers will need training and an understanding of human dignity in the areas just mentioned. The institute suggests training should be standardized with a 2-week course of study at a probation and parole academy. Once the rookie officer has graduated, he or she should be assigned a mentor in the department.

Each officer must recognize the role played by other agencies in supervision. Community partnerships should develop in program planning, resource development, and cooperative partnering. These partnerships should include neighborhood groups, schools, local businesses, faith communities, law enforcement, and other criminal justice agencies. Connections should be made with human services, treatment programs, and nonprofit agencies as they impact offender assessment, diagnosis, treatment, and supervision. Comprehensive education campaigns are needed to alert communities of crime, steps taken to deal with it, and the need for community involvement. Caseloads must be reduced if probation is to achieve the goals of greater public safety. The cost reduction achieved by reducing prison populations and less use of central offices will ease resource demands. A greater use of technology—especially laptop computers—will enable around the clock supervision, provide greater offender regulation, increase officer accountability, and reinforce the outcomes sought by the agency's mission.

Complex Work

loosely coupled organizations such as the court and the probation system, are responsive to one another but at the same time maintain independent and diverse identities and operational separateness.

Probation work is very complex, requiring a great deal of discretion, and is exercised by officers who differ considerably in personality, ideology, training, and education. Probation work takes place in **loosely coupled organizations** (Hagan 1994). The imagery of the loosely coupled system is meant to convey the impression that the court and the probation subsystems are responsive to one another but that at the same time they maintain independent and diverse identities and operational separateness (Weick 1976). Meyer and Rowan (1977) point out that loosely coupled formal organizations have organizational elements that are only slightly linked to one another's activities. Rules are often violated, decisions often go unimplemented or if implemented have uncertain consequences, and techniques are often subverted or rendered so vague as to provide little coordination. Glassman (1973) put forward the argument that court subsystems are loosely coupled to the extent that they share few influences in common. He suggests the influence they share differs substantially in the degree of influence they have over one another, and these shared influences are weak when compared to other influences also operating there. Loosely coupled organizations are not administered and directed by a set of hard and fast rules but are, instead, organizations that are managed as loosely articulated subsystems in which control is internal and external to the subsystem (Reiss 1971, 114–121). In other words, a loosely coupled organization may have a set of rules set by the leadership that is intended to regulate organizational behavior but within organizational subunits employees determine for themselves the rules that are actually adhered to. These rules are determined by persons outside the subsystem and by those who work within the subsystem. In a very real sense, each probation officer operates as a subsystem providing his or her own system of justice. Probation requires a loosely coupled system to provide individualized treatment for the offender. Officer discretion was an artifact of the historical roots of probation when departments were granting considerable freedom to officers to do their work as they deemed necessary. It was also a means of accommodating the diverse political interests that impinged on the system while at the same time preserving a measure of officer autonomy and the impression of impartiality. This leads to the impression that the United States has a haphazard probation system.

For the most part, probation officers are dedicated professionals who care a great deal about what they do and only hope that other people will come to recognize it. Officers have taken a great deal of pride in the conducting of the investigation, taking reports, field visits, filing violations, and discharging and closing cases. These tasks require the officer to acquire different skills. Much attention today is directed toward conducting investigations and supervising the caseload. Some officers have found these duties to be overwhelming and believe they have been let down by the rest of the system and society in general.

Violations

Probationer violations will be discussed at length in another chapter. For the moment it is must be remembered that probationer violations involve new crimes, absconding, and the failure to comply with the conditions of probation. In general at the federal level about 10 percent of probationers are considered to have violated their probation (Bureau of Justice Statistics 1996). Some officers violate as many as 25 probationers per year. Some of them are violations because the offender cannot be located.

Many probation officers are hesitant to bring a probationer to court for a violation. First of all, a new charge may be unfounded and dismissed by the court so it is a waste of time. Secondly, the officer may seek time to develop an alternative treatment plan. This is important if the officer wishes to maintain the relationship with the probationer and is concerned that a hearing will reverse the process. Finally, the officer may feel somewhat responsible for the client's failure. This opinion can develop out of recognition of the lack of time available for each case with rising caseloads and greater numbers of presentence reports.

The probation officer, public defender, district attorney, and judge all work together to form a courtroom work group (Cole 1989). Cole assumes that officials work regularly with one another and develop a working relationship out of this continuous contact. In many instances, however, the probation officer is caught in the middle of a process in which the interests of the different actors are not in consort. Quite often the officer opposes the positions worked out by these participants. He or she would like stricter enforcement and support for his or her supervision but finds the court and lawyers have agreed to something else.

Discharges and Closings

Discharges and closings are the end product of probation. This is the time to make the offender feel good for having accomplished something for which he or she should be proud. These processes involve notifying the court of the status of the probationer and asking the court to approve the recommendation of the probation officer. The probationer who has done well will more often be discharged early. These are the probationers who make the job worthwhile. Closings occur when someone has maxed out his or her time on probation. In other words, the court ordered a three-year period of probation and the three years are over.

During interviews Danielle, a juvenile officer, said this about the procedures used in discharges: "I have a 17 year old African-American youth who should have received a discharge letter focusing on progress made in school, work, family relations, treatment, drugs, alcohol, and any other areas. I look to see if he has completed the court order, paid the fine, been reporting and proven himself by his behavior. They have to be working, if not in school. And the last thing that I do on a discharge is to call the wife or the parents and see if they agree with me."

Harry, a juvenile officer, said, "Usually when you discharge somebody you have a feeling who will make it and who is coming back." Personal experience helps some probation officers to develop an intuitive sense as to who will succeed and who will fail after leaving probation. Probationers are discharged before they are ready for release from supervision but the officer's authority over the person has ended with the fulfillment of the term of probation.

■ Models of Supervision

Smykla (1984) has offered four case management strategies a probation agency may adopt in dealing with the offender. Changes in clients, organizations, and environments all require the officer to make adjustments in the case management strategy. Ignoring this concern furthers organizational disintegration. For example, some clients may need controlling before they are ready for any rehabilitation. Others will simply need rehabilitation, because they already understand the trouble they are in. The key officer models are casework, program, advocacy, and brokerage.

casework model is predicated on the belief that internal staff in the department are capable of providing the necessary care for the probationer.

The traditional **casework model** is predicated on the belief that staff members are capable of providing the necessary care for the probationer. The agency's counseling skills are directed toward rehabilitation and surveillance.

The **program model** involves assigning probationers to officers who specialize in dealing with particular offenders. Clients are assigned to officers who specialize in dealing only with substance abusers, sex offenders, property offenders, perpetrators of domestic violence, or some other category, which is considered relevant at the time. Need-assessment instruments and risk-assessment instruments are used in these programs.

The **advocacy model** calls for a generalist staff, which uses external resources to deal with client needs. According to this model, the community is responsible for the client's problems and thus, the people in the community who the have the skills and the experience to deal with these offenders should be used in addressing their needs. The staff is expected to work with the probationers to see that they are attending various community programs. These resources include family and child guidance clinics, job training programs, and drug treatment facilities.

The **brokerage model** uses external resources but combines them with the program model. The brokerage approach emphasizes the assessment of client needs and the linkage of available community services with those needs. The primary task of the brokerage probation officer is to locate existing community resources, which can be used to benefit the probationer and to bind the probationer to community social service agencies (Dell'Apa et al. 1976; Rubin 1977). Accordingly, the probation officer uses external resources for a specialized caseload.

program model involves assigning probationers to officers who specialize in dealing with particular offenders.

advocacy model calls for a generalist staff, which uses external resources to deal with client needs. The community is responsible for the client's problems.

brokerage model emphasizes the assessment of client needs and the linkage of available community services with those needs.

Case Management

A critical element in supervision is the process of case management. Putting an offender on probation is far more than simply demanding that the conditions of probation be adhered to over time. Offenders, the communities they live in, and the social context under which they interact with others are constantly changing. Even important considerations found in the presentence report may not be true anymore. For the most part, the two major concerns for supervision are (1) offender compliance with the law and the conditions of probation and (2) the provision of services to assist in the offender's rehabilitation. In a case method in which community resource management, intensive supervision, team supervision, and risks assessment and classification are taken into consideration, the case method shifts from the potential harm posed by the offender to problems that instigate criminal acts. It is assumed that crime is not freely chosen but is rather the inevitable outcome of social disadvantages acting upon people without emotional or family strengths to protect them from developing criminal associations and then criminal behavior (Parsloe 1976, 73).

Correctional case management is a systematic process by which identified needs and strengths of the offender are matched with selected services and resources in corrections (Enos and Southern 1996, 1). The case management model of treatment affords enhanced protection of human dignity and the facilitation of

correctional case management a systematic process by which identified needs and strengths of the offender are matched with selected services and resources in corrections.

growth. Case management was designed to provide both the structure and the opportunity not found in other schemes by organizing comprehensive, individually oriented services with a structured stepwise model of treatment. It is especially valuable as a tool to be employed each time a probation officer comes in contact with a new probationer. In the face of persistent offender problems, community-based correctional case management provides a means of providing relapse prevention and multiple treatment options for a variety of offenders. This is achieved through the goals of reduced recidivism, reintegration, and systematic monitoring of performances through the use of systematic and integrative approaches. Enos and Southern suggest that case management has the following components.

Advocacy

advocacy is meant to trigger the correctional process by instigating changes in the offender and in the service delivery. True advocacy would promote the rights and interests of the offender in dealing with service providers.

<u>Advocacy</u>, the first stage of the process, is meant to trigger the correctional process by instigating changes in the offender and in service delivery. True advocacy would promote the rights and interests of the offender in dealing with service providers. The goal is to have the service provider recognize these interests and to develop a stake in the intervention. There are several different types of advocacies required of probation officers. A probation officer provides advocacy services when testifying and making recommendations to the court, negotiating pro bono services for the client, or securing priority placement at programs with waiting lists. The probation officer may also provide advocacy in regard to child custody or negotiating bureaucratic procedures. However, at a broader level, the officer can advocate for organizational change, interagency cooperation, and community development. Advocacy is limited only by the officer's self-imposed limitations.

Intake

intake clients are processed into the system or referred to other agencies. During this intake step, an orientation takes place and rapport building develops between the offender and the probation officer.

<u>Intake</u> is the second stage of the process. For the most part, these are involuntary clients receiving services from understaffed agencies. Clients are processed into the system or referred to other agencies. During this step, an orientation takes place and rapport building develops between the offender and the probation officer. This stage may involve crisis intervention or an ongoing readjustment to a problem. There may be a crime involved or there may not. The youth who is on probation may have had a difficult argument with a parent or the youth may have trouble with a condition of probation. Many of these clients have multiple needs and have particular difficulty with authority, stress, and dealing with threatening and unfamiliar environments. Knowing that one will be treated with dignity and respect under these conditions goes a long way toward processing the paperwork and developing a system of effective communication where appointments are kept and problems reduced.

Assessment

assessment attempts to answer questions raised during the intake phase. This is the phase in which there is a matching of services to the identified needs of the offender.

<u>Assessment</u>, as the third step, attempts to answer questions raised during intake. This is the phase in which efforts are made to match services with the identified needs of the offender. Assessment, through the use of the presentence report, includes information from the family, other persons, and organizations that have some knowledge of the offender. Specialized assessments are needed for sex or violent offenders as well as the substance-abusing offender.

Assessment depends on the adequacy of the information provided. Correctional programs have often published their results using the Pearson Product Correlation Coefficient, which generates an r-value. An r-value is a measure that estimates the strength and direction of a linear association between two variables. Pearson's r-values range from -1.0 to $+1.0$ (Walsh and Ollenberger 2001). It is argued that when presenting results of an analysis of the magnitude of the relationship between a predictor variable (substance abuse) and an outcome variable (recidivism) one must recognize that r-values of .30 or less are of little consequence. If the r-value is squared one finds that it explains only 9 percent of the variance. In other words, substance abuse, in this case would account for only 9 percent of the reason for the offender's recidivism. A great deal is left unexplained. More importantly, a squared r-value tends to underestimate the magnitude of the effects produced and for the most part is an approximation of the percentage difference in outcome between individuals who have more or less of a particular characteristics (Gendreau et al. 1996, 18). In other words, an r-value would account for the difference between offenders who are on average high and low substance abusers.

Classification

<u>Classification</u>, the fourth step, helps to direct offenders to the programs which will have maximum effect. Amenability to treatment is considered the principal determiner of whether or not the person goes to prison. Where possible, differential intervention should match the offender to specific programs and specific services. Input from a variety of professionals is used to achieve this. Simple classification schemes involve a checklist, while the more complicated involve reports from outside professionals and the data are then organized and presented into a meaningful classification scheme. The reliability of this classification depends on the quality of the assessments and the ability of the case manager to integrate the information into a specific intervention. The presentence report is a good example of a classification stage activity (Enos and Southern 1996, 11). This instrument combines information developed from the probation department's questionnaire, criminal history, evaluations and diagnosis from psychiatrist, psychologist and substance abuse specialist, and findings developed from interviews, records, and contacts with individuals who have reliable information about the offender.

classification a system for separating offenders based on their risk of reoffending.

Referral Referrals are the means by which classification decisions are implemented. Resource brokering and liaison with service providers are essential because no probation officer can provide quality services to every probationer. Referrals are accomplished through knowledge of the quality of available services and the willingness to network and link with various agencies and service providers. This work also requires case monitoring and tracking to ensure the client is complying with the treatment order. Effective officers try to get out of the office and meet with these service providers, maintain telephone contacts, gather written reports, and complete record keeping. All of these are essential to good liaison and client performance. Many officers enjoy meeting with other professionals to discuss client performance. Knowledge is shared and a sense of camaraderie and mutual support develops.

Intervention

According to Enos and Southern (1996, 13–14), intervention comes in a variety of formats and can be understood as having two essential attributes: who is responsible for the problem and who is responsible for the solution. In general the medical model tends to view the problem in terms of a basic constitution, a physical ailment, or to apply the model to social-adjustment problems in terms of identifying the problem, prescribing a treatment, and assessing when a cure has been effected. Enos and Southern (1996, 13) point out that the moral model considers the offender as responsible for the problem and the solution. Individual choice and personal commitment to change are emphasized. In the enlightenment model, the person is considered responsible for the problem but not the solution. Chemical dependence is viewed in these terms. This model is closely linked to the medical model in that chemical dependence is viewed as a chronic illness that is inherited. Part of the cure under this model calls for a reliance on God. The compensatory model is the major perspective in rehabilitation (Enos and Southern 1996, 14). The offender is the product of a dysfunctional family and social disadvantages. This model calls for offenders to gain control of their lives by planning and acting responsibly in resolving problems. Inequality or discrimination is considered an excuse with the principal concern with matching needs with resources to overcome disadvantages and lifestyle problems. The client is to go through the change and the correctional agent is to identify the existing resources.

Relapse Prevention

Intervention effectiveness is enhanced through relapse prevention. Criminal justice professionals establish behavioral boundaries for the offender. At the same time, the probationer is granted a limited measure of freedom and responsibility to test out his or her behavior, especially as it leads to improvements in education, vocational training, psychology, and interpersonal skills. Both the professional and the client assume responsibility for change. The introduction of behavioral structures or boundaries is designed to decrease over time, resulting in increased levels of freedom. In due course, the responsibility for change shifts increasingly toward the offender so that prior to release from probation, the probationer becomes more self-regulatory. The offender comes to recognize criminogenic needs and associates as possible trouble and directs his or her behavior away from them. No longer are offenders told what to do but do it on their own. As the offender progresses from high structure to low structure and social regulation to self-regulation, office visits and field visits become increasingly rare and other restrictions on behavior are reduced. This does not mean the offender is free to act as before the offense but that the offender develops new behavior that provides an alternative to the self-destructive behavior exhibited earlier.

Offender Supervision | **191**

Offender Supervision | **191**

Evaluation

Evaluation is the last component of the case management strategy. Corrections require demonstrable results. Classification can determine treatment amenability versus differential intervention; outcome evaluation can determine program effectiveness and professional accountability. Differential treatment selection is the key to program effectiveness (Beutler and Clarkin 1990). Differential treatment calls for matches being made relative to the offender's characteristics, the targeted behavior, and steps in correctional intervention as they relate to the offender's learning style and the instructor's teaching style responsivity. To further the evaluation, it is necessary to do both process evaluations and outcome evaluations. These evaluations answer the questions of what you are doing and how you are doing. Once the evaluation is conducted, it is important to present appropriate information to outsiders who are responsible for the program. Governmental authorities and granting agencies all need appropriate information they can use.

■ Treatment Strategies

In *Asylums,* Goffman (1961) points out that while in prison, the offender is to undergo a transformative experience that causes a radical shift in the offender's moral career. This radical shift of self is the essence of rehabilitation. It is less of a problem on all levels when the offender undergoes a transformation in the self and no longer desires to commit crime in the future. Rehabilitation certainly operates as a preventive measure. Support for rehabilitation can be found at both the empirical and at the normative level. Rehabilitation is supported in order to cut criminal justice system cost, to promote the concept of human dignity, to maintain the integrity of the profession, and to support reform in the criminal justice system. Rehabilitation is cheaper than imprisonment. Rehabilitation also promotes the concept of human dignity by recognizing that all offenders can change for the better. The integrity of the profession is maintained when higher level purposes, other than retribution, are sought when dealing with the offender. Lastly, rehabilitation utilizes various schemes that are considered improvements over the traditional punitive approaches.

Gendreau and Ross (1987) have provided a comprehensive assessment of rehabilitation programs. They found that many studies reported reductions in the offender's behavior. "Simply put, there have been significant gains from the perspective of theory development, clinical practice, treatment outcome literature, and policy development," said Cullen and Gendreau (1992, 238). More recently, Gaubatz (1995) identified support for nonincarcerative penalties, particularly for the property offender. Gaubatz found support for rehabilitation among people who oppose capital punishment, who believe too much use is made of imprisonment, and who believe that greater resources should be put into solving human problems. In 1984, 79 percent of a national sample chose the statement that society would be better served if nonviolent offenders were not jailed but were put to work and made to repay their victims, over the assertion that nonviolent criminals must be kept in jail because allowing them out represents too great a risk to society (Maguire and Pastore 1995). In another survey, 64 percent of the respondents indicated that most violent offenders could be rehabilitated if given the right rehabilitation program (Maguire and Pastore 1995, 176).

In the Public's Eye . . .

Applegate, Cullen, and Fisher (1997) report that although the public wants to see the offender punished, the public is not interested in punishment alone; most of the public support the rehabilitation of offenders. In reviewing 27 studies that asked respondents to rate, rank, and choose rehabilitation in comparison to other options, Applegate, Cullen, and Fisher found rehabilitation was considered important in 20 of the studies—and if rehabilitation was not found to be the primary purpose of corrections, the citizens ranked it second. Punitive attitudes vary dramatically depending on whether they are measured with broad opinion poll-type questions or by more specific questions. Applegate, Cullen, and Fisher also report that many polls present a misleading picture of public opinion. Single-item questions tap only surface views and not the complexity of what the public wants done with crime. The public is fairly rational in their views; they favor a balanced approach to dealing with crime. The public seems interested in imposing fair punishments and providing treatment. They support punishment and getting tough but they believe it is important to rehabilitate offenders. They support imprisonment, but mainly for serious and violent offenders. Community corrections should be used, especially if it involves more than just putting offenders on the street with no supervision or treatment. The public is very supportive of rehabilitation for juveniles including early intervention programs, even favoring using tax dollars for these programs over building more prisons. As for habitual offenders, they found that the public did not support lenient punishment of habitual offenders. (Applegate, Cullen, and Fisher 1997)

Continued Support

Support for community-based programming must continue because it costs less than sending someone to prison. *The Corrections Yearbook* (Camp and Camp 2000) reports that in 1999 the annual cost of probation ranged from $452 per year to $1,275 per year. It is generally believed that imprisonment costs at least $20,000 per year. Petersilia (2002) points out that although the cost of probation is less than imprisonment, it is difficult to calculate what one receives for a per diem cost rate because probation services vary so much across the nation. The cost of treatment obviously varies with the type and quality of treatment given. The rich, and those with insurance, can take advantage of these programs. Sometimes, county social services will assume a portion of the cost.

Rehabilitation maintains the integrity of the profession. Probation was founded on providing support for those who were in trouble with the law but who, with some help, could alter their lives and become contributing members of society. Many probation officers support rehabilitation because of the good they do. Moreover, many probation officers continue to take up the profession because they believe that they have a chance to help someone, particularly juveniles. In earlier studies by Glaser (1969) and Harris, Clear, and Baird (1989) to just name two, it was argued that there is still considerable support for rehabilitation among the officers. Ellsworth (1990) provides further support for the rehabilitation principle. His findings indicated that even when given a choice to reconfigure the probation system, to meet the needs of the public for community protection, probation professionals rise to the historical challenge of providing rehabilitation services to the offender.

Juvenile offenders under the doctrine of *parens patriae* (the state assumes the duties of parent) have a right to treatment. If the state intervenes in the lives of a probationer, then among other purposes, that intervention must be offered for the probationer's good, too. Many serious juveniles offenders come from backgrounds that are so brutalized, alienated, and bizarre that they truly have problems that are not of their own making. Efforts to rehabilitate require substantial support. Society may feel bad for them but not sorry enough to set aside punishment in favor of a serious commitment to support rehabilitation programs. According to Feld (1999), people seem to care more about their own children than about the children of another race or ethnicity.

If *parens patriae* provides the motive for the provision of treatment to juveniles, then the concept of the social contract provides a rationale for providing treatment for adult probationers. On moral grounds, rehabilitation is the only justification of punishment that obligates the state to care for an offender's needs (Cullen and Gilbert 1982). According to Locke (1988), a political society is brought about by a social contract, a hypothetical accord by which people agree to forgo some of their independence in exchange for peace and a set of reciprocal working arrangements. Under the contract, the state assumes the responsibility for charging, convicting, and punishing the offender as outlined in the laws of that time. The social contract is based on the assumption that society is a voluntary agreement amongst those who wish to be bound by the compact they have formed. The authority of the system stems from the free consent of those who compose it. Individuals have certain inalienable rights that the contract is intended to secure. The contract calls for the punishment of those who have violated the contract and forfeited their rights; but it also calls for the support and nurturing of those who are in need of help because they share common human qualities with each member of society. And although the outlaw may have violated the contract, rarely is it so completely violated that little good is found in the person. This person, too, deserves to receive the solicitude of the society so that the person can reintegrate back into society. Rousseau (1988) provides further comment on the subject. He argues that after punishment for any violation of the social contract, offenders regain their original rights and resumes their natural liberty. Frequent punishments are always a sign of weakness or failure on the part of the government. Furthermore, it is thought that there is no single ill doer who could not be turned to some good. The state has no right to put someone to death, even for the sake of making an example of them, unless it is very dangerous for others to keep the person alive.

More on Rehabilitation

Rehabilitation provides an alternative view that more severe punishments than probation are inappropriate responses to crime and delinquency (McAnany 1984). It is therefore recognized that social and personal circumstances often compel someone to violate the law, and unless efforts are made to help offenders escape these conditions, little relief from the effects of crime can be anticipated. Whatever the available resources, probation continues to deploy community assets in a fashion that centers on the offender (client) and sees the probation officer (therapist) as responsible for developing, through referrals, the resources necessary to meet the client's needs. Convicted offenders may be shown leniency because the diagnosis (presentence report) is optimistic about their prognosis for law-abiding behavior, provided a treatment plan is implemented. It is, therefore, a theory that focuses on the offender, rather than the offense (McAnany 1984, 68).

The final reason offered for continuing support of rehabilitation is that, historically, efforts to establish treatment programs have often led to reform in the criminal justice system. Because of the argument that it is beneficial to reform the offender, reasons have been found for improving services to victims, witnesses, and the public in general. Support for rehabilitation could also come from those who believe that it will augment public safety.

Serious rehabilitation programs were previously attempted sporadically on a scale that could never have truly tested rehabilitation's potential. According to Currie (1985), these programs lacked people, resources, and the time to do the job (p. 237). Programs didn't do what they were designed to do on paper. Most lacked therapeutic integrity in that they failed to follow through on their theoretical assumptions about what rehabilitation would require. Programs were underfunded, understaffed, poorly trained, and unmotivated. Often, it was not possible to separate the better programs from the truly poor programs operating in shattered communities (Currie 1985, 239). Before presenting what is considered to be a successful intervention, it is important to identify what are not likely to be successful strategies. Cullen and Gendreau (1992) believe ineffective programs employ the medical model, are nondirective, and use behavior modification inappropriately. Moreover, behavior modification is an imposed strategy, it emphasizes punishment too much, and it fails to incorporate the inherent strengths of the peer group.

New Studies on Rehabilitation

Support for rehabilitation is found among the newer studies, which more carefully evaluated programs. Experts learned more about why rehabilitation fails, and that when it does work, the reason is not solely with the nature of the clients but with the programs and with the larger community (Currie 1985, 238–239). According to Currie, what must be kept in mind is that no program is a complete failure. Spending any time, no matter how small, with an offender has a benefit. More specifically, it is important to recognize the conditions under which a program is delivered. The strength and integrity of the treatment must be maintained. This means that society must follow through on the theoretical assumptions about crime and what is required to change offender behavior (Gendreau and Ross 1979). One cannot assume, for example, that crime is caused by social learning experiences and that the solution is to offer intensive psychotherapy. Whatever the specific technique used, the most important factor is that it is implemented intensively, seriously, and for a reasonable length of time. The program need not be punitive but it must be linked with other community resources including schools, employers, social service agencies, networks with relatives, and neighborhood organizations. This concept of offender treatment maintains that if the offender is to change, a comprehensive effort must be employed that addresses the individual and his or her family and the influences directed toward that family. The probationer must be linked to a range of services involved in the community and tied to the family. The goal is to strengthen the individual, the family, and the community. Communities must be stable and offer a decent and dignified existence as the fruits of respectable and cooperative behavior.

Andrews and colleagues (1990) at Carlton University conducted a meta-analysis of 154 correctional programs. A meta-analysis examines the findings of different studies and tries to establish consistencies of measurement among different studies. The value of the meta-analysis is that it identifies contradictory findings and reduces the needed for duplicative studies. For example, the researcher may examine, among many other considerations, the gender makeup of the different sample populations of similar offenders to see if the researchers report similar findings for gender differences. In the Andrews and colleagues (1990) meta-analysis each assessment involved an exploration of the size of the link between reduced recidivism and either an experimental or a comparison condition. Overall, the meta-analysis found that the average correlation between the 154 tests of correctional intervention and reduced recidivism was r = .10. This represents a reduction of only 10 percent relative to the comparison group, that is, the control group reported recidivism rates of 55 percent and the experimental group reported a 45 percent recidivism rate. The argument that nothing works would have had a correlation of .00. One source of variability was consideration of correctional treatment versus punishment values. Correctional punishment produced no results, but 40 percent of the 124 studies of correctional treatment produced results of at least r = .20. Treatment services may be further differentiated by application of the principle of responsivity. This suggests that approaches emphasizing specific behavioral changes are more promising than less structured services. Behavioral approaches require the offender to either do something or cease doing something. One may, for example, ask the offender to attend school or cease drinking alcohol. The idea is to have something the offender can do and can understand. Correctional treatment that emphasizes actions (behavioral), certain verbal expressions or thought processes (cognitive), or role modeling approaches (social learning) use good role modeling, reinforcement of positive behavior, and practice of positive behavior until it becomes habitual and the negative behavior is extinguished. More specifically the average effect of the behavioral approach was r = .29 as compared to an r = .07 for the non-behavioral approach. When the Carlton group looked further into these 124 tests of correctional treatment by employing a content analysis of risk, needs, and responsivity, it was learned that the mean recidivism effect of appropriate clinical or psychological treatment was 35 percent as compared to 65 percent for the comparison condition. The Carlton study concluded that correctional treatment did work when applied appropriately (Andrews et al. 1990, 13). The therapeutic integrity was considered to be vital to success in reducing recidivism but also to be crucially linked to clinical and psychological appropriate treatment. **Therapeutic integrity**, in this sense, has come to mean that specific modeling of appropriate behavior is targeted at linking offenders to specific treatment interventions, intermediate targets that can reasonably be

therapeutic integrity is a specific modeling linking intervention, intermediate targets, and reduced recidivism with trained workers and clinically supervised workers.

achieved, and reduced recidivism, as well as treatment that employs sufficiently trained workers who experience clinical supervision of their own behavior (Andrews et al. 1990, 13).

Sometimes, the probation officer is the only person there is to deal with the offender's problem. This is why it is suggested that officers should have some understanding of the anticriminal modeling, cognitive therapy, and motivational interviewing. These approaches are presented in subsequent sections.

Anticriminal Modeling

In teaching probationers to respond constructively to comments about their own behavior, it is possible to correct behavior that does not respect others. Modeling is the key to effective cognitive learning processes associated with thoughts, beliefs, values, and perceptions (Bandura 1977). Good modeling and good interpersonal skills have proven to be most effective, especially for probation officers. Andrews (1980) found that probation officers who modeled anticriminal behaviors and sentiments, but also possessed good relational skills, had lower recidivism scores than others who represented the converse.

A growing body of research indicates that the qualities of good role modeling are attractiveness, competence, and receiving rewards for one's behavior (Bandura 1977; Bandura and Walters 1963). The communication skills needed for a good counselor include listening, empathy, genuineness, concreteness, self-disclosure, probing, feedback, summarizing, confrontation, and immediacy (Masters 1994, 168). This does not mean the probation officer does not get angry with the probationer who skips treatment. Officers can be honest in their anger and yet limit comments to the behavior of the offender and its consequences. The officer can retain the belief in the client's ability to succeed and in his or her inherent worth as an individual. The relationship qualities of good role modeling also involve maintaining an environment of mutual liking, respect, and caring in which openness, warmth, and understanding are offered within the limits of an appropriate interpersonal boundary (Van Voorhis 2000, 152).

Probation officers must take into account the manner in which their prosocial behavior is presented and antisocial behavior is discouraged. As suggested by Van Voorhis (2000, 152), appropriate models must be reinforced by clear and vivid expressions of concern. This is done with public displays of recognition or through behaviors that clearly exhibit trust, warmth, and interest in others. Good behavior must be reinforced through recognition and praise. Positive reinforcement is conveyed through emphatic and immediate expressions of warmth and understanding but also by eye contact, hand shakes, smiles, the sharing of experiences, holding timely meetings, and making every effort to give the probationer undivided attention when in the office. Conversely, probationers should receive a clear explanation of the counselor's reasons for approval or disapproval with suggestion for the appropriate behavior as an alternative.

In the modeling process and in conjunction with efforts to attack dysfunctional thoughts, beliefs, and attitudes, special consideration should be made to support and encourage ideas promoting human dignity in consideration of past actions and future behavior. Probationers should be discouraged from statements that express disrespect. Appropriate recognition should be given to statements expressing individual value and worth. Such expressions are particularly relevant as they pertain to the victim.

Cognitive Therapy

Offenders often engage in a set of thinking processes, which make it difficult for them to identify the harm they have inflicted on the victim. By denying the humanity in the victim, the offender is able to rationalize crimes in ways not otherwise possible. Cognitive therapies focus on the offender's thinking process by targeting dysfunctional perceptions, attitudes, and beliefs that support dysfunctional behavior. In corrections, cognitive restructuring programs seek to change offender thinking errors that support criminal behavior (Van Voorhis et al. 2000, 109).

A handout from the Minnesota Department of Corrections (undated) lists various thinking errors. Such thinking errors include closed thinking where probationers reject the idea that there is anything wrong with themselves. They are also not interested in any new ideas or any suggestion that they improve in some way. The probationer can also attend only to positive personal attributes thus denying any destructive behavior. As part of these thinking errors probationers can clam up. They can make no disclosures about themselves, thus becoming passive aggressive. Another thinking error involves role reversal. The probationer can incorrectly assume the role of the victim thus arguing that he or she is not responsible for the crime. The crime would not have occurred if not for the alcohol or drugs the offender used. Errors in thinking are also found in a lack of effort because something is seen as boring, unexciting, or unsatisfying. Such people seek immediate gratification with little sense of obligation. A desire for immediate gratification leaves the probationer with a lack of time perspective in understanding how much time things take, failure to learn anything of the past, and expectation of others to react immediately to demands. The offender may even think of himself or herself as better than or different from others and that other people should do what he or she fails to do. Thinking errors can also occur when decisions are made on the basis of assumptions, not fact. The person can also have a fear of fear, death, injury, or putdowns, but refuses to admit it. The probationer may even try to reduce the sense of fear by being overly optimistic but when things get tough the person easily quits. Distortion in thinking is also found when the offender feels worthless when held accountable. Such individuals may compensate for these feelings by needing to be in control, or by being manipulative or deceitful, and refusing dependency unless the probationer believes there is some later advantage. In conjunction with this view is an ownership attitude in which the probationer perceives that all persons or things are objects to be possessed but others do not have any similar rights. Finally, errors of thinking may be found in the use of sex for power and control, not intimacy.

Rational Emotive Therapy

Rational emotive therapy (Ellis 1973) is concerned with emotions and thoughts that impair a person's existence. First, there is the activating experience, something that occurs that is unpleasant. In the unhealthy thought system, there follows a set of irrational beliefs that decrease happiness, increase pain, and set one up for personal failure. In a healthy thought system, the unpleasantness is followed by rational beliefs that increase positive feelings and minimize pain. They are related to observable, empirically valid events (Lester and Van Voorhis 2000, 169).

Rational emotive therapy involves teaching the client that emotional states are the result, not of the activating experience, but of irrational beliefs. The client must be taught to challenge irrational beliefs.

Burns (1980) has identified some irrational ways of thinking:

1. *All-or-nothing thinking.* The individual views things in black or white. A less-than-perfect performance is a failure.

2. *Overgeneralization.* One negative event is seen as a never-ending pattern of defeat.

3. *Mental filter.* Dwells on negative details and filters out the positive.

4. *Disqualifying the positive.* Positive experiences are labelled as not counting for some reason.

5. *Magnification or catastrophizing.* The importance of something is exaggerated.

6. *Jumping to conclusions.* One assumes one knows what another person is thinking but fails to check with that person.

7. *"Shoulding."* Motivates oneself by saying "I must" or "I ought" and so feels guilty when they do not.

Rational-emotive therapy does not dwell on the stuff of psychotherapy such as the client's early history, unconscious thoughts or desires, nonverbal behavior, dreams, or any transference that occurs in the counseling setting. Quite the contrary, the counselor plays an active role in persuading, educating, directing, and sticking to his or her position. The counselor's job is to teach rational emotive theory by challenging irrational beliefs. The counselor shows how irrational beliefs affect all aspects of life and are current and observable. Perpetuating earlier experiences only exacerbates the problems. The client is taught to observe and challenge his or her own belief system and to act and understand. The counselor teaches the theory, points out irrational beliefs, and interprets quickly and with no pretense that the interpretation is difficult to accept. The counselor must be confrontational but at the same time allow the client to openly express himself or herself and bring out his or her own feelings. This is all done within the context of unconditional acceptance. Attention focuses on the beliefs and not the client. To achieve this, the counselor will use a variety of techniques including role-playing, modeling, stories, behavior therapy techniques, philosophic discussion, and audiovisual aids. Anything reasonable is employed to point out the irrational beliefs and the harm they bring. Clients must come to understand that they are in charge, can assume responsibility for what they believe, and can choose to like and accept themselves. The idea is to develop within the client the ability to self-observe and self-assess (Lester and Van Voorhis 2000, 170–171).

More on Cognitive Skills

While cognitive restructuring attempts to change the content of reasoning, cognitive skills programs seek primarily to change the structure of one's reasoning. Understanding structure is found in an example of impulsivity. Cognitive restructuring pays attention to what the person is not thinking. Cognitive behavioral coping skills are developed through self-instructional training in self-talk.

The process begins with the counselor talking his or her way through a task or situations, which include behavioral tasks as well as instructions to go slowly, to concentrate on what is happening, and to self-praise. The client verbalizes to the counselor the same thing with another task. The client then does a task on his or her own but is careful to talk through the process. In the last phase, the client does the assignment individually by saying the instructions to himself or herself (Lester and Van Voorhis 2000, 176).

Cognitive behavioral approaches recognize that cognition, as well as behaviors, is learned. Behavior is also prompted, supported, mediated, and reinforced by cognition (Bandura 1973). Furthermore, a considerable amount of modeling and role-playing, the tools of the social learning model, is noted in the practice of cognitive behavioral psychology.

Cognitive skills programs with offenders stem from Ross and Fabiano's (1985) and Robinson's (1995) research. Their research indicates that as a result of a variety of causes that include poverty, abuse, inadequate schooling, and others, many offenders are deficient in the cognitive skills needed for effective social adaptation. Such skills include self-control; the ability to take the perspective of others; problem solving; developing short- or long-term plans; avoidance of high-risk situations; anticipating the consequences; decision making; coping; and flexible thinking strategies (Freedman et al. 1978).

Treatment strategies involve a number of different activities. These include games, journal activities, reasoning exercises, didactic teaching methods, audiovisual aids, and group discussions (Lester and Van Voorhis 2000, 179). Moreover, eight different cognitive treatment program components are social skills development, interpersonal problem solving, cognitive style of thinking, social perspective taking, critical reasoning, values analysis, meta-cognition (or the ability to understand what someone is doing and what the behavior means), and self-control. Of importance is the process of self-talk to help the offender stop old thinking patterns and practice new thinking skills (Bush and Bilodeau 1993). Cognitive group treatment leaders teach the offender to develop a perspective on high-risk situations. Group members are asked to consider what part of the process for which they are responsible, to consider what it must be like to be the other person in this situation, to change any dehumanizing thoughts about the victim into humanizing thoughts, to consider similar situations and the negative consequences that were derived from it, to remind the offender of the new person he or she wants to become, and to identify any favorable attitudes or sentiments that they can routinely cut off or suppress (Lester and Van Voorhis 2000, 180). The central idea is to teach the offender to think before talking or acting. Between sessions, clients are encouraged to keep a diary of an experience in which they used this strategy to solve a problem—what types of thoughts did they have, did they see the other person's viewpoint, did they control their emotions, did they assert their own position in a nonviolent manner, did they examine the beliefs around the situation, and what were their true feelings.

During later sessions, the offenders learn skills for preventing adverse outcomes. This attends to dysfunctional thoughts, setting new goals, making and carrying out plans, self-talking one's way through new plans, practicing new thinking, and reminding oneself of the consequences of incorrect action. In the more expansive version, the offender is also taught to live without violence, to develop parenting skills, and the importance of community reintegration (Lester and Van Voorhis 2000, 181).

Motivational Interviewing

Motivational interviewing is a technique that has been applied to substance abusers and to others. According to Miller and Rollnick (2002), motivational interviewing (MI) is a strategy that works toward the client building a commitment and reaching a decision to change. MI is a directive, client-centered counseling style that elicits behavior change by helping clients to explore and resolve ambivalence (Miller and Rollnick 2002). In comparison to nondirective counseling, it is more focused and goal oriented.

MI uses open-ended questions, affirmations, reflective listening, and summaries. Open-ended questions allow the client to approach the meeting with the probation officer as the probationer desires rather than as determined by the probation officer. The probationer provides the opportunity for moving forward. Affirmation or approval of thoughts and current behavior is necessary for people who have had little success in their lives and frequently encounter people who view them only as having problems. Affirmations require that one recognize the human dignity in people by telling them that their fear of failure is quite real. Recognizing that they are self-motivating, self-assessing, and self-correcting grants the offenders recognizable qualities that can be turned into strengths to achieve a measure of success. For an affirmation to work, it must be congruent and genuine.

Reflective listening is the key to this method (Miller and Rollnick 2002). Reflective listening requires that one listen carefully, patiently, and unemotionally as one stays on the topic. Summaries result from what is observed and understood about the client. If the probation officer understands, the clients will say, yes, that is what I mean. This builds rapport, expresses interest in the client, gives attention to prominent factors, and allows a shift to new topics. Offenders will say what has worked in the past and what has not. One must not be too quick to tell offenders what is good for them in the discussion in dealing with life issues.

Miller and Rollnick (2002) also point out that understanding the spirit of motivational interviewing is axiomatic to its implementation. Motivation for change is elicited from the client and not imposed from the outside. Motivational interviewing relies on identifying and mobilizing the client's intrinsic values and goals to stimulate behavior change. For MI to work, the therapist must understand the client and offer encouragement. This process grants the probationer a measure of autonomy. The counselor is not there to provoke the probationer, but rather the counseling style calls for the counselor to be quiet and eliciting. To officers with large caseloads who seek to influence every probationer, motivational interviewing may appear to be hopelessly slow and a passive process. The counselor, however, is directive in helping the client to examine and resolve the ambivalences of daily life. Once the ambivalence is resolved, most other tactics may appear unnecessary because the client is prepared to use existing skills to deal with life's circumstances. Under this methodology, readiness to change is not a client trait but a fluctuating product of interpersonal interaction. Client resistance is often a sign that the counselor is assuming a greater readiness for change than the client is prepared to undertake and it is a clue that the counselor should modify his or her motivational strategies. Finally, the therapeutic relationship is more like a partnership or companionship than expert/recipient roles (Miller and Rollnick 2002). To carry the process further, the therapist should be trained to understand the client's personal frame of reference, particularly through reflective listening. Through the use of acceptance and affirmation, the therapist elicits and reinforces the client's self-motivational statements concerning expressions of problem recognition, concern, desire, and the intention to change and ability to change. Monitoring a client's readiness for change guards against jumping ahead of the client. Finally, the therapist, in a manner that respects the qualities of human dignity the offender possesses, is to affirm the client's freedom of choice and self-direction (Miller and Rollnick 2002). It is the spirit of MI that once again points out the importance of treating the offender with human dignity. The principles of human dignity require one to recognize the rational qualities of each offender especially as one views each one as a self-assessing and self-correcting individual.

Motivational interviewing recognizes completely that offenders are highly ambivalent about changing. Ambivalence takes the form of a conflict between two courses of actions, indulgence versus restraint, each of which has cost and benefits attached to it. Many offenders realize they should stop using drugs, alcohol, or tobacco products because of the harm inflicted on themselves and others. However, clients get some satisfaction from this behavior in that temporarily, at least, they get some relief from their emotional pain or trauma. Many clients have not had the opportunity to express the confusing, contradictory, and uniquely personal elements of the conflict. The counselor's job is to facilitate expression of both sides of the ambivalence impasse and guide the client toward an acceptable resolution. Direct persuasion, aggressive confrontation, and argumentation are the conceptual opposites of motivational interviewing and are explicitly proscribed in this approach.

■ Summary

Probation's lack of identity can be interpreted to reflect the ambivalence present in the rest of society. The American ethos has, over the years, developed a set of beliefs that emphasized that no problem is insurmountable if the proper effort has been put behind it. What this means, too, is that when solutions do not work, something else needs to be done. This does not mean that one should reject the concept of rehabilitation, but it does mean that one should establish procedures to see that everything possible is done in these cases. Too often, by the time people arrive on probation, they have been through other service networks that have either failed or have been rejected by these services. One needs to be realistic about one's expectations and what can be achieved with the officer and with the client.

Rehabilitation has been criticized, but in the long run, one needs to recognize that it is needed and will continue to help some people. Rehabilitation continues to receive public support but not as much as it once did. The public needs to understand that there is value in probation. Probation is still cheaper than incarceration, officers believe that it serves a purpose, and many of them would rather make referrals than provide surveillance. Rehabilitation also provides a justification for the state to care for the offender and has been instrumental in encouraging humanitarian reforms, too.

One of the main findings that emerge from research on the topic is the differing perceptions that probation officers and probationers have in relation to the theory and practice of probation. Although probation officers may see their work as helpful and client focused, probationers may take the opposite view and argue that the probation officer treats them like any other person and is every bit the controlling agent. In truth, the probationer's perception of the matter may be the only one that really matters.

Effective programs are possible if they emphasize the proper techniques and engage problem solving, utilize community resources and interpersonal relations, enforce the rules, and prevent relapse. Casework is still important, particularly if it promotes self-esteem and human dignity, deals with resistant probationers, and provides a contractual agreement.

Probation officers can supply different strategies for providing services. They can do it themselves through the casework or the program model, or the officers can utilize external resources through the advocacy or the brokerage model. There is ample evidence of the use of the brokerage model in the present section. Reality therapy and crisis intervention, when melded to the brokerage model, provide the officer with some ammunition to fight the problems of probationer.

No program or strategy is completely successful; thus, one is in need of a means for assessing its effectiveness. The problem is that probation does not have a consistent measure that is tied to program mission statements or the risk-needs assessment, is consistent across the field, addresses organizational variables including the performance of individual officers, or includes measures of social adjustment. In other words, one evaluates programs on the basis of what is available and not what would provide the best information. Much of the responsibility for not developing the appropriate measures must rest with the requesters who have apparently not found too much fault with the way the data are collected and presented. What must be kept in mind is that these data are often analyzed with political purposes in mind. Those who use these data, then, find that they are not accountable to anyone else so there is no reason to refine or improve the data collection enterprise.

While there is much concern about whether probation does any good, it should be kept in mind that the problems these people have will not go away and that the probation system may be their last chance. If it is possible to do something to alleviate their misery, one has an obligation to do so. Both risk-needs assessments and performance contracts provide a means for controlling the probation officer's discretion and maintain a balance between the surveillance and control.

REFERENCES

Allen, H., E. Carlson, and E. Parks. 1979. *Critical issues in adult probation.* Washington, DC: U.S. Department of Justice, USGPO.

Allen, H., C. Eskridge, E. Latessa, and G. Vito. 1985. *Probation and parole in America.* New York: Free Press.

Andrews, D. 1980. Some experimental investigations of the principle of differential association through deliberate manipulation of the structures of service systems. *American Sociological Review* 45: 448–462.

Andrews, D., and J. Bonta. 1998. *The psychology of criminal conduct.* Cincinnati, OH: Anderson.

Andrews, D., I. Zinger, R. Hoge, J. Bonta, P. Gendreau, and F. Cullen. 1990. Does correctional treatment work? A psychological informed meta-analysis. *Criminology* 28: 369–404.

Applegate, B. K., F. Cullen, and D. S. Fisher. 1997. Public support for correctional treatment: The continuing appeal of the rehabilitative ideal. *Prison Journal* 77: 237–258.

Bandura, A. 1977. Self-efficacy: Toward a unifying theory of behavioral change. *Psychological Review* 94: 191–215.

Bandura, A. 1973. *Aggression: A social learning analysis.* Englewood Cliffs, NJ: Prentice Hall.

Bandura, A., and R. Walters. 1963. *Social learning and personality development.* New York: Holt, Rinehart and Winston.

Beutler, L., and J. Clarkin. 1990. *Systematic treatment selection: Toward targeted therapeutic interventions.* New York: Brunner/Mazel.

Bottoms, A. E., and W. McWilliams. 1979. A nontreatment paradigm for probation practice. *British Journal of Social Work* 9: 159–202.

Brewer, D., G. Becket, and H. Holt. 1981. Determinate sentencing in California: The first year's experience. *Journal of Research in Crime and Delinquency* 18: 200–231.

Bureau of Justice Statistics. 1996. *Federal crime case processing, 1982–1993.* Washington, DC: U.S. Department of Justice, USGPO.

Burns, D. 1980. *Feeling good.* New York: Morrow.

Bush, J., and B. Bilodeau. 1993. *Options: A cognitive change program.* Washington, DC: National Institute of Corrections.

Camp, C., and G. Camp. 2000. *The corrections yearbook. Adult corrections.* Middletown, CT: Criminal Justice Institute.

Clear, T., and R. Corbett. 1999. Community corrections of place. *Perspectives.* Winter. 23(1): 24–31.

Clear, T., and K. Gallagher. 1983. Screening devices in probation and parole. *Evaluation Review* 7: 217–234.

Clear, T. R., V. B. Clear, and W. D. Burrell. 1989. *Offender assessment and evaluation: The presentence report.* Cincinnati, OH: Anderson Publishing.

Cole, G. 1989. *American system of criminal justice.* Pacific Grove, CA: Brooks Cole.

Cullen, F., and P. Gendreau. 1992. The effectiveness of correctional rehabilitation and treatment. In D. Lester, M. Brasswell, and P. Van Voorhis, eds., *Correctional counseling.* Cincinnati, OH: Anderson.

Cullen, F., and K. Gilbert. 1982. *Reaffirming rehabilitation.* Cincinnati, OH: Anderson.

Currie, E. 1985. *Confronting crime: An American challenge.* New York: Pantheon.

Dell'Appa, F., T. Adams, J. Jorgensen, and H. Sigurdson. 1976. Advocacy, brokerage, community: The ABC's of probation and parole. *Federal Probation* 40: 37–45.

Ellis, A. 1973. *Humanistic pyschotherapy.* New York: Julian.

Ellsworth, T. 1990. Identifying the actual and preferred goals of adult probation. *Federal Probation* 54: 10–15.

Enos, R., and S. Southern. 1996. *Correctional case management.* Cincinnati, OH: Anderson.

Feld, B. 1999. *Bad kids: Race and the transformation of the juvenile court.* New York: Oxford University Press.

Fogel, D. 1978. Foreword. In R. McCleary, *Dangerous men: The sociology of parole.* Beverly Hills, CA: Sage.

Freedman, B., L. Rosenthal, C. Danohoe, D. Schlundt, and R. McFall. 1978. A social behavioral analysis of skills deficits in delinquent and nondelinquent adolescent boys. *Journal of Consulting and Clinical Psychology* 46: 1448–1462.

Gaubatz, K. 1995. *Crime in the public mind.* Ann Arbor: University of Michigan.

Gendreau, P., C. Goggin, and M. Paparozzi. 1996. Principles of effective assessment for community corrections. *Federal Probation* 60: 18–24

Gendreau, P. and Ross, R. 1979. Effective correctional treatment: Bibliotherapy for cynics. *Crime and Delinquency* 25: 463–489.

Gendreau, P., and R. Ross. 1987. Revivification of rehabilitation: Evidence from the 80s. *Justice Quarterly* 4: 349–407.

Glaser, D. 1969. *The effectiveness of a prison and parole system.* Indianapolis, IN: Bobbs-Merrill.

Glassman, R. 1973. Persistence and loose coupling in living systems. *Behavioral Science* 18: 83–98.

Goffman, E. 1961. *Asylums: Essays on the social situation of mental patients and other inmates.* Garden City, NY: Anchor Books.

Hagan, J. 1994. *Crime and disrepute.* Thousand Oaks, CA: Pine Forge Sage.

Hagan, J., J. Hewitt, and D. Alevin. 1979. Ceremonial justice: Crime and punishment in a loosely coupled system. *Social Forces* 58: 506–527.

Harris, P., T. Clear, and S. Baird. 1989. Have community supervision officers changed their attitudes toward their work? *Justice Quarterly* 6: 233–462.

Hennepin County Minnesota probation officer in discussion with author, August, 1998.

Jacobs, M. 1990. *Screwing the system and making it work.* Chicago: University of Chicago.

Jester, J. 1990. Technologies for probation and parole. In D. Duffee and E. McGarrell, eds. *Community corrections.* Cincinnati, OH: Anderson.

Karp, D., and T. Clear, eds. 2002. *What is community justice? Case studies of restorative justice and community supervision.* Thousand Oaks, CA: Sage.

Kingsnorth, R., and L. Rizzo. 1979. Decision making in the criminal courts: Continuities and discontinuities. *Criminology* 17: 3–14.

Lester, D., and P. Van Voorhis. 2000. Cognitive therapies. In D. Lester, M. Braswell, and P. Van Voorhis, eds., *Correctional counseling and rehabilitation,* 4th ed. Cincinnati, OH: Anderson, pp. 167–190.

Lipsey, M. November 1989. *The efficacy of intervention for juvenile delinquency. Results from 400 studies.* Paper presented to the 41st meeting of the American Society of Criminology. Reno, Nevada.

Locke, J. 1988. *Concerning civil government: Great books of the Western world.* Chicago: Britannica Great Books.

Maguire, K., and A. Pastore. 1995. *Bureau of justice statistics: Sourcebook of criminal justice statistics– 1994.* Washington, DC: US. Dept. of Justice, USGPO.

Manhattan Institute Policy Reseach (MIPR). 2003. *Broken windows for probation: Next steps in fighting crime.* New York: Center for Civic Innovation at Manhattan Institute.

Masters, Ruth E. 1994. *Counseling criminal justice offenders.* Thousand Oaks, CA: Sage Publications.

McAnany, P. 1984. Mission and justice: Clarifying probation's legal context. In P. McAnany, D. Thomson, and D. Fogel, eds., *Probation and justice.* Cambridge MA: Oelgeschlager, Gunn & Hain.

McAnany, P. D., D. Thomson, and D. Fogel. 1984. *Probation and justice: A reconsideration of mission.* Cambridge, MA: Oelgeschlager, Gunn & Hain.

Meyer, J., and B. Rowan. 1977. Institutionalized organizations: Formal structure as myth and ceremony. *American Journal of Sociology* 83: 340–363.

Miller, W., and S. Rollnick. 2002. *Motivational interviewing: Preparing people for change,* 2nd ed. New York: Guilford Press.

Minnesota Department of Corrections. Not dated. Handout. Offender Thinking Errors.

National Institute of Corrections. 1999. *Promoting public safety using effective interventions with offenders.* Longmont, CO: U.S. Department of Justice.

Neubauer, D. 1974. *Criminal justice in middle America.* Morristown, NJ: General Learning Press.

O'Leary, V. 1985. Reshaping community corrections. *Crime and Delinquency* 31: 349–366.

Parent, D., J. Byrne, V. Tsarfaty, L. Valade, and J. Esselman. 1995. *Day reporting centers: Volume I.* Washington, DC: National Institute of Justice, USGPO.

Parsloe, P. 1976. Social work and the justice model. *British Journal of Social Work* 6: 71–89.

Petersilia, J. 2002. *Reforming probation and parole.* Lanham, MD: American Correctional Association.

Reiss, A. 1971. *The police and the public.* New Haven, CT: Yale University Press.

Rhine, E. H. 1998. Probation and parole supervision: A time of a new narrative. *Perspectives* 22: 26–29.

Rhine, E., W. Smith, and R. Jackson. 1991. *Paroling authorities: Recent history and current practices.* Laurel, MD: American Corrections Association.

Robinson, D. 1995. *The impact of cognitive skills training on post-release recidivism among Canadian federal offenders.* Ottawa, Ontario: Correctional Service of Canada.

Rosencrance, J. 1987. A typology of presentence probation investigators. *International Journal of Offender Therapy and Comparative Criminology* 31: 163–177.

Rosencrance, J. 1986. Probation supervision: Mission impossible. *Federal Probation* 50: 25–31.

Ross, R., and E. Fabiano. 1985. *Time to think: A cognitive model of delinquency prevention and offender rehabilitation.* Johnson City, TN: Institute of Social Science and Arts.

Rousseau, J. 1988. *The social contract: Great books of the Western world.* Chicago: Britannica Great Books.

Rubin, H. 1977. The new directions in misdemeanor probation. *Judicature* 60: 435–441.

Schmolesky, J. and T. Thorson. (1982). The importance of the presentence investigation report after sentencing. *Criminal Law Bulletin* 18: 406–441.

Smith, M., and W. Dickey. 1998. *Reforming sentencing and corrections for just punishment and public safety. Sentencing and corrections: Issues for the 21st century.* Washington, DC: U.S. Department of Justice, National Institute of Justice, OJ Programs.

Smykla, J. 1984. *Probation and parole: Crime control in the community.* New York: Macmillan.

Van Voorhis, P. 2000. Social learning models. In D. Lester, M. Braswell, and P. Van Voorhis, eds., *Correctional counseling and rehabilitation,* 4th ed. Cincinnati, OH: Anderson, pp. 149–166.

Van Voorhis, P., Braswell, M. and Lester, D. (2000). *Correctional counseling and rehabilitation.* 4th ed. Cincinnati, OH: Anderson.

Walsh, A., and J. Ollenburger. 2001. *Essential statistics of the social and behavioral sciences.* Upper Saddle River, NJ: Prentice Hall.

Weick, K. 1976. Educational organizations as loosely coupled system. *Administrative Science Quarterly* 21: 1–19.

Wright, K., T. Clear, and P. Dickson. 1984. Universal applicability of probation risk assessment instruments. *Criminology* 22: 113–134.

KEY POINTS

1. Effective correctional programming requires probation officers to get into the field, to put an offender in a worthwhile program for a period of time as to be effective, and to have a theory of crime that explains what is taking place in order to understand what is driving the offender into crime.

2. Active community-centered supervision requires that probation officers work in the neighborhood with the greatest concentration of offenders.

3. Failure of the offender in the community is more often the result of the failure of the program than the person who has been attending.

4. The psychology of criminal conduct is based on the assumption that crime is the result of an individual being in a particular situation at a particular time. Crime occurs when the person has reason to commit the crime, his or her objections have been neutralized, and the offender believes he or she has the self-efficacy to commit the crime.

5. Offender supervision is the principal area in which human dignity is exhibited especially because it is difficult to develop a set of behaviors consistent with social expectations when the officer is not doing what is expected of everyone else.

6. Among experienced officers, there is a sense that almost anyone can find his or her way onto probation.

7. One of the critical components of human dignity is the recognition that humans are self-correcting; thus, probation affords an opportunity for the person to test reality under conditions that grant more and more freedom.

8. A good presentence investigation provides a detailed description of someone's life and offers an explanation for the behavior.

9. Risk-needs assessment is one method of controlling organizational drift and a lack of organizational goal clarity.

10. The general conclusion from research conducted on specialized caseloads indicates that they can be relatively effective with the target population if probationers are referred to appropriate services they can afford.

11. When taking reports, officers are interested in the probationer's home life, work, school, treatment programs, required payments, and whether any important areas have changed.

12. Community-centered supervision activities call for the development of supervision strategies that carefully monitor offender behavior by altering working hours, doing most of the work in the field, using flexible schedules, employing location specific selection criteria, and training for those in leadership positions to understand the role of human dignity.

13. Intervention comes in a variety of formats and can be understood as having two essential attributes: who is responsible and who is responsible for the solution.

14. Anticriminal modeling provides a source of social reinforcement, which promotes the acquisition of prosocial and anticriminal attitudinal, cognitive, and behavioral patterns.

15. Motivational interviewing is a directive, client-centered counseling style eliciting behavior change by helping clients to explore and resolve ambivalence.

KEY TERMS

advocacy is meant to trigger the correctional process by instigating changes in the offender and in the service delivery. True advocacy would promote the rights and interests of the offender in dealing with service providers.

advocacy model calls for a generalist staff, which uses external resources to deal with client needs. The community is responsible for the client's problems.

assessment attempts to answer questions raised during the intake phase. This is the phase in which there is a matching of services to the identified needs of the offender.

brokerage model emphasizes the assessment of client needs and the linkage of available community services with those needs.

casework model is predicated on the belief that internal staff in the department are capable of providing the necessary care for the probationer.

classification a system for separating offenders based on their risk of reoffending.

correctional case management a systematic process by which identified needs and strengths of the offender are matched with selected services and resources in corrections.

hooking occurs when the probation officer continues to supervise someone who is viewed by the unit supervisor as either beyond help or no longer in need of supervision.

intake Clients are processed into the system or referred to other agencies. During this intake step, an orientation takes place and rapport building develops between the offender and the probation officer.

loosely coupled organizations such as the court and the probation system, are responsive to one another but at the same time maintain independent and diverse identities and operational separateness.

program model involves assigning probationers to offices who specialize in dealing with particular offenders.

therapeutic integrity is a specific modeling linking intervention, intermediate targets, and reduced recidivism with trained workers and clinically supervised workers.

working the caseload means the officer examines his or her caseload from time to time to see who can be released.

REVIEW QUESTIONS

1. What constitutes effective supervision and what does it require of a probation officer?

2. How is human dignity preserved in community corrections?

3. Why is a good presentence investigation important?

4. List the changes that the Manhattan Institute recommends for offender supervision.

5. How do the different models of supervision impact the probationer?

6. List the errors in offender thinking addressed in cognitive restructuring programs.

7. How might an offender's dignity be affected by the use of motivational interviewing?

8

Restorative and Community Justice

> **Chapter Objectives**
> In this chapter you will learn about the importance of:
>
> - Balancing the needs of everyone affected by the crime
> - Holding the offender accountable
> - Having the offender make amends
> - Transforming the offender through shaming
> - Providing a chance for healing the wounds of the crime
> - Building the community

In transforming the corrections system to a peacemaking perspective, there are a number of ideologies, policies, and practices that must change. There is a tendency to gravitate toward explanations and assumptions about offenders that focus on retribution, punishment, deterrence, rehabilitation, and incapacitation but not restoration of the victim, of the community, or the offender. The treatment of victims and offenders as human beings who deserve respect and dignity is hard to sell in the criminal justice system. Society tends to demonize lawbreakers and view them as different, thus deserving the most horrific punishments to be devised. It always seems politically correct to be prejudiced against, or even hate, inmates (Braswell et al. 2001, 74–75).

Offenders vary considerably in the degree to which they are blameworthy or concerned that the victim was able to avoid the harm. Some offenders act purposely, others knowingly, yet others are reckless, and some just negligent. Such technical distinctions do not take into account how shameful the offender is once caught. For some offenders, the shame relates more to the embarrassment and stigmatization associated with getting caught. Others are glad they are apprehended so they can get some help and offer amends. The criminal justice system makes such actions possible. What is important is not to forget about the *person* when describing the offender.

The essential teaching of Christianity concerning peacemaking is that each is a child of God and therefore able to love one another. This foundation illustrates that all are brothers and sisters who are to treat each other with loving kindness, dignity, and respect (Braswell et al. 2001, 12). Recognition of the inherent worth and value of the person is most evident in the restorative justice model for community corrections. This model attends to the offender's ability to reason and act in a self-determining fashion. It recognizes the victim and offender must have the freedom to make moral choices. The victim can decide whether to meet with the offender and the offender can decide to make amends. Everyone involved in the process must recognize that the person sitting across from him or her has similar attributes. This is true of the victim or the offender. Their dignity or worth is the kind of value that all human beings have equally and essentially. The deepest, least empirical, way in which to express the moral egalitarianism of people is by reference to their inherent dignity; to their self-activating, self-directing, self-criticizing, self-correcting, self-understanding, and self-determinate capacities. They can evaluate, calculate, organize, predict, explain, conjecture, justify, appraise things and situations, and thus choose not only the means to ends but also the ends themselves.

Any attempt to transform corrections into a more effective and humane institution requires an awareness of the political and financial interests in the status quo. With the prison-industrial complex so entrenched in the opinion-making process, it is difficult to get a fair hearing for alternatives to punishment. Both restorative justice measures and rehabilitative treatment suffer from being perceived as soft on crime and from challenging the vested interests of those who control the criminal justice system. It is suggested that there are some issues and concerns that make the correctional system more effective and can ensure that justice is being served, although these issues and concerns will typically be met with resistance. In evaluating this resistance, one must distinguish between vested interests and objective differences of opinion. The logic and eventual outcomes of the peacemaking perspective can overcome the skepticism of those who honestly doubt its relevance. However, the transformation of such doubters will require that they be convinced that their careers will not suffer as the process evolves from a punishment-centered institution to a justice-centered one (Braswell et al. 2001, 74).

While incarceration is clearly a better option than physical torture, it fails to make the offender less likely to commit future crimes, and it does a poor job of satisfying society's desire for harsh punishment. In the move toward a peacemaking perspective, the creation of ways to deal with criminal offenders can satisfy people's desire to see offenders pay or experience consequences for their crimes. It will be necessary eventually to recast the entire concept of justice from one of punishment to one of restorative justice. Citizens will always be frustrated with the criminal justice system that uses punishment as its primary goal. There is simply no way to satisfy the lust for punishment of someone who has had a family member murdered. The healing and recovery from such an event cannot be attained from watching someone else suffer. No matter how severe the punishment, the emptiness remains. What is needed is another way of healing the wounds of crime. Peacemaking criminology and restorative justice represent such a way (Braswell et al. 2001, 75). An important principle of restorative justice that guides such processes is that all human beings have dignity and worth (Zellerer and Cannon 2002, 92).

Restorative Justice

Restorative justice is a distinct and unique response to crime and has to be distinguished clearly from rehabilitative and retributive responses to crime. Although rehabilitation has some of the features of restorative justice, its purposes are quite different when applied to the offender (Walgrave 1994). The *rehabilitative process* takes place in the societal context of a welfare state, focuses on the offender, provides treatment to him or her, seeks conforming behavior, and ignores the victim. The *retributive process* to crime takes place in a societal context of state power, focuses on the offense, inflicts harm (punishment), seeks just desert, but ignores the victim, too. On the other hand, the *restorative justice process* takes place in the societal context of empowering the state, focuses on losses, repairs the damage inflicted, seeks satisfied parties, and views the victim as the central person in the whole process (Weitekamp 1999, 75).

Restorative justice focuses on repairing harm caused by crime and reducing the likelihood of future harm. This is achieved by encouraging the offender to take responsibility for the crime and to identify with the victim's loss by providing redress and promoting reintegration back into the community of both the offender and victim. Communities and the government can work together in this matter. Restorative justice is different from conventional formulations of criminal justice in various ways. It views crime comprehensively and involves more parties by considering not only the crime but also the harm inflicted on victims and the community. It also measures success differently. Rather than measuring how much punishment has been inflicted, it considers how much harm has been repaired or prevented. It recognizes that the government and community must work together to reduce and respond to crime (Van Ness and Strong 2002, 49).

Restorative justice is an attempt to address the crime victim's grief by touching on the shaming sentiments present in the offender brought out by reintegrating him or her back into the community. The idea is to make anew the offender and those harmed. Restorative justice involves parties who can make a claim on the events and their outcomes. This means the victim, offender, community, and criminal justice system all have a stake in the success of the encounter. Restoration itself is dependent on whatever issue matters to the victim, offender, and the community. Unlike in the past, stakeholder deliberation determines what restoration means in a specific context, not the actors of the criminal justice system.

There is a need to understand who or what is being restored, including the core values of healing, moral learning, community participation, community caring, respectful dialogue, forgiveness, responsibility, apology, and making amends (Nicholl 1998). The restoration involves restoring property loss, injury, a sense of security, dignity, a sense of empowerment, deliberative democracy, community harmony in a feeling that justice has been done, and social support (Braithwaite 1996).

■ Social History

Durkheim's (1968) concept of mechanical solidarity is characterized by community homogeneity in values and behavior, strong social constraint, and loyalty to tradition and kinship. These are small nonliterate societies displaying a simple division of labor, little specialization, few social roles, and little tolerance for individuality. When deviance occurs, it is addressed directly at perpetrators, later extending to their families. Accordingly, punishment in the less-cultured societies constitutes an emotional response. When punishment is applied to the person, it extends beyond the guilty person and strikes even the family or neighbors. This is because the passion that lies at the heart of punishment is only extinguished when it is spent. Lukes and Scull (1983) argue that the emotional character of punishment is most visible with shame that doubles the impact of most punishments. To disgrace the offender makes sense when there is no other punishment available or when it is necessary to supplement some other penalty. Society reverts to major penalties when shame and minor penalties prove ineffective. One may say that society resorts to legal punishments when others are inadequate.

The historical origins of restorative justice have existed since humans began forming communities. Michalowski (1985) argues that human society can be categorized along two distinct lines: nonstate and state societies. The nonstate acephalous society is the earliest, dating back 30,000 years. According to Hartman (1995), acephalous societies are distinguished as nomadic tribes and segmental societies. Nomadic societies are hunter-gathers and segmental societies evolve when they become food producing. Essentially, these societies are small, economically cooperative, egalitarian, and use simple technology. Such societies are typified by Toennies' (1940) *gemeinschaft* concept, which clearly indicates that even in very stable and basic societies, there are occasions when deviance occurs.

Michalowski (1985) points out that in an acephalous society, individuals were bound closely to the group because of their diffuse structure, kin-based social organization, and concept of collective responsibility. This both reduced egoistic interests and the potential for trouble. If trouble did arise, the acephalous society resolved it collectively without formal legal actions. After evaluating the harm, the society was required to do something for either the offender or the victim. Unrest existed until the offender was made right again. Resolution was achieved through blood revenge, retribution, **restitution**, or a symbolic public demonstration of the offender's guilt (Weitekamp 1999).

restitution is a form of payment in kind, labor, or money in compensation for a wrong.

It is easy to assume from the literature that punishment is the most universal way of responding to violators. However, by expanding the analysis to acephalous societies, one finds that restitution to victims takes precedence over taking action against the offender and that the reestablishment of peace was central to their concerns. A stateless society maintained order in a number of ways. These societies were egalitarian with each member having equal access to materials and opportunities to develop a sense of personal worth. This might explain why there was little basis for the development of property crimes in these societies. Because each member was necessary for the life of the community, deviant members were neither devalued nor disgraced, nor were they stigmatized for even a short period of time. Because these communities were small, social relations were personal, leading to the development of strong communal bonds and a reduction in deviant behavior. Viewed in this light, deviant behavior was viewed as both a community problem and a community failure; thus, everyone was motivated to resolve the conflict (Weitekamp 1999, 81).

An Historical View

Restorative justice has been around in various forms for centuries. It is grounded in the traditions of justice found in Arab, Greek, and Roman civilizations (Van Ness 1986). Early examples of the restorative approach can be found from 6000 to 2000 B.C. in Indian Hindus (Beck 1997), in the ancient Buddhist, Taoist, and Confucian tradition that one sees blended in North Asia (Haley 1996), and in the public assemblies of German peoples following the fall of Rome (Berman 1983). Much of it is found in restitution, a form of payment in kind, labor, or money in compensation for a wrong done. The Code of Hammarabi (circa 2380 B.C.) espoused the practice of individual compensation for the victim of the harm, especially in property crimes. The early Hebrews used restitution and various forms of restorative justice for personal crimes (Gillin 1935). Michalowski (1985) points out that the ancient Germans used restitution in compensation for personal crimes as well. Diamond (1935) found that restitution in the form of payment of people was accepted for homicide in many parts of the Western world (Weitekamp 1999). The transition from blood vengeance to restitution is seen in Arabia in as much as the tribes continued the feud but the people living in the cities understood the need for restitution. The Semitic people used the fine throughout the Turkish Empire. Restitution and atonement were common with Indian Hindus. One ancient punishment was the *wergild*, which was money paid to a family for the death of one of their members. The *bot* was money paid for injuries not leading to death, and the *wite* was money paid to a mediator to cover the cost of overseeing the compensation plan. Some crimes were viewed as *botless* in that no compensation could be paid, making it necessary to resort to the blood feud (Weitekamp 1999). One of the more elaborate accounting systems was developed under the laws of Ethelbert of Kent (circa A.D. 600). Each part of the body was worth some compensation. The four front teeth, for example, were worth six shillings. The Saxons' law had a catalog for almost all injuries. This is also true of the Franks (Weitekamp 1999).

A Shift in Obligation

Restitution was an important means of resolving conflict and maintaining peace, especially for personal crimes. For societies without a strong chief or that lacked a central authority figure, the main reason for restitution was to avoid a blood feud. Such feuds had the potential to seriously endanger the safety of the community. Earlier societies were characterized by rudimentary technology, simple division of labor, some form of control over property, and limited material inequality. Rulers, even though they held limited powers, exploited or controlled the labors of others through a system of kinship enforcers. Rules were enforced by the relatives of the ruler. These relatives were people who were required to work in support of the family's kinship system.

As the rulers took an interest in maintaining a costly peace, the needs of the victim became less important and progressively the needs of the state took prominence. The king collected the restitution instead of the victim or the victim's family. The decline of the victim's role in settling disputes signified an important change in the nature of social control. Responsibilities became increasingly individualized rather than collective, thus making more abstract the obligation to conform to social rules (Weitekamp 1999).

In Anglo-Saxon law, the increasing power of the king uniting large areas and different peoples marked a radical shift in social structure: the communitarian tribal society was supplanted by a hierarchical feudal system. In A.D. 843 following the Treaty of Verdun, a fine assessed by a tribunal, which was collected and kept by the state, replaced restitution. Eventually an elaborate system was developed to collect monies and properties that were to be given to the crown or the church. By the end of the 12th century, the erosion of restorative justice was complete, because the common victim of crime could no longer expect to receive compensation from the offender. After the 12th century, restitution was utilized most often by the wealthy who wish to avoid the consequences of the law (Weitekamp 1999). The rich were able to avoid harsh penalties by promising to compensate their victims lavishly.

The concept of victim restitution as a criminal sanction, however, never completely ended. In the late 18th century, Bentham (1748–1832) advocated for the use of restitution whenever possible. One hundred years later, international symposiums and penal congresses discussed the idea as well (Schafer 1970). Albert Eglash (1975) is credited with providing the first articulation of restorative justice as a restitutive alternative.

The family-group conferencing in Australia, Singapore, the United Kingdom, Ireland, South Africa, the United States, and Canada also influenced restorative justice. Other influences were healing and sentencing circles in Canadian First Nations (James 1993) and Navajo Justice and Healing ceremonies (Yazzie and Zion 1996). The concept of victim restitution as a criminal sanction never really died.

More Modern Alternatives

Recent interest in restorative justice began with the establishment of a victim-offender reconciliation program in Kitchener, Ontario, in 1974 (Peachey, 1989). According to John Braithwaite, one the most influential works offered in support of restorative justice is Nils Christie's 1977 work "Conflicts as Property." Christie argues that conflicts are important elements in social systems. They should be organized so as to be nurtured and visible, and yet the professional does not monopolize the solution. Crime victims should regain their right to participate in the court's process. Particular attention should be given to what can be done for the victim, first by the offender, then by the local neighborhood, and finally, by the state. The central goal is to reduce reliance on professionals for community crime control.

Restorative justice was popularized in North America and Britain by Howard Zehr (1990), Mark Umbreit (1994), Kay Pranis (1996), Daniel Van Ness (1986, 1999), and Tony Marshall (1985). New impetus came from New Zealand and Australia as restorative justice became an emerging social movement there.

Restorative justice was furthered by various justice traditions including making amends (Wright 1982), reconciliation (Marshall 1985; Dignan 1992), peacemaking (Pepinsky and Quinney 1991), redress (De Haan 1990), transformative justice (Moore and Forsythe 1995), real justice (McDonald et al. 1995), and republican justice (Braithwaite and Pettit 1990). Moreover, feminist thinking about crime has the dialectic of the ethic of justice versus care (Heidensohn 1986).

◼ A Comprehensive Model

A comprehensive model of restorative justice offered by Van Ness and Strong (2002) recognizes that there are four parties affected by crime: the victim, the offender, the community, and the government. It is a model that in many ways combines various aspects of civil and criminal law. The government and the community have a need for public safety. The victim and the offender are to achieve a resolution of their conflict. In the past, this might have been achieved by filing a civil action against the offender. In this model, this is done through understanding and a measure of reparations. Through the efforts, in part, of government-imposed order, community safety is achieved by forming strong, stable, peaceful relationships among its members forming well-integrated communities. The victim seeks a measure of vindication from the government, too. This means the government recognizes the victim is not responsible for the pain and loss and that the victim's claims are legitimate. The government, for its part, demands order from the offender by adhering to the precepts of the law. The offender is expected to provide communal recompense. In addition to paying restitution to the victim, the offender is to take an active role in mending the damages. At the same time, the community makes every effort to put the victim at peace. The community is to provide the victim with sufficient support in overcoming the loss so the victim can start the healing process. It is crucial that the government redresses the victim's complaints and that it treats the offender with fairness. This is the beginning of the process of rehabilitating and reintegrating the offender into the community.

Restorative Justice

Bazemore and Umbreit (1994) have provided the most detailed description of the restorative model. The three components of restorative justice—**accountability**, community protection, and competency development—need to be assessed in terms of the roles played by the criminal justice system, the offenders, and the community. Each of these roles will be considered in terms of purpose and intended outcome.

Responsibility and accountability are key actions needed by offenders to repair the harm they have inflicted upon the victim. Correctional intervention, as considered here, focuses on ways that offenders can learn and demonstrate prosocial and responsible behavior (Ferns 1994). Offenders are responsible for their choices, behaviors, and lives. As said earlier, they are capable of moral choices, both in terms of the means and the goal that they seek. The restorative philosophy emphasizes cost-effective sanctions, while deemphasizing the retributive use of incarceration. The model attends to building on strengths instead

accountability means the offender needs to understand and take responsibility for what he or she has done. This can be achieved through cognitive restructuring, allowing offenders to understand their actions, their feelings, and the outcomes that are derived from these feelings.

of identifying weaknesses. The emphasis on specific interventions with offenders is not restricted to examining the lack of insight but the capacity to act responsibly and to think clearly about past choices.

A fundamental objective of restorative case management is to insist the offender be given a meaningful opportunity to change. Simply put, offenders are expected to exit the system more capable of living a viable, productive, and responsible life than they were when they entered the system (Ferns 1994).

Accountability

One central issue of restorative justice lies in how it is defined (Ferns 1994). According to Zehr (1990), genuine accountability means, first of all, the offender needs to understand and take responsibility for what he or she has done. This can be achieved through cognitive restructuring, allowing offenders to understand their actions, their feelings, and the outcomes that derive from these feelings. The criminal justice system's accountability role is to ensure that the offender fulfills commitments to the victim and completes other requirements. The intended outcome is to establish efficient, fair, and meaningful restorative justice practices, as well as to increase responsiveness to the victim. The offender's role is to actively work to restore the victim's losses and to participate in activities that increase empathy for the victim. The community is responsible for assisting in the process by providing paid work opportunities for the offender, helping to develop community work service programs, supporting victim awareness programs. One dimension of accountability is understanding and taking ownership for wrongdoing (Zehr 1990, 73). Accountability has been associated with holding the offender answerable for crimes committed. In the retributive sense, the offender is asked to pay via suffering or compensation. The current system employed for establishing guilt encourages the offender to make rationalizations and the key actors in the system see themselves as simply carrying out the law. The restorative model would argue that a broader interpretation be made. When a crime occurs, a debt results. Justice requires that, when possible, every effort be made by offenders to restore losses suffered by the victim. Accountability develops by recognizing the obligation to the victim resulting from the crime. Restitution, community service, and victim offender mediation are intended to foster awareness in the offender of the deleterious consequences of the crime. This requires the offender to take action to make amends to victims and the community, and, whenever possible, involve the victims in the process.

Careful consideration must be given to the quantity and quality of sanctions, degree of culpability, probability of future offending, and the associated risk of offending. Factors that come to impinge on the degree to which accountability is effective depend on individual differences relative to the meaning of the punishment, the feasibility of completing the punishment, and the ability of the criminal justice system to provide it as desired. Is the punishment unwelcomed and doable?

Community Protection

The restorative model emphasizes the use of expanded community supervision systems as a primary method of providing for community protection (Ferns 1994). The criminal justice system's role is to ensure that offenders are carefully supervised in the community, that the offender's time is carefully organized into productive activities, and that a range of restrictive options is available. The intent is to increase public support for community supervision. The offender is to become involved in competency building and restorative activities, which should lead to the avoidance of further crime. The intended outcome is to reduce recidivism when supervision ends. The community is to provide input regarding public safety but also share responsibility for offender control and reintegration. This was addressed earlier under the concept of guardianship. The plan is to increase community feelings of safety and increased confidence in the system by attacking fear and indifference, thereby rekindling a new spirit of public support.

The public has the right to a safe and secure community. To accomplish this, a progressive response system is needed to ensure offender control in the community. With the refusal to completely address various social-economic problems, there is a corresponding increase in fear that is brought about by ignorance. What is not known is feared.

range of sanctions is a series of unwelcomed experiences that are designed to increase in intrusiveness as they match the risk of further harm.

According to the restorative model, community protection is the outcome of an understanding that the public has a right to live in a safe and secure community and must be protected during the time the offender is under supervision. These sanctions include an intermediate **range of sanctions** that includes electronic and intensive surveillance schemes that channel the offender's energy into productive activities. Failure to comply with these conditions leads to even more intrusive levels of surveillance and greater intrusion into the probationer's life. Further attention is also given to competency skill development. Problems are less difficult when it is known how to deal with them.

To accomplish this, probation provides a range of sanctions, which are geared to the different risks posed by probationers (Harland 1993). From what is known of traditional sentencing schemes, it is possible to apply a range of sanctions that have a distinctively restorative approach by addressing the victim and the community (Harland 1993, 12). Range of sanctions is a series of unwelcomed experiences, which are designed to increase in intrusiveness as they match the risk of further harm. Harland is careful to warn that a range of sanctions cannot be adopted without maintaining a sense of fairness. Through a continuum of sanctions, one is provided with a sense of order as to how various sanctions can be interchanged as equivalent penalties for different offenses, especially in consideration of the equivalence of economic measures vis-à-vis work-related or physical confinement measures. These discussions are necessary to impose standardized procedures in order to avoid the discretionary abuses found in indeterminate punishments. Klein (1988) has provided a host of alternative sentences that can be applied to many different offenses, many of which in the past have been earmarked for imprisonment. Authorities need to recognize that there are pains attached to various forms of rehabilitation and not punishment alone.

Competency Development

Today, probation officers who are interested in achieving a measure of occupational significance must develop a perspective that reconciles their concern for control with their interest in helping the probationer. Offenders are no longer presented as victims, as they were in the 1960s. During that time, major legislation prohibiting discrimination and assuring medical care for the poor was enacted. Employment programs also were common. Today there are such programs but they are not as large scale nor are they available to as many people as they once were.

One of the roles of the criminal justice system is to assess the individual's needs and strengths and to identify community resources to reinforce existing competencies. Partnerships with employers, educators, and community agencies are meant to develop opportunities for growth. The offender is to become involved in these activities, thus making a positive contribution to the community while building life and educational skills. Increased competency and enhanced self-esteem are essential if the offender is to progress. The community is responsible for developing opportunities for the offender, assuming partial ownership of the crime problem, and improving the quality of life in the community.

The development of competency results from the belief that upon leaving the system, the probationer is capable of being a productive and responsible citizen. Instead of merely receiving treatment and services aimed at suppressing problem behavior, the offender should have a chance to make measurable improvements in the ability to function in a free society. Work experience, active learning, and public service provide opportunities for offenders to develop skills, interact positively with conventional citizens, earn a wage, and demonstrate publicly that they are capable of productive behavior (Bazemore and Umbreit 1994). The basis for many of these beliefs is found in terms of a person's resources or human capital. Humans are resources that should be developed to their fullest. Included under the rubric of human resource development are all policies designed to enhance the effectiveness of human beings in their productive activities (Parnes 1984). The most important of these is the development of vocational and educational skills of all kinds, both those that are on the job and those that are learned before and after employment. This process also includes the development of skills that are needed by those who have experienced poverty, frustration, and futility in their work careers and who have attitudes that are incompatible with mainstream employment. Human resources have to be continually redistributed as needed. In this regard, employment agencies are crucial.

Human capital refers to human productive capabilities. This concept encompasses the abilities and know-how of people who have acquired their skills at some cost and who can command a price in the labor market. At the societal level, there are investments made in education and training. At the individual level, people invest in themselves by financing their educations. Investment in human capital is worthwhile only if the present value of potential benefits is as large as the present value of costs. Many social programs that can be justified on humanitarian grounds can also have economic payoffs. Measures that fight discrimination and improve the human capital value of the individual also have the value of improving economic prosperity for all.

Greater probationer competence can be achieved through human resource development as found in the community-based vocational network (Tomlinson 1994). The community-based vocational networks are inexpensive to operate because they use existing resources. These networks provide training, education, and jobs to probationers who qualify. Programs are found that give attention to problems involving addiction and other interpersonal problems, many of which involve the family. Once these problems have been addressed, the offender is expected to find and obtain education and training for a job. From this point, the probationer is expected to develop job-finding skills. These include learning how to fill out applications, write resumes, and participate effectively in the interview. The community college is the source of much of this education. The network then moves forward in finding the person a job.

With the aid of these programs, greater human capital is developed and community agencies address problems together instead of competing with one another for resources. Effective planning and program development is addressed as agencies and communities cooperate together.

■ Crime as a Loss

Restorative justice responds to crime even though it remains a function of the criminal justice system. Crime control is viewed as a larger problem that is best addressed as a social system problem. The criminal justice system can respond to crime and attempt to repair the harm, but it can only have a marginal impact on the actual level or occurrence of crime (Ferns 1994).

According to Zehr (1990), according to **retributivists**, crime is defined as a violation of a rule in technical and legal terms whereas harm is defined abstractly. Crime is distinguished from other harms, such as civil harms, because the state is viewed as a victim. The state and the offender are the only parties, with the needs of the victim ignored. The relationship between the victim and the offender is considered largely irrelevant. The crime is viewed as resulting from a conflict that found no outlet other than harming another person. No interest is shown in the injuries suffered by the offender.

According to Zehr (1990), the **restorativists** view crime much more broadly, especially as the harm impacts the relationship between people and where it is related to other harms and conflicts. Harm also must be understood within its full moral, social, economic, and political context. The victims of crime are the people and their relationships. The victim and the offender are primarily and secondarily related; the state has a tertiary role. Interpersonal relations between the victim and the offender are viewed as a form of conflict relationship. In short, the restorativists have a communal sense of the crime, harm, and what must be done to achieve offender integration.

If crime is a harm, what should be done with the offender and the victim? Instead of defining crime as necessitating retribution, restorationists define crime as an injury. Justice repairs the injury and promotes healing. Acts of restoration are meant to counterbalance the harm of the crime. The primary obligation is toward the victim of the offense. The offender has an obligation to make things right. This means encouraging offenders to understand and acknowledge the harm they have done. According to the just deserts model, neither the victim nor the offender is eligible for any special consideration. This is indicated as much in the discussion of less eligibility and its application to the offender. Less eligibility would suggest that the offender should be treated no better than the treatment given the members of the lowest significant social

retributivists define crime as a violation of a rule in technical and legal terms whereas harm is defined abstractly. Crime is distinguished from other harms, such as civil harms, because the state is viewed as a victim.

restorativists view crime much more broadly, especially as the harm impacts the relationship between people and where it is related to other harms and conflicts. Harm also must be understood within its full moral, social, economic, and political contexts.

class. This becomes a problem during periods of economic decline and cuts in services. Offenders are considered to be the least deserving segment of persons in need. Society's interest dictates that the many social needs discussed earlier are directed to those who have not broken the law. However, identifying and addressing offenders' needs are key elements in restorative justice because by ignoring these needs one fosters additional crime and suffering among all.

In the restorative model the correctional system is not based on punishment but, instead, is based on the extent to which the victim is restored. Of course the offender is to experience a degree of suffering in this process but this is only to be expected in that a punishment is defined, in part, as an un-welcomed experience. The restorative model emphasizes the expanded use of cost-effective community supervision systems. Any intervention should build on the strengths instead of the weaknesses of the offender. The stress in specific interventions with offenders is not restricted to examining their lack of insight but their capacity to act responsibly and their capacity to make choices (Ferns 1994, 36). If the process works effectively, the offender will experience a radical shift in the self. The offender should understand him- or herself as never before and come to understand others as never before. The offender should be able to recognize he or she is a self-activating, self-directing, self-criticizing, self-correcting, self-understanding, and self-determinate individual who has the capacity to do good acts as well as do harm.

■ Grief

To understand the grief experienced by others, one must understand the grief within oneself. Grief is certainly an outcome of criminal victimization. One feels a deep sense of loss, anger, and guilt. This loss comes in the form of feeling responsible for one's own physical, mental, or economic problems. Once the offender is arrested and charged, the victim is responsible for getting to the hearing and trial. Sometimes this entails hardships, such as missing work or having to find child care. Once the trial begins, the victim must relive the incident, undergo cross-examination, and experience the whole process as a piece of evidence. Following the conviction of the offender, the victim must carry on with fears, damages, injuries, and traumas (Reiff 1979).

Crime victims pay in a number of other ways: emotionally, economically, and/or physically. As a result of the crime, the victim may suffer extensive and permanent injuries resulting in loss of earning potential and increased impoverishment for life. These conditions are especially problematic for the elderly because their bodies take longer to heal and they may never fully recover. When a murder or assault causing serious physical injury occurs, entire families become victims of a single violent crime. If the victim is economically disadvantaged, even relatively minor injuries can result in disastrous consequences. The cost of medical care can be catastrophic to those who are already medical indigents. The loss of money for food or rent may mean starvation, eviction, or having the utilities cut off. Offenders who threaten more serious harm if the crime is reported or prosecuted often worsen the situation. Even if the offender is jailed, the victim cannot be sure of his or her safety (Reiff 1979, 4–5). Victims also make themselves invisible. The fear of revictimization accompanied by strong emotional shock often generates high levels of suspicion and distrust. Victims often isolate themselves (Reiff 1979, 4–5).

Most people consider individuals who suffer the disastrous effects of violent crimes as unfortunate victims of their own lifestyle. They are thought to be unlucky and are often forgotten. Once blaming begins, people fix their attention on the cause of their disaster and become indifferent, often fatalistic, to the effect on its victims. If catastrophe strikes beyond human responsibility and control, it tends to produce compassionate and often heroic behavior toward victims. However, if responsibility and blame are placed upon the victim, people behave as if aid to the victim is solely a matter of the perpetrator making amends. The victim's needs for compassion and aid are considered the exclusive responsibility of the blamed (Reiff 1979, 12).

Nolen-Hoeksema and Larson (1999) propose three different phases of grief (pp. 3–6). The first is an initial period of shock, disbelief, and denial, which can last for hours or several weeks. Bereaved people feel numb and paralyzed and may not believe that the loss is real. In the case of losing a loved one, they may actively search for the deceased, may imagine hearing and seeing them, or may simply yearn and pine for them. The second phase begins when the loss or death is acknowledged cognitively and emotionally. This phase of acute mourning includes intense feelings of sadness, despair, loneliness, anxiety, and anger. The full syndrome of depression may occur with a loss of interest in life, disruption in sleep and appetite, inability to concentrate or make decisions, a sense of hopelessness and helplessness, and even suicidal wishes. Bereaved people may withdraw from others and be preoccupied with their loss. Even when they try to engage in everyday living, they may have intrusive, painful thoughts about the loss. This phase may last several months. Eventually, the acute mourning phase is replaced by a restitution phase in which the bereaved return to a feeling of well-being and an ability to go on living. They come to some understanding or acceptance of the loss, and most of the time they will be able to engage in everyday life in a positive way—yet grief can reappear from time to time for years and throughout one's life. Grief is lessened with closure that is made possible by reconciling the facts in the case. This is achieved by meeting with the offender.

■ Encounter Conferencing

Restorative justice is a powerful mechanism for change because it requires the offender to humanize the crime. In the conventional court setting, the victim rarely has any contact with the offender, and if such contact takes place, it is often unwanted. Encounters are restricted by the activities of lawyers, practical considerations, and the rules of evidence (Launay and Murray 1989). There are four different approaches used to structure an encounter between the offender and the victim. They are mediation, conferencing, circles, and impact panels.

Victim-Offender Mediation

victim-offender mediation (VOM) is a process that provides the victim with the opportunity to meet the offender in a safe setting.

<u>**Victim-offender mediation (VOM)**</u> has been around since the 1960s. The year 1960 saw the advent of the neighborhood dispute resolution experiments (Umbreit et al. 2000, 2). Sander (1976) has identified various means of conflict res-

olution including ombudsman, mediation/conciliation, negotiation, and avoidance. These programs are designed to use informal processes outside the court to resolve a dispute. The earlier programs were called victim-offender reconciliation programs with full knowledge that complete reconciliation may never be achieved (Van Ness and Strong 2002, 58). Others such as Bazemore and Umbreit (1994) prefer to use offender dialogue or mediation.

The first type of restorative justice conferencing, VOM has a 25-year history with over 1,300 programs in North America and Europe. VOM has been used to handle pre- and postdisposition cases and involves crimes that are petty to serious including assault and murder (Umbreit et al. 2000, 2). VOM is closely connected to victim offender reconciliation programs. These programs focus on humanizing the criminal justice process, changing lives, and providing assistance to the victims.

Victim-offender mediation is a process that provides the victim with the opportunity to meet the offender in a safe setting. The goal is to hold the offender accountable for his or her behavior while providing important assistance to the victim (Umbreit et al. 2000, 5). With the assistance of the mediator, victims let offenders know how the crime affected them, receive answers to questions they have, and are directly involved in a restitution program plan. Offenders take full responsibility for their behavior, learn the full impact of what they did, and make a plan for making amends. In some cases, these programs operate as diversion from prosecution programs, and in others, the programming starts after the court accepts an admission of guilt. Mediation is a condition of probation if the victim so desires. Authorities at all levels of the criminal justice system can make referrals for mediation. Once mediation has been agreed upon, a trained mediator will meet with the participants, listen to their stories, invite their participation, and then share what is likely to be the process. The mediation processes includes the victim, the offender, the mediator, and sometimes family members. The mediator's role is to facilitate a discussion so that all issues and questions are addressed. Eventually a restitution plan may emerge in the form of a contract. Although forms of mediation are settlement driven, victim-offender-reconciliation programs (VORP) are dialogue driven with an emphasis on victim healing, offender accountability, and restoration of losses. Any agreement is secondary to the initial dialogue between the parties that addresses emotional and informational needs of the victim. This is important not only for the victim's healing but also to develop victim empathy in the offender. One goal is to reduce future criminal behavior (Umbreit et al. 2000, 5).

Family Group Conferencing

<u>Family group conferencing (FGC)</u> is another method involving victim-offender encounters. These programs are sometimes referred to as *restorative justice conferencing*. Family group conferencing began as an outgrowth of recognizing the inherent problem-solving practices of the Maori culture, an indigenous New Zealand group, and the mandate of the 1989 New Zealand Children's, Young Persons, and Their Families Act. The whole idea was to increase family and extended family involvement and responsibility, supporting children's rights, recognizing New Zealand's cultural diversity, and promoting partnerships among the family, the community, and the state (Hassall 1996).

family group conferencing (FGC) is a process involving the bringing together of the offender, the offender's immediate and extended family members, support persons, justice system representatives, and the victims of the crime and their support persons.

The primary functions of the FGC are to reach a decision as to whether or not the offender should be prosecuted and make other decisions that are appropriate to resolve the dispute (Hassall 1996). Accordingly, youth are referred to conferencing unless the nature of the crime mandates that a judge hear the case. It is assumed that the youth admits to guilt if the matter is to go forward through conferencing. The primary aim of these programs is to strengthen the moral bonds between the offender and the community (Sherman and Strang 1997).

The family group conferencing process involves bringing together the offender, the offender's immediate and extended family members, support persons, justice system representatives, and the victims of the crime and their support persons. The conference begins with introductions, followed by a discussion of the details of the offense as understood by the victim and the offender. Both parties have opportunities to describe their feelings and experiences, which then results in a plan for handling the situation. Reparations, apologies, community work, and restitution may be part of the plan.

Circle

circle is one form of a victim-offender encounter involving the victim, offender, families, and community members.

The basic model of a **circle** is derived from aboriginal peacemaking traditions in North America, group consensus decision-making principles, and insights gained from mediation programs. A circle is one form of a victim-offender encounter involving the victim, offender, families, and community members. The description of circles as performed in the aboriginal territories provides a clear understanding of how they work (Lilles 2002). Circles require an application to the court by the offender. As such, the circle has all of the legal safeguards present in other hearings. A transcript is made and the decision can be appealed to higher courts. Instead of the victim attending alone, a community of victims attends instead. The procedure is a straightforward, open, nonhierarchical process in which the 15 to 50 people in attendance know either the offender or the victim. A judge or a village elder chairs the circle. Following the introduction of everyone at hand, the prosecutor presents the facts in the case. The defense then makes his or her statement, which is then followed by the circle's statements. The offender is required to speak from time to time, which can be a difficult process, as he or she attempts to respond to the statements offered by persons familiar with the victim. Emotions run high. It may take some time for the offender to reach a level of comfort in such a setting.

Whether he or she is a judge or village elder, the facilitator is a community member. Facilitators are primarily interested in maintaining order and periodically summarizing the activities for the benefit of the group. The idea is to create a place where everyone, including the offender, victim, family members and supporters, community members, and criminal justice officials, all can speak from their heart and be heard. Much of the discussion is about community norms and expectations, which leads to a shared affirmation of theses norms and values (Sivell-Ferri 1997). Participants speak on wide-ranging issues related to the crime, the community, and their concerns as to why the crime occurred and what can be done about it. Quite often, they recognize the importance of forming a support group to help the offender address future problems. The focus is on a constructive outcome where the dignity of the victim is preserved and the interests of the community understood and acknowledged, along with the needs and obligations of the offender. When a consensus on the sentence is achieved, the process goes forward. The disposition is considered successful when the offender's lifestyle changes, the sentence is complete, and the offender appears as a community member at a later time. The process extends the concept of human dignity beyond the offender but to include the victim and the community.

Impact Panels

<u>Impact panels</u> are comprised of groups of victims who meet a group of offenders who are linked by a common type of crime, although they are not each other's victim or offender. The purpose of such meetings is to find resolution and to expose offenders to the damage caused by their crime, especially when the direct victim is not interested in meeting. In the United States, the largest group of participants in impact panels is the organization Mothers Against Drunk Driving (MADD). The court or probation officer usually orders offenders to participate in the panels. The victims are chosen from a list of victims or their survivors. The selection of victims is based on two criteria: whether telling their story will help more than harm the victim and whether they are able to speak without blaming or accusing the offender. This is a difficult assignment. The victim has a chance to express any feelings during a 60- to 90-minute meeting. Offenders are selected on the basis of their speaking ability, their sense of genuine remorse, completion of all aspects of their sentence, and the agreement that participation will benefit in reducing their sentence. The Sycamore Tree Project brings groups of five or six victims into prison to meet with similar numbers of unrelated prisoners. This is an intensive 8- to 12-week program that incorporates discussions about the effects of the crime, the harm it causes, and how to make things right. The studies done of victim-offender programs indicate that everyone can benefit from the process. Victims found their anxiety and anger reduced and offenders developed a better understanding of the impact of their crime. Drunk driving research indicates these programs are very successful in reversing prodrinking attitudes (Vanness and Strong 2002, 67–68).

impact panels are comprised of groups of victims who meet a group of offenders who are linked by a common kind of crime, although they are not each other's victim or offender. The purpose of such meetings is to find resolution and to expose offenders to the damage caused by their crime, especially when the direct victim is not interested in the meeting.

Additional Thoughts

Victim-offender conferencing has been examined in various settings. Are victims interested in meeting the offenders? In one study (Pranis and Umbreit 1992), four out of five Minnesotans expressed interest in meeting the offender. In a British survey (Reeves 1989) less than a third of the violent crime victims and approximately two-thirds of property offense victims were willing to participate. Gehm (1990) reported that victims are more likely to meet with an offender if the offender is white, if the offense is a misdemeanor, and if the victim represents an organization. Wyrick and Costanzo (1999) found that the longer the time lapsed between the crime and the referral to the VOM, the less like the victims of property crime are to reach mediation. The reverse is true of personal crimes. There are additional findings suggesting that the greater the number of incentives to participate, the more likely the victim is to participate. People are also motivated to participate if they feel they are helping the juvenile offender. Family group conferencing is also important.

The importance of voluntary victim participation is found in the summary of participation reported by Umbreit and Coates (2000, 18). Umbreit and Coates found that 83 to 100 percent of the victims in their studies voluntarily participated. The percentages of victims who felt adequately prepared to meet the offender range from 68 to 98 percent. Their satisfaction with the justice system's response to the case ranges from 50 to 90 percent. Low rates of victim satisfaction are related to low rates of completion of the negotiated restitution agreements.

Victim-offender conferencing results are also important. Studies conducted by Umbreit and Bradshaw (2000) found that victim satisfaction was dependent on the victim's positive attitude toward the mediator, the victim's perceived fairness of the restitution agreement, and the importance of meeting the offender. Victim satisfaction with the outcome is seen not just in the satisfaction of restitution but also in a change in the offender's attitude. It helped to have a mediator who was thought to be fair. Over and over, the importance of preparation was emphasized as important to the success of the process.

Recidivism, although an important indicator for retributive or rehabilitative punishments, does not play a central role in restorative justice. Further research is necessary to determine program effectiveness in this respect. The studies of mediation among juveniles indicate the program offered some success. Schneider (1986) found a recidivism rate of 53 percent for program participants as compared to 63 percent for those on regular probation. Stone, Helms, and Edgeworth (1998) found no overall difference in recidivism rates between youth who participated in VOM and a similar sample who were not referred. Youth who completed their mediation program were less likely to recidivate than those who did not. Studies of California VOM participants found that in five out of six programs, the recidivism rate was at least 10 percent lower for program participants than for others (Evje and Cushman 2000, 22). Taken as a whole, these results suggest that many juvenile restorative justice conferencing programs do in fact make an impact on the future behavior of the participating youth (Umbreit and Coates 2000, 31).

Negative results were indicated among a minority of participants. For example, one participant in family group conferencing said that it made him mad to see the offender sitting there: "I was being taken advantage of and it was a waste of time" (Umbreit 1995). Victims have also complained about the amount of time it takes, the delay between the offense and resolution, and the lack of follow-up (Coates and Gehm 1989; Perry et al. 1987; Strode 1997; Umbreit 1995).

■ Encounter and Shaming

Criminal behavior is determined by biological, psychological, and social structural variables over which the criminal has little control. The theory of reintegrative shaming, however, adopts a much more active view of the offender. Consistent with the notion of human autonomy and dignity, the offender is viewed as making choices about crime, joining a criminal subculture, or adopting a deviant self-concept, but also choices relative to societal pressures brought about by shaming (Braithwaite 1999, 9). The offender is constrained by the moralizing qualities of social control (i.e., shaming). In other words, the offender obeys not for fear of punishment but for dread of the loss of esteem in the eyes of those about which he or she cares. Shaming is a tool used to get the offender to recognize the moral claims of the criminal law, to encourage compliance, and to instruct the offender as to the harmfulness of the conduct. The offender is free to reject all of this, too.

Braithwaite (1999) believes moralizing social control is more likely to secure compliance with the law than repressive social control. Because criminal behavior is harmful by any moral yardstick, moralizing appeals treat the citizen as someone with the responsibility to make the right choice. Society grants the offender the autonomy to make a moral choice, even if it is a bad choice. Such appeals are generally, though not invariably, responded to more positively than repressive controls, which deny human dignity by treating people as amoral calculators. A culture impregnated with high moral expectations of its citizens, publicly expressed, will deliver superior crime control compared with a culture that sees control as achievable by inflicting pain on its "bad apples."

Shaming is in theory a means of making citizens actively responsible for their behavior by informing the offender on how justifiably resentful other citizens are of the wrong done (Braithwaite 1999, 10–11). In practice, shaming is effective in limiting offender autonomy because of the emphasis given to community values and in recognition of the fact that moral claims can be made by any citizen who reasonably expects to express disgust should violations of these values occur. This process includes specific words and gestures that bring into question the value of the behavior. It may be a snide comment, laugh, tut-tut, or a direct verbal confrontation. It would seem that sanctions imposed by relatives, friends, or a personally relevant collectivity have more effect on criminal behavior than sanctions imposed by a remote legal authority (Braithwaite 1999, 69). Only a small proportion of the informal sanctions that prevent crime are coupled with formal sanctions (Braithwaite 1999). Legal authorities also have diminished effect when they are considered unfair or prejudicial. In other words, shaming is the route to freely chosen compliance, while repressive social control is a route to coerced compliance. However, in the absence of any coercion, compliance is less likely to be achieved. Shaming invites compliance by bringing to the offender's attention what an offense means to the victim, the offender, and the community. One sees that the offender in meeting with the community has a chance to agree to comply but also has an opportunity to express his or her concerns and negotiate or appeal for mercy. Moralizing social control restricts autonomy by inviting one to see that one cannot be a moral person by reflecting only on one's own interests. One is shamed if one exercises one's own autonomy in a way that tramples on the autonomy of others (Braithwaite 1999, 10–11). One violates the human dignity of others when one denies them a chance to act as autonomous individuals.

Braithwaite's (1999) theory of reintegrative shaming distinguishes between shaming that leads to stigmatization and shaming that is reintegrative. Stigmatizing pushes the offender further away from the community as an outcast and deviant and closer to a criminal subcultures. Reintegrative shaming, however, maintains bonds of respect, dignity, or love and sharply terminates disapproval with forgiveness. This type of shaming controls crime. Individuals are more susceptible to shaming when they are enmeshed in multiple relationships of interdependency; societies shame more effectively when they are communitarian

(Braithwaite 1999). As Znaniecki (1971) says, shaming punishments reinforce agreements and solidarity among those who actively or vicariously participate in the meeting.

Healing

An important function of restorative justice is making the victim anew. With the commission of the crime, there is an opportunity to correct the injustice and reestablish a sense of equity through reparations and reconciliation. The outcomes lead to participants feeling safer, respected, empowered, and more trusting. The importance of this healing means victims have fewer problems in the future and reduced medical cost. It is a time when the victim can achieve some closure on the act. It is these residual costs that bring the most pain.

Victims can suffer from posttraumatic stress disorder. With this problem, victims are going to have physical, psychological, and emotional problems that will follow them until closure is achieved and the event can be put behind the victim. This may not be achieved without professional counseling. Meeting with the offender may or may not be an important step along the process. If the victim is a child, the problem may be much more severe.

Amends and Forgiveness

Jesus taught forgiveness and the love of one's enemies. This doctrine of forgiveness is part of the basis for victim reconciliation in the current restorative justice movement (Braswell et al. 2001, 12–13).

Mahatma Gandhi, Desmond Tutu, Myanmar's Noble Peace Prize winner Aung San Suu Kyi, and the Dalai Lama have preached that crime permits an opportunity for transformation of the evil doer. The Dalai Lama is quoted as saying (Eckel 1997, 135):

> *Learning to forgive is much more useful than merely picking up a stone and throwing it at the object of one's anger, the more so when the provocation is extreme. For it is under great adversity that there exists the greatest potential for doing good, both for oneself and for others. Crime is an opportunity to prevent greater evils, to confront crime with grace that transforms human lives to paths of love and giving.*

The importance of love for one's fellow human beings is voiced in the Bible by the writer of John who wrote: "If someone says they love God but hate their brother, he is a liar; for the one who does not love his brother whom he has seen, cannot love God whom he has not seen" (I John 4:20). In other words, loving those persons around oneself who are visible, shows that one also loves God, who is invisible. In one of the central teachings of the Sermon on the Mount, Jesus enjoined his followers to be peacemakers because peacemakers will be called children of God (Matthew 5:9). Likewise, he encouraged his followers to be merciful and to hunger and thirst for righteousness (Matthew 5:6–7) (Braswell et al. 2001, 12–13).

Many of the victims and offenders who complete VOM processes do not become friends with one another. They do come to a new understanding and with that comes closure. People have to move on with their lives. Apology and forgiveness after a relatively brief meeting can be offered in only a limited way (Van Ness and Strong 2002, 59). There is great power in the ability to forgive; there is great pain in the power of vengeance.

■ Social Integration

Communities play an important part in the restorative justice process (Braithewaite 1999, 35). Without a community, there can be no restorative justice. Community concerns are central to everything. On the one hand, there can be concern that venting victim anger will tear at the fabric of the community. Yet again, while families may be strong elsewhere, the worst offenders are alienated and alone; their families are so dysfunctional and uncaring that they do not participate meaningfully in any community. Hudson and colleagues (1996) have concluded, nonetheless, that many of the concerns about the ineffectiveness of dysfunctional families have not proven to be well-founded. Braithwaite (1999, 36) has identified various studies that consider the level of satisfaction of community members who extend beyond the offender and the victim and who participated in the process. People representing the police and the public have come away with a high level of satisfaction. This group included parents of offenders and representatives in the community. A study by Schneider (1990) found that completing restitution and community service was associated with enhanced sense of commitment to the community, feelings of citizenship, and reduced recidivism. A crime offers a community an opportunity to reassess its social relations, to consider where these relations have deteriorated, and to mend fences so it can be rejuvenated. It is an opportunity to promote community solidarity.

The restorative model, as offered by Zehr (1990), Bazemore and Umbreit (1994), Bazemore and Maloney (1994), Maloney and Umbreit (1995), Karp and Clear (2002), Braswell et al. (2001), and Van Ness and Strong (2002), argues that community protection, offender accountability, and competency development are crucial to a balanced approach to probation. The community also becomes much more important in this model. Probation's attachment to the community was truncated when its ties to volunteers were severed and the system became more professionalized and formalized as it developed over the years. The restorative model calls for probation to become more proactive in its dealing with the public and in providing support for building accountability, community protection, and competency development.

■ Problems of Restorative Justice

Restorative justice has a number of problems to deal with if it is to achieve the full measure of respect and implementation it desires. For one, VOM is a time-consuming process; preparing the participants and holding the conference can be lengthy processes. It is also believed that each VOM may be fairly expensive. According to the author's calculation, if a single individual earning

$35,000 annually devotes 8 hours to one VOM, the cost is about $135 in salary alone, not to mention administrative expenses. One also has to consider the expenses associated with travel and the victim's cost. It is believed the cost could rise to $250.

Restorative justice also has faced obstacles in the court (Zellerer and Cannon 2002). Judges and prosecutors alike fought the initiative because they did not understand the principles and process. It was also clear that the restorative justice people did not understand how the court works; they insisted on seeing the offender within a week of the filing of charges. Once these differences were ironed out, the program worked much more effectively. Restorative justice is not likely to succeed if it is imposed on unwilling participants.

Restorative justice research fails to speak to the classic measure of criminal justice program success—recidivism rates. Much of the material collected on program success points to participant satisfaction and to the restitution completion payment rate. There is not a sufficient number of studies to say that restorative justice works to achieve a reduction in recidivism. At this point, most recidivism research focuses on juvenile offenses. Long-term research is needed in this area.

Braithwaite (1999) has identified several areas where restorative justice might be in trouble. There is a belief that restorative practices offer no benefits to most of the white-collar and victimless crime victims. Furthermore, most offenses in the United States do not lead to the identification of an offender. The FBI reports (Federal Bureau of Investigation 2003) that the clearance rate (the percentage of offenses where there is a known perpetrator) for murder was 63 percent, aggravated assault, 56 percent, larceny-thefts 18 percent, and burglary 14 percent. With clearance arrest rates so low, it is no surprise that VOM programs seem so irrelevant. It is also believed that restorative justice can increase victim fears of revictimization. Although victims often are surprised about the meek behavior of many perpetrators, some offenders can be intimidating (Braithwaite and Mugford 1994). This is where preparation of the victim and the offender is so crucial. Another identifiable problem is that restorative practices can make victims little more than props for attempts to rehabilitate the offender. During the process, victim anger may be perceived as too destructive. There is also the issue of the shaming machine as crucial in understanding the damaging effects of sarcasm, moral superiority, and moral lecturing, especially when it is repetitive and out of control. Moral indignation interferes with identifying with the offender. The best way to deal with this is to invite a large group of supporters (Braithwaite and Mugford 1994). Even though the offender may have his or her supporters present, there is the further problem of shaming offenders who have a history of humiliating experiences behind them, especially as a child and youth, who see the restorative process as just another effort to further devalue them. The offenders are asked to seek forgiveness when no one has given consideration to the pain experienced in their lives unless the encounter is truly revealing. Another problem is that restorative justice might work in communities that are somewhat integrated but not in those where there is less a sense of community. Community building may be the first step in any restorative program. Certain practices including verbal lynching are possible if isolated rural communities take on restorative justice practices and exceed the limits of appropriate practice. Restorative justice practices can widen the net of social control. Restorative justice does little to reduce poverty and unemployment. Finally, restorative justice practices are prone to being captured by the dominant group in the process; for example, restorative practices may be dominated by a well-organized group of mothers concerned about bullying in school. Other matters seem to be appropriate, too.

Domination in the Process

Braithwaite (2000) argues that restorative processes must seek to avoid domination. What this means is that any stakeholders who want to attend a conference or circle and have a say must not be prevented from doing so. If they have a stake in the outcome, they must not be prevented from attending and speaking. Any attempt by a participant to silence or dominate another participant must be countered. The restorative process must be structured to minimize any power imbalance. Young offenders must not be led into a situation where they are upbraided by a roomful of adults. Similarly, a group of offender supporters cannot dominate a group of women victims. People should recognize the importance of consulting attorneys about their rights but attorneys should not have the right to speak on behalf of their clients. Most importantly, the process should be constrained so as not to impose a sentence that exceeds limits set by law. The offender should also have the right to appeal.

Brooks (2000) cautions further about problems with the restorative model. He argues that programs that emphasize restitution over reconciliation can give rise to several problems. First, a lack of remorse may lead to revictimizing the offender. Secondly, the offender may not think of reparations as an expression of genuine remorse or of his or her desire to make things right. As far as the offender is concerned, the whole thing is about having the victim have a say in what kind of punishment the offender is required to serve. The offender essentially fakes his or her way through the program. Lastly, it is widely believed among observers of mediation or other restorative processes that the claims made about restorative justice ring true; people do believe they receive a higher quality of justice, the offender is shamed within a continuum of love and respect, and they do enable victims to experience forgiveness. The problem is that experts do not know how to test such claims.

Relying on the Community

Restorative justice puts a great deal of stock in the community's interest in and ability to develop competency. Essential to this model is the balancing of accountability with community protection and competency development. There is a great deal of uncertainty as to whether the model can maintain itself. Any community has a wide variety of needs and demands placed on its resources. Accountability and community protection will certainly develop more community interests. Competency development is another challenge. It would seem that many people would interpret competency as just another umbrella under which to hide the promotion and protection of community-based rehabilitation services. Competency must be clearly understood as reducing tax burdens and increasing tax rolls.

Specifics of the Process

The problems associated with compassion fatigue and botheration/toleration have to be addressed before going further in this direction. Many people may feel they are unwilling to forgive the offender even after meeting and discussing the case. These people cannot be forced to do something they have little interest in. Only time may make a difference here.

The restorative model has little to say on how to deal with specific offenders. For example, the model is unclear if the crime is essentially victimless such as in the case with drugs, gambling, and other vice offenses. Much discussion is taking place about the importance of expanding the understanding of victimhood. Quite obviously there are people who are injured by drug-related activities, in particular activities associated with the protection of neighborhood turf. However, for the most part, most of the offenders are consensual offenders who do not believe that they are hurting anyone by their actions.

This restoration model also suffers from the fact that it has never been truly tested using an experimental design. This is particularly apparent when it comes to making any claims about success in reducing crime or delinquency. Obviously maintaining a quality of life is a central factor for everyone but if the model is to achieve full recognition and public support, an experiment is necessary to evaluate its performance and acceptance in the community.

Empirical assessment is just one of the means used to evaluate any activity. For the most part, the restorative model is normative in nature, basing much of its support on the imperative claim that all people deserve just treatment because of their essential human qualities. As is now known, just because something seems the right thing to do, that does not mean that it gains wide acceptance. Both the civil rights movement and opposition to the Vietnam War achieved wide public support but it took years for desegregation to be achieved and for the American involvement to end in Vietnam.

■ Conclusion

There is no Marshall Plan for the ghetto. Political and economic realities preclude this. Positive attitudinal change toward the criminal underclass will likely take place only if the ghetto poor, despite their social and economic disadvantages, subscribe to the traditional American values of a strong family, individual initiative, self-sufficiency, responsibility, discipline, and normative order, and if they eschew self-destructive behaviors (Kasarda 1992, 86). This may be virtually impossible to achieve without outside support. Greater support is not likely to be forthcoming because the rift between the "haves" and the "have-nots" is increasing, resulting in greater social distances between them. This means an increase in fear and less trust. People one knows one tends to care about but those not known are only feared.

Feeley and Sarat (1980) have claimed that the U.S. political system has engaged in the process of "politics by promise." Political campaigns are full of this rhetoric. The criminal justice system has been the focal point of much of this activity. Politicians have promised a great deal without understanding the system-wide implications. They have passed get-tough legislation but they do not recognize, much as in disciplining a child, that if the offender is motivated solely by fear, compliance with the law is ephemeral.

Probation must learn to deal with the question of whether it will succumb to external or internal political wrangling or whether it will offer as many services as before, and press on with an agenda it will be proud of in 50 years. Whether the officers provide restoration, supervision, support, therapy, or referrals, they must decide which consideration is a priority and for what kind of probationer. For juveniles, the probation officer clearly is going to provide greater remedial services, but at the same time, the officer is going to be watching very carefully the progress of the probationer. For the adult offender, the officer is more likely to act in a role that is similar to a parole officer or even police officer. What does this then mean for restorative justice?

Probation officers must be anchored in a set of values that protects the interests of the officer, the agency, the victim, the offender, the community, and the state. This is a problem because probation officers are not saints who have supernatural powers. Probation officers, like anyone else, are subject to the same turbulence as their probationers.

REFERENCES

Bazemore, G., and D. Maloney. 1994. Rehabilitating community service: Toward restorative service sanctions in a balanced justice system. *Federal Probation* 58: 24–35.

Bazemore, G., and M. Umbreit. 1994. *Balanced and restorative justice.* Washington, DC: Office of Juvenile Justice Delinquency Prevention, U.S. Government Printing Office.

Beck, G. 1997. Fire in the Atman: Repentance in Hinduism. In A. Etzioni and D. Carney, eds., *Repentence: A comparative perspective.* New York: Rowan and Littlefield.

Bellah, Robert N. 1959. Durkheim and history. *American Sociological Review* 24: 447–461.

Benekos, P. 1990. "Beyond reintegration: Community corrections in a retributive era." *Federal Probation* 54: 52–56.

Berman, H. 1983. *Law and revolution: The formation of the Western legal tradition.* Cambridge, MA: Harvard University Press.

Braithwaite, J. 2000. Standards for restorative justice. United Nations Crime Congress, ancillary meeting. Vienna, Austria. www.restorativejustice.org/rj3/UNBasicprinciples/ancillarymeetings.

Braithwaite, J. 1999. *Crime, shame, and reintegration.* New York: Cambridge University Press.

Braithwaite, J. 1996. Restorative justice and a better future. *The Dalhousie Review* 1: 9–32.

Braithwaite, J., and S. Mugford. 1994. Conditions of successful reintegration ceremonies: Dealing with juvenile offenders. *British Journal of Criminology* 34: 138–171.

Braithwaite, J., and P. Pettit. 1990. *Not just deserts: A republican theory of criminal Justice.* Oxford University Press.

Braswell, M., J. Fuller, and B. Lozoff. 2001. *Corrections, peacemaking, and restorative justice.* Cincinnati, OH: Anderson.

Brooks, D. 2000. Evaluating restorative justice programs. United Nations Crime Congress, ancillary meeting Vienna, Austria, 2000. www.restorativejustice.org/rj3/UNBasicPrinciples/AncillaryMeetings/Papers/RJ_Un_Dbrooks.htm.

Burnside, J., and N. Baker. 1994. *Relational justice: Repairing the breach.* Winchester, UK: Waterside Press.

Christie, N. 1977. Conflict as property. *British Journal of Criminology* 17(1): 1–14.

Coates, R., and J. Gehm. 1989. An empirical assessment. In M. Wright and B. Galloway, eds., *Mediation and criminal justice.* London: Sage.

De Haan, W. 1990. *The politics of redress: Crime, punishment and penal abolition.* London: Unwin Hyman.

Diamond, A. S. 1935. *Primitive law.* London: Longmans, Green and Co.

Dignan, J. 1992. Repairing the damage: Can reparation work in the service of diversion? *British Journal of Criminology* 32: 453–472.

Durkheim, E. 1968. *The division of labor in society.* New York: Macmillan.

Eckel, M. 1997. A Buddhist approach to repentence. In A. Etzioni and D. Carney, eds., *Repentence: A comparative perspective.* New York: Rowan and Littlefield.

Eglash A. 1975. Creative restitution. In J. Hudson and B. Galaway, eds., *Restitution in criminal justice.* Lexington, MA: Lexington Books.

Evje, A., and R. Cushman. 2000. *A summary of the evaluation of six California victim-offender reconciliation programs.* San Francisco, CA: Judicial Council of California, Administrative Office of the Courts.

Federal Bureau of Investigation. 2003. *Crimes cleared.* Uniform Crime Reports. Available at: http://www.fbi.gov/ucr/.

Feeley, M., and A. Sarat. 1980. *The policy dilemma: The crisis of theory and practice in the law enforcement assistance administration.* Minneapolis, MN: University of Minnesota Press.

Ferns, R. 1994. Restorative case management. *Perspectives* 18: 36–41.

Gehm, J. 1990. Mediated victim-offender restitution agreements: An exploratory analysis of factors related to victim participation. In B. Galaway and J. Hudson, eds., *Criminal justice, restitution, and reconciliation.* Monsey, NY: Willow Tree.

Gillin, J. L. 1935. *Criminology and penology,* rev. ed. New York: Appleton-Century.

Haley, J. 1996. Crime prevention through restorative justice: Lessons from Japan. In B. Galaway and J. Hudson, eds., *Restorative justice: International perspectives.* Monsey, NY: Criminal Justice Press.

Harland, A. 1993. Defining a continuum of sanctions. *Perspectives* 17: 6–16.

Hartman. A. 1995. Schlichten oder Richten. Der Tater-Opfer-Ausgleich und das (Jugend) Strafrecht. Translated by Weitekamp. Munich, Germany: Willem Fink Verlag.

Hassal. I. 1996. Origins and development of family group confernces. In J. Hudson, A. Morris, G. Maxwell, and B. Galaway, eds., *Family group conferences: Perspectives on policy and practice.* Monsey, NY: Criminal Justice Press.

Heidensohn, F. 1986. Models of justice: Portia or Persephone? Some thoughts on the equality, fairness, and gender in the field of criminal justice. *International Journal of the Sociology of Law* 14: 287–298.

Hudson, J., A. Morris, G. Maxwell, and B. Galaway, eds. 1996. *Family group conferences: Perspectives on policy and practice.* Monsey, NY: Criminal Justice Press.

James, T. 1993. *Circle sentencing.* Yellowknife: Supreme Court of the Northwest Territories, Canada.

Karp, D., and T. Clear, eds. 2002. *What is community justice? Case studies of restorative justice and community supervision.* Thousand Oaks, CA: Sage Publications.

Kasarda, J. D. 1992. The severely distressed in economically transforming cities. In A. V. Harrell and G. E. Peterson, eds., *Drugs, crime, and social isolation.* Washington, DC: Urban Institute, pp. 45–98.

Klein, A. 1988. *Alternative sentencing.* Cincinnati, OH: Anderson.

Launay, G., and P. Murray. 1989. Victim/offender groups. In M. Wright and G. Galaway, eds., *Mediation and criminal justice.* Thousand Oaks, CA: Sage Publications.

Lilles, H. 2002. *Circle sentencing: Part of the restorative justice continuum.* Third International International Institute for Restorative Practices, Minneapolis, MN, August 8–10, 2002.

Lukes, S., and A. Scull. 1983. *Durkheim and the law.* Oxford: Martin Robertson.

MacDonald, J., K. Moore, T. O'Connell, and M. Thorsborbe. 1995. *Real justice training manual: Coordinating family group conferences.* Pipersville, PA: Pipers Press.

Maloney, D., and M. Umbreit. 1995. Managing change: Toward a balanced and restorative justice model. *Perspectives* 19: 43–47.

Marshall, T. 1985. *Alternatives to criminal courts.* Aldershot: Grover.

Michalowski, R. J. 1985. *Order, law and crime.* New York: Random House.

Moore, D., and L. Forsythe. 1995. *A new approach to juvenile justice: An evaluation of family conferencing in Wagga Wagga.* Wagga Wagga: Charles Stuart University.

Nicholl, C. 1998. *Implementing restorative justice.* Washington, DC: U.S. Department of Justice, Office of Community Oriented Policing Services.

Nolen-Hoeksema, S., and J. Larson. 1999. *Coping with loss.* Mahwah, NJ: Lawrence Erlbaum Associates.

Parnes, H. 1984. *People power: Elements of resource policy.* Beverly Hills, CA: Sage Publications.

Peachey, D. 1989. The Kichener experiment. In M. Wright and B. Galaway, eds., *Mediation and criminal justice: Victims, offenders, and community.* Thousand Oaks, CA: Sage Publications.

Pepinsky, H., and R. Quinney, ed. 1991. *Criminology as peacemaking.* Bloomington: Indiana University Press.

Perry, L., T. Lajeunesse, and A. Woods. 1987. *Mediation services: An evaluation.* Manitoba, Canada: Research, Planning and Evaluation Office of the Attorney General.

Pranis, K. 1996. A state initiative toward restorative justice: The Minnesota experience. In B. Galaway and J. Hudson, eds., *Restorative justice: International perspectives.* Monsey, NY: Criminal Justice Press.

Pranis, K., and M. Umbreit. 1992. *Public opinion research challenges perception of widespread public demand for Hasher punishment.* Minneapolis, MN: Minnesota Citizens Council on Crime and Justice.

Reeves, H. 1989. The victim support perspective. In M. Wright and B. Galaway, eds., *Mediation and criminal justice: Victim, offenders, and community.* Thousand Oaks, CA: Sage Publications.

Reiff, R. 1979. *The invisible victim.* New York: Basic Books.

Sander, F. 1976. Varieties of dispute processing. *Federal Rules Decisions* 70: 111–134.

Schafer, S. 1970. *Compensation and victim restitution to victims of crime.* Montclair, NJ: Patterson Smith.

Schneider, A. 1990. *Deterrence and juvenile crime: Results from a national policy experiment.* New York: Springer-Verlag.

Schneider, A. 1986. Restitution and recidivism rates of juvenile offenders: Results from four experimental studies. *Criminology* 24: 533–552.

Sherman, L., and H. Strang. 1997. *The victims perspective.* RISE working papers 2, Canberra ACT, Australian National Univesity.

Sivell-Ferri, C. 1997. The Ojibwa circle: Traditions and change. In Aboriginal Corrections Policy Unit, eds., *The four circles of hollow water.* Ottawa: Soliciter General.

Stone, S., W. Helms, and P. Edgeworth. 1998. Cobb County (Georgia) Juvenile Court Mediation Program Evaluation.

Strode, E. 1997. Victims of property crimes meeting their juvenile offender: Victim participants evaluation of the Dakota Co. (MN) Community Corrections Victim Offender Meeting Program. Masters thesis. Smith College School of Social Work, Northampton, MA.

Sycamore Tree Project. 2005. Prison Fellowship International. Available at: http://www.pficjr.org/programs.

Toennies, F. 1940. *On sociology: Pure, applied, and empirical.* Chicago: University of Chicago Press.

Tomlinson, T. 1994. Reintegrating the criminal offender through community-based vocational networks. In C. Fields, ed., *Innovative trends and specialized strategies in community-based corrections.* New York: Garland Publishing.

Umbreit, M. 1995. *Mediation of criminal conduct: An assessment of programs in four Canadian provinces.* St. Paul, MN: Center for Restorative Justice and Mediation.

Umbreit, M. 1994. *Victim meets offender: The impact of restorative justice & mediation.* Monsey, NY: Criminal Justice Press.

Umbreit, M., and W. Bradshaw. 2000. Factors that contribute to victim satisfaction with mediated offender dialogue in Winnipeg: An emerging area of social work practice. *The Journal of Law and Social Work.*

Umbreit, M., and R. Coates. 2000. *Victim impact of restorative justice and mediation.* Fort Lauderdale, FL: Community Justice Institute, Florida Atlantic University.

Umbreit, M., R. Coates, and B. Vos. 2001. Victim impact of meeting with young offenders: Two decades of victim offender mediation practice and research. In A. Morris and G. Maxwell, eds., *Restorative justice for juveniles: Conferencing, mediation and circles.* Portland, OR: Hart Publishing.

Van Ness, D. 1999. Legal issues in restorative justice. In G. Bazemore and L. Walgrave, eds., *Restorative juvenile justice: Repairing the harm of youth crime.* Monsey, NY: Criminal Justice Press.

Van Ness, D. 1986. *Crime and its victims: What we can do.* Downers Grove, IL: Intervarsity Press.

Van Ness, D., and K. Strong. 2002. *Restoring justice.* Cincinnati, OH: Anderson.

Walgrave, L. 1994. Beyond rehabilitation: In search of a constructive alternative in the judicial response to juvenile crime. *European Journal on Criminal Policy and Research* 1: 57–75.

Weitekamp, E. 1999. The history of restorative justice. In G. Bazemore and L. Walgrave, eds., *Restorative juvenile justice: Repairing the harm of youth crime.* Monsey, NY: Criminal Justice Press.

Wright, M. 1982. *Making good: Prisons punishment and beyond.* London: Hutchinson.

Wyrick, A., and M. Costanzo. 1999. Predictors of client participation in victim-offender mediation. *Mediation Quarterly* 16: 243–267.

Yazzie, R., and J. Zion. 1996. Navajo restorative justice: The law of equality and justice. In B. Galaway and J. Hudson, eds., *Restorative justice: International perspectives.* Monsey, NY: Criminal Justice Press.

Zehr, H. 1990. *Changing lenses.* Scottsdale, AZ: Herald Press.

Zellerer, E., and J. Cannon. 2002. Restorative justice, reparation and the South Side project. In D. Karp and T. Clear, eds., *What is community justice? Case studies of restorative justice and community supervision.* Thousand Oaks, CA: Sage.

Znaniecki, F. 1971. *Nauki o kulturze.* Warsaw, Poland: PWN.

KEY POINTS

1. Restorative justice focuses on repairing harm caused by crime and reducing the likelihood of future harm.

2. The concept of victim restitution as a criminal sanction has been around for centuries in various forms.

3. A comprehensive model of restorative justice recognizes that there are four parties affected by crime: the victim, the offender, the community, and the government.

4. Three components of restorative justice are accountability, community protection, and competency development in which the offender is given a meaningful opportunity to change.

5. Restorative justice emphasizes a safe and secure community during the time the offender is under supervision.

6. Offender needs and strengths matched to community resources aids in the development of offender competencies.

7. In the restorative justice model, the correctional system is not based on punishment, but instead is based on the extent to which the victim is restored and the offender is to experience something unwelcomed.

8. There are four different approaches used to structure an encounter between the offender and the victim: mediation, conferencing, circles, and impact panels.

9. Shaming is conceived in theory for making the offender actively responsible for their behavior by informing the offender on how justifiably resentful the citizen is of the wrong done.

10. Reintegrative shaming avoids stigmatization, maintains bonds of respect or love, and sharply tempers disapproval with forgiveness.

KEY TERMS

accountability means the offender needs to understand and take responsibility for what he or she has done. This can be achieved through cognitive restructuring, allowing offenders to understand their actions, their feelings, and the outcomes that are derived from these feelings.

circle is one form of a victim-offender encounter involving the victim, offender, families, and community members.

family group conferencing (FGC) is a process involving the bringing together of the offender, the offender's immediate and extended family members, support persons, justice system representatives, and the victims of the crime and their support persons.

impact panels are comprised of groups of victims who meet a group of offenders who are linked by a common kind of crime, although they are not each other's victim or offender. The purpose of such meetings is to find resolution and to expose offenders to the damage caused by their crime, especially when the direct victim is not interested in the meeting.

range of sanctions is a series of unwelcomed experiences that are designed to increase in intrusiveness as they match the risk of further harm.

restitution is a form of payment in kind, labor, or money in compensation for a wrong.

restorativists view crime much more broadly, especially as the harm impacts the relationship between people and where it is related to other harms and conflicts. Harm also must be understood within its full moral, social, economic, and political contexts.

retributivists define crime as a violation of a rule in technical and legal terms whereas harm is defined abstractly. Crime is distinguished from other harms, such as civil harms, because the state is viewed as a victim.

victim-offender mediation (VOM) is a process that provides the victim with the opportunity to meet the offender in a safe setting.

REVIEW QUESTIONS

1. What are the advantages of addressing crime using restorative justice?

2. Discuss the history of restorative justice.

3. Compare retributive and restorative justice.

4. What is VOM? Give some examples.

5. What are some of the drawbacks of restorative justice?

6. What role does restorative justice play in human dignity?

9

Regulatory Probation

Chapter Objectives

In this chapter you will learn about:

- What happens to offenders who fail to meet the conditions set for them
- The forces at work that make supervision difficult
- The deterrence model of supervision versus the regulatory model
- The importance of human dignity during this process
- Gaining offender compliance through inspection, discipline, and normalization

Who's in Charge?

One of the questions being asked in probation today is how much authority probation officers should have to impose punitive conditions or lessen the rigors of existing sanctions without review of a sentencing authority. The American Probation and Parole Association (2001) believes officer authority to impose conditions of supervision is valid and deserves support. Under proper conditions, it promotes consistency in the response to violations. Detailed policies and procedures should be established and included in a comprehensive training program. Absent these, agent-imposed sanctions on an informal basis can result in vague, misunderstood, and often misapplied discretion instead of a policy-driven, risk-based violation process (Stroker 1991).

The American Probation Parole Association Board (2001) reports that less than half (46 percent) of the respondents in their study indicated that field officers have the authority to modify conditions of supervision. However, a substantial number (69 percent) felt that officers modified conditions informally. It is apparent in some jurisdictions that line officers feel justified in altering some aspects of an offender's supervision strategy, regardless of whether this is a matter of policy. Two states, Oregon and South Carolina, have programs that provide specific guidelines for the officer increasing imposed sanctions. In South Carolina, for example, field officers have a range of options that include placing the offender in a halfway house, or in a treatment facility, restructuring the plan of action, increasing contacts, and ordering additional community service. The primary purpose is to increase punitive sanctions. There appears to be little interest in lessening the severity of conditions of supervision without some type of judicial review. It is believed that by permitting the officer to react quickly by modifying supervision conditions, the officer avoids the time-consuming task of obtaining a warrant and scheduling a case before a judge. It also gives the officer some flexibility to explore treatment options that hold the offender accountable and increase the officer's effectiveness. On the other hand, there are those who argue that granting the officer additional authority only confuses the offender as to who has jurisdiction. There is also some belief that court-imposed sanctions have a greater impact. Moreover, there is concern that such a system will lead to abuses of discretion and lead to greater liability for the officer. Lastly, there is the concern that such activities would only diminish the existing relationship with the judiciary.

Violations

Ethical and legal problems arise when the probationer's behavior reaches the point that a violation is filed with the court (Smith and Berlin 1979). The technical violation is a transgression against the conditions by which the probationer was ordered to abide. Not reporting is one such violation; new arrest and absconding are two other types of violations. A technical violation is the most difficult to handle because of the discretion granted the officer, the prosecutor, and the court. If the probationer has rejected every available community resource and continues to pose a threat to the community, there is reason enough to bring the probationer back into court. If the probationer refuses to report, the officer needs to understand the reason for this failure. The problems could be related to work, transportation, and substance abuse; the officer's attitude toward the probationer; or a breakdown in communication. Further investigation is warranted to sufficiently address the problem. It may be necessary for the probationer to report to another officer.

Research conducted by the author found that many probation officers are hesitant to bring a probationer to court for a violation.

1. A new charge may be unfounded and dismissed by the court so it is a waste of time.

2. The officer may seek time to develop an alternative treatment plan. This is important if the officer wishes to maintain the relationship with the probationer and is concerned that a hearing will reverse the process.

3. The officer may feel somewhat responsible for the client's failure. This opinion certainly can develop out of recognition of the lack of time available for each case with rising caseloads and greater numbers of presentence reports.

4. The officer may come to recognize that he or she is outside the sphere of influence in the matter.

A Group Effort

The probation officer, public defender, district attorney, and judge all must work together. Cole (1989, 417–426) considers this a courtroom work group. Cole assumes that officials work regularly with one another and develop a working relationship out of this continuous contact. However, not all relationships in the group are equal. In many instances, the probation officer is caught in the middle of a process in which the interests of the different actors conflict. Quite often, the officer opposes the positions worked out by these others.

Interviews conducted by the author with probation officers reveal that not all officers are likely to be concerned with violating the probationer and that something else might be happening. By the time the officer has brought the case to court for a violation, there have been numerous instances in which the probationer chose to act contrary to the law and conditions of probation. Most officers take violations very seriously and only do so after an administrative hearing has been held and other warnings have been issued. Often there appears to be no other alternative. One juvenile officer said:

> Sometimes we have kids who are placed on probation who should never be on probation. You can also be fooled by it because the ones who you think should have gone away to jail sometimes work out and the ones that you think have everything going for them fail.

Another added:

> If I violate the probationer, it is not because I don't like him. This is the responsibility that we both have. If we meet these responsibilities we won't have any problems.

One adult officer spoke of the frustrations of violations:

> Violations are the most frustrating part of this job. It is extremely time consuming. When he violates probation, he is violating the judge's order and yet the judge says we have a probation officer who is accusing you of having violated your probation. He gets a lawyer and we go to trial. The DA prosecutes and I am the witness for the prosecution. The judge is trying to decide if I am telling the truth or the probationer is telling the truth. A lot of times, arrangements have been made beforehand. Then it is a question of what will we do. Fifty percent of the time or more the defense attorney talks the judge into continuing him on probation. The defense attorney's thinking is just the opposite of mine. His thinking is, that if the judge didn't lock this guy up for his original crime, why would you even consider locking him up for something as insignificant as not reporting to a probation officer. They make me look like a schmuck!

One ISP officer had this to say:

> I almost never violate on "just not reporting." It is a bullshit technical violation. If he has a consistent record of failing to report, usually he will become an absconder, and I will get him with a warrant. If they are not reporting, they are not going to counseling, they are

not going to the clinic, they are not following up on any other conditions of probation. Sometimes a violation is the only way to get their attention. He has a couple of missed reports, he has a few positive urine tests for cocaine, marijuana, and you go into court for a violation on all of these things. That process will take you a month and a half. By the time that you get an arraignment, a lawyer is assigned, you come back, conduct a hearing, and adjournments— usually he is out because they set bail. Now in that month-and-a-half process, if you chose to refer him back to the clinic, you start working with a preexisting relationship with the clinic, you know some of the counselors and you ask, what do you think of this guy's chances? If I get some positive feedback from the counselor, even if I am in a violation process on the guy, I will send him back there. If during that violation, he does pretty well, you have some options open to you.

Alternatives

Probation operates under differential enforcement practices. There are various typologies of community supervision officers (Baird et al. 1985; Czajkoski 1973; Glaser 1964; Katz 1982; Klockars 1972; Miles 1965; Rosencrance 1987; Sigler and McGraw 1984; Tomaino 1975; Van Laningham et al. 1966). Most of the models put probation decision making on a bipolar continuum between offender treatment and offender control. Of particular note are the probation officers' quasi-judicial functions. Many times during the day a probation officer must make a decision affecting his or her probationers. Ideally, the public wants officers to treat like cases alike but it also wants the officer to display the wisdom necessary to handle unique situations. Probation officers, moreover, must interpret the conditions set by the court, instruct offenders as to how to follow the conditions, inspect offenders to see that they are in line, discipline them when they aren't, and attempt to bring offenders back from the edge by seeing that they attend mandatory treatment programs. In an effort to achieve a measure of individualized justice and fairness, attorneys follow the process as never before. The attorney attempts to mediate the severity of punishment, the intrusiveness of the inspections, the enforcement of the conditions of probation, and the extent to which the offender is to participate in mandatory treatment programs. The attorney attempts to reduce the severity of the sanctions when he or she cannot defeat the prosecution at trial.

Various studies reported by Harris, Clear, and Baird (1989) revealed that the majority of the officers accepted treatment or assistance as the most important of community supervision objectives. More importantly they found despite the weakness of the data, concern for authority has increased and is now a more meaningful concept in supervision than either assistance or treatment. Authority easily translates into a hardening of attitudes toward the offender. In addition, probation officer authority has become important as a means for expressing concerns about incapacitation, dangerous work experiences, and criticism directed at probation for being "soft on crime." This hardening of attitudes is expected in light of probation's prime directive to protect the community, especially when a substantial number of serious offenders are granted probation (Bureau of Justice Statistics 1997). Holding officers accountable for the actions of probationers is one of the reasons for officers giving more emphasis to law enforcement functions (del Carmen 1986).

The Probation System

Probation is more sophisticated and plays a more integral role in the system of punishment than ever before. It is now considered an essential alternative to incarceration for some offenders. Rhine (1998) argues that a plausible narrative of community-based corrections is needed which suggests what must be done to ensure the viability of the probation system. In other words, a model for probation is necessary which is relevant to the discretionary conditions under which probation operates. This chapter discusses the effort and forces at work that encourage officers to use discretionary decision making to handle a host of issues including getting tough on the offender while also managing the caseload. The officer cannot consistently fulfill a get-tough mission because it is widely understood that the system has self-imposed limits and when overloaded, will not accept the officer's violation of the offender but will recycle the offender back through probation. It is also known that certain offenders respond better to the carrot than the stick and instead of punitively approaching the offender, the officer is more concerned with getting the offender to comply with the conditions of probation. Some officers realize that certain conditions are excessive or needless and only encourage the offender to react negatively.

deterrence models include elements such as postmonitory, formal, and accusatory, emphasizing a rational choice perspective of crime, employing mission statements, and taking an adversarial approach to the offender.

regulatory models include elements such as premonitory, informal, and bargained. The major emphasis is on probation technical violations. Crime is viewed as a social construction, is discretionary, and the response to it involves negotiations.

This chapter outlines a theory of probation supervision that focuses on the handling of technical violations and the use of a regulatory model of probation that employs the concepts of inspection, discipline, and normalization to keep the probationer in line. This process is counter to the **deterrence model** of probation, which is concerned that the offender clearly understands the cost attached to committing crime. Of central importance to this **regulatory model** are the various conditions set for probation and the emphasis given each within the officer's caseload. One of the main features of community supervision is the importance attached to rules governing the behavior of the offender. The probationer's performance, movements, and attitudes are measured against the conditions of probation. The deterrence model makes a violation of a condition of probation a criminal offense because the offender is a threat to the community. The regulatory model interprets a violation as a technical problem, especially as probation officers view many offenses from the social constructionist perspective. Field supervision, office visits, collateral phone calls, drug testing, and electronic surveillance provide an expanded system of inspection, allowing violations to be recognized and dealt with according to the officer's ideological leaning toward either deterrence or compliance. If one were to categorize an officer as oriented toward either emphasizing deterrence or regulation in the handling of the officer's caseload, consideration could be given to how he or she view violations of the conditions of probation.

In 1973, the federal probation system used various generic requirements as conditions of probation (see **Table 9-1**). These conditions have the obligatory refrain that the probationer should not violate the law. The conditions specify that the probationer must only associate with certain people, that he or she must

| Table 9-1 | Federal Probation Conditions, 1973 |

1. The offender should refrain from the violation of any law. If arrested, the probationer is to report to the probation officer.
2. The probationer should associate only with law-abiding persons and maintain reasonable hours.
3. The probationer should regularly work at a lawful occupation and support their dependents to the best of their ability.
4. The probationer, when unemployed, should notify the officer at once who should be consulted prior to job changes.
5. The probationer should not leave the jurisdiction without permission.
6. The probationer should notify the officer of any changes in address.
7. The probationer should follow the officer's instructions.
8. The probationer should report as directed.

Source: Dillingham, S., Montgomery, R. and Tabor, R. 1990. *Probation and parole in practice.* 2nd ed. Cincinnati: Anderson.

work, maintain regular contact with respect to where he or she is when about, and where he or she lives. Lastly, the conditions admonish the offender to abide by the orders of the probation officers. There is not much here to suggest that probation is interested either in deterrence or regulation. By 1994, the list of probation conditions had lengthened, but was still not yet oriented toward deterrence (see **Table 9-2**).

By 2004, the conditions of probation had become much more elaborate, specific, and deterrence oriented. The United States Code Title 18, Section 3563 from 2004 provides a list of various conditions of probation and supervised release (**Table 9-3**). If a term of probation is ordered, the court can impose a condition that the offender cannot commit another federal, state, or local crime during the term of probation. The domestic violence offender also gets some attention and required treatment. Another condition deals with the requirement that the offender submit to drug testing if thought necessary. Probationers can also be required to pay restitution and assessments in light of the offender's ability to pay. The offender must also provide the addresses for residence and employment, and must also register with authorities. The offender is to cooperate in the collection of DNA evidence. And lastly, the offender can be required to work out a payment schedule for any fines. The discretionary conditions allow for or indicate financial support of dependents, restitution, victim notices, conscientious work ethic, refraining from working in specified occupations that are related to the original offense, refraining from frequenting certain places, refraining from alcohol or drugs, and refraining from possessing firearms and dangerous weapons. Offenders are also to undergo treatment, remain in the custody of the Bureau of Prisons, participate in selected programs, perform community service, reside in certain places, remain within the court's jurisdiction, be permitted visits to home or elsewhere, answer probation officer questions, notify the probation officer if arrested, remain in residence during certain hours, comply with court order, submit to deportation, and satisfy such conditions as the court may impose.

Table 9-2 Federal Probation Conditions, 1994

1. The defendant shall not leave the judicial district or other specified geographic area without the permission of the court or probation officer.
2. The defendant shall report to the probation officer as directed by the court or probation officer and shall submit a truthful and complete written report within the first 5 days of each month.
3. The defendant shall answer truthfully all inquiries by the probation officer and follow the instructions of the probation officer.
4. The defendant shall support their dependents and meet other family responsibilities.
5. The defendant shall work regularly at a lawful occupation unless excused by the probation officer for schooling, training, or other acceptable reasons.
6. The defendant shall notify the probation officer within 72 hours of any change in residence and employment.
7. The defendant shall refrain from excessive alcohol and shall not purchase, possess, use, distribute, or administer any narcotic or other controlled substance, or any paraphernalia related to such substances, except as prescribed by a physician.
8. The defendant shall not frequent places where controlled substances are illegally sold, used, distributed, or administered, or other places specified by the court.
9. The defendant shall not associate with any person engaged in criminal activity and shall not associate with any person convicted of a felony unless granted permission to do so by the probation officer.
10. The defendant shall permit the probation officer to visit him or her at any time at home or elsewhere and shall permit confiscation of any contraband observed in plain view by the probation officer.
11. The defendant shall notify the probation officer within 72 hours of being arrested or questioned by a law enforcement officer.
12. The defendant shall not enter into an agreement to act as an informer or a special agent of law enforcement agency without permission of the court.
13. As directed by the probation officer, the defendant shall notify third parties of risks that may be occasioned by the defendant's criminal recorded personal history or characteristics and shall permit the probation officer to make such notification and to confirm the defendant's compliance with such notification requirements.

Source: Dillingham, S., Montgomery, R. and Tabor, R. 1990. *Probation and parole in practice.* 2nd ed. Cincinnati: Anderson.

Caution is needed in reading Table 9-3, because it is wrong to assume that all conditions of probation stand equal. Probation officers attend to those conditions that initially aid in the resolution of a crisis, and later to those that are directed by policy directives.

Conditions of Probation

Probation conditions are an important feature of probation supervision. In the Bureau of Justice Statistics 1995 Survey of Adults on Probation (SAP), a record check of over 4,000 cases offers some important information on the conditions of probation (Bureau of Justice Statistics 1999). These findings indicate that 82 percent of probationers are given three or more conditions on their sentence.

Table 9-3 — Federal Probation Financial Penalties

U.S Code Title 18: Sec. 3563. – Conditions of probation

1. (a) Mandatory Conditions. –

The court shall provide, as an explicit condition of a sentence of probation –

(1)

for a felony, a misdemeanor, or an infraction, that the defendant not commit another Federal, State, or local crime during the term of probation;

(2)

for a felony, that the defendant also abide by at least one condition set forth in subsection (b)(2), (b)(3), or (b)(13), unless the court finds on the record that extraordinary circumstances exist that would make such a condition plainly unreasonable, in which event the court shall impose one or more of the other conditions set forth under subsection (b);

(3)

for a felony, a misdemeanor, or an infraction, that the defendant not unlawfully possess a controlled substance;

(4)

for a domestic violence crime as defined in section 3561(b) by a defendant convicted of such an offense for the first time that the defendant attend a public, private, or private nonprofit offender rehabilitation program that has been approved by the court, in consultation with a State Coalition Against Domestic Violence or other appropriate experts, if an approved program is readily available within a 50-mile radius of the legal residence of the defendant;

(5)

for a felony, a misdemeanor, or an infraction, that the defendant refrain from any unlawful use of a controlled substance and submit to one drug test within 15 days of release on probation and at least 2 periodic drug tests thereafter (as determined by the court) for use of a controlled substance, but the condition stated in this paragraph may be ameliorated or suspended by the court for any individual defendant if the defendant's presentence report or other reliable sentencing information indicates a low risk of future substance abuse by the defendant;

(6)

that the defendant –

(A)

make restitution in accordance with sections 2248, 2259, 2264, 2327, 3663, 3663A, and 3664; and

(B)

pay the assessment imposed in accordance with section 3013;

(7)

that the defendant will notify the court of any material change in the defendant's economic circumstances that might affect the defendant's ability to pay restitution, fines, or special assessments;

(8)

for a person described in section 4042(c)(4), that the person report the address where the person will reside and any subsequent change of residence to the probation officer responsible for supervision, and that the person register in any State where the person resides, is employed, carries on a vocation, or is a student (as such terms are defined under section 170101(a)(3) of the Violent Crime Control and Law Enforcement Act of 1994); and

(9)

that the defendant cooperate in the collection of a DNA sample from the defendant if the collection of such a sample is authorized pursuant to section 3 of the DNA Analysis Backlog Elimination Act of 2000.

Continued

Table 9-3 **Federal Probation Financial Penalties (Continued)**

If the court has imposed and ordered execution of a fine and placed the defendant on probation, payment of the fine or adherence to the court-established installment schedule shall be a condition of the probation.

(b) Discretionary Conditions. –

The court may provide, as further conditions of a sentence of probation, to the extent that such conditions are reasonably related to the factors set forth in section 3553(a)(1) and (a)(2) and to the extent that such conditions involve only such deprivations of liberty or property as are reasonably necessary for the purposes indicated in section 3553(a)(2), that the defendant –

(1)

support his dependents and meet other family responsibilities;

(2)

make restitution to a victim of the offense under section 3556 (but not subject to the limitation of section 3663(a) or 3663A(c)(1)(A));

(3)

give to the victims of the offense the notice ordered pursuant to the provisions of section 3555;

(4)

work conscientiously at suitable employment or pursue conscientiously a course of study or vocational training that will equip him for suitable employment;

(5)

refrain, in the case of an individual, from engaging in a specified occupation, business, or profession bearing a reasonably direct relationship to the conduct constituting the offense, or engage in such a specified occupation, business, or profession only to a stated degree or under stated circumstances;

(6)

refrain from frequenting specified kinds of places or from associating unnecessarily with specified persons;

(7)

refrain from excessive use of alcohol, or any use of a narcotic drug or other controlled substance, as defined in section 102 of the Controlled Substances Act (21 U.S.C. 802), without a prescription by a licensed medical practitioner;

(8)

refrain from possessing a firearm, destructive device, or other dangerous weapon;

(9)

undergo available medical, psychiatric, or psychological treatment, including treatment for drug or alcohol dependency, as specified by the court, and remain in a specified institution if required for that purpose;

(10)

remain in the custody of the Bureau of Prisons during nights, weekends, or other intervals of time, totaling no more than the lesser of one year or the term of imprisonment authorized for the offense, during the first year of the term of probation;

(11)

reside at, or participate in the program of, a community corrections facility (including a facility maintained or under contract to the Bureau of Prisons) for all or part of the term of probation;

(12)

work in community service as directed by the court;

(13)

reside in a specified place or area, or refrain from residing in a specified place or area;

(14)

remain within the jurisdiction of the court, unless granted permission to leave by the court or a probation officer;

Table 9-3 Federal Probation Financial Penalties (Continued)

(15)

report to a probation officer as directed by the court or the probation officer;

(16)

permit a probation officer to visit him at his home or elsewhere as specified by the court;

(17)

answer inquiries by a probation officer and notify the probation officer promptly of any change in address or employment;

(18)

notify the probation officer promptly if arrested or questioned by a law enforcement officer;

(19)

remain at his place of residence during nonworking hours and, if the court finds it appropriate, that compliance with this condition be monitored by telephonic or electronic signaling devices, except that a condition under this paragraph may be imposed only as an alternative to incarceration;

(20)

comply with the terms of any court order or order of an administrative process pursuant to the law of a State, the District of Columbia, or any other possession or territory of the United States, requiring payments by the defendant for the support and maintenance of a child or of a child and the parent with whom the child is living;

(21)

be ordered deported by a United States district court, or United States magistrate judge, pursuant to a stipulation entered into by the defendant and the United States under section 238(d)(5) of the Immigration and Nationality Act, except that, in the absence of a stipulation, the United States district court or a United States magistrate judge, may order deportation as a condition of probation, if, after notice and hearing pursuant to such section, the Attorney General demonstrates by clear and convincing evidence that the alien is deportable; or

(22)

satisfy such other conditions as the court may impose.

(c) Modifications of Conditions. –

The court may modify, reduce, or enlarge the conditions of a sentence of probation at any time prior to the expiration or termination of the term of probation, pursuant to the provisions of the Federal Rules of Criminal Procedure relating to the modification of probation and the provisions applicable to the initial setting of the conditions of probation.

(d) Written Statement of Conditions. –

The court shall direct that the probation officer provide the defendant with a written statement that sets forth all the conditions to which the sentence is subject, and that is sufficiently clear and specific to serve as a guide for the defendant's conduct and for such supervision as is required.

(e) Results of Drug Testing. –

The results of a drug test administered in accordance with subsection (a)(5) shall be subject to confirmation only if the results are positive, the defendant is subject to possible imprisonment for such failure, and either the defendant denies the accuracy of such test or there is some other reason to question the results of the test. A defendant who tests positive may be detained pending verification of a positive drug test result. A drug test confirmation shall be a urine drug test confirmed using gas chromatography/mass spectrometry techniques or such test as the Director of the Administrative Office of the United States Courts after consultation with the Secretary of Health and Human Services may determine to be of equivalent accuracy. The court shall consider whether the availability of appropriate substance abuse treatment programs, or an individual's current or past participation in such programs, warrants an exception in accordance with United States Sentencing Commission guidelines from the rule of section 3565(b), when considering any action against a defendant who fails a drug test administered in accordance with subsection (a)(5).

Source: United States Code, Title 18, Crimes and Criminal Procedures, Part II – Criminal Procedure, Chapter 227 Sentences, Subchapter B – Probation, Section 3563. Available online at http://www.caselaw.lp.findlaw.com.

Probationers are given such conditions as fees, drug testing, employment, and requirements for treatment. Monetary requirements were the most common condition (84 percent). Note that 61 percent were required to pay supervision fees, 56 percent were to pay a fine, and 55 percent were to pay court cost. Another 33 percent were to pay restitution to the victim. One in 10 probationers were restricted from any contact with the victim. One in four were required to perform community service; two of every five were required to maintain employment or to maintain or enroll in an employment or educational program. Ten percent of the probationers were under some form of monitoring or restriction of movement. Because so many probationers were convicted of public order offenses, especially those related to alcohol abuse, it is not surprising that two out of five probationers (40 percent) were required to enroll in substance abuse treatment. Alcohol treatment was required more frequently for misdemeanants as for felons (41 percent compared to 21 percent), while drug treatment was required more often for felons (28 percent compared to 15 percent). Nearly a third of all probationers were subject to mandatory drug testing (Bonczar 1997, 9).

Probationers who violate a condition of probation by being arrested for a new offense are called before the court to review the circumstances of their violation. Such occasions may call for the issuance of an arrest warrant for the probationer who has absconded, a jail sentence, or reinstatement of probation with or without new conditions. It is estimated, using the SAP data, that 18 percent of all adults on probation had experienced one or more formal disciplinary hearings. The data also indicate that of the probationers who had served 36 months or more on probation, 38 percent had at least one formal hearing, compared to the 5 percent who had served less than 6 months on probation. Disciplinary hearings were more common among probationers who were unemployed and those with prior sentences. Failure to maintain contact was the most frequent reason for the hearing. Despite what might be expected with violations, over 40 percent of the probationers received new conditions rather than incarceration (40 percent vs. 29 percent) (Bonzcar 1997, 9–10).

Years ago, the rates of recidivism of probationers were historically low due to the selection of persons who were likely to succeed on probation. Today, however, there are felons on probation who have much higher rates of recidivism (Petersilia et al. 1985). Based on federal data alone, there were 20,956 probation terminations; 81 percent had no violations, 10 percent experienced technical violations, 3.5 percent were charged with new crimes, and 5 percent had administrative case closures (Bureau of Justice Statistics 1997). **Table 9–4** provides further data on probation hearing outcomes.

The 1995 Survey of Adults on Probation (SAP), a record check of over 4,000 cases, revealed 2,172 technical violations (Bureau of Justice Statistics 1999). With a history of getting tough on offenders, one would expect that offenders are given jail time when they fail to comply with the conditions of probation. This is not true. It seems clear that probationers are given new conditions when they have problems during supervision. If the offender is convicted of a new offense, he or she is likely to be given a new condition (37 percent) more frequently than being incarcerated (28 percent). Also, those arrested for a new offense were more likely to receive new conditions over jail time. Of the offenders who absconded, 25 percent received jail time but slightly more, 28 percent, were given new conditions. There is a reluctance to put offenders in jail for their noncompliance. To

Regulatory Probation | 247

Table 9-4 Probation Revocation Hearing Outcomes

Reasons for Hearing	Incarcerated	Charges Not Sustained	New Conditions	No New Conditions	Hearing Continued	Other Outcome	Still Pending	Totals
Convicted	44 (28%)	1 (.0001%)	58 (37%)	20 (13%)	6 (.04%)	15 (10%)	11 (.07%)	155
Arrest for New Offense	73 (21%)	25 (7%)	120 (35%)	38 (11%)	19 (5%)	54 (16%)	11 (3%)	340
Absconded	39 (25%)	1 (.006%)	44 (28%)	31 (20%)	5 (.031%)	21 (13%)	16 (10%)	157
Positive Drug Test	20 (18%)	0 (0%)	35 (31%)	16 (14%)	10 (9%)	17 (15%)	14 (13%)	112
Failure to Appear	62 (16%)	3 (.007%)	94 (25%)	76 (20%)	22 (6%)	61 (16%)	61 (16%)	379
Failure to Pay Fines	57 (12%)	9 (2%)	126 (27%)	97 (21%)	26 (5%)	88 (19%)	65 (14%)	468
Failure to Attend and Complete Program	43 (17%)	2 (.008%)	52 (21%)	53 (21%)	16 (6%)	40 (16%)	43 (17%)	249
Other Technical Violations	46 (15%)	3 (1%)	64 (20%)	64 (20%)	16 (5%)	70 (22%)	49 (16%)	312 (100%)
Totals								2,172

Source: Bureau of Justice Statistics. 1999. *Survey of adults on probation, 1995.* International Consortion of Political and Social Research. Ann Arbor: University of Michigan.

some degree, there is a sizeable proportion of offenders who experience no new conditions in response to their technical violations. This pattern continues with a positive drug test, failure to appear, failure to pay fines, failure to attend and complete a program, and other technical violations. The data indicate that the courts are approaching violations not as a means to deter the offender but to gain the offender's compliance with the law.

Clearly, offenders on probation have a responsibility to comply with the conditions of supervision. When they do not, then it is up to probation to enforce compliance with such terms. It is here that the practice of probation frequently breaks down. Clear and Cole (1990) point out that once a person has been granted probation, it is not the case that he or she will be held accountable for or removed from the community for serious misbehavior or even for failing to maintain contact with his or her probation officer. The enforcement of the conditions of probation remains all too often sporadic and ineffectual. Over 90 percent of probationers are ordered by the courts to get substance abuse counseling, abide by house arrest, perform community service, or meet other court-ordered conditions. Unfortunately, studies have found that nearly half of all probationers do not comply with the terms of their sentences, and only a fifth of those who violate their sentences ever go to jail for their noncompliance (Langan 1994).

■ Recidivism

Two studies that have reported a high level of probationer recidivism are the Rand Study (Petersilia et al. 1985), which found that 40 months after being sentenced to probation, 65 percent of the offenders had been rearrested and 51 percent had been reconvicted, and a U.S. Department of Justice study (Langan and Cunniff 1992) that reported 43 percent of probationers were rearrested for a felony within 3 years of receiving their probation sentence. Overall, 46 percent of the probationers were classified as failures (Langan and Cunniff, 1992). In terms of public safety, about two thirds of probationers commit another crime within 3 years of their sentence (Bennett et al. 1996). Many of these crimes are crimes of violence. The roughly 162,000 probationers returned to state prison and incarcerated in 1991 were responsible for 6,400 murders, 7,400 rapes, 10,400 assaults, and 17,000 robberies. It has also been shown that 156 of 1,411 persons convicted of murder in Virginia from 1990 to 1993 were on probation at the time of the crime. Reaves and Smith (1995) report that nearly one in five felony defendants arrested and 15 percent of felony offenders charged with violent crime were on probation at the time they committed the new crime. About half of all probationers have a history of criminal violence (Bonczar and Glaze 1999). Glaze and Palla (2004) report that 50 percent of all probationers are felony probationers. Furthermore, about three in five of the more than 2 million adults discharged from probation in 2003 had successfully met the conditions of supervision. The percent of probationers discharged from probation supervision because of incarceration due to rule violations or new offenses varied from 21 percent in 1995 to 16 percent in 2003.

Probation is ineffective in helping probationers learn to read, avoid drugs, obtain jobs, or reconnect with prosocial peers. The researchers at the Manhattan Institute for Policy Research (Olsen et al. 1999) also found that many probationers are not fulfilling the court orders mandating treatment. Although research indicates over half of the offenders were using drugs at the time of the offense, the obvious need for community-based drug treatment is only achieved for 37 percent of the probationers nationally who are required to participate in any type of drug treatment program—32 percent are being tested for drug use once they receive treatment (Bonczar 1997). Where caseloads are in excess of 100 offenders officers are completely overwhelmed by their responsibilities. With probation spending less than $200 per year per probationer, there are too few resources directed toward the task to make any real difference. In some jurisdictions, extremely high caseloads (from 100 to 500 per probation officer) have made supervision ineffectual (Nessman 1997). This has contributed to failure rates and recidivism. All too frequently, offenders on probation come to the realization that some conditions of probation are not consistently enforced whether they are "dirty" urine samples, electronic monitoring violations, or failure to comply with the supervision conditions. Violations do not lead to revocation and removal from supervision (Clear and Cole 1990). In addition hundreds of thousands abscond by breaking off contact with the probation officer.

■ Absconders

Many probationers do not stay in contact with their probation officer. The Manhattan Institute for Policy Research (Olsen et al. 1999) reported that by year-end, some 288,000 probationers had absconded and were out of contact with their officer, out of compliance with their orders, and free from any control or monitoring. The latest national survey of probationers reveals that 10 percent of the probationers—340,000—have officially absconded (Bonczar and Glaze 1999). The system makes little effort to find those who have absconded, serve them with warrants, or otherwise bring them to justice. In many jurisdictions, nothing is being done to apprehend the scofflaws. For probation to be meaningful, this permissiveness and laxity in enforcement practice must be reversed. In its place, swift, consistent, and strong enforcement of all conditions of probation is necessary. A critical component of enforcing the conditions of probation is the cooperation of the courts in applying appropriate and proportional responses to the crime but also it is necessary to apply additive sanctions to reporting, curfew, house arrests, electronic monitoring, and mandatory treatment (Morris and Tonry 1990; Petersilia 1999). Programs that have strictly enforced the conditions of supervision and enjoy a supportive relationship with the court tend to have fewer problems with offender compliance (Olsen et al. 1999, 2–13). A program in Iowa established a willingness to deal with violations of conditions of probation, thus increasing the deterrent value of the program. A residential drug treatment program located in the state made a decision to revoke the probation of all offenders placed in the facility who later tested positive for drug use. Initially officials feared this approach would lead to prison crowding but that proved not to be the case. In actuality, compliance with program rules increased, drug abuse subsided, and the number of revocations for drug violations dropped by 70 percent (Olsen et al. 1999, 2–14).

■ Forces at Work

The language of the **new penology** is risk assessment, resource allocation, internal management processes, and aggregate justice. In turn, the offender loses individual characteristics and becomes a member of an aggregate offender category. Offenders are then stigmatized in terms of their probable association with violence, substance abuse, sexual predation, and so forth. The new penology is not about punishment or about rehabilitation; it is about identifying and managing obstreperous groups by employing a system-wide coordinated process (Feeley and Simon 1992; Garland 1990). This is a system-wide risk-based paradigm that can essentially operate as a technological device principally concerned with controlling the offender's behavior. Social control (Reiss 1984) is achieved either through deterrence or compliance.

new penology is not about punishment or rehabilitation; it is about identifying and managing obstreperous groups by employing a system-wide coordinated process.

offender control models
seek to incapacitate the
offender through various
means that emphasize
authority and control.

A model that has received a lot of attention in various forms desires to incapacitate the offender through various means. Because of its interests in authority and control, it is known as the **offender control model**. This model uses a duel system of supervision whereby offenders are considered capable of self-control or subject to informal controls such as the family. They are assigned to a risk category involving various levels of surveillance and control in which many offenders are likely to fail and will be sent on to prison (Simon 1993). Finally, the criteria for success has been reversed where apparently there is no longer interest in the successful rehabilitation of the offender as there is interest in the number of offenders who are held accountable and find their probation revoked.

The mission of community corrections has shifted to the identification and cost-effective management of high-risk offenders ultimately destined for imprisonment. Organizational visions, mission statements, policy directives, procedural manuals, and stated goals and objectives imbue an agency with benchmark activities that grant the organization a certain level of legitimacy and community acceptance. No organization worth its salt operates without these because they are too important. First, they provide guidance in how the probation law is to be interpreted and applied. They offer a means of controlling the officer's discretionary power. Secondly, they are tools for reordering organizational and individual priorities. Regarding federal probation, the U.S. probation and pretrial service unit's mission statement says:

> Our primary goal is to ensure the protection and safety of the community on behalf of the court through investigation and supervision of the criminal offender. . . . We are dedicated to providing quality services and accountability in the enforcement of court ordered sanctions. We are committed to identifying the needs of persons under supervision by referring them to a full spectrum of services.

The most influential experts on crime today are conservatives who are more concerned with the victims of crime than offenders and more concerned with punishment than rehabilitation (Lehman 1998, 25). These views are influenced by the fear of crime, an exasperation with and loss of confidence in the criminal justice system, and the opinion that offenders are no longer unfortunate victims of the social system (Flanagan 1996). The denial of the offender-as-victim status is made possible by the failure of the government to deliver adequate services (Jacobs 1990).

The negation of the offender's victim status was the result of three factors:

1. social fragmentation
2. a lack of an authoritative capacity for achieving valued social goals
3. a civic philosophy incapable of appointing individual or institutional responsibility

The deterioration of mutual aid that once bonded people together has been almost totally displaced by professionalism, self-reliance replaced by laws, neighborliness by a service economy, and the sharing of gifts and hospitality by payment and insurance plans (Sullivan 1980, 13). The culmination of these social attitudes was the passage of stiffer criminal penalties and major changes for federal probation.

As the criminal justice system becomes more dependent on statistics to explain criminal behavior, criminologists have deprived black criminals of the empathy given them by the Chicago Sociology School's explanation of criminal behavior (Miller 1996). In establishing policy, the government should be careful to apply the least restrictive measures possible, to act in good faith in imposing the risk measure, and to firmly establish the principle that the proof of the effectiveness of the risk measure rests with the government and not the offender (Clear 1992, 37).

Deterrence Model

Few people could have foreseen the sweeping changes in the federal probation system that resulted from the enactment of the Comprehensive Crime Control Act of 1984 (Hughes and Henkel 1997, 103). As a result of this law and the previously discussed social sentiments, probation is considerably different from the dichotomous enforcement-social welfare model put forward by others earlier (Hughes and Henkel 1997). The virtual replacement of rehabilitation by a just deserts model and the phasing out of parole marked a definitive end to an era that began with such optimism for the ideals of "human reclamation." Sentencing guidelines and mandatory minimum sentences now set the tone and the probation officer-as-caseworker role is no longer predominant. While the pendulum yet may swing back from crime control to individualized treatment, the system has undergone a profound transformation (Hughes and Henkel 1997, 103).

Early forms of probation supervision followed a simple officer/clerk model for supervision. In fact, some places such as California have been forced to return to this model due to extremely large caseloads. In many places, however, officers specialize in their assignments to match the growing complexity of the work by employing sentencing guidelines, substance abuse treatment, mental health treatment, and electronic monitoring. Decentralization of personnel and the assignment of financial management from the administrative office of the courts to the individual courts have given rise to a variety of administrative support specialties such as budget and fiscal reporting, procurement, property management, personal administration, accounting, and contracting (Hughes and Henkel 1997, 103).

The deterrence model finds support in the theory of rational choice (Cornish and Clarke 1986). This theory views crime from the perspective of the rationally deliberative criminal capable of voluntary decision making. It assumes offenders make choices and decisions about crime, which are restrained only by time, ability, and relevant information. People make rational decisions based on the extent to which the choice will maximize the benefits and minimize the losses. The decisions are based on the offender's expected effort and reward compared to the likelihood and severity of punishment and other costs of crime (Cornish and Clarke 1986). By shifting the focus from the criminal to the law, the rational choice theory forsakes traditional determinism and assumes it is no longer necessary to understand individual motivation but only necessary to achieve some mechanism for convincing the offender that his or her behavior is not productive whether one emphasizes deterrence or incapacitation.

Table 9-5	Models
Deterrence Model	**Regulatory Model**
Postmonitory	Premonitory
Formal	Informal
Accusatory	Bargaining
Crimes	Technical Violations
Rational Choice	Social Construction
Mission Statements	Discretionary
Adversarial	Negotiations

Probation officers are responding to criticisms that probationary sentences have failed to be proportional to the harm inflicted by the crime or that it is being lenient (Feld 1981; von Hirsch et al. 1989). Closer examination of the workings of a probation office indicates that probation officers have an opportunity to provide some measure of self-determined proportionate sentencing. Officers are permitted to apply the philosophy of just deserts to supervision by taking advantage of the discretion allotted them. The officer no longer identifies the offender as "sick" but sees him or her as a rational moral agent deserving of blame. The officer influences the length of the probationary period to fit the officer's own assessment of the extent of harm inflicted by the crime. The court may, for example, order a 5-year probationary sentence but the officer has the discretion to ask the court to shorten the penalty by writing a complimentary letter to the judge seeking an early discharge. Conversely, a probationer may be given a 3-year probationary sentence but the officer who believes it does not correspond with the harm visited by the crime can, through careful supervision, accumulate evidence to support the violation of the probationer and thus an extension of the sentence. In the final analysis, many officers who begin work as "bleeding heart" liberals develop a more realistic, if expedient, perspective on the various issues affecting their work.

■ Social Control

Social control institutions take an approach that either emphasizes the deterrence of crime or the regulation of crime. The deterrence model sees crime as an aberration. This model wishes to eliminate crime through a formal response where the offender is presumed guilty and deserving of harsh penalties. The regulatory model accepts the inevitability of crime and the necessity of recognizing the impossibility of effectively responding to each offense because of a lack of time and resources. The deterrence model of probation is applied to those who are considered "beyond the pale." Gaubatz (1995) has argued that some offenders are considered to be beyond the pale in that they cannot be reformed or rehabilitated. This includes serious drug offenders and pedophiles. The system goes into action after the offense has taken place; thus, it is postmonitory. The procedures involved are formal and recorded for the purpose of appeal. Because the deterrence model relies heavily on plea bargaining, it is essentially accusatory.

There is a strong presumption of guilt. Bad behavior is always interpreted as a crime and not as simple mischief or a violation. The offender is considered to have committed the crime in response to faulty cost-benefit analysis. At the organizational level mission statements and policy directives determine organizational goals and operational procedures. Finally, because attorneys are involved, the processes become adversarial as attorneys battle for the offenders' freedom. According to Reiss (1984), to the extent that enforcement relies more heavily on formal legal processes, it depends less on private negotiations and more on proving violations of the law.

If the community is to feel safe, the probation officer's records and performance must withstand scrutiny. It is suggested here that we have an offender control model that actually is engaged in a regulatory process. This model attempts to incapacitate the offender through various means by use of authority and control. Instead of rehabilitating, the offender is regulated. Regulation is made necessary by high caseloads requiring perfunctory contact and discretionary decision making. Rehabilitation is relegated to secondary or tertiary importance. To further understand this, we need to look at the concepts of social control, provide a definition of social regulation, and recognize the importance of organizational uncertainty and the methods used to achieve offender compliance with the regulatory process.

The regulatory model of probation is **premonitory** in that it attempts to intervene before a violation of the law has occurred. The process is essentially informal, allowing the officer a great deal of discretion to achieve his or her goals. Most of the officer's time is given over to handling technical violations but not criminal offenses. These technical violations are understood by officers as constituting not inherently criminal behavior but behavior declared as such by the state. Experienced officers have come to understand that those who engage in the worst behavior do not always end in prison and those who engage in minor offenses do not always find their way onto probation. As a result of this, many officers take it upon themselves to act outside of directives to achieve what they believe is in the best interest of the probationer and still treat the person with a measure of dignity. The officer's biggest concern is how to get the offender through probation without reappearing in court. Negotiations and bargaining with attorneys and the probationer allow the officer to recognize the human dignity of the probationer if the offender is treated with respect and is granted a certain measure of autonomy. **Table 9-5** compares the main features of the deterrence and regulatory models.

premonitory compliance systems are concerned with a law violation as it develops rather than after it is a formal crime.

■ Human Dignity

When the regulatory process is consistently and fairly applied, the probationer is also treated with an appropriate measure of dignity. This means the offender through negotiations is allowed to express himself or herself. One must remember that human dignity is intimately related to human autonomy. Autonomy in moral matters is achieved through exercising rational natures. As stated previously, an autonomous creature is a self-activating, self-directing, self-criticizing, self-correcting, and self-understanding creature. Autonomous individuals are self-reflective. Fully autonomous creatures do not merely pursue ends; they create them and confer value on them. More typically, a person violates the autonomy (dignity) of another when exercising patronizing and condescending supervision and control over the other or (worse yet) manipulates the other by using force or fraud in order to achieve some good or end chosen without regard to the other's welfare or capacity for autonomy. Negotiations and bargaining also recognize that the offender possesses a self-conscious rationality, with the capacities to evaluate, calculate, organize, predict, explain, make conjecture, justify, and so forth, and to prize and appraise things and situations. In lacking self-conscious rationality, a creature lacks dignity; only rational creatures can have that.

■ Regulation

self-regulation is manifested in the personal acceptance, through socialization, of various norms, customs, values, and traditions, which were designed to reinforce conventional social practices.

group regulation is the imposition of social control over the behavior of group members through the establishment, enforcement, and punishment of group normative behavior.

state regulation is a process imposed by the courts and is, in theory, based on statutory law, case law, and constitutional law.

In the United States, workplace dangers are monitored through corporate <u>**self-regulation**</u> (Fisse and Braithwaite 1993). A regulatory agency begins most leniently, with advice, warnings, and persuasions. If this fails, fines may be imposed, and corporate remedial actions requested. When these methods do not suffice, court-ordered remedies are sought, and, if warranted, criminal sanctions. The severest criminal penalty—corporate capital punishment—requires the firm's liquidation. Fisse and Braithwaite stress trying to avoid the deterrence trap, punishing the corporate offense so severely as to force a firm into bankruptcy. Such an extreme outcome penalizes all the firm's employees and the communities in which they are established.

Crime control is achieved through a combination of three forms of social regulation: self (internal processes), group (family, clan, gang, clique, workgroup, etc.), and state regulatory mechanisms. Self-regulation is manifested in the personal acceptance, through socialization, of various norms, customs, values, and traditions, which were designed to reinforce conventional social practices (Nadel 1953). <u>**Group regulation**</u> is the imposition of social control over the behavior of group members through the establishment, enforcement, and punishment of group normative behavior. Group regulation occurs in settings employing informal mechanisms to control the activities of neighbors, children's groups, gangs, work groups, and many behaviors exhibited in public. The willingness to intercede is linked with familiarity, security, and a sense of responsibility connected with the neighborhood setting (Greenberg et al. 1982). Group regulation is very similar to the concept of guardianship that will be discussed in the chapter on prevention. <u>**State regulation**</u>, as exemplified in the criminal justice system, is a tertiary social control mechanism that becomes necessary after self-regulatory and group regulatory mechanisms have failed.

State regulation as imposed by the courts is, in theory, based on statutory law, case law, and constitutional law. The court system, especially the federal system, regulates the criminal justice agencies. In making sure the criminal justice system operates within the law, the courts are theoretically blind to the demands of the general public or cultural changes or other environmental factors. However, a significant body of research suggests that judges, whether elected or appointed, make decisions congruent with the values they bring to the office. Their decisions often reflect the regional and political values they have acquired more than a strict interpretation of the law (Cole 1988; Frazier and Block 1982; Kolonski and Mendelsohn 1970).

Correctional institutions, parole agencies, and probation departments are all being asked to protect society from criminals; in addition, they are expected to do something productive with offenders so that criminal propensities are reduced. These are lofty expectations. Nevertheless, such expectations are altering the context within which correctional agencies as well as other criminal justice organizations are functioning. Newer models of employee supervision have been proposed to augment the functioning capabilities of employees to meet these new challenges. One model that has shown promise is the human service model of employee supervision (Stojkovic et al. 1998, 199).

Interviews conducted with probation officers indicate that although some continue to emphasize some aspect of rehabilitation, many officers develop a supervision style that can best be characterized as regulatory. The Tomaino (1975) model of supervision offers an indication of the regulatory model. Tomaino (1975) offers a paradigm of probation supervision that considers rehabilitation on one vertical axis and control on the horizontal axis. The "let-him-identify" (with the values of the probation officer) position places the offender at the midpoint of both rehabilitation and control. Sentiments expressed toward rehabilitation and control are neither very high nor low. Probationers are thought to keep the rules if they like the probation officer and identify with him or her and his or her values (i.e., if the probation officer presents himself or herself as a good role model). More importantly, the probation officer must work out solid compromises in his or her relations with the probationer. These compromises result from negotiations taking place between the probationer and the probation officer, especially within the context of organizational and environmental uncertainty and the officer's need to use discretion. Regulation, therefore, is affected by concerns for uncertainty, decoupling, discretion, and compliance.

Uncertainty

Probation agencies, as coupled organizations operating in a field of uncertainty, are characterized by structural elements that are loosely linked to each other, rules that are often violated, decisions that go unimplemented, technologies that are problematic, and evaluations that are subverted or rendered so vague they provide little coordination (Meyer and Rowan 1977, 343). The often tumultuous and uncertain political environment forces criminal justice administrators to stress accountability and control of employees. Employee concerns, meanwhile, center on task completion. Often there is conflict between the organization's search for control and certainty and the desire to accomplish "soft" organizational objectives and goals. Organizations such as probation departments cannot observe their own outcomes and outputs. It is often difficult to identify what tasks are actually related to the accomplishment of specific goals in coping organizations (Stojkovic et al. 1998, 202). In other words, it is difficult for a probation department to identify what specific task was responsible for the offender's change in behavior. Many factors come into play.

The concept of regulatory uncertainty implies an obligatory tolerance of conduct. This tolerance is exhibited in the choice of which harmful activity is subject to control and how the rules developed around this activity are enforced. For example, a probation officer is not able to completely restrict all of the possible illegal activities available to a probationer; thus, he or she has to make choices about which rules are enforced and the consequences for violating these rules. Secondly, regulatory agencies are charged with a particular policing mission. However, there is still the question as to the objective: should the mission be eradication or the repression of the problem? If the behavior is not considered serious, it is to be repressed and handled with a measure of discretion. How much attention is given to each violation depends on the resources available (Kagan 1978, 11).

One source of uncertainty stems from the moral ambivalence surrounding the regulatory (probation) agency's mandate. Most of the research indicates a lack of consensus as to whether probation should achieve law enforcement or treatment objectives (Harris 1989). The perception of uncertainty in the environment is the result of three conditions: a lack of information about environmental factors important to decision making, an inability to estimate how probabilities will relate to a decision until it is implemented, and a lack of information about the cost associated with an incorrect decision (Duncan 1972). In other words, there is a great deal of important missing information; there is little understanding on what will actually happen and how much it will cost. No viable business would ever operate with such uncertain conditions.

A high degree of uncertainty about the mission of probation offers clear evidence of how the social construction of the definition of a problems leads to problems (Hawkins and Thomas 1984, 17–18). Social constructionists focus primarily on the interpretation of reality according to individual bureaucrats. Under circumstances of high caseloads, complicated offender treatment needs, and harsh and seemingly unfair sentences, there are few objective indicators of successful performance except when referring to the mission statement or policy guides. Again, individualized punishments present a different picture. This means that at the individual level some rules are enforced and others are not. This activity is mediated by the probation officer's relationship with the regulated. The officer makes a personal assessment of the harm and the motives of those involved.

Probation work involves *mala en se* and *mala prohibita* offenses and technical violations. How these are handled varies considerably depending on the person, time, and place, thus leading to a great deal of uncertainty. Political and moral ambivalence surrounding regulatory activity presents problems for policy making and street-level enforcement. An initial zeal for a policing mission may generate certain expectations about appropriate strategies of control. However, enforcement activity in practice must contend with seemingly endless good grounds for noncompliance or partial compliance put forward by those who find themselves unwilling or unable because of financial circumstance, technology, or time to conform to the law (Hawkins and Thomas 1984, 9).

Decoupling

Large organizations tend to become decoupled; that is, they face multiple environments and interact with each environment at different organizational levels. One sector of the organization might be unresponsive to another. To complicate matters further, an environment may have two subenvironments to which to respond: the political-legal and the service-delivery subenvironments. Large organizations tend to break into overlapping subgroups, dominant coalitions, and the work proces-sors. Within the context of the political-legal environment, the dominant coalition is a small group of employees who oversees the organization and dictates policy decisions. The dominant coalition is responding to the demands resulting from mission statements, public image concerns, and financial constraints. When done well, the output is political satisfaction. The work processors, probation officers, are the bulk of the organization's members and are directly involved with its pri-mary clientele (Nokes 1960). The decoupling occurs when the probation officers who must implement the decision are unable to do so due to high caseloads.

Discretion

Officers are recruited on the basis of departmental screening criteria but later are free to develop, within reasonable limits, their own concepts of reintegration, risk assessment, punishment, and offender management. As officers acquire ex-perience, their expectations of their clients and of themselves change and their supervision styles evolve into a working style. This working style is comprised of various notions of offender supervision including when and where to bring the offender back into court. This decision considers the officer's attitude toward the offense, the seriousness of the offense, the victim's involvement, the proba-tioner's prior behavior, the time left on probation, and the plans made for the fu-ture. Some officers are known to become pragmatic and expedient, employing whatever values are necessary to resolve the problem. Others develop a hard line approach to their work (Rosencrance 1987).

Public service workers who interact with citizens in the course of their jobs and who have substantial discretion in the execution of their work are called *street-level bureaucrats* (Lipsky 1980, 4). Typical street-level bureaucrats include teachers, police officers and other law enforcement personnel, social workers, judges, public lawyers and other court officers, health workers, and many other public employees who grant access to government programs and provide serv-ices within them. People who work in these jobs tend to have much in common.

Street-level bureaucrats deliver benefits and sanctions that structure and de-limit people's lives and opportunities. Street-level bureaucrats have a consider-able impact on people's lives. They socialize citizens as to the expectations of the government services and determine the eligibility of citizens for government sanctions. They oversee the treatment (the service) citizens receive in those pro-grams. Thus, in a sense, street-level bureaucrats implicitly mediate aspects of the constitutional relationship of citizens to the state (Lipsky 1980, 4). Street-level bureaucrats make decisions about people that affect life chances. For example, to designate or treat someone as a juvenile delinquent affects the relationships of others to that person and also affects the person's self-evaluation. As a result, street-level bureaucrats must deal with personal reactions to their decisions, however they choose to cope with the implications. Clients of street-level bu-reaucrats react angrily to real or perceived injustices (Lipsky 1980). They de-velop strategies to ingratiate themselves with workers by acting grateful, with elation, sullenly, or passively in reaction to various decisions. Through the development of a personal relationship with street-level bureaucrats, clients hope their problems will be given more consideration than the person who walks off the street seeking information and support. Finally, street-level bureaucrats, including probation officers, play a crucial role in regulating social conflict by virtue of their roles as social control agents. Probation officers convey the expectations established by the conditions of probation. In the final analysis, street-level bureaucrats are at the center of controversy because a divided public perceives that social control in the name of public order and acceptance of the status quo are social objectives with which proposals to reduce the role of the street-level bureaucrat (probation officers) would interfere (Lipsky 1980, 12).

It would seem that officers use their discretion not so much to deter the offender but to regulate the offender's behavior. This is done in full recognition that rehabilitation may not be needed nor always possible and that acceptable levels of incapacitation can only be achieved within certain limits. The assertion that street-level bureaucrats exercise considerable discretion is fairly obvious. There are limits, however, to this discretionary decision-making process. Policy elites and political and administrative officials shape the major dimension of public policy. Occupational and community norms also structure policy choices of street-level bureaucrats. Rules, however, may be impediments to effective supervision in that individualized justice would indicate a different course of action than the one called for by policy. Many of these rules are impossible to enforce because they are contradictory or voluminous. With limited resources and a proliferation of rules and responsibilities, there is a limit to what can be expected of probation officers. Given the estimated 11,900 officers who were supervising 2.9 million adult probationers in 1994, the average caseload was a whopping 258 adult offenders per line officer (Petersilia 1997). One of the central questions asked of any probation agency is how does it deal with large caseloads.

Compliance

Much of the difficulty brought on by large caseloads is the need to maintain probationer compliance with the conditions of probation. The distinction between compliance and deterrence systems of social control is fundamental to the problem of implementing regulatory policy (Hawkins and Thomas 1984, 13). Compliance and uncertainty are principal features of the regulatory model. Tables 9-2 and 9-3 provide evidence that authorities desire, through the enforcement of conditions, to establish varied measures of inspection, discipline, or normalization. There is much diversity with respect to these conditions. Under the deterrence model, one would expect that more attention would be given to inspection and discipline functions. However, as noted, when taken individually more of the conditions of probation are targeted at the normalization functions. Normalization plays such a large role because of the vestiges of the medical model and the complicated problems and uncertainty faced by many probationers. More importantly, many of the normalization conditions have disciplinary and inspection components built into them, especially as they involve mandatory drug treatment. Nonetheless, when inspection and discipline functions are combined, joint effects exceed that of normalization.

The principle objective of a regulatory law enforcement system is to secure compliance with the law. The regulatory model is applied to those who are considered redeemable, determined by the offender's prior record, attitude toward the offense, and community resources. The core violation in a compliance system is dubbed a *technical violation*, behavior that violates a condition or standard that is designed to prevent harm or unwanted conditions. The system creates standards for monitoring noncompliance that define a host of technical violations. Whether or not the penalties are actually invoked to secure leverage for compliance or rather to punish for failure to negotiate a reasonable agreement in good faith is another thing. The levying of a penalty in the private sector is a mark of failure to get an agreement on compliance, whereas the levying of a penalty in the criminal justice system is a mark that the system means what it says.

Premonitory Compliance

Compliance systems are premonitory; they attend to a set of conditions prior to any violation in order to induce conformity. The idea is to prevent the violation rather than punish it. The threat of penalty and a system of reward are essential to the process. Once compliance is indicated, the sanction is typically suspended or withdrawn. The idea is to manipulate the reward structure and to impose penalties only after a period of long negotiations has failed. Bargaining and informal negotiations are central to the process. This is most evident in the daily supervision of the offender and in making the decision as to what to do when a new offense or new violation of a condition of probation has been uncovered. It is axiomatic that the more one attends to the offender, the more often one will uncover questionable behavior. Fully realizing this, officials are most concerned with conserving resources and minimizing interference with the routines of their office and the courtroom work groups. Any excessive legalism, including mandatory sentencing, in the enforcement of rules can preclude effective bargaining. What this means is that bargaining between the officer and probationer can take place outside of the public interest. The legitimacy of bargaining is diminished if it occurs as a result of resource constraints, unclear policy objectives, agency conflict, or inadequate incentives. In other words, if the impetus to bargain stems from organizational inadequacies, it will eventually be depreciated in the same manner as plea bargaining is today.

Further problems arise if compliance is excessively routinized and does not deal with the fundamental problems underlying the causes of the offense. To the extent that bargaining promotes trust, it furthers the rehabilitative process. When it does not, there is likely to be greater recourse to the deterrence model. The following is an example taken from the author's field observation as a case in point.

An Example from the Field

An officer has a probationer who has been on intensive supervision for an extended time and has a short period remaining before a transfer to regular probation. Despite this, the probationer is frustrated by his lack of freedom and is desperate to get some relief. The officer has seen the probationer's frustration increase over the last few months. He also knows the probationer has survived previous crises, some more successfully than others. One night, the probationer decides to stay out late, smoke some marijuana, and celebrate a friend's birthday. The next time the probationer reports, the officer is supposed to test the probationer for drugs. He can overlook the violation itself, hoping that no one else finds out about it and work toward getting the probationer ready for transfer. He also knows that violations of probation do not always lead to convictions or revocation of probation even if the person is brought into court; the court often just continues the case. The officer also knows that some people respond better to carrots than sticks and that some probationers are doing everything they can to avoid problems but no matter what they do, they still have trouble. Officers can anticipate problems with careful supervision, letting the probationer speak about his frustrations, earning some slack from the officer, and buying some time. The officer's goal is to "cool out the mark" or settle the offender down so he doesn't violate probation. Negotiations between the officer and probationer take place in terms of what conditions are most important to uphold. Bargaining takes place between upholding conditions and rewarding the probationer with early release from probation.

◼ Maximizing the Regulatory Process

The regulatory model of probation requires elaboration of the compliance concept. Maximization of the regulatory process is achieved by applying Garland's (1990, 132) concepts essential to the regulatory process: inspection, discipline, and normalization.

Inspections

Officer inspections of the clients are accomplished by field visits at home and work, blood and urine tests for drugs and alcohol, and checks conducted with various collateral sources. These sources, such as employers, have knowledge of and responsibility for the offender. Inspections are conducted for the purpose of seeing if the offender is in compliance with the conditions set by the court. Inspections are achieved through the use of technology. Federal probation employs an automated case tracking system, an information management system, cellular phone systems, and a host of other devices intended to monitor offenders in the community. These systems are designed to increase probationer accountability while at the same time allow for a reduction in personal contact. Skilled automation staff is now needed to keep a probation office running (Hughes and Henkel 1997, 103).

Discipline

According to Simon (1993), employment in the private labor market was the primary source of discipline for parole (p. 45). Industrial labor offers a mechanism for disciplining individuals who submit to a schedule of work and the demands of machines. A highly industrialized society offers the optimal environment in which the released offender can be supervised. This is especially true of the federal probationer who is under supervised release. What this means for probation is that probationers are disciplined by the work they do but also by the conditions set by the court. Discipline is maintained through inspections to determine if the condition set by the court is being met. This includes the requirement of working and submitting to drug tests. Compliance occurs through the officer's discretionary tolerance for the probationer's misbehavior.

During periods of a large number of caseloads, the intensity of discipline can be allowed to operate as a safety valve for releasing offenders. It functions as a carrot and a stick in terms of offering the probationer an inducement to stay clear of trouble when the probationer is poorly motivated. The actual sanctions tend to bring conduct into line and help make the individual more self-controlled (Garland 1990, 145).

Normalization

Inspections and discipline are intended to further the process of bringing the offender back from being considered irredeemable. The real work of normalization is to further the reintegration process. Parole shifted toward the clinical model to fill the gap between the ideal of the industrial order and the conditions found in the offender's community (Simon 1993, 104). Probation also must fill the gap between what the offender lacks in order to participate in the workforce and what is provided in the probationer's community. Normalization is achieved by providing the offender with a combination of employment, job training, schooling, or counseling. It is hoped that with these skills the offender will become more self-controlled, self-motivated, compliant, and once again, a full-fledged member of the community.

These three components of regulation provide the means for supervising the offender according to the reordered emphasis given to control, supervision, and management. They allow the officer who desires to treat the probationer as something more than a mere object of punishment, as someone who does command respect, support, and understanding—as someone deserving dignified treatment.

■ Conclusion

Many organizations opt for mixed strategies of selectively using a system based on compliance and deterrence. Compliance and deterrence systems are enforcement responses to contrasting kinds of rule breaking. A compliance strategy emerges in the context of some degree of personal relationship between the enforcement agent and his or her clientele. Compliance is preferred when detecting and sanctioning violations are so complex, protracted, and costly that they are regarded as inadequate remedies for continuing harms. Although it is known that the police adopt a compliance strategy when they are involved in continuing relationships with certain kinds of rule breakers (drunks, vagrants, and prostitutes, for example), this approach is much more evident in the enforcement of regulations. This is also true of probation. The deterrence system tends to be associated with incidents or acts of wrongdoing that by their very nature are relatively unpredictable, thus allowing no personal relationship to be established between enforcement agent and rule breaker.

There is clearly a desire for more control over the offender and more control over the officer. Officers as street-level bureaucrats have a great deal of discretion in dealing with their clients. In dealing with their clients, officers have become regulators. They deal with the client in terms of compliance and bargaining in a field permeated by uncertainty. These street-level bureaucrats (Lipsky 1980, 5) are the essence of the criminal justice system, and how these employees are supervised and evaluated is one of the most pressing issues facing criminal justice administration in the new century. Probation has entered a period of postmodern maturity where it might consider becoming more introspective, self-assessing, and politically active. For many officers, the job has moved into a new era requiring new initiatives reestablishing their own priorities. This may be accomplished by doing three things. First, officers might engage in a campaign to understand what the public wants. An example would be holding a series of public focus groups in each jurisdiction that can culminate in regional and a national meeting to establish a charter of probation priorities. Secondly, a national conference sponsored by the American Probation and Parole Association should include representatives from probation, law, social sciences, social work, and the public. Lastly, probation departments must establish lobbying mechanisms designed to support probation initiatives and national standards. Probation has always found itself playing second fiddle to the court or to some other branch of the correctional establishment. The public must be educated on the important work of probation and the role it has in today's society.

REFERENCES

American Probation and Parole Association. 2001. Pros and cons of increasing officer authority to impose or remove conditions of supervision. Issue Papers 1–2.

Baird, S., T. Clear, and P. Harris. 1985. The use and effectiveness of the behavior control tools of probation officers. Unpublished report to National Institute of Justice.

Bennett, W., J. Dilulio, and J. Walters. 1996. *Body count: Moral poverty and how to win America's war against crime and drugs.* New York: Simon Schuster.

Bonzcar, T. 1997. *Characteristics of adults on probation, 1995.* Washington, DC: U.S. Department of Justice, Bureau of Justice Statistics, U.S. NCJ 164267.

Bonzcar, T., and L. Glaze. 1999. *Probation and parole in the United States, 1998.* Washington, DC: U.S. Department of Justice, Bureau of Justice Statistics.

Bureau of Justice Statistics. 1999. *Survey of adults on probation, 1995.* International Consortion of Political and Social Research. Ann Arbor: University of Michigan.

Bureau of Justice Statistics. August 1997. *Nation's probation and parole population reached almost 3.9 million last year.* Press release. Washington, DC: U.S. Department of Justice, Bureau of Justice Statistics.

Clear, T. 1992. Punishment and control in community supervision. In C. Hartjen and E. Rhine, eds. *Correctional theory and practice.* Chicago: Nelson-Hall.

Clear, T. R., and G. Cole. 1990. *American corrections,* 2nd ed. Pacific Grove, CA: Brooks/Cole Publishing.

Cole, G. 1989. *The American system of criminal justice.* Pacific Grove, CA: Brooks/Cole Publishing.

Cole, G., ed. 1988. *Criminal justice: Law and politics,* 5th ed. Pacific Grove, CA: Brooks/Cole Publishing.

Cornish, D., and R. Clarke. 1986. *The reasoning criminal.* New York: Springer-Verlag.

Czajkoski, E. H. 1973. Exposing the quasi-judicial role of the probation officer. *Federal Probation* 37: 9–13.

del Carmen, R. 1986. *Potential liabilities of probation and parole officers.* Cincinnati: Anderson.

Dillingham, S., R. Montgomery, and R. Tabor. 1990. *Probation and parole in practice,* 2nd ed. Cincinnati: Anderson.

Duncan, R. 1972. The characteristics of organizational environments and perceived environmental uncertainty. *Adminstrative Science Quarterly* 17: 313–327.

Federal Probation. 1997. U.S. probation and pretrial service western district of New York mission statement. Unpublished report.

Feeley, M., and J. Simon. 1992. The new penology: Notes on the emerging strategy of corrections and its implications. *Criminology* 30: 449–474.

Feld, B. 1981. Juvenile court legislation reform and the serious young offender: Dismantling the "rehabilitative ideal." *Minnesota Law Review* 65: 167–242.

Fisse, B., and J. Braithwaite. 1993. *Corporations, crime, and accountability.* Cambridge: Cambridge University Press.

Flanagan, T. 1996. Community corrections in the public mind. *Federal Probation* 60: 3–9.

Frazier, C., and W. Block. 1982. Effects of court officers on sentencing severity. *Criminology* 20: 257–272.

Garland, D. 1990. *Punishment and modern society.* Chicago: University of Chicago Press.

Gaubatz, K. 1995. *Crime in the public mind.* Ann Arbor: University of Michigan Press.

Glaser, D. 1964. *The effectiveness of a prison and parole system.* New York: Bobbs-Merrill.

Glaze, L., and S. Pella. 2004. *Probation and parole in the United States 2003.* Washington, DC: U.S. Department of Justice, Bureau of Justice Statistics.

Greenberg, S., W. Rohe, and J. Williams. 1982. The relationship between informal social control, neighborhood crime, and fear: A synthesis and assessment of research. Paper presented to the annual meeting of the American Society of Criminology, Toronto, Canada.

Harris, P., T. Clear, and S. Baird. 1989. Have community supervision officers changed their attitudes toward their work? *Justice Quarterly* 6: 233–246.

Hawkins, K., and J. Thomas. 1984. The regulatory process: Issues and concepts. In K. Hawkins and J. Thomas, eds. *Enforcing Regulation.* Hinghamm, MA: Kluwer, pp. 3–22.

Hughes, J. M., and K. Henkel. 1997. The federal probation and pretrial services system since 1975: An era of growth and change. *Federal Probation* 61: 103–111.

Jacobs, M. 1990. *Screwing the system and making it work.* Chicago: University of Chicago Press.

Kagan, R. 1978. *Regulatory justice.* New York: Russell Sage.

Katz, J. 1982. The attitudes and decisions of probation officers. *Criminal Justice and Behavior* 9: 455–475.

Klockars, C. 1972. A theory of probation supervision. *Journal of Criminal Law, Criminology, and Police Science* 63: 550–557.

Kolonzki, H., and R. Mendelsohn. 1970. *The politics of local justice.* Boston: Little, Brown.

Langan, P. A. 1994. Between prison and probation: Intermediate sanctions. *Science* 6: 795.

Langan, P. A., and M. Cunniff. 1992. *Recidivism of felons on probation, 1986–1989.* Washington, DC: U.S. Department of Justice, Bureau of Justice Statistics.

Lehman, N. 1998. Justice for blacks. *New York Review of Books* XLV: 25–28.

Lipsky, M. 1980. *Street-level bureaucracy.* New York: Russell Sage.

Meyer, J., and B. Rowan. 1977. Institutionalized organizations: Formal structure as myth and ceremony. *American Journal of Sociology* 83: 340–363.

Miles, A. 1965. The reality of the probation officer's dilemma. *Federal Probation* 29: 18–23.

Miller, J. 1996. *Search and destroy: African-American males in the criminal justice system.* New York: Cambridge University Press.

Morris, N., and M. Tonry. 1990. *Between prison and probation.* New York: Oxford University Press.

Nadel, S. F. 1953. Social control and self-regulation. *Social Forces* 31: 265–273.

Nessman, R. 1997. Probation caseloads driving agents to triage system. *Pittsburgh Post-Gazette.* March 23, 1997.

Nokes, P. 1960. Purpose and efficiency in human social institutions. *Human Relations* 13: 141–155.

Olsen, H., J. Dilulio, W. Bratton, M. Paparozzi, and R. Corbett, 1999. *Transforming probation through leadership: The "broken windows" model.* Manhattan Institute for Policy Research. Available online at http://www.manhattan-institute.org.

Petersilia, J. 1997. Probation in the United States: Practices and challenges. In M. Tonry, ed., *Crime and justice: A review of research.* Chicago, IL: University of Chicago Press.

Petersilia, J., S. Turner, J. Kahan, and J. Peterson. 1985. *Granting felony probation: Public risk and alternatives.* Santa Monica, CA: Rand Corporation.

Reaves, B., and P. Smith. 1995. *Felony defendants in large urban counties, 1992.* Washington, DC: U.S. Department of Justice, Bureau of Justice Statistics.

Reiss, A. 1984. Selecting strategies of social control over organizational life. In K. Hawkins and J. Hingham, eds., *Enforcing regulation.* New York: Kluwer, pp. 23–27.

Rhine, E. H. 1998. Probation and parole supervision: A time of a new narrative. *Perspectives* 22: 26–29.

Rosencrance, J. 1987. A typology of presentence probation investigators. *International Journal of Offender Therapy and Comparative Criminology* 31: 163–177.

Sigler, R., and B. McGraw. 1984. Adult probation and parole officers: Influence of their weapons, role perceptions, and role conflict. *Criminal Justice Review* 9: 28–32.

Simon, J. 1993. *Poor discipline.* Chicago: University of Chicago Press.

Smith, A. B., and L. Berlin. 1979. *Introduction to probation and parole.* St. Paul, MN: West.

Stojkovic, S., D. Kalinich, and J. Klofas. 1998. *Criminal justice organizations,* 2nd ed. Belmont, CA: West/Wadsworth.

Stroker, R. 1991. A reassessment of violations policy and practice. *Community Corrections Quarterly.*

Sullivan, D. 1980. *The mask of love: Corrections in America.* Port Washington, NY: Kennikat Press.

Tomaino, L. 1975. The five faces of probation. *Federal Probation* 39: 42–45.

United States Code, Title 18, Crimes and Criminal Procedures, Part II – Criminal Procedure, Chapter 227 Sentences, Subchapter B – Probation, Section 3563. Available online at http://www.caselaw.lp.findlaw.com.

Van Laningham, D., M. Taber, and R. Dimants. 1966. How adult probation and parole officers view their job responsibilities. *Crime and Delinquency* 12: 97–108.

von Hirsch, A., M. Wasik, and J. Greene. 1989. Punishments in the community and the principles of desert. *Rutgers Law Journal* 20: 595–618.

KEY POINTS

1. One of the main features of community supervision is the importance attached to rules governing the behavior of the offender.

2. The Survey of Adults on Probation data indicate that 82 percent of probationers are given three or more conditions that often include fees, drug testing, employment, and requirements to work.

3. The Manhattan Institute reports that as many as 288,000 probationers were absconders and were not fulfilling the court orders mandating treatment. Thus probation is ineffective in helping probationers learn to read, avoid drugs, obtain jobs reconnect with prosocial peers.

4. Many officers are reluctant to bring a probationer to court for a violation because the new charges may be dismissed, an alternative treatment approach may be tried, and the officer may feel responsible for what has happened.

5. The regulatory model of probation recognizes the power of professional discretion at work.

6. Technical violations are seen as not inherently criminal.

7. Regulation is a concept of probation that suggests that probation is not so much interested in seeing the offender sent to prison for a violation but recognizes that there is a great deal of tolerance for organizational uncertainty.

8. Regulatory probation occurs in a decoupled organization where the officer is seeking compliance to the rules achieved through inspection, discipline, and normalization.

KEY TERMS

deterrence models   include elements such as postmonitory, formal, and accusatory, emphasizing a rational choice perspective of crime, employing mission statements, and taking an adversarial approach to the offender.

group regulation   is the imposition of social control over the behavior of group members through the establishment, enforcement, and punishment of group normative behavior.

new penology   is not about punishment or rehabilitation; it is about identifying and managing obstreperous groups by employing a system-wide coordinated process.

offender control models   seek to incapacitate the offender through various means that emphasize authority and control.

premonitory compliance systems are concerned with a law violation as it develops rather than after it is a formal crime.

regulatory models include elements such as premonitory, informal, and bargained. The major emphasis is on probation technical violations. Crime is viewed as a social construction, is discretionary, and the response to it involves negotiations.

self-regulation is manifested in the personal acceptance, through socialization, of various norms, customs, values, and traditions, which were designed to reinforce conventional social practices.

state regulation is a process imposed by the courts and is, in theory, based on statutory law, case law, and constitutional law.

REVIEW QUESTIONS

1. Discuss how the conditions placed on a probationer affect his or her life and what happens when those conditions are violated.

2. Compare the deterrence with the regulatory model of probation.

3. Offender compliance can be improved through the use of inspection, discipline, and normalization. Discuss what those terms mean.

4. How is regulation affected by concerns for uncertainty, decoupling, discretion, and compliance?

10

Public Safety and Collaborative Prevention

Chapter Objectives

In this chapter you will learn about:

- The need for probation officers to be in the field
- Problem communities
- Preventive collaborations
- Guardianships, partnerships, and leaderships

■ The Importance of Probation

As discussed in Chapter 5, the number of offenders is quite large and growing. It has been shown that the resources devoted to probation do not reflect the importance given its assignments. As the primary sentencing disposition of the justice system affecting both adults and juvenile offenders, probation is well positioned strategically to contribute to <u>public safety</u> and community well-being. As a matter of social policy, probation occupies a place between law enforcement and human services. As a criminal sanction, probation has at its disposal wide-ranging leverage to influence the conduct of offenders. Its strength lies in its power to help the victim and hold the offender accountable. Its weakness lies in its lack of financial support. Probation is weakly funded and woefully understaffed despite staggering caseloads (MIPR 1999, 1–10). Since 1977, spending for probation has shown a steady decline, while spending for imprisonment has increased. The disparity between prison and probation budgets becomes most visible by comparing per-offender amount spent. According to Petersilia (1997), most states spend between $20,000 and $50,000 a year for each person in their prison system. Petersilia (1997) notes that some jurisdictions spend as little as $200 per year per probationer for supervision. There is no jurisdiction that invests in probation at the level of funding comparable to that available for housing felons in state prison

public safety means that offenders living in the neighborhood are accounted for and properly managed. Problems are attended to before they lead to violations.

(Camp and Camp 1998, 184). At a national level, even though probation alone is responsible for supervision of six out of ten offenders under some form of correctional supervision, it receives less than 10 percent of state and local government funding earmarked for corrections (Petersilia 1997; 150 MIPR 1999, 1–11). This means that many probationers are not given the attention they warrant. Even though imprisonment is the backbone of the correctional enterprise, probation is the paramount sanction, in terms of sheer numbers.

Clear (1999) believes that correctional leaders must embrace three major attitudinal shifts if they are to be effective:

1. move toward targets that enhance the community's quality of life
2. move beyond professionalism to citizen participation
3. move beyond case management to problem solving

This can be achieved with collaborative prevention and partnerships.

The central focus is developing a strategy based on a broken-windows concept of probation. As with the police, the broken-windows approach for probation attempts to deal with small problems before they become large. According to Wilson and Kelling (1982), the idea is that small disorders and criminal violations if left unattended will eventually lead to more serious offenses and greater social disorder. More attention is given to minor offenses that take place in public places and in developing partnerships with the community so that there is a sense of shared ownership of the process. Broken-windows probation is based on the notion that public safety comes first, supervision of the offender should take place in the community, resources should be rationally allocated, violations of probation conditions should be enforced quickly and strongly, partnerships should be established, and effective leadership is crucial (Olsen et al. 1999). This chapter discusses the failure of probation to be in the field and discusses several measures intended to improve probation including public safety, collaborative preventive measures, community partnerships, resource allocation, performance-based assessments, and the development of leadership skills that maximize the talents of the workforce in furthering the cause of justice and dignified treatment of the offender.

■ Public Safety

For all probation officers, public safety is a prime concern. No officer wants responsibility for an offender who commits a major offense. For the purposes of community corrections, *public safety* is defined as the condition of a place, at times when people in that place are justified in feeling free from the threat to their persons and property (Olsen et al. 1999). Public safety means that offenders living in the neighborhood are accounted for and properly managed. Problems are attended to before they lead to violations. Public safety requires a systemic, yet local focus on the social ecology of crime. The social ecology of crime considers various actors present in the community as responsible for crime. It means that probation's approach is community centered and neighborhood based (MIPR 1999, 2–8). Under this broken-windows model, probation officers extend their commitment by proactively approaching supervision and giving a

partnership is a term that can be used interchangeably with *networking, collaboration,* and *coordination.* Partnership occurs where people have joint interests. People who have common interests will often collaborate in order to exchange information, alter their activities, share resources, and enhance the capacity of another for the mutual benefit of all to achieve a common purpose.

fair amount of attention to victim safety. By forming a <u>**partnership**</u> with law enforcement, the courts, human services, community and neighborhood groups, the faith community, and local stakeholders, probation can provide effective public safety and offender reform (Olsen et al. 1999, 1–4).

The paradox of public opinion (Doble 1999) is that the public wants more punishment; it wants violent offenders in prison, but it favors alternatives to incarceration. It wants to feel safe from violent predators; to know that all offenders are held accountable for their offenses and that damages are repaired, but that offenders receive treatment and education; and especially it wants to be involved with decisions making. The public wants restorative justice to be a real factor. Offenders should assume responsibility for their crimes, understand the harm involved, acknowledge the wrong done, offer an apology, and repair the harm. Victims of crime do not want their experience trivialized. They want to see that punishment has been handed down and that some rehabilitation or education has also been done. Most importantly, the victim wants to be treated with respect (Olsen et al. 1999, 1–17).

The American Probation and Parole Association (APPA 2001) has generated a vision for the future of community corrections:

> *We see a fair, just, and safe society where community partnerships are restoring hope by embracing a balance of prevention, intervention, and advocacy.*

Intervention and advocacy have been discussed in earlier chapters. Preventing crime is a goal that can unite neighborhoods, open doors, and facilitate communication between people who have little in common with one another. It can energize a community and offer a measure of assurance for citizens who have experienced crime and have come to fear it. As has been said for decades, the prevention of crime makes good economic sense, especially because it saves money in the long run. According to the National Center for Education Statistics, the nation on average spends $6,900 per year per student. That compares quite favorably with the $20,000 spent per year per prison inmate.

■ Restorative Justice

Restorative justice removes crime prevention from the back burner. It also provides the incentive and the community participation crime prevention needs to work. Most importantly, deterrence and incapacitation work most effectively when they are enhanced through restorative justice programs. Both restorative justice and public safety incorporate similar features. The central concerns are for the victim, the offender, and especially for the community because it plays an active role in the process. Communities determine the rules, understand that rules must be enforced, and appreciate that rules are essential to social life. This is conceptualized as <u>**normative affirmation**</u> (Karp 2002). Normative affirmation resets the moral order of the community by getting the offender to see the offense as an individual effort to repeal the community's code of conduct and that the act was a truly deviant act the offender should not repeat. As Goffman (1967) writes:

normative affirmation reaffirms the moral order of the community by getting the offender to see the offense as an abrogation of the community code and an aberration of the offenders so they will not repeat.

The suspected person shows that he is capable of taking the role of the others toward his own identity . . . that the rules of conduct are still sacred, real, and unweakened.

Problem Areas

With respect to promoting safety, there are considerable problems with large offender numbers, the problem of legitimacy for the criminal justice system, and a clear measure of crime. First of all, there are over 4 million offenders on probation (Glaze and Pella 2004). Despite the fact that a small percentage commit serious crimes while on probation, about 20 percent of them commit another serious crime within 3 years of their sentence (Langan & Cunniff 1992). According to a study conducted by the Manhattan Institute (Olsen et al. 1999), 162,000 probationers returned to state prisons and were incarcerated in 1991. They were responsible for 6,400 murders, 7,400 rapes, 10,400 assaults, and 17,000 robberies. They also report that 156 of 1,411 persons convicted of murder in Virginia from 1990 to 1993 were on probation at the time of their offense. The Manhattan Institute concludes that if probation had done a better job, fewer people would have been killed or harmed.

A critical assessment of probation must begin by placing its problems within the more encompassing and deeper crisis of legitimacy affecting the entire system of justice (LaFree 1998). For nearly three decades, commentators have expressed heightened anxiety about the problems of crime. Simon (1998) calls these sentiments "populist punitiveness," reflecting fear, moralism, and a belief in the need to restore punishments at the center of crime control policy. This is expressed most directly in different forms of increased severity of punishments such as mandatory minimums and "three-strikes-and-you're-out" legislation. These reforms are premised on the belief that punishment and incapacitation are the only appropriate goals in a system apparently unable to change offenders' criminality (Olsen et al. 1999, 1–4).

It is apparent that the probation officers' tradition of passive supervision is inadequate in achieving public safety goals (MIPR 1999, 1–11). One of the key problems with probation occurs when an officer places a paramount emphasis on administrative paperwork and processing required reports. As Smith and Dickey (1998) point out, this produces a passivity in supervision that elevates an approach to case management referred to as "harvesting failures" (Olsen et al. 1999). As was emphasized in the chapter on offender regulation, increasingly managerial and organizational demands reward timely submission of reports and the ability to document minimum compliance with contact standards for supervision, not outcomes that contribute to public safety. Passive probation supervision undermines rigorous enforcement of the conditions of probation. Months may go by from the time a violation is detected to the point at which corrective action, if any, is taken. Drug testing is done but the results of the test may take weeks to obtain or testing is done so infrequently that it is an ineffective deterrent or tool to prevent drug use. These practices encourage noncompliance and other crimes (Olsen et al. 1999). Additionally, too many agencies do not encourage field-based activities that provide meaningful face-to-face supervision in their neighborhoods. Probation has become disconnected from such communities. In turn, it fails to draw on the leverage and resources of the community. The operation of probation in too many jurisdictions today is far removed from community concerns and needs (Clear and Corbett 1999).

◼ Differential Supervision

It is suggested that a new approach is required using probation and parole as public safety mechanisms that do not emphasize going after probation violators but instead emphasize order in the community or offender discipline through close supervision thereby reducing the offender's propensity for crime (**Figure 10.1**). Supervision does not take place in the office but out in the community where offenders live. The central office should be a tool, not a base of operation. Understanding offenders, their families, and the social milieu can only be achieved through off-hour visits (outside of the traditional 9–5 work hours) in an assigned area of the community. Understanding the community is enhanced by the use of minority probation officers. Public safety improves with the use of differential supervision programs.

Differential supervision allocates resources to offenders based on their level of risk for reoffending. This includes sex offenders, drug offenders, mentally ill offenders, gang members, domestic violence perpetrators, and other high-risk offenders. As discussed in Chapters 7 and 9, due to the discretionary nature of probation work, there are large numbers of probationers who are given special consideration. In some jurisdictions, probationers believe they are allowed "free" dirty urine samples, electronic monitoring violations, and failures to comply with the conditions of probation orders. Little good is served when an offi-

Figure 10.1 Supervision does not take place in the office but out in the community where offenders live.

cer discovers that an ISP probationer has violated for the first time the conditions of his or her probation only 2 weeks before readjustments are made in the level of supervision. Some officers would attempt to head off such behavior. Many officers realize that despite their efforts to bring the matter before the court, the court is unresponsive. Attorneys negotiate deals that return offenders to the community under the supervision of the probation officers who just tried to send them to prison.

Problem Communities

A *community* is a gathering of people living in the same area who share common interests. A residential neighborhood, a high-rise apartment or office building, a school, a church, a professional society, or a civic network can be a community. Communities are central to the concept and practice of crime prevention. To thrive, the community must offer its members a sense of security. Community members must feel free to interact with each other, but in the presence of crime, citizens experience fear, reduce their use of public spaces, participate less in civic activities, decrease their economic and social activity, and undergo a diminished respect for duly constituted authority (i.e., the criminal justice system). Victims encounter the loss of productive time and incur the costs of injuries. For the criminal justice system, there is the expense of apprehending, prosecuting, and jailing the offender.

Fear of crime, in particular, is a vicious force that can cause residents to change their behavior dramatically, disrupt community life, and force residents into isolation. A parent refuses to attend a PTA meeting; a single person declines to engage in sociable conversation with a polite stranger; a business closes at 5:00 P.M. instead of 9:00 P.M.; older residents venture outside only briefly at the height of daylight; cultural, sports, and civic events suffer as concerned patrons forego attendance to avoid the prospect of victimization; and children are kept out of playgrounds and parks by worried adults. One further consideration the public needs to make is a true measure of criminal activity, not only in terms of crime rates but more importantly, in terms of clearance rates. Cleared offenses in general reflect trends in reporting crime. Most of all, they tell about the number of reported crimes that have been solved, which is a better indicator of police activity and workload. Considerable resources will have to be directed toward crime if the clearance rate for murder, for example, is to achieve the levels it held during the 1960s when 80 percent of the murders were cleared as opposed to some 60 percent today (FBI 2003). Certainty of punishment, brought on by a high clearance rate, makes it possible to punish the offender frequently but parsimoniously. Failure to pay heed to the crime-clearance rate differential is like asking the beekeeper how many bees he has when he knows that he can only manage so many effectively. Beyond that number the bees are on their own.

With a safer neighborhood, many people are willing to meet the challenge of community-wide action. Community policing intrinsically recognizes that security must extend beyond self-protection, that the community must be safe for the individual to be secure living there. It also works to enhance the sense of cohesion and the partnerships that enable communities to prevent crime.

Victimization or Offense?

An interesting connection exists between offending and victimization. Throughout the world, there seems to be a close connection between crime and victimization. In general, victims tend to come from the same backgrounds and areas as their perpetrators. Crime is generally found in areas where there are persistent social and economic problems. According to Loeber and Farrington (1998), it also appears that a small percentage of offenders are responsible for a majority of identifiable crimes. For example, 6 percent of the young males are responsible for 50 to 70 percent of all crimes (Loeber and Farrington 1998). It is also estimated that violence against women and children is widespread. In developing countries, it is estimated that between 33 percent and 50 percent of all women are victims of violence from male partners (Heise et al. 1994). In the United States, the number of children who are abused or neglected almost doubled between 1986 and 1993. Violence in the family can often lead to other problems including crime and ill health (Shaw 2001, 6).

According to Shaw (2001) evidence is accumulating about the factors that put people, especially children, at risk of crime and victimization. These include poverty and a poor environment, poor parenting practices, family conflict and violence, early signs of aggressive behavior, too much time with friends without adult contacts, doing poorly at school or dropping out, failing to learn good work skills, having few employment opportunities, living in areas that lack services and facilities, and having access to drugs (p. 7).

Failing to address these issues is a costly proposition. Tougher sentencing laws only postpone the inevitable need to address the causes of the problems. Most prisoners are released from prison. Children who grow up in poverty without close parental supervision and lack sufficient support services are subject to long-term drug use and crime. There are considerable cost savings in addressing these problems through means other than long prison sentences. Preventive action can be up to 10 times more cost-effective than traditional measures such as incarceration. Money invested in prevention also aids in improved education, job skills, and health (Shaw 2001, 10). Traditionally, crime prevention has been regarded as the responsibility of the police and prosecutors, yet despite increased expenditures over the last 40 years, there are still high crime rates. In many countries, the public has lost confidence in the criminal justice system (Shaw 2001, 10). Carefully planned approaches building on prior knowledge reduce both crime and risk factors. Effective programs involve community organizations, families, police departments, school systems, labor unions, social service agencies, youth groups, housing developments, and elements of the justice system (Shaw 2001, 9).

■ Preventive Collaboration

Crime prevention has become an urgent policy goal because state and local governments are overwhelmed by the joint demands of managing a criminal justice system and providing homeland security. These governments are also faced with the competing demands for providing quality education systems and efficient infrastructure systems.

In recent years, increases in crime and violence have affected countries worldwide. The responses of most governments have been to toughen their legal systems and to increase spending on law enforcement and corrections to unprecedented levels. At the same time, crime prevention has played a minor role in the justice system. Furthermore, crime prevention was seen as a police function. According to Shaw (2001), investing in crime prevention is much more productive. Despite the fact that crime and violence rates in the United States decreased for the 8 consecutive years prior to 1999, these levels are still higher than they were 30 years ago. Shaw also stated there have been marked changes in the way that local and national governments have come to understand and tackle the problem of crime, violence, and insecurity. This new focus has given attention to the underlying problems based on careful analysis and planning in collaboration with citizens.

Early intervention is crucial in addressing these problems. Sherman and colleagues (1997) and the International Centre for the Prevention of Crime (1999) have identified successful projects aimed at high-risk families and children. Preschool home visits and giving children a head start in school have shown reductions in delinquency, lower school dropout rates, and an improved quality of life for children and parents. Parent training and family therapy projects designed to strengthen child-rearing practices have shown similar results (Shaw 2001, 8). Moreover, widespread intervention can help to reduce bullying, improve school climate and academic performance, and reduce school disruption and dropout rates. Reintegration into the community can be achieved for dropouts and excluded students through mentoring, job training, and work skills development.

It has also been shown that cleaning up the environment and situations that encourage crime is very effective in reducing crime. Cleaning up rundown streets, changing the design of buildings or public spaces, and improving lighting and surveillance has been noted to reduce the opportunities for crime. According to Shaw (2001), studies of programs using this approach in the Netherlands, England, and Wales indicated a reduction in household burglaries by 75 percent when employing neighborhood watch programs, improving security, and marking personal property. Vandalism has been reduced by increased surveillance on public transportation, the addition of closed circuit television cameras, and requiring bar owners to change their serving practices (Shaw 2001, 9).

There is a need for a plausible narrative for community-based supervision that can be translated to the public as to what probation does and how well it is done. Probation must show that it can control offenders and reflect important public values through the work of probation in the field (Burrell 1999). **Community justice** is a concept closely related to but clearly distinguishable from restorative justice (Barajas 1995, 1998; Carey 1999; Clear and Karp 1998). Both perspectives share the focus of repairing the harm and directing attention to the victims' needs and issues. However, as defined in a recent position statement by the APPA (2000), "community justice is a strategic method of crime reduction and prevention, which builds or enhances partnerships with communities." The crime-fighting policies that are called for under this approach emphasize proactive, problem-solving practices intended to prevent, control, reduce, and repair crime's harm. The overriding goal of community justice is to create and contribute

community justice is a strategic method of crime reduction and prevention, which builds or enhances partnerships with communities.

to a healthy, safe, vibrant, and just community and to improve the citizen's quality of life. According to the Manhattan Institute (1999), there are probation departments that are doing an effective job of putting public safety as a number one priority. These proactive departments are results oriented with key decisions made on the basis of research and other findings.

Agency adjustments and organizational reforms will have some impact on prevention, but in truth, they are only part of the solution. A satisfactory role for probation requires a broader approach. The preventive strategy being proposed here emphasizes the importance of probation officers engaging members of the community in their own protection. If public safety is to be achieved, the public must, with the help of the criminal justice system, take charge of their environment. Together, they can achieve the goal of public safety and people can reclaim their communities. Probation officers can feel more secure when they go out in the community and the public will feel more secure knowing that whatever they do the criminal justice system stands behind them.

Since the 1970s, crime prevention has developed a track record that demonstrates its success in reducing crime, reducing fear, and restoring the citizens' sense of security (Olsen et al. 1999). Crime prevention has produced benefits beyond changing attitudes and behaviors, mobilizing communities, and reducing crime rates. It has built better working relationships among government agencies in Knoxville, Tennessee; enabled once confrontational groups to develop solid working partnerships in Waterloo, Iowa; created strong community groups; generated police-community partnerships via Neighborhood Watch and numerous other programs; and saved businesses money and other crime losses (Olsen et al. 1999). The public and the criminal justice system are working harder at crime prevention.

In 1990, the Crime Prevention Coalition of America (CPCA) formulated the following definition of crime prevention:

> *A pattern of attitudes and behaviors directed both at reducing the threat of crime and enhancing the sense of safety and security, to positively influence the quality of life in our society and to help develop environments where crime cannot flourish.*

This definition clarifies the importance of community as a base for prevention. It also recognizes that there is a dual task: (1) reducing crime's threats to the community and (2) developing communities that discourage crime.

Crime prevention deals with both immediate situations and causes that are far removed in time and space. It provides know-how for individuals, neighborhoods, or whole cities; it addresses the physical and social needs of communities, from redesigning streets to formulating social programs. It deals with fear that paralyzes communities and their residents and saps civic lifeblood. This definition also acknowledges the importance of community perceptions. One task of **community crime prevention** is to help people overcome the crippling effects of unwarranted fear while acknowledging their legitimate concerns and helping to resolve these problems. Like community policing, crime prevention seeks to understand local needs and perceptions and solve problems in local contexts (APPA 2001).

community crime prevention is a type of crime prevention premised on the idea that changing the community may change the behavior of the people who live there.

Prevention of crime is a complex problem. Sex offenses, robberies, thefts, arson, vandalism, drug trafficking, and domestic violence are motivated by different factors. Crimes of impulse, emotion, or intoxication, and crimes resulting from socialized deviance are not likely to be well-controlled by law enforcement. A comprehensive governmental strategy should include situational, developmental, and community approaches (Tonry and Farrington 1995, 7). Crime is considered a community problem that must be dealt with beyond the offender. The community needs to address efforts that may prevent new juvenile and criminal offenders from emerging. Community mobilization initiatives seek to instill a sense of personal safety and security in those most directly confronted with the reality of not moving freely in the neighborhood (prevention and community safety). Probation must take a community justice approach in which probation officials will know what is in the mind of the public. Doing a market analysis of public expectations will prepare probation to better serve the community's quality of life issues. Enlisting the support of the community as a viable contributing partner in the supervision and management of probationers can enhance the guardianship capabilities, by investing in community members' expertise and drawing on their diversified resources. This requires proactive community involvement within a problem-solving philosophy that engages the community in problem-solving partnerships involving the community, law enforcement, public health service providers, economic development organizations, private sector businesses, community advocacy organizations, and others.

■ Situational Crime Prevention

Situational crime prevention is based on the premise that much crime is contextual and opportunistic. In response to the perceived risk of harm, people routinely alter their behavior, even using animals and technologies to increase their sense of security. In response, offenders change their tactics, too. **Situational prevention** is expressed in the military vernacular of target hardening (making it more difficult to destroy or victimize a target) and is operationalized in the efforts commonly found in the private security industry. Greater use of fire, health, and police licensing powers to inspect various locations could increase the security level of various environments. Victims could also receive specific training designed to reduce further victimizations. What is unique in the present discussion is the systematic effort in the last decade to develop and test situational techniques, by fostering cooperation between probation and law enforcement. Despite claims of any displacement effect (pushing crime from one environment to another) a consensus seems to be building suggesting that situational prevention is effective in some cases (Tonry and Farrington 1995, 8).

situational prevention is expressed in the military vernacular of target hardening and is operationalized in the private security industry. Greater use of fire, health, and police licensing powers to inspect various locations could increase the security level of various environments.

■ Developmental Prevention

U.S. **developmental prevention** is the new frontier for prevention. Developmental prevention is a highly diverse field in which individuals in health, medicine, psychology, and the like have entered into the discussion. Much of the

developmental prevention is a highly diverse field in which individuals in health, medicine, psychology, and the like have entered into the discussion. Much of the attention is focused on risk factors that are predictive of antisocial behavior.

attention is focused on risk factors that are predictive of antisocial behavior. Reducing risk factors or immunizing children from risk could have broad implications for offenders and others with similar needs. Interventions that improve parenting skills, a child's physical and mental health and school performance, and reduce child abuse not only prevent crime but they also provide benefits to noncriminal populations. Interventions intended to improve the life chances of children-at-risk warrant support independent of any crime prevention consideration. Evaluation of such programs has demonstrated either delinquency-reducing effects or beneficial effects on other indicators (Tonry and Farrington 1995, 9–10).

Chapter 7 on supervision considered various risk factors, especially risk-needs assessment because developmental prevention is associated with reducing known risk factors. The goals of prevention may be accomplished by direct efforts to reduce exposure to risk factors or by enhancing protective factors that moderate or mediate the effects and exposure to risk. Prevention efforts should specify what risk factors are targeted and the mechanism or process within which these risk factors are thought to operate. Sherman, Farrington, and MacKenzie (2003) have a complete list of studies that have identified risk factors. They are clear to point out that dynamic risk factors are the most important because they are capable of changing; thus, over time one can see a change in the offender's behavior or risk. Some risk factors may not be causal but may be useful in identifying high-risk populations for intervention. Causal risks factors should be the objects of preventive interventions that seek to modify the level of risk (Hawkins et al. 1995, 388–393).

While addressing risk factors, it is important to enhance known protective factors. Strength may be added to preventive interventions by enhancing changeable protective factors that moderate risk. For example, even in families with an alcoholic parent, it may be possible to moderate the effects of parental alcoholism on children by interventions that provide supports for good family management, school achievement, and abstinence from alcohol use by children (Hawkins et al. 1995, 388–393). Furthermore, interventions that focus on reducing family management problems should do so in ways that enhance family bonding and a conventional or healthy belief structure in the family. In this way, not only is the negative risk reduced, but also bonding is strengthened to provide motivation to continue sound management and to obey family rules (Hawkins et al. 1995, 388–393).

Predictors

Some risks and protective factors appear to be relatively stable predictors across the life span, while others appear to predict dysfunction at specific periods of development. For example, poor parental monitoring appears to predict conduct disorders across childhood, while association with drug using peers is predictive of drug use only in adolescence (Dishion 1990). Conduct and behavioral problems in early elementary school signal risk for eventual health and behavior problems. Early intervention is warranted in these children. If children experience academic difficulties in grades 4 to 6, they are more likely to be at risk for abusing drugs later on. Tutoring and academic enrichment programs are, thus, indicated during the elementary period (Hawkins et al. 1995, 388–393).

Early Intervention

Early intervention is necessary before the target behavior stabilizes. Early initiation of drug use is a predictor of a prolonged course of involvement with drugs and drug abuse. This suggests that preventive intervention should be delivered before the initiation of drug use. A viable goal for preventive intervention may be to delay the onset of initiation of alcohol and other drugs. This is the immediate goal of many recent drug abuse prevention initiatives, though few have been followed long enough to determine whether early delays in initiation translates into later reductions in diagnosable substance abuse disorders (Hawkins et al. 1995, 388–393).

It is also important to include those at high risk. Given the additive or perhaps multiplicative effect of exposure to multiple risk factors, it is important to design preventive interventions to reach those exposed to them. This may be accomplished by selecting for intervention those communities or schools in which there are elevated levels of risk or by identifying individuals exposed to multiple risks for special attention (Hawkins et al. 1995, 388–393).

Multiple Risks

It is also necessary to address multiple risks with multiple strategies. A viable prevention strategy may require attention to individual vulnerabilities, poor child rearing, school achievement, social influences, social skills, and broad social norms, all of which are implicated in the development of adolescent drug abuse. Because risks are present in several social spheres and cumulate in predicting drug abuse, multicomponent prevention strategies focused on reducing multiple risks and enhancing multiple protective factors may be required. Such strategies would be designed to increase protection while reducing or moderating risk exposure (Hawkins et al. 1995, 388–393). Unfortunately, the evidence for community crime prevention is not as convincing as it is for situational or developmental prevention (Tonry and Farrington 1995, 8). However, there are results that indicate some success.

■ Community Crime Prevention

Community crime prevention is premised on the idea that changing the community may change the behavior of the people who live there. Community crime prevention goes back to the Shaw and McKay (1969) studies of the Chicago Area Projects. The hope is that by altering the physical and social organization of the community, crime will be reduced. Tonry and Farrington (1995) argue that crime prevention efforts include altering building and neighborhood designs to increase natural surveillance and guardianship. This is achieved by improving an area's physical appearance, organizing community residents to take preventive action, soliciting political and material resources, and by organizing self-conscious community crime prevention strategies such as recreational programs for youth.

In reviewing 11 evaluations described in *Community Crime Prevention: Does It Work?* Robert K. Yin (1986) observed that police involvement in community crime prevention has demonstrated effectiveness in 6 key areas that include increasing knowledge, changing attitudes, altering actions, mobilizing communities, reducing crime rates, and enhancing quality of life. According to Yin, "The evaluations and their largely positive outcomes do point to the fact that crime can be prevented, under a variety of circumstances." Following are some examples of how some of these key areas have been used by police departments to effectively decrease crime within communities.

- In Lincoln, Nebraska, a major outreach effort was conducted by police officers to teach members of a Vietnamese community how to understand the law and prevent crime. It was found that increasing their knowledge of the law not only reduced victimization among that group, but also increased the level of respect and understanding between law enforcement and the community.

- Community-based programs by police in Houston, Texas, and Newark, New Jersey, helped to reduce residents' fear of crime and led to a more positive attitude toward law enforcement officials.

- In Columbus, Ohio, a crime prevention coordinator altered the actions of the community by reducing the number of drug houses in the community from 251 to 5 in just 2 years.

- In Baltimore, Maryland, a deep and strong partnership among residents, city government officials, the police department, community organizers, probation and parole officers, treatment services, and foundations reinvigorated the safety and vitality of 6 of the city's toughest neighborhoods. This extraordinary commitment to mobilizing the community is another hallmark of this now citywide strategy, which has reduced crime by as much as 50 percent in some neighborhoods.

- Boston, Massachusetts, also set a new national standard for community mobilization. The collaboration among law enforcement, criminal justice system components, and the community has saved countless young lives and brought a new atmosphere to residents throughout the city by embracing a research-based, neighborhood-focused, and fully balanced intervention strategy. A strong commitment to strategic planning helped to point out priorities, which remain the focal point of the city's successful efforts. Between 1990 and 1999, the homicide rate dropped from 150 to 17.

- Hartford, Connecticut, has reduced crime rates by creating a comprehensive crime prevention program. The community court; the 16 neighborhood-based, multi-agency and resident problem solving committees; and partnerships with businesses are creating a city with a safer and brighter future. In 1997, neighborhoods experienced drops in reported crime of 20 to 40 percent as compared to 1995 and 1996. The strategy is supported by a local government committed to finding the points where the program can have the greatest influence on change from a more community-oriented perspective.

- Columbia, South Carolina, residents formed a partnership among police, the city's community development agency, residents, and area churches to close down and remove drug houses. In their wake, this partnership strived to improve the quality of life for residents of these neighborhoods by building new housing that attracted several new businesses, including a grocery store. In one of the city's public housing neighborhoods, a similar commitment to crime prevention and safety has resulted in the resumption of pizza and other food delivery to the neighborhood for the first time in recent memory. These results signal that residents are more active and secure in their communities and value the return to "normal" life.

Mobilizing Leaders

Community prevention has some similarities with problem-oriented policing (Goldstein 1990) especially when efforts are made in mobilizing community leaders who can form community prevention boards, identifying risk factors in the community, choosing local strategies, implementing the strategy, and evaluating the effects. Community policing emphasizes a law enforcement process that works in conjunction with local residents and institutions working in collaboration rather than confrontation. The ultimate goal of problem solving and collaboration is to prevent further crimes. The energies of law enforcement and criminal justice agencies are better invested in resolving problems rather than continually reacting to the same calls for service and repeat offenders.

■ Guardianship

According to Clarke (1995), criminal opportunities have three components: targets, victims, and facilitators. The supply of targets is offered by the physical environment, consisting of the layout of cities, building design, technology (sensors and lights) and communication, transportation, retailing establishments, vehicles, and supply of drugs and alcohol. He points out that victim lifestyles and routine activities, including patterns of work, leisure, residence, and shopping, either hinder or facilitate support from members of the community. Facilitators are people and situations in which crime is made possible through lax enforcement or through the public's apparent indifference to the occurrence of crime.

Some of the nation's best policy thinkers on criminal justice have strongly endorsed the concept of community-based crime prevention (Rosenbaum 1988). The basic premise is that citizen participation in maintaining order is essential to a cost-effective and community-sensitive response to crime. Rosenbaum's "co-production of public safety" is used to describe the idea that just as everyone shares the benefits of a well-ordered social life, so must everyone take part in establishing them. Crime prevention and community policing both appreciate that civic participation, social activity, and individual freedom cannot flourish if crime is rampant, and that informal social standards must play a major role in reducing crime and fear. The community must assume ownership of these standards and further develop control mechanisms if these informal rules are to be truly effective. Crime prevention also encourages and embraces various processes including community-building activities such as installing lights; cleaning up graffiti and litter; creating positive opportunities by providing mentoring, recreation, transportation, and job training; and developing industries, making infrastructure improvements, and giving aid to small businesses. Crime prevention seeks to build and sustain the kinds of communities that can keep themselves healthy through a sensible combination of formal (legal) and informal (social) controls and safeguards. Through regulations, laws, and sanctions, the community provides explicit standards and expectations and establishes official punishment for those who violate the rules. The concept of guardianship is central to understanding crime prevention. Guardianship is premised on the belief that local residents can develop a stake in their communities.

A Change

The role of probation changes considerably when the concept of guardianship is considered. Instead of focusing on offender management, guardianship shifts the emphasis to identifying unofficial, naturally occurring people who are willing to participate in a normative reaffirmation process designed to reestablish norms, values, and ideals that are representative of the community (Karp and Clear 2002). Unofficial attitudes and actions by community members are expressed as guardianship when peer pressure is exerted to establish neighborhood standards and defines, teaches, and encourages acceptable behavior. In other words, **guardians** exhibit the acceptable means for appropriate informal intervention. Guardians maintain a protective relationship to vulnerable targets, but they are also people who can have an intimate or supervisory relationship to potential offenders (whether the offenders are under correctional supervision or not), and they are people who are responsible for places where the guardians and the public may come together. Guardians may be parents, spouses, children, friends, neighbors, employers, local shopkeepers, and security guards. By mobilizing them, probation and parole agents can most effectively increase and preserve public safety (Smith 2001).

Examples of guardianship include the willingness of friends, neighbors, coworkers, and others to call the police when witnessing a crime; testifying in court; stopping a child from vandalizing a street sign; increasing the number of children who refuse drugs and report pushers; encouraging friends to stay out of gangs. It also takes the form of neighbors questioning strangers, watching over each other's property, and intervening in local disturbances (e.g., scolding children for fighting). These are all examples of informal social control and expressions of guardianship. The basis for these behaviors is a shared set of norms for appropriate public behavior. Informal social controls in a community are extremely important in preventing crime (Greenberg et al. 1985, 1–2).

guardians maintain a protective relationship to vulnerable targets, but they are also people who can have an intimate or supervisory relationship to potential offenders. Whether the offenders are under correctional supervision or not, they are people who are responsible for places where the guardians and the public may come together. Guardians may be parents, spouses, children, friends, neighbors, employers, local shopkeepers, and security guards.

■ Partnerships

Partnership is a term that can be used interchangeably with *networking*, *collaboration*, and *coordination*. Partnership occurs when people have joint interests. People who have common interests will often collaborate in order to exchange information, alter their activities, share resources, and enhance the capacity of another for the mutual benefit of all to achieve a common purpose (Woodward 2001). Partnerships are becoming essential to the daily activities of the criminal justice system. Officials realize that effective collaborations have a clear goal, principled leadership, results-driven structure, competent team members, unified commitment, standards of excellence, collaborative climate, and external support (Woodward 2001).

The following section is about the creation of a community justice system in which there are community partnerships, rationally allocated resources, performance-based initiatives, accountability, and effective leadership. These five elements comprise the essential core of the partnership movement.

Criminal justice agencies are increasing their involvement with collaborative efforts in the community and with other criminal justice agencies. Courts have promoted or approved a variety of neighborhood dispute resolution systems to help settle conflicts peacefully in the community and with relative informality. Prosecutors are working with community groups to gather evidence on drug dealers, to provide victim and witness support, and to build prevention systems. Probation and parole departments are working with police departments, prosecutors, and defendants in new partnerships to reduce recidivism and enhance community safety. Probation is locating in neighborhoods and developing special mentoring and monitoring relationships with offenders. The probation-community partnership is enhanced when the public is surveyed as to its concerns, guardianship opportunities are identified, and partnerships are established with the community, law enforcement, and successful treatment programs. Probation is also in the unique position through the use of various databases to create a good understanding of the criminogenic influences in a community and then offer leadership as to what strategies would have the biggest impact on crime reduction.

Community Partnerships

Within the community justice framework, the need to establish enduring partnerships with citizenry, other agencies, and local interest groups is critical to the success of probation. Forming such partnerships increases probation's ability to garner support and the promotion of co-ownership of the problems in the community. Active participation from the public is premised on the belief that public participation is essential to the success of probation (Rhine and Hinzman 2000). In other words, community participants should be treated with respect and dignity because they truly have something to contribute. Partnerships are developed with thoughtful individuals who have an intimate knowledge of the community; they have reasonable expectations for how they should be treated by government officials, and they understand what needs to be done. They know they are using nontraditional problem-solving approaches in their decision-making capacity (Clear and Karp 1998). Employing the nonhierarchical approach presented by restorative justice furthers this process. Administrators must recognize they have obligations to share what they understand to work with others (Olsen et al. 1999, 2–17). Each form of collaboration contributes to the provision of greater public safety and a growing set of probation practices that are regarded as more credible given their deepening ties to the social ecology of the neighborhood and community relations. These collaborations allow the officer to take advantage of the existing social capital furnished by the local community members (Olsen et al. 1999).

Collaboration

Collaboration will not be easy because it is likely that over time a pattern of practices has led to suspicion and distrust. Proper planning is needed to resolve any outstanding issues and to anticipate upcoming ones. Program developers must consider formal reciprocal or sharing agreements for resources, personnel, operations, information, communication systems, treatment strategies, and the use of treatment resources. Most of all, there must be a joint vision and mission to create an environment in which there are fewer victims in the future (Olsen et al. 1999, 2–20).

One Example Community collaboration is essential to effective partnerships. The National Institute of Corrections (Kuehl 2001) believes that successful partnerships require the involvement of the community. A good example is Iowa's sixth judicial district located in Cedar Rapids. To create a series of partnerships, action groups were formed in six areas: community education, victim-sensitive practices, community/criminal justice, invest-in-children, creating community, and offender education action groups. To further the partnership process, time was spent on publicity, alliances were built that focused on trust and relationship development, principles were developed on how people should work together, patience was encouraged, and education was understood as essential. People were encouraged to practice what was preached, to take risks, to sustain their efforts, to maintain a vision, to advertise success, and to monitor and evaluate outcomes (Kuehl 2001). An outcome of these activities was the development of a comprehensive computer program to assess offender needs for supervision and treatment. The sixth district also established partnerships with law enforcement and neighborhood groups to develop an intensive supervision program in collaboration with the local Community-Oriented Police Service (COPS) program. Along with a police task force, probation officers targeted certain anticriminal activities, especially in encouraging neighbors to participate in restorative justice reparation boards. The evaluation of the program produced a 5 percent failure rate during the subsequent year. This program reduced crack or disorderly houses in the neighborhood from 92 in 1998 to 23 1 year later in 1999.

Another Example In "How to Make Partnerships Work," Valentine (2001) focuses on the use of partnership programs dealing with managing 1,400 sex offenders in downtown Houston, Texas. Faced with an increasing number of unfunded legislative mandates dealing with sex offenders, the law enforcement community, probation department, and other groups formed an interagency coordinating council composed of 35 representatives from agencies involved with sex offenders. These agencies addressed treatment, registration, abuse investigations, polygraph tests, criminal defense, restitution, public education, law enforcement, prosecution, jail, and probation and parole supervision. More specifically, probation established a sex offender tracking system requiring the probation department to fax an information sheet to the police patrol division asking them to conduct random drive-by visits of an identified sex offender's residence to check on any compliance order. Results were then reported to probation or parole.

Programs That Work

According to Valentine (2001), workable programs require various approaches. There must be clearly defined visions, missions, and goals that key officials can buy into; everyone must benefit; stakeholders must be identified and invited to participate at the beginning; information must be produced that explains the task, its importance, and how stakeholder participation is useful; scheduled meetings must be set; and at these meetings relevant information must be gathered and distributed that identifies priorities. Moreover, publicity must be generated about proactive and collective accomplishments that engages the media; attention must be given to seeking out multiple sources of funding, taking advantage of training and technical assistance opportunities, getting involved with the legislature, and maintaining momentum. The idea is to keep people informed even if they are not involved.

In "Providing Strategic Direction Through Community Council Justice Boards," Amanda Hayes (2001) describes a collaborative criminal justice planning process brought on by the establishment of community criminal justice boards throughout Virginia. Boards involving officials from the police, courts, and corrections met regularly to review criminal justice issues. The Williamsburg area board, composed of five agencies from six different localities, reviewed pretrial programs, conducted local agency needs assessments, monitored and evaluated any implemented programs, developed and amended criminal justice plans, reviewed grants, and facilitated local responses to changing criminal justice needs. Programs under review included those addressing drug addiction, at-risk youth, domestic violence, and victim assistance.

Operation Neighborhood Shield (Pender-Roberts and Domurad 2001) combines the services of probation and the New York City police. In an effort to restructure adult probation, the focus shifted from highlighting the number of contacts to a program emphasizing risk, need, and probationer responsivity. Cognitive-behavioral groups and automated reporting kiosks for thousands of low-level risk offenders were developed. The probation department, moreover, began to attend to criminogenic environmental factors known to foster antisocial activities. The idea was to develop a strong crime prevention and reduction program that emphasized the balanced restorative justice approach based on what was learned from the concept of broken-windows probation.

In 1999, New York City (Pender-Roberts and Domurad 2001) established a community-based response team (CBRT) located in a high crime neighborhood of Brooklyn. Working as a team, the probation officers and police officers contacted the probationers at their homes, conducted compliance checks, talked to and worked with families, met with treatment providers, obtained and acted on warrants, and served as the eyes and ears of the case management probation officers. Case management officers frequently traveled to the CBRT site to meet with families and probationers, to discuss case management, problem solving, and decision making.

In addition, members of the CBRT team also conducted general police operations, especially when visiting a housing authority building where vertical patrols were used to apprehend law violators. The CBRT team also participated in meetings to discuss crime trends and map out other policing functions. The success of this program was indicated by the willingness of the public to seek out the police to share strategic information about criminal activities in the building. Eventually, community activists took a more active role in the CBRT. Community asset maps were drawn up to help the participants understand the resources available to them in their local communities. More importantly, their participation was facilitated with the promulgation of two principles: (1) there was no issue presented to the team that was outside of its purview, and (2) the bureaucratic process delaying any response to a citizen complaint had to be curtailed. Constant collaboration and communication was the key to the project's success.

Another program is the Parole Enhanced Policing Program (Moran and Guglielmi 2001). They maintain that a collaboration effort is necessary to correct the jurisdictional disconnection that often exists between loosely coupled agencies such as the community, the police, and the parole agencies. This particular program attempted to bond community-based policing and parole supervision through an extensive system of communication. Effective communication was considered essential so that parole could understand the goal of the police to put offenders behind bars and the police could understand the goal of parole to keep the offender in the community. It was common for both sides to deal with repeat offenders. The community policing units share their knowledge with parole regarding the community, its leaders, and their concerns. The result was the development of a program that increased interagency contacts. Police accompanied parole on home visits, parole rode with police patrols in known areas of drug or gang activity, parole became involved in community meetings, the police maintained information on each parolee, parole officers attended certain police officer staff meetings, parole used some police facilities, parole participated in certain police operations, and the police were notified of any parole operation in their jurisdiction. Joint fugitive task forces were developed and joint sex offender teams formed.

Further evidence of this collaboration is found in Storm's (2001) report of a sex offender program that combines the efforts of probation and parole, the district attorney, public defender, center for community solutions, relationship training institute, county sheriff and police, and the local association of governments. Central to this process was the recognition of the presence of competing interests in addressing the problem of sex offender management.

Fitzgerald (2001) reports on a fatherhood program involving a partnership between the district court, probation, and the Asuza Christian community. The purpose of the program is to teach young fathers on probation the importance of involvement with their own children. The program teaches the participants the importance of giving affection, being gentle, providing financial support, displaying respect to the mother, and setting a good example. Each participant is required to address these areas as they are put into effect. Frequently attention is given to the problems of parenting.

Frank (2001) reports on a collaborative effort addressing domestic violence in Prince William County, Virginia. The county developed a joint program involving the police, the courts, community corrections, a rape crisis center, the domestic violence center, social services, child protection agencies, the victim/witness unit, and the office of the commonwealth attorney. The working group was established to identify and address gaps in domestic violence services at all levels. Particular achievements include ensuring that protective orders are entered into a statewide computer system, offender compliance is monitored, effective information is given to the public, protective orders are included in probation officer files, and repeat offenders are targeted.

Moran (2001) describes a Hennepin County, Minnesota, partnership program involving a probation officer, social worker, and family worker in a coordinated effort to address female substance abuse in the Rebound program. The team coordinated the probation order, the child protection case plan (if any), and the woman's own goals for herself and her family. Each woman is visited in her home and meets with the team once a month to review goals and assess progress. The client is also required to attend parenting classes, a women's support group, and a treatment program. Careful attention is provided by the child protection agency. Successful women maintain sobriety, gain skills in parenting and basic living, and learn to access resources, successfully completing probation and gaining the return of their children.

Central to all of these partnerships programs is the importance of communication and team building. Partnerships are a primary concern but it is also necessary to carefully allocate resources so that more is done with existing monies and personnel.

Rationally Allocated Resources

Partnerships must be guided by a commitment to thoughtful distribution of staff and resources where they are needed most. Probation must demonstrate how its actions contribute to public safety by focusing on offenders who are most at risk to violate their conditions of probation and on those whose offenses or affiliations pose a safety risk (e.g., sex offenders, gang members, drug dealers, and those with histories of violence). This approach could benefit greatly from a modernized management information system, because it requires comprehensive presentence reports, juvenile records, psychological evaluations, and risk-and-need assessments. Effective placement decisions require a variety of assessment instruments for special offenders to maintain the proper match for programming. One such program is found in Dallas County, Texas. There, a Comprehensive Assessment and Treatment Services program was implemented to address the gap in substance abuse and mental health treatment for probationers. Early assessment and treatment are used to increase the successful completion of the program. Those who cannot afford services receive county assistance. Of those who were screened, 63 percent were referred for drug treatment and another 9 percent were referred for mental health (Olsen et al. 1999, 2–10). Early treatment reduces overall cost.

Place-based supervision, or supervision where the offender lives and work, recognizes that the rate of crime actually reflects the aggregation of many different crime problems that are scattered about in hundreds of neighborhoods, and are located within jurisdictions that may display sharply different characteristics. The threats offenders pose to public safety are by definition local in nature, disproportionately affecting some neighborhoods, bedrooms, street corners, and public buildings and parks, far more so than others (Dickey and Smith 1998). Place-based supervision is one method of rationally allocating resources to address this issue.

Place-Based Supervision

Place-based supervision offers an excellent chance for partnerships with law enforcement to jointly supervise the offender in the community (Clear and Corbett 1999). Joint supervision, working with neighborhood groups, sharing data, and cooperating in other ways achieves public safety. In Spokane, Washington, and Hillsboro, Missouri, program departments have developed important partnerships with their police departments and have strategically placed probation officers so as to achieve greater operational efficiency (MIPR 1999). In this model, an officer is responsible for a particular district and the offenders who reside there. New cases are assigned as they are identified as being in that neighborhood. A recurring problem is the maldistribution of cases because an officer may work an area that has an outbreak of offenses and will have a caseload that is much higher than comparable neighborhoods. Place-based supervision, nonetheless, counters passivity in case management, because the officer must be responsive to local crime problems and community concerns. Placement in the community of staff and officer is essential. Place-based supervision requires that resources be allocated with a sustained focus on managing risk of harm posed by probationers at those times and places where community and victim vulnerabilities are greatest. A good example is Nashville, Tennessee, which has its operation in, and placed many officers in, housing projects, community centers, schools, and mental health centers. Officers work in self-directed work teams (MIPR 1999, 2–12).

Place-based supervision is also beneficial due to its openness. The public can appreciate what is being accomplished. Probation must prove itself by employing measures the public understands as punishments. The public understands the importance of recording free time available to offenders; curfew requirements; the occurrence of electronically monitored house arrests; the intensity of reporting requirements; rates of collection of fines, penalties, and supervision fees; compliance with employer notification requirements; compliance with sex offender notification laws; and mandated public works projects, to name just a few (MIPR 1999, 3–5). These requirements address the old adage that an idle mind is the devil's workshop.

Performance-Based Initiatives

For partnerships to work and to know if resources are being rationally allocated, it is necessary to understand what is working or not. Achieving public safety within the community justice framework is enhanced significantly through effective programming. For the last several years, the probation system has had financial problems, and with it, has come a greater need for accountability.

Achieving public safety under these conditions means reducing the risk of harm by connecting the offender to environments that have prosocial supports and structures (MIPR 1999, 2–20). To find such environments there is a need for information-based decision making. Information-based decision making also requires comprehensive presentence reports, juvenile records, psychological evaluations, and risk-and-need assessments. Sound assessment at the front end is needed to make placement decisions and uses a variety of assessment instruments for special offenders so as to maintain the proper match for programming. Good evaluation models call for clearly defined program outcomes, but equally important, they call for planning and implementation strategies associated with the administration of the program. There is a need to pay close attention to program design, implementation, and evaluation (MIPR 1999, 2–20).

As discussed earlier, using meta-analytic techniques of controlled evaluations of community probation studies has shown substantial reductions in recidivism. Probation has been proven to offer the greatest reductions associated with any community-based programs. The best programs reduced offender recidivism rates beyond the mean an average of 30 percent below traditional programs (Andrews and Bonta 1998). Probation administrators must be attentive to the level of support given programmatic initiatives adopted by their agency. This calls for assessing staff attitudes toward the tools used for offender assessment, treatment, and program goals and outcomes. It also means assessing officer attitudes toward human dignity. To what extent is the offender to be treated with respect and why? How strongly does the officer hold these attitudes? To achieve all of this, it is necessary for probation to routinely collect baseline data, make program and staff assessments, establish time frames for management and implementation of action plans, provide oversight to prevent program drift, and guard against informal staff efforts to change the original goals and program design. These are no small accomplishments.

Performance Measures

Performance measures for crime prevention should include programs that involve offenders and nonoffenders alike. The inclusion of nonoffenders is essential to understanding the prevention of crime. Excluding nonoffenders means the program is essentially a treatment strategy for offenders and does little to aid those who have yet found themselves involved with the law. Performance-based measures could include the number of referrals and completions of parenting programs, literacy programs attended, participation in civic and neighborhood watch meetings, community redevelopment programs, reparative community service programs, mentoring programs, partnerships with law enforcement, probation staff involvement with economic redevelopment programs, social services, public health initiatives, probation officer cross-training with other professionals, and linkages with the faith community (MIPR 1999, 3–8).

Accountability

Holding probation accountable is crucial to public safety. To be effective, performance-based initiatives require accountability (Rhine and Hinzman 2000). As a long-term goal, accountability is needed for designing supervision strategies and programs that target the reduction of recidivism (Olsen et al. 1999, 3–4). If recidivism is reduced, performance measures should be employed. The list of performance measures relative to recidivism has multiple factors. According to the Manhattan Institute for Policy Research (Olsen et al. 1999) attention should be given to the rates of technical probation and parole violations; absconder rates; the proportion of positive to negative test results; the amount of time to an offender's new arrest(s); the nature of the new charges; the quantity and quality of individual risk-and-need assessments; the relevance of offender case management plans to risk-and-need assessments; and offender participation and completion of appropriate treatment programs. More importantly, however, there must be an effort to go beyond these activities, to measure outcomes that reflect the public's concerns in the short and long term. Performance-based initiatives call for a thorough market analysis on the steps taken to reduce crime by incorporating continual community feedback. It calls for not only an analysis of program outcomes but also an analysis of the program's impact on the community. Consideration should be given to the types of programs that reduce the fear of crime, enhance security, aid in referrals to other service providers, establish businesses, and build or revitalize homes. The central idea is to generate value for the public (Olsen et al. 1999, 3–7). Probation must demonstrate how its actions address the public's need to live free of risk or harm in their neighborhoods, at work, at play, and as they travel about (Rhine and Paparozzi 1999).

To satisfy the public's concerns for achieving a measure of punishment, probation must assess the free time available to the offender, curfew requirements, electronically monitored house arrests, intensity of reporting requirements, rates of collection of fines, restitution, penalties, supervision fees, compliance with employer notification requirements, compliance with sex offender notification laws, and mandated public works projects. All of these activities are designed to structure time so that there is less available for antisocial activities and criminal associations (reduce time and reduce criminal contacts) (Olsen et al. 1999, 3–5).

Leadership

Probation executive leadership has changed a great deal in the past years. A leadership void is due to several factors (Seiter 1999). The presence of leadership is harder to identify today than in the past. This is because the process of leading organizations and agencies is more long-term and less situational. Also, as many leaders of the public sector have found, their personal character is often challenged, and their flaws or failings are used to undermine their good faith efforts to produce meaningful change. Finally, given the close scrutiny correctional leaders experience from legislators and the public alike, those who attempt to go too far too quickly in terms of innovation run the risk of becoming controversial, if not vulnerable, to removal from their position (Olsen et al. 1999, 2–22).

Today leadership is more diffuse than in years past—less command- and control-centered. Public managers must be explorers committed to discovering, defining, and marshalling resources to produce public value. This commitment goes well beyond figuring out how to accomplish the various purposes mandated for the agency. It requires that the leadership discover and define, with the help of the workforce as a whole, what the public wants. Leaders must be innovators who seek to change what the organization does, thereby increasing operational efficiencies by responding to new public and political needs and redefining the mission or redirecting resources, but ultimately conducting the agency in such a way as to produce a clear public value. Public value embraces accountability by connecting clearly articulated organizational goals to the values of those who oversee the operation, thus committing the agency to achieve objectives responsive to these goals. As probation embraces public inspection, its actions become more transparent, but it also garners greater public support (Olsen et al. 1999, 2:22–23).

Community justice not only requires managers to develop partnerships and to think outside of the box, but to be sensitive to the intricacies of community organization and development. It is likely that some department heads will look at community justice as a real opportunity to do something they have desired to do for some time. Initiating true innovation is not the kind of role some leaders are suited for by personality or experience. To some of them, any effort to change may be just another fad that has the attention of the political leadership for the time being. They ask themselves: Why change anything? This, too, will pass.

Leadership is the most important element in reengineering probation toward a system with clear values that emphasize public safety, rationally allocated resources, meaningful supervision, quick responses to violations, inclusiveness, and accountability. Beto, Corbett, and DiIulio (2000) point out that leadership comes from individuals who care about probation and are not satisfied with the status quo. Leaders possess the courage to acknowledge that all is not well and have the vision and dedication to do something about it. Much of the leadership talent in the field remains unchallenged, untapped, and misdirected. If probation is to assume its rightful place in the criminal justice system, then it is incumbent on practitioners to step up to the task of leadership (Beto et al. 2000).

■ Conclusion

Crime prevention, regulatory probation, offender supervision, community policing, and restorative justice share much in common. Each strategy attempts to regain control of the community, endeavors to attend to the needs of the public, and seeks input from the public on the utilization of resources. Restorative justice is premised in part on restoring the community. This is most evident in reflecting on what harms have come to the community and how the community is rebuilding. Harm comes in the form of fear, destruction, apathy, and alienation, as well as a substantial loss of public safety. Public safety and restorative justice will each achieve their goals if they can be merged into a common set of practices. Of central importance is that restorative justice and community corrections must enlarge their operational capacity. Penal laws will need to change. Probation will have to redeploy personnel and resources and establish collaborative relationships with other agencies. Agencies will have to do more than simply provide routine casework. Probation will have to develop detailed knowledge of problems in the neighborhoods they serve. Incremental investment in current strategies will not work. Radical restructuring will be needed to address public safety concerns.

Central to this change will be the utilization of management information systems capable of digesting all of the information presentence reports and case management records to identify ongoing community problems and trends in routine activities. There is little reason for probation to have access to huge data files and not fully utilize this information in a systematic format. Annual reports should be highly detailed and carefully scrutinized rather than an account of compliance and daily reporting activities. One limitation to this will be found in partnerships where some information is not available except in an aggregate form. As a function of the partnerships established with probation, it is possible to share data so that different social agencies working with the same population can compare records to better serve their clients and learn to anticipate problems before they become major difficulties. Ultimately, prevention means probation will become a political force as it has never been in the past.

Community corrections views normalizing offenders as a process whereby one tries to render offenders harmless by securing their adherence to community norms. If public safety were seriously pursued as the strategic objective, community corrections would be trying to normalize places where known offenders are found. If community corrections were fully to embrace restorative principles, it would take upon itself the much larger task of normalizing communities. It is difficult, if not impossible, for a single agency to be effective in pursuing all three strategic ideas, any one of which would tend to consume its entire operational capacity.

REFERENCES

American Probation and Parole Association (APPA). 2001. Vision statement. www.appa-net.org.

American Probation and Parole Association (APPA). 2000. Position statement on community justice. *Perspectives* (Spring) 24 pp. 18–20.

Andrews, D. A., and J. Bonta. 1998. *The psychology of criminal conduct.* Cincinnati, OH: Anderson.

Barajas, E. 1998. Community justice: An emerging concept and practice. In K. Dunlap, ed., *Community justice: Concept and strategies.* Lexington, KY: American Probation and Parole Assocation, Council on State Governments.

Beto, D. R., R. P. Corbett, and J. J. DiIulio. 2000. Getting serious about probation and crime problems. *Corrections Management Quarterly* 4: 1–8.

Burrell, W. D. 1999. Facing up to the critical task of rehabilitating probation's public image. *Community Corrections Report* May/June: 49–60.

Camp, C. G., and G. M. Camp. 1998. *The corrections yearbook.* Middletown, CT: Criminal Justice Institute.

Carey, M. 1999. Building hope through community justice. *Perspectives* 23(2): 32–37.

Clarke, R. V. 1995. Situational crime prevention. In M. Tonry and D. Farrington, eds., *Building a safer society: Strategic approaches to crime prevention.* Chicago: University of Chicago Press.

Clear, T. R. 1999. Leading from and leading toward. *Corrections Management Quarterly* 3(1): 14–18.

Clear, T. R., and R. P. Corbett. 1999. Community corrections of place. *Perspectives* 23(1): 24–31.

Clear, T. R., and D. R. Karp. 1998. Community justice: An essay. *Corrections Management Quarterly* 2(3): 49–60.

Crime Prevention Coalition of America. Available online at http://www.cipleanton.ca.us/police.

Dickey, W. J., and M. E. Smith. 1998. *Rethinking probation: Community supervision, community safety.* Washington, DC: U.S. Department of Justice.

Dishion, T. J. 1990. The peer context of troublesome behavior in children and adolescents. In P. Leone, ed., *Understanding troubled and troublesome youth.* Beverly Hills, CA: Sage Publications.

Doble, J. 1999. *Restorative justice and community-based reparative boards: The view of the people of Vermont.* Englewood Cliffs, NJ: Doble Research Associates.

Federal Bureau of Investigation. 2003. Crimes Cleared. *Uniform Crime Reports.* Available online at http://www.fbi.gov/ucr/.

Fitzgerald, B. 2001. Fatherhood program forges links between probation and faith community. In *Topics in corrections, annual issue 2001, collaboration: An essential strategy.* Longmont, CO: National Institute of Corrections.

Frank, C. 2001. Prince William working group talks domestic violence prevention. In *Topics in corrections, annual issue 2001, collaboration: An essential strategy.* Longmont, CO: National Institute of Corrections.

Glaze, L., and S. Pella. 2004. *Probation and parole in the United States, 2003.* Washington, DC: United States Department of Justice, Bureau of Justice Statistics.

Goffman, E. 1967. *Interaction ritual.* Garden City, NY: Anchor.

Goldstein, H. 1990. *Problem-oriented policing.* New York: McGraw-Hill.

Greenberg, S., W. Rohe, and J. Williams. 1985. *Informal citizen action and crime prevention at the neighborhood level.* Washington, DC: U.S. Department of Justice, National Institute of Justice.

Hawkins, J., M. Arthur, and R. Catalano, 1995. Preventing substance abuse. In M. Tonry and D. Farrington, eds., *Building a safer society: Strategic approaches to crime prevention.* Chicago: University of Chicago Press, pp. 343–428.

Hayes, A. 2001. Providing strategic direction through community criminal justice boards. In *Topics in corrections, annual issue 2001, collaboration: An essential strategy.* Longmont, CO: National Institute of Corrections.

Heise, L., J. Pintanguy, and A. Germain. 1994. *Violence against women: The hidden health burden.* Washington, DC: World Bank.

International Centre for the Prevention of Crime. 1999. *Crime prevention digest II.* Montreal, Canada: International Centre for the Prevention of Crime.

Karp, D. 2002. The offender/community encounter: Stakeholder involvement in the Vermont community reparative boards. In D. Karp and T. Clear, eds., *What is community justice? Case studies of restorative justice and community supervision.* Thousand Oaks, CA: Sage Publications.

Karp, D., and T. Clear, eds., 2002. *What is community justice? Case studies of restorative justice and community supervision.* Thousand Oaks, CA: Sage Publications.

Kelling, G., and J. Wilson. 1982. Broken windows: The police and neighborhood safety. *Atlantic Monthly.* 3: 29–38.

Kuehl, J. 2001. Putting the community back into corrections: A partnership in accountability. In *Topics in corrections, annual issue 2001, collaboration: An essential strategy.* Longmont, CO: National Institute of Corrections.

LaFree, G. 1998. *Losing legitimacy: Street crime and the decline of social institutions in America.* Boulder, CO: Westview Press.

Langan, P., and M. Cunniff. 1992. *Recidivism of felons on probation, 1986–1989.* Washington, DC: Bureau of Justice Statistics.

Loeber, R., and D. P. Farrington. 1998. *Serious and violent crime offenders.* Thousand Oaks, CA: Sage Publications.

Manhattan Institute for Policy Research (MIPR). 1999. *Broken windows probation: The next step in fighting crime.* Available online at http://www.manhattan-institute.org.

Moran, M. 2001. Partnership helps mothers with substance abuse problems rebound. In *Topics in corrections, annual issue 2001, collaboration: An essential strategy.* Longmont, CO: National Institute of Corrections.

Moran, R., and A. Guglielmi. 2001. Parole enhanced policing program has statewide support. In *Topics in corrections, annual issue 2001, collaboration: An essential strategy.* Longmont, CO: National Institute of Corrections.

National Center for Education Statistics. *Expenditure per pupil and average teacher salary and pupil/teacher ratio, 2000.* Available online at http://www.ed.gov/nationsreportcard.

Nessman, R. 1997. Probation caseloads driving agents to "triage" system. *Pittsburgh Post-Gazette,* March 23, 1997.

Olsen, H., J. DiIulio, W. Bratton, M. Paparozzi, and R. Corbett. 1999. *Transforming probation through leadership: The "broken windows" model.* Manhattan Institute for Policy Research. Available online at http://www.manhattan-institute.org.

Pender-Roberts, C., and F. Dumurad. 2001. Operation Neighborhood Shield creates community trust and reduces crime. In *Topics in corrections, annual issue 2001, collaboration: An essential strategy.* Longmont, CO: National Institute of Corrections.

Petersilia, J. 1997. Probation in the United States. In M. Tonry, ed., *Crime and justice: A review of research.* Chicago: University of Chicago Press.

Rhine, E. E., and G. R. Hinzman. 2000. Probation and parole: The value of reinvesting in community expertise. *Corrections Management Quarterly* 2: 61–67.

Rhine, E. E., and M. Paparozzi. 1999. Reinventing probation and parole: A matter of consequence. *Corrections Management Quarterly* 3(2): 47–52.

Rosenbaum, D. 1988. Community crime prevention: A review and synthesis of the literature. *Justice Quarterly,* 5(3): 324.

Seiter, R. P. 1999. The leadership and empowerment triangle. *Corrections Management Quarterly* 3: iv–v.

Shaw, C., and McKay, H. 1969. *Juvenile delinquency and urban areas.* Rev. ed. Chicago: University of Chicago Press.

Shaw, M. 2001. *The role of local government in community safety.* Washington, DC: U.S. Department of Justice, Bureau of Justice Assistance.

Sherman, L. W., D. P. Farrington, B. C. Welsh, and D. L. MacKenzie (Eds.). 2003. *Evidence based crime prevention: Markets and meaning.* New York: Routledge.

Sherman, L. W., D. Gottfredson, D. MacKenzie, J. Eck, P. Reuter, and S. Bushway. 1997. *What works: What doesn't work, what's promising.* Washington, DC: National Institute of Justice.

Simon, J. 1998. Between prison and a hard place: Public confidence in community supervision and the future of the prison crisis. *Corrections Management Quarterly* 2(3): 1–11.

Smith, M. 2001. Alternatives to incarceration: What future for "public safety" and "restorative justice" in community corrections? In *Research in brief.* Washington, DC: National Institute of Justice.

Smith, M. E., and W. J. Dickey. 1998. What if corrections were serious about public safety? *Corrections Management Quarterly* 2: 12–30.

Storm, S. 2001. San Diego County collaborative team develops a plan for managing sex offenders. In *Topics in corrections, annual issue 2001, collaboration: An essential strategy.* Longmont, CO: National Institute of Corrections.

Tonry, M., and D. Farrington. 1995. Strategic approaches to crime prevention. Preventing substance abuse. In M. Tonry and D. Farrington, eds., *Building a safer society: Strategic approaches to crime prevention.* Chicago: University of Chicago Press, pp. 1–20.

Valentine, K. 2001. How to make partnerships work: Suggestions from the field. In *Topics in corrections, annual issue 2001, collaboration: An essential strategy.* Longmont, CO: National Institute of Corrections.

Wilson, J. and G. Kelling. 1982. Broken windows: The police and neighborhood Safety. *Atlantic Monthly* 3: 29–38.

Woodward. B. 2001. Collaboration: What it takes. *Topics in corrections, annual issue 2001 collaboration: An essential strategy.* Longmont, CO: National Institute of Corrections.

Yin, R. K. 1986. Synthesis of eleven evaluations. In D. Rosenbaum and M. Cahn eds., *Community crime prevention: Does it work?* Beverly Hills: Sage Publications, chapter 11.

KEY POINTS

1. Programs that have strictly enforced the conditions of supervision and enjoy a supportive relationship with the courts tend to have fewer problems with offender compliance.

2. Public safety should come first, supervision of the offender should take place in the community, resources should be rationally allocated, violations of probation condition should be enforced quickly and strongly, and partnerships should be established and supported by effective leadership.

3. By forming partnerships with law enforcement, the courts, human services, community and neighborhood groups, the faith communities, and local stakeholders, probation can significantly enhance its public safety mission.

4. It is suggested that a new approach is required using probation and parole as public safety mechanisms that do not emphasize going after offending probationers but instead emphasize order in the community or offender discipline through close supervision, thereby reducing the offender's propensity for crime.

5. Prevention offers the prospect of heading off many of the criminal justice costs while at the same time avoiding other costs of crime.

6. The prevention strategy being proposed emphasizes the importance of probation officers engaging members of the community in their own protection.

7. Situational crime prevention is based on the premise that much crime is contextual and opportunistic.

8. Poor parental monitoring appears to predict conduct disorders across childhood, while association with drug using peers is predictive of drug use only in adolescence.

9. Community crime prevention may be premised on the idea that changing the community may change the behavior of the people who live there and it has some similarities to problem-oriented policing.

10. Guardianship shifts the emphasis to identifying unofficial, naturally occurring people who are willing to participate in a normative reaffirmation process designed to re-establish norms, values, and ideals representative of the community.

11. Partnerships must be guided by a commitment to thoughtful distribution of staff and resources where they are needed. Probation must demonstrate how its actions contribute to public safety.

KEY TERMS

community crime prevention is a type of crime prevention premised on the idea that changing the community may change the behavior of the people who live there.

community justice is a strategic method of crime reduction and prevention, which builds or enhances partnerships with communities.

developmental prevention is a highly diverse field in which individuals in health, medicine, psychology, and the like have entered into the discussion. Much of the attention is focused on risk factors that are predictive of antisocial behavior.

guardians maintain a protective relationship to vulnerable targets, but they are also people who can have an intimate or supervisory relationship to potential offenders. Whether the offenders are under correctional supervision or not, they are people who are responsible for places where the guardians and the public may come together. Guardians may be parents, spouses, children, friends, neighbors, employers, local shopkeepers, and security guards.

normative affirmation reaffirms the moral order of the community by getting the offender to see the offense as an abrogation of the community code and an aberration of the offenders so they will not repeat.

partnership is a term that can be used interchangeably with *networking, collaboration,* and *coordination.* Partnership occurs where people have joint interests. People who have common interests will often collaborate in order to exchange information, alter their activities, share resources, and enhance the capacity of another for the mutual benefit of all to achieve a common purpose.

public safety means that offenders living in the neighborhood are accounted for and properly managed. Problems are attended to before they lead to violations.

situational prevention is expressed in the military vernacular of target hardening and is operationalized in the private security industry. Greater use of fire, health, and police licensing powers to inspect various locations could increase the security level of various environments.

REVIEW QUESTIONS

1. What is the "broken-windows" concept of probation?
2. Why are communities central to the concept and practice of crime prevention?
3. Explain how guardianship enhances crime prevention.
4. What are community partnerships? How do they promote the value of human dignity? Give some examples of partnerships.

11 Juvenile Probation

Chapter Objectives

In this chapter you will learn that:

■ Juveniles deserve to be treated with dignity
■ Juveniles can make moral choices and should be held accountable for those choices
■ Juveniles have rights that need protection

parens patriae is the right and responsibility of the state, as a common guardian, to substitute its own control over children for that of the natural parents when the latter appear unable or unwilling to meet their responsibilities or when the child poses a problem for the community.

Over the past three decades, judicial decisions and legislative amendments have transformed the juvenile court from a nominally rehabilitative social welfare agency into a scaled-down criminal court for young people (Feld 1999, 3). The initial juvenile court was conceptualized as an informal welfare system in which judges acted in the best interests of the child under the theory of **_parens patriae_**. The court was to act in the best interests of the child much as a parent would. Today, changes in the court have created a formalized juvenile court in which offenders are held responsible for their offenses.

This chapter is a discussion of the history of juvenile probation. It offers a presentation of the value placed on juveniles today, and an overview of the juvenile justice system, the juvenile in court, juvenile court processing, and juvenile court waivers. Also discussed are special problems including juvenile violence and juvenile drug offenses, juvenile drug courts, runaway adolescents, minorities in the juvenile justice system, and juvenile probation supervision.

■ The Value of Children

The worth placed on children is an important consideration in how they are treated and how society views itself. Thousands of children are abused, neglected, and abandoned by their parents, other responsible adults, and the welfare system that is designed to protect them. Problems with the foster child care system have become well publicized. Many of these children, in order to seek love and safety, run away. The National Incidence Studies of Missing, Abducted, Runaway, and Throwaway Children (NISMART) (Hammer et al. 2002) reported that in 1999, an estimated 1,682,900 youth had a runaway/throwaway episode. A *runaway episode* is one that involves a child who is no more than 14 years old and leaves home without permission for at least 1 night or if the child is 15 years old or older is away from home and chooses not to come home and stays away 2 nights. A *throwaway episode* is one that involves a child who is told to leave home by a parent or other household adult without any consideration of alternative overnight care. The child may even be prevented from returning home even if he or she desires to do so.

This NISMART report noted that 68 percent of the runaway/throwaway children were 15 to 17 years of age. There was an equal proportion of male and female of these members, 57 percent were white, 17 percent were black, 15 percent Hispanic, and 11 percent were other races or mixed race. Of these youth, 37 percent were missing from their caretakers and 21 percent were reported to the authorities for the purpose of locating them. Seventy-one percent of these runaway/throwaway children were considered to be endangered by the use of hard drugs, sexual and physical abuse, or the presence of criminal activity, or were at an extremely young age (13 years or younger).

What is particularly interesting is that the authorities were notified the child was missing in only a little more than two-thirds of the cases. This means that in one out of every three cases of a missing child, no one took the time to notify authorities. What is striking is that many of the episodes were relatively brief and the child stayed close to home. Most of these caretakers did not see the episode as serious enough to warrant formal notification. Some of these parents may be comfortable with their child away from home. A number of parents may be engaging in an expression of tough love; they are trying to teach the child a lesson about complying with the rules of the household. In some instances, reporting the child as missing may increase the chance an investigation is conducted into who is responsible for precipitating the episode. Based on the reported cause of the runaway/throwaway episode, assistance to these youth must extend far beyond simply returning the children to their homes. Returning them, in fact, may only increase rather than decrease their danger. Because many juveniles are considered status offenders, parents may feel that the only solution is to put the child in the hands of the juvenile court.

Feld (1999) adopted the phrase "other people's children" to describe the standing of many current juvenile offenders. Other people's children are considered problems if they are someone else's children but not if they are family members or people who share a common background. Making a distinction between what "my" children deserve and how they should be treated is different than what "your" children deserve and how they should be treated.

The discretionary powers of the juvenile court allow it to respond differently to other people's children. The last three decades have seen increased evidence of this. The recent changes in the juvenile court, such as increased procedural formality, **diversion** of status offenders, waiver of serious offenders

diversion is the process of channeling a referred juvenile from formal juvenile court processing to an alternative form for resolution of the matter and/or a community-based agency for help.

to adult criminal court, and harsher punishments for delinquents constitute a form of criminological triage to distinguish between "our" children and "other people's" children. This strategy, which selectively manipulates the alternative conception of young people as dependent and vulnerable or as autonomous and responsible, removes many middle-class, white, and female noncriminal status offenders from the juvenile justice system (Feld 1999). The middle-class white child is assigned greater worth and dignity than children with other characteristics. The white middle-class juvenile is sent to the private social service system, thereby consigning persistent, violent, and disproportionately minority youth to criminal courts. Here increasingly punitive sanctions are imposed on middle-range offenders who remain within the jurisdiction of the juvenile courts (Feld 1999, 7). "Other people's" children are not the only problem; minorities continue to assume a greater portion of punishment.

Juveniles in Corrections

An Office of Juvenile Justice and Delinquency Prevention National Report Series, *Juveniles in Corrections* (Sickmund 2004), offers some interesting information on juveniles in corrections. She reports that there were more than 7,600 juveniles under 18 serving time in adult jails, and more juveniles in detention in 1999 than in 1991. Thirty-five percent of them are in for person offenses, 9 percent for drug offenses. Minorities comprise 7 of the 10 offenders held. All states report a disproportionate share of minorities in their detention facilities, and for that matter, at various decision points in the criminal justice system. Black youth comprise 15 percent of the U.S. population but they make up 34 percent of the violent juvenile offenders, 26 percent of juvenile arrests, 49 percent of arrests for violent offenses, 31 percent of delinquency cases in court, 40 percent of the delinquency cases involving detention, 37 percent of petitioned cases, 35 percent of adjudicated cases, 36 percent of cases resulting in residential placement, and 52 percent of cases waived to adult court (Sickmund 2004). Racial discrimination is one possible explanation for these findings. Overrepresentation can also be attributed to behavioral and legal factors such as the amount and type of crimes committed. Much of the literature suggests when bias has occurred, it may take place at any stage of the system but it was also noted that racial disparities can accumulate and became more pronounced as the minority youth proceed through the system.

Of particular note is that if the family composition is controlled for, one finds a reduced level of difference. In other words when comparing similar families, one finds reduced levels of difference. Families comprise a key attribute in the class structure. Single-parent households, as noted earlier, have the highest levels of poverty. Often when considering racial disparity, one may be comparing class difference, too. One way to examine this is to consider private residential facilities. One would expect to find that private residential facilities have fewer minority youth because of cost of placement. If a youth from any race has the economic tools to fight legal battles, as with adults, the youth is much less likely to be in the criminal justice system and may be sent to a private facility as part of a plea agreement. According to Sickmund (2004), in 1999, there were 31,599 juveniles in private residential facilities. A private facility is operated by private nonprofit or for-profit corporations or organizations. Workers in the facilities are employees of private corporations or organizations. Private facilities tend to be more numerous than public programs but they also have smaller juvenile populations. Private facilities tend to hold more juveniles who are in residential placement as part of a diversion agreement. Also 65 percent of the status offenders were held in private facilities (Sickmund 2004). On any given day, the 65 percent of the youth in public facilities were minorities while minority youth comprised 55 percent of the youth in private facilities (Sickmund 2004). In all states, minorities were disproportionately represented in residential placements.

Private residential facilities are in high demand today, especially as the problems experienced by male and female youth are more clearly identified. What must be noted is that private facilities may offer a host of programs not available to state-operated programs but they can be very expensive. Some programs run as high as $100,000 per resident per year. Payment for such programs is provided by state, county, and local government funds and by insurance programs. The indigent offender (or minority offender) is unlikely to have the type of health insurance necessary to cover a detailed diagnosis and treatment plan that calls for private residential placement.

■ History

To understand juvenile probation, one needs to understand both the history of juvenile probation and the juvenile court. The history of the juvenile court must be understood as an institution designed to provide distinct treatment for the youth between the approximate ages of 10 and 18 years. The movement toward the juvenile court, and thus juvenile probation, was not an inevitable outcome of the Enlightenment. There was a period of time when juveniles were considered young adults and exposed to all of the harsh realities of adult life at a very early age. Today, however, some might say that some youth have a period of extended adolescence lasting until they are sometimes in their late 20s.

Childhood has gone through various changes over the last millennium. Prior to the Renaissance, children in Western societies were viewed as miniature adults (Aries 1962). Boys and girls were needed to fill adult labor roles as soon as possible due to labor shortages in the peasant economy. Getting a child through to adulthood was an important consideration. Reaching adulthood was not a given due to illnesses, famine, and war. Considering a young person as different from an adult are social constructs or cultural artifacts (Berger and Luckman 1967). For centuries following the Renaissance, children were raised in extended families comprised of various relatives, servants, and apprentices. Everyone was treated alike. For the most part, children were not separated into distinctive age groups, setting them off from one another and adults. For some of these children, however, their early years were a nightmare in that they were denied any worth except as an additional labor source. Some were treated worse. Centuries ago, some children found their early years to be traumatic, especially as they were killed, abandoned, beaten, terrorized, and sexually abused (deMaus 1974, 1). If the child survived these hardships, the child was integrated at an early age into an adult group where the child had a role in work, recreation, and community life.

During the colonial period, huge labor shortages increased the value of children as workers. Children were quickly integrated into various social, economic, religious, and educational institutions. Apprenticeships performed the important social control function of training and educating younger workers, adding to the skilled workforce and functioning as a system of social welfare.

By the early 19th century, significant legal, social, and economic changes affected how children were viewed. On the legal front, there were concerns for family rights.

Parens Patriae

Parens patriae is the right and responsibility of the state, as a common guardian, to substitute its own control over children for that of their natural parents when the latter appear unable or unwilling to meet their responsibilities or when the child poses a problem for the community (Cogan 1970; Curtis 1976; Pisciotta 1982). Native Americans, blacks, and Catholic children subject to *parens patriae* were put in houses of refuge, houses of reformation, and reform schools (Bremmer 1971).

One of the earliest discussions of *parens patriae* is found in the *Ex parte Crouse* (1838). In this case, Mary Ann Crouse, an incorrigible youth, on the request of her mother and over the objections of her father, was committed to the Philadelphia House of Refuge. The Pennsylvania court dismissed the father's petition by noting that the object of the house of refuge was reformation, imbuing its residents with moral and religious principles, furnishing them with the means to earn a living, and separating them from the corrupting influences of improper associates. The court went on to say that when the parents are not up to the task of educating or are considered unworthy of such, their rights are superseded by *parens patriae*. Schlossman (1977, 17) argues that the *Crouse* opinion is another instance of the belief at that time that universal education was considered a panacea, that poor people had few rights, lacked appropriate moral character, were incapable of appropriately raising their children, and any government action was superior. Unlike the middle class, the poor understood that they could no longer feel secure in maintaining custody of their children despite doing everything they could to raise their children. The training and control evident in the apprenticeship system broke down when large numbers of unskilled children began to work in mills and plants (Cochran 1972; Finestone 1976). Traditional family structures were also seriously impacted, because children were required to respond to the authority of the workplace rather than their parents. If things didn't work out in the family, they headed to large cities or to the wide open West. The demand for workers was so high that young people could readily find work. Such conditions led to a decrease in social control and contributed to youth crime, drinking, and drug use (Hawes and Hiner 1985).

■ Immigration and Juveniles

Immigration changed cities and social arrangements in the 19th century. Early on, immigrants coming into this country were principally comprised of Anglo-Protestants or Irish Catholics but after the Civil War, a greater number of immigrants came from other parts of Europe and Asia. Many of them flocked together to create communities of similar peoples. To some Americans already here, these foreigners were a dangerous group. Their presence was often associated with poverty and crime because they were required to live in the sections of cities where these social problems were evident before their arrival. As the industrial revolution made farming less labor-intensive, people migrated to the cities in even larger numbers. The shift to an industrial economy meant that work and home was no longer one unit.

By the 19th century, children in middle-class families with sufficient resources were now understood as vulnerable, innocent, and dependent beings whose parents protected them from the harsh realities of life (Hawes and Hiner 1985; Kett 1977; Platt 1977). Setting up barriers to outside family influences became an important means of protecting the children. Women were given the main responsibility for maintaining order in the household and seeing to it that the children were protected well beyond the age when they would otherwise go to work (Lasch 1977). As public health care improved and as greater amounts of leisure time came available, middle-class parents could devote more time and energies to raising their children according to accepted moral principles and class standards (Kett 1977, 116). For the middle-class family with the time and resources, these practices suited them fine, but for the poor, minority, and immigrant family, white middle-class values proved to be a burden and oppressive. Traditional old-country family practices were no longer sufficient to raise a child.

■ A Shift in a Look at Juveniles

As the Progressive era played itself out from 1890 to 1920, a major shift in analysis of the juvenile's problems occurred. Changes in the concept of childhood and how children grow and develop, and alterations in social control philosophies brought about by the advent of college programs and other writings during the 19th century led progressive reformers to think of alternatives to the adult courts. Progressive reforms were directed toward political reform and administrative efficiency, but more crucially, toward the family including child development, inadequate and broken families, dependent and neglected children, poverty and welfare, education, work, crime, delinquency, recreation, and play. These reforms were motivated by racial intolerance, desires to reassert control of the social and economic environment, and the need for administrative efficiency (Feld 1999, 34). The impetus for more acceptable motives, in a large part, was the advent of various degree programs that included sociology, political philosophy, and education then being introduced at various colleges and the new land grant universities.

During this era, children were thought to be reacting to a lack of moral direction that could be corrected through proper reform. By the 1890s, it was believed that children from the lower middle and lower classes (the classes lacking effective political representation) needed additional protection to adequately deal with the future. These needs could be provided only by people outside of the family. Ideal families offered a "household refuge" from the troubles of the outside world (Feld 1999). The middle-class woman's responsibility was to tend to the home, care for a husband, and serve as the moral guardian of the home. In doing so, she was to exhibit modesty, obedience, and dependence, a message that was pounded home from the church pulpit. Without the power to vote, most women could do little to deflect these requirements placed on them. They had few more rights than the children. The white middle-class cult of domesticity was, of course, very distinct from the lives of the struggling working- and lower-class women who by necessity had to enter the labor force.

Because middle-class women were considered capable of managing their own domestic lives and fighting off the evils of modernity, with their free time, they could direct their efforts toward lower-class children. The child-saving movement broadened the women's domestic responsibilities to include "other people's children" in the roles of caretakers and carriers of moral virtues (Feld 1999, 18). These efforts were not wholly accepted because many recipients of these services were actually caught up in matters of cultural conflict rather than truly aberrant behavior.

■ The Juvenile Court

The juvenile court also came into existence because of the deficiencies of the adult court. Prior to the juvenile court, the adolescent brought before court was considered an adult offender who possibly could be excused from the crime because he or she lacked sufficient means or criminal intent (Feld 1999). As the child became older (7 to 14 years old), the prosecutor could contest the claim of diminished responsibility and, if successful, the child would still be tried as an adult (Feld 1999). Children over 14 were tried as adults (McCarthy 2000). It was left to the judge and jury to dismiss the charges or to nullify the verdict in order to save the child from an overly severe punishment (Fox 1970; Platt 1977). If convicted in adult court, the child often received a sentence that seemed excessively harsh. Juveniles with real needs and problems were left to fend for themselves; nothing was done for them because they were no longer under the jurisdiction of the court.

In 1899, the Illinois state legislature established a special court in Cook County (Chicago) that had broad powers and informal procedures designed to promote the welfare of dependent, neglected, or delinquent children. The idea was to avoid the stigma of the criminal court and to offer aid, encouragement, and guidance to children in need (Trattner 1999). The court managed to cobble together different features of other courts and present them as a new institution: the juvenile court (Griffin and Torbet 2002, 7). Among its distinctive features was the reliance on probation and the belief that the place for the child was not an institution but the child's own home (Mack 1907).

The juvenile court of 1899 was the result of the efforts of many different organizations, agencies, and persons interested in juvenile offenders, women's rights, child labor laws, mandatory education, alcohol consumption, and social welfare laws. The juvenile court was looked on as a welfare agency to treat children rather than a criminal court to punish them. Thus, the idea of the juvenile court was supported by schools of thought that understood criminal behavior to be the result of antecedent deterministic conditions; developmental psychology promoting the notion of childhood dependence and malleability; utilitarian notions of punishment that viewed the punishment in terms of what can be accomplished in the future; and a reliance on informality over due process considerations to get around the problem of finding the child innocent but bereft of any reason to help the child. Thus, sociology, psychology, and law merge to bring the juvenile court into existence.

A Beginning

From the start, the juvenile court tended to focus its attention on obstreperous children charged with truancy, sexual promiscuity, and incorrigibility (Sutton 1988). Children were eventually found guilty of either living a particular lifestyle or committing a criminal act. By allowing deviant but noncriminal behavior to trigger the intervention, the juvenile court was sending a message to the outside community that it intended to intervene in the lives of lower-class families as never before. Legal rectitude was added to a dose of moral persuasion. What was apparent was the continued use of the court to uphold conservative middle-class values. The themes of the juvenile court movement further reflected this conservative and middle-class bias. Delinquents needed firm control, restraints, and isolation from the evils of the community, and if that could not be achieved in the community, the youth could be sent to a reformatory or be removed from the family. In effect, only lower-class families were so evaluated as to their competence whereas middle-class families were exempt from investigation and recrimination (Feld 1999).

One of the unique features of the new juvenile court was the attention given to future problems of female morals as presented by prostitution and white slavery. From the start, girls found themselves before the juvenile court charged with immorality and waywardness (Chesney-Lind 1971; Schlossman and Wallach 1978; Shelden 1981). As a result of such charges, girls were sent to reformatories at a rate higher than boys.

The juvenile court began as essentially a civil court. Moreover, there was no presumption of innocence, to the extent that it was thought the child wouldn't be in court if not for some problem. Moreover, it was thought that too much research identified key antecedent conditions that were beyond the child's control. Child savers believed delinquency was the result of a variety of social, psychological, and biological factors (Chesney-Lind and Shelden 1992). Child savers, especially in Chicago, were middle-class women at the beginning of the 20th century who believed children should be removed from the harmful circumstances of city life, which created too much temptation (Platt 1977). The presentence report, which considered various dimensions of these factors, was to offer a carefully thought out analysis of the facts and a full understanding of the youth's character and lifestyle, thereby revealing an accurate diagnosis and appropriate response to the offenders' problems. Analysis was to be provided by social workers and psychologists. The idea was to address the problem leading to the trouble. As a result, the court proceedings were more like a meeting of concerned citizens than a determination of guilt, much like restorative justice sentencing circles today. Few courts, however, were able to generate the necessary level of professional expertise to fully diagnosis the problem and execute the plan. For not the last time, the rhetoric about the possibilities of the courts' achievements exceeded the realities of these courts (Platt 1977; Rothman 1980; Ryerson 1978; Schlossman 1977; Sutton 1988).

20th Century Juvenile Courts

The first half of the 20th century saw little criticism directed at juvenile probation (Griffin and Torbet 2002, 8). For the most part, the juvenile court operated behind a veil of obscurity; it seemed to suit the purposes for which it was designed and few people had any problems with it. Furthermore, few people really understood how it worked. Judges welcomed it as an alternative to harsh unnecessary punishments and parents felt their children were not lost in a system of unreasonably punitive punishments. The juvenile court was not, as some writers have suggested, a "radical" reform but rather a politically compromised reform that consolidated existing practices (Platt 1977, 135). It was similar to the coalescence of forces that led to the revision of sentencing laws during the 1980s.

The role model of the juvenile court judge was doctor-counselor rather than lawyer (Platt 1977, 142). This "judicial therapist" was expected to establish a one-on-one relationship with "delinquents" in the same way that a country doctor might give his or her time and attention to a patient. The courtroom was arranged like a clinic and the vocabulary of the participants was largely composed of the medical metaphor that required a thorough examination and private family conference (Platt 1977, 143).

The second half of the 20th century saw intense pressure placed upon the juvenile justice system as baby boomers came of age and moved through the system. The treatment techniques used in earlier forms of probation no longer proved effective, because they could no longer keep up with the number of offenders. One of the abiding concerns of the juvenile justice system was a desire to limit the "labeling" of juveniles. It was thought that the more the court responded to juvenile delinquency, the more it stigmatized the youth and actually promoted delinquency. By the 1960s, stigmatization was central to any approach to any national antidelinquency policy (President's Commission 1967).

Additional fuel was heaped on the fire by the Martinson (1974) article in which the now-infamous "nothing works" statement originated. However, the larger study conducted by Martinson and others never made the claim that "nothing works." Nevertheless, the phrase took on a life of its own as a hue and cry heard throughout the field of corrections. The truth of the matter was that Martinson was writing about prison reform and not probation, even though for political purposes, the notion was applied across the board to all kinds of rehabilitation programs. By the 1980s, there was widespread belief that juvenile courts were soft on delinquency and juvenile probation responded to it. Officers who previously hesitated to express punitive recommendations were now speaking openly about what needed to be done. This was necessitated in part by the explosion in use of crack cocaine and the collateral violence associated with the unregulated drug industry. New statutes were passed waiving violent juveniles on to adult criminal courts. These measures were augmented with design and procedural changes that made the juvenile court resemble the adult criminal court (Griffin and Torbet 2002, 9).

Moving Ahead

Today, the argument is made for the need for a balanced approach to juvenile justice. The probation department is now responding to the competing demands for safety, retribution, incapacitation, deterrence, and restitution. At the same time, efforts are increased to protect the community, hold offenders accountable, and develop the competency needed to integrate the offender into the community. The victim rights and the restorative justice movements spurred on much of this effort. No longer were the victim and the community to be excluded from the decision-making process—and no longer is the probation officer only to see the offender once a month in the office (Griffin and Torbet 2002, 9).

Eventually the concept of social equality began influencing probation and the juvenile court. The system was asked to consider its treatment of juveniles in light of changes taking place in the adult system. By the 1970s, substantial reforms had taken place in the adult system. The accused had more rights and greater protections once convicted of an offense. No longer could an offender, for example, be convicted without legal representation.

■ Legal Reform

Juvenile probation officers do not need to be lawyers, but there are times when knowledge of the law is important, especially when either attorneys or judges fail to comprehend various issues. It is also important for probation officers to have some understanding of the facts behind the decisions in major juvenile rights cases.

Juvenile codes give jurisdiction over a delinquent to the court. A *delinquent* is defined as a minor who commits an act that would be considered a crime if committed by an adult. There are also states requiring the juvenile to be in need of treatment, supervision, or rehabilitation. The youngest for original juvenile court jurisdiction in delinquency matters is age 6 in North Carolina; 7 in Maryland, Massachusetts, and New York; 8 in Arizona; and 10 in Arkansas, Colorado, Kansas, Louisiana, Minnesota, Mississippi, Pennsylvania, South Dakota, Texas, Vermont, and Wisconsin. Other states rely on case law or common law. The upper age limit for juveniles varies from 18 to 24. The oldest age for which the juvenile court may retain jurisdiction for disposition purposes in delinquency matters is age 18 in Alaska, Iowa, Kentucky, Nebraska, Oklahoma, and Tennessee; 19 in Mississippi and North Dakota; 20 in Alabama, Arizona, Arkansas, Connecticut, Delaware, the District of Columbia, Florida, Georgia, Idaho, Illinois, Indiana, Louisiana, Maine, Maryland, Massachusetts, Michigan, Minnesota, Missouri, Nevada, New Hampshire, New Mexico, New York, North Carolina, Ohio, Pennsylvania, Rhode Island, South Carolina, South Dakota, Texas, Utah, Vermont, Virginia, Washington, West Virginia, and Wyoming; 22 in Kansas; and 24 in California, Montana, Oregon, and Wisconsin. In Colorado, Hawaii, and New Jersey, the youth is under the juvenile court's jurisdiction until the full term of the disposition (Sickmund 2003).

State laws also determined the purpose and philosophy of the juvenile code: case processing, arrest and detention, diversion, disposition powers, and confidentiality. The powers and duties of juvenile probation officers are often spelled out in state codes. The juvenile code may give juvenile probation officers the powers to receive and examine charges and complaints of delinquency and make initial decisions regarding whether they should be formally processed. Probation officers also have powers to conduct investigations, file reports, make recommendations regarding dispositions, supervise offenders, make referrals to public and private agencies, and make arrests (Griffin and Torbet 2002, 11).

■ Juvenile Rights

The history of juvenile rights is an examination of the problem of promoting juvenile dignity over time. As the history of childhood indicated, children earlier in history were often considered mere chattel to be exploited as needed. It was not until the 19th century that an awareness of childhood as something special seemed to develop. It was not so much that children were considered to have more worth than previously but a new understanding of developmental psychology led to a new understanding of how children should be treated. It was, however, only since 1945 that an appreciation of the value and worth of all citizens of the world became an issue of relevance to many. Following World War II, positions in support of racism, anti-Semitism, sexism, and the like seemed inherently flawed. As a result of the push to expand the rights of African Americans, one sees a corollary expansion of rights being pursued by women, the disabled, and then juveniles. What is crucial to this understanding is that juveniles should be treated with dignity, as if they were adults. The problem is that juveniles are treated as they are because they have a diminished capacity to understand their rights and to respond rationally to problems, and easily succumb to the pressures inherent in the power differential existing between adult and child. Age, class, or ethnic differences and linguistic or cognitive deficits render young people more vulnerable than adults in formal legal proceedings (Feld 1999, 127).

According to J. R. Lucas (1980), a right has an imperative quality to it in that someone can force another person to recognize a right. Rights are also first personal in that only a person can exercise his or her rights. One can have someone protect his or her rights but that person cannot have someone else exercise his or her rights on his or her behalf. Rights are concerned with everyone all the time. They are not specific to a time or person but affect everyone equally all of the time. Rights expand into interests after sufficient recognition is given to the concern that they must be safeguarded. Over time, these interests will become a part of the everyday vocabulary of justice. A good example of this is the role of the attorney in a juvenile court proceeding. For years, it was thought necessary to have an attorney only if there was a possibility that the offender would be sent to a reformatory. Today, it is axiomatic that one considers the importance of an attorney anytime one appears before a court.

The Courts and Juvenile Rights

In *Kent v. United States* (1966), it was decided that juveniles could be waived to adult court if they were granted adult due process protections. An attorney who has access to the juvenile's records must represent the child. *In re Gault* (1967) is probably the most important juvenile court decision in the last 50 years. The court ruled that a juvenile must receive notice of the charges in writing. The notice must spell out the offense charged and conduct alleged. Sufficient advance notice must be granted prior to the hearing to allow preparation for the hearing. The juvenile must also be notified of the right to counsel, the right to confront the accuser, the right to avoid self-incrimination, and the right to cross-examine witnesses. In both of these cases, significance is given to the role of due process.

The role of the attorney is a reflection on the increased value and worth we have come to recognize in the juvenile. No juvenile, despite the offense, is the sum total of his or her worst deeds. Juveniles now have many due process rights. We are now very concerned that a juvenile's due process rights are protected. The importance of due process is found in recognizing that juveniles are given their due as human beings because they have value and worth and are provided a certain process that is consistent with the value and worth of the person. Juveniles have worth because they have the potential for doing good, they have a lifetime ahead of them, and there are many decent things they can do for others. Finally, juveniles have worth because of their uniqueness as rational creatures that are capable of self-initiating, self-directing, self-assessing, and self-correcting their activities. Juveniles can make important decisions about their lives.

Due process requires not just giving people their due but also necessitates that certain procedures be granted. For the most part, juveniles are denied the right to a jury trial and, in some jurisdictions, hearings are not the formal procedure they should be. Nonetheless, the *Gault* decision and others have made it possible for procedures to be in place that allow the juvenile to be heard. These procedures are designed to ensure that justice is served by giving the juvenile a chance to test the evidence and by protecting the innocent from wrongful conviction.

Various cases play a prominent role in spelling out the rights of the juvenile. They include:

In re Winship (1970): the court ruled that the standard for proof in juvenile proceedings is proof beyond a reasonable doubt.

McKeiver v. Pennsylvania (1971): this decision established that a juvenile had no right to a jury trial.

Breed v. Jones (1975): double jeopardy attaches with the adjudication of juvenile delinquency.

Swisher v. Brady (1978): double jeopardy does not attach to *de novo* hearing (a second, new hearing), an order for a new trial, or supplemental findings by a judge after a trial before a master.

Fare v. Michael C. (1979): the juvenile's request for a probation officer rather than an attorney during questioning does not trigger application of the *Miranda* rule; police are not required to stop questioning a juvenile.

Schall v. Martin (1984): New York state statute permitting the preventive pretrial detention of a juvenile is valid under the due process clause of the 14th amendment.

Thompson v. Oklahoma (1984): Eighth and Fourteenth Amendments prohibit the execution of a person who is under the age of 16 years at the time of the offense.

Stanford v. Kentucky (1989): execution of a person who was 16 or 17 years of age at the time of the offense does not offend the Eighth amendment's prohibition against cruel and unusual punishment.

Victims of juvenile offenses have rights, too. Expansion of probation officer duties has included responsibility for victims' rights. From 1992 through 1997, for example, 32 states enacted laws that extended certain rights to victims of juvenile offenders. Typically, state laws have opened hearings to victims; given notice of the hearing to the victim and given notice of final adjudication, release, or escape; created separate waiting areas; taken victim impact statements; offered explanations of plea agreements; provided compensation for violent crimes; made restitution; allowed victim advocates a chance to speak; and kept the address of victims confidential (Griffin and Torbet 2002, 16).

Much of the concern for juvenile rights, as it plays out for the probation officer, is vis à vis the role of the counselor. Juveniles waive their *Miranda* rights, even though there is ample evidence that they do not possess the competence of an adult to knowingly and intelligently waive these rights. Juveniles have trouble understanding the legal language and the justice process (Smith 1985), and their parents are often no better equipped to understand what has happened. In many cases, it falls on the probation officer's shoulders to explain what has happened in court. It is only then that the juvenile completely understands the consequences of what occurred. However, often a sense of accountability is diminished when juveniles think they have avoided full responsibility for their crime by pleading guilty to a lesser offense, when in fact they are being held accountable for the offense they committed.

Attorneys and Juveniles

Attorneys working in the juvenile justice system are caught in a serious dilemma. Grisso (1983) reported that even if a juvenile has an attorney, many offenders do not expect to receive much help. Problems of confidentiality and offering a vigorous defense are the most pressing issues. The attorney is caught in a conundrum in many cases. First of all, there are barriers getting in the way of effective communication. The lawyer may not clearly understand the juvenile's case and background. There are class, race, and language barriers that interfere with a complete understanding of the case and the offender. Lawyers are also concerned with addressing the problem of community safety and holding the offender accountable. As part of a courtroom workgroup, the attorney works on a team that handles similar cases. Through the accumulation of activities, a routine presumption of guilt is formed that affects the manner in which the case is viewed. This, in turn, affects how the juvenile views the quality of the defense. In a study by Huerter and Saltzman (1992, 354), it was reported that about one-third of the delinquents interviewed had something positive to say about their attorneys. Many of them believed their attorneys had given up, would not explain things fully, would not convey to the judge the juvenile's desires, and were not on the juvenile's side.

Attorneys often are ineffective in their representation of a juvenile offender. Organizational pressure to cooperate, judicial hostility to adversarial litigants, role ambiguity created by the dual role of rehabilitation and punishment, reluctance to help juveniles "beat the case," or internalization of the court's treatment philosophy compromises the adversarial role that counsel plays in court (Bortner 1982; Feld 1989; Stapleton and Teitelbaum 1972). Expert witnesses may unduly sway attorneys who are working with the best interests of the youth in mind. Attorneys also know that if they are too adversarial, in some courts the judge is going to issue a punitive sentence. A significant body of research suggests that procedural formality and the presence of an attorney aggravate the sentence a youth receives (Bortner 1982; Clark and Koch 1980; Feld 1988, 1989; Stapleton and Teitelbaum 1972). Even when controlling for the offense, juveniles represented by attorneys are more likely to receive a harsher sentence and be removed from the home if represented by an attorney than if they represent themselves (Bortner 1982).

Feld (1999) argues that attorneys can lead to stiffer sentences for a variety of reasons, including the incompetence of the attorney, the appointment of an attorney simply as a procedural formality, or if the sentence is attributable to enhanced procedural formality. Additionally, the presence of counsel enhances the sentence if variables within the case file are likely to suggest that out-of-home placement and a stiffer sentence are likely to be imposed. In other words, stiffer sentences occur when the case is considered more serious and will result in a more drastic outcome.

Much of what is taking place reflects the role of *parens patriae*. The concept of *parens patriae* and the desire to respond to the needs of the juvenile restricts the attorney who sees the juvenile court hearing as an adversarial proceeding— either the attorney works to gain an acquittal or he or she ends up appearing indifferent to the needs of the client for the sake of working in the juvenile's best interests.

■ Juvenile Probationers

By 2000 U.S. courts with juvenile jurisdiction handled an estimated 1.6 million cases involving delinquency charges (OJJDP 2003). More than half (55 percent) of these cases were processed formally, either by filing a delinquency petition in the juvenile court or by waiving the case to criminal court. According to Stahl (1999), a ten-year trend analysis from 1986 to 1995 indicated a significant shift in the handling of informal versus formal processing of cases. There was a 69 percent increase in actual caseloads over this same time period as numbers increased from 554,000 to 938,000 cases. Between 1986 and 1992, juvenile courts handled a greater number of delinquency cases informally, although the proportion remained fairly steady from 1989 to 1992. Beginning in 1993, however, formally processed delinquency cases outnumbered those handled informally. By 1995, the formal delinquency caseloads exceeded the informal caseloads by 21 percent (Stahl 1999).

Juvenile probation is the oldest and most widely used vehicle through which a range of court-ordered services is rendered. Probation may be used at the "front-end" of the juvenile justice system for the first-time, low-risk offenders or at the "back-end" as an alternative to institutional confinement for more serious offenders. In some cases, probation may be voluntary; the youth agrees to comply with a period of informal probation in lieu of formal probationary status.

■ Law Enforcement

Any description of juvenile processing must of necessity be general. The process begins with the police. Police officers are given wide discretion in the handling of young people who are accused of crimes. Frequently, the police make "street adjustments, or settle the issue where it is found," in lieu of arrests. They may release juveniles unconditionally after arresting them, release them with a warning, release them into the custody of their parents or guardians, or release them on the condition that they report to entities other than the juvenile court such as citizen hearing boards where private citizens review the case and the offender's progress. The extent to which juveniles are diverted varies from jurisdiction to jurisdiction (Griffin and Torbet 2002, 34). Law enforcement agencies divert many juvenile offenders out of the justice system. At arrest, a decision is made either to send the matter further into or to divert the case out of the system, often into alternative programs. Generally, law enforcement agencies make this decision after taking into consideration the victim, the juvenile, the parents, and the juvenile's prior contacts with the juvenile justice system (Sickmund 2003).

Of all delinquency cases referred to juvenile court in 1998, 84 percent were referred by law enforcement agencies. The remaining referrals were made by parents, victims, schools, probation officers, and others (Sickmund 2003, 2). Nearly one in four juveniles arrested in 1998 were handled within the police department and then released; nearly 7 in 10 arrested juveniles were referred to juvenile court (Sickmund 2003, 2). A referral occurs when someone files an arrest report or a complaint with the juvenile court alleging that a young person has violated the law.

■ Intake Decision Making

When juveniles are referred to juvenile court, they are first required to meet with a probation officer or prosecutor who will make an intake decision on the handling of the complaint against the juvenile.

Specialized intake units or "ordinary" probation officers may do the screening in one department. Intake can also have important considerations as a gatekeeper for the juvenile justice system. Intake units can act as valves to control the number of cases reaching the juvenile court. They also can function to handle complaints quickly, equitably, and consistently in the least restrictive means possible, consistent with public safety. A unit can hold the juvenile accountable even when the case is diverted, addressing the needs of the victim, and finally, giving consideration to the underlying causes of the problem. These often competing goals make this process particularly difficult (Griffin and Torbet 2002, 41). Intake decisions can lead to dismal, informal supervision; resolution in some manner or form; or filing a formal petition with the court. It is important to control unfettered discretion. Intake decisions should be directed toward specific goals, guided by explicit criteria, and based on pertinent information (Gottfredson 2000). Clearly written policies and procedures can establish guidelines for various criteria, questions to be answered, circumstances to be considered, and weights to be assigned in particular cases, thus giving both structure and consistency to decision making while respecting professional discretion. These policies and goals should be found in documents that are subject to open review, criticism, and comment, and periodic assessment where modifications are made as needed (Griffin and Torbet 2002, 42).

Cases handled informally by the intake unit include minor offenses, offenders with no prior record or pattern of offending, those with no apparent need for services, juveniles who have learned their lesson simply by being arrested, and cases in which the victim is satisfied. Diverted cases often include the juvenile who doesn't deny the allegations, who is not considered a threat to the community, whose family is willing to cooperate in services, and cases in which the needed services are best provided by a nonjudicial agency. Formally petitioned cases might include serious offenses in which there has been serious harm to the victim, there is a belief the juvenile is a threat to the community, and in cases in which the juvenile denies the charges and desires a hearing. The juvenile is also a good candidate for formal processing of the case when he or she has a prior record of referrals, and in the instances of the young offender who is in need of services and the juvenile or family is unwilling to accept them (Griffin and Torbet 2002, 43).

■ Diversion

Diversion is defined as the process of channeling a referred juvenile from formal juvenile court processing to an alternative forum for resolution of the matter and/or a community-based agency for help (Kurlycheck et al. 1999, 55). A properly employed diversion program provides a mechanism for holding a youth accountable while meeting the needs of the community, the victim, and the offender. The benefits of diversion include the avoidance of stigma, the involvement of the victim and the community in the process, a reduction in the demands on court resources, and the exercise of wise restraint as most juveniles who are referred to juvenile court never return (Snyder and Sickmund 1999).

Because of the various issues that confront local agencies, each jurisdiction by necessity must establish its own criteria for diversion based on laws, policy, resources, and sensitivity to local traditions. Successful diversion policies depend on the long-term support of law enforcement, social services, schools, and community stakeholders. Success depends on all parties understanding and agreeing to the policies. It is apparent, nonetheless, that diversion decisions should be structured by explicit guidelines that serve agency goals. Such guidelines should be clear, firm, and definite enough to be of use but flexible enough to address the various contingencies facing decision makers. The guidelines should function to limit any "net-widening" effect (taking in youth whose cases would otherwise simply be dismissed). They should ensure the exclusion of the first-time inconsequential offender who has no serious prior criminal record, and those whose parents willingly accept services and sanction. Finally, the victim must be given a say in this process because it is vitally important for the victim to be appropriately vindicated by the sanction and services required of the offender. To maintain an appropriate level of respect for the victims, they should have the right to ask for a reconsideration of the diversion plan if they so desire.

To the extent the process is formalized, it is necessary to have a clear and complete diversion agreement. According to the National Center for Juvenile Justice (Griffin and Torbet 2002), a good diversion agreement is established in an adjustment conference held among the juvenile, the parents, an attorney if desired, and a probation officer. The conference should produce an agreement that has the following characteristics: clarity, specificity, informed consent, and a definite time period to establish closure. Positive-active statements should make reference to community service, restitution, letters of apology, victim awareness classes, offense-specific classes, law-related education, participation in prosocial groups, mentoring, and tutoring programs.

According to the National Council of Juvenile and Family Court Judges (1989), diversion programs fall into two broad categories: alternative dispute resolution (ADR) programs and community-based programs (C-B). ADR programs can be either participatory or adjudicatory programs. **ADR-participatory programs** employ a neutral facilitator to help discuss issues and develop mutually acceptable resolutions. The idea is to preserve and enhance an ongoing relationship in the family, school, neighborhood, or community. The parties themselves define the issues and engage in a search for solutions. With the aid of a facilitator, the disputants arrive at a mutually acceptable agreement. When handled effectively, the process teaches conflict-resolution and problem-solving techniques. As participation and inclusion increase, the process becomes increasingly informal. These types of programs are victim/offender mediation, circle sentencing, and family group conferencing.

The **ADR-adjudicatory process** intends to insert a moral or legal message in the process and impose a solution. The facilitator or panel imposes all decisions after assessing the facts and culpability involved with the event under consideration. The idea is to teach accountability by employing increasingly more formal processes as the problem becomes more serious. Examples of such enterprises include teen courts, peer juries, citizen hearing boards, and youth aid panels.

Community-based diversion programs can include mentoring programs, work programs, educational programs, skill-development programs, counseling programs, and programs that work with families. These programs provide closer supervision, accountability, and some sense that someone cares about the youth.

Dryfoos (1990) argues that effective diversion programs must provide intensive, comprehensive, and appropriate services presented by well-trained, experienced staff working in carefully designed programs, offering specific services targeted at specific offender populations. The idea is to enhance the responsivity of the process. Diversion programs must establish clear policies relative to the locally appropriate options, age-specific criteria for involvement, parental participation, those who may make the decision to refer youth to the diversion program, program diversion, and concerns for participant noncompliance. It is vitally important that the process be fair to all of the parties including the victim, the offender, and support services. For this to occur not only must there be an appearance of fairness but the offender and the victim must come to accept the outcome even if they are not completely satisfied. For this, there should be a formal legal status, and the purpose, goals, and procedures must be clearly articulated in accessible documents. They should outline referral protocols that emphasize (NCJFCJ 1989):

1. the importance of voluntary participation
2. the necessity for training
3. clearly understood agreements
4. the role of monitoring compliance
5. appropriate incentives
6. fair sanctions if the offender fails to live up to the agreement

ADR-participatory programs employ a neutral facilitator who works with families to discuss issues and develop mutually acceptable resolutions that preserve and enhance ongoing relationships in the family, school, and community. The parties involved define the issues and search for resolutions with the aid of a facilitator.

ADR-adjudicatory process is a mechanism which intends to assert a moral or legal message in the settlement of the dispute and to impose a solution when one cannot be reached.

Preadjudicatory

There is greatest variation from state to state in case-processing procedures in the preadjudicatory phase. Consistently present in most states are such processes as the filing of a petition that identifies (1) the juvenile, (2) the alleged offense being charged, and (3) the type of possible disposition of the juvenile. **Arraignment** is a special hearing to give the juvenile formal notice of the charges and notice of his or her rights, to ascertain if the juvenile has or needs an attorney, and to give a statement of plea. **Probable cause hearings** are held to determine if sufficient reason exists to believe the allegations in the petition. These hearings can protect the juvenile from unwarranted prosecutions while saving the state the expense of a prosecution. Probable cause hearings can be held in conjunction with arraignments. If insufficient evidence is indicted, the charges against the youth should be dismissed. Probable cause hearings are indicated if there is a motion to transfer the juvenile to criminal court, the juvenile is held in custody, or the juvenile is held in emergency custody (Griffin and Torbet 2002, 35).

arraignment is a special hearing to give the juvenile formal notice of his or her rights and the charges against him or her, to ascertain if the juvenile has or needs an attorney, and to give his or her statement of plea.

probable cause hearings are held to determine if sufficient probable cause exists to believe the allegations in the juvenile petition. These hearings can protect the juvenile from unwarranted prosecutions while they also can save the state the expense of a prosecution.

Detention

In some instances, law enforcement must detain a juvenile in an adult facility for a brief period in order to contact parents or guardians or to arrange transportation to a juvenile detention facility. Federal regulations discourage holding juveniles in adult jails and lockups. As reported earlier, there are thousands of juveniles serving time in jail. In order to receive certain federal funding a state must agree to comply with four criteria relative to detaining juveniles (Snyder and Sickmund, 1999):

1. Status offenders must be deinstitutionalized.
2. Juveniles may not be held where they can see or hear incarcerated adults.
3. Juveniles cannot be held in a jail or lockup unless for a brief period while other arrangements are being made unless they are being tried as an adult.
4. States must determine the extent to which minorities are overrepresented.

While the chief purposes of detention is community protection, a 1995 census of detention facilities revealed that most juveniles were held for short periods for nonviolent and minor offenses. Historically, juveniles were held in detention for reasons that had little to do with absconding, harming themselves, or reoffending. Too often when considering offender absconding, the criteria used to make the decision are subjective, unreliable, inconsistent, and biased. Moreover, this process leads to overcrowding. By 1995, 62 percent of the public detention centers were operating above capacity. As with prisons, overcrowded detention facilities are unhealthy, dangerous, chaotic, and expensive. The staff feels overburdened and services cannot meet the demands placed on them. The risk of violence and suicide increase accordingly (Orlando 1999; Snyder and Sickmund 1999).

A juvenile probation officer or a detention worker reviews the case to decide whether the youth should be detained pending a hearing before a judge. The officer must determine if the facts are legally sufficient, then hold a face-to-face interview with the juvenile, apply detention criteria, and decide whether to detain, release, or offer some form of diversion. If the juvenile is to be detained, the officer must put in writing his or her findings relative to the charges, the reason for the detention, an explanation as to why release is inappropriate, the alternatives that were considered, and the recommendation for interim status. In all states, a detention hearing must be held within a 24- to 72-hour time period (Griffin and Torbet 2002, 58). At the detention hearing, a judge reviews the case and determines whether continued detention is necessary. In 1998, juveniles were detained in 19 percent of delinquency cases processed in juvenile courts. Detention may extend beyond the adjudicatory and dispositional hearing. If residential placement is ordered and no placement beds are available, detention may continue until a bed becomes available (Sickmund 2003, 3).

As with bail for adults, detention can be imposed under the following conditions:

- to ensure the juvenile's appearance in court
- to prevent the juvenile from inflicting serious harm on somebody or on property
- to protect the juvenile from imminent harm

While in custody, it is expected that the juvenile will receive a wide range of helpful services that support the juvenile's physical, emotional, and social development. Juvenile detention can include a system of clinical observations and assessments that can be reported to complement the services (Roush 1996). It is important that detention not be used for purposes for which it was not intended (Griffin and Torbet 2002, 58):

1. teaching the juvenile a lesson
2. punishing the juvenile
3. rehabilitating the offender
4. allowing parents to avoid their responsibilities
5. satisfying the desires of a victim, the police, or a community
6. providing greater administrative access to the juvenile
7. furthering investigative efforts
8. because more appropriate facilities are not available

The decision to detain a juvenile should follow explicit guidelines. These factors, whatever they may be, must be related to the purposes of detention, easily measured, correlated with risk, weighted but flexible, and subject to ongoing review. Specific attention should be given to the present offense, the circumstances of the arrest such as whether there was a weapon or resistance to arrest, court history, current criminal justice status, and reoffense or flight record. Detention officials should have a variety of decision options tailored to meet the juvenile's needs and circumstances in light of the declared purposes of detention. With the aid of electronic monitoring, it is possible for a juvenile to experience home detention along with supervision, attend day or evening reporting centers, or take advantage of a shelter.

There are critics (Roush 1996) who feel that detention has its share of problems. For example, although there is an emphasis on programming while in detention, the length of stay for any child often determines the quality of the experience. Too often, juveniles are not kept in detention long enough to have a significant programming impact, especially in the area of mandated education. Probation officers and judges unnecessarily extend the time in detention or impose it as sanction for children who do not need a secure facility. To some critics, a sentence to detention of 30 to 120 days is proof that detention centers have been used as a form of punishment. When doing so there is the additional problem of crowding. If detention center rehabilitation programs are to have any effect, detainees will have to have an extended stay, which will result in overcrowded conditions, confusion about the mission of such facilities, and allow the true purpose of detention to take a back seat to rehabilitation. Despite these concerns, time in a detention center can be used for needs assessments, finding placements, victim empathy classes, mentoring, value clarification, and promoting the value of human dignity.

■ Case Processing

Puzzachera et al. (2002) have outlined the typical outcome of 1,000 cases that have been referred to juvenile court. These outcomes have been categorized by their most restrictive outcome. At the start, we see that 57 percent of the cases are petitioned to the court. A small percentage (0.005) were waived to adult court. Of those petitioned, 36 percent were adjudicated, 9 percent would be placed, 20 percent were put on probation, 0.04 percent were given other sanctions, and 0.019 were released. Of the 20 percent not adjudicated, only 0.005 percent were placed in a program, 0.030 percent were placed on probation, 0.032 percent were given other sanctions, and 13 percent were dismissed. For juveniles who were not petitioned, 43 percent of the cases were not petitioned, 0.002 percent were placed, 14 percent were still placed on probation, 10 percent were given other sanctions, and 18 percent were dismissed.

Juvenile court intake is the stage at which somebody must decide whether a referral merits a petition, whether the matter described in the complaint against the juvenile should become the subject of formal court action and whether the juvenile should be held in detention. Intake may be the most crucial point in case processing because so much follows from that decision. Intake is generally the responsibility of the probation department or the prosecutor's office, but some of the larger departments have special intake units. Whoever makes the intake decision has considerable discretionary power regarding who enters the juvenile system (Griffin and Torbet 2002, 34). Intake decides whether to dismiss the case, handle it informally, or to request formal intervention by the juvenile court. To make this decision, the intake officer or prosecutor reviews the facts of the case to determine whether there is sufficient evidence to prove the allegation. If not, the case is dismissed. If there is sufficient evidence, intake then determines whether formal intervention is necessary.

Although 55 percent of the juvenile cases are adjudicated formally, most informally processed cases are dismissed if the juvenile successfully completes the informal disposition. In such informally processed cases, the juvenile voluntarily agrees to specific conditions for a specified time period. These conditions are outlined in a written agreement, generally called a consent decree. It may include conditions such as victim restitution, school attendance, drug counseling, or a curfew or other specified referrals (Sickmund 2003, 2). If, however, the juvenile fails to comply, the case is referred for formal processing and proceeds as if the initial decision had been to refer the case to an adjudicatory hearing. The juvenile justice system has been criticized for excessive use of informal probation. Rather than simply diverting juveniles away from formal processing (which is frequently indistinguishable from doing nothing at all), the better practice is to divert them to informal sanctions and services.

If the case is to be handled formally in juvenile court, intake files one of two types of petitions: (1) a delinquency petition requesting an adjudicatory hearing or (2) a petition requesting a waiver hearing to transfer the case to criminal court. A delinquency petition states the allegation and requests the juvenile court to adjudicate the youth a delinquent, making the juvenile a ward of the court. This language differs from that used in the criminal court system, where an offender is convicted and sentenced. In response to the petition, an adjudicatory hearing is scheduled. At this hearing, witnesses are called and the facts of the case are presented. In nearly all adjudicatory hearings, the judge determines whether the juvenile is responsible for the offense. In some states, the juvenile has the right to a jury trial (Sickmund 2003, 2).

Formal Hearing

The adjudication hearing is a fact-finding proceeding in which the juvenile's responsibility for the alleged offense must be established. The allegation must be proven—as in a criminal trial—beyond a reasonable doubt. If not, the juvenile must be released. At the adjudication hearing, all interested parties and necessary witnesses are convened in a courtroom. Evidence and witnesses are generally presented in court by the prosecuting attorney. However, in some jurisdictions, when the case is uncontested, the probation officer may present the case to the judge with no prosecutor in attendance. The juvenile may present evidence and cross-examine witnesses if not represented by an attorney.

As in criminal court cases, most juvenile cases are handled by plea agreements made between the prosecutor and the juvenile and his or her lawyer prior to appearing before the judge. At the conclusion of the adjudication hearing, the judge may amend the petition if it is in error, dismiss the petition due to a lack of evidence, continue the case without a finding (to be dismissed later at a specific date if the juvenile complies with the court's orders), allow the juvenile to admit to the charges, or make a finding of delinquency (Griffin and Torbet 2002, 36).

One of the central problems facing juvenile offenders is provision of adequate counsel as ordered by the 1967 *In re Gault* case (Puritz et al., 1995). In a report to the American Bar Association, Puritz and associates outline various problems present in the juvenile court. They state that the stakes for children are much higher than in the past because:

1. Many states have changed the purpose clause of their juvenile codes to emphasize punishment and public safety considerations rather than treatment.

2. Sanctions have become more punitive and longer in duration.

3. More juveniles are locked up in secure detention facilities, training schools, jails, and prisons than ever before.

Their research indicates that heavy caseloads are a significant barrier to effective legal representation. Often, defenders have little or no time to meet with their clients prior to a detention hearing. Resources are often inadequate to investigate the charges and gather critical information from families, schools, or social service agencies. Children represented by overworked lawyers frequently do not understand what is happening in court and come away with the impression that their attorney did little for them. Attorneys feel burned out, anxious, dissatisfied with the their ability to have enough time to do the job as they know it must be done (Puritz and Shang 1998).

High-quality legal representation programs for indigent juveniles have one or more of the following characteristics:

- Ability to limit or control the caseload
- Support for entering cases early and the flexibility to represent, or refer, clients in related collateral matters such as special education
- Comprehensive initial and ongoing training and available resource material
- Adequate nonlawyer support and resources
- Hands-on supervision of attorneys
- Work environment that values and nurtures juvenile court practices

Programs supporting these initiatives are found in the office of the public defender in the state of Maryland (Puritz and Shang 1998).

Maryland formed a series of special units within the office of the public defender to address the problems presented by indigent juvenile offenders (Puritz and Shang 1998). In 1995 a special program was established to handle cases waived to the criminal court. In part, the program comprised a youth defendant unit that was designed to provide information for lawyers representing juveniles tried in criminal court. Important information was provided to public defenders and their clients about programs available to a juvenile if a transfer motion back to juvenile court succeeded. Another unit, the detention response team, comprised lawyers and social workers who identified children held in detention who could benefit from placement in private homes, group homes, or nonsecure facilities. The social worker conducted assessments of the youths' needs and identified appropriate residential and community services plans for addressing mental, behavioral, and educational needs. The attorney investigated the case from the legal standpoint to determine if the detention could be modified in light of community alternatives. The educational development unit concerned itself with the educational needs of youth who were expelled, suspended, or dropped from the school rolls. It also provided advocacy for parents who wanted to understand their rights and options with respect to future school placement. The educational unit also provided assessments and referrals. The client assessment recommendation and evaluation (CARE) unit used social workers to develop treatment plans and dispositional alternatives for juveniles aged 12 to 17. The CARE unit accepted referrals of juveniles who had a wide range of problems. Especially critical were the transfer summaries prepared by the unit to advocate for transfer of the case back to juvenile court where it is believed the juvenile could be better served.

Juvenile Waiver

juvenile waiver occurs when a juvenile accused of a serious delinquency has the hearing switched from juvenile court to a trial in adult criminal court.

Known as **juvenile waiver**, one of the major issues facing juvenile probation is the juvenile who is charged with a violent crime, waived out of juvenile court, and then sent to adult criminal court. The escalation of homicide, especially among young African-American males in the late 1980s, provided the impetus for legislative strategies to "crack down" on youth crime (Feld 1999). Public fear of youth crime and political desires to get tough instigated legislation authorizing the transfer of more young offenders to criminal courts for prosecution as adults and to stiffen the penalties authorized for the juvenile court. A juvenile's case can be transferred to criminal court for trial through prosecutorial discretion, statutory exclusion from juvenile court, or judicial waiver. A juvenile or his or her parents can also request a transfer if the youth meets the age, offense, or offense history requirements; or the treatment amenability. Prosecutorial discretion is employed in states where prosecutors are given the authority to file certain juvenile cases in either juvenile or criminal court under concurrent jurisdiction statutes. Thus, both criminal and juvenile courts share original jurisdiction. Often concurrent jurisdiction is limited to charges of serious, violent, and repeat offenders. Legislatures transfer a large number of young offenders to criminal court by statutorily excluding them from juvenile court jurisdiction. Statutes limit judicial waiver by age, offense, or offense history. By the early 1990s, most states had revised their waiver laws by restricting judicial discretion, encouraging the transfer of more youths to criminal court, expanding prosecutors' authority to transfer youths, or removing certain categories of offenses from the jurisdiction of the juvenile court. These various legal trends have resulted in the prosecution of a greater number of younger youths in the criminal justice system (Podkopacz and Feld 2001). Adjudication in juvenile court and waiver to criminal court are considered the most serious court actions in delinquency cases. Despite increases in the use of formal processing, the proportion of delinquency cases that were either adjudicated or waived to criminal court did not change substantially. Waivers increased 68 percent from 1988 to 1992 but by 1998, less than 1 percent of all petitioned delinquency cases were waived to criminal court (Sickmund 2003).

Although not typically thought of as a transfer, large numbers of youth under the age 18 are tried as adults in the 11 states where the upper age of juvenile court jurisdiction is lower than 18. Nationwide, an estimated 17,600 cases involving youth under the age of 18 were tried in criminal court in 1991 because they were considered adults by state law (Sickmund 1994). Juveniles who have committed certain serious crimes, have been previously waived to criminal court, or convicted in criminal court are excluded from juvenile court jurisdiction. Exclusion from juvenile court may depend on the offender's age, the seriousness of the offense, and if there was a prior felony conviction. Juveniles convicted under these terms may be given juvenile or criminal court sanctions (Sickmund 1994).

■ Extended Juvenile Jurisdiction

In 1995, Minnesota revised its juvenile waiver laws by refocusing the judge's attention primarily on offense-based public safety criteria rather than the youth's amenability to treatment in making transfer decisions and mandating criminal prosecution of older juveniles charged with first-degree murder. Public safety is thought to be served by considering the following issues: offense seriousness, offender culpability, prior record, a willingness to participate in programs, adequacy of programs and punishment, and available dispositional options (Podcopacz and Feld 2001). Unlike most states that sought criminal prosecution of such youth, Minnesota also expanded the authority of juvenile court judges to impose longer juvenile dispositions and provide more extensive treatment than was previously available to delinquents. The Minnesota innovation, **extended jurisdiction juvenile (EJJ) prosecution**, allows judges to simultaneously impose a delinquency disposition and an adult criminal sentence, the execution of which the judge stays pending successful completion of the delinquency sentence (Podcopacz and Feld 2001).

According to Podcopacz and Feld (2001), when a Minnesota prosecutor files a delinquency petition alleging a felony offense, a motion must accompany the petition indicating whether the prosecutor also seeks an EJJ designation or an adult certification. EJJ has become another way for the prosecutor to get around the problem he or she faces when a judge refuses to certify a juvenile for criminal prosecution. The prosecutor does not want the offense to be ignored, but to receive the attention he or she feels it deserves. EJJ is based on the assumption that judges will certify to adult court the very worst offenders. For those juveniles whose crimes are not quite so serious, it is also assumed that a mandatory EJJ disposition for an older juvenile offender who has committed a crime with a presumptive prison sentence attached will subject the not quite so serious juvenile offender to more stringent controls than ordinarily imposed on a juvenile. Essentially, the juvenile is placed in an intensive supervision program in which the juvenile is accountable to a probation officer and a community service worker. Now a judge's decision not to certify to adult court is based on the determination that the youth is amenable to probation.

Prosecutors can get around the judge by charging a 16- or 17-year-old youth with a presumptive-certification felony court offense. This automatically designates the case as an EJJ prosecution without any further judicial review (Podcopacz and Feld 2001). Because the only alternative to waiver available to a judge following a presumptive-certification hearing is to designate the case as an EJJ prosecution, the law allows the prosecutor to maintain preeminence to designate the case as an EJJ proceeding. Thus, the prosecutor can quickly abjure pro forma certification motions and still obtain greater plea bargaining leverage. Lastly, instead of filing a certification motion against a nonpresumptive-certification youth, a prosecutor may file a motion for the court to elevate the youth to an EJJ prosecution. Just as a judge may deny a motion to certify and designate a 14- to 17-year-old charged with a felony as an EJJ when public safety requires, similarly a judicial hearing on a prosecutor's motion for an EJJ designation provides the same result. At the EJJ hearing, the prosecutor must prove by clear and convincing evidence that public safety warrants designating the

extended jurisdiction juvenile (EJJ) prosecution allows judges to simultaneously impose a delinquency disposition and an adult criminal sentence, the execution of which the judge stays pending successful completion of the delinquency sentence.

proceedings as an EJJ prosecution, using the same public safety criteria specified in the certification legislation. The EJJ affords greater procedural protections than those available in ordinary juvenile delinquency proceedings, including the right to a jury trial. The EJJ conviction is also part of any computation done for calculating a sentencing guideline criminal history score. To complicate matters further, it is possible for a youth to be charged with an EJJ-qualified offense, but be convicted of a lesser included offense at trial, and thus be sentenced as an ordinary delinquent. However, to expedite plea bargaining, a youth may enter a guilty plea to a nonpresumptive-commitment offense and still receive an EJJ disposition. Finally, the law raised the juvenile court's dispositional jurisdiction from age 19 for ordinary delinquents to age 21 for EJJ youths. This was done to allow the youth one last chance for success in the juvenile justice system (Podcopacz and Feld 2001), thus creating some flexibility in the law.

An evaluation of the EJJ program found that because every EJJ youth received a stayed criminal sentence and probation was revoked, nearly half (48 percent) of these youth were sent to prison. A vast majority of these revocations were not the result of new criminal charges. Judges sent nearly as many youths to jail or prison following judicial revocations of EJJ probation as they did directly through certification proceedings. These EJJ youth were offenders whom judges already had determined in the context of a waiver hearing to be inappropriate candidates for adult criminal prosecution or sentencing (Podcopacz and Feld 2001). In one final note, it should be noted that EJJ programs are only as good as the funding they receive and like so many others, they are subject to political forces in operation. Minnesota, for example, may consider the EJJ program supportable in one session of the legislature but when budgetary cuts are necessary during a following session, this program is no more immune to cuts than any other state-funded program.

■ Investigations

Juvenile courts rely on probation officers to investigate and assess juvenile offenders and recommend an appropriate disposition. Due to limitations on resources, probation departments avoid conducting wasteful, unnecessary, and redundant predispositional investigations. Most cases referred to juvenile court do not require a full-blown predispositional investigation. In 1998, for example, only about 36 percent of all cases referred to intake actually resulted in an adjudication of delinquency. About 43 percent of the cases were never petitioned at all, and about 20 percent were dismissed or resolved without a finding of delinquency (Griffin and Torbet 2002). Management information systems should aid this process greatly. Critically important is the time available for investigations. Despite the *Gault* decision and other safeguards built into the process since the 1960s, there still are judges who desire to make a disposition of the case almost immediately after a finding of delinquency. This is done for convenience or organizational pressure. Although there may be good reasons to quickly administer a sentence, there are lingering concerns that fairness will not be served when a judge does not give the defense a sufficient amount of time to develop an alternative sentencing proposal.

Effective dispositions should consider risk assessment, accountability, and rehabilitation (Griffin and Torbet 2002). States vary in terms of the emphasis given these different goals. Obtaining basic documents, checking records, conducting interviews, and making collateral contacts are standard predisposition investigative techniques. The facts gathered at intake or during the detention phase are crucial, especially the information relative to the offense, court history, and victim input. Official documents relative to the offender will have to be gathered. Through in-home interviews, information will be gathered from the juvenile and his or her parents or guardians regarding living conditions and the neighborhood, missing information regarding the offense, assessing the parents' or guardians' attributes, and determining where additional information can be gleaned about the juvenile. Signing release forms for health and school records is also done at this time. The officer must also consider any previous records and reports done on the family.

The number one concern of any probation officer is community safety. As such, assessing risk is vital to the process (Griffin and Torbet 2002, 65). In this assessment the investigator should refer, in part, to the Level of Service Inventory (LSI) and other instruments and departmental policies. Careful examination should be made of the offense, the circumstances, the offender's motivation, and the offender's previous history. Although these are subjective assessments, they do give the officer some sense of who the offender is and what is the likelihood of future events. The availability of a range of sanctions and services determines, for the most part, whether a juvenile can be safely kept in the community. It must be noted that most juveniles serve their sentence in the community.

Such questions as to whether the juvenile accepts responsibility for the crime, regrets its occurrence, understands the consequences, and has remorse all play an important role (Griffin and Torbet 2002, 66). Culpability establishes the extent to which the delinquent intended to commit the offense. Establishing the level of intent is obscured by the frequent use of plea bargaining. If a plea bargain has been reached, it is virtually impossible to hold the offender fully accountable without ascertaining the degree to which the delinquent tried to avoid the harm inflicted on the victim. Victim impact statements and the offender's attitude toward the offense are relevant here. Rehabilitative goals are achieved through careful consideration of the juvenile's strengths and weaknesses. The key questions are:

- What skills and competencies are needed for the juvenile to break out of his or her cycle of offending?
- What skills are needed to break free from old patterns?
- What strengths and resources does the juvenile possess?
- How responsive is the juvenile to any intervention?

Through the acquisition of living, learning, and coping skills, juveniles learn to end destructive behavior and improve their understanding and decision-making skills. With the acquisition of such skills, many juveniles are able to establish significant relationships with conventional groups and institutions (Griffin and Torbet 2002, 66).

Well-designed, thorough, flexible departmental guidelines for disposition recommendations should reflect the emphasis the department gives to public protection, offender accountability, and rehabilitation (Griffin and Torbet 2002, 66).

Assessments should consider risk, needs, the juvenile's attributes, family attributes, performance, substance abuse and mental health, juvenile and family strengths, school or work performance, and accountability factors. Each of these considerations should reflect local resources. In other words, a department writes a report to reflect the resources available to it in light of how the judiciary has handled cases.

Available Alternatives

There is a range of possible dispositions available to a juvenile court judge. A juvenile can be sent to a secure institution, a juvenile prison, or a residential placement in the community in a private or public facility; referred to a nonresidential program for day treatment; or assigned various levels of probation supervision, payment of fines, restitution, or the performance of community service. Puzzachera et al. (2002) found that in 1998, probation was the most serious disposition in about 58 percent of the more than 600,000 cases in which juveniles were adjudicated nationwide. About 26 percent of adjudicated cases resulted in placement outside of the home. Another 11 percent were ordered to pay fines, give restitution, perform community service, or participate in day treatment or counseling programs. Lastly, 5 percent were adjudicated delinquent but released without sanctions (Puzzachera et al. 2002).

The National Center for Juvenile Justice (2002) recommends that probation officers should always recommend what is in the best interests of the juvenile despite what is available or impractical. Secondary recommendations can address what is available. Future planning can address the existing shortcomings. Finally, it is the job of the probation officer to propose a program of supplemental restrictions, sanctions, and services that form the backbone of a case plan (Griffin and Torbet 2002).

■ Supervision

The probation supervision plan is a blueprint for action serving as a contract between the offender and the probation officer. The plan is developed by balancing the considerations of the victim, the community, and the offender by setting out the activities and responsibilities to be performed, the benefits to be gained, and the consequences to be faced if the plan is to be fulfilled or is derailed. This plan should have clear goals and meaningful objectives outlining various activities the juvenile should complete during a specified time period. The plan is also a tool that guides the offender, his or her parents, and the probation officer through major and minor objectives (Carey et al. 2000). If the juvenile complies with the conditions and acts to meet the objectives, then he or she should be discharged from probation in a timely manner.

An appropriate sentence achieves three different goals: (1) community safety, (2) offender accountability, and (3) practical rehabilitation. Every supervision plan should emphasize community safety. This is the principal function of probation. Safety is achieved through calculating the overall risk posed by the juvenile and considering how the day's activities are structured to promote incapacitation such as how many and what type of contacts will be made with the juvenile. Offender accountability is spelled out in the juvenile's efforts to make amends. This can be done through the stipulation of restitution or community service, victim-offender mediation, victim impact panels, sentencing circles, victim awareness classes, and apologies. Effective reintegrative shaming uses a variety of approaches to sensitize the offender to the harm done and to have the offender recognize the pain caused others without pushing him or her further along the path of crime. Practical rehabilitation addresses behaviors, thought processes, and skill deficits that further the juvenile's risk of re-offending. In many ways, these concrete measures are designed to promote the offender's well-being. These programs include, but are not limited to, conflict resolution and anger management; living, learning, and working skill-building classes; tutoring and mentoring programs; cognitive interventions; counseling; treatment programs; parent education; skills training; and family therapy. These approaches are backed by a series of graduated sanctions.

Taxman, Soule, and Gelb (1999) identified the following as essential to a good system of graduated sanctions:

Certainty in responding to every transaction

A swift response

Consistency in seeing that like cases are treated alike

That the chosen response is the minimum punishment likely to produce the desired result

That the level of response matches the seriousness of the offense

Progressiveness with more severe responses accompanying future failures to comply

Responses are objective and are impartial reactions to the offense

Graduated responses should also correspond with the principles of human dignity in that people are to be treated as though they are the sum total of their worst deeds or that they lack any value as human beings.

■ Conclusion

Human dignity is supported by the expansion of juvenile rights but there are times when the needs of the child are secondary to the achievement of legal acquittal at the expense of denial of service for the needy. Society must remember that children have value and worth regardless of their background and what they have done. One should not forget that young people are not the sum total of their worst deeds. They have worth because they are still capable of doing well. They can make rational and moral choices about the means they choose and the ends they seek. They grow into people who are capable of being self-directed, self-assessing, self-criticizing, and self-correcting. Of course mistakes will be made, but that is the reason they are considered juveniles and not adults. One tends to reduce the claim of culpability because of a lack of maturity. However, bear in mind that although juveniles may be committing more serious offenses and they may appear to be more sophisticated in their criminal efforts, they still do not possess the necessary maturity to make the appropriate decisions. They must be treated with dignity so they can learn to treat others with dignity.

REFERENCES

Aries, P. 1962. *Centuries of childhood: A social history of family life.* New York: Vintage.

Berger, P., and T. Luckman. 1967. *The social construction of reality.* New York: Anchor Books.

Bortner, M. 1982. *Inside a juvenile court.* New York: New York University Press.

Breed v. Jones. 1975. 421 U.S. 519; 95 S.Ct. 1779.

Bremmer, R. 1971. *Children and youth in America: A documentary history,* vol.1–II, Cambridge, MA: Harvard University Press.

Carey, M., D. Goff, G. Hinzman, A. Neff, B. Owens, and L. Albert. 2000. Field service case plans: Bane or gain? *Perspectives* Spring: 30–41.

Chesney-Lind, M. 1971. *Female juvenile delinquency in Hawaii.* Master's thesis. University of Hawaii.

Chesney-Lind, M., and R. Shelden. 1992. *Girls: Delinquency and juvenile justice.* Belmont, CA: Wadsworth.

Clark, S., and G. Koch. 1980. Juvenile court: Therapy or crime control, and do lawyers make a difference? *Law and Society Review* 14: 263–308.

Cochran, T. 1972. *Business in American life: A history.* New York: McGraw-Hill.

Cogan, N. 1970. Juvenile law, before and after the entrance of *parens patriae. South Carolina Law Review* 22: 147–181.

Curtis, G. 1976. The checkered career of *parens patriae:* The state as parent and tyrant. *DePaul Law Review* 25: 895–915.

de Maus, L. 1974. The evolution of childhood. In *The history of childhood.* New York: Harper Books.

Dryfoos, J. 1990. *Adolescents at risk: Prevalence and prevention.* New York: Oxford University Press.

Ex parte Crouse. 4 Whart. 9, Pa. (1838).

Fare v. Michael C. 1979. 442 U.S. 707; 99 S.Ct. 2560.

Feld, B. 1999. *Bad kids: Race and the transformation of the juvenile court.* New York: Oxford University Press.

Feld, B. 1989. The right to counsel in juvenile court: An empirical study of when lawyers appear and the difference they make. *Journal of Criminal Law and Criminology* 79: 1185–1346.

Feld, B. 1988. *In re Gault* revisited: A cross-state comparison of the right to counsel in juvenile court. *Crime and Delinquency* 34: 393–424.

Finestone, H. 1976. *Victims of change: Juvenile delinquency in America.* Westport, CT: Greenwood.

Fox, S. 1970. Juvenile justice reform: An historical perspective. *Stanford Law Review* 22: 1187–1239.

Gottfredson, D., ed. 2000. *Juvenile justice with eyes open: Methods for improving information for juvenile justice.* Pittsburgh, PA: National Center for Juvenile Justice.

Griffin, P., and P. Torbet, eds. 2002. *Desktop guide to juvenile probation practice.* Pittsburgh, PA: National Center for Juvenile Justice.

Grisso, T. 1983. Juveniles' consent in delinquency proceedings. In *Children's competence to consent.* Gary B. Melton, Gerald P. Koocher, and Michael J. Saks (Eds.). New York: Plenum.

Hammer, H., D. Finkelhor, and A. Sedlak. 2002. *NISMART: National incidence studies of missing, abducted, runaway, and thrownaway children.* Washington, DC: U.S. Department of Justice, Office of Justice Programs.

Hawes, J., and N. Hiner (Eds.). 1985. *American childhood: A research guide and historical handbook.* Westport, CT: Greenwood.

Heuter, R., and B. Satzman. 1992. What do they think? The delinquency court process in Colorado as viewed by the youth. *Denver University Law Review* 69: 345–358.

In re Gault. 1967. 387 US 1.; 87 S.Ct. 1428.

In re Winship. 1970. 397 U.S. 358; 90 S.Ct. 1068.

Kent v. United States. 1966. 383 U.S. 541; 86 S.Ct. 1045.

Kett, J. 1977. *Rites of passage: Adolescence in America, 1790 to the present.* New York: Basic Books.

Kurlycheck, M., P. Torbet, and M. Broznyski. 1999. *Focus on accountability: Best practices for juvenile court and probation.* Juvenile Accountability Incentive Block Grant Bulletin. Washington, DC: Office of Juvenile Justice and Delinquency Prevention.

Lasch, C. 1977. *Haven in a heartless world: The family besieged.* New York: Basic Books.

Lucas, J. R. 1980. *On justice.* New York: Oxford University Press.

Mack, J. 1907. Prevention and probation: Proceedings of the National Prison Association, 27–28, 32 in Bremmer Vol. 2, p. 533.

Martinson, R. 1974. What works? Questions and answers about prison reform. *The Public Interest* 35: 22–54.

McCarthy, F. 2000. *Pennsylvania juvenile delinquency practice and procedure*, 4th ed. Suwanee, GA: The Harrison Company.

McKeiver v. Pennsylvania. 1971. 403 U.S. 528; 91 S.Ct. 1976.

National Council of Juvenile and Family Court Judges. 1989. *Court-appointed alternative dispute resolution: A better way to resolve minor delinquency, status offense, and abuse/neglect cases.* Reno, NV: NCJFCJ.

Office of Juvenile Justice Delinquency Prevention (OJJDP). 2003. *Juvenile court cases.* Washington, DC: National Criminal Justice Reference Service.

Orlando, F. 1999. *Controlling the front gates: Effective admissions policies and practices.* Baltimore, MD: Annie E. Casey Foundation.

Pisciotta, A. 1982. Saving the children: The promise and practice of *parens patriae, 1838–98. Crime and Delinquency* 28: 410–425.

Platt, A. 1977. *The child savers: The invention of delinquency.* Chicago: University of Chicago Press.

Podcopacz, M., and B. Feld. 2001. The backdoor to prison: Waiver reform, blended sentencing, and the law of unintended consequences. *Journal of Criminal Law and Criminology* 91: 997–1071.

President's Commission on Law Enforcement and Administration of Justice. 1967. *Task force report: Juvenile delinquency and youth crime.* Washington, DC: U.S. Government Printing Office.

Puritz, P., and W. W. L. Shang. 1998. *Innovative approaches to juvenile indigent defense.* Washington, DC: U.S. Department of Justice, Office of Justice Programs.

Puritz, P., S. Burrell, R. Schartz, M. Soler, and L. Warboys. 1995. *A call for justice: An assessment of access to counsel and quality of representation in delinquency proceedings.* Washington, DC: American Bar Association.

Puzzachera, C., A. Stahl, T. Finnegan, N. Tierney, and H. Snyder. 2002. *Juvenile court statistics 1998.* Washington DC: Office of Juvenile Justice and Delinquency Prevention.

Rothman, D. 1980. *Conscience and convenience: The asylum and its alternative in progressive America.* Boston, MA: Little, Brown.

Roush, D. 1996. *Desktop guide to good juvenile detention practice.* East Lansing, MI: National Juvenile Detention Association.

Ryerson, E. 1978. *The best-laid plans: America's juvenile court experiment.* New York: Hill and Wang.

Schall v. Martin. 1984. 467 U.S. 253; 104 S.Ct. 2403.

Schlossman, S. 1977. *Love and the American delinquent: The theory and practice of progressive juvenile justice.* Chicago: University of Chicago Press.

Schlossman, S., and S. Wallach. 1978. The crime of precocious sexuality: Female delinquency in the progressive era. *Harvard Educational Review* 48: 65–94.

Shelden, R. 1981. Sex discrimination in the juvenile justice system: Memphis, Tennessee, 1900–1917. In *Comparing male and female offenders,* M. Q. Warren, ed. Newbury Park, CA: Sage Publications.

Sickmund, M. 2004. *Juveniles in corrections.* OJJDP National Report Series. Washington, DC: U.S. Department of Justice.

Sickmund, M. 2003. Juveniles in court. *Juvenile offenders and victims: National report series bulletin.* Washington, DC: U.S. Department of Justice.

Sickmund, M. 1994. *How juveniles get to criminal court.* OJJDP update on statistics. Juvenile Justice Bulletin. Washington, DC: U.S. Department of Justice.

Smith, T. 1985. Law talk: Juveniles' understanding of legal language. *Journal of Criminal Justice* 13: 339–353.

Snyder, H., and M. Sickmund. 1999. *Juvenile offenders and victims: 1999 national report.* Washington, DC: Office of Juvenile Justice and Delinquency Prevention.

Stahl, A. 1999. *Juvenile court processing of delinquency cases, 1986–1995.* Office of Juvenile Justice and Delinquency Prevention Fact Sheet. Washington, DC: U.S. Department of Justice.

Stanford v. Kentucky. 1989. 492 U.S. 361; 109 S.Ct. 2969.

Stapleton, V., and L. Teitlebaum. 1972. *In defense of youth: A study of the role of the counsel in American juvenile courts.* New York: Russell Sage.

Sutton, J. 1988. *Stubborn children: Controlling delinquency in the United States.* Berkeley: University of California Press.

Swisher v. Brady. 1978. 438 U.S. 204; 98 S.Ct. 2699.

Taxman, F., D. Soule, and A. Gelb. 1999. Graduated sanctions: Stepping into accountable systems and offenders. *Prison Journal* 79(2): 182–205.

Thompson v. Oklahoma. 1984. 487 U.S. 815; 108 S.Ct. 2687.

Trattner, W. 1999. *From poor law to welfare state.* New York: Free Press.

KEY POINTS

1. Youth have not always held a position of importance in society. For centuries, they were considered nothing more than chattel to be bought and sold like slaves.

2. *Parens patriae* gave the state a doctrine in support of its efforts to intervene in family life when it was thought a child was in need of support.

3. The juvenile court came into existence when the Progressives decided that family problems, poverty, education, and crime could be dealt with by experts outside of the family.

4. The child saving movement was spearheaded by middle-class women with enough time on their hands to take on the needs of other families who were not so fortunate despite the apparent cultural conflict it would breed.

5. From the start, the juvenile court was charged with dealing with children who were truant, sexually promiscuous, and incorrigible.

6. The intense pressure has been put on juvenile probation by baby boomers following World War II but also by the civil rights movement, which led to major reforms in juvenile justice.

7. Juvenile offenders have rights but they lack the ability to express those rights on their own. Quite often the attorneys representing juvenile offenders are ineffective and can bring about a stiffer sentence.

8. The process of a juvenile case goes through many phases from intake and diversion through sentencing.

9. Juvenile waiver to adult court has become a principal concern.

10. Adjudication in juvenile court and waiver to criminal court are considered the most serious court actions in delinquency cases. Still less than 1 percent of all petitioned delinquency cases are waived to criminal court.

11. EJJ is intended as a form of intensive supervision rendered to a specific population of high-risk offenders who have committed serious offenses.

12. Well-designed, thorough, flexible departmental guidelines for disposition recommendations should reflect the emphasis the department gives to public protection, offender accountability, and rehabilitation.

KEY TERMS

ADR-adjudicatory process is a mechanism which intends to assert a moral or legal message in the settlement of the dispute and to impose a solution when one cannot be reached.

ADR-participatory programs employ a neutral facilitator who works with families to discuss issues and develop mutually acceptable resolutions that preserve and enhance ongoing relationships in the family, school, and the community. The parties involved define the issues and search for resolutions with the aid of a facilitator.

arraignment is a special hearing to give the juvenile formal notice of his or her rights and the charges against him or her, to ascertain if the juvenile has or needs an attorney, and to give his or her statement of plea.

diversion   is the process of channeling a referred juvenile from formal juvenile court processing to an alternative form for resolution of the matter and/or a community-based agency for help.

extended jurisdiction juvenile (EJJ) prosecution   allows judges to simultaneously impose a delinquency disposition and an adult criminal sentence, the execution of which the judge stays pending successful completion of the delinquency sentence.

juvenile waiver   occurs when a juvenile accused of a serious delinquency has the hearing switched from juvenile court to a trial in adult criminal court.

parens patriae   is the right and responsibility of the state, as a common guardian, to substitute its own control over children for that of the natural parents when the latter appear unable or unwilling to meet their responsibilities or when the child poses a problem for the community.

probable cause hearings   are held to determine if sufficient probable cause exists to believe the allegations in the juvenile petition. These hearings can protect the juvenile from unwarranted prosecutions while they also can save the state the expense of a prosecution.

REVIEW QUESTIONS

1. What is *parens patriae*? How did it reflect the status of children around the time it was first used?

2. How did the Progressive era affect ideas about lower-class children?

3. What were the main reasons for the creation of the juvenile court? What was its main purpose during the late 1890s and early 1900s?

4. Why might attorneys often be ineffective in their representation of juveniles?

5. What is diversion? How do diversion programs operate?

6. How do extended jurisdiction juvenile prosecutions address juvenile delinquency proceedings? What are they intended to do?

12 Parole: Its Evolution and Current Status

If one is to have a complete understanding of community corrections, understanding the current uses of **parole** is necessary. With the generally accepted view that prisons are meant to house dangerous persons, it also must be understood that most of these people, even though they are serving long sentences, will one day be released from prison. Parole is a unique enterprise that is required to address the important issues of danger, public safety, social reintegration, and state regulation all within the guise of treating the parolee with a measure of dignity. Parole or supervised release has to use the possibility of returning the offender to prison as a means of controlling a population of offenders who have served their time. They may have experienced community indifference to their plight and faced few chances of support once on the outside. They know that there is an increased possibility of returning to prison if things do not work out.

parole is given the duty to act as an independent, citizen-oriented board that carefully reviews each prisoner nearing the end of a prison term, to demand that all prisoners demonstrate they are no longer a danger to society before they are permitted to return to the community, and to set specific conditions that must be met before release.

The Role of Parole

Parole was founded primarily as a means of reducing the sentence of those offenders who had earned an early release from prison through good behavior. Parole is a complex institution that has evolved into a major instrument of social control. To further an appreciation of the role played by parole today, various issues need to be considered including the history of parole, its organization and administration, parolee characteristics, life on the outside, revocations, and the reform of parole.

Parole can be defined in different ways according to its responsibilities. As identified by the American Parole and Probation Association (Burke 1995), parole is given the duty to act as an independent, citizen-oriented board that carefully reviews each prisoner nearing the end of a period of incarceration mandated by court, to extend the time of imprisonment for the more violent and dangerous offenders, to demand that all prisoners demonstrate they are no longer a danger to society before they are permitted to return to the community, and to set specific conditions that must be met before release. Parole also carefully plans for the offenders' safe return to the community for those who have met the requirements for release by setting specific requirements for the prisoner. These might include restitution to victims, mandatory employment, electronic monitoring, house arrest, continuing drug treatment, appropriate residence, and a whole range of strategies to minimize risk. In addition, this requires monitoring offenders carefully through a network of professional parole officers who work in the community and returning offenders to prison whenever community safety is threatened. Parole is also careful control and supervision of offenders after they have earned release from prison and while they are demonstrating their worthiness to remain in the community, including the careful monitoring of the offender's home, job, activities, and associates. This supervision is an early warning system designed to alert the board to the necessity for returning the prisoner to prison. Finally, parole is a legal framework that empowers judges, prison officials, and parole boards to work together to administer a flexible system for punishing offenders and protecting the community.

Parole Versus Probation

Parole is different from probation. A New York parole officer noted that the difference between probation and parole was that parole involves a much higher level of supervision. The parole officer must conduct mandated visits in the office, home, job, and program sites. In New York, this process calls for intense risk assessment as well as the use of weapons. Each officer is required to qualify twice a year in the use of firearms, train in street survival, review the prosecution of violations, and conduct detective work. Parole officers clearly make a distinction between probation·and parole. Parole officers, for example, consider the difference between probation and parole to be similar to that of dentistry and brain surgery; probation is "dentistry" and parole is "brain surgery." This distinction is based on the fact that parole officers believe probation is too general; the officer is expected to be all things to all offenders and they must enforce the conditions of probation and provide casework. What is clearly a difference is that parole deals with stigmatized offenders who have spent time in prison, an institution geared far more toward punishment. Prisons deny the offender a sense of worth, dignity, and fair play. For many offenders, prison teaches them nothing more than the idea that society cares little for them as a people and much less as ex-offenders. Thus, many parolees have major problems after

prisonization is the process by which inmates adapt to life in prison, reflecting a prison subculture, influencing the inmates' language, role, group structure, and sexual behavior.

serving time in a prison. This requires special treatment of the offender. Most prisoners have undergone considerable pressure brought on by the effects of **prisonization**. The prison experience teaches the offender to be suspicious and manipulative, traits that serve little real purpose in daily activities on the outside.

A 1985 Rand study (Petersilia et al. 1985) that compared parolees with a matched sample of probationers found that a higher proportion of parolees had been on parole before, on juvenile probation, were armed during the crime, and were drug users. Parolees were also more likely to recidivate; however, their new crimes were not more serious than those committed by probationers. What was also interesting was that those who were incarcerated seemed to have a higher rate of recidivism (Pertersilia et al. 1985). To further understand parole, it is necessary to consider its history.

■ The History of Parole

The modern system of parole evolved from several measures including the frankpledge system (a form of social organization in a small community in which ten community members take responsibility for one another), pardons, indentures, and the **ticket of leave** of prisoners transported from England to the colonies (Goldfarb and Singer 1973, 257; Simon 1993). The history of parole can be divided into four periods: surety parole, disciplinary parole, clinical parole, and the modernist period.

Surety Parole

ticket of leave is a conditional pardon that frees the prisoner from governmental supervision during good behavior as long as the offender lawfully supports himself or herself.

suretyship system requires a citizen of good reputation to be obligated for the good behavior of another person.

recognizance bonds good behavior bonds were issued against persons who did not have a good reputation, e.g., persons considered lazy, transients, and parents of illegitimate children.

As an alternative to capital punishment for minor offenses and before the advent of imprisonment, the **suretyship system** was in operation. The suretyship system required a citizen of good reputation to be obligated for the good behavior of another person (Simon 1993, 18). One form, the frankpledge system, was issued in a large portion of England from the 10th to the 15th centuries. One of these obligations was to provide collective security through a requirement to report offenses committed by other members of the community and assume a financial obligation if the offender failed to appear at court (Morris 1910). The **recognizance bond** was used to keep the peace and supervise the dangerous person (Samaha 1981). Recognizance bonds included the peace bond for actions that threatened community peace and personal violence and good behavior bonds that were issued against persons who did not have a good reputation (e.g., persons considered lazy, transients, and parents of illegitimate children) (Simon 1993, 22).

Another form of early parole arose from the transporting of offenders from England to America or Australia where they served time in a penal colony and were later paroled. In 1790, according to Goldfarb and Singer (1973, 258), a British enabling act gave prison authorities the power to discharge and grant land to prisoners who displayed good conduct. Out of this, the prison authorities developed a form of the conditional pardon that came to be known as the ticket of leave that freed the prisoner from governmental supervision during good behavior as long as the offender lawfully supported himself. Prisoners serving 7-year terms were eligible after 4 years, those serving 14-year terms after 6 years, and those with life sentences after 8 years.

Alexander Maconochie (1787–1860) has been called the "father of parole" (Goldfarb and Singer 1973, 258). Maconochie applied the ticket of leave and the mark system temporarily during his term as administrator of the Norfolk Island penal colony. To facilitate reform of the offender, Maconochie proposed that sentences should be for the performance of a specified amount of labor; the quantity of labor must be expressed in a number of marks that he must earn by improvement in conduct, frugality of living, and habits of industry before he can be released; while in prison, the prisoner should earn everything he receives, all else should be added to his debt of marks; when qualified by discipline to do so, he should work in association with a small number of other prisoners and the whole group should be answerable for the conduct and labor of each other member; and, in the final stage, the prisoner should be given proprietary interest in his labors and should be subject to less rigorous discipline (Barry 1973, 91).

Murton (1976) describes the principles in action. The prisoner was transported to Norfolk Island where he was engaged in various labors. Each day the prisoner was paid 10 marks for his labor. With these marks, the prisoner could purchase food or could save some money and pay for a day toward release. Release was granted when a number of marks had been earned. As the prisoner moved to the next stage, he was granted a ticket of leave that became a rudimentary form of parole. If he served his time satisfactorily, the prisoner then moved into a conditional pardon. The next phase was penal settlement in some type of communal setting and then transportation to England and restoration of the prisoner's status as a freeman. This system is an example of the cyclical process of expulsion, mortification, penitence, reconstitution, and reacceptance back into society.

An Historical Review

It is generally believed that the first person to articulate the doctrine of commutation of sentence for good behavior as a principle was Archbishop Whatley of Dublin, Ireland. In an article published in 1829 in the *London Review,* he argued that definite sentences should be replaced with flexible sentences that could be earned by industrious labor. In the 1850s, Sir Joshua Jebb introduced a progressive stage system in Ireland that combined indeterminate sentences with parole. Later, the Irish system, under Sir Walter Crofton, introduced the intermediate stage. In the Crofton system, the prisoner spent 9 months in solitary confinement and was then transferred to a public works project. Afterward, he moved into a stage of unsupervised work while residing in a halfway house. After completing these stages, the person was placed on parole in the community. In addition to the obvious requirement to obey the law, the parolee could not associate with bad characters, thieves, and prostitutes nor could the person lead an idle life (Goldfarb and Singer 1973; Murton 1976).

The principles and methods established by Maconochie and Crofton provided the foundation for the birth of parole in the United States (Rhine et al. 1991). Just as probation began out of the recognition of its practical value, parole developed more out of a realistic understanding of the experience of prison and life afterward (Lindsey 1925).

One of the earliest examples of the commutation of sentence for good behavior appears in a New York law passed in 1817 for application in the Auburn prison. Widespread concern for the social disorder brought on by the New York

City Civil War race riots, along with disillusionment with the effectiveness of congregate prisons (Pisciotta 1983), led New York State in 1869 to pass legislation authorizing the construction of an industrial reformatory. The year 1877, nevertheless, marks the official birth of parole, the reformatory, and the indeterminate sentence. This activity was supported with the passage of a set of governing principles set forth by the newly formed American Prison Association's meeting held in Cincinnati, Ohio, in 1870 that called for a more humane treatment of the offender. The Cincinnati meeting promoted the notion that the treatment of the offender is for the protection of society, and, as such, the object of any punishment should be reformation through the moral regeneration of the offender. The prisoners' destinies should be placed in their own hands where they are able through their own exertion to better themselves by applying a concept of regulated self-interest. The primary means for applying these principles is through the indeterminate sentence (Lindsey 1925). These principles were exemplified in the reformatory.

Zebulon Brockway, a Michigan penologist, is given credit for implementing the first parole system in the United States. In 1876, he was appointed the first superintendent of the Elmira, New York, reformatory. He employed various elements in managing the prison population including indeterminate sentences, a marking system, early release for those with good records, and a suitable plan for employment. The decision to release the offender was made by the board of managers in consultation with the superintendent. Jurisdiction was maintained over the released offender, and if conditions were violated the offender could be returned to prison. Police chiefs, district attorneys, New York Prison Association members, and citizen volunteers provided initial supervision. If, after the initial 6-month period, the offender led a law-abiding life, the board of managers had the authority to recommend the offender's absolute release from imprisonment (Rhine et al. 1991, 9).

Despite these efforts, the period following the Civil War and leading up to the 20th century were characterized by practices that emphasized harsh treatment of the offender, especially the use of fixed-term sentences. Prisons continued to be crowded, inmate discipline was inconsistent and often brutal, and to reduce the problems of overcrowding, wardens continued to rely on good-time statutes, governor's pardons, and corporal punishment (Rhine et al. 1991, 9).

Disciplinary Parole

The basic form of prison release under the indeterminate sentence became disciplinary parole (Simon 1993). By 1898, about 25 states had a parole law (Johnson 1988, 228). The growth in parole was brought on by the need to rationalize the pardoning process and by the need to restore institutional discipline caused by the demise of the convict labor system (Simon 1993, 35). More importantly, parole was welcomed as a tool to keep prisons under control, as a means for relieving population pressures, and as a way of rewarding inmate cooperation (Simon 1993, 48). More importantly, prison officials could continue to maintain extremely harsh regimes because they assumed parole was responsible for normalizing and reintegrating the offender, a process that continues to this day.

The political leaders during the Progressive era of the early 20th century were ardent supporters of broad-scale reform efforts directed at social problems caused by the unregulated demands placed on the industrial economy: child labor abuses, dangerous occupations, poorly ventilated factories, dilapidated settlement houses, and slums (Rothman 1980). Support for parole came from citizens, social workers, criminologists, psychologists, psychiatrists, charitable societies, judges, district attorneys, wardens, and superintendents (Rothman 1980). In 1931, the Wickersham Report (Rhine et al. 1991) characterized parole as the safest means for releasing the offender into the community and for completing the work of reforming the offender. Despite this backing, parole still proved to be highly controversial (Rhine et al. 1991, 11). Opposition was at times harsh and unyielding, because it continued to be viewed as an act of leniency. Criticism was all the more easily directed if attention focused on the offender's performance record. Neither the decision to release nor the supervision of the offender was carried out with any degree of competence (Rothman 1980).

Clinical Parole

The rehabilitative ideal dominated the correctional system from the 1940s to the 1970s; this period has been termed the clinical parole period. This model relied on the professional abilities of the parole officer to develop a program to meet the individual needs of the parolee (Simon 1993, 69). The practice was based on a series of assumptions (Allen 1981):

1. It assumed human behavior is the product of identifiable antecedent conditions.
2. It assumed this knowledge provides the means for controlling human behavior.
3. It assumed the offender should be exposed to treatments that can alter his or her behavior, not only for the sake of building public safety but to enhance the offender's own happiness, health, and satisfaction.

The concluding program in this rehabilitative process was parole. Prisoners under this model were released at the discretion of the paroling authority. According to the ideal, parole boards should use their power to release prisoners when rehabilitated. However, prisoners were often unsure as to why they were granted or denied release. As far as rehabilitation's effect on prisoners is concerned, the experts lacked the ability to identify and correct criminal behavior, the prison culture mitigated offender change, and the parole board was more concerned with the offender's record of adjustment to the prison than actual preparation for the outside.

Modernist Period

By 1975, the American correction system was predicated on the indeterminate sentence and parole release. Every state had some form of the indeterminate sentence. In 1977, over 70 percent of the prison releases came by way of parole. Parole was considered an effective tool for dealing with the offender by encouraging offenders to participate in prison programming; assisting in the maintenance of institutional control and discipline in as much as prisoners responded to good-time laws (earning reduced time with good behavior); and providing a means for maintaining a system of discriminatory control through treatment programming while appearing to offer fair treatment to prisoners.

Finally, parole was an excellent means of controlling the size of the prison population (Petersilia 2000). Crowded conditions meant low-risk offenders and those with short prison times could be given an early exit. On all of these fronts, there is ample evidence to suggest that parole was a problem. Indeterminate sentencing, when combined with parole release, gave both rationale and authority to parole boards comprised of experts in behavioral sciences who were to pinpoint the moment the offender was rehabilitated and prepared for release. Parole boards, however, were composed not of "experts" but political appointees who expressed interests in parole despite their previous backgrounds. Instead of truly understanding if the offender was prepared for release as a rehabilitated offender, the board considered the seriousness of the offense in deciding to grant parole. Andrew von Hirsch's just-deserts model (1976) simply formalized the procedure and gave the boards something concrete to consider. Even with sentencing guidelines, there is little consensus from state to state on what constitutes a serious offense and how much time it merits. These matters only highlight the various forms of disparity experienced by prisoners.

Parole was based essentially on the medical model and one has to question the ability of anyone to apply it effectively to prisoners. If crime has to be seen as a disease, one has to be able to identify and treat the disease, to know when the treatment regime has been effective, and to know when to discharge the patient-offender. None of these issues were certainties. As with medical treatment in general, one treatment does not suit all types of diseases nor is it appropriate for all offenders. Far too much was made of the ability to change the thinking and behavior of the unwilling offender who believed his or her treatment had more to do with race, class, and gender than with the apparent malady he or she suffered. More importantly, the offender had trouble participating in a treatment plan that blamed him or her for the brutalization he or she experienced at the hands of the family, the school system, the state, and society in general.

■ Abolition of Parole

By the late 1970s, it had become somewhat popular among academicians, politicians, and prisoner advocates to call for the abolition of parole. Parole decisions came under severe scrutiny during the 1970s and 1980s (Fogel 1975; Gottfredson 1970; Kastenmier and Eglit 1975; Schmidt 1977; Talarico 1984; von Hirsch 1976) and there were a number of reasons for this. These reasons include the decision to release being dispersed across many decision makers, the process being invisible to the public, it lacked public standards, and it was without a guarantee of objectivity or accountability (Burke 1995, 19). Parole boards were functioning as unsupervised, autonomous quasijudicial bodies answerable neither to institutional authorities nor to the court (Pogrebin et al. 1986). Parole was considered unjust, capricious, arbitrary, and lacking explicit standards and should be replaced by a measure reflecting the harm of the offense and not the reform of the offender (von Hirsch and Hanrahan 1978). Fogel (1975) argued that parole boards had too much unbridled discretion under the flag of treatment and he felt treatment programming should be voluntary. What's more, it should be noted that the attack on parole was in part a product of ideological/political times with the rise of the right and get-tough policies that emphasized longer sentences and harsher prison conditions. In parole, this meant tighter scrutiny for the released offender who is subject to a greater number of post-release supervision requirements.

Parole board members have been criticized for lacking the appropriate qualifications, a particularly perilous situation considering the board must weigh the importance of protecting the community against the prisoner's right to freedom. Accurate prediction of the offender's recidivism and the monitoring of the offender's progress are beyond the scope of the system's powers (von Hirsch and Hanrahan 1978). It is also difficult to predict serious violent behavior with any high degree of accuracy (Bennett 1995). In order to identify a sizable proportion of predicted serious offenders, one has, by necessity, to include a large number of persons who are false positives, those persons predicted to engage in future criminal behavior but, if given the choice between being a criminal and noncriminal, choose to be crime free. Aside from considerations of effectiveness, it is unjust to base decisions about the severity of punishments on what the offender is expected to do in the future (von Hirsch and Hanrahan 1978).

Beginning in 1976, the experiment with the abolition of parole release had by 1998 included Arizona, Delaware, Illinois, Indiana, Kansas, Maine, Minnesota, Mississippi, New Mexico, North Carolina, Ohio, Oregon, Virginia, and Washington, and federal parole. Maine and Virginia went so far as to abolish parole supervision. In Virginia, the judge must impose a split sentence if the offender is not to walk away from the prison altogether following the end of the sentence. Several states that claimed to have abolished discretionary release have instead given parole a new name; Florida continued the post-release supervision by calling it "controlled release authority." Other jurisdictions, Minnesota and the U.S. Bureau of Prisons, changed the name of parole to "supervised release" and Ohio changed it to "community control" (Petersilia 2000). Colorado abolished discretionary release, but reinstated it after officials learned that prison sentences had actually decreased and high-risk offenders were left without any supervision (Gainsborough 1997). Since these changes, various activities performed under the guise of protecting the community changed from focusing on offender rehabilitation to programs grounded in punishment, incapacitation, and the enforcement of conditions (Benekos 1990; Byrne 1989; Cochran et al. 1986; Lipschitz 1986; O'Leary 1987). With further information about what is working in corrections, administrators are shifting to integrate their intervention strategies with their public safety concerns. It is important to recognize the distinction between measures that promote long-term behavioral change and short-term control (Boone et al. 1995, 71–72).

The ethics of parole release necessitate a reconsideration of what happens to the offender once released from prison. Quite often, a prisoner will not have changed sufficiently to warrant parole. Nonetheless, a prisoner does not deserve continued incarceration beyond the given prison term if he or she has failed to accomplish the impossible—to reform himself or herself while living in the most procriminal environment ever devised by humankind. Can the prisoner be kept when the system has not allowed him or her to change (Manocchio and Dunn 1982, 226)? These measures require further consideration. How is it possible to identify an appropriate psychological adjustment to such an environment?

Parole has historically provided job assistance, family counseling, and chemical dependency programs, although arguably, parole has never provided enough of these services. Campaigns to increase punishments and diminish social services have resulted in fewer services provided to parolees. This led to parole recidivism rates of around 60 percent (Hughes et al. 2001) that cost states dearly. A greater number of parolees are failing parole and being returned to prison, thus putting greater pressure on the prison system. In California, parole violators account for 65 percent of all prison admissions with 41 percent representing technical violations (Austin and Lawson 1998). Recycling offenders costs the system huge sums of money, does nothing to reduce community crime, demoralizes the prison population, and leads to staff cynicism. Legislators and the public alike must come to realize the parolee's failure is also their failure.

■ Administration of Parole

Petersilia (2000) reports that parole costs an average of $2,200 a year but is still considerably less than the $20,000 or more it costs on average to house a prisoner. Parole was first established as a diffuse agency. In some states, it was under the authority of the governor or board of pardons and was viewed as a form of executive clemency. In other states, parole was tied to prison administration. Currently, only 14 states have separate paroling agencies. The contemporary organization of the parole agency is quite complex and varies according to state preferences. For the most part, parole has been administered by state departments of corrections; departments of corrections administer 35 out of 51 paroling authorities. Probation is joined in a common department with parole in only 4 states under departments of parole and probation (Maguire and Pastore 1994, 117). Some experts believe it is hard to sustain a unified probation and parole system (Clear and Cole 1997).

An Example: New York

The history of the administration parole in New York State offers some understanding of how parole has shifted from one administrative structure to another in an effort to clarify its role and meets the needs of a rising prisoner population. Established in 1930, the New York Division of Parole had a board consisting of three members who had responsibility for conducting all parole hearings. At that time, paroling functions were then transferred from the Department of Corrections to the Division of Parole. In 1945, all paroling functions involving training schools, mentally disabled prisoners, and the women's reformatory were consolidated under the Division of Parole. By 1967, paroling functions in New York were under the authority of the Board of Parole. At that time, New York's City's paroling functions were also transferred to the state.

In 1971, the New York Department of Correctional Services (DOCS) was formed with the consolidation of the Division of Parole and the Department of Corrections. It was thought that a coordinated effort involving institutional and community supervision would have a higher impact on crime. This consolidation lasted until 1977 when the parole division was again reestablished as a separate agency. At this time, parole guidelines were mandated to structure the parole board's decision-making process involving minimum sentences and the granting and denying of parole. By 1992, the number of people on parole in New York had grown from 4,000 in 1930 to 50,000. To handle these numbers, the parole board expanded to 19 full-time members. In New York, the governor has the power to appoint up to 19 members who must meet the approval of the state senate. Each member serves a term of 6 years. The members of the New York parole board must have earned a baccalaureate degree and have at least 5 years of experience in criminology, administration of criminal justice, law enforcement, sociology, law, social work, corrections, psychology, psychiatry, or medicine (Rhine et al. 1991, 36)

In a majority of states, the governor nominates people to the parole board and has a great deal of latitude in selecting the people to serve. Only 6 states require the parole board member to possess a 4-year college degree, and 9 states require some experience in the criminal justice system. Appointment to the parole board underscores the political nature of the work. Parole becomes particularly politicized in the appointment process, when new legislation is being considered, and when a controversial case is under review. While the political influence on parole is quite evident, there must be a recognition that parole operates, for the most part, as an independent agency. In principle, parole makes decisions autonomously without consideration of another agency (Rhine et al. 1991, 48).

Parole Operations

In some states (especially New York), parole operations are supported by various staff functions, administrative services, policy analysis and information units, and public information offices. Parole officers write reports and offer release recommendations on each offender. Legal counsel provides advice on policy and legislation and administers due process hearings. The executive clemency unit investigates applications for pardons and commutation of sentences. The victim impact office provides advice to victims and assists them in having an impact at parole hearings (Russi 1992).

Parole Officers

Parole officers are comprised of individuals of various races, creeds, and political persuasions. Some states, such as Tennessee, have almost as many female (88) as they have male (98) officers. New York, however, has 847 male officers and 392 female officers (Maguire and Pastore 1995). Parole officers come from a variety of backgrounds, but many of them have prior experience in law enforcement, probation, or corrections. Their motives for leaving their previous jobs and becoming a parole officer are revealing. If they came from law enforcement, the parole officer likes the independence found in parole. If the officer comes from corrections, the officer likes the increased professional stature. Coming from probation, the officer enjoys the additional emphasis given to law enforcement. Many officers like the job security. In interviews conducted by the author with New York parole agents, one officer mentioned he became a parole officer because it provided an interesting alternative to going to law school. Another became a parole officer after losing his fourth grade teacher's post due to staff reductions at school. Another became a parole officer after working in corrections and construction work. Another joined the parole service because it offered him an opportunity to use his experience gained in corrections working with sex offenders. This officer enjoyed the additional flextime found with the job and the additional money.

Working as an Officer

Parole officers operate within a system of norms that regulate how the work is done. Discussion held with officers for this work reinforced the earlier findings of McCleary in *Dangerous Men* (1992). For example, various norms regulate the supervision of the officers. Officers do not interfere with each other's caseloads nor do they overly criticize each other's style of supervision. Often but not always, two officers may even work as a team but each officer recognizes the importance the other adds to their work.

When dealing with parolees, many officers combine a sense of fairness with skepticism. The officer wants to treat the offender in a manner that is according to legal standards and policies but that also respects the parolee's dignity. At the same time, the parole officer will carefully supervise the parolee knowing that something may go wrong at any time. Experienced officers come to recognize the qualities of the person they are supervising. These officers come to recognize parolees who are and are not going to make it on parole. Some parolees will do just fine on parole and during the period that follows, some will fail while on parole and some will fail after the person has been discharged from parole. Whether the parolee succeeds or not sometimes depends on factors that are beyond the parolee's control such as family problems, employment difficulties, or a lack of training.

Good officers also realize that it does them no good to treat the parolee with scorn, derision, and contempt; the parolee received plenty of that while in prison. What is important is to reinforce the importance of treating everyone with dignity. The officer has to show respect for the parolee as a human being who has served his or her time and deserves to be treated as someone of value. The officer also knows treating parolees badly only increases their chances of returning to prison. Lastly, through adopting a dignified approach, the officer is giving the parolee a chance to gain some experience treating others with dignity and learning how to think for himself or herself, how to make mistakes, make corrections, and gain some confidence in the "outside" world.

Releases

Since 1990, discretionary releases to parole have dropped while mandatory releases have risen. Discretionary releases to parole supervision by parole boards have decreased from 50 percent of adults entering parole in 1995 to 39 percent in 2003 (Glaze and Palla 2004). Mandatory releases to parole supervision have risen from 45 percent in 1995 to 51 percent in 2003 (Glaze and Palla 2004).

The parole release decision is fraught with public and political concerns that are not found in most probation cases. Meyer (2000) offers an interesting account of the parole board at the community-level decision-making process. In the state where she served on the board, there was a two-tier release process. First, prisoners petitioned the state-level parole board with a parole plan detailing their employment and housing plans. This board reviewed the petition and, if accepted, the case was transferred to the local selection panel that was responsible for determining the suitability of release into a specific community. The local selection panel used the same criteria as the state-level panel. However, it was composed of unpaid members who were appointed by the state's secretary of corrections based on recommendations by the local community corrections program director. If the local selection panel refused a candidate, the person had to submit a new parole plan or submit an application to another community. There was no opportunity to appeal the local selection committee's decision.

Meyer (2000) learned that local selection panelists were selected from a variety of backgrounds. Although many were associated in one way with the state's probation and parole division for adults, other members represented local law enforcement agencies, social service agencies, or the community-at-large as private citizens. Women tended to outnumber men on the panel. Meetings were quite informal because there was no requirement for note taking, but in Meyer's experience, notes were often taken. Most of the panel members arrived before the meeting to review the 10 files that were routinely up for examination. On more than one occasion, a panelist voted without having read the file. Community acceptance of the offender's release is in some cases a function of the publicity given recent similar offenses. Offenses committed by other offenders that are considered heinous certainly work against the decision to grant parole. There is little that the prisoner can do about it.

Meyer's (2000) description of the decision-making process was particularly enlightening in view of an understanding of small-group dynamics, especially juries. Acceptance of an applicant's file for parole was fairly routine; it called for little discussion. However, in the case of a rejected candidate, discussions were much more elaborate. Panelists generally made their decision following the discussion based on material supporting their conclusion. Occasionally, a panelist would switch gears after hearing other remarks or after being directed toward certain facts in the case. Acceptance was based on whether the prisoner deserved to be approved. This related to the level of culpability. If the offender had served what was considered an appropriate amount of time or did not deserve to be incarcerated to begin with, he or she could be approved. At the second step of the process, panelists attempted to fashion the most appropriate level of supervision in light of the community's resources and the offender's needs. If they did not match well, the offender could be denied parole. Concerns might be expressed about public safety, at which point, conditions were designed to reduce the likelihood of recidivism. Lacking such conditions, the offender remained in prison. The panel reviewed the severity of the offense, prior record, prison misconduct, and aggravating and mitigating factors. Aggravating factors included the feeling that the appropriate amount of time had not been served or that the offender was from a community outside of the local panel's purview. Outsiders were considered someone else's problem and a drain on local resources. Moreover, aggravation could be attached to the sentence despite the fact the offender had not been convicted but was charged with a particular offense. Mitigating factors might include experiencing a difficult childhood or having drug and alcohol problems. Mitigation was relevant only if an appropriate treatment program could be put into place.

Parole Techniques

Meyer's (2000) local parole panels discussed various techniques for granting parole. The first technique was sponsorship in which an individual panel member advocated for the acceptance by the board. Potentially unsatisfactory applicants were certain to be accepted if they were sponsored by at least one member of the panel. Sponsorship meant that a board member chose to speak on behalf of the applicant. Sponsors may redefine the level of culpability, use euphemisms to describe some behavior, and speak of the inherent general problems with incarceration for any offender. Inasmuch as parole members may read each file differently, sponsorship plays a major role in seeing that applicants' files are given a full measure of consideration. In Meyer's study, sponsorship involved bringing information to the board's attention that was not in the file, attempting to minimize the offender's culpability or prior life experiences, however difficult that may be, offering a personal diagnosis of the offender's problems, and providing an exoneration of prison conduct reports. Most importantly, sponsorship made a difference if it was presented by the board's chairperson especially through oral presentations not available to other members of the board.

The second assessment technique relied on a "magical variable" to substantiate votes and influence others to grant or deny parole (Meyer 2000). One magic variable was prison behavior. When decision makers desired to think outside of the acceptable criteria they relied on the magic variable prison conduct to support or deny release. Magic variables were used to acquit decision makers of any responsibility for their decisions. Magic variables play an important role in overcoming the rigidity of sentencing guidelines. Sentencing guidelines diminish in importance if an offender proves to be a model prisoner or very troublesome to authorities. If the offender acts out and causes trouble while in prison, the authorities can reduce the amount of earned good time but they cannot sentence the offender to additional time unless there is a true violation of the law. If the offender's behavior is exemplary the offender may still serve a lengthy sentence, especially if the offender lives in a truth-in-sentencing state where he or she has committed a crime of violence and is required to serve 85 percent of the sentence in prison before release (Hughes and Wilson 2003).

The last technique the panel used for granting or denying parole was a form of "justice roulette" (Meyer 2000) in which the panel tried to anticipate the future actions of judges and offenders as to how likely they were to accept the conditions set for parole release. Quite often, the major concern was that the applicant might wait until he or she could be paroled without any conditions. When this problem arose, the panel tended to fall back on the question of whether the offender had served enough time. Frequently, offenders were paroled simply because they were due for release soon and the panel believed some supervision was better than none at all. **Table 12-1** details the percent of parolees who have been released from state prisons through discretionary parole, mandatory parole, and expiration of the sentence.

Table 12-1 indicates that the method in which prisoners are released from prison is changing. Prisoners today are more likely to be released through mandatory parole or expiration of their sentences than they were in 1980. Discretionary releases to parole dropped from 39 percent of releases in 1990 to 24 percent in 2000. *Discretionary parole* exists when a parole board has authority to condition-

Table 12-1	Percent of Releases from State Prison by Method, 1980–2000		
	Discretionary Parole	**Mandatory Parole**	**Expiration of Sentence**
1980	54.76%	18.63%	14.25%
1981	51.44%	20.15%	13.06%
1982	50.28%	23.63%	13.92%
1983	46.32%	25.86%	15.50%
1984	45.23%	28.25%	16.03%
1985	42.55%	30.36%	16.66%
1986	42.65%	30.68%	14.65%
1987	40.07%	30.78%	16.00%
1988	39.82%	30.26%	16.58%
1989	38.36%	30.28%	15.25%
1990	39.40%	28.83%	12.65%
1991	39.72%	29.94%	10.83%
1992	39.54%	29.48%	11.38%
1993	38.82%	31.61%	11.88%
1994	34.99%	35.61%	12.47%
1995	32.33%	38.98%	14.50%
1996	30.35%	37.95%	16.74%
1997	28.19%	39.67%	16.80%
1998	25.98%	40.45%	18.67%
1999	23.71%	41.13%	18.09%
2000	23.87%	38.78%	19.60%

Sources: Bureau of Justice Statistics, *Trends in state parole, 1990–2000,* 2001, and National Corrections Reporting Program. Available online at http://www.ojp.usdoj.gov/bjs/abstract/tsp00.htm.

ally release prisoners based on a statutory or administrative determination of eligibility. Mandatory releases to parole steadily increased from 116,857 in 1990 to 221,414 in 2000 (from 29 percent of all state prison releases to 39 percent). *Mandatory parole* generally occurs in jurisdictions using determinate sentencing statutes in which inmates are conditionally released from prison after serving a specified portion of their original sentence minus any good time earned. About 112,000 state prisoners were released unconditionally through an expiration of their sentence in 2000, up from 51,288 in 1990. Sixteen states have abolished discretionary parole for all offenders (Hughes and Wilson 2003).

Presently, too much can be made of the 22-month average prison sentence for initial release. Many inmates serve additional time due to parole violations and others are released due to completing the sentence. Furthermore, many inmates serve as much as half a year waiting in a jail to go to prison. Adding the additional 6 months to the sentence would bring the total to 28 months of imprisonment. Lastly, these inmates are no reflection of the population of offenders who have received stiff sentences and will not be included in the data for some time (Irwin and Austin 1997).

Prison sentences have increased as a result of the restrictions on parole boards, the "three-strikes-you're-out" laws, truth-in-sentencing laws, mandatory minimum sentence laws, and sentencing guidelines that employ risk-assessment instruments to determine that the lower-risk offender is given the first opportunity to be released. Such instruments reduce the disparity by eliminating subjective assessments done by caseworkers.

Parole Conditions

When an inmate is approved for parole or conditional release, he or she must agree to certain conditions of parole (Executive Department—Division of Parole 1997). In New York, for example, parole is considered voluntary; thus, the parolees and their property are subject to search and inspection. New York parolees also understand that violations of these conditions may result in the revocation of their release. The parolees are to report to parole authorities within 24 hours of their release. They agree to:

- Report as scheduled
- Not leave the state
- Allow the parole officer to visit where he or she lives or works or has a treatment program
- Report any changes in those three areas
- Reply promptly to any inquiry
- Notify if there is an arrest
- Not associate with anyone known to have a criminal record
- Not violate the law or endanger the public
- Not possess a gun or dangerous weapon
- Not leave the jurisdiction, or waive their right to extradition
- Not possess any drug paraphernalia
- Respond to special conditions
- Comply with all conditions of parole

■ Parolees

The Bureau of Justice Statistics in its parolees summary, *Probation and Parole in United States 2003* (Glaze and Palla 2004), reported that the correctional population was at an all-time high of 6.9 million offenders with 4.8 million offenders on probation and parole. These offenders comprised 70 percent of all offenders under correctional supervision. There were 774,588 offenders on parole, an increase of 3.1 percent or 23,654 parolees over 2002. The increase in number was the largest since 1995. Women comprised one in eight parolees or 96,800 offenders. Blacks (41 percent) and whites (40 percent) were evenly distributed among parolees but blacks were clearly overly represented by national population data. There were roughly 136,000 Hispanics on parole. At the end of the year 2003, more than four out of every five parolees were under active supervision and were required to maintain regular contact with the paroling agency. About 9 percent of the parolees were absconders and could not be located. Two out of five parolees discharged from supervision returned to prison. Among those returned to prison, 38 percent were for rule violations or new offenses (Glaze and Palla 2004).

Life on the Outside

For anyone coming home and trying to fit in, whether it is after a stint in the Peace Corps, in the military, or in prison, there are certain critical adjustments to be made for a smooth and successful transition. The person who has been away wants to know what's going on and the person who is being asked has no idea what the person wants to hear. There are all kinds of information to be shared, but it must be clear that the time away cannot be made up; it is simply lost. This realization comes after much struggle and disappointment. In many of these cases, however, with a little help, this period does not have to be so painful. In some ways, the pain of re-entry is worse than the struggle to survive daily prison life. It is at this juncture that the humanity of the parolee must be recognized. A stigma (Goffman 1963) is the application of an unwarranted negative label on a person. Drug offenders, sex offenders, and the mentally ill are three heavily stigmatized offenders, but all offenders are to some degree stigmatized. It is this stigmatization that denies the offender his or her human dignity. We must remember that no person is the sum total of his or her worse deeds. As Bedau (1992) earlier outlined Kant's position on human dignity, a person's dignity is another way of referring to a person's worth. A person's worth must be kept distinct from other attributes of the person, in particular, the person's merit, value, or usefulness. Above all, a person's dignity is not the product of decent conduct, virtuous behavior, moral rectitude, or respect for the moral law. Rather, dignity is granted because people are seen to have the capacity for virtuous conduct. People have value because they have the capacity to do good. Parole officers must come to recognize the potential in each of their parolees. Second, parolees do not vary in their dignity or worth. Human dignity is shared equally, essentially as a form of moral egalitarianism where human dignity is invariably inherent and complete but not contingent or circumstantial (Bedau 1992, 153–154). Third, human dignity is intimately related to human autonomy. A parolee who has served his or her sentence deserves to experience autonomy. An autonomous creature is a self-activating, self-directing, self-criticizing, self-correcting, and self-understanding creature. Autonomous individuals are self-reflective. Fully autonomous creatures do not merely pursue ends, they create them and confer value on them (Bedau 1992, 154).

Parole officers who emphasize social integration have to balance individual freedoms of expression with expectations of conformity especially with youth, minorities, and nonconformists in general (Karp and Clear 2002). At this point, the parole officer must walk a thin line between careful supervision and allowing the offender to experiment with decision making. Ultimately, rehabilitated offenders are ones who can make appropriate decisions on their own. Moreover, dignity is inseparably connected to an individual's capacity to evaluate, calculate, organize, predict, explain, conjecture, and justify, and to prize and appraise things and situations, thus to choose not only the means to ends but the ends themselves. Despite a pattern of poor choices, parolees are self-conscious, rational individuals whose thoughts must be understood as a rational story or explanation of what happened to them and is going on inside of them. It is when this presentation as someone offering an honest appraisal is rejected that essential dignity is most likely to be denied. Too often, it can be assumed that an explanation is a justification or excuse when it is all someone has to offer. Finally, human dignity provides the basis for equal human rights. After the successful conclusion of parole, offenders should have all of their civil rights reestablished because they have served their time and no longer deserve to be punished. Only creatures with rights (not merely positive legal rights, but the rights that sound moral theory confers) have dignity. In the preamble to the 1948 Universal Declaration of Human Rights (United Nations 1948), explicit reference is made to the "inherent dignity of all members of the human family" and to "the dignity and worth of all human persons" as part of the rationale for universal human rights. These rights are the sword and shield that secure humanity's interests and sense of worth in the political arena. Equal human rights are a necessary consequence of equal human worth and dignity. Whatever inequalities (socioeconomic, psychological, physical) may arise owing to the natural lottery or to the contingencies of the social environment, they do not efface, override, or undermine equal human rights (Bedau 1992, 155).

Family

Spending time in prison and on parole may make it difficult for offenders to maintain contact with their families. The number of children whose parents are in prison is astounding. More than 1.5 million children in the United States have parents in prison (Hagan and Dinowitzer 1999). Two out of three women offenders and more than half of the men in prison have minor children.

Mumola (2000) reports that the 1.5 million figure for children under 18 whose parents were in prison is a figure that has increased by over 500,000 since 1991. There were 667,000 fathers and 53,600 mothers of minor children held in state and federal prisons. Of the nation's 72 million children, roughly 2.1 percent of them had a parent in prison in 1999. Black children were nine times more likely to have a parent in prison than white children. Only 43 percent of the male and 64 percent of the female prisoners lived with their children prior to incarceration. Approximately 22 percent of these children whose parents were in prison were under the age of five. Over 90 percent of the fathers said that at least one of their children lived with their mother; 28 percent of the mothers said that the father was the current caregiver. Ten percent of the mothers and 2 percent of the fathers said that their child was now living in foster care. A majority of fathers and mothers reported never having a personal visit with their children since imprisonment began. This is due in part to the fact that over 60 percent of the parents reported being held in a facility that was over 100 miles from where they last lived.

Whether released offenders are rejoining a family or trying to get by on their own, they face major problems. Their host communities are not interested in their return. In fact, if the offender has committed a crime that has recently drawn a lot of attention, the wrath of the public will be directed at them. More importantly, family reintegration is not a principal concern for many people. Because public policy does not support family reintegration, rejoining prior families is quite difficult. Furthermore, many prisoners live in high crime communities, but with few job opportunities or few social services. These communities find it more important to give attention to fighting drugs than to providing social services. More attention is given to police surveillance, housing and job prohibitions, voting disenfranchisement, and welfare/child reform stipulations (Hairston 2003, 20).

The ability to provide food, shelter, clothing, and medical care is a fundamental concern for any family that is reuniting (Hairston 2003, 20). Because public policy assures that offenders do not leave prison with any significant resources, they must rely on extended family relatives and close friends for support. For many parolees, the extra room waiting for them is a sofa or chair. There is little additional money for food, clothing, transportation, and personal items. Under these conditions, it is unlikely parolees will stay with their hosts for a long time. They, in turn, become peripatetic as they move from one associate to another. Quite often, when they refer to home, they are talking about where their mothers live and not where they currently live (Hairston 2003, 21). In fact, the only thing for certain is that the offender has a place to live and a permanent legal address.

Planning for release does not usually include any consideration of the financial burdens placed on the host family. Often from low-income families, any additional person is a real burden on the family unless he or she can contribute immediately to the family's overall well-being through paid employment. Temporary assistance is found in welfare benefits, food stamps, and Medicaid. Unfortunately, the war on drugs has placed these benefits beyond the reach of former prisoners, especially those with drug convictions (Brown 2000; Hirsch 2000).

Parolees face additional problems with respect to finding work. An important component of doing well on parole is finding a job.

Work

One of the reasons that the national unemployment rate has stayed so low and why the current level underestimates the problem is that the 2 million low-skilled offenders in prison and jail are not counted among the unemployed. If they were, the unemployment rate would stand another 2 percentage points higher than it is now (Western and Beckett 1999).

As far as finding work is concerned, many parolees have exaggerated impressions of what they will do once they are released. Many parolees want to catch up with the life they lost and finding a good job is a requisite for that. Today, if a good job cannot be found, there is always the possibility of going into the drug trade. Moreover, if law-abiding citizens are going through economic turmoil, the parolee will also experience a similar, if not worse, fate. Research indicates that offenders have no clear idea as to whether they should report that they have a criminal record to the employer. Many offenders do not have the type of training, work experience, or social networks that are needed to secure or hold work. Prison work does not prepare the offender for work in the public or private sector. Community-based training is as rare and prison-based industries have no obligation to provide the offender with employment on the outside (Hairston 2003, 23).

Parolees are not entitled to any unemployment benefits. In a study by Holzer (1996), during a particular year, as many as 60 percent of the parolees were not employed in legitimate occupations. With the shift of manufacturing to second- and third-world nations, there are few opportunities for parolees seeking work in the inner cities (Petersilia 2000, 3). In a study of employers, it was learned that they are increasingly reluctant to hire ex-offenders. In a survey of five major U.S. cities, it was learned that 65 percent of all employers were not interested in knowingly hiring an ex-offender regardless of the offense and another 20 to 40 percent said they had begun to check the criminal records of new hires.

Shelley Albright (1996) has pointed out that traditionally offenders have been destined for low-paying, low-skilled, and menial work. With a lack of education and other job-related skills, the added burden of a criminal record makes gainful employment a daunting achievement. Recycling low-skilled offenders between freedom and imprisonment is simply another method of regulating the surplus population.

Employment provides the person with an organizing and stabilizing resource that eases a variety of household tensions (Curtis and Schulman 1984, 512). Rossi and associates (1980, 211) note that employment provides an individual with a valued position in society and a set of supporting social contracts. It also provides direct competition for the time spent on illegal activity. At the very least, employment provides the person with a measure of self-worth and personal respect. Even for those who are on the margins of society, knowing that they are paying their own way through life offers them a measure of dignity they would not achieve were they to lose their jobs or receive public assistance. For some people, this measure of dignity is all to which they can cling.

It has been assumed that ex-offenders are deficient in human capital and that improvements in skills, attitudes toward work responsibilities, and self-esteem will lead to increases in post-release employment opportunities. It is not hard to imagine that employers are unwilling to hire ex-offender. Albright (1996) points out that post-release employment is affected by a multitude of factors associated with the employer and larger community. The effects of the ex-offender's educational level, government incentives, the type of offense, and the job-crime relationship can all affect the probability of employment as far as employer attitudes are concerned (Albright 1996). A study conducted by Hulsey (1990) found that 30 percent of the employers would hire an ex-offender. Albright's study also found low rates of interest in hiring ex-offenders. Albright's study notes that as the ex-offender's level of education increases, so does the offender's chances of gaining employment. Government incentives have a positive effect on employment. Employers are more likely to hire ex-offenders who are bonded, insured, and licensed. Ex-offenders who commit murder, robbery, arson, and sexual offenses against children have a considerably lesser chance to gain employment. Lastly, state laws and parole regulations make it imperative that ex-offenders stay clear of certain occupations related to their declared offense. In California, for example, Pertersilia (2000) reports that ex-offenders are restricted from occupations in law, real estate, medicine, nursing, physical therapy, and education. Colorado prohibits them from becoming dentists, engineers, nurses, pharmacists, physicians, and real estate agents. Forgers and those charged with embezzlement, for example, are not going to be working with payrolls.

In an effort to clarify the analysis, criminal offenders are identified by the convicted offense while little attention is given to the criminal lifestyle that may have remained unknown to the parole agent or employer. One must recognize that offenders, despite the prison experience, will make some changes from the time of entry to discharge. In some cases, offenders are willing to work at jobs no one else will take and will do exemplary work.

According to Petersilia (2000), unemployment is correlated with drug and alcohol abuse as well as child abuse and family violence. Moreover, the unemployed offender is unable to meet his or her restitution and other court-ordered payments.

Housing

A key problem that has come to light lately is housing for ex-offenders. In California, 10 percent of all parolees are homeless (Petersilia 2000). Public housing and subsidized housing rules prohibit individuals convicted of drug offenses, for example, from residing in that type of housing (Brown 2000). Rental agreements and leases in private housing often restrict the tenants to those who are actually renting or leasing. If the returning prisoner was not living in the unit at the time of the arrest, it is unlikely that he or she will be listed on the lease. Rental applications ask questions about arrest records and convictions to screen out potential residents with criminal histories. With the rise in the establishment of crime-free housing programs, the offender has fewer opportunities for housing than before entering prison. If the offender is required to register as a sex offender, there is also the problem that the family residence will also be put on a public register as a place housing a sex offender, leading to problems of stigmatization. This can lead to the family experiencing a great deal of unwanted attention and cause family members to be needlessly humiliated as an associate of the offender. Such singling out puts them at risk of social isolation, hostility, verbal abuse, and demonstrations by neighbors who seek to drive the offender out of their neighborhood (Hairston 2003, 21).

Families who are caring for relatives' children under formal arrangements with child welfare departments are in jeopardy of having the children removed from the home if they allow the criminal to reside there. An occupant's criminal history, including that of the child's parent, could lead to loss of a foster home license and removal of the child to the home of unrelated individuals.

Doing Well on the Streets

It is clear that making a successful reintegration back into the community is greatly enhanced by connecting the offender with family, community, and mentors. The data indicate that parolees who make it on the outside can be categorized as either sincere (McCleary 1992) or "tired dudes" (Irwin and Austin 1997). The sincere parolee, besides sharing common goals with the officer, is trouble free, cooperative, honest, and informative. Officers find it rewarding to work with the bright, articulate, and more pleasant parolee. The parolee willingly gets involved in programming. There is a willingness to accept the parolee as a counselee and the officer, in turn, is accepted as a counselor. If the parolee is not considered a problem, he or she may be "banked" or "papered," meaning the person is on parole but is seen only three or four times a year. Many of these parolees are targeted for special programs. Some officers consider addicts and the educationally handicapped parolees as noncriminal types and deserving of different consideration. Special treatment programs get rid of the problem non-criminal parolee without labeling the person as dangerous. Mandatory treatment provides additional support and supervision where needed. Administrators have come to believe the sincere parolee is given too much consideration and requires greater constraint. Nonetheless, the officer has the final say in how the parolee is typed.

There is also the older parolee who responds well to warnings and admonitions and doesn't want any trouble or hassles. These parolees have witnessed their friends and relatives die or move away, have established valued relationships with others, and do not want to return to prison. They have a job and modest living quarters, and eat inexpensive meals. They value their outside existence regardless of how modestly they must live. They realize that it takes time to get back on track. They also know how vulnerable they are to the wishes of an officer or problems from an old offender friend.

Mental Health

Another problem sometimes experienced by parolees is mental illness. There are estimates that say as many as 283,000 jail and prison inmates reported experiencing a mental illness (Ditton 1999). Many of these prisoners are also suffering from some form of substance dependence. Furthermore, continued confinement in maximum security and super-max prisons exacerbates depression and anxiety problems, especially when spending long hours in solitary confinement or segregation. Many prisoners fail to use the mental health facilities because they do not trust the mental health system (Petersilia 2000). Prisoners also come to recognize that a superficial diagnosis means they can be prescribed heavy doses of drugs simply by asking for them (Hassine 1999).

Parole officials will have to come to some understanding of the kind of treatment these people will need after they get out of prison. The use of prisons to manage the mentally ill is obviously related to the efforts in the 1960s to deinstitutionalize mental health patients. Following the debate as to labelling the mentally ill, what they require, and how they can best receive care, it was decided that the local community was to provide additional outreach and community-based treatment services augmented by a host of newly discovered medications intended to reduce their symptoms.

Some prisoners diagnosed as suffering from a mental illness receive meaningful treatment that is characterized by a reliable and valid diagnosis. What is troublesome is the prisoner who receives drugs that are prescribed to deal with the symptoms, a regimen that must be continued while on parole if the parolee is to remain effective in the community. This regimen of drugs can be expensive, uncomfortable, and difficult to obtain. Because of this, parolees then stop taking their medication. Parole officers have to remain vigilant about this possibility. When conditions become extreme, the parolees need to be rehospitalized.

Supervision

Many parole officers view their work in terms of enforcing the conditions of parole. Parole officers are responsible for the supervision and reintegration of the offender. Eighty percent of the returning prisoners are placed on parole and assigned a parole agent (Petersilia 2000). The remaining prisoners will complete their sentence and will receive little in the way of postrelease supervision. Ironically, it is this latter population who needs the most attention even though they are ineligible for services. Parole officers play an important role as a source of support, helping the offender adjust to the community. Although the officer may enforce the conditions of parole, he or she should understand the difficulties of adjusting to a new life on the outside. The officer also serves as an information source for the victim so that he or she is kept fully informed of the conditions of supervision and other safety-related concerns of the victim (Petersilia 2000).

The burdens placed on the parole officer have increased dramatically over the last 25 years. Not only is the officer expected to fully understand the psychology of the parolee and the effects on the family and victim, but the officer is also expected to understand the law, work a caseload that is twice as large as it was 25 years ago, and work in an environment that is much more dangerous. Although caseloads may have expanded from 45 to over 70 parolees, officers are required to maintain contact with all parolees. This means that quite often there is less than two 15-minute face-to-face contacts per month. The lack of time means that there are problems with parolees absconding. Nationally, about 7 percent of all parolees have absconded (Glaze and Palla 2004).

Either institutional parole staff or field staff carry out parole supervision. Institutional officers are assigned for the purpose of guiding the inmate during incarceration. They are responsible for helping inmates develop positive attitudes and behavior, motivating inmates to participate in the appropriate programs, and preparing inmates for their board interviews and eventual release from the prison. Assignments to the field entail supervising and guiding parolees during the period of adjustment following incarceration (Russi 1992).

There are many different types of supervision. Good field officers are described as fair and competent, have the ability to solve problems, and work long hours. They are informed about their parolees, fair in their interactions with the parolee, and selective in terms of which parolee they support (McCleary 1992). These factors become particularly important in light of limited resources and when dealing with a variety of other agencies. There are also informative officers who, as part of their law enforcement function, provide information to the rest of the criminal justice system. These officers collect information that is used selectively in reports in order to appear insightful and current. This builds a sense of indebtedness on the part of the parolee. Discretion is selectively applied in that the officer helps the prosecutor at the parolee's expense or chooses to help the parolee. Some officers are criticized, however, for playing social worker. For example, the New York State parole department wants team players who can work together and are effective communicators. Parole requires a combination of skills not found in other professions. The demands presented by the parolee require that officers work as social workers, police officers, detectives, lawyers, and medical specialists. Many officers believe the public does not understand the nature of their work nor does the public appreciate the difficulties associated with working with such a diverse population of offenders.

Supervision of the offender continues to be the principal means of reintegrating the offender back into the community in states that employ determinate and indeterminate sentencing models. It must be remembered that the largest

COMMUNITY CORRECTIONS & HUMAN DIGNITY

number of states still use the indeterminate sentence model (Bennett 1995). Despite the deficiencies in the release process, the greatest problem by far is the supervision of the offender. Again, there is no clear evidence about the effectiveness of this process.

In a study conducted in Minnesota, parolees were classified and assigned to either light, medium, or intensive supervision categories. These parolees were then assigned to regular or special supervision models. The parolees classified as low-risk and assigned to a low level of supervision seemed to do well regardless of whether they had any supervision or not. There was also no difference for the medium-risk offender. Those classified as high-risk and receiving intensive supervision and high levels of services did much better in terms of employment, adjustment to the community, and managing their social and family lives but did not show a significant difference in their recidivism (Bennett 1995, 16).

Not Making It

The revocation of parole is one of the major responsibilities for every paroling agency (Rhine et al. 1991, 122). To justify its existence, parole evolved into a law enforcement agency rather than an agency interested in the parolee's adjustment to the world. The conditions of parole have achieved renewed prominence, especially during the revocation hearing. Parole revocation is affected by due process considerations, prison crowding, parole guidelines, intermediate sanctions, and parole recidivism (Rhine et al. 1991, 123).

All of these decisions are influenced by the availability of intermediate sanctions, including electronic monitoring and house arrest, and by the competence of the parole officer in convincing the court that certain actions are most appropriate. According to McCleary (1992), an officer's competence is indicated by the ability to lie about the client in a way that fulfills the officer's goals for the client. If the officer wants the parolee returned to prison, he or she will present the offender as worse then he or she is and if the officer wants to keep the parolee in the community, he or she will describe the offender as better than he or she is. Parole success is difficult to achieve for a variety of reasons. Some parolees do well when released, and yet others have problems with the effects of prisonization, getting into special treatment programs, finding a job, dealing with supervision, drug testing, intensive supervision, and electronic monitoring.

Making the transition to the "free" world from a total institution is quite difficult. Donald Clemmer's *The Prison Community* (1958) provides an insightful analysis of prisoners' subculture. Prisonization, the process by which inmates adapt to life in prison, reflects a prison subculture influencing the inmate's language, role, group structure, and sexual behavior. The parolee coming out of prison has to completely remake himself or herself in terms of trusting people and understanding that many people are motivated to be kind and helpful rather than by exploitation or manipulation. Prisonization contributes to the parolee feeling disorganized, depressed, and disoriented. Upon getting out of prison, the parolee must engage in the difficult process of developing a network of friends. Some parolees solve this problem by associating with other ex-cons. During the height of their loneliness, many parolees actually long for the former days of imprisonment when they had many friends (Irwin 1970).

Increased funding for the construction and operation of prisons has not meant more dollars spent on prison programming. With the demise of the indeterminate sentence, there is less incentive for prisoners to participate in rehabilitation and the state sees this as another reason not to fund existing programs. This means that fewer inmates are leaving prison having met their programming needs in the area of work, substance abuse, and education. Because the increase in the prison population is largely attributed to increasing arrests for drug offenses (Blumstein and Beck, 1999), questions are raised as to why so much attention is given to drug offenses if the drug offender is not treated (Petersilia 2000).

Failures

Parolees fail because they do not find work, they do not establish positive social relations, and they do not establish contacts with the opposite sex (Irwin and Austin 1997). Just meeting the exigencies of life overwhelms some of them. It is likely that without a trade or some formal education, finding work can be difficult. The economic system can change dramatically from the time an offender enters the prison to the time he or she is released. A parolee must be careful about seeking work on the outside considering the possibility of recessions, economic downturns, and the relocation of jobs. These problems are made worse if there is no major improvement in a parolee's skills during imprisonment. Data on parole entries indicate that only 40 percent had finished high school or had some college education (National Corrections Reporting Program 1992, 55). They find work in dead-end jobs with little chance for advancement. Mental and physical health problems may further affect their employment. Some parolees find themselves in a rut (Irwin 1970).

The stigma of imprisonment is a further impediment to reintegration. Understandably, certain positions involving financial responsibilities or dealing with women or children may be inappropriate for a parolee. Because many people have been sent to prison who have minor criminal backgrounds, employers may be willing to overlook their prior record. Parole officers who have learned to screen parolees also make finding work possible for parolees. The employer comes to trust the officer's recommendation. Even when things are going well, parolees sooner or later find their dreams collapsing (Irwin 1970). They realize that their ambitions will not be fulfilled and that their difficulties are much more complicated than they anticipated. For example, a parolee who has little experience with computers may be overwhelmed with their use today. When confusion sets in and the parolee realizes he or she is not doing well, fear sets in or resignation develops. At this critical point, the parolee can either move forward with the help of the parole agent or backslide into a life of crime.

Parole officers have a difficult time dealing with parolees who are in crisis. Besides having to manage a caseload of parolees who are coming and going with their own issues and problems, the officer now has to spend precious time on the crisis. Surmounting the problem is made easier if the parolee has some experience with handling prior difficulties, the officer has sufficient experience with similar problems, the officer has some understanding of the parolee, and the parolee is willing to make an effort to deal with the problem. The officer must have some understanding of who the parolee is and appreciate the parolee's quality of life.

Parole Revocations

Parole officers categorize some parolees as troublemakers (McCleary 1992). These parolees have little interest in doing well and require additional work and challenge the status quo. Further problems appear when any behavior is no longer rational and predictable, because it appears the parolee cannot be controlled. The parolee does not respond to threats, contingencies, or incentives. The rewards of early discharges are not valued by such parolees (McCleary 1992).

Parole revocations are receiving attention because of the changing nature of parole supervision and the imposition of increasingly more severe conditions on parolees (Irwin and Austin 1997). One would expect that once parole supervision practices stabilize, the rate of parolees returned to prison would remain the same over time. Since 1926, however, the percent of state prison admissions who are on parole or other conditional release when admitted to prison increased from around 5 percent to around 30 percent in 1992. This figure adds appreciably to the growing prison population (Petersilia 2000). Langan (2002) reports that among 300,000 prisoners released from 15 states in 1994, 67 percent were rearrested within 3 years; 46 percent were reconvicted of a new offense; and 25 percent were sent back to prison. Released prisoners with re-arrest rates that were higher than 70 percent were robbers, burglars, larcenists, motor vehicle thieves, possessors of stolen property, and those selling illegal weapons. Those with lower rates included homicide (40 percent), rape (46 percent), sexual assault (41 percent), and driving while under the influence (51 percent).

Technical violations committed while under community supervision offers some insight into what parolees are doing (**Table 12-2**). New offenses and drug

Table 12-2	Technical Violations Committed While Under Community Supervision
Type of Violation	**On Parole (%)**
Arrest for new offense	43
Positive test for drug use	10.2
Failure to report for drug testing/treatment	4.4
Failure to report for alcohol treatment	2
Failure to report for counseling	2.3
Failure to report to parole officer/absconded	34.2
Left jurisdiction without permission	4.1
Failure to secure or maintain employment	2.8
Failure to pay fine, restitution, obligations	2.9
Maintained contact with other known offenders	2.5
Failure to report change of address	2.5
Alcohol or drug use	2.3
Weapons	2.5
Other reasons	17.0

Sources: Robyn Cohen. *Probation and parole violators in state prisons 1991.* Washington, DC: U.S. Dept. of Justice, Bureau of Justice Statistics, 1995.

offenses account for over half of the technical violations. Failure to report to treatment was tied to approximately 4 percent of the cases. Another 34 percent had absconded or left the jurisdiction.

Throughout the 1960s, parolees had virtually no legal standing to question the actions of the parole officer who pursued revocation or of the parole board who returned the offender to prison. One officer characterized those days as "rough and tumble." In some states, parole revocation could even be dangerous. Physical altercations between the parole officer and the parolee broke out when the officer sought to have the parolee sent back to prison. Quite often the only proof provided in the case was the word of the parole officer. Much of this information could be hearsay or unsubstantiated evidence.

Morrisey v. Brewer

The 1972 *Morrisey v. Brewer* decision changed all of this. Essentially, the court determined that parolees were not different from other people in that they should be afforded due process considerations. For the most part, aside from living under a state of conditional liberty, the parolee had the same responsibilities as others. The court believed that the denial of these interests would amount to a grievous loss for the parolee.

The result of *Morrisey v. Brewer* requires due process protection in two phases. In the first phase, the parolee is given a written notice of the charges, is informed of the right to an attorney, and is subject to a preliminary hearing in which the evidence of a violation is disclosed. Within 15 days, the preliminary hearing should take place before a hearing officer. The hearing officer, often a representative of the state's parole agency, is usually a supervisory class parole officer. If sufficient probable cause is found at a preliminary hearing, then a final hearing is heard before an administrative law judge. At this hearing, the parolee has an opportunity to be heard in person, present evidence as well as witnesses, and confront adverse witnesses. The standard of proof is a preponderance of the evidence. If an adverse decision against the parolee has been made, the parolee receives a written statement of the reasons for revoking parole as well as the evidence used in arriving at this decision. In some states, the case is prosecuted by lay prosecutors who are former senior parole officers. The quality of these prosecutions can be quite high. Parolees now have the right to council in some cases. Instead of viewing revocation as an in-or-out matter, the parole board has many different options. Besides returning the offender to prison, the board may make no change, it may modify the conditions of parole, it may require the parolee to serve an out-of-state sentence as a new sentence, it may require the offender to serve an out-of-state sentence consecutively with the new sentence, it may extend the term of parole, it may incarcerate the offender for an extended term, it may discharge the person from parole, and it may incarcerate the offender for a new term (Rhine et al. 1991). If parole is revoked, the parolee is required to serve the remainder of what remains of the prison sentence minus the time served in the community.

Reintegrative Parole

The task of parole includes rebuilding solid ties between the offender and the community, integrating and reintegrating the offender into community life. This requires not only efforts directed toward changing the individual offender, but also mobilizing the community and its institutions. These efforts must be undertaken without giving up the important control and deterrent role of corrections, particularly as applied to dangerous offenders (President's Commission 1967, 7).

To achieve reintegration, programs must be located within the community; provide community-based education, training, counseling, and support services; offer opportunities to assume normal multiple roles of the citizen; and have opportunities for personal growth (McCarthy and McCarthy 1997, 5–6). This process is quite daunting for some parolees. The parole staff have responsibilities for supervision, support, and therapy. Acting as resource brokers, they link offenders to the appropriate services and monitor their progress after assistance has been initiated. Often it will be necessary to act as an advocate, working to ensure that the offender's rights are protected, and that a high quality of service delivery is maintained (McCarthy and McCarthy 1997).

Social integration for the parolee is a lofty goal in as much as the community's exclusion of the offender is inevitable. In a great many cases, the needed services are simply not there. Resources for adult education and drug treatment may have extended waiting list. In the past, integration was possible as long as someone was white, the government cared, economic avenues were still open, and professionals were trained to accept the concept. Because many criminal justice practitioners have come to believe that changing an offender is difficult and/or impossible, a more manageable goal is to help the parolee adjust to society.

More recently a shift has occurred that emphasizes incapacitation, deterrence, and retribution, all of which mean greater efforts directed toward program efficiency and management of the dangerous offender (Hagan 1994, 158). According to Hagan, the new focus is on subgroups and their risks of crime. Offenders are seen as responsible individuals who make choices. Target offender categories are "high-rate offenders," "career offenders," "the underclass," and the "dangerous class" (Hagan 1994, 163). In many respects, risk-assessment scales have replaced community service directories as key office resources. When parolees consistently make bad choices, they are viewed as in need of regulation. Regulation takes hold when the offender is considered "beyond the pale" or incapable of rehabilitation (Gaubatz 1995). The offender becomes responsible for changing himself or herself. People often run out of sympathy for someone who has been in prison. Counselors assume reactive stances and provide little more than surveillance, which is frequently considered a police responsibility. Some take little to no initiative in helping parolees solve their problems, leaving parolees to their own devices.

A New Model
Criminal justice professionals often feel frustrated because they are unable to work with clients. In response to these conditions, a new model of parole has emerged. Restorative justice is currently being discussed in community corrections. As stated earlier, restorative justice is concerned with protecting the interest of the victim, the offender, and the community. The offender meets his or her obligation to the victim by repairing the harm done; the parolee also should leave the system in a better condition than when he or she entered it, and lastly, the public has a right to a feel safe and to live in a secure community. These notions can also be applied to parole, especially where parole has been revised to ensure that the community is safe, the offender exhibits the appropriate behavior prior to release, and the community is willing to accept the offender back.

Jeremy Travis (2000) has outlined a restorative parole process that considers the importance of first having someone in the role of the judge in a re-entry court. The judge would establish with the offender the prison sentence and the length of time on parole. A plan would be put into effect early on, stipulating the preparation to made in prison and the conditions later on to be served in restorative parole. The judge would also ask any stakeholders what they might do for the offender when he or she returns to the community. While in prison, the offender would receive the needed support to overcome any identified deficiencies in his background that have contributed to his or her criminal lifestyle. These could be related to drugs, education, mental health, work, and so on. During his or her prison sentence, the offender would pay restitution and maintain ties to his or her family. When released, the offender would be brought back to court where a ceremony would be held to honor the completion of his or her prison term and to introduce the offender to the next phase. At this point the parolee would be presented with a set of parole conditions under which he or she must live. The full powers of the court would be applied to keep the offender in line, much as they are in a drug court where judges move quickly to address problems presented by the offender. With the involvement of family, friends, and interested parties, the positive impact of re-entry is enhanced and the re-entry shock is eased somewhat. The offender is essentially being supervised by the judge who would review the offender's progress in a timely manner. The offender would be expected to remain drug free, make restitution and reparations to the community, work to make the community safer, participate in programs that were begun in prison, avoid situations that pose a risk of re-offending, and refrain from committing crime (Travis 2000). Substantial barriers to this restorative parole model are found at the societal, organizational, and individual levels.

The Principle of Less Eligibility
Regardless of how dangerous the offender appears to be, it is always possible to argue that the offender is less deserving than free citizens of social services. Drawing upon the regulations that came out of the English poor laws, it was felt that in order to fend off idleness, the system of public relief must always provide assistance that is less than what could be obtained by working at the lowest-paid job available. Thus developed the principle of less eligibility (Sieh 1989, 160). Closely tied to the system of poor relief was the system of punishment. When applied to punishment, less eligibility became crucial to solving the problem of class discipline and control (Hogg 1980, 64). Crime was viewed as arising from idleness and impoverishment. The principle of less eligibility stipulates that if a punishment is to act as a deterrent, the treatment given a prisoner should not be superior to that provided a member of the lowest significant social class in the free society (Sieh 1989).

The Principle of Nonsuperiority
Rehabilitation programs such as counseling, free college educations, and other benefits are affected by the principle of less eligibility. Once the offender has served his or her time, the principle of nonsuperiority comes into effect. The principle of nonsuperiority is defined as the requirement that the condition of the offender upon release should be at least not superior to that of the lowest classes of the non-criminal population (Mannheim 1939). There are three implications of this theory. First, it means that the parolee is not likely to be given a chance to accumulate

a significant amount of wealth while in prison. Secondly, it means the released inmate is not likely to receive any meaningful support, and thirdly, he or she will experience reduced opportunities when returned to the free society. Nonsuperiority provides the mechanism for assuring that the ex-convict's sigma makes a lasting impression on the former inmate and the public as well. It does, however, provide an incentive for the ex-convict to return to a criminal lifestyle (Sieh 1989). The principles of less eligibility and nonsuperiority provide a link with the noncriminal population by establishing the foundation for the ex-prisoner's social standing. Although the person is no longer an outlaw, the connection to the rest of society is tenuous and negative. The ex-convict is still not permitted to fully integrate back into society without a maximum of effort (Sieh 1989).

Social Regulations

Risk assessment, electronic monitoring, and surveillance of the underclass involves gathering knowledge that can be used to act against the subject. This strategy ignores the perceived necessity to do more than simply watch and react to offender behavior. Because the urban client is very likely to be viewed as the undeserving, any additional treatment often comes in the form of increased control, as social regulation.

To regulate means to govern or direct according to a rule or to bring under control of constituted authority, to limit and prohibit, to arrange in proper order, and to control that which already exists (Black 1979, 1156). Social regulation reflects two different concerns. First of all, social regulation is based on the notion that certain aberrant behaviors must be eliminated. If the behavior cannot be completely eradicated, it must be controlled. Control is possible through the use of state and individual regulatory mechanisms. Regulation is a tertiary social control mechanism that becomes necessary after self-control and group pressure have failed. Regulation is another means of controlling a population others deem unworthy of rehabilitating or believe have never been habilitated. The second concern is the belief that more stringent control measures are necessary during periods of social, economic, and technological change. For political purposes, the public is made to believe that not enough is done about crime and that harsher penalties are necessary, especially for a population of offenders who are considered disreputable. Regulation then offers a means of controlling this population others deem unworthy of rehabilitating.

Technological changes in the workplace mean that there has been a reduction in the human element at work; less concern for individual considerations; and greater interests in rationality, cost reductions, efficiency, and standardization as found in mandatory sentencing and sentencing guidelines.

■ Conclusion

Parole has gone through many changes since surety and the ticket of leave. Society has moved from the disciplinary to the clinical and back to the disciplinary form of parole. The administration of parole is complex because it has been under the authority of the state in most jurisdictions. However in some states, including New York, the agency itself is under the authority of the department of corrections and then given autonomy to run its own affairs.

Parole officers are also complex and diverse; they have many different reasons for choosing this work. Many of them are dedicated to doing a difficult job. One of the biggest problems has been the release of offenders from prison. Too often, the process has lacked any rational or predictable qualities. The use of sentencing guidelines, salient factor scores, and mandatory release dates have all increased the predictability of the process. However, there are still some people who are not satisfied, believing that parole is unable to do the job well. They feel that parole must be abolished. Regardless of whether parole continues as originally conceived or is significantly altered, what is important is whether the parolee makes it in the community. To do well on parole requires of the offender a great deal of determination, support, and good luck. Too often, the cards are stacked against an offender. For many parolees, release simply is a continuation of the pains of imprisonment. To meet the present situation head on, it is important to incorporate a renewed concern in the offender, the victim, and the community. Restorative justice can be applied to parole as easily as it can be to probation. The future of parole is likely to be tied to the future of technology and the need to deal with massive prison populations.

REFERENCES

Albright, S. 1996. Employer attitudes toward hiring ex-offenders. *The Prison Journal* 76: 118–138.

Allen, F. 1981. *The decline of the rehabilitative ideal: Penal policy and social purpose.* New Haven, CT: Yale University Press.

Austin, J., and Lawson. 1998. *Assessment of California parole violations and recommended intermediate programs and policies.* San Francisco: National Council of Crime and Delinquency.

Barry, J. 1973. Alexander Maconochie. In H. Mannheim (Ed.), *Pioneers in criminology.* Montclair, NJ: Patterson-Smith.

Bedau, H. 1992. The Eighth Amendment, human dignity, and the death penalty. In M. Meyer, and W. Parent, ed. *The constitutional rights: Human dignity and American values.* Ithaca, NY: Cornell University Press.

Benekos, P. 1990. Beyond reintegration: Community corrections in a retributive era. *Federal Probation* 54: 52–56.

Bennett, L. 1995. In defense of parole—Is it worth the effort? *Perspectives* 19: 14–18.

Black, H. 1979. *Black's law dictionary.* St. Paul, MN: West.

Blumstein, A., and A. Beck. 1999. Population growth in United States prisons, 1980–1996. *Crime and Justice: A Review of Research* 26: 20–22.

Boone, H., B. Fulton, A. Crowe, and G. Markley. 1995. *Results-driven management: Implementing performance-based measures in community corrections.* Lexington, KY: American Probation and Parole Association.

Brown, R. 2000. Helping low income mothers with criminal records achieve self-sufficiency. *Welfare Information Network News Issue Notes* 4: 13.

Burke, P. 1995. *Abolishing parole.* Lexington, KY: American Probation and Parole Association.

Byrne, J. 1989. Reintegrating the concept of community into community-based corrections. *Crime and Delinquency* 35: 471–497.

Clemmer, D. 1958. *The prison community.* New York: Rinehart and Co.

Cochran, D., R. Corbett, and J. Byrne. 1986. Intensive probation supervision in Massachusetts: A case study in change. *Federal Probation* 50: 32–41.

Cohen, R. *Probation and parole violators in state prisons, 1991.* Washington, DC: U.S. Dept. of Justice, Bureau of Justice Statistics.

Cole, G., and T. Clear. 1997. *American corrections.* Albany, NY: Wadsworth.

Curtis, R., and S. Schulman. 1984. Ex-offenders, family relations, and economic support: The significant women's study of the TARP project. *Crime and Delinquency* 30(4): 507–528.

Ditton, P. 1999. *Mental health and treatment of inmates and probationers.* Bureau of Justice Statistics Special Report. Washington, DC: U.S. Department of Justice, Office of Justice Programs.

Executive Department—Division of Parole. 1996. *General rules governing parole.* Albany, NY.

Fogel, D. 1975. *We are living proof: The justice model for corrections.* Cincinnati, OH: Anderson.

Gainsborough, J. 1997. Eliminating parole is a dangerous and expensive proposition. *Corrections Today* 59: 23.

Gaubatz, K. 1995. *Crime in the public mind.* Ann Arbor: University of Michigan.

Glaze, L., and S. Palla. 2004. *Probation and parole in the United States, 2003.* Washington, DC: U.S. Department of Justice, Bureau of Justice Statistics.

Goffman, E. 1963. *Stigma: Notes on the management of spoiled identity.* Englewood Cliffs, NJ: Prentice Hall.

Goldfarb, R., and L. Singer. 1973. *After conviction: A definitive and compelling study of the American correction system.* New York: Touchstone.

Gottfredson, D. 1970. Assessment of prediction methods. In N. Johnston, L. Savitz, and M. Wolfgang, eds., *The sociology of punishment and corrections.* New York: John Wiley.

Hagan, J. 1994. *Crime and disrepute.* Thousand Oaks, CA: Pine Forge Sage.

Hagan, J., and R. Dinowitzer. 1999. Collateral consequences of imprisonment for children, communities, and prisoners. *Crime and Justice: A Review of Research.* 26: 121–162.

Hairston, C. 2003. Families, prisoners, and community reentry: A look at issues and programs. In Vivian Gadsden (Ed.), *Heading home: Offender reintegration into the family.* Lanham, MD: American Corrections Association.

Hassine, V. 1999. *Life without parole.* Los Angeles: Roxbury.

Hirsch, A. 2000. The impact of welfare reform on women with drug convictions. Pennsylvania: A case study. *Women, Girls, and Criminal Justice* 13: 33–34.

Hogg, R. 1982. Imprisonment under British capitalism. In T. Platt and P. Takagi, eds., *Punishment and penal discipline: Essays on the prison and the prison movement.* San Francisco: Crime and Social Justice Association.

Holzer, H. 1996. *What employers want: Job prospects for less-educated workers.* New York: Russell Sage.

Hughes, T., D. Wilson, and A. Beck. 2001. *Trends in state parole 1990–2000.* Washington, DC: Bureau of Justice Statistics, U.S. Department of Justice.

Hughes, T and D. Wilson. 2003. *Reentry trends in the United States.* Washington, DC: Bureau of Justice Statistics, U.S. Department of Justice.

Hulsey, L. 1990. Attitudes of employers with respect to hiring released prisoners. Unpublished doctoral dissertation, Texas A & M University, College Station, Texas.

Irwin, J., and J. Austin. 1997. *It's about time: America's imprisonment binge.* Albany, NY: Wadsworth.

Irwin, J. 1970. *The felon.* Englewood Cliffs, NJ: Prentice Hall.

Johnson, H. 1988. *History of criminal justice.* Cincinnati, OH: Anderson.

Karp, D., and T. Clear (Eds.). 2002. *What is community justice? Case studies of restorative justice and community supervision.* Thousand Oaks, CA: Sage.

Kastenmier, R., and H. Eglit. 1975. Parole release decision making. In W. Amos and C. Newman (Eds.), *Parole: Legal issues and decision making research.* New York: Federal Legal Publications.

Langan, P. 2002. *Recidivism of prisoners released in 1994.* Washington, DC: U.S. Department of Justice, Bureau of Justice Statistics.

Lindsey, E. 1925. Historical sketch of the indeterminate sentence and parole system. *Journal of the American Institute of Criminal Law and Criminology* 16: 9–126.

Lipschitz, J. 1986. Back to the future: An historical view of intensive probation supervision. *Federal Probation* 50: 78–81.

Maguire, K., and A. Pastore, eds. 1995. *Sourcebook of criminal justice statistics 1994.* Washington, DC: U.S. Department of Justice, Bureau of Justice Statistics.

Mannheim, H. 1939. *The dilemma of penal reform.* London: Allen and Unwin.

Manocchio, A., and J. Dunn. 1970. *The time game.* Beverly Hills, CA: Sage.

Masters, R. 1994. *Counseling: Criminal justice offenders.* Thousand Oaks, CA: Sage.

McCarthy, R., and B. McCarthy. 1997. *Community-based corrections.* Albany, NY: Wadsworth.

McCleary, R. 1992. *Dangerous men: The sociology of parole.* New York: Heston.

Meyer, J. 2000. Strange science: Subjective criteria in parole decisions. *Journal of Crime and Justice* 24: 43–70.

Morris, W. 1910. *The frankpledge system.* New York: Columbia University Press.

Morrisey v. Brewer. 1972. 408 U.S. 471

Mumola, C. 2000. *Incarcerated parents and their children.* Washington, DC: U.S. Department of Justice, Office of Justice Programs, Bureau of Justice Statistics.

Murton, T. 1976. *The dilemma of prison reform.* New York: Holt, Rinehart and Winston.

O'Leary, V. 1987. Probation: A system in change. *Federal Probation* 51: 8–11.

Petersilia, J. 2000. When prisoners return to the community: Political, economic, and social consequences. *Research in Brief,* Washington, DC: National Institute of Justice.

Petersilia, J., S. Turner, J. Kahan, and J. Peterson. 1985. *Granting felons probation: Public risks and alternatives.* Santa Monica, CA: Rand.

Pisciotta, A. 1983. Scientific reform: The new penology of Elmira, 1876–1900. *Crime and Delinquency* 29: 613–630.

Pogrebin, M., E. Poole, and R. Regoli. 1986. Parole decision making in Colorado. *Journal of Criminal Justice* 14: 147–155.

President's Commission on Law Enforcement and Administration of Justice. 1967. *Task force report: Corrections.* Washington, DC: U.S. Government Printing Office.

Rhine, E., W. Smith, and R. Jackson. 1991. *Paroling authorities: Recent history and current practices.* Laurel, MD: American Corrections Association.

Rossi, P., H. Berk, and K. Lenihan. 1980. *Money, work, and crime: Experimental evidence.* New York: Academic Press.

Rothman, D. 1980. *Conscience and convenience: The asylum and its alternatives in progressive America.* Boston: Little, Brown.

Russi, R. 1992. *New York State: Parole handbook.* Albany: Division of Parole.

Samaha, J. 1981. The recognizance bond in Elizabethan law enforcement. *American Journal of Legal History* 25: 189–204.

Schmidt, J. 1977. *Demystifying parole.* Lexington, MA: D.C. Heath.

Sieh, E. 1989. Less eligibility: The upper limits of penal policy. *Criminal Justice Policy Review* 3: 159–183.

Simon, J. 1993. *Poor discipline.* Chicago: University of Chicago Press.

Talarico, S. 1984. *The dilemma of parole decision-making.* In G. Cole, ed., *Criminal justice law and politics.* Belmont, CA: Brooks/Cole.

Travis, J. 2000. *But they all come back: Rethinking prisoner reentry.* National Institute of Justice. Washington, DC: U.S. Department of Justice, Office of Justice Programs.

United Nations. 1948. Universal Declaration of Rights, General Assembly, resolution 217 A (III) of 10 December, 1948.

von Hirsch, A. 1976. *Doing justice.* New York: Hill and Wang.

von Hirsch, A., and K. Hannrahan. 1978. *Abolish parole?* Washington, DC: National Institute of Law Enforcement and Criminal Justice.

Western, B., and K. Beckett. 1999. How unregulated is the U.S. labor market? The penal system as a labor market institution. *American Journal of Sociology* 104: 1030–1060.

KEY POINTS

1. Parole is a unique enterprise that is required to address the important issues of danger, public safety, social reintegration, and state regulation within a context of treating the parolee with a measure of dignity.

2. Parole has moved through phases of surety parole, disciplinary parole, clinical parole, and modernist parole.

3. Alexander Maconochie is called is the father of parole. He faced tremendous opposition to make parole more rational and humane.

4. The growth of parole was brought about by the need to rationalize the pardoning process and the need to restore institutional discipline.

5. Clinical parole is based on the belief that knowledge is available to control human behavior.

6. The modernist period of parole brought into question the ability of parole to effectively apply the medical model.

7. It is unjust to base decisions about the severity of punishments on what the offender is expected to do in the future.

8. The success rate among those discharged from parole dropped from 50 percent in 1990 to 46 percent in 2000 but the percent of reincarcerated offenders also dropped.

9. Parolees suffer re-entry shock when they return to the community.

10. Finding work and a place to live are the two major needs of a parolee. Some parolees also have to deal with mental illness.

11. More than 1.5 million children in the United State have parents in prison.

12. Parolees sometimes fail because they do not find work, they do not establish positive social relations, and they do not establish contacts with the opposite sex.

13. Restorative parole is possible where officials connect the victim with the offender. Rigorous review considering community safety and concerns for the victim is essential.

KEY TERMS

parole is given the duty to act as an independent, citizen-oriented board that carefully reviews each prisoner nearing the end of a prison term, to demand that all prisoners demonstrate they are no longer a danger to society before they are permitted to return to the community, and to set specific conditions that must be met before release.

prisonization is the process by which inmates adapt to life in prison, reflecting a prison subculture, influencing the inmates' language, role, group structure, and sexual behavior.

recognizance bonds good behavior bonds were issued against persons who did not have a good reputation, e.g., persons considered lazy, transients, and parents of illegitimate children.

suretyship system requires a citizen of good reputation to be obligated for the good behavior of another person.

ticket of leave is a conditional pardon that frees the prisoner from governmental supervision during good behavior as long as the offender lawfully supports himself or herself.

REVIEW QUESTIONS

1. Parole can be defined in different ways. Discuss the four definitions referred to in the text.

2. Give a brief history of parole from its early use to the modernist period.

3. What problems do parolees face when adjusting to "life on the outside"?

4. Who carries out parole supervision?

5. How did the *Morrisey v. Brewer* decision affect the nature of parole revocations?

6. What are the implications of the principles of less eligibility and nonsuperiority?

Community Corrections: Human Dignity and Future Times

Chapter Objectives

In this chapter you will learn about:

- The possible future for probation
- The implications of that future
- The role of technology in the future
- The notion of punitive probation
- The social factors affecting the future

I believe that we are headed towards a medieval technological society.

Milton Brooks

Probation has come a long way since John Augustus first offered his services. It has become more formalized, rationalized, and scientific. It is now a major institution offering society a considerable amount of social protection. It deals with real people from all walks of life who have made mistakes.

Probation and parole are political institutions subject to the whims of local and state political institutions. Probation thus may be destined to reinvent itself according to its past images. In a study of the cyclic nature of correctional reform, Murton (1976) suggests that institutions are reinvented and real change is permitted as long as it does not threaten the status quo or the existing agenda of the power elite. Despite probation's pulse on the community, it has never been a strong advocate of community change, action programs, or programs that empower community leaders. In fact, among all of the criminal justice agencies, probation is probably the least politically active.

■ Probation of Today

Once probation managed to survive a major attack on its existence during the 1920s, it quickly took on the guise of other social work agencies by focusing on support and supervision. Many changes have taken place in the practice of probation since the beginning of the 20th century. Technology has played a major part and will continue to do so for the remainder of probation's existence.

The social-economic context of probation is in a constant state of change and is highly unpredictable. There will always be an underclass and other categories of people who have great needs. Probationers will continue to come from a variety of social classes but will always be populated by people who have various criminogenic needs. These needs will become more apparent as the service providers become more selective in who gets quality care and who is delegated to state-sponsored apparatuses.

Offender classification systems have progressed immeasurably since first employed. Today, with the aid of ever-improving management information systems, it is possible for each department to develop a classification system that truly represents its clients. Technological innovation is limited only by expense and imagination. Supervision has become much more than simply determining the whereabouts of the offender. Today, not only is it important to know where the offender is, but also what the offender is doing and his or her state of mind. In the future, technology will provide much additional information needed to improve this information.

One promising and innovating approach is the use of restorative justice. Despite the problems associated with it, few can argue against its basic premise. Reintegrative shaming is intended to hold the offender accountable, while full recognition of the victim's complaint is given. The offender must be armored with the skills necessary to survive in society. The offender needs to be considered as someone of worth if for no other reason than the consequences for doing otherwise can be detrimental.

■ The Future of Probation

At this time, it seems appropriate to ask what the probation system may look like in 25 or 30 years. Based on the difficulty in predicting criminal behavior and other social variables, it is expected that looking into the future of probation is, at best, an exercise in conjecture. However, it is worthwhile to consider the future of probation in order to prepare for certain scenarios which may arise.

Social and economic conditions in the 21st century are expected to remain the same or may even get worse. Today, the changes in cities are important to consider because more and more people are moving to urban areas all over the world. Cities suffer from many intractable social problems including public drunkenness, corner gangs, street harassment, drug usage, noisy neighbors, homelessness, prostitution, physical decay, vandalism, dilapidation and abandonment of buildings, and accumulated rubbish. These problems lead to increased anger, demoralization, fear, and alienation of their citizens.

The public may decide that certain segments of the population are more deserving than others. Special interest groups may make it virtually impossible for politicians to make a rational decision reflecting the needs of all constituents. With the current emphasis on governmental cost reductions, there seems to be little reason why any governmental program will alter these conditions at least in the immediate future.

Probation has never established its own independent identity where it is recognized as a key element of the criminal justice system. In some respects, it has marginal status and a poor image because it is considered soft on crime. More importantly, probation has lacked a constituency. It has no national partisans and no great national leaders (Cushman 1984). For the most part, it is dominated by judges or members of the board of supervisors. Probation has not crawled out from under their shadow. Therefore, probation can make few claims on public monies, resources, or reciprocal support from other agencies. Its funding is discretionary, not mandated, and the front loading of resources means the police and courts have gotten the first crack at the money (Lemert 1993, 457–458).

Speculations about probation's future are derived from other writers who suggest that probation will be much different from what it was originally conceived to be and much different from what it is today. One must consider some of the major influences that will direct the actions of the future to have any understanding of what the future has in store for probation.

Thirty years from now, instead of a probation system based on concern for the client, more than likely, the system will be influenced by a desire for increased accountability brought on by a greater use of technology. The focus of concern will shift from the needs of the client to the needs of the system. It is believed that technological advances will dominate the field and that probation officers will have a job that is much different from what it is today.

■ Historical Precedent

If historical precedent offers any clues, community attitudes toward criminals may continue to harden. It is expected that more crimes will be capitalized and that few new solutions directed toward meeting the offender's needs will be tried except where advances in technology are employed.

It appears that whenever great social unrest and high levels of criminal activity take place, the solution calls for greater police activity or renewed interest in the death penalty. Patrick Colquhoun's (1745–1820) *Treatise on the Police of the Metropolis* claimed that well over 50,000 inhabitants of London composed a class of habitual criminals. Effective police activity was seen as essential to gain control of the anarchy. By the time of the American Revolution, the police were less effective in preventing crime because the death penalty was considered a solution to the crime problem (Johnson 1988, 175).

Population growth and economic activity were evident on the eve of the American Revolution. Population density in colonial cities, coupled with a shifting itinerant labor supply, resulted in a growing crime rate, riots, and other disorders (Johnson 1988, 130). Because the British considered their system of justice to be superior to that available on the European continent, the liberal use of the death penalty was thought to be applied only to the guilty and never the innocent. Disquiet over rampant crime in the American colonies first led to increased use of the death penalty but later the ineffectiveness of traditional penalties led to the development of the U.S. penitentiary (Hirsch 1992, 39–40). When the public became reluctant to impose the death penalty, the use of the penitentiary became the likely alternative.

When the public was disinclined to use the house of refuge and other institutions as monuments to social control, it accepted the notion of probation. Probation was eventually institutionalized across the country, providing an accepted alternative to imprisonment for many adults and youth. When probation itself was seen as inadequate it, too, was reinvented.

Authoritarian Response

Since 1975, probation has been the subject of debate and controversy, often centering on the construction of new models of supervision (Lemert 1993, 448). McWilliams (1987) submits that probation has moved from an early missionary stage in which it was mainly a plea for mercy through a scientific/treatment stage to a current bureaucratic/managerial stage. Today, postmodernists would argue that probation has lost its sense of direction. Instead of responding to the uniqueness of the individual, probation has become preoccupied with objective considerations of facts about the client without maintaining the essence of the job as John Augustus performed it. In the pursuit of order and security, probation has lost its verve.

Harris, Clear, and Baird (1989) have documented this change in attitude. Their data suggest that concern for authority among community supervision officers has increased, and that authority is now a more meaningful concept in supervision than either assistance or treatment. This means that service delivery is a more rigid enterprise dominated by concern for the client's risk of recidivism. This change in attitude is attributable to a change in the clients served by probation, the thought that some deserve imprisonment, the influences of ISP units, civil actions holding officers accountable for the actions of their clients, and a decline in public confidence in rehabilitation (Harris et al. 1989, 245). Individual officers support these values through volunteering for ISP programs; displaying symbols of authority available to the job such as side arms, target silhouettes, flack jackets, and handcuffs; and conducting search-and-seizure raids with the police. Some of these probation officers are "wanabee" police officers who for reasons such as color blindness could not pass the entrance examinations. Lemert suggests that the officers who support these new developments are most likely to deny what probation has meant and that they are now organized to expect the client to fail. What has been accomplished with this new image is a dramatic presentation of themselves to the community and not greater increments of social control (Lemert 1993, 456).

Feeley and Simon (1992) have observed that penal ideology and practices have become more conservative with identifying and managing unruly groups. This transformation is reflected in more concern for probability and risks, greater regard for system efficiency, and more thought to targeting offenders through aggregate stereotypes but not individual characteristics and problems. Accordingly, probation no longer is an individual product of court action but rather an instrument of national policy. The offender has become a unit in a class defined by policy categories (McWilliams 1987). There is now the policy-guided management of offenders (Lemert 1993, 449).

The significance of the emphasis on risks under this mechanistic model means greater attention is given to crime control, rationality, and accountability. The goal is not to eliminate crime but to make it tolerable through systemic co-ordination of activities intended to deal with it (Feeley and Simon 1992, 455). The idea is not to eliminate recidivism but to control crime and emphasize the additional number of persons under control. Risk management becomes important through frequent drug testing and for application with low-risk offenders for whom the more secure forms of custody are judged too expensive or unnecessary (Feeley and Simon 1992, 461). Any assessment of the outcome will indicate much greater success. This process is easier to achieve, and as opposed to rehabilitation, it is more definitive. It is similar to the difference among churches in which one tries to count the number of souls saved while the other simply wants to count collections. It also reflects one of the basic tenets put forward by Durkheim (1964), who views crime as a normal aspect of social life much as traffic accidents are now.

Broad (1991) predicts the social control model will dominate where regulation and prevention are important. The social control model is concerned with viewing the probationer as a deviant who engages in pathological behavior. This behavior originates in a population in need of regulation. The goal of probation is to punish and control the behavior; thus, the primary function of probation is to operate as a policing agent. Under the guise of prevention, state control is extended when probation is directed toward inappropriate behavior leading to delinquency and crime. Ecologically speaking, when an area deteriorates enough, a social control response followed by sanctions is thought necessary. Social control emphasizes individual responsibility while also limiting the resources available to the probationer. Whatever needs are identified are met by local agencies presumably equipped to meet the task. Particular emphasis is given to self-help initiatives that emphasize local responsibility. Rather than advocate for client services or operate as a community change agent, probation service will become more like police work in that it will be concerned with reducing social conflict and disorder. Police officers have always made referrals, provided some form of crisis intervention counseling, and encouraged people to follow the law. Probation will do the same. The idea is to reassert the dominance of the state in a situation where authority may be lacking or is considered irrelevant (Broad 1991, 178).

The social control approach has the potential for leaving the poor and more vulnerable sectors of the working class far worse off, reproducing a state of affairs that already exists in the worst American ghettos (Downes 1979). The best that can be said about social control is that its usage has changed from a progressive concern with the scientific reconstruction of society to a revisionist's interest in how a hypothetical social order is maintained through the control of socially defined deviance (Lemert 1993, 447). The changes in the way that probation work is conducted are also reflected in the way penal institutions operate. What very well may occur is a diminution in the value of the person's worth. Concerns for human dignity are replaced by concerns for fairness and equality. It is still possible to treat people fairly by treating everyone badly.

■ Alternative Futures

Changes in America's political environment have indicated a growing dissatisfaction with government programs dealing with the nation's marginal or deviant populations (the poor, the criminal, and the uneducated) (O'Leary 1987, 8). Society increasingly is seeking stability at the expense of harmony and consensus building is replaced by conflict, change, and the need for constraint or coercion (Dahrendorf 1967, 161–162). Conflict is greatest where material interests arising from economic exploitation are evident and compromise is illusory and limited. This results in a pattern of adaptation, compromise, and containment (Raynor 1985). The practice of containment has meant that probation officers are pushed to become less interested in the client's welfare and more interested in exercising authority. The job has been redesigned to emphasize these features over the possibility of change, even when there is evidence of the value of rehabilitation.

The Probation World According to Raynor

Raynor (1985) offers two scenarios of the future of probation, one being more punitive than the other. In the first scenario, prisons will continue to be overcrowded and unemployment will remain high. Civil disturbances and riots will be common, particularly among unemployed youth. Proposals will be offered that merge prison and probation functions. In the future, Raynor sees the community probation officer performing traditional tasks, such as being concerned with victim programs, community-work service, restitution, conditional discharges, probation orders, and liaisons with community agencies. The officer's duty will involve matching the client's needs to a particular program. Volunteer organizations will play such a large part that officers will have a caseload of volunteers. The officers will receive training in community development, social work techniques, and research methods. Computers will play a much larger role. Computerized programs will track sentencing patterns and objectives and will identify cases that need attention. A decentralized office will mean the officer will be more accessible and can have greater influence over community development, but it will be harder for some probationers to get direct treatment.

In his second scenario, Raynor (1985) believes probation officers will become community control specialists. Crime is thus viewed as a result of personal problems for which there are few solutions. Bureaucratic control, discipline, and credibility will be evident. Only about 20 percent of the caseload will be given traditional treatment. The officer will spend most of his or her time ensuring probationers meet the restrictions and work requirements of probation. Anyone who fails to meet a deadline for payment of a fine, restitution, or fee payment is quickly identified. This new system permits little discretion.

Clear's Forecast

Clear (1994) predicts a probation system that is completely privatized. The work will be difficult and dangerous. Officers consider flack jackets, field boots, stun guns, and electric pistols to be de rigueur. The automobile will become a mobile office with all the latest gadgetry. Work will be completely dominated by the computer. Daily schedules will be determined by preset computerized priorities. Specialized caseloads, intermediate sanctions, and cosupervision of offenders will be common. Officers will not have caseloads but will be assigned to do certain things with different clients. Accountability will dominate the situation for both the client and the officer. Computers will make it easier to know the current state of the client and will measure the performance of the individual officer. Officers will be assessed in terms of arrests, group and client progress, and policy adherence. The officers will also be held accountable in the civil courts where their strategies will be challenged either by clients or by victims of future crimes.

Rhine

Rhine reports on a similar future-oriented approach, but this one is in operation. Many probationers don't report on time if at all. An interesting response to this problem and to the future of probation is the mobile intervention supervision team (MIST) (Rhine 1998). MIST is a program that supervises offenders ordered to community placement by the court at the time of their sentencing. Each offender in the program is under strict probation with specific conditions that address drug use, alcohol use, contact with the victim, and the required completion of treatment. Other conditions may apply, too. The MIST team is equipped with a vehicle, computers, and cell phones. A community-based, small office serves as a headquarters for the unit. The idea is to meet the offender in the community by working as a mobile self-directed work team. What is different is the officers have greater access, through the computers, to information. As with community justice, the officers are expected to forge relationships with various sectors of the community and with the police.

Feld's Work

Feld (1999) believes that in the future social welfare should be uncoupled from the social control function in the juvenile court. According to Feld, the juvenile court should try juveniles as adults and mitigate the punishment accordingly. He also believes that the social welfare needs of the offender should be addressed with the appropriate policies to help the client. The client should be forced to comply with the punishment but the social work treatment should be kept distinct from the punishment. Feld's approach would likely require a wholly new nonsocial work-based community surveillance agency. The problem is that for many offenders the crime is symptomatic of many other troubles that must be addressed before any criminal conduct ceases. What is done is better described as help rather than treatment. Thus, what is done requires a reconceptualization of probation (McWilliams 1984, 208).

The Five Futures of Dickey and Smith

Walter Dickey and Michael Smith (1998) offer five futures for community corrections. They are:

1. muddling along
2. principled minimalism
3. enforcing court orders
4. community and restorative justice
5. public safety

Muddling Along

The first, muddling along, occurs when probation offices are demoralized and confused because their work is done without clear purpose, programs are under-resourced and lack political support, and it is uncertain as to who is the client. Labeled a shutdown future, caseloads can run as high as 500 to 1 with expectations to match. Resources finally vanish. Muddling along occurs because difficult decisions on what the public desires are made without clear guidelines. A muddle results when officers are confused about enforcing court orders, holding offenders accountable, how much attention to give to reducing recidivism, reforming offenders, and maintaining public safety. Is restorative justice still important and should the officer continue to collect restitution and try to restore victims? The officer may not know what to do to prevent crime, reduce fear and harm, and involve the public in decision making. Muddling along leaves no one with any responsibility. To move out of this dilemma, community corrections requires a strategy for producing public value, maintaining authority, and maximizing resources through partnering the community and government agencies.

Principled Minimalism

Principled minimalism, the second option, suggests that the future is stark but survival can be achieved with enough attention to detail. It results from rejecting responsibility for public safety, restoring the community, and attending to victims. The possibility of failure is reduced by concentrating on one easily measured but valuable product or assuming responsibility for catching backsliders and delivering them to custody. For instance, one such approach would focus on the need for offender sobriety. This is a single purpose and single value. This would require that sobriety be understood and that one understands how to achieve it, how to teach it, and how to monitor it. Probation would provide vouchers for services that would aid the offender to stay straight and sober. Doing away with much of what is known of probation would leave other money for services dealing with drugs, employment, education, and the like. Leftover funding would go toward primary prevention. This would leave no room for innovation in supervision and promotion of public safety or for probation to work with other guardians in the community. The appeal of this future seems too weak among the public. In addition, agencies with something to gain with additional client populations may find that the funds are not there, either.

Enforcing Court Orders

The third option, enforcing court orders, would mean the future might be left to sentencing courts alone. The future would evolve around the enforcement of court orders, especially when probation is housed under the judiciary. Because court orders can be quite varied, probation agencies need to work harder to specify the court's purpose and choice of supervision in the case. Under this model, the court might lend its energies toward reengineering community corrections. The court, community corrections, and the prosecutor's office must come together on this matter. Major problems arise here if court orders are meant not for supervision but as a shield against court criticism for having done nothing to the offender. Under the circumstance, the order itself is the principal value, not its actual enforcement.

Community and Restorative Justice

The fourth option, community and restorative justice, reiterates the issues presented in Chapter 8. The idea again is to develop greater community involvement in the solution to crime; restore the offender and restore the community. Neighborhoods must become meeting places for concerned citizens who believe the government has made a commitment to making their lives better. Relationships must be built between citizens in the community and the offender, and not just with the probation staff. This would require that probation grant more power to the informal means of social control and social cohesion processes in the community. Value is created by the relationship between the offender and victim and offender and community, and not between the offender and the criminal justice system.

Public Safety

The fifth and final option would emphasize public safety (discussed in Chapter 10). The nature and character of supervision should be tied to the perception of the offender's harm; the more grave the harm, the more active the supervision. Staff will need both legal authority and resources to do the job. Work to reduce the offender's anonymity. Engage the offender in the setting that finds housing, labor market, support systems. Use local social control agents where they are found.

In the final analysis, the future would be a combination of minimalism and collaborative approaches to community and restorative justice.

■ Discussion

These projections into the future do not offer hope. Raynor's models emphasize community volunteers, control, computers, and cars. Clear also speaks of privatization, cars, and computers. Rhine believes mobile units with additional technology will become the wave of the future. Feld thinks social welfare for juveniles is unreasonable. Dickey and Smith offer several scenarios that cover a variety of perspectives. Of central concern is the muddling along and principled minimalism approaches that offer stark assessments of the future of probation. It is possible probation will be reinvented to conform to a set of community values that are subject to change and influence. On an informal level, there is a battle being waged for dominance of the value structure that will determine the direction probation will take over the next several years.

Each of these authors proposes a model for probation agencies that suggests that they are headed toward greater complexity or conversely greater simplicity as they become more technologically driven. This will happen whether the agency desires this change or not, for the simple reason that change may be driven not locally but on a statewide basis. No longer do some states stand behind their rights and declare they are the experts when determining what they need. Governors are too sensitive of appearing provincial in the face of a national press corps. The models just discussed, nonetheless, must account for regional variations in how community corrections is understood in different parts of the country. Various parts of the country are going to respond to the future in the different ways. In fact, it appears that it is important to be careful that solutions are not sought that are simplistic and convenient while attempting to conceal real complexities. These prospects for the future of probation are essentially influenced by technology, concepts of punishment, and social and economic conditions.

Technology

The most important factor influencing the future of probation is technology. Technology will give probation a tool to meet multiple challenges. The measures of civilization are the access people enjoy to certain technologies—cars, television, refrigerators, and so on. Equally, it is commonly assumed that, with suitable technology, any problem can be solved (Street 1992, 158).

There is almost no correctional organization without some kind of computerization. Computers are used to track, record, summarize, and analyze data. It is also possible that there will be smaller, more decentralized offices with greater telecommunication systems (Felson 1994). Managers have the power to assess the performance of organizations, divisions within organizations, and the work of separate individuals, all without directly observing performance. Staff can now be held accountable in ways not previously done (Cohn 1995).

Probation managers in the future will have to understand the implications of working in a system, the criminal justice system. The use of technology to achieve administrative and management goals will require highly skilled and flexible staffs who can work as teams to solve problems. Decentralized authority will be necessary as work units are given greater autonomy, working units will not have clear hierarchical structures, and management information systems will provide performance and outcomes measures at a moment's notice. Work-related experience may not prove as valuable as information gathering and processing. For example, a well-written presentence report will have a positive influence on supervision. The possibility of writing the better-quality report is made possible when management understands that reports can be written more rapidly, and with a higher degree of validity, if information can be accessed directly from a computerized network.

Research and development continue to play a large role in the electronics industry. Along with this have come some changes such as increased miniaturization. Cellular phones and satellite technology will make phone lines obsolete.

This leads to possibilities that a far more imaginative system of electronic monitoring is possible than presently marketed. Electronic monitoring devices that measure not only someone's location but also measure pulse rate, blood pressure, adrenalin level, and blood-alcohol or blood-narcotic level are a real possibility. However, moving too quickly in this direction may have dire consequences.

Corbett and Marx (1992, 86), for instance, warn that we "appear to be moving toward a maximum security society." No longer are there barriers such as distance, darkness, time, walls, windows, and even skin. Moreover, while directors of departments that use technology are viewed as progressive, there are some serious concerns. Technology has been used to enhance the perception that probation is a punishment. People are required to participate in their own monitoring. It is most effective when it is combined with other measures. On the down side, due to limited assets, traditional approaches will be deprived of needed resources as other expense are realized.

Advances in technology are occurring so rapidly that what is state-of-the-art one day is, in only a few years, anachronistic. Several things are likely to occur. First of all, it is possible to have an innovation race where one technology becomes soon outdated by a new advancement and everyone considers it too important to reject the newest innovation. It is also possible that society might be hustled and lobbied into accepting a particular model that would mean huge profits for one company that wants to dominate the market regardless of the effectiveness of the device. Thirdly, it is quite possible that the cost, despite the advantages of economy of scale, will eventually match the cost of incarceration, particularly if prisons become more cost efficient.

It is important to note that the value of technology lies in its application to preexisting practices or imagined ends. In other words, it is an instrument; it does not add anything except speed, convenience, and economy to practices and goals. Technology may help to solve problems, but those problems are posed by, and spring from, prior political decisions and choices (Street 1992, 174). Any failure to understand the instrumental nature of technology can open the door to political oppression. As Adorno and Horkheimer (1979) claim, the logical rationale is the rationale of dominance. It is the coercive nature of society alienated from itself.

Technology is not neutral because it shapes the ends it is supposed to serve. Efficiency, for example, is not altogether an objective rationale for the use of technology. The notion of efficiency rests on assumptions on how social relations ought to be ordered. By focusing on efficiency, one can adopt procedures where human beings are manipulated into more compliant behavior. According to Street (1992), "Whenever efficiency and effectiveness are used, they beg the questions as to what end is being sought and how are we to assess the relative efficiency/effectiveness of any one method over another."

Rehabilitative Probation?

Probation in some circles is seeking to redefine itself because it has found that the old system was too costly and offenders were not held accountable for their actions. This discovery permitted the critics of probation to suggest that probation had better prove itself if it is to remain an option. In response, probation has offered performance-based programming. Probation was not required to do this before because it was accepted, not on the basis of its proven efficacy, but because it offered a morally superior choice. It permitted officers to provide mercy and to offer care to the offender.

Cullen and Gilbert's (1982) argument for the continued support for rehabilitation is still relevant, saying that it is important to not forget that rehabilitation obligates the state to care for the offender's needs, counters the rationale that increased repression will reduce crime, is still supported in the community particularly for juveniles, and has been an important force in support of reform of the criminal justice system. Andrews and Bonta (1998) assert that critical findings about the general outcome of treatment cannot be ignored—the evidence is too strong. Certain treatment programs do work and these positive outcomes should not be overlooked. Positive outcomes have been obtained for day-training centers and other non-custodial innovations (McWilliams 1984). McWilliams also states it is important to realize that too much can be made of writings on the future of probation that have failed to grasp the central importance of the theoretical basis of probation in their explication of the future of probation.

In an effort to appear more accountable, probation has made overtures to the new penology, which has infiltrated probation departments as officers are becoming more vocal in complaining about the lack of progress in fighting crime, with the court's coddling of probationers and with the lack of public recognition. This backdrop provides a very receptive environment for a theory of crime control based on risk management. When there is no accepted theory on crime causation, classification and risk management have become nothing more than a hope and prayer (Lemert 1993).

The regulatory model of probation, discussed in Chapter 9, has its limitations. First of all, lawyers will challenge any effort to regulate behavior that is too broadly defined or is in violation of the equal protection clause of the Constitution (probation regulations could be more strictly applied to a particular minority or social class). Furthermore, despite the efforts of officials to carefully build in controls of the probation officer's tasks, a certain amount of discretion is still necessary. For example, what happens when a client who is forbidden to use alcohol apparently has but does not test positive for being drunk? Probation under these conditions can be used to harass people who are stigmatized. If public order is the concern of the probation system, will probation services find the courts receptive to handling increased caseloads? The judicial system may become overwhelmed with petty offenses. If the probationer is not convicted, it can be interpreted as a form of extra-legal harassment.

Social Factors

The models of probation discussed thus far suggest that in the future there will be a more unitary system, one dominated by a centralized technology network. Probation, nevertheless, will continue to operate as a part of a complex social system operating in a rapidly changing turbulent environment. This situation prevents rational, long-range, and macro-planned change (Wright 1990, 32).

This means that it is difficult to identify and specify a set of goals and to bring about change to remodel the system (Duffee 1980; Emery and Trist 1965; Terryberry 1968).

Probation may mean different things whether it is provided in a large city, in the suburbs, or in a rural county. "Before we attempt to change actual operating agencies to conform to a unitary conception of criminal justice, we may wish to ask why such variations occur, whether these variations are functional equivalents, or whether the contrasting practices provide important functions in the locality in which they are observed, on make contributions to social order that might be lost if all criminal justice agencies everywhere behaved appropriately to the expectations of the analyst" (Duffee 1980, 101–102). Caution must be taken so that an important element of the probation process is not rejected in efforts to adapt to the new penology.

A New World

The organizational structure and bureaucracy, the probation officer union, and the probationer may come to resist the new probation scheme. A probation department may still believe that through increased management techniques, officials can provide increased community protection while also providing adequate client casework. Should these departments be required to redefine their missions? The staff certainly may resist an increasing emphasis on accountability and workload while also curtailing their discretion. Older officers may feel that it is not worth the effort.

Some officers find value in nonlogical practices. For example, some officers may find advantages in the social interaction that takes place in the file room that would not be available to them if everything were found on a computer screen. Some officers also take pride in their ability to do traditional "people work." Job satisfaction should not be measured by indicators that are tied too closely with technology.

The probation officer's association will have something to say about privatization of corrections. The officers may want more training, lower caseloads, more safety measures, and greater benefits. More importantly, officers will probably want greater public recognition for the job they are doing. If these measures are not forthcoming, it is very likely job slowdowns and other pressures will be applied to the courts. The corporations responsible for managing the probation service will probably divide the probation system and gradually introduce officers who are accommodating to their demands while weeding out officers who refuse to comply with their initiatives. The same type of person who worked in the field years ago may not make the same choice of career. Many of these people had backgrounds in one of the social sciences. The probation officer in the future may be a graduate of a law school or a school of criminal justice. These individuals may have little understanding of social-psychological problems and may defer to experts whenever a problem is exhibited. Accountability will increase but understanding certainly may not. More importantly, proper cautions must be taken so that this new control ideology is not used as an excuse to further dehumanize the client.

Equal Treatment

It is important to incorporate the notion of human dignity in the future of probation. There will always be problems with those who are willing to express attitudes or exhibit behavior that denies the dignity of the offender. If social change leads to improvements in the treatment of women offenders or women at work, it is then possible that another, different set of scapegoats will be targeted. Probation officials may lose sight of the offender as a person and begin to treat him or her as a number with few other acceptable qualities. Those in probation and parole need to find a unifying agenda that allows people who are concerned with the offender as a person to have a strong voice in the process. Probation and parole must consider the notion of human dignity according to the idea that all offenders, regardless of the charge, must be presumed innocent. The presumption of innocence is not so much a matter of what is expected to be the result of the case as it is a matter of how the accused are treated before guilt is established. Probation will also have to recognize that as humans each is unique and the court of law is established to maintain each one's dignity before the state.

moral egalitarianism is the concept that everyone is to be held accountable for the same offenses in the same way.

<u>Moral egalitarianism</u>, the concept that everyone is to be held accountable for the same offenses in the same way, plays a major part in probation. Regardless of the level of technology applied to the level of supervision, the offender's dignity is maintained if one recognizes that all probationers are to be treated equally before the bar and while on probation, regardless of what they are accused of doing, what level of supervision they are under, or what services they receive. The current use of fees means that some offenders with resources will have a much easier time on probation than those accused of similar offenses but lacking sufficient resources to pay the fees. Additional punishments are likely to be given to these offenders. The deepest way in which to express the moral egalitarianism of the probationer is to recognize his or her inherent dignity as a self-activating offender who can choose to act and not act, that the probationer's choice of action can take several directions, that the probationer can assess how he or she is doing after being placed on probation, and that he or she is capable of making the appropriate adjustments himself or herself. Finally, human dignity provides the basis for equal human rights. These rights are the sword and shield that secure one's interests and one's sense of self-worth in the political arena. The equal worth and capacity for autonomy and rationality of all persons, a status not shared with other things or creatures, constitute this status.

Changes Ahead

There are many possible changes ahead for community corrections. Will these changes increase the status of the job and provide a rational source of employment consistent with their training? It will be seen. Probation will provide a method of supervision that is consistent with emphasizing legal requirements and restrictions.

■ Conclusion

Political communities get the quality of justice they deserve. If attention is not paid to the people elected, communities find themselves supporting policies they do not like. The United States may have to enter a correctional Dark Age before once again recognizing the importance of individual human dignity—not just in the abstract, but in very real, concrete terms. What is particularly noteworthy is the absence of any utopian vision for correction. Americans are living in a time when no one is offering a commonly accepted vision of the future, but the vision of the future is essentially bleak, foreboding, and nihilistic. Society seems overwhelmed by the dimensions of the many problems in its communities, but there seems to be little consensus on what to do about them. Demands on society, however, are not likely to diminish. If these trends continue, solutions may be sought that are more authoritarian in the face of increased social disorganization. These solutions ultimately are limited in their effectiveness. As the work becomes more uncertain, there will be a greater desire for concrete solutions. When combining technology, cynicism, and fear, one becomes the answer for the other. Who can blame the officer who would like to know that something is being accomplished? If the task becomes impossible, why seek to do it?

A probation system operating under fear and cynicism must consider strategies that provide additional resources. The obvious solution that has been mentioned earlier is to privatize the entire criminal justice system and to charge fees and service charges. This works only to the extent that the offender is employed—but many of these clients may be permanently unemployed. Privatization has some important risks, not the least of which is the fear that in the name of profits, administrative decisions will be based on expedience. The use of preprofessional and retired volunteers offers some hope, but unions and others will resist any suggestion that unpaid personnel can do the job as well as the paid civil servant.

If agencies do not build in change mechanisms, some programs become moribund, while others that have change mechanisms can be in constant turbulence with every new political appointee leading to some rocking of the boat. Actions need to be based on sound evaluations involving the entire organization. At each level of the organization, deficient workers need training in all aspects of the job. Probation needs reinventing but it must be done with a measure of kindness, understanding, and concern for others. After all is said and done, society must decide whether it can continue to require probation officers to perform as saints or at least atheistic altruists. Is there another John Augustus out there?

REFERENCES

Adorno, T., and M. Horkheimer. 1979. *Dialectic of enlightenment*. London: Verso.

Andrews, D., and J. Bonta. 1998. *The psychology of criminal conduct*. Cincinnati, OH: Anderson.

Broad, B. 1991. *Punishment under pressure: The probation service in the inner city*. London, England: Jessica Kingsley.

Clear, T. 1994. Ophelia the CCW: May 11, 2010. In J. Klofas and Stan Stojkovic (Eds.), *Crime and justice in the year 2010*. Belmont, CA: Wadsworth.

Cohn, A. 1995. The failure of correctional management: Recycling the middle manager. *Federal Probation* 59: 10–16.

Corbett, R., and G. Marx. 1992. Emerging technofallacies in the electronic monitoring movement. In J. Byrne, A. Lurigio, and J. Petersilia (Eds.), *Smart sentencing: The emergence of intermediate sanctions*. Newbury Park, CA: Sage Publications, pp. 85–102.

Cullen, F. T., and K. E. Gilbert. 1982. *Reaffirming rehabilitation*. Cincinnati, OH: Anderson.

Cushman, R. C. 1984. Probation in the 1980s—A public administration viewpoint. In P. D. McAnany, D. Thomson, and D. Fogel (Eds.), *Probation and justice*. Cambridge, MA: Oelgeschlager, Gunn & Hain, pp. 327–346.

Dahrendorf, R. 1967. *Class and class conflict in industrial society.* Stanford, CA: Stanford University Press.

Dickey, W., and M. Smith 1998. *Rethinking probation: Community supervision, community safety.* Washington, DC: U.S. Department of Justice, Office of Justice Programs.

Downes, D. Praxis makes perfect: A critique of critical criminology. In D. Downes and P. Rock (Eds.), *Deviant interpretations.* Oxford, England: Martin Robertson, pp. 1–16.

Duffee, D. 1980. *Explaining criminal justice: Community theory and criminal justice reform.* Cambridge, MA: Oelgeschlager, Gunn & Hain.

Durkeheim, E. 1964. *The rules of sociological method.* New York: Free Press.

Emery, F., and E. Trist. 1965. The causal texture of organizational environments. *Human Relations* 18: 21–31.

Feeley, M., and J. Simon. 1992. The new penology: Notes on the emerging strategy of corrections and its implications. *Criminology* 30: 449–474.

Feld, B. 1999. *Bad kids: Race and the transformation of the juvenile court.* New York: Oxford University Press.

Felson, M. 1994. *Crime and everyday life.* Thousand Oaks, CA: Pine Forge Press.

Harris, P., T. Clear, and S. Baird. 1989. Officers changed their attitudes toward their work. *Justice Quarterly* 6: 233–246.

Hirsch, A. J. 1992. *The rise of the penitentiary: Prisons and punishment in early America.* New Haven, CT: Yale University Press.

Irwin, J. 1985. *Jail: Managing the underclass in American society.* Berkeley: University of California Press.

Johnson, H. 1988. *History of criminal justice.* Cincinnati, OH: Anderson.

Lemert, E. 1993. Visions of social control: Probation considered. *Crime and Delinquency* 39: 447–461.

McWilliams, W. 1987. Probation, pragmatism, and policy. *The Howard Journal* 26: 97–121.

Murton, T. 1976. *The dilemma of prison reform.* New York: Holt, Rinehart and Winston.

O'Leary, V. 1987. Probation: A system in change. *Federal Probation* 51: 8–11.

Raynor, P. 1985. *Social work, justice and control.* Oxford, England: Basil Blackwell.

Rhine, E., ed. 1998. *"Mobile Intervention Supervision Team" best practices: Excellence in corrections.* Lanham, MA: American Corrections Association.

Street, J. 1992. *Politics and logy.* New York: Guilford.

Terryberry, S. 1968. The evolution of organizational environments. *Administration Science Quarterly* 12: 490–513.

U.S. Bureau of Census. 1990. *Cities of the United States.* Washington, DC: U.S. Government Printing Office.

Wright, K. 1990. The desirability of goal conflict with the criminal justice system. In S. Stojkovic, J. Klofas, and D. Kalinich (Eds.), *The administration and management of criminal justice organizations.* Prospect Heights, IL: Waveland Press, pp. 30–42.

KEY POINTS

1. The future of community-based corrections may become dependent on political forces dominated by conservative and punitive agendas.

2. Instead of responding to the uniqueness of the individual, probation has become preoccupied with objective considerations of facts about the client without maintaining the essence of the job as John Augustus performed it.

3. The goal is not to eliminate crime but to make it tolerable through systemic coordination of activities intended to deal with it.

4. Probation will become more interested in management information systems at the expense of greater understanding of the offender.

5. Raynor predicts that probation officers will use volunteers so extensively that they will have caseloads of volunteers.

6. Clear believes that probation officers will utilize a great amount of technology in their mobile office vehicles.

7. Feld believes that probation should devoid itself of trying to address the problems of the youth and instead focus on the legal requirements of doing juvenile probation work.

KEY TERMS

moral egalitarianism   is the concept that everyone is to be held accountable for the same offenses in the same way.

REVIEW QUESTIONS

1. What some of the major influences that will direct the actions of probation in the future?

2. How do the different scenarios offered for the future of probation compare with one another?

3. What do Dickey and Smith see as the future of probation?

4. How will technology affect the future of probation?

5. Considering the author's discussion of the future of probation, how might human dignity as employed in probation work be endangered?

Index

generic requirements of probation, 240–242
group effort, as a, 238–239
group regulation, 254
human dignity, and, 253–254
inspections, conduction of, 260
maximization of the regulatory process, 260–261
new penology, 249–250
normalization process, 261
offender control model, 250
premonitory compliance, 259
recidivism, and, 248–249
regulation, role of, 254–260
regulatory model, 240
revocation hearings, outcomes of, 247
self-regulation, 254
social control institutions, role of, 252–253
state regulation, 254
uncertainty, impact of, 255–256
Rehabilitation
assessment of rehabilitative functions, 21
implementation challenges, 19–20
indeterminate sentence, 20–21
intentions of, 19
medical model, 20
Rehabilitation model, 62–63
Rehabilitation programs, 191–196
Rehabilitative probation, 369–370
Reintegration into the community, 345–346
Reintegration model
assumptions of, 64–65
challenges to, 65–66
community corrections, and, 63–64
development as a result of the medical model failure, 64
education, role of, 67
employment, role of, 66–67
family, emphasis on, 66
objectives, achieving, 64
offender, emphasis on the, 63
resource brokers, staff as, 64
"underclass," and the, 67–68
Reintegrative parole, 351–354
Reintegrative shaming, 225–226
Relapse prevention, 190
Releases, discretionary, 336–340
Religious fervor, rise in, 43–45
Renaissance, role of the, 5
Resistance from probationers, role of, 158–159
Resource brokers, staff as, 64
Responsivity, 148, 156–157, 159–160
Restitution, 210
Restorative justice
accountability, 214, 215
amends and forgiveness, role of, 226–227
challenges of, 227–230
community, role of, 227
community protection, 214, 215–216
competency development, 214, 216–218
components of, 214–215
comprehensive model, 214

contemporary usage of, 360
correctional intervention, 214
crime as a loss, 218–219
encounter and shaming, 224–226
encounter conferencing, 220–223
grief, role of, 219–220
healing, role of, 226
historical development of, 211–213
modern approaches, 213–214
range of sanctions, 216
reintegrative shaming, 225–226
restorativist view, 218, 219
retributivist view, 218
role of, 268–269
social integration, 227
Restorative justice conferencing, 221
Restorative parole process, 353
Restorativist view, 218, 219
Restraint model, 63
Retributive process, 210
Retributivist view, 218
Retrospectivity, 70
Reviving Cities: Think Metropolitan, 93
Revocation hearings, outcomes of, 247
Revocation of parole, 348–351
Rights, history of juvenile, 304–306
Right to treatment, 91
Risk, evaluation of, 156
Risk-assessment tool, 146
Risk-needs instruments
Community Risk-Needs Management Scale, 150
conducting assessments, 155
differential supervision, 150
Level of Service Inventory-Revised (LSI—R), 150–155
Wisconsin Risk and Needs Assessment, 149–150
Risk principle, 148
Runaway episode, 295

S

Salient Factor Score (SFS), 148–149
Savage, E.H., 38
Schall v. Martin, 305
Security threat group (STG), 22–23
Self-correction, role of, 13
Self-possession, role of, 24
Self-regulation, 254
Severity of current offense and prior sentence, probationers by, 118
Sexual victimization, role of, 21–22
Shaming, 224–226
Situational crime prevention, 275
Sketch for a Historical Picture of the Progress of the Human Mind, A, 40
Smith, Adam, 40
Smith, Reginald, 55
Social capital, 79, 95–96
Social contract, concept of a, 25
Social control institutions, role of, 252–253